T0388448

PROPORTIONATE SHARE IMPACT FEES AND DEVELOPMENT MITIGATION

After decades of evolving practice often tested in court, development impact fees have become institutionalized in the American planning and local government finance systems. But, they remain contentious, especially as they continue to evolve. This book is the third in a series of impact fee guidebooks for practitioners, following *A Practitioner's Guide to Development Impact Fees* and *Impact Fees: Proportionate Share Development Fees*.

Proportionate Share Impact Fees and Development Mitigation is the culmination of the authors' careers devoted to pioneering applications of the dual rational nexus test. That test requires (1) establishing the rational nexus between the need for infrastructure, broadly defined, to mitigate the impacts of development and (2) ensuring that development mitigating its infrastructure impacts benefits proportionately. The book elevates professional practice in two ways. First, it shows how the rational nexus test can be applied to all forms of development infrastructure impact mitigation. Second, it establishes the link between professional ethics and equity as applied to proportionate share impact fees and development mitigation.

The book is divided into four parts, with the first reviewing policy and legal foundations, the second detailing the planning, calculation, and implementation requirements, the third exploring economic, ethical, and equity implications, and the fourth presenting state-of-the-art case studies.

Proportionate Share Impact Fees and Development Mitigation sets new standards for professional practice.

Arthur C. Nelson, PhD, FAcSS, FAICP, is emeritus Professor of Urban Planning and Real Estate Development at the University of Arizona, as well as emeritus Presidential Professor of City and Metropolitan Planning at the University of Utah, where he was also Adjunct Professor of Finance. He has authored more than 20 books and more than 300 other publications. Recent books include *Foundations of Real Estate Development Financing*, *Reshaping Metropolitan America*; *The TDR Handbook* (with Julian Conrad Juergensmeyer and James C. Nicholas and others), and the critically acclaimed *Megapolitan America* (with Robert E. Lang). Nelson's expert testimony helped frame urban sprawl as a legal concept in Florida, guide the Georgia Supreme Court to establish affordable housing case law, and support the rationale used by the US Supreme Court when it established the "rough proportionality" exaction doctrine in *Dolan v. City of Tigard*, 512 U.S. 374.

James C. Nicholas, PhD, is emeritus Professor of Urban and Regional Planning and emeritus affiliate Professor of Law at the University of Florida. He has written widely on the subject of land, environmental policy, and growth management. Nicholas has authored eight books, three monographs, and over 60 articles in the professional literature, dealing primarily with growth and local governmental finance of infrastructure. He is author of *The Calculation of Proportionate-Share Impact Fees*, the American Planning Association's first impact fee guide. Nicholas is also co-author of *A Guide to Impact fees and Housing Affordability* (with Julian Conrad Juergensmeyer and Arthur C. Nelson), editor of *The Changing Structure of Infrastructure Finance,* and author of *State Regulation and Housing Prices.* Together with Juergensmeyer, he pioneered the *Rational Nexus Test,* which has become the guiding principle for development mitigation such as impact fees in the United States.

Julian Conrad Juergensmeyer, a BA and JD graduate of Duke University and a member of the Ohio Bar, is emeritus Professor and emeritus Ben F. Johnson, Jr. Chair in Law at Georgia State University, where he served as Co-Director of the Center for the Comparative Study of Metropolitan Growth and Editor in Chief of the *Journal of Comparative Urban Law and Policy.* He was also Adjunct Professor in City and Regional Planning at the Georgia Institute of Technology and is emeritus Professor of Law at the University of Florida. Juergensmeyer is the co-author of the widely cited *Land Use Planning and Development Regulation Law; Impact Fees: Principles and Practice of Proportionate Share Development Fees* (with Nelson and Nicholas); and over 100 other books and articles. He has consulted with local governments and attorneys on matters relating to impact fees and other infrastructure finance policies as well as development mitigation in 29 states.

Clancy Mullen, AICP, is president of Duncan Associates. Having prepared more than 300 impact fee studies, he is one of the nation's foremost authorities on professional impact fee practice. Prior to joining Duncan Associates, Mullen served as a zoning planner for Austin. He is a contributing author to two American Planning Association publications, *Principles and Practice of Proportionate-Share Development Fees* and *Growth Management Principles and Practice.* He is also a co-founder of the National Impact Fee Roundtable (now the Growth and Infrastructure Consortium).

PROPORTIONATE SHARE IMPACT FEES AND DEVELOPMENT MITIGATION

ARTHUR C. NELSON, JAMES C. NICHOLAS,
JULIAN CONRAD JUERGENSMEYER, AND
CLANCY MULLEN

Routledge
Taylor & Francis Group

NEW YORK AND LONDON

Cover image: "A bouquet of new development." Drawing by Susan Leeb, Chapel Hill, North Carolina, based on a conceptualization by Raymond J. Burby, FAICP. © 1988 by the American Planning Association.

First published 2023
by Routledge
605 Third Avenue, New York, NY 10158

and by Routledge
4 Park Square, Milton Park, Abingdon, Oxon, OX14 4RN

Routledge is an imprint of the Taylor & Francis Group, an informa business

© 2023 Arthur C. Nelson, James C. Nicholas, Julian Conrad Juergensmeyer, and Clancy Mullen

The right of Arthur C. Nelson, James C. Nicholas, Julian Conrad Juergensmeyer, and Clancy Mullen to be identified as authors of this work has been asserted in accordance with sections 77 and 78 of the Copyright, Designs and Patents Act 1988.

All rights reserved. No part of this book may be reprinted or reproduced or utilised in any form or by any electronic, mechanical, or other means, now known or hereafter invented, including photocopying and recording, or in any information storage or retrieval system, without permission in writing from the publishers.

Trademark notice: Product or corporate names may be trademarks or registered trademarks, and are used only for identification and explanation without intent to infringe.

Library of Congress Cataloging-in-Publication Data
Names: Nelson, Arthur C., editor.

Title: Proportionate share impact fees and development mitigation / [edited by] Arthur C. Nelson, James C. Nicholas, Julian Conrad Juergensmeyer, and Clancy Mullen.

Description: New York, NY: Routledge, 2023. | Includes bibliographical references and index.

Identifiers: LCCN 2022023925 (print) | LCCN 2022023926 (ebook) | ISBN 9781032372563 (hardback) | ISBN 9781032372587 (paperback) | ISBN 9781003336075 (ebook)

Subjects: LCSH: Impact fees–United States. | Real estate development–United States.
Classification: LCC HJ4182.A6 .P76 2023 (print) | LCC HJ4182.A6 (ebook) | DDC 336.22–dc23/eng/20220603

LC record available at https://lccn.loc.gov/2022023925

LC ebook record available at https://lccn.loc.gov/2022023926

ISBN: 9781032372563 (hbk)
ISBN: 9781032372587 (pbk)
ISBN: 9781003336075 (ebk)

DOI: 10.4324/9781003336075

Typeset in New Baskerville
by Deanta Global Publishing Services, Chennai, India

To those we have served over our careers and from whom we have learned so much.

CONTENTS

ILLUSTRATIONS

FIGURES

TABLES

BOXES

ACRONYMS

CDD	community development district
CIE	capital improvements element
CIP	capital improvements program (or capital improvements plan)
CPI	Consumer Price Index
EDU	equivalent dwelling unit
EMS	emergency medical service
EPA	Environmental Protection Agency
ERU	equivalent residential unit
FOIA	Freedom of Information Act
GO	general obligation [bond]
HUD	[US Department of] Housing and Urban Development
ITE	Institute of Transportation Engineers
LOS	level of service
MSA	metropolitan statistical area
NAICS	North American Industrial Classification System
NEPA	National Environmental Policy Act
O&M	operations and maintenance
DOT	[US] Department of Transportation
SDC	systems development charge
SFE	single-family equivalent
TIF	tax increment financing
TOD	transit-oriented development
TUF	transportation utility fee
VMC	vehicle-mile of capacity
VMT	vehicle-mile traveled

FOREWORD

DWIGHT MERRIAM

What comes to mind in reading *Proportionate Share Impact Fees and Development Mitigation* is *magnum opus*. My favorite dictionary, Merriam-Webster, defines it as "a great work; especially: the greatest achievement of an artist or writer."

It sounds pompous, perhaps, to hang that label on a practitioner's guide to impact fees. Impact fees can be dry stuff, complicated by the dark science of development economics. Even one of the co-editors, Prof. James Nicholas, a PhD economist and Emeritus Professor of Urban Planning and Law at the University of Florida, describes economists as accountants without personalities, thereby deftly poking fun at two professions at once. The point he makes is that the work of the economist, especially important in this business of determining defensible impact fees, is beyond the ability of most people to fully comprehend and appreciate.

One of the very first things I learned from Jim Nicholas decades ago was that impact fees have an advantage over in-kind exactions, such as intersection signalization or a turning lane. "Exactions are lumpy," he said. "A turning lane comes in one size. You can't just go out and pave seven inches on a 12-foot-wide turning lane if that seven inches is your proportionate share, but you can make a payment equal to that impact." That is a major selling point for impact fees. They can mitigate proportionate shares with precision. That should be good for developers, and I have made the argument to my developer clients, to little or no avail. They often see impact fees as

yet another way of getting more money out of them. In some cases, they may be right.

As the lead co-editor, Prof. Arthur C. (Christian "Chris") Nelson, Emeritus Professor of Urban Planning and Real Estate Development at the University of Arizona as well as Emeritus Presidential Professor of City and Metropolitan Planning at the University of Utah, notes in the Preface, this book can trace its origins to 1988, and is the eighth in a series stretching back over professors Nelson's and Nicholas's storied careers, touched on in the biographies of the editors and contributors you will find in the list of contributors. The economics are essential but of no use if not coupled with planning. Planning asks: What do we have, what do we want, and how do we get it? Planners consider impact fees at all three steps in the planning process. Chapter 6, "In Accordance with the Plan," provides an overview, but woven throughout the book are considerations of what we have in assessing infrastructure needs and how we fund them. What we want follows from that.

The Nelson–Nicholas duet might seem enough, but where would we be without a lawyer? We are a democracy based on the Rule of Law. Law is critical from the commencement of planning to the ribbon-cutting of the newest capital improvement. Enter Prof. Julian Juergensmeyer, Emeritus Professor of Law at the University of Florida and Georgia State University after over 55 (not a typo) years of teaching, but still very much a thought leader in the law of impact fees.

There is no individual and no collectivity of experts other than the Nelson–Nicholas–Juergensmeyer triumvirate who know more about impact fees. Individually and together, they taught, they researched, they wrote, they lectured, and they consulted. But, an important perspective was missing, that of a planner immersed in the daily work of a consultant. Enter Clancy Mullen, President of Duncan Associates in Austin, with whom they had worked over many years, joining them as a co-editor to bring that experience to this book.

Together, they could have written it all by themselves, but they took on the more difficult job of identifying the most influential impact fee innovators and practitioners to author key chapters. Contrary to what someone who has not written or edited a book might believe, editing a collection such as this is far more difficult. Identifying the best authors, enlisting them, coordinating the work for seamless consistency, and packaging it all is hard work, but the rewards are great, as they are here. The truism is true: The sum is greater than the parts.

You can read this book straight through. But, it is so well organized and partitioned that it is useful to go to just a single chapter or the artfully drafted Chapter 15 Coda or the ruminative Epilogue. Either way, do start with the Prologue, which is a rather complete overview of what proportionate share impact fees are, their origins in, and relationship with, the many other ways we address meeting the needs created by development, how they relate to planning to protect the public interest, and why impact fees transcend being just another revenue source. Front and center is the nettlesome issue of who must bear the burden of existing inadequate capital improvements and new development.

Just as *Gallia est omnis divisa in partes tres, Impact Fees* is fundamentally three parts— Foundations, Context, and Practice—with an added fourth, Innovations, that attempts, successfully, to identify new and improved ways to use impact fees.

Part 1, Policy Rationale and Legal Foundations, covers revenue needs and sources; legal foundations, the statutory basis for impact fees; a comparison of Texas and Georgia, two leaders in the field; and a national survey of a sample of jurisdictions as to whether impact fees are levied, in what amounts, for what facilities, and how they vary by land use.

As someone who gets to read thousands of land use decisions a year as a co-author of a law school casebook on land use law and the co-editor of the leading treatise on land use law, I can safely attest that there is little uniformity among the states and the local governments using impact fees. Part of this is because the basis for impact fees, as the authors note in several areas, can come from state statutory enabling law giving local governments the authority to impose impact fees under the police power, that power to protect, preserve, and promote the public health, safety, and general welfare. That grant of power is shaped by the common law, the law the judges make in rendering decisions. The common law itself might be the sole basis for local governments undertaking impact fee programs when there is no enabling legislation, instead relying on their home rule powers. Prof. Juergensmeyer argues for this in the Epilogue. Home rule itself varies greatly across the country and is sometimes misunderstood by planners, land use lawyers, and local government lawyers, thus making it difficult to find any order in the chaos of public policy and implementation regarding impact fees.

What is lacking and might be helpful would be a uniform law that states across the country could consider for adoption. There is a Uniform Law Commission to develop such laws.[1] Also known as the National Conference of Commissioners on Uniform State Laws, it was created in 1892 to provide states with nonpartisan, well-conceived and crafted legislation to bring clarity as well as stability to many critical areas of state statutory law.[2]

The Common Interest Ownership Act (CIOA) is an example. It, and an earlier version, the Uniform Condominium Act (UCA), have made the creation of common interest ownership communities, such as condominiums and cooperatives, much easier, more regular, and more uniform in several states. Consequently, the case law that has developed interpreting the enabling statute has been beneficial across the states.

A remarkable example of how a uniform law can shape state and local law is the Uniform Partition of Heirs Property Act (PHPA),[3] helping to preserve family wealth passed on to the next generation. There is a long and shameful history in this country of African Americans, who have died intestate and whose property thus passed to their heirs as tenants-in-common, only to have the property taken away from those heirs by speculators who acquired a small interest of the property as the number of tenants-in-common expanded over generations. The need for a law to protect these families became obvious. In just a decade after the creation of this uniform law, 19 states have adopted it, and seven others have introduced it.

A uniform law for impact fees, if widely adopted, could solve many of the problems that we have in planning for and implementing impact fees, and interpreting state and local impact fee law.

Developers mostly want two things: certainty and speed. The present, Balkanized approach of state-by-state statutory and common law impact fee planning and regulation precludes both certainty and speed and hamstrings economic development, development that would be beneficial to everyone.

The Policy Rationale and Legal Foundations section of *Impact Fees* makes it patently evident that a concerted effort must be made to create consistency, currently utterly lacking, in the planning and implementation of impact fees.

Part 2, Foundations of Planning, Calculation, and Implementation, in four chapters takes up the comprehensive plan,

methodologies, a model impact fee ordinance with commentary, and implementation based on independent fee studies and available relief from the strict application of an impact fee program.

Part 3, Efficiency, Ethics, Equity, Policy Options and International Perspectives, brings in seven new authors in six chapters of the nine in this Part, including two older pieces from the 1988 book (see Preface) brought up to date. Among others, the perspectives include impact fees in the context of public finance, impacts of the fees, supply-side theory, value capture, ethical issues, standards for professional practice, and impact fees internationally.

The chapters are all worthwhile, but two deserve special note: Chapter 14 by Timothy Beatley on "Ethical Issues in the Use of Impact Fees to Finance Community Growth," and Chapter 15, "Planning Ethics and Impact Fee Equity," by Mary Kay Peck Delk and Susan A. Wood along with Nelson.

Prof. Beatley's work is foundational in recognizing intertemporal equity as a potential barrier to entry for some people: "We must face up to the possibility that impact fees may be used to intentionally exclude certain groups, communities of color in particular, much in the way that zoning has been used in the past."

Mary Kay Peck Delk and Susan Wood developed an equity analysis and suggested questions that must be asked. The issues are important, and more so considering the recent release of a substantially revised "AICP Code of Ethics and Professional Conduct" of the American Planning Association's American Institute of Certified Planners with a greater emphasis on diversity, equity, and inclusion.[4] The ethical concerns are addressed later in Chapter 23, relating to "Innovations in Affordable Housing Impact Fee Policy", which candidly offers only partial solutions.

Richard Rothstein's book *The Color of Law* (2017) grabbed the attention of planners and so many others and led them to consider the government's role in racial segregation and what we can do to right the wrong. With impact fees, an orderly approach to avoid unintended consequences is to focus our analysis on equity and environmental justice. Achieving intertemporal equity will limit the potential for segregative effects. Ensuring environmental justice in infrastructure planning, for example, will give some protection from segregative effects and social, economic, and racial inequity. Once we can say that there is intertemporal equity, and the impact fee program is environmentally just, we are still only part way there. As Prof. Beatley acknowledges:

We must also be concerned with the broader spatial implications of impact fee use. Situations may arise where some localities in a region or state are using impact fees while others are not. Again, where the fees involved are quite high, impact fees may constitute a sort of membership or admittance fee, in turn creating or exacerbating the social and economic differences between communities.

The next step after the threshold equity/justice determination is to make sure that an impact fee program is not a bar to entry. That bar may be one of economics, and that, in turn, is likely to have segregative effects. In the end, it may be that impact fees are not what is needed but instead, a change in how we pay for local capital improvements, and beyond that, even how local government is funded generally.

Take schools, for example. There is no question that exclusionary zoning, such as large lots, in most instances results in higher-priced housing, and that, in turn, not only has segregative effects but creates greater funding for schools and better education for those not excluded.[5] It may be more complicated than that, however, and it may not be exclusionary land use practices alone that have segregative effects.

"A National Study of Public School Spending and House Prices" published in 2020 found that "both increases in salary expenditure per teacher and teachers per student are capitalized into higher house prices, suggesting that parents value both the increased quality and quantity of school personnel made possible by higher spending on salaries." The study also revealed "that the combination of higher house prices and increased school spending affects who sorts into a school district."[6] "Sorts into a school district" is odd phrasing, but it must mean who gets to live there and have access to the high-quality education.

While the researchers found no significant correlation between capital expenditures (that impact fees might fund) and house prices, the total expenditures, driven by salary spending, were highly correlated. If impact fees are paid by those moving in, they get no benefit in terms of higher house prices, and the impact fees levied on them free up other local funds to be used to increase salaries, benefiting the existing homeowners with increased house values and increasing the barrier to entry.[7] Gregory Burge and Trey Dronyk-Trosper in Chapter 11, "Impacts of Proportionate-Share Development Fees," get as deeply into this issue as they can, given the paucity of research. We need to know more, much more.

Part 4, Innovations in Practice, spans 13 chapters, a third of the book, and covers a broad landscape, including transportation and parking, workforce housing, affordable housing innovations, conservation fees, public institutions, flexible funding, and even a new way to engage the public. There is a lot to be learned here, particularly with workforce and affordable housing generally. The takeaway is that there are opportunities to expand the use of impact fees in ways that neutralize exclusionary effects and support economic development. Resort and other vacation destinations often struggle to house the workers who support the industry. Everyone benefits when adequate housing is available for them and the nexus, both qualitative and quantitative, is typically strong. Indeed, one can consider workforce and affordable housing as infrastructure.

The four case studies in Chapters 26 through 29 pick up on the equity concerns that first surfaced in Chapter 14 (Ethical Issues in the Use of Impact Fees to Finance Community Growth), Chapter 15 (The Ethics of Impact Fee Equity), and Chapter 15 Coda (A Standard of Professional Practice for Proportionate Share Impact Fees and Development Mitigation). These four studies point the way to improving equity by a more thorough analysis of the adverse impacts of fee programs and ways to mitigate them, and by using house size in setting fees. They do more than that, however; they whet the appetite for knowing more. The understanding of how to plan and implement impact fees is in its refined third or fourth generation, which enables highly beneficial and defensible programs. The next pursuit in research should be to learn more about how to measure, determine cause and effect, and completely mitigate the unintended exclusionary effects of impact fees.

What if the Town of McPhee[8] determines to build new schools and parks? Developers are required to pay impact fees. Housing consequently may be priced higher. Developers do not absorb new costs like impact fees if they can avoid it. They will pass them back to the seller of the land in bargaining for a lower price, given the new development costs, or they will pass them on to the homebuyer or renter. If the developer cannot pass the costs back or forward, and the project does not work financially, they will go elsewhere, gingerly leapfrogging to some more hospitable place without impact fees, or investing in other ventures instead of building. Developers are not eleemosynary institutions; they build to make money.

Gregory Burge and Trey Dronyk-Trosper in their Chapter 11, Impacts of Proportionate-Share Development Fees, provide a thorough analysis of the literature. They note deadpan: "Impact fees have complex effects on housing prices and land prices." They find that increased house costs are not the result of passing costs forward but reflect the increased value of being in a good town and appreciating the present value of reduced taxes in the future. I agree with the former, but I doubt that homebuyers do any sort of present value analysis of lower, future tax bills. I have tried to help people with that analysis for home solar, and it is difficult. Still, it is important to recognize that for a host of reasons, too complex and varied to spell out here (please read Chapter 11) and beyond my complete grasp, there is good evidence that impact fee programs can enhance values. The avoided future taxes, for example, apparently do get capitalized in the value of the land, and improved infrastructure enables more development and a larger tax base, with beneficial tax consequences.

House values are up because the fee-based infrastructure improvements in place have made the community more desirable in the eyes of the homebuyers, or market demand and pricing have begun to reflect an infrastructure program that is firmly in the process (fee program funding locked in, planning done, contracts being signed up …). The houses are built and sold at a higher price because of the perceived higher value of the community, which has created greater demand. The builders can make a profit even with the fees. In the end, it matters not which came first. The salient fact is that houses in McPhee now cost more.

The impact fee program goes forward, and now, the schools and public recreational facilities are considered the best in the region. The demand of homebuyers and renters to live in McPhee continues to grow, and home prices and rents increase. Homeowners are willing to spend even more through general revenue taxes for great schools; after all, that is why they bought in McPhee. Landlords, begrudgingly, complain about the taxes, but they know that the premium they get in rents is because of the desirable schools and recreation opportunities available in McPhee.

What have we done? Our impact fees made McPhee a wonderful place in which to live, but in doing so, we have excluded a good part of the middle class and all those with lower income. No one intended there to be a segregative effect, but there is. One of the most critical social, economic, and racial equity issues today is the disparity in wealth by race and how to create opportunities for intergenerational wealth for those have been deprived of equal opportunity. Homeownership is key. Median wealth is $215,000 for white parents, $35,000 for Hispanic parents, and $14,400 for Black parents.[9] Nationally, 83% of white parents own their own homes, while 49.3% of Black parents are homeowners, and 65.2% of Hispanic parents are homeowners. In some areas, the disparity is even greater. In Massachusetts, 67% of white families own homes, while only 36% of Black families do, and Latino households are owners only 28% of the time.[10] These numbers have not changed much since 1968. The gap remains large and has not narrowed.

The unanswered question, one that demands our full attention, is: In making our communities better through improved infrastructure funding, are we exacerbating exclusion and limiting opportunities to create intergenerational wealth for families that have suffered discrimination?

There are many other challenges in the use of proportionate share impact fees. We should always consider the null alternative and ask the toughest question first: Are impact fees the best approach, especially as to housing equity? Should fee programs be coupled with other initiatives, creating hybrid approaches? For example, can we preserve Naturally Occurring Affordable Housing (NOAH)[11] without always requiring developers to build new? Should impact fees be more widely used to fund housing for the homeless? Sometimes, municipalities will exempt affordable housing developments from fees. Sometimes, fees go to supportive housing, but even where there are trust funds, it is not always readily apparent what the pass through is to house the homeless. In 2020, 580,466 people experienced homelessness in the United States on a single night.[12] Might government commit itself to matching impact fee levies with general funds or borrowing to subsidize low-income housing that impact fees are incapable of funding?

Proportionate share impact fees are here to stay. They will remain important tools to mitigate the adverse effects of new development and will continue to evolve. Other mitigation measures may be better suited to some infrastructure needs, such as water offset programs,[13] and should be considered as alternatives. This book, *Proportionate Share Impact Fees and Development Mitigation*, is an important contribution to our understanding of how we got where we are, where we are headed, and what opportunities lie ahead. It deserves to be recognized as the *magnum opus* of the editors and contributors, who have devoted a major part of their lives' work to the subject.

Well done.

Dwight Merriam, FAICP
December 29, 2021

NOTES

1 www.uniformlaws.org

2 www.uniformlaws.org/aboutulc/overview

3 www.uniformlaws.org/committees/community-home?CommunityKey=50724584-e808-4255-bc5d-8ea4e588371d At 34

4 https://planning.org/ethics/ethicscode/ Revised November 2021, effective January 1, 2022.

5 Jonathan Rothwell, Housing Costs, Zoning, and Access to High Scoring Schools (April 2012). https://www.brookings.edu/wp-content/uploads/2016/06/0419_school_inequality_rothwell.pdf

6 P. Bayer, et al., A National Study of Public School Spending and House Prices, www.hks.harvard.edu/sites/default/files/Taubman/PEPG/colloquium/2021-02-18-pepg-colloquium-blair-et-al.pdf. See also House Prices and Local Spending on Public School Teachers, National Bureau of Economic Research, NBER, The Digest: No. 3, March 2021, www.nber.org/digest-202103/house-prices-and-local-spending-public-school-teachers; Yi Y, et al., Linkage among School Performance, Housing Prices, and Residential Mobility, Sustainability (Switzerland) (2017) 9(6), www.mdpi.com/2071-1050/9/6/1075

7 See US Congress Joint Economic Committee, "Zoned Out: How School and Residential Zoning Limit Educational Opportunity" (Nov. 19, 2019) ("[T]he

average ZIP code associated with an A+ public elementary school has a median home value of $486,104, which is roughly four times higher than a D or lower public elementary school ($122,061)).” www.jec.senate.gov/public/index.cfm/republicans/2019/11/zoned-out-how-school-and-residential-zoning-limit-educational-opportunity

8 Such a town, owned by the New Mexico Lumber Company, existed in Dolores, Montezuma County, Colorado from 1924 to 1948. Library of Congress, “Town of McPhee, McPhee Road, Dolores, Montezuma County, CO.” www.loc.gov/item/co0095/

9 In 2015 dollars. Jung Hyun Choi, Jun Zhu, and Laurie Goodman, “Intergenerational Homeownership,” Urban Institute (Oct. 2018) p. 6; see also Alanna McCargo and Jung Hyun Choi, “Closing the Gaps: Building Black Wealth through Homeownership,” Urban Institute (Nov. 2020, update Dec. 2020) Closing the Gaps (urban.org)

10 Jon Corey, “How is it that the average Boston-area house ‘made’ more than a minimum wage earner last year?” *The Boston Globe* (Feb. 3, 2021) www.bostonglobe.com/2021/02/03/magazine/how-is-it-that-average-boston-area-house-made-more-than-minimum-wage-worker-last-year/

11 See https://noahimpactfund.com/

12 HUD Releases 2020 Annual Homeless Assessment Report Part 1: Homelessness Increasing Even Prior to COVID-19 Pandemic (Mar. 18, 2021). www.hud.gov/press/press_releases_media_advisories/hud_no_21_041
See Net Blue, for example. www.allianceforwatereff iciency.org/resources/topic/net-blue-supporting-water-neutral-growth

13 See Net Blue, for example. https://www.allianceforwaterefficiency.org/resources/topic/net-blue-supporting-water-neutral-growth

PREFACE

Between us, *Proportionate Share Impact Fees and Development Mitigation* is our eighth book on or related to impact fees. The first, *The Calculation of Proportionate-Share Impact Fees*, was penned for the American Planning Association as a Planning Advisory Service report by Nicholas in 1988. All books since have used this as their foundation. Following a special symposium on impact fees at the American Planning Association's (APA) 1987 conference in New York City and two themed issues of the *Journal of the American Planning Association* organized by Nelson on impact fees generally (Volume 54, Issue 1, 1988) and linkage fees in particular (Volume 54, 1988), APA published Nelson's edited work, *Development Impact Fees: Policy Rationale, Practice, Theory and Issues.* Several contributors to that book have encore chapters in this one. In 1991, the APA published the first comprehensive guide for professionals: *A Practitioner's Guide to Development Impact Fees*, written by Nicholas, Nelson, and Juergensmeyer. This was followed by Nelson's 1995 book on *System Development Charges for Water, Wastewater and Stormwater Charges*, published by Routledge. In the same year, 1995, Nelson and Mullen (with Dames B. Duncan and Kirk Bishop) coauthored *Growth Management Principles and Practices* for the APA, which outlined the role of impact fees in capital improvements planning; key elements of that book are included in the planning-related chapters of this book. In 2007, for the US Department of Housing and Urban Development, Nelson, Nicholas, and Juergensmeyer co-authored *Impact Fees & Housing Affordability: A Guide for Practitioners.* This was followed in 2008 by Island Press's book *A Guide to Impact Fees and Housing Affordability*, also co-authored by them. A year later, in 2009, Nelson, Nicholas, and Juergensmeyer wrote *Impact Fees: Principles and Practice of Proportionate-Share Development Fees* for the APA. We concluded this book with our own call for the next edition to advance the broad practice of proportionate share development mitigation and especially social equity through proportionate share impact fees.

Arthur C. Nelson, FAICP
Tucson, Arizona
James C. Nicholas
Gainesville, Florida
Julian Conrad Juergensmeyer
Fernandina Beach, Florida
Clancy Mullen, AICP
Austin, Texas
September 2022

PROLOGUE

Proportionate Share Impact Mitigation

These newcomers arrive in our community seeking opportunity. They come seeking a new beginning, a new start with hope, or a final fulfillment of life's just reward.

They come for the same reasons that we came. They stay for the same reasons that we stay in this community and state we all love.

These newcomers bring with them all their fondest dreams of the future. They bring dreams that are the same as ours—dreams of a better life and a better future.

What they don't bring with them are the roads, the bridges, the schools, the hospitals, the libraries, the parks, the utilities, the sewers, the waterlines, and all the vast and varied human services that will be needed to realize our dreams.
(adapted from Florida State Comprehensive Plan Committee 1987: 6)

These words, written in the last century, still capture the angst local government has in meeting the challenges of new development while also ensuring a desired quality of life. Various "tax revolts," federal and state unfunded mandates, court cases mandating higher-quality facilities, and increasing demand by citizens for facilities and services of high quality put locally elected officials into a bind. They often cannot raise taxes, either because of tax limits or because voters will not let them—or both. They cannot raise new revenues through exotic or risky ventures because of statutory limitations. They cannot borrow their communities out of infrastructure deficits because of statutory and common-sense limitations. But, they want to make their communities better.

Our book, *Proportionate Share Impact Fees and Development Mitigation*, focuses on the use of impact fees to mitigate the impact of new development on infrastructure broadly defined. We argue that the proportionate share impact mitigation methodology underpinning impact fees should be applied to all forms of development impact mitigation for three reasons. First, it is a rational way in which to establish the nexus between development and its impact on infrastructure broadly defined. We use the term "broadly defined" because in our view, infrastructure means not only water and sewer lines, roads, schools, parks, and so forth but also clean air and water, preservation of community heritage, the housing needed by local firms to house their workers, and really anything that a community depends on for its existence and well being.

Second, the method ensures that development mitigating its impact on infrastructure through impact fees or other means also benefits proportionately. This has location and timing elements that we discuss in Chapter 2, "Legal Foundations."

Third, and perhaps more pragmatically, "dual rational nexus" proportionate share impact mitigation has become institutionalized through legislation and professional practice.

There is common ground for this perspective. Christina M. Martin (2015:15) writes on behalf of the Pacific Legal Foundation, which assists plaintiffs in takings claims, that mitigating the impact of development on communities is a legitimate exercise of government as long as mitigation does not exceed the impact of development. Had this been done by the City of Tigard, Oregon, for instance, there might not have been the need for *Dolan v. Tigard*[1] litigation and the court's fabrication of the "rough proportionality" standard for administrative decisions. That said, we will show in Chapter 2, "Legal Foundations," and elsewhere that the proportionate share impact mitigation methodology used to craft impact fees is itself a higher standard than "rough proportionality." By extension, if all forms of mitigation, whether administrative or legislative, were based on principles of proportionate share impact mitigation, there would be more certainty in how to calculate mitigation and maybe less litigation.

But, herein lies an unresolved issue. Judicial guidance has been limited to mostly administrative decisions where local governments exercise their discretion to shape the nature of individual development proposals. So far, local governments seem to have been immune from "takings" challenges when such mitigation measures as impact fees are based on such legislative actions as comprehensive plans, capital improvement plans, and the impact fees needed to implement them. This raises important equity and ethical issues covered in Chapter 15, "The Ethics of Impact Fee Equity," when local governments use the legislative process to require mitigation from some development that is in excess of its impact on infrastructure. In a particular application, Chapter 15 shows that in one jurisdiction, school impact fees—which generate funds for new or expanded schools proportionate to the new students generated by new development—are the same for studio apartments as for single-family detached homes despite data showing clear differences in impact. It may

be only a matter of time before the Supreme Court agrees with Justice Thomas that:

> [U]ntil we decide this issue, property owners and local governments are left uncertain about what legal standard governs legislative ordinances and whether cities can legislatively impose exactions that would not pass constitutional muster if done administratively.[2]

We worry that it would take just a few local governments, or maybe just one, that abuse proportionate share impact mitigation principles to such an extent as to attract the attention of courts. In turn, courts may decide to extend administrative takings tests to legislative actions. Maybe that would be a good thing, because it could require that legislative actions make individualized determinations of the nature and extent of impacts to be mitigated, and that may best be done through the proportionate share principles as advanced in this book.

With this admonition as a starting point, the Prologue offers opening perspectives on the need for such mitigation measures as impact fees. It then offers a brief history of development mitigation in the United States, including key legal advances. As an aside, readers may notice that we use the term "mitigation" instead of "exaction" because mitigation implies a calculus to correct a harm imposed by change, while exaction implies open-ended conditions of development approval, sometimes euphemistically called "extortions." The first section frames the context for the five chapters comprising Part 1: Policy Rationale and Legal Foundations.

The second section outlines the four chapters comprising Part 2: Foundations of Planning, Calculation, and Implementation, which focuses on the planning, methodology, and implementation. Skipping a little, the fourth section provides an overview of the 13 chapters comprising Part 4: Innovations in Practice. The reader will see many ways in which proportionate share analysis can be used to establish what may be needed to mitigate the adverse effects of new development on the community.

The third section summarizes the issues presented in Part 3: Efficiency, Ethics, Equity, Policy Options, and International Perspectives. In particular, how do impact fees relate to public finance theory, and what are the market outcomes from them? What are the value-added implications of impact fees that may lead to efforts to capture value created by public decisions and investments to be reinvested back into communities? What are the effects of impact fees on urban form, noting that while impact fees promise to create market discipline whereby new development internalizes its adverse impacts on facilities, which according to standard urban economics, results in more efficient development patterns, in practice, impact fees can actually exacerbate urban sprawl. What are the ethical and equity implications of impact fees? And, what are the practical alternatives to impact fees? We finish with a review of the political alternatives to impact fees.

The Prologue finishes with perspectives about the role of development mitigation in managing community impacts to the middle of the twenty-first century and beyond.

WHY IS MITIGATION NEEDED?

The over-arching concern is that it costs money, sometimes a lot of money and more money than local governments have, to mitigate the impacts of new development. The cost of providing a residential dwelling unit with new or expanded public facilities including water, sewer, drainage, police, fire, library, school, park, recreation, and other public facilities in a new development is considerable, routinely being more than $100,000 per new home in many metropolitan areas. Nonresidential development is equally costly on communities, with impacts reaching into the millions of dollars or even tens of millions of dollars for large projects. In this section, we remind readers why development mitigation tools such as impact fees are needed. We then offer brief historical perspectives.

RISING COSTS AND DECLINING REVENUES

As we show in Chapter 1, "The Past, Present, and Future of Impact Fees," infrastructure costs are rising at a pace that exceeds local government's revenue-generating capability. The increasing cost of maintenance of existing infrastructure, combined with declining public support for raising taxes, has forced local jurisdictions to seek alternatives such as impact fees.

Impact fees are defined as one-time charges on new development to generate revenue to mitigate its proportionate share impact on community infrastructure net of new revenues it generates. While impact fees are used mostly to help finance water and wastewater, school, road, park and recreation, and other types of physical infrastructure, Part 4, "Innovations in Practice," shows that they are used for workforce and affordable housing, habitat conservation, and even operations and maintenance. In effect, the proportionate share methodology can be applied to mitigate any development impact that can be measured reasonably.

It is very difficult to estimate the number of communities that assess impact fees (see Chapter 5, "National Impact Fee Survey"). One of the complications is the lack of standard terminology. In some communities, these developer charges are called impact fees, while in others, they may be called benefit assessments or connection charges. Developers tend to call them "exactions" or "extortions," while local governments call them mitigations, which is the correct technical term through formal legal construction (see Chapter 2, "Legal Foundations" and Chapter 3, "State Impact Fee Legislation").

Earlier studies indicated that impact fees were relatively common in California, Florida, Oregon, and growth spots of other states including Colorado and Texas (Nelson, Nicholas, and Juergensmeyer 2009). Our more recent, albeit nonscientific, study, reported in Chapter 5, suggests that impact fees in some form are probably assessed in every state, with the number of communities assessing them ranging well into the thousands. In very large measure, impact fees have become institutionalized as a common source of revenue.

Impact fees are imposed as a condition of development approval. As such, they fall within the rubric of land development regulation as contrasted with revenue-raising (taxation) programs. The objective of impact fees is not to raise money but rather, to ensure that adequate capital facilities are available concurrently with the impact of new development. The adequacy of capital facilities is critically important to the entire system of land development regulation. Where capital facilities are not adequate, permitting development may be contrary to the responsibility of a local government to protect public health, safety, and welfare. For instance, if the local water supply is incapable of serving new development, the public may be harmed when new development reduces water pressure or forces rationing to meet collective needs. Protecting the public from this form of harm imposed by new development falls within the police power function that all states grant to local governments, although such grants of authority by states will vary in nature and extent.

To advance the public health, safety, and general welfare, local governments may deny new development proposals unless that development mitigates its impacts. One form of mitigation would be to have it build new or expanded water facilities. Another form would be to pay impact fees to the community for the same purpose, albeit apportioned to the impacts associated with the new development. These options can also work together. For instance, if a proposed development mitigates its impact on facilities for which impact fees are assessed, such as constructing water facilities ahead of the community's schedule, no impact fees would be due, and there may even be a credit against future impact fee payments, or this may be sold to others under certain conditions.

Before it establishes regulations to protect against harm, however, local government must define the harm, its source, and how it needs to be mitigated. For its part, impact mitigation is rooted in the economic concept of "internalizing externalities." An externality occurs when, for instance, a new development increases impervious surface, which then moves stormwater off the development's property onto neighbors. Few would assert an owner's right to harm others in the use of their land in this fashion. It is the specifics of what constitutes "harm" that are often a matter of contention. While most would agree that inadequate roads provide a reasonable basis for denying an owner a proposed change in land use, some find it unreasonable to impose a charge on that owner to remedy or mitigate the impact. The issue, then, is who should be financially responsible for paying to achieve adequacy?

Three possible candidates for mitigating the cost of impacts are: the local government; the property owner; or "someone else." The latter category would include entities like the state and federal governments. In general, local governments and property owners can readily agree that "someone else" should bear the cost of roads or other capital facilities. But, their agreement has not resulted in funding. Moreover, it flies in the face of modern fiscal reality. With all due respect given to it during the early 2020s, the federal government is not going to provide sustained funding for local infrastructure over the long term. On the contrary, federal support has been declining (see Chapter 1). The states have generally not filled the vacuum created by the federal withdrawal. The simple reality is that the community and the property owner are the only available candidates to bear the financial burden. The issue then becomes which of these should bear this burden and how the burden should be borne.

On the one hand, it may be argued that the community should be financially responsible for needed facilities because it is the principal beneficiary. Land development is part of the creation of socially and economically beneficial products such as new housing and jobs that satisfy needs of the community. Land development creates jobs and enhances the tax base. Moreover, it may be argued that impact fees are fundamentally unfair, in that they shift to new development costs that were formerly borne by the community.

It may be argued that imposing such costs upon an unwilling community is harmful. It is harmful to the extent that higher taxes and fees must be paid by those who had no part in the decision to develop the property, whether or not they benefit from the development. This argument has been going on for a number of years and will undoubtedly continue. Clearly, a community may pay for needed facilities. But, must it? Increasingly, the answer is that a community need not absorb all costs but may impose a proportionate, or fair, share of such costs upon new development. This is a permissive rule, and certainly, individual communities may elect not to follow it.

Let us next review how we got here through a brief, historical perspective.

FROM EXACTIONS TO PROPORTIONATE SHARE MITIGATION: A BRIEF HISTORY

How did we get to formalized approaches to mitigating the impacts of development on communities? To begin with, impact fees are a product of evolution in public policy toward land use and provision of public facilities. Before the US Commerce Department's model planning and zoning enabling acts of the 1920s, most growing communities had no effective land use controls. It was not uncommon to find speculators, for example, subdividing vast tracts of land considerable distances from cities in anticipation that purchasers and home builders would eventually receive city services (Nelson 1988). There were no land use regulations controlling the

location, timing, or dimensions of those developments; nor were public facility extension policies linked to land use regulation. The model acts are the genesis of modern land use regulation. They were adopted by most states, many verbatim. Today, a person can travel to virtually any state and find commonalities in land use regulation process and substance that are rooted in the model acts.

An immediate outcome of the model acts was regulations requiring developers to provide necessary facilities on site. Prior to the model acts, developers often demanded and received street, water, sewer, and drainage facilities to their development at the expense of the local community. The model acts gave public officials legal rationale for requiring developers to internalize that cost.

It must always be remembered that development impact fees are a form of land use regulation, and they have evolved just as the regulation of land development has evolved (see Chapters 1 and 2). The object of development regulations is to protect the public. In some circumstances, protecting the public from harm has required the prohibition of certain types of developments in certain locations.

Requiring developers to provide adequate facilities is common now, but this was not always the case. From the time the US was formed and well into the last century, there was no control over the practice of subdividing land into parcels for sale to those who assumed they could build on them. It was not the subdivider to whom buyers looked for roads and water systems, not to mention the schools, public safety services, and parks new residents wanted—that responsibility fell to local government. So pervasive was this thinking that one of us (Nelson) got first-hand experience through a studio he conducted in the 1990s for a city in central Georgia. The mayor bemoaned the obligation of his city's taxpayers to incur the cost of extending roads, water, sewer, and drainage to new subdivisions within the city limits. After all, was it not the right of the landowner to subdivide their land and the obligation of the city's taxpayers to incur the cost to serve the needs of new residents who bought and built homes on them? While that is no longer the case, it took a studio comprised of Georgia Tech planning students in the 1990s to change long-standing city philosophy and policy.

Nowadays, most states have subdivision control enabling acts that allow local governments to require that developers install all infrastructure needed by those buying and building on subdivision lots. This includes not only water, wastewater, stormwater, roads, sidewalks, signs, special lanes, and intersections connecting the subdivision to the main streets, along with traffic lights and the like, but sometimes pocket or other parks where subdivisions are large, and occasionally sites for schools, fire stations, and so forth. Aside from the example noted earlier, it is probably the very rare case that new development is not required to install onsite infrastructure at its own expense.

But, what about the adequacy of public facilities extending beyond the limits of the development? As zoning and other land use regulatory forms evolved, so also did the methods to mitigate off-site impacts of development. While these requirements were found to be within the authority of a local jurisdiction if there was a valid public purpose and the result was reasonable, it took more than a century to establish.

FIRST ERA: MANDATORY LAND DEDICATION AND IN-LIEU FEES

From the turn of the last century to the Baby Boom (1946–1964), public officials wrestled with providing facilities outside the boundaries of the development. For example, local officials discovered that fiscal resources could not satisfy the appetite generated by new development for new parks and schools. The initial resolution of this problem was requiring developers of residential subdivisions to dedicate land for park and school use, which is usually facilitated by state enabling legislation.

But sometimes, land dedicated by development was in the wrong place, was too small, or for other reasons could not be used to satisfy community demand for parks and schools. As an adjunct to subdivision dedications, therefore, a system of payment in lieu of dedication came into use. Payment in lieu is employed when actual dedication or provision of land or improvements is not practical or feasible. For example, under a requirement to set aside 5 percent of a development's land area as open space, a 5-acre subdivision would reserve one-quarter of an acre. Such a site might prove to be totally impractical for both the subdivision and the community. The alternatives are either to exempt smaller subdivisions from such requirements or to allow a payment to be made in lieu of dedication. This resulted in local governments requiring money in lieu of land dedication. The money exacted was to equal the value of the land that would have been dedicated.

By the 1940s, local government's power to demand land or money for facilities located off site was firmly established. But, mandatory dedication and in-lieu laws did not necessarily enable modern impact fees. This is because in-lieu fees are related to mandatory land dedication. There is usually no mandatory land dedication for water, sewer, drainage, roads, and many other facilities. The need for these facilities and services would have to be satisfied on a different, but related, basis.

SECOND ERA: RECONSIDERING THE GROWTH ETHIC

Until the 1960s and 1970s, most communities believed that growth and new development were fundamentally good. This is because they brought an improved tax base that could be used to build better facilities that all community residents enjoyed. Growth meant improving services at declining average cost to taxpayers. Challenges to the growth ethic emerged in the 1960s, however, as residents of desirable, rapidly growing communities discovered that unbridled growth caused pollution, congestion of streets, overuse of other facilities, and a general lowering of the quality of life. Furthermore, cost-revenue studies showed that in many cases, new development resulted in incremental demands for community facilities that actually increased average tax burdens for existing taxpayers. Citizens concluded that growth was inimical to their reasons for choosing to live in their communities. A new land use regulation ethic emerged, calling for new development to internalize all the costs it imposes on existing residents.

Regulations based on such logic have been found to be within the power of local jurisdictions provided that there is a clear public purpose and that the regulations are reasonable. Protecting the public also commonly requires that certain types of developments be denied because the necessary supporting facilities are lacking. The development would become acceptable once the needed facilities were provided.

THIRD AND CONTINUING ERA: SUSTAINED LOCAL GOVERNMENT FISCAL STRESS

A number of changes in the attitude toward financing public facilities emerged in the 1970s and continue to the present. At the forefront of these changes was the fiscal revolt of the 1970s and 1980s. Other factors included inflation, rising facility standards, and rising expectations of existing residents on the preferred range of public services.

The fiscal revolt manifested itself in rejection of new general obligation and revenue bonds for capital improvements needed to accommodate new development. It also manifested itself in electorates imposing on local government severe restrictions on the taxation of real property. Propositions 13 in California and 2-1/2 in Massachusetts are only two of the more visible outcomes of this revolt.

The fiscal revolt extended to state and federal levels as well. When combined with inflation, the result was dramatically declining public fiscal support for public facilities. As a result, government capital financing has not kept pace with either inflation or population growth since about 1965. Government capital financing was 3.4 percent of gross national product in 1965, for example, but by 2020, it had fallen to just 1.5 percent. Much of this is attributable to the fiscal revolt.

Coupled with the fiscal revolt are rising facility standards and rising expectations for facilities by existing residents. Improved water and wastewater treatment, and larger and better-designed highways, are not so much demanded by the public as they are required by state and federal regulatory agencies. But, new arts centers, public day care centers, and expanded parks facilities are examples of the rising public appetite for new or expanded facilities. The bottom line is that local governments are forced to consider all possible revenue-enhancing sources. These include new or higher user fees, privatization of some services, negotiated exactions of new development requiring planning approval, and development impact fees.

Sustained fiscal stress, however, does not give local government license to demand more from development than is needed to mitigate its impact on communities. We illustrate key limitations next.

THE RISE OF PROPORTIONATE SHARE MITIGATION

Exaction noun
ex·ac·tion | \ ig-'zak-shən
1a : the act or process of exacting
1b : extortion
2 : something exacted especially : a fee, reward, or contribution demanded or levied with severity or injustice

Merriam-Webster's Dictionary

As Chapter 2 shows, the evolution of requiring new development to mitigate its community impacts is reflected in court decisions that, to be very simplistic, have moved from the privilege theory to the mitigation theory. Early cases found that development was a privilege and not a right. This emboldened local governments to exact from new development benefits to the community that went beyond what was needed to mitigate impacts. This brings us to a critical distinction between the terms "exaction" and "mitigation" from *our* perspective.

From our perspective, an *exaction* occurs when there is no rational basis for requiring it. Another way to put it is that there is no reasonable relationship between the impact of new development and the conditions required of it. Some might call this "extortion in the public interest." In contrast, *mitigation* occurs when analysis is done showing the impacts of new development and what is needed as conditions of approval to mitigate those impacts.

Chapter 2 fleshes these concepts out in terms of the evolution of development and property rights law. In *Nollan v. California Coastal Commission*,[3] the Supreme Court held that the California Coastal Commission's required lateral beachfront easement along Nollan's property was a taking because there was no "essential nexus" between the impact of Nollan's proposed building permit (to remodel an existing home) and its impact that would require the easement. In *Dolan v. City of Tigard*,[4] another easement case in which Dolan was required to dedicate unbuildable floodplain land to the city as a condition of expanding a plumbing goods store, the court held the condition must be "roughly proportional" in nature and extent to the impact of the proposed land development. While those cases involved granting easements as a condition of approval, the court held in *Koontz v. St. Johns River Water Management District*[5] that *Nollan* and *Dolan* applied to money and implicitly, any other type of condition that did not meet the "essential nexus" or "rough proportionality" tests.

Figure 0.1 illustrates the evolution of development and property rights law. The left side conceptualizes the extent to which local government could impose conditions of development approval without showing necessarily the reasonable relationship between the impacts of new development and what was being exacted. The right side shows the effects of the *Nollan, Dolan,* and *Koontz* (N-D-K) cases in moving away from exactions toward identifying impacts and requiring conditions to mitigate them. The illustration does not mean that a certain share of conditions that were constitutional before N-D-K are not such afterward, only that the scrutiny incurred by local government to show that its conditions are constitutional has been raised (See Chapter 2 for details).

But, this begs the question: Are proportionate share mitigations such as impact fees even subject to the kind of takings analysis used by the court in N-D-K? Perhaps not, for reasons explained in Chapter 2 and based on the analytic approaches described throughout our book. Indeed, if local governments in all three of these cases had used the rational nexus impact mitigation approaches presented in our book, their decisions might never have been litigated, at least successfully.

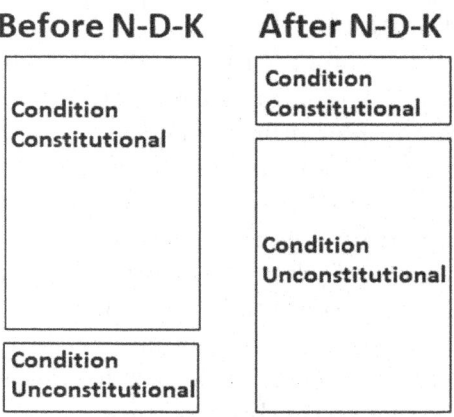

FIGURE 0.1 Constitutional conditions of development approval before and after Nollan-Dolan-Koontz (N-D-K).

POLICY RATIONALE AND LEGAL FOUNDATIONS

Much of the foregoing discussion is the focus of Part 1, "Policy Rationale and Legal Foundations." These foundational chapters provide an overall policy perspective about "The Past, Present, and Future of Impact Fees" (Chapter 1), "Legal Foundations" (Chapter 2), an overview of "State Impact Fee Legislation" (Chapter 3), including a "Tale of Two States: Texas and Georgia Impact Fee Legislation Compared" (Chapter 4) that provides a detailed comparison of two models of legislation that have been adapted by most states, and implications revealed in a "National Impact Fee Survey" that reports pre-, during-, and post-Great Recession impact fee trends (Chapter 5).

We turn next to a review of Part 2, which focuses on the foundations of planning, calculation, and implementation.

FOUNDATIONS OF PLANNING, CALCULATION, AND IMPLEMENTATION

Part 2 is devoted to the practice of impact fee policy making, planning, programming, calculation, and implementation. It builds on the foundational material presented in Part 1 and is used to guide perspectives presented in Part 3.

"In Accordance with the Plan" is the title of Chapter 6. As impact fees are an integral part of the planning process, this chapter is devoted to reviewing that process as it relates to impact fee design. It begins with an overview of planning goals, which includes a characterization of what constitutes urban sprawl as well as the potential role of impact fees in helping rein it in or perpetuate it. Most of the chapter is an overview of procedural planning steps focusing on how planning influences impact fee design. The chapter also includes key elements of capital improvement planning and the role of impact fees in implementing it.

Chapter 7, "Impact Fee Methodology," ties everything together from establishing level of service (LOS) standards based on a planning process to assessing the need for new or expanded infrastructure based on those standards, which then drives the capital improvement element (CIE). Identifying the shortfall in revenues needed to finance the CIE becomes the basis for impact fees, which are calculated based on different methodologies that depend on the type of infrastructure, the degree of flexibility needed to raise and expend funds, and limitations of state legislation. A critical element of calculating impact fees is accounting for the extent to which new growth and development generates new tax and fee revenues that may be used to help finance the same infrastructure that is financed in part by impact fees. Impact fee calculations thus include a credit provision to guard against double charging new development, once through impact fees and again, through new revenues used to help finance the same infrastructure.

Chapter 8, "Model Proportionate Share Impact Fee Ordinance," provides sample language for crafting impact fees ordinances.

We conclude this part with Chapter 9, "A Word About Independent Fee Calculations, Variances, Exemptions, and Waivers." This chapter has two elements. The first discusses the role of independent fee calculations to help ensure proportionality in impact mitigation. Independent fee calculations occur either when a particular development activity is not addressed or addressed adequately in the impact fee schedule, or when the feepayer asserts that a different (usually lower) fee should be assessed. We identify issues that are rarely raised but may become sources of future litigation, perhaps drawing the attention of courts for reasons noted in Chapter 2. The second element explores issues relating to variances, exemptions, and waivers. We define exemptions as situations where a development activity does not increase its impact on infrastructure, and therefore, no impact fees are due. Rebuilding a home that recently burned down with no increase in size may be an example. Finally, waivers occur when a new development is charged an impact fee, but local policy makers want to eliminate all or a part of it. Elected officials are especially keen to advance their key interests, in part by waiving impact fees for such laudable activities as affordable housing and economic development. But, who pays for the fees not collected? Waivers can be especially problematic to implement financially.

EFFICIENCY, EQUITY, AND ETHICAL CONCERNS WITH POLICY OPTIONS AND INTERNATIONAL PERSPECTIVES

At their heart, impact fees are one of many tools available to communities to finance the infrastructure needed to mitigate the impacts of new growth and development. But for many facilities, they are not the "best" tool for reasons explained in Chapter 10, "Evaluation of Impact Fees Against Public Finance Criteria," written by Douglas B. Lee, Jr. Indeed, this is an update to his chapter in *Development Impact Fees: Policy Rationale, Practice, Theory and Issues* (Lee in Nelson 1988). One criterion to consider in public finance is whether some types of infrastructure serve the broad public interest and thus, provide a "public good," such as education for everyone regardless of their ability to pay. Where public goods exist, such as in the case of parks and public safety as well as education, general taxation is a more appropriate method of financing than impact fees. Still, if communities are limited in their ability to raise taxes, impact fees may be a necessary, albeit second-best, solution. On the other hand, because impact fees are limited in most states to physical infrastructure but not its operations and maintenance, impact fees may be an appropriate method of mitigating the impact of new development on physical infrastructure, while it is the community as a whole that pays for ongoing operations, maintenance, repairs, and eventual replacement. In the case of education, for instance,

the largest share of school budgets goes to personnel and support services, which are financed from general taxes.

From the beginning of impact fees, there has been debate on whether and the extent to which they affect development patterns and community well-being. Some early studies suggested that each dollar of impact fee raised housing prices by more than 20 dollars, while other studies showed that impact fees reduced building permit applications. The impact of impact fees on prices, economic development, housing production, and other concerns is addressed by Greg Burge and Trey Dronyk-Trosper in Chapter 11, "Impacts of Proportionate-Share Development Fees." Not surprisingly, impact fees behave as they should in economic systems. That is, in normal markets, the sellers of land absorb the cost of the fees as lower land prices, while the value of homes may rise more than the fees paid because of numerous value-added benefits. Furthermore, because economic development needs the very infrastructure financed from impact fees, there is a strong correlation between impact fees and economic development. There are sustainability benefits as well.

The special case of the role of impact fees in affecting the supply of land to advance housing affordability is presented in Chapter 12, "Toward a Supply-Side Theory of Development Impact Mitigation." The standard theory of development impact mitigation suggests that development supply will be reduced, thus putting upward pressure on housing prices. But, impact fees generate the revenue needed to build the very infrastructure needed to support growth. As such, they are a supply-side mechanism. Moreover, when calibrated to reflect the costs of housing—where smaller homes on smaller lots in areas that cost less to serve are assessed at a lower value than larger homes on larger lots—impact fees can improve housing affordability.

As impact fees increase infrastructure investments by the community, they also create value that is capitalized in the market. This is shown in Chapter 11 with implications explored in Chapter 13, "Good Planning, Value-Added Planning, and Value Capture." This chapter begins with the proposition that bad planning can lead to a misallocation of land needed to meet market needs, thus resulting in less development. In the absence of "misallocation planning," the private market likely does a better job of allocating resources, including land, to meet development needs. But, the private market may be unable to marshal the resources needed to sustain development, such as water and wastewater systems, road networks, and schools and parks, that makes a community attractive for development. We call this "good" planning. While impact fees are part of the value-added equation, their ability to leverage other resources as shown in Chapter 12 creates value over and above the cost that is paid by new development. It is this increment of value-added caused by good planning that can be tapped through recoupment, with the proceeds reinvested into the community to create even more value, which itself may be captured. Lessons from the United Kingdom's betterment and planning gain experience are highlighted. We call this a virtuous cycle.

The purpose of mitigation is to force development to internalize its externalities. For example, most local governments require new development to prevent downstream flooding from stormwater runoff occurring on the impervious surface it creates upstream. That used not to be the case, meaning that people downstream often suffered the consequences of upstream development. Mitigation of adverse impacts would seem to be a good thing. It is, however, fraught with important ethical questions that are raised by Tim Beatley in Chapter 14, "Ethical Issues in the Use of Impact Fees to Finance Community Growth," which is an update of his chapter in *Development Impact Fees: Policy Rationale, Practice, Theory and Issues* (Beatley in Nelson 1988). One of the key issues is that development creates benefits for the entire community, perhaps elevating the

quality of life for everyone, yet the costs of creating positive externalities may be borne only by tenants and occupants of new development. Moreover, those who decide to impose such mitigations as impact fees are not those who pay the fees. And, to what extent are future generations affected? These and many more ethical issues are addressed.

We expand on Beatley's over-arching concerns in Chapter 15, "The Ethics of Impact Fee Equity," written by Mary Kay Peck Delk and Susan A. Wood along with one of us (Nelson). Combined with adopted policy directives by the American Planning Association, they show that the Code of Ethics of the American Institute of Certified Planners *requires* that planners address equity implications in their professional practice as related to impact fees. A key passage of the AICP Code states that as planners:

Seek social justice by identifying and working to expand choice and opportunity for all persons, emphasizing our special responsibility to plan with those who have been marginalized or disadvantaged and to promote racial and economic equity. Urge the alteration of policies, institutions, and decisions that do not help meet their needs.[6]

Although this passage applies technically to just members of the AICP, in our view, it ought to be a guide to all other professionals as well as elected officials in everything they do in their professional and official capacities. Besides, AICP planners are likely involved in at least some stages of impact fee development and implementation. Delk, Nelson, and Wood adapt real examples of impact fee design, showing how they may fail to advance the AICP Code of Ethics.

Chapter 15 includes a "Coda: A Standard of Professional Practice for Proportionate Share Impact Fees and Development Mitigation," which synthesizes issues raised through this Part. It offers a checklist that outlines the standard of practice needed to ensure that impact fees are consistent with professional planning ethics.

Chapter 16, "The Option of Impact Fees," implores officials not to take impact fees lightly. The decision about whether to engage in impact fees, considering options and challenges, needs to be taken seriously, and impact fees must fit into the larger scheme of advancing community well-being. Indeed, despite the considerable benefits of impact fees, the decision to pursue them may alter community priorities and foreclose options of future officials. As Aesop in one his fables admonishes: *Be careful what you wish for.*

In Chapter 17, "Impact Fees in an International Context: Comparisons and Similar Fiscal Tools," David Amborski, the author of a chapter on Canadian development fees in *Development Impact Fees: Policy Rationale, Practice, Theory and Issues* (Amborski in Nelson 1988), updates his prior work and provides a survey of applications internationally. The principles of nexus and proportionate share calculations are not just American inventions; the underlying logic has become an international standard.

We devote the last part of our book to the always evolving innovations to impact mitigation through such formulaic approaches as impact fees.

INNOVATIONS IN PRACTICE

Impact fees are a dynamic field. The reason is that once the foundations have been established—namely, establishing the nexus between the impact of new development on infrastructure broadly defined and that which is needed to mitigate that impact—it is a straightforward exercise to calculate what is needed to mitigate the impact. The mitigation itself is based on a formula, so that all similar developments are held to the same standard.

Because transportation impact fees are among the highest impact fees charged, and considering that among all types of infrastructure, transportation is among the most multifaceted as well as arguably the most

dynamic in terms of change, we devote the first four chapters to it. The first of these chapters, Chapter 18, presents a "A Framework for Estimating Multimodal Transportation Impacts for Sustainable Development," which technically does not present an impact fee but rather, presents how transportation impact fees of the future may be transformed to improve sustainability. It is written by Kristina Currans and Kelly Clifton.

Taking the queue using some of the advances outlined in Chapter 18 are "Mobility Fees," which are presented conceptually in Chapter 19, written by Jonathan Paul. Unlike conventional road-based impact fees, mobility fees can include several transportation modes, such as transit bikeways, walkways, and roads, as well as operations and maintenance, especially of transit systems. They can also be tailored to different kinds of landscapes, such as urban service areas, where multi-modalism is feasible, and suburban and rural service areas, where transportation options are limited. They can also be layered, so some service areas have multiple mobility fee components, while others have as few as one. Mobility fees can also be designed to encourage more efficient transportation choices through service area and fee design. This chapter outlines many, though not all, the ways in which mobility fees may be the future of transportation-related impact fees.

While nearly all the impact fees reviewed in this book are used for new or expanded infrastructure, the impact mitigation methodology can be applied broadly for other purposes. Chapter 20, "Operations and Maintenance Mitigation Fees, and Transportation Utility Fees with Implications for Improving Impact Mitigation," reports two important applications. The first is extending development mitigation to include recovery of operations and maintenance (O&M) costs. Literature shows that many development patterns do not generate sufficient revenues to cover O&M costs, which leads to deferred maintenance issues. One alternative is to calculate the difference between revenue generated and revenue needed to create an endowment that over time will generate sufficient (or at least, less insufficient) O&M revenues. The second innovation is to create a utility-like billing system in which an annual (or more frequent) fee is charged to real property, often on the property tax bill, reflecting its proportionate share of the cost of maintaining road systems in the community. The method works successfully for many transportation systems, not to mention water, wastewater, and stormwater systems, and can be adapted to other types of infrastructure.

Chapter 21, "Parking In-Lieu Fee Incentivizes Development in Downtown Oxnard, California" by Alison Bouley, is yet another application of the nexus-based mitigation fee approach, in this case to encourage development and redevelopment in a suburban center.

The next two chapters present innovations in development mitigation to advance workforce and affordable housing. Chapter 22, "A Rational Nexus Approach Supporting Development Mitigation to Increase Workforce Housing Supply," presents an approach to mitigating the workforce housing impacts associated with new development in the city of Jackson and Teton County (Jackson/Teton), Wyoming. This is an in-lieu fee program in that new development has the option of mitigating its impact on workforce housing or paying a fee in lieu to Jackson/Teton, which uses the money for the same purpose. It is also a "project improvement" as opposed to a "system improvement," which has important impact mitigation nuances. In many states, impact fee legislation limits fees to a list of infrastructure types (see Chapter 3) called system improvements. The mitigation of impacts caused by specific development projects is addressed through conditions of approval that are called project improvements. For instance, a new streetlight required to mitigate the transportation impacts of a specific development project

may be a condition of approval. Project-related impacts on workforce housing are an extension of this project-related impact mitigation rationale. This chapter includes the legal rationale as well as the calculation methodology.

Chapter 23, "Innovations in Impact Fee Adjustments to Advance Housing Affordability," summarizes findings of the Florida Housing Finance Corporation into the wide range of ways in which Florida local governments adjust impact fees to advance housing affordability. We believe this is the only study that catalogues the range of techniques used by local governments to offset potential adverse impacts of impact fees on housing affordability. We note that one of the best techniques is simply calculating impact fees based on the type and size of residential units, which we advocate especially in Chapters 1, 15, 22, and 26–29.

While impact fees are used commonly for parks, open space, beach access, and other purposes where people may enjoy active or passive recreation activities, they can also be used to preserve wetlands, habitats, and other sensitive landscapes not accessible to the public. Robert Spencer provides an example of this for California in Chapter 24, "Western Placer County, California: Habitat Conservation Fee."

Sometimes, local planners and officials need to be nimble to manage unexpected changes in the market. Alison Bouley presents an example of this in Chapter 25, a case study of "Flexible Development Funding for Large-Scale Development." When the Great Recession ended, the city of Tracy, California, targeted several areas for development, in one of which a developer proposed residential, mixed-use, commercial, and light industrial land uses. For its part, the city did not have the funds to install infrastructure concurrent with the impacts of development. The city and the developer created agreements that outlined the funding mechanisms for infrastructure impacted by the development, including impact fees and bond funds. Notably, the developer was required to pay the costs of certain improvements upfront, for which it received a credit against its impact fees.

The next four chapters address *impact fees as if equity matters*. In Chapter 26, J. Richard Recht describes the logic and calculation of "Residential and Nonresidential School Impact Fee Nexus: Case Study of Fremont Union High School District, California." Outside of California, it is unusual for communities to extend school impact fees to nonresidential development, because offices and warehouses do not send children to schools. Recht reasons that because nonresidential jobs bring families and children to the community who need school services, nonresidential development must mitigate its reasonable share of school facility impacts.

Carson Bise extends this to Chapter 27, "Parks and Recreation Impact Fees for Residential and Nonresidential Development," which is a case study of Tucson, Arizona. Bise uses similar reasoning to that offered by Recht to extend parks and recreation impact fees to nonresidential development. The logic can be extended to library impact fees as well.

All too often, impact fees are not scaled to the size of residential units, even though census and other data show clearly that smaller homes have smaller impacts on facilities than larger ones. For instance, impact fees for water facilities are often based on just the size of the meter connecting the home to the system without any variation based on demand, which varies by size. In Chapter 28, Bise addresses this through "Water Impact Fees for Residential Development Based on House Size: Case Study of Bozeman, Montana." This shows how water impact fees can be scaled by the size of the residential unit.

Bise completes his trilogy with Chapter 29, which addresses "Transportation Impact Fees Scaled to Residential Unit Size in

Tucson, Arizona." Many communities have a one-size-fits all approach to assessing transportation impact fees on residential development. Others vary fees by the type of residential unit. Very few calibrate transportation impact fees based on the size of residential units. Bise shows how this can be done.

All four of these case studies show practitioners how equity can be advanced by (a) extending impact to all sources of impact, such as new nonresidential development that generates new jobs that bring people to the community, and (b) scaling impact fees to the size of the residential unit. This addresses efficiency in land use patterns, because economic logic holds that over-charging smaller homes means that fewer will be built, but under-charging larger homes means that more will be built, which can eventually create local fiscal stress.

Kevin Burnett concludes our set of case studies on innovations with Chapter 30, "Impact Fee Focus Groups: Case Study of Town of Queen Creek, Arizona." While all state impact fee legislation requires a public process, and many require impact fee advisory committees, we should always worry about whether we are doing enough to engage the citizens in impact deliberations. Burnet shares a novel way in which to improve engagement of the public in impact fee policy decision making.

We finish our book with an Epilogue. Each of us has devoted our entire career to advancing fairness and equity in government decision-making processes through proportionate share mitigation analysis, with impact fees being a key focus. We use the Epilogue to offer our personal observations about the evolution and future of impact fees as a form of proportionate share impact mitigation.

Before offering closing perspectives, we wish to acknowledge Garrett B Aldrete's assistance in formatting most of the figures for our book.

CLOSING PERSPECTIVES

A word of caution is in order. Our book addresses a dynamic issue that is always evolving. Relying upon actual experience, as it does, it necessarily draws examples only from communities where impact fees as a form of proportionate share impact mitigation have been found to be an acceptable form of land development regulation. Both case law and local authority with respect to development regulation vary considerably across the states. This book will not discuss the jurisdictional variation in regulatory or home rule powers, even though they are critical to the outcome of any impact fee program. In attempting to develop and implement impact fees, one must note the nature of local regulatory powers.

Nor does this book go into the detail of the calculations of impact fees, with a few exceptions. As most of our other books on impact fees (see Preface) do so, we refer readers to them. This book instead looks to the broader issues surrounding the mitigation of impacts of new development on infrastructure through such tools as impact fees. Those issues include efficiency, especially in the context of public finance, equity, the benefits of growth and how to capture them for mitigation purposes, and how good planning elevates overall prosperity and well-being, among others.

In the latter regard, we observe that there is concern among some that impact fees slow new growth and development. For the most part, this is not supported by the evidence. States where impact fees are commonplace are also those where residential permitting exceeded demand during the 2000s, leading to the financial collapse—often called the Great Recession—of the latter 2000s that extended well into the 2010s (Nelson, Marshall, Nicholas, and Juergensmeyer 2017). Our view, shared by economists who have studied the political economy of impact fees (see Chapters 10, 11, and 12), is that impact fees are often the grease that facilitates new

growth and development. Simply, without the revenue impact fees generate to help pay for infrastructure, growth and development stalls or stops.

Looking ahead, to the middle of the twenty-first century, America will add about 60 million people and about 25 million homes. More than 30 billion square feet of nonresidential development will accommodate more than 50 million new jobs. Private development will top $30 trillion, while public investment in infrastructure will approach $10 trillion. Raising a substantial share of the money needed to finance new and expanded infrastructure through higher taxes is unlikely. Instead, local governments must look to new growth and development to mitigate its proportionate share impact on infrastructure costs. When done in ways offered in our book, we believe it also advances good planning.

NOTES

1 *Dolan v. City of Tigard, Oregon*, 512 US 374 (1994).
2 *California Bldg. Indus. Ass'n v. City of San Jose, Calif.*, 136 S. Ct. 928, 194 L. Ed. 2d 239 (2016) (THOMAS, J., dissenting).
3 483 U.S. 825, 841-42 (1987).
4 512 U.S. 374 (1994).
5 133 S. Ct. 2586 (2013).
6 www.planning.org/ethics/ethicscode/

REFERENCES

Amborski, D. P. (1988). Impact fees Canadian style: The use of development charges in Ontario. In A. C. Nelson (Ed.), *Development impact fees: Policy rationale, practice, theory and issues* (ch. 4, pp. 52–63). Routledge.

Beatley, T. (1988). Ethical issues in the use of impact fees to finance community growth. In A. C. Nelson (Ed.), *Development impact fees: Policy rationale, practice, theory and issues* (ch. 27, pp. 339–361). Routledge.

Florida State Comprehensive Plan Committee (1987). *The keys to Florida's future: Winning in a competitive world*. Department of Community Affairs.

Lee, D. B., Jr. (1988). Evaluation of impact fees against public finance criteria. In A.C. Nelson (Ed.), *Development impact fees: Policy rationale, practice, theory and issues* (ch. 24, pp. 290–312). Routledge.

Martin, C. M. (2015). Nollan and Dolan and Koontz: Oh my! The exactions trilogy requires developers to cover the full social costs of their products, but no more. *Willamette University Law Review, 51*(1), 39–72.

Nelson, A. C. (Ed.) (1988). *Development impact fees: Policy rationale, practice, theory and issues* American Planning Association.

Nelson, A. C., Duncan, J. B., Mullen, C. J., & Bishop, K. R. (1995). *Growth management principles and practices*. American Planning Association.

Nelson, A. C., Nicholas, J. C., & Juergensmeyer, J. C. (2009). *Impact fees: Principles and practice of proportionate-share development fees*. American Planning Association.

Nelson, A. C., Marshall, J. T., Juergensmeyer, J. C., & Nicholas, J. C. (2017). *Market demand-based planning and permitting*. American Bar Association.

PART 1

Policy Rationale and Legal Foundations

In the beginning there was no mitigation of the adverse impact of new development on communities. Those communities were left holding the bag when developers came to town, subdividing and selling lots to buyers who assumed (perhaps being told by developers) that the community would provide free infrastructure. Eventually, to protect themselves from the "negative externalities" of new development, communities exacted concessions from developers, often arguably in excess of the impact. A privilege theory emerged whereby communities deemed development approval to be a privilege and not a right. Communities in some states cultivated this into an art. In Virginia, for instance, a "voluntary proffer" system emerged that was anything but, as it forced developers to "proffer" sufficient contributions to the community to gain approval of such discretionary approvals as zone changes, conditional use permits, subdivisions and other discretionary approvals.[1] The terms "exaction" and even "extortion in the public interest" were used commonly the characterize the privilege theory.

Over time, the privilege theory gave way to interpretations of the Constitution, leading to the mitigation theory. Chapter 1, "The Past, Present and Future of Impact Fees," lays the foundation for development impact mitigation from economic and policy perspectives. Two key observations are made. First, the methods and applications of impact mitigation are becoming more sophisticated and broader in scope, and they are becoming more sensitive to ethical and equity concerns, as we show in Parts 3 and 4.

"Legal Foundations" are offered in Chapter 2. It traces the evolution of relevant law from exactions (as we characterize them based on the privilege theory) to mitigation. It then frames the legal foundations of mitigation to guide planning, economic analysis, policymaking, and implementation.

During the 1980s and through the 1990s, there was a flurry of state legislation to guide the process and calculation of impact fees. This is the subject of Chapter 3, "Overview of State Impact Fee Legislation." Although most legislation gives sound guidance about public engagement and deliberative processes, it also restricts the application of impact fees, usually to a narrow subset of facilities.

We add context to the discussion about legislation in Chapter 4, "A Tale of Two States: Texas and Georgia Impact Fee Legislation Compared." These were among the earliest states to adopt impact fee legislation, but their approaches are very different. One lesson from this chapter is that despite differences in approaches, both states use impact fees extensively to help finance the infrastructure needed to sustain growth and economic development.

We conclude Part 1 by summarizing results from a "National Impact Fee Survey," presented in Chapter 5. We are indebted to our co-author, Clancy Mullen, who has conducted these surveys since the 2000s, from their heyday of rapid adoption and fast-rising fees through the Great Recession and then recovery into a new era of increased adoption and rising fees.

Part 2 applies these foundations to the planning, methods, and implementation of impact fees as a common form of development impact mitigation.

DOI: 10.4324/9781003336075-1

NOTE

1 For details of these and other uses, and perhaps abuses, of discretionary land use decisions, see Brian W. Blaesser, *Discretionary Land Use Controls: Avoiding Invitations to Abuse of Discretion*, Clark Boardman Callahan (2016). For elaboration, in Virginia, local officials often withhold a decision on a discretionary permit but would not reveal conditions under which it might. Eventually, if the voluntary proffers were raised high enough, approval would be given with development agreements reflecting the voluntary nature of the proffers. One wonders whether the mistake by local officials in Florida leading to *Koontz v. St. Johns River Water Management District*, 570 US 595, was that they revealed what would be needed for them to approve Koontz' discretionary permit before the application was field formally.

1 THE PAST, PRESENT, AND FUTURE OF IMPACT FEES

Oliver Wendel Holmes wrote that "taxes are what we pay for a civilized society."[1] Part of this civilization is the sum of things we call "infrastructure." Typically, infrastructure, the underpinning of society, is provided by government and paid for by some form of taxation. Table 1.1 shows the source of state and local government revenue for 1993, 2000, and 2018.

Over this 25-year period, total state and local revenues increased by 221 percent; state by 226 percent and local governments by 113 percent. Accepting education and transportation as two primary functions of state and local government, the resulting fiscal "squeeze" is apparent, especially on local governments. Table 1.2 presents these same data on a per capita basis, assuming that local governments are populated by the total population. The per capita data follow the general pattern of the total, given that the total population grew by 27 percent over this period. However, inflation also occurred. Table 1.3 shows real per capita revenues for 1993 and 2018, and the percentage change. These data show the fiscal dilemma facing local governments:

- Real per capita revenues are declining for local governments;
- Educational expenditures exceed the growth of total revenues for both states and local governments;
- Non-educational and transportation revenues to local governments declined by 34 percent between 1993 and 2018.

These data show that both tax and property tax revenues have grown, but at rates less than education, with a resulting pressure on sectors other than education or transportation. What is apparent is that local governments are faced with insufficient revenues from traditional sources to meet the needs of a growing population. Various movements have resisted and frequently restricted taxation, especially property taxation. Such movements have not actually reduced either taxes or property taxes, but they appear to have imposed limits on their usage

This opening chapter serves as a background to impact fees and how they have evolved over time. It also includes data on how impact fees are assessed today, with tables summarizing national data and several useful local examples illustrating specific impact fee structures. This chapter concludes by introducing the concept of equity as applied to impact fees and the impact on housing.

1.1 THE NEED FOR INFRASTRUCTURE FINANCING TOOLS

The financing of basic community infrastructure in the United States has become more complex and more expensive as each year passes. It has become more complex because we are continually expanding our urbanized areas and, thereby, requiring increased quantities of infrastructure. Table 1.4 shows some basic trends for the US from 1980 to 2020. The urbanization of the nation's population has continued and with continued urbanization comes increasing numbers of people and households looking to government for services, including the provision of infrastructure. The population continues its shift to metropolitan areas,[2] although at a lower rate

DOI: 10.4324/9781003336075-2

TABLE 1.1   State and Local Government Revenue: 1993, 2000, 2018

	1993	2000	2018	Percent Change
Total Revenue	$1,270,748,009	$1,942,328,438	$4,081,253,658	221.2
State	$805,196,100	$1,280,829,249	$2,630,221,402	226.7
Local	$681,780,357	$1,013,824,631	$1,451,032,256	112.8
Taxes	$594,299,587	$872,351,114	$1,761,402,148	196.4
State	$353,849,819	$539,655,337	$1,022,783,253	189
Local	$240,449,768	$332,695,777	$738,618,895	207.2
Property Tax	$189,743,134	$249,177,604	$547,038,543	188.3
State	$7,796,392	$10,996,021	$17,457,845	123.9
Local	$181,946,742	$238,181,583	$529,580,698	191.1
Charges & Misc	$248,677,334	$377,021,617	$788,897,979	217.2
State	$111,458,679	$170,746,508	$387,057,415	247.3
Local	$137,218,655	$206,275,109	$401,840,564	192.8
Educational Expenditures				
State	$90,367,707	$138,329,956	$322,250,848	256.6
Local	$251,919,383	$383,282,151	$774,016,015	207.2
Transportation Expenditures				
State	$43,673,625	$61,941,936	$116,397,678	166.5
Local	$37,204,079	$39,393,974	$107,557,530	189.1
Revenue Minus Education & Transportation				
State	$671,154,768	$1,080,557,357	$2,191,572,876	226.5
Local	$392,656,895	$591,148,506	$569,458,711	45

Source: Bureau of the Census, State, and Local Government Finances, yearly.

TABLE 1.2   State and Local Government Revenue per Capita: 1993, 2000, 2018

	1993	2000	2018	Percent Change
Total Revenue	$4,927	$6,902	$12,475	153.2
State	$3,122	$4,551	$8,039	157.5
Local	$2,643	$3,603	$4,435	67.8
Taxes	$2,304	$3,100	$5,384	133.6
State	$1,372	$1,918	$3,126	127.9
Local	$932	$1,182	$2,258	142.2
Property Tax	$736	$885	$1,672	127.3
State	$30	$39	$53	76.5
Local	$705	$846	$1,619	129.4
Charges & Misc.	$964	$1,340	$2,411	150.1
State	$432	$607	$1,183	173.8
Local	$532	$733	$1,228	130.9
Educational Expenditures				
State	$350	$492	$985	181.1
Local	$977	$1,362	$2,366	142.2
Transportation Expenditures				
State	$169	$220	$356	110.1
Local	$144	$140	$329	127.9
Revenue Minus Education & Transportation				
State	$2,602	$3,840	$6,699	157.4
Local	$1,522	$2,101	$1,741	14.3

Source: Bureau of the Census, State and Local Government Finances, yearly.

TABLE 1.3 State and Local Government Revenue Real per Capita: 1993–2018 (2018 = 100)

	1993	2018	Percent Change
Total Revenue	$8,580	$12,475	45.4
State	$5,437	$8,039	47.9
Local	$4,603	$4,435	−3.7
Taxes	$4,013	$5,384	34.2
State	$2,389	$3,126	30.8
Local	$1,624	$2,258	39.1
Property Tax	$1,281	$1,672	30.5
State	$53	$53	1.4
Local	$1,228	$1,619	31.8
Charges & Misc.	$1,679	$2,411	43.6
State	$753	$1,183	57.2
Local	$926	$1,228	32.6
Educational Expenditures			
State	$610	$985	61.4
Local	$1,701	$2,366	39.1
Transportation Expenditures			
State	$295	$356	20.6
Local	$251	$329	30.9
Revenue Minus Education & Transportation			
State	$4,532	$6,699	47.8
Local	$2,651	$1,741	34.3

Source: Bureau of the Census, State and Local Government Finances, yearly.

TABLE 1.4 Metropolitan Population and Cities by Population Categories: 1980, 2000, 2020

	1980	2000	2020	Percent Change, 1980–2020
Population (000)				
Total (000s)	227,226	282,162	329,938	45.2
Metropolitan (000s)	209,936	263,924	311,770	48.5
Non-Metropolitan (000s)	17,289	18,238	18,168	5.1
Percent Urban	78.2	81.4	82.7	
Cities 500K and Over				
Number	22	29	37	68.2
Population (000s)	28,400	35,888	44,894	58.1
Per City (000s)	1290.9	1237.5	1213.3	−6
Cities 100K to 500K				
Number	147	213	289	96.6
Population (000s)	28,400	40,193	52,151	83.6
Per City (000s)	193.2	188.7	180.5	−6.6
Cities Under 100K				
Number	18,513	19,214	19,188	3.6
Population (000s)	83,800	98,800	111,724	33.3
Per City (000s)	4.5	5.1	5.8	28.6

Source: Bureau of the Census.

than in the past.[3] Both the number and the populations of urban areas have continued to grow, with growth of the medium-sized cities being the greatest. In both the medium and largest cities, the population per city declined, simply indicating that the cities added to that size grouping would be at the lower end of the size range, thus reducing the average size.

But increased numbers of people in cities alone understates the demand. As incomes have increased, the public's expectations of and demand for public facilities have grown. Schools are no longer aggregations of classrooms but have become multimedia learning and social/cultural centers. This transition has greatly increased the cost of providing educational facilities. The same is true for parks and recreational facilities. Gone are the days when a ballfield was simply an otherwise vacant area where ball was played. Now they are stadiums with all the accoutrements, including red dirt. A fire department no longer simply puts out fires; today, it offers advanced life support. These evolutions are responses to public demands. Few would doubt that the quality of modern public services is greatly improved.[4] Few would doubt that the cost of these services has greatly increased.

The federal government has long since reached a peak in being a source of growth revenue for state and local governments. Since 1987, the federal portion of state and local revenues has remained constant at about 20 percent, leaving state and local governments to rely on their own revenue-generating abilities to meet the demands of the public.[5] It might be argued that the federal government failed in its responsibilities for many of the increased costs being borne by local governments.[6]

A series of events during the 1970s and 1980s reshaped local public finance. First of all, inflation became an issue.[7] Prior to the 1970s and 1980s, this was not the case. One of the more pernicious aspects of inflation is that it significantly weakens the effective revenue of fixed-base taxes, such as the motor fuel tax. Inflation increases the cost that fixed-base revenue sources are to cover without increasing the means to pay those costs. Inflation increases the cost of road construction and maintenance but does nothing to the proceeds derived from a 6-cent or 8-cent per gallon levy. In the face of such a problem, the logical thing to do is to raise the fixed-base tax. Property taxes, while not fixed-base as such, still require action to be increased. The action required is an increase in the assessed or taxable value of the property.

Inflation was an especially important consideration during the period 1970 through 2004. These were also the formative years of impact fee experimentation and judicial review. During this period, inflation averaged 4.95 percent per year or about twice the long-term rate of inflation. Inflation peaked in 1980 at 13.5 percent, while the year-over-year 1979–1980 rate peaked at over 17 percent. Such rates of price growth meant that the purchasing power of fixed-base taxes, such as the motor fuels tax, declined by 13.5 percent during 1980 while costs grew at the rate of inflation.

One of the commodities most responsive to inflation is real estate, including development property. In fact, real property inflation tends to proceed faster than general inflation.[8] General inflation increased public facility operating and capital costs, but it also increased the prices of both new and existing homes, thereby increasing the property taxes on those properties. It should not be surprising that California's Proposition 13 was enacted in 1978, during a period of unprecedented inflation. Proposition 13 rolled back taxable property values to 1975 and capped their rate of increase.[9] Massachusetts soon followed in 1980 with Proposition 2½, which took its name from the limit on property taxes being no more than 2.5 percent of the taxable value.[10] Since the referendum enactment of these two limits, all states have taken some action on limiting property taxes.[11] Thus, property taxes tend to act like fixed-base taxes because of the limitations imposed by legislation or constitutional amendment.

It was during this period that local governments found themselves faced with conflicting demands:

- Increase the supply of facilities, especially infrastructure, to larger populations;
- Increase the quality of public facilities, also to larger populations; and
- Avoid tax increases in meeting these demands.

As these events unfolded, the philosophy of taxation moved more toward the use of the *Benefit Principle* and away from the *Ability to Pay Principle*.[12] This shift, combined with continuing urbanization and inflation eroding the tax base, set the stage for "alternative" sources of revenue.

Local jurisdictions were also being compelled by federal government to make massive investments in water pollution control facilities.[13] These investments were originally funded up to 85 percent by federal grants. They are now funded by federal loans amounting to only 45 percent. The highway system that was funded primarily by federal sources has fallen into disrepair with increasing congestion because of the inadequacy of federal funding. States elected not to assume the primary role that the federal government was abandoning for precisely the same reason that the federal government was abandoning it: The cost. The responsibility for these and other major public investments has fallen to local jurisdictions by default. Where local governments attempted to assume these responsibilities, they were met with the "taxpayers' revolt," a reaction to the increase in property taxes that resulted from increasing local absorption of these responsibilities. Clearly, some other means of funding were needed. When the power to tax proved ineffective, local jurisdictions looked to their police powers as a means to address the problem.

American local jurisdictions have great discretion in the exercise of their power to protect the public's health, safety, and welfare. By contrast, they have almost no discretion in the exercise of their power to tax. It was natural then that the police powers would be turned to as an alternative. Local communities found that growth and development meant that more traffic, wastewater, and school children somehow had to be accommodated. Absent the funds to make physical improvements, congestion resulted and with congestion came citizen outrage. Increasingly, local elected officials faced a public demand to reduce taxes and maintain or even increase services. In such an environment, growth and development came to be viewed by many as detrimental rather than beneficial.[14] The detrimental aspects of urban growth provided the basis to invoke police powers and protect the public against the congestion and loss of "quality of life" that further growth and development would entail.

The impact fee arose not out of any great thought or plan, but simply from desperation resulting from conflicting demands placed on local officials. Citizens demanded quality public services and taxpayers insisted on lower taxes. Builders demanded that they be allowed to serve the clearly apparent market for their products and those that earned their livings from development fought for their jobs. Local governments were vested with the authority to impose reasonable conditions on new developments that were consistent with the protection of public health, safety and welfare in all of its manifestations. The impact fee filled this role.

Impact fees were not the first option turned to. Developers were required to make dedications, initially of land and later of cash or land. In states where required dedications were seen as unacceptable, developers were allowed to proffer—"voluntarily" offer—land or cash payments to offset infrastructure costs. While dedications and proffers addressed the problem, they were, at best, an incomplete approach. Required dedications or proffers could only be made by large developers while the scale of most development is small, thus assuring that insufficient resources were being directed to infrastructure. Additionally, it places larger-scale developers at a competitive disadvantage, something that was contrary to good planning. The payment in lieu of dedications became the basis for the impact fee. But unlike payment in lieu of a required dedication, the impact fee would be a required payment of money by all new developments, thus eliminating any competitive advantages or disadvantages. While required dedications and proffers remain, today the impact fee, by whatever name, is the evolving alternative to taxes.

To understand the evolution of the impact fee it may be helpful to understand the state of urban infrastructure by considering a representative example. The small community of Key West, Florida, originally a pirate enclave, which still maintains certain of those traditions today, is an island jutting out into the Straits of Florida. The city had been dumping its untreated sewage into the Straits. In order for the City of Key West to fund an Environmental Protection Agency mandated sewage treatment system, it would have to raise the monthly bill for each homeowner by $65 to fund the expansion with revenue bonds.[15] An increase of $65 per month was considered to be outrageous, and the citizens turned it down, thus creating an environmental and funding crisis. This crisis ultimately became an issue in the further development of the city, in that the City was barred from making new sewer connections, and thus new construction could not proceed. A cost-sharing agreement was struck between the City and the development interests that included a monthly bill increase of $15, which, combined with an impact fee, funded the sewage treatment system, and development was allowed to proceed. Everyone located north-east of Key West should be eternally grateful that it solved this problem, for the City was pumping its raw sewage into the Gulf Stream.

A number of policy issues are raised in this simple Key West example. The community had to be threatened with a shut-down of the construction industry before they would address the water pollution problem and, at the same time, the water pollution problems within the Straits of Florida and the Gulf Stream were redefined from being a national problem to being solely a problem for Key West.[16] Beginning with the Reagan Administration, the federal government suggested that there was a need for a conservative reform program and that responsibilities were going to be shifted from what was seen as an inefficient federal government to the much more efficient and responsive states and local governments. Of course, funding did not follow this shifting of responsibility. The states elected to absent themselves from this affair, leaving the funding problem to the mayors and councils. This is not to suggest that the states played no role. Quite the contrary. The states joined the federal government in filing suits against the local jurisdictions that failed to meet either federal or state mandated standards.

As sanitary and road systems were falling apart, public school facilities became increasingly over-crowded in the growing areas of the nation. Like sanitary and road infrastructure, school construction tended to be financed from inelastic revenue sources, and these too failed to keep pace with need. The result has been public schools where maintenance has been grossly postponed, and facilities crowded to an extent never thought possible. Certainly, the question needs to be asked: Why would enlightened people allow such conditions to continue?

While there are long, complex, and most likely wrong answers to this question, it must be noted that this type and pace of growth is not experienced nationwide or even statewide. In rapidly growing Florida, the actual growth areas are confined to no more than 10 percent of the geographic area of the state. For the state to step in and provide funding would mean taxing both the growing and the non-growing (and therefore poorer[17]) areas, with the result being taxing the poor to subsidize the rich. The state's legislatures joined the federal government in the position that if the needs were great enough, the prosperous growth areas had the ability to fund the improvements needed to serve growth. What they lacked was the willingness to raise the funds.

Now, given this situation, what are the alternatives? Obviously raising taxes did not get very far. This is not to suggest that taxes were not raised, for some were. But the increases were simply insufficient to respond to the magnitude of the needs. There was quite a movement to restrict growth to that level which could be accommodated by existing infrastructure. This position was hotly opposed by the building industry. Impact fees were an alternative to further congestion or the shutting down of new construction. Impact fees charged new construction and generated revenue that the community could use to expand the physical infrastructure needed to accommodate growth.

However, impact fees, like all financing mechanisms, have drawbacks. Capital improvements and infrastructure are needed "up front," but impact fees dribble in.[18] Roads, schools, parks, and utilities are all needed ahead of development. The problem is that funding is not available "up front" unless it is put up by the developer or borrowed from the host local government. Both of these actions are assiduously avoided by developers and local governments. Impact fees, while becoming an important component of local government finance, do not address the timing problem. Impact fees, as they are commonly implemented, charge new development when the construction is actually permitted. Thus, the impact fee receipts "dribble in" as construction occurs. While jurisdictions prefer revenues "dribbling in" to no revenues at all, what is needed are up-front revenues so that facilities can be constructed and be available as new development occurs. Alpharetta, Georgia, solves

this problem with bonding. The city received public approval of a general obligation bond issue for road and fire facilities improvements. A large portion of this debt was for growth accommodating improvements that would be paid for by impact fees. The impact fees collected were used to pay debt service, thereby reducing the necessary tax rate. The key to this program was the public's willingness to support a general obligation bond. This support facilitated an impact fee funding program that provided road and fire protection improvements "up front" and did so at the lowest possible cost.

The key to resolving the "dribble in" problem is bonding, but bonding requires a secure source of revenue that can be pledged. Impact fees are not considered to be secure because their receipt will rise and fall with the level of construction in a community. The solution is to create some type of security, borrow against that security, and then use impact fees to make the required payments.

1.2 IMPACT FEE AMOUNTS

How much are impact fees? This is not an easy question to answer because there is no single repository of what impact fees are assessed by which jurisdiction and for which facilities and land uses. Chapter 4 reports our own efforts to do this, but it is subject to numerous qualifications. Average impact fees for 2019 are reported in Table 1.5. For a single-family detached home, the average fees for each facility total $13,627. But note that not all jurisdictions charge all these fees and indeed many states restrict fees to a limited number of facilities (see Chapter 3). The average total of impact fees for multi-family units are considerably less, at $8,034. Yet, as we will show in Chapter 12, many jurisdictions charge the same impact fees for residential units regardless of their type and size. We show further in Chapter 5 that impact fees continue to increase over time.

TABLE 1.5 Average Fees by Land Use and Facility Type, 2019

Facility	Sample Size	Single-Family (Unit)	Multi-Family (Unit)	Retail (1,000 sf)	Office (1,000 sf)	Industrial (1,000 sf)
Roads	218	$3,691	$2,493	$5,970	$3,772	$2,143
Water	128	$4,249	$1,680	$654	$854	$889
Wastewater	138	$3,896	$1,986	$852	$1,217	$1,662
Drainage	56	$1,622	$852	$1,011	$815	$962
Parks	195	$2,993	$2,283	na	na	na
Library	62	$455	$344	na	na	na
Fire	130	$484	$370	$523	$503	$359
Police	103	$395	$295	$404	$270	$173
General Government	57	$1,573	$1,197	$665	$649	$388
Schools*	114	$5,395	$3,134	na	na	na
Total Non-Utility **	261	$9,887	$6,476	$6,439	$4,640	$2,877
Total*	270	$13,627	$8,034	$6,760	$5,407	$3,942

* Rarely charged to non-residential land uses, with the exception of school fees in California

** Average of total fees charged by jurisdictions, not sum of average fees by facility type (non-utility fee excludes water and wastewater fees)

Source: See Chapter 4.

1.3 TOTAL IMPACT FEE REVENUES

While it would be nice to know the total impact fee revenues generated by jurisdiction, by state, by year, and by facility, these data do not seem to exist. Instead, to get a sense of impact fee trends over time, we defer to a 2006 study reported by the Florida Legislative Committee on Intergovernmental Relations (LCIR). The study has not been updated.

The LCIR compiled data on impact fee revenues reported annually by counties, municipalities, independent special districts, and school districts during the period 1993 through 2004. Table 1.6 shows the growth in the number of counties, municipalities, special districts, and school districts reporting the collection of impact fees annually. For all but school districts, the growth in jurisdictions assessing impact fees grew by a third to half. School districts saw explosive growth, rising from nearly none through the 1990s to double-digits in the early 2000s. Table 1.7 breaks down impact fees by type of facility for which fees were collected, showing similar trends. Although these data are from a few decades ago, they illuminate past trends that help frame the current and future reliance on local governments on impact fees.

Table 1.8 reports impact fee revenues collected by category and total for each year. In 1993, reported impact fee revenues in Florida totaled $177 million. Eleven years later, in 2004, impact fee revenues totaled $1.07 billion. This growth in impact fee revenues represents a 505 percent increase with much of the accelerated growth since the late 1990s. This is an annual rate of increase of 17.8 percent per year. Cumulatively, from 1993 through 2004, reported impact fee revenues totaled nearly $5.3 billion. This represents approximately 23 percent of all local government infrastructure spending in the state of Florida at the time.[19]

Impact fee revenue collections vary by type of governmental entity. Between 1993 and 2004, counties accounted for the largest amount of impact fee revenue collections at $3.5 billion. Municipalities follow with $1.2 billion in impact fee revenue collections. Prior to 2002, school districts reported very few impact fee revenue collections. Since 2002, however, school districts have become

TABLE 1.6 Number of Governmental Entities Reporting Impact Fee Revenues for Fiscal Years 1993–2004

Year	Counties	Municipalities	Special Districts	School Districts	Annual Totals
1993	28	100	32	2	162
1994	26	108	32	1	167
1995	34	108	30	3	175
1996	34	125	32	2	193
1997	34	118	35	1	188
1998	35	134	33	3	205
1999	36	139	31	0	206
2000	34	148	37	1	220
2001	37	150	36	1	224
2002	40	155	44	15	254
2003	39	150	46	14	249
2004	39	154	46	19	258

Sources: Counties, municipalities, and independent special districts from the Florida Department of Financial Services and school districts from the Florida Department of Education, Office of Funding and Financial Reporting.

TABLE 1.7 Number of Governmental Entities Reporting Impact Fee Revenues by Fee Category, 1993–2004

Year	Public Safety	Physical Environment	Transportation	Economic Environment	Human Services	Culture and Recreation	Other (excl. School)	School	Annual Totals
1993	79	54	55	1	3	48	27	2	269
1994	77	63	55	4	2	51	30	1	283
1995	87	57	58	3	2	67	31	3	308
1996	89	62	70	2	2	70	36	2	333
1997	97	59	70	1	2	72	35	1	337
1998	110	64	71	2	3	83	38	3	374
1999	106	68	80	5	3	84	35	0	381
2000	112	75	82	5	2	89	42	1	408
2001	108	95	85	4	3	90	43	1	429
2002	115	97	87	3	3	87	55	15	462
2003	123	96	90	4	3	91	53	14	474
2004	128	111	83	4	2	97	48	19	492

Sources: Counties, municipalities, and independent special districts from the Florida Department of Financial Services and school districts from the Florida Department of Education, Office of Funding and Financial Reporting.

a major beneficiary of impact fees, with $500 million in impact fee collections, and the amount expected to grow substantially in the future. This increase in impact fee revenues is a result of Florida's rapid population growth, the growing number of local governments imposing impact fees, and the rising cost of land and building infrastructure.

The LCIR also reported impact fee revenues by fee category, notably transportation, physical environment, and public safety, among others, during the same time period. As a percentage of total cumulative revenues, transportation impact fees represented the largest impact fee category, totaling $2.2 billion or 38 percent of the total. Physical environment

TABLE 1.8 Annual Impact Fees Collected by Category, 1993–2004 (figures in thousands of dollars not adjusted)

Year	Public Safety	Physical Environment	Transportation	Economic Environment	Human Services	Culture and Recreation	Other (excl. School)	School	Annual Totals
1993	$13,359	$47,065	$84,797	$257	$3,104	$21,859	$6,426	$51	$176,918
1994	$17,962	$76,250	$91,299	$364	$5,900	$18,815	$8,222	$92	$218,904
1995	$13,516	$52,447	$91,767	$295	$9,233	$15,252	$26,401	$1,127	$210,038
1996	$12,085	$53,460	$91,115	$492	$8,706	$14,097	$26,320	$1,275	$207,549
1997	$26,750	$44,193	$137,231	$246	$10,055	$30,971	$13,804	$2,199	$265,448
1998	$28,283	$71,480	$133,889	$302	$11,374	$33,248	$18,123	$2,295	$298,995
1999	$31,270	$95,143	$163,352	$5,285	$19,887	$37,293	$22,255	na	$374,484
2000	$36,281	$86,835	$194,807	$312	$22,165	$51,724	$31,492	$3,429	$427,045
2001	$51,230	$161,538	$194,780	$762	$26,578	$51,131	$36,098	$3,505	$525,622
2002	$49,208	$197,441	$204,438	$1,269	$30,156	$61,187	$73,757	$124,451	$741,908
2003	$61,765	$173,228	$281,112	$2,133	$30,836	$73,717	$59,367	$117,673	$799,831
2004	$76,675	$210,580	$352,461	$2,322	$39,184	$88,200	$42,496	$258,581	$1,070,499
Total	$418,385	$1,269,661	$2,021,048	$14,037	$217,178	$497,493	$364,760	$514,680	$5,317,241

Source: Florida Legislative Committee on Intergovernmental Relations (2006).

impact fees represented the second-largest category, totaling $1.3 billion or 24 percent of the total.

1.4 IMPACT FEES OF THE FUTURE

Although more will be said about how impact fees of the future may be shaped to be sensitive to housing affordability and represent sound fiscal decision-making, in this section we introduce the topic in light of historical perspectives, emerging practices, and lingering realities.

Impact fees began as minor supplements to traditional sources of capital improvement finance. The water and sewer impact fees that were the issue in the 1975 case of *Contractors and Builders Association of Pinellas County v. City of Dunedin*[20] were $325 for water and $475 for sewage.[21] These 1975 amounts are substantially below the $4,320 of today.[22] Similarly, the "transportation" fee litigated in *Broward County v. Janis Development Corp.*[23] was $100, which is very much less than the average road impact fee of $2,326, even after considering inflation.[24] The amounts of impact fees thus began small and became much larger. The role of impact fees began as supplemental and is now primary. But the impact fee debate continues. That debate has evolved, however, from *whether* impact fees should be assessed at all to *how* they are assessed.

Between 2004 and 2006, the average impact fee for a single-family home grew by 41 percent, an annual rate of growth of 12 percent. In order for impact fees to assume the role that they have in local government finance, this type of growth has been necessary. But what about the future? A 2006 impact fee of $8,879 for a single-family home will grow to $15,910 in 5 years, $31,610 in 10, and $99,247 in 20 years. (See Figure 1.1, which illustrates this.) While this amount of money would yield substantial

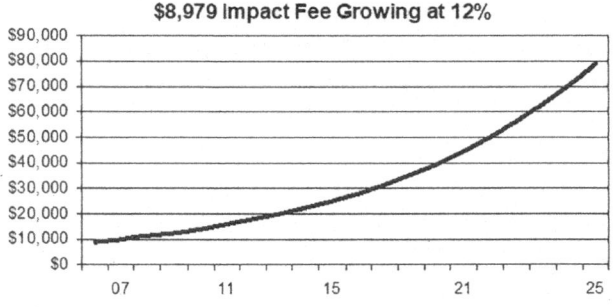

FIGURE 1.1 Compounded growth at 12 percent per year.

revenues to local governments, certain consequences with respect to housing costs would be expected to follow. However, the trends observed today suggest that impact fees will continue to rise at rapid rates until market forces or legislative restrictions rein them in. We discuss these issues in Chapter 5.

Such levels of impact fees elicit concerns about societal matters, especially the goal of home ownership and matters of equity. Impact fees are here to stay, so doing away with them in the name of home ownership or equity is not an option. But the manner and form of impact fees can be structured in order to have very different consequences on home ownership and equity. While these concepts of equity are important, the focus of this guidebook is how to address proportionate equity—that is, the extent to which an impact fee reflects the actual impact different housing units have on community facilities.

A critical aspect of proportionality is the extent to which impact fees are based on the impact of new development on facilities. Many impact fee programs assume that each residential unit has the same impact on facilities regardless of size, type, density, location, or other factors. Hence, the impact fee for a large single-family detached home is the same as for a small efficiency apartment despite the fact that census figures clearly show substantial differences in occupancy rates. These impact fees are described as "flat rate" fees and are inherently unfair. The result is that flat rate impact fees thus designed have a "regressive" effect; that is, they fall disproportionately on those with lower incomes than with higher ones.

1.5 THE PROBLEM OF REGRESSIVITY

Regressivity: a burden falling more heavily upon those with less income. This book focuses on methodologies for calculating impact fees that would help to ensure that regressive effects are minimized if not eliminated. Through taking an approach that correctly allocates the proportionate share, the resulting fees are not regressive. When done properly, impact fees, as presently practiced in many if not most places, would be reduced for smaller units on smaller lots, in locations where facilities currently exist, including public transit, and in configurations that economize, especially on vehicular trips.

A special concern is the effect of impact fees on housing cost and affordability. A common practice has been to charge residential impact fees based on the type of residence: single-family detached, single-family attached, multi-family, mobile home, etc. This method implicitly assumes that the only relevant distinction among dwellings is the type of unit and that there is at least some degree of homogeneity within unit types. Both of these implicit assumptions are simply incorrect. The net effect of the unit-type approach to levying impact fees has been to ignore all characteristics other than the type of dwelling unit. The result has been that while multi-family and mobile home units tend to have lower fees than detached units, a modest single-family detached unit of 1,200 square feet will pay the same amount as a mansion of 10,000 square feet or more. The problems inherent with such an approach led some jurisdictions to look for other variables that when applied can result in more equitable fee structures. Recently,

several jurisdictions have set impact fees that look to the size rather than the type of unit as the basis for assessing impact fees.[25] The premise of this approach is that it is the size of the dwelling, rather than its type, is the better predictor of impact on the need for infrastructure. Three examples illustrate the benefit of this approach.

One of the first jurisdictions to address the regressivity problem was Palm Beach County, Florida. Palm Beach County had been using a unit-type approach to residential impact fees and was dissatisfied with the relative burden on that approach between less expensive and more expensive dwellings. In response, the County incorporated unit size in calculating its residential impact fees. An example is its school impact fee, as shown in Table 1.9. Had the traditional unit-type approach been used, the single-family detached fee would have been around $5,000. Smaller and presumably more affordable units receive a substantial reduction in the fee paid. We explore this issue as it relates to school impact fees in Chapter 12.

Canton, Georgia, adopted park and recreation impact fees that also use unit size as the basis for fees, as shown in Table 1.10. It applies the fees to all development, not just residential land uses. The arguments are that nonpresidential development both benefits from park and recreation facilities as they attract new jobs, and they impact those facilities through a variety of organized events. As shown in the table, the park impact fee in

TABLE 1.9 Palm Beach County, Florida, School Impact Fees

Unit Size	Impact Fee
800 Square Feet and Under	$2,362
801–1,399	$4,330
1,400–1,999	$6,153
2,000–3,599	$6,608
3,600 and Over	$6,506

Source: Palm Beach County, Florida.

TABLE 1.10 Canton, Georgia, Impact Fees

Calculation Step	Figure
Total Growth Cost	$42,054,887
Residential	$26,094,512
Non-Residential	$4,349,086
Net Growth Cost*	$12,233,362
Residential	$10,485,738
New Residential Square Feet	$19,905,404
Cost per Square Foot	$0.53
Non-Residential	$2,250,246
New Non-Residential Square Feet	12,972,159
Cost per Square Foot	$0.17

*After amount paid by taxes

Canton is simply 53 cents per square foot of living area, regardless of the type of dwelling. It is also 17 cents per square foot for nonpresidential development.

These and several other jurisdictions have been shifting away from unit type and toward assessment bases that reduce the regressivity of impact fees while still properly assessing fees based on impact. These attempts have been rather cautious and have tended to be incremental steps rather than giant leaps. Each jurisdiction has tended to build upon the experience of the previous one and to extend anti-regressive methodologies. This evolution has not been without its criticisms. Some criticisms have been based on statistical analysis and others on the basis of dislike of the resulting fees. See later chapters for a much more detailed discussion of these issues.

In summary, impact fees are here to stay. But the role and scope of impact fees will continue to evolve. The task is to continue the expansion of new methodologies that satisfy the legal criteria for impact fees while accommodating both the interests of cities and counties looking to finance an ever-increasing share of capital costs and the legitimate concerns of the shelter industry for equity in the application of impact fees. This book deals with the regressivity problem and suggests methods of developing impact fees that are progressive and sensitive to the impact on affordability.

NOTES

1 *Compania General De Tabacos De Filipinas v Collector of Internal Revenue*, 275 US 87 (1927).
2 There is a circularity here as new metropolitan areas continue to be created, thus adding to the metropolitan population by the simple act of creating more metropolitan areas.
3 In 1920 the urban population first equaled the non-urban population in the US Since then, urbanization has grown to more than 80 percent in 2020.
4 Nostalgia notwithstanding.
5 For a review, see www.taxpolicycenter.org/taxvox/census-governments-illustrates-declining-aid-localities-other-trends-state-and-local-finance.
6 For instance, the Clean Water Act required massive expenditures to be made largely by local governments. Of course, it could be argued that it was those local jurisdictions that dirtied the water so the burden of clearing that same water should be borne by them.
7 From 1929 (the first year of consistent price indices) to date, the annual increase in prices has averaged 3.3 percent. Excluding two periods of rapid inflation, the long-term rate of inflation drops to about 2 percent.
8 Between 1980 and 2000, all prices rose at 3.8 percent per year while shelter costs rose at 4.4 percent. See *Stat. Abstract of the U.S.*, 2001, p. 454. The median sales price of a new single-family home grew by 4.9 percent per year. See *Ibid*. p. 598. The median price of existing home sales rose by 4.1 percent per year.
9 See John Kirlin. *The Political Economy of Fiscal Limits*. Lexington, MA: Lexington Books.
10 *Ibid.*
11 Therese J. McGuire, "Proposition 13 and Its Offspring: For Good or Evil?", 52 *National Tax Journal*, 1999, 129–138.
12 Musgrave, Richard A., and Peggy B. Musgrave. 1989. *Public Finance in Theory and Practice*. 5th ed. New York: McGraw-Hill.
13 The "Water Pollution Control Act," commonly known as the Clean Water Act, PL 92-500.
14 See William K. Reilley, *The Use of Land*, New York: Crowell, 1972.
15 One of the authors (Nicholas) served as a consultant to the City of Key West during this period and these facts are from the author's on-site observations.
16 Ultimately the federal government did agree to finance a portion of the improvement costs.
17 In Florida, the per capita incomes of the non-growing portions of the state amount to approximately 50 percent of those of the growth areas. See *Florida Statistical Abstract*, 1995, pp. 199–204.
18 Sometimes this is referred to as "trickle in."
19 See J. Nicholas et al, "Impact Fees in Florida: Their Evolution, Methodology, Current Issues and Comparisons with Other States," prepared for the Florida Impact Fee Task Force, Tallahassee, September 2005, citing data from the 2003 Census of Government.
20 329 So. 2d 314.
21 *Ibid.* at 315. These fees are for a single-family detached unit.

22 The 1975 water fee of $325 would be $1,265 after adjustment for changes in the CPI, and the $475 sewer fee would amount to $1,603. These indicate that the relative amount of Dunedin's fees has remained about the same.

23 311 So.2d 371

24 Adjusting the $200 from 1974 to 2002 by the CPI yields a 2002 value of $683.

25 See J. Nicholas, "On The Progression of Impact Fees," *Journal of the American Planning Association*, Vol. 58, No.4, 1992.

2 LEGAL FOUNDATIONS[1]

In one form or another, impact fees now exist in nearly all states and are a common technique used to generate revenue for capital funding necessitated by new development.[2] To date, approximately half of the states have enacted impact fee legislation,[3] and in most other states impact fees are adopted pursuant to home rule powers or pursuant to individual local government enablement. Impact fees are charges imposed by local governments that take the form of a predetermined monetary payment—a fee—and are required of developers as a condition for development permission to fund capital expansion of large-scale public facilities and services. Such fees play an integral part in giving local governments the ability to cope with many burdens of rapid population growth, such as the need for new parks, roads, schools, jails, public buildings, sewer and water treatment facilities, and public facilities, and public safety (fire, police, and EMS) facilities.[4]

Historically, it has been a primary function of state and local governments to construct, operate, maintain, and improve the basic physical infrastructure of American communities. However, as a result of three significant events in American history, this traditional approach began to break down. The first of these events was the sharp rise in inflation in the 1970s[5] and the decimation of fixed-based taxes such as the motor fuel tax. The next was the federal government's fiscal retrenchment that began in 1982 and has continued since then, thus reducing the funds made available to local jurisdictions. The third factor leading to the breakdown of the traditional approach was the general hostility to the taxation of real property, thus forcing local jurisdictions to look elsewhere to fund the ever-increasing quantity and quality demands of constituents.[6]

Because these factors were occurring at a time when the pace of urban development was increasing, both the demand for and the cost of investment in public infrastructure began to climb at a time when the available financial resources were falling. As a result, there arose an increasing need for investment concurrent with declining means.

Due to the lessening of federal and state funding for such infrastructure facilities as water pollution control and highway system expansion and repairs, an increasing share of the responsibility to pay for these and other public investments fell directly on local jurisdictions by default.[7] In order to assume control of providing these infrastructure needs, local governments were forced to pay the associated costs, commonly by raising local property taxes. In turn, they were then hit by the "taxpayers revolt." Increasingly local elected officials faced a public demand to increase public services without increasing taxes. After failing to remedy this dilemma through taxation, many jurisdictions looked to their police power as a means of addressing the problem.

In terms of police power, most local governments have great discretion to regulate in order to protect the public's health, safety, and welfare. In contrast, local governments have almost no discretion in the exercise of their power to tax. It was natural, then, that local governments would turn to police power, where they had discretion, in order to finance infrastructure needs.[8] Negative aspects of urban growth, including congestion and loss of quality of life that further growth and development would entail, provided the framework for invoking the police power to protect the public. Thus, in order to make up for the public service funding lost as a result of the conditions mentioned above, local governments

DOI: 10.4324/9781003336075-3

began to impose conditions on development that were consistent with the protection of the public's health, safety, and welfare. This was accomplished through the implementation of the impact fee.

To see how impact fees originated, however, it is necessary to understand the division of public services that had arisen in American public administration, namely governmental and proprietary services. Governmental services were those needed in order to promote the health, safety, and welfare of the public but not provided for by private entities (e.g., police and fire protection and the maintenance of public roads and parks). Proprietary services, on the other hand, are those services created for the same purposes but which can be and frequently are provided by the private sector and for which service charges are imposed by the party performing the service (e.g., trash collection and water service).

Local governments had long charged for proprietary services, and these charges— often called "user fees"—were extremely common. These user charges were possible because the benefit of providing a service could be isolated to individual users and, if the individual user failed to pay the charge, the user could be excluded from use or consumption.[9] Governmental services, on the other hand, are classified differently because the cost of performing a service cannot be identified with a single user, nor can individuals be easily excluded from use or benefit. Under this framework, initial proponents of the impact fee had the objective of applying the principles of public finance, which had hitherto been applied only to proprietary services, to governmental services. This type of application had the effect of reducing, if not eliminating, the distinction between proprietary and governmental services.[10]

The legal implications of enacting a program such as this were unknown at the time. Fearing that the fees would be seen as an unconstitutional tax, many impact fees to pay for governmental services were initially set very low. For example, the "land-use fee" used in Broward County, Florida,[11] imposed for road improvement, was $100 per residence. Even so, this particular charge was struck down by a Florida court as an unconstitutional tax.[12] The court based its holding on the theory that the fee exceeded the county's cost of regulation, which would have justified its collection.[13] This holding, like court holding in many other states, demanded that fees or charges assessed under the police power for the impact of new development be no greater than the costs borne by the governmental entity in "regulating" new development; otherwise, such a fee would be considered a tax.

Ultimately, both the definition of regulation and a detailed accounting of the "costs of regulating" development allowed local governments to base the imposition of impact fees on police power and avoid the tax label.[14] Once at this stage, local governments were able to have their impact fee programs classified as regulatory by demonstrating that the new development creates the need for new and expanded facilities, and then collecting from the new development its proportionate share of the cost of expanding facility capacity. Even though local governments labeled impact fees as regulatory, courts still required local governments to produce calculations and other data to support the reasonableness of their fees.[15]

2.1 EVOLUTION OF IMPACT FEES

Required dedication was the earliest significant land-use regulation developed to shift a portion of the capital expense burden to developers. The practice of local governments conditioning their approval of a subdivision plat upon the developer's agreement to provide and dedicate certain improvements is now a well-accepted part of subdivision regulation and generally approved by the courts.[16]

The "in-lieu" fee was developed as a refinement of required dedications. For example, requiring each subdivision to dedicate land for educational purposes would not solve the problem of providing school facilities for developing suburban areas because the sites would often be inadequate in size and imperfectly located. The in-lieu fee sought to solve this problem by substituting a money payment for dedication of land when the local government determined that the latter was not feasible.[17]

Although the impact fee owes its origin to the impact analysis concepts of federal environmental law, it is functionally similar to the in-lieu fee in that both are required payments for capital facilities. In fact, the terms are sometimes used interchangeably.[18] Impact fees are, however, a more flexible approach to private funding of public infrastructure. Impact fees are designed to apportion the cost of new infrastructure among the new residents who create the need for these improvements. The fees, at least in theory, represent the pro rata share of the cost of providing a public service to an individual residential, commercial, or industrial unit.

The distinction between in-lieu fees and impact fees results in several decided advantages for impact fees. First, impact fees can be utilized to fund types of facilities and capital expenses, which are not normally the subject of dedication requirements and can more easily be applied to facilities to be constructed outside the development (extra-developmental or system infrastructure) as well as those inside the development (intra-developmental or project infrastructure). For example, since in-lieu fees are predicated on dedication requirements, they can be used only where required dedications can be appropriately utilized. In the case of sewer and water facilities, public safety facilities, and similar capital outlays, required dedications frequently are not an appropriate device for shifting a portion of the capital costs to the development because one facility (and parcel of land) can service a very wide area, and there is little need for additional land to extend these services.[19]

Second, impact fees can be applied to developments platted before the advent of required dedications or in-lieu fees and thus impose on new development its fair share of these capital costs. This advantage is particularly important in a state such as Florida, where hundreds of thousands of vacant lots were platted prior to the use of required dedications by local governments.[20]

A third advantage is that impact fees can be applied to condominium, apartment, commercial, and industrial developments, which create the need for extra-developmental capital expenditures, but which generally escape dedication or in-lieu fee requirements because of the small land area involved or the inapplicability of subdivision regulations.

Finally, impact fees can be collected when building permits are issued, when the growth creating a need for new capital facilities occurs, rather than at the time of platting.[21]

2.1.1 Constitutionality of Impact Fees

Developer funding of public capital facilities—whether in-lieu fees, required dedications, or impact fees—has been justified by several theories. Shifting the burden of the cost of new facilities from the general public to the people who create the need for the facilities has been viewed as a logical and fair method of accommodating growth. Commentators have argued that, absent developer exactions, the developer may reap a windfall at the expense of the general public, which must bear the costs generated by the new development. Others have extolled the "privilege" theory, which holds that, in exchange for the privilege of developing, the developer must be responsible for the costs of public facilities necessary to service the project.[22]

In spite of these conceptual supports, impact fees are generally subjected to a two-tiered constitutional attack. The preliminary objection is that they are not authorized by state statute or constitution and therefore are void as *ultra vires*. If statutory authority is found or unneeded, the local impact fee ordinance is alternatively challenged as an unreasonable regulation exceeding police power or as a disguised tax which violates various state constitutional strictures.[23]

Additionally, impact fees have been challenged as discriminatory and a violation of equal protection principles since different types of development may pay varying amounts and those who developed prior to the enactment of the impact fee may have made no contribution toward infrastructure. Finally, impact fees have been challenged as violations of property rights and therefore as regulatory "takings" without just compensation.[24]

2.1.2 Land-Use Regulation or Taxation?

Because impact fees are conceptually and functionally similar to dedications and other land-use regulations, they can be considered land-use regulations, which are generally considered valid exercises of police power. Arguably, however, impact fees could also be classified as taxes, particularly if a court considers simplistic distinctions between taxes and regulations, and does not look closely at the purposes of impact fees and the restrictions placed on their collection and use.

The choice a court makes between these two classifications is important since this issue will often determine the validity of the exaction at issue. If the tax label is adopted, the impact fee will be invalidated unless express and specific statutory authorization for the tax exists. Even if statutory authorization is present, constitutional limitations on taxation may still invalidate the statute. Alternatively, if the impact fee is construed as a police power regulation, very broad legislative delegation will suffice.

The clear trend among state courts is to validate such extra-developmental capital funding payment requirements as a valid exercise

of police power. Nonetheless, the issue will not go away, and several recent cases return to the fee-versus-tax dispute, which was resolved many years ago in most states by judicial decision or impact fee enabling statutes.[25]

Those courts applying the tax label to impact fees either implicitly or expressly rely on two rationales. The first is the simplistic observation that impact fees are a positive exaction of funds and therefore a tax. This criterion is an untenable basis for distinction because it exalts form over function. It ignores similar police power regulations, which mandate that the developer expend considerable funds for streets, sewers, and other capital project improvements within the development. Also, distinctions between impact fees and similar police power regulations, made on the basis that impact fees are imposed prior to the issuance of building permits rather than as part of the plat approval process, are distinctions without a difference. In either case, funds must be expended by the developer prior to development

The second rationale used to label system infrastructure impact fees "taxes" is the theory that funds for educational, recreational, and public safety purposes cannot be raised under police power.[26] This assertion is based on the conviction that such facilities should be financed solely from general revenues provided by the community as a whole. There is no constitutional mandate, however, that educational, recreational, and other facilities be underwritten by the general population rather than by the new development creating the need for additional improvements. Furthermore, this rationale employs an unduly restrictive and inflexible conception of local land-use regulatory power.[27]

Finally, some courts avoid this classification issue altogether by viewing some impact fees as charges for services rendered rather than as either police power regulations or invalid taxes. Impact fees under this analysis are generally upheld as authorized under general and broad statutory authority. Utah decisions, for example, have upheld sewer connection fees and similar charges as neither "taxes nor assessment but payments for services rendered."[28]

2.1.3 Tests for Impact Fee Validity

Two early landmark decisions placed an almost insurmountable burden on local governments seeking money payments for system infrastructure capital spending from developers whose activities necessitated such expenditures. In *Pioneer Trust & Savings Bank v. Village of Mount Prospect*,[29] a developer challenged the validity of an ordinance requiring subdividers to dedicate one acre per 60 residential lots for schools, parks, and other public purposes. In determining whether required dedications or money payments for recreational or educational purposes represented a valid exercise of the police power, the Illinois Supreme Court propounded the "specifically and uniquely attributable test." The court focused on the origin of the need for the new facilities and held that, unless the village could prove that the demand for additional facilities was "specifically and uniquely attributable" to the particular subdivision, such requirements were an unreasonable regulation not authorized by police power. Thus, where schools had become overcrowded because of the "total development of the community," the subdivider could not be compelled to help fund new facilities that his activity would necessitate.[30]

The New York court in *Gulest Associates, Inc. v. Town of Newburgh*[31] delineated a related and equally restrictive test. In that case, developers attacked an ordinance that charged in-lieu fees for recreational purposes. The amounts collected were to be used by the town for neighborhood park, playground, or recreational purposes, including the acquisition of property. The court held that the money payment requirement was an unreasonable regulation tantamount to an unconstitutional taking because the funds collected were not used solely for the benefit of the residents of the particular subdivision charged but rather could be used in any section of town for any recreational purpose.[32]

In essence, the *Gulest* "direct benefit" test required that funds collected from required payments for capital expenditures be specifically tied to a benefit directly conferred on the homeowners in the subdivision that was charged. If the recreation fees were used to purchase a park outside the subdivision, the direct benefit test was not met, and the ordinance was invalid.

Perhaps the reason for this initial restrictive approach was an underlying judicial suspicion that payment requirements for system capital expenditures were, in reality, a tax. Unlike zoning, payment requirements did not fit neatly into traditional conceptions of police power regulations. By applying the restrictive *Pioneer Trust* and *Gulest* tests, courts imposed the restrictive requirements of a special assessment on such payment requirements. This was consistent with perceiving them as a tax. Unfortunately, it effectively precluded their use for most system capital funding purposes. The *Pioneer Trust* and *Gulest* tests, therefore, quickly became difficult to reconcile with the planning and funding problems imposed on local governments by the constant acceleration of suburban growth. This restrictiveness also became difficult to rationalize with the judicial view of zoning ordinances as presumptively valid. As public policy concerns about the burden of economic growth became even more evident, the state courts turned away from the stringent *Pioneer Trust* and *Gulest* standards. Although the results of these decisions are progressive, the measure of police power criteria developed by the courts is far from enlightening.

Some courts nominally retained the *Pioneer Trust* test but reached patently contrary results without any explanation of the discrepancy. Other courts adopted a privilege theory, under which granting the privilege to subdivide entitles local governments to require payments for extra-developmental capital spending in return; the imposition of these payment requirements is viewed more as a part of a transaction than as an exercise of the police power. Still other courts have deferred to legislative judgments and eschewed constitutional analysis of such payment requirements.[33]

In contrast to these results-oriented techniques, the Wisconsin Supreme Court in *Jordan v. Village of Menomonee Falls*[34] suggested a more rational constitutional approach. A two-part "rational nexus" test of reasonableness for judging the validity of extra-developmental impact and in-lieu fees can be discerned in the decision. In response to a developer's attack upon the ordinance as unauthorized by state statute and as an unconstitutional taking without just compensation, the *Jordan* court addressed the constitutionality of in-lieu fees for education and recreational purposes. After concluding that the fee payments were statutorily authorized, the court focused first on the *Pioneer Trust* "specifically and uniquely attributable" test.

The Wisconsin Supreme Court expressed concern that it was virtually impossible for a municipality to prove that money payment or land dedication requirements were assessed to meet a need solely generated by a particular subdivision. Suggesting a substitute test, the court held that money payment and dedication requirements for educational and recreational purposes were a valid exercise of the police power if there was a "reasonable connection" between the need for additional facilities and the growth generated by the subdivision. This first "rational nexus" was sufficiently established if the local government could demonstrate that a series of subdivisions had generated the need to provide educational and recreational facilities for the benefit of this stream of new residents. In the absence of contrary evidence, such proof showed that the need for the facilities was sufficiently attributable to the activity of the

particular developer to permit the collection of fees for financing required improvements.[35]

The *Jordan* court also rejected the *Gulest* direct benefit requirement, declining to treat the fees as a special assessment. It imposed no requirements that the ordinance restrict the funds to the purchase of school and park facilities that would directly benefit the assessed subdivision. Instead, the court concluded that the relationship between the expenditure of funds and the benefits accruing to the subdivision providing funds was a fact issue pertinent to the reasonableness of the payment requirement under the police power.

The *Jordan* court did not expressly define the "reasonableness" required in the expenditure of system capital funds; however, a second "rational nexus" was by implication required between the expenditure of the funds and benefits accruing to the subdivision. The court concluded that this second rational nexus was met if the fees were to be used exclusively for site acquisition, and the amount spent by the village on the construction of additional school facilities was greater than the amounts collected from the developments creating the need for additional facilities.[36]

This second rational nexus requirement inferred from *Jordan*, therefore, is met if a local government can demonstrate that its actual or projected system capital expenditures are greater than the capital payments required of those developments. Such proof establishes a sufficient benefit to a particular subdivision in the stream of residential growth so that the system payment requirements may be deemed to be reasonable under the police power. The concept of benefits received is clearly distinct from the concept of needs attributable. As the *Jordan* court recognized, the benefit accruing to the development, although it need not be direct, is a necessary factor in analyzing the reasonableness of payment requirements for system infrastructure capital funding. Simply stated, the rational nexus tests—i.e., the dual rational nexus test, has two components: (1) impact fees may be no more than the government's infrastructure costs which are reasonably attributable to the new development, and (2) the new development required to pay impact fees must benefit from the expenditure of those fees.

With the adoption by most state courts of the dual rational nexus test, the focus of impact fee controversies shifted to the calculation of impact fees so as to meet the first prong of the test. Since the test provides that a developer can be charged no more than her proportionate share of the cost of new infrastructure, the calculation process must take into account not only the cost of the new infrastructure that the new development requires but credits for payments that have been or will be made by the developer outside the impact fee program. Furthermore, the developer cannot be required to pay for the unmet infrastructure costs of previously permitted development.

Another court addressing the difficult issue of the reasonableness of an impact fee has identified seven factors to evaluate the validity of an impact fee. The Utah Supreme Court, in *Banberry Development Corp. v. South Jordan City*,[37] suggested the following as the most important factors for a local government to consider when determining the burden borne and to be borne by a new development:

1. The cost of existing infrastructure.
2. The method of financing existing facilities (e.g., user charges, bonds, special assessments, general taxes, and federal grants).
3. The extent to which new developments and existing projects have already contributed to the cost of existing facilities (e.g., through property taxes and special assessments).
4. The extent of future contributions (e.g., user charges).
5. The extent to which developers may be entitled to credit because of required common facilities.
6. The extraordinary costs, if any, in providing service to new development and

7. The time–price differential inherent in the comparison of amounts paid at different times.

The *Banberry* criteria were promulgated in an attempt to deal with two problems of the proper cost apportionment in an impact fee rate determination. The first problem (recoupment) occurs because impact fees are sometimes required in situations in which a local government seeks to recoup a portion of the money spent previously on capital facilities with excess capacity. The second problem (double charging) occurs when infrastructure is financed by more than one revenue source. These criteria are designed to ensure that developers pay their fair share and are not overcharged by local governments.[38]

2.1.4 Equal Protection Issues

Another challenge to the validity of impact fees is that they violate the constitutional guarantees of equal protection. A fee levied only on new development, it is argued, denies the equal protection of the law guaranteed by the United States Constitution. In an opinion letter addressing a proposed beach restoration impact fee, for example, the Maryland attorney general noted that developers of new beachfront projects (and therefore the ultimate buyer or lessees) would pay all of the cost of restoring the beachfront despite the fact that all residents would benefit by the restoration. However, the attorney general concluded that, since the plan was supported by a rational basis, an equal protection attack would probably not be successful.[39]

If a court accepts the principle of impact fees, it is likely to reject equal protection attacks. For example, in California, a city's impact fee plan was upheld as reasonable despite its varying rates for residential developers and builders.[40]

In *Ivy Steel and Wire Co. v. City of Jacksonville*,[41] the Jacksonville, Florida, ordinance at issue imposed a water pollution control charge on those persons connecting to the city sewer system after a specified date. Plaintiff challenged the ordinance on the theory that the equal protection clause of the US Constitution was violated by the fact that those people connected before the specified date would be exempt while those who connected afterwards would have to pay the fee. The federal district court found no denial of equal protection.

The Florida Supreme Court considered but rejected an equal protection challenge in its landmark decision in *Contractors and Builders Assn. of Pinellas County v. City of Dunedin*,[42] which is discussed later in this chapter. The Supreme Court of Colorado also rejected an equal protection-based challenge in *City of Arvada v. City and County of Denver*.[43]

In *Cherokee County v. Greater Atlanta Home Builders Ass'n*,[44] Cherokee County's impact fee program, adopted pursuant to the Georgia Development Impact Fee Act, was challenged on equal protection grounds because the fees were imposed only on development within the unincorporated area of the county but also benefited development in the incorporated areas. The court upheld the fees and stated:

The county's authority to require development approval through a building permit, however, is restricted to development in unincorporated portions of the county. OCGA Section 36-13-1. Thus, the General Assembly has limited Cherokee County's authority to impose impact fees on the unincorporated portions of the county. It has authorized but not required counties to enter into intergovernmental agreements with municipalities to jointly collect impact fees to pay for system improvements benefiting both. OCGA Section 36-71-11 … The County has imposed an impact fee on all new developments within the unincorporated portions of the county, which is all it has the power to do. It has not made a "classification" exempting incorporated developments from the fees, for by statute the county simply has no power or control over developments within municipal limits. The reason new developments in

municipalities do not pay the fees is not because of any legislative distinction or action by the county but results from decisions by the municipalities not to impose such fees and not to enter into optional intergovernmental agreements with the county regarding such.[45]

2.2 THE TAKING ISSUE: THE RATIONAL NEXUS TEST REVISITED?

Challenges by landowners that a land-use regulation constitutes a taking of property without compensation are frequently made. Certainly, many land-use regulations—including developer funding requirements —decrease the market value of land or the potential profits from its development. Nonetheless, the taking attack is one of the least successful and hardest to establish by landowners in suits against local governments. In theory, the concept does place limitations on the power of local governments to require mitigation, and the issue is frequently raised in impact fee litigation.

The US Supreme Court has admitted that it quite simply has been unable to develop any "'set' formula" for deciding whether there has been a taking.[46] The test used by the reviewing court indicates whether the regulation imposes too heavy an economic burden on the landowner to be sustained as an exercise of police power. The requirement of the courts (i.e., that mandatory dedications, in-lieu fees, and impact fees benefit the developments paying them) seems at the same time a limitation within the taking jurisprudence and an answer to such a challenge. In other words, to be valid, such exactions must be required by and be of benefit to the development. If the exactions are for infrastructure necessitated by the development and are used to benefit it, then the regulation would arguably have not gone too far, since value would have been returned to the development by the provision of infrastructure. So-called "linkage" programs for social infrastructure such as affordable housing or childcare facilities would seem to be the most susceptible of all mitigation requirements to a taking challenge since the link between the development and the benefit of the fees paid are at times less direct. Again, however, the reasonableness of the amount charged and the economic analysis of the connection between the development and the linkage program would seem to be the key.[47]

Two cases decided by the US Supreme Court set out the federal constitutional standards that must be met by programs requiring developer funding of infrastructure by way of required dedications or physical exactions: *Nollan v. California Coastal Commission*[48] and *Dolan v. City of Tigard*.[49] A look at *Dolan* will provide the opportunity to consider the effect of both cases on the rational nexus standards for impact fees.

In *Dolan v. City of Tigard*,[50] the Supreme Court of Oregon used the "reasonable relationship" test to uphold the validity of the city's requirement that a landowner dedicate land for improvements of a storm drainage system and for a bicycle/pedestrian pathway. The Oregon court considered its usage of the "reasonable relationship" test consistent with the "essential nexus" language contained in *Nollan*. In a 5–4 decision, the US Supreme Court reversed the Oregon decision. Chief Justice Rehnquist, writing for the majority, first explained that the court granted *certiorari* to resolve a question left open by *Nollan* "of what is the required degree of connection between the exactions imposed by the city and the projected impacts of the proposed developments."[51]

Chief Justice Rehnquist went on to characterize the attack by the landowner Dolan on the constitutional validity of the city's actions as being grounded in the contention that the Supreme Court in *Nollan* "had abandoned the 'reasonable relationship' test in favor of a stricter 'essential nexus test'"[52] and further commented that the Supreme Court of Oregon had read *Nollan* "to mean that an exaction serves the same purpose that a denial of the permit would serve."[53]

The majority had no problem, as it had in *Nollan*, with finding an essential nexus between the governmental action and the governmental interest furthered by the permit condition, and therefore reached the second issue (i.e., "whether the degree of the exactions demanded by the city's permit conditions bear the required relationship to the projected impact of petitioner's proposed development"[54]).

In answering this question, the majority first turned to state court decisions because, as Chief Justice Rehnquist phrased it, "they have been dealing with this question a good deal longer than we have ..."[55] The examination of state court decisions began with *Billings Properties Inc. v. Yellowstone County*[56] and *Jenad, Inc. v. Scarsdale*.[57] Without any discussion of what standard was used in those cases or why it was deficient, the majority opinion rejected the standard used as "too lax to adequately protect petitioner's right to just compensation if her property is taken for a public purpose."[58]

The opinion next turned to a case previously discussed, *Pioneer Trust & Savings Bank v. Village of Mount Prospect*,[59] and, in a comment of considerable potential importance to local governments that enact impact fee programs, concluded that the federal constitution does not require such exacting scrutiny as the *Pioneer Trust* court's "specific and uniquely attributable test" requires.

Chief Justice Rehnquist then turned to state court decisions of which he approved. One of these is *Jordan v. Village of Menomonee Falls*,[60] the important Wisconsin decision that established the dual rational nexus test. Surprisingly, the chief justice did not refer to the *Jordan* test by its usual name—the dual rational nexus test—but instead referred to it as a "form" of the reasonable relationship test. This part of the decision seems to leave us with the specific and uniquely attributable test being stricter than the constitution requires, the "generalized statements as to the necessary connection between the required dedication and the proposed development"[61] required by a few state courts being too lax, and the form of the reasonable relationship test adopted by the majority of state courts being the constitutionally acceptable standard.

As previously stated, instead of calling the "acceptable test" the "dual rational nexus test," the Court comes up with a new label, to wit:

We think the "reasonable relationship" test adopted by a majority of the state courts is closer to the federal constitutional norm than either of those previously discussed. But we do not adopt it as such partly because the term "reasonable relationship" seems confusingly similar to the term "rational basis" which describes the minimal level of scrutiny under the Equal Protection Clause of the Fourteenth Amendment. We think a term such as "rough proportionality" best encapsulates what we hold to be the requirement of the Fifth Amendment. No precise mathematical calculation is required, but the city must make some sort of individualized determination that the dedication is related in nature and extend to the impact of the proposed development.[62]

To the extent that *Dolan* applies to impact fees, the majority may have actually liberalized the standard required of local governments in most states since Chief Justice Rehnquist concludes, "No precise mathematical calculation is required, but the city must make some effort to quantify its finding in support of ... [its] dedication requirement."[63] Most state courts and statutes require local governments enacting impact fee and other mitigation programs to have precise mathematical calculations and to make considerable efforts to quantify their findings.

Arizona and California courts, and a few others, have considered the applicability of *Nollan* and *Dolan* to developer funding fees. The Arizona and California cases intertwine. The Arizona Court of Appeals in *Home Builders Ass'n of Central Arizona v. City of Scottsdale*[64] deduced that the US Supreme Court's remand of *Ehrlich v. City of Culver City*[65] (a case in which the city required a developer to pay an impact-type fee for recreational facilities when it sought approval to build apartments to replace a private tennis club) for reconsideration in light of the *Dolan* decision implied that the *Dolan* tests can apply to impact fee cases. However, the court of appeals proceeded to distinguish *Dolan* and determined that a *Dolan* analysis was not appropriate in the *Scottsdale* case:

Unlike Tigard's ordinance, Scottsdale's [ordinance] allows its staff no discretion in setting the fees which are based upon a standardized schedule. The fees are tailored to the type of development involved and are uniform within each class of development. Because the fees are standardized and uniform, and because the ordinance permits no discretion in its application, a prospective developer may know precisely the fee that will be charged. The Scottsdale ordinance, therefore, does not permit a Dolan-like *ad hoc*, adjudicative determination.[66]

Although the Supreme Court of Arizona unanimously affirmed the court of appeals decision,[67] the court saw the *Dolan* issue somewhat differently. It agreed with the language just quoted but added:

We note, however, that there may be good reason to distinguish the Dolan adjudicative decision from the Scottsdale legislative one. *Ehrlich v. City of Culver City**** dramatically illustrates the differences between the two exactions.*** On remand from the United States Supreme Court for reconsideration in light of Dolan, the California Supreme Court held the record insufficient to show that the fee was roughly proportional to the public burden of replacing recreational facilities that would be lost as a result of rezoning Ehrlich's property. The California court suggested that the Dolan analysis applied to cases of regulatory leveraging that occur when the landowner must bargain for approval of a particular use of its land. ... The risk of that sort of leveraging does not exist when the exaction is embodied in a generally applicable legislative decision.

Dolan may also be distinguished from our case on another ground. There, the city demanded that Mrs. Dolan cede a part of her property to the city a particularly invasive form of land regulation that the court believed justified increased judicial protection for the landowner. Here, Scottsdale seeks to impose a fee, a considerably more benign form of regulation.[68]

As indicated in the quoted language from the *Scottsdale* case above, following the remand of its decision in *Ehrlich* by the US Supreme Court, the California Court of Appeal, in a divided and unpublished opinion, reaffirmed its earlier ruling in favor of *Ehrlich*. In a long, rambling decision made especially confusing by the "concurring in part—dissenting in part" statements of several justices, the Supreme Court of California reversed and remanded.[69]

The holding starts out with a direct statement responsive to the speculation over the impact of *Dolan*, to wit:

We conclude that the tests formulated by the high court in its Dolan and Nollan opinions for determining whether a compensable regulatory taking has occurred under the takings clause of the Fifth Amendment to the federal constitution apply under the circumstances of this case, to the monetary exaction imposed by Culver City as a condition of approving plaintiff's request that the real property in suit be rezoned to permit the construction of a multiunit residential condominium. We thus reject the city's contention that the heightened taking clause standard formulated by the court in Nollan and Dolan applies only to cases in which the local land-use authority requires the developer to dedicate real property to public use as a condition of the permit approval.[70]

Unfortunately for those seeking a clear answer to the speculation over the meaning of *Dolan*, the California Supreme Court ties its above-quoted conclusion to its interpretation of the California Mitigation Fee Act.[71]

The Supreme Court of California revisited the issue in *San Remo Hotel v. City and County of San Francisco*,[72] which involved the required payment of a substantial in-lieu fee pursuant to the San Francisco Residential Hotel Unit Conversion and Demolition Ordinance regulating the conversion and demolition of single-room occupancy units. The court held that the heightened scrutiny requirements of *Nollan/Dolan* did not apply because the in-lieu fee was generally applicable and nondiscretionary.

In 2006, the Supreme Court of Washington weighed in on the applicability of *Nollan/Dolan*[73] principles to impact fees. In *City of Olympia v. Drebick*,[74] the amicus parties argued that *Nollan/Dolan* was the applicable standard and had been violated. The court totally and no doubt properly rejected this contention but with an analysis much less clear than some of its sister state supreme courts, such as those of Arizona and California.[75] The Washington Court of Appeals had found *Nollan/Dolan* not only applicable to the impact fees in question but also found the fees in violation of them. The state supreme court disagreed and opined as follows:

[T]he dissent takes the … view that local governments must base GMA impact fees on individualized assessments of the direct impacts each new development will have on each improvement planned in a service area. … the dissent does not explain that neither Nollan nor Dolan concerned the imposition of impact fees but addressed instead the authority of a local government to condition development approval on a property's owner's dedication of a portion of land for public use; nor does the dissent mention that neither the United States Supreme Court nor this court has determined that the tests applied in Nollan and Dolan to evaluate land exactions must be extended to the consideration of fees imposed to mitigate the direct impacts of a new development, much less to the consideration of more general growth impact fees imposed pursuant to statutorily authorized local ordinances.[76]

The debate continues over whether or not and to what extent *Nollan/Dolan* principles of essential nexus and rough proportionality apply to all or some impact fees or only required dedications (i.e., physical exactions). From that, four principles emerged. Some advocated the full application of taking principles, including *Nollan/Dolan*, to impact fees and all other forms of developer funding requirements. Their position is based upon the assertion that the *Dolan* test is well established, it is logical in its outcome, and it seems to work reasonably well for both developers and local governments.[77] Others considered that *Nollan/Dolan* should be applied only to mandatory dedications of land.[78]

A third position is that *Nollan/Dolan* should apply to administratively determined impact fees but not to those legislatively set.[79] This approach centers on the *Ehrlich* decision by the California Supreme Court, previously discussed. A fourth view of the issue that impact fees should not be subject to the *Nollan/Dolan* test because, in virtually all states, they are subject to the dual rational nexus test, which is more stringent than *Nollan/Dolan*. It guarantees that exactions, which meet the dual rational nexus test, could not be takings. If an impact fee is valid (i.e., it satisfies the dual rational nexus test), then it cannot destroy property rights. If an impact fee violates the nexus test, it is invalid. Therefore, no takings analysis is appropriate or necessary.[80]

The relevance of *Nollan/Dolan* to required dedications and monetary exactions, such as impact fees, took a new twist with the 2005 decision of the US Supreme Court in *Lingle v. Chevron, USA, Inc.*[81] In overruling *Agins*,[82] the *Lingle* court retained the holdings of *Nollan* and *Dolan* but disclaimed the "substantially advances" rationale used in those opinions. While recognizing that "it might be argued that [the *Agins*] formula played a role in [those] decisions,*** the rule those decisions established is entirely distinct"[83] from *Agins*'s "substantially advances" test. Rather the Court says, those cases "involved dedications of property so onerous that, outside the exactions context, they would be deemed

per se physical takings"[84] under the *Loretto*[85] doctrine. Thus, whether an exaction is justified and thus exempt from *Loretto*'s *per se* takings rule depends on whether the exaction is a condition for the granting of development permission and that, qualitatively and quantitatively, the exaction is reasonably necessary to prevent or counteract anticipated adverse public effects of the proposed developments.

Prior to *Lingle*, lower courts differed on the question of whether *Nollan* and *Dolan*'s intermediate scrutiny should be extended to regulations such as impact fees that do not cause physical invasions. By directly tying those cases to *Loretto*, and in disclaiming use of the "substantially advances" test to explain them, *Lingle* appeared to answer that question in the negative; however, the US Supreme Court did not choose to affirmatively answer this question in *Lingle*, instead waiting for another case to do so.

Finally, in *Koontz v. St. Johns River Water Management District*,[86] the US Supreme Court attempted to answer this issue. There, Florida law mandated that a landowner create or preserve wetlands elsewhere in the event a landowner wished to build on wetlands. When Koontz applied for a permit to develop 3.7 acres of wetlands, the St. Johns River Water Management District advised Koontz that he could not develop the 3.7 acres of wetlands unless Koontz significantly downsized his development plans or offset the loss of wetlands by providing the funds to create culverts or fill in ditches in parcels to enhance the 50-acres of wetlands owned by the district. Rather than fulfill the district's requests, Koontz brought suit in state court and claimed that, under Florida law, the district's actions were an unreasonable exercise of the state's police power, which constituted a takings clause violation.

In a 5–4 decision, the *Koontz* Court held that monetary exactions are subject to *Nollan* and *Dolan* scrutiny. In its opinion, the majority first addressed the procedural posture of the case. The Florida Supreme Court previously decided against Koontz under the rationale that *Nollan* and *Dolan* did not apply because the district did not refuse to grant the permit subject to the condition, but rather had denied the permit because Koontz had refused to meet the district's conditions. The Florida Supreme Court rationalized that *Nollan* and *Dolan* applied only where a government approved permits on the condition that a property owner meet the exaction. The US Supreme Court subsequently rejected this rationale, asserting that

[t]he principles that undergird our decisions in *Nollan* and *Dolan* do not change depending on whether the government approves a permit on the condition that the applicant turn over property or denies a permit because the applicant refuses to do so.[87]

In both the case of "approval subject to" and "denial due to refusal," the Supreme Court stated that the government cannot attempt to leverage its power to grant land development permission for reasons not related to the applicant's proposal given that a lack of the *Nollan/Dolan* nexus and a requisite showing of rough proportionality, the government would coerce an individual into consenting to an unconstitutional taking. While the Florida Supreme Court questioned how the taking clause could be violated where a government demands property even though "no property of any kind was ever taken." However, the US Supreme Court resolved the Florida Court's confusion by using the unconstitutional conditions doctrine.

Next, the Supreme Court turned to the question of whether a requirement to pay—e.g., fees, impact fees, in-lieu fees, or monetary exactions—constitutes a takings violation. Unlike in *Nollan* and *Dolan*, where only physical exactions were involved, the Supreme Court in *Koontz* claimed that such an approach would lead to precarious results. More specifically, the Supreme Court asserted that by limiting the rule to real property—e.g., *Nollan*

and *Dolan*—then governments would have the ability to circumvent the takings clause of the Fifth Amendment. Per the Supreme Court in *Koontz*, "a permitting authority wishing to exact an easement could simply give the owner a choice of either surrendering an easement or making a payment equal to the easement's value."[88] In essence, the Supreme Court was not willing to give governments the ability to coerce landowners into either ponying up the cash or giving the government their land.

The takeaway from *Koontz* is that when a takings claim

rests on the more limited proposition that when the government commands the relinquishment of funds linked to a specific, identifiable property interest such as a bank account or parcel of real property, a "per se [takings] approach" is the proper mode of analysis under the Court's precedent.[89]

In essence, monetary exactions must be distinguished from taxes, with the former subject to the *per se* takings approach. However, the dissent and majority strongly disagreed over governments' ability to determine this distinction, with the dissent chastising the majority for a lack of guidance on the issue. Furthermore, as we will discuss in the proceeding paragraphs, it is notable that neither the *Koontz* majority nor the *Koontz* dissent addressed the issue of whether *Nollan* and *Dolan* applies to legislatively enacted, generally applicable impact fees. Going forward, it seems as if the Supreme Court will continue to kick the proverbial can down the road as it pertains to this issue.

For example, in *California Building Industry Ass'n v. City of San Jose*,[90] the California Supreme Court upheld the City of San Jose's conditions on housing development permits—i.e., that the developer sell 15 percent of the units for less than market value or pay an in-lieu fee. The crux of the issue, the California high court found, was whether inclusionary zoning requirements fell within the confines of "exactions," which, if so, would implicate the unconstitutional conditions doctrine of the *Nollan/Dolan/Koontz* trilogy. However, the court held that the city's housing development permits did not constitute an exaction and thus did not implicate the unconstitutional conditions doctrine.

Nollan and *Dolan* arose in adjudicatory settings, and the courts have grappled with whether the doctrine of those cases applies to legislative action as well. The legislative/adjudicatory question arises because exactions are imposed on development in two distinct settings that may call for different levels of review. As Chief Justice Rehnquist said in *Dolan*, the burden is on a challenger to prove the invalidity of a generally applicable law, but where an adjudicative decision is made, the burden must switch to the government. Where property owners must bargain on a case-by-case basis, in what is essentially an adjudicatory setting, the safeguards of the open legislative process are lost, and concern arises that the individual may be compelled to give more than a fair share. Taking their cue from *Dolan*'s emphasis on the fact that the case involved an adjudicative decision, most lower courts in addressing the issue have found heightened scrutiny inapplicable to broad-based legislative conditions. Other courts take the position that heightened scrutiny applies to legislative as well as adjudicative acts. The question remains open and likely will continue to be disputed until the Court answers it.[91]

Much to the chagrin of local governments across the country, the Supreme Court has continuously refused to take up the issue of whether *Nollan* and *Dolan* applies to legislative action, given that *Nollan* and *Dolan* arose in adjudicatory settings. The question of whether the fee is adjudicatory or legislative is important because exactions can arise in two different settings, with each setting receiving its own level of review. Per Chief Justice John Roberts, the burden is on a challenger to prove the invalidity of a generally

applicable law, but where an adjudicative decision is made, the burden must switch to the government. In an adjudicatory setting where the property owner must bargain on an *ad hoc* basis, the safeguards from an open legislative process are nonexistent, and the property owner is more susceptible to being compelled to give more than his or her fair share. As such, many lower courts in the post-*Dolan* era have held that the heightened scrutiny from *Nollan/Dolan* applies to adjudicatory settings and not to broad legislative conditions. On the other hand, many other lower courts have taken a more far-reaching approach by applying the heightened *Nollan/Dolan* scrutiny to broad legislative conditions as well as adjudicative acts.

In *Dabbs v. Anne Arundel County*,[92] the Maryland Court of Appeals discussed this very issue. The *Dabbs* Court retained the holding in *Koontz*, requiring that certain monetary exactions meet the nexus and rough proportionality elements of *Nollan* and *Dolan*. However, in upholding the validity of certain Anne Arundel County impact fees, the Maryland Court of Appeals held that the impact fees imposed by legislation applicable on an "area-wide basis" are not subject to *Nollan/Dolan* scrutiny. The Court reasoned that, unlike the fees imposed in *Koontz*, the local ordinance in *Dabbs* did not direct a specific property owner to make a conditional monetary payment to obtain approval of a permit application, nor did the local ordinance impose the condition on a particularized or discretionary basis.[93] Thus, because the legislatively imposed impact fee was predetermined—based on a specific monetary schedule and applied to any person wishing to develop property in the district on a uniform basis—the *Dabbs* Court held that the Anne Arundel County impact fee fell in line with *Dolan*'s recognition that generally applicable impact fees are not subject to a rough proportionality or nexus analysis.[94] As such, the *Koontz* rule regarding the requirement that certain monetary exactions be subject to the nexus and rough proportionality elements of *Nollan/Dolan* is inapplicable to generally applicable legislatively imposed impact fees such as the one found in *Dabbs*.[95]

After the Maryland Appellate Court's decision upholding the validity of the impact fees, Dabbs filed a petition for a writ of certiorari to have the case heard in the US Supreme Court, which the high court subsequently declined. As a result of the *Dabbs* decision, Maryland joins Alabama, Alaska, Arizona, California, Colorado, and the Tenth Circuit regarding jurisdictions that limit the *Nollan/Dolan/ Koontz* trilogy to administratively imposed conditions.[96]

In contrast, Texas, Ohio, Maine, Illinois, New York, Washington, and the First Circuit Court of Appeals have all applied the nexus and rough proportionality tests to generally applicable permit conditions, choosing not to distinguish between legislatively and adjudicatory imposed exactions.[97]

The US Supreme Court's current reluctance to address this jurisdictional split places property owners and local governments throughout the US in a state of uncertainty. Justice Thomas voiced his disapproval of not addressing the issue in his dissenting opinion regarding the Supreme Court's denial of *certiorari* in *CBIA*, contending that:

until we decide this issue, property owners and local governments are left uncertain about what legal standard governs legislative ordinances and whether cities can legislatively impose exactions that would not pass constitutional muster if done administratively. These factors present compelling reasons for resolving this conflict at the earliest practicable opportunity.[98]

Despite Justice Thomas' statements, the Supreme Court's denial of the *Dabbs* petition signals the court's reluctance to address the applicability of the *Nollan–Dolan–Koontz* trilogy to these types of impact fees—a sentiment further echoed in their recent denials of several other petitioners raising the issue, with *Dartmond Cherk v. Marion County* serving as the most recent example of the Supreme Court's reluctance.[99]

Finally, in *Alpine Homes, Inc. v. City of West Jordan*,[100] the Utah Supreme Court highlighted another limitation regarding the applicability of *Koontz*. In *Alpine Homes*, a group of developers challenged the validity of impact fees imposed by the city of West Jordan. The developers argued that because the city failed to spend some of the impact fees it collected within six years and spent some of the fees on statutorily prohibited expenditures, the city violated the property owners' rights under the takings clause.[101] The Utah Supreme Court recognized that, under the *Koontz* standard, an applicant may challenge the validity of an impact fee by asserting that it lacks either an essential nexus or rough proportionality. However, the Utah Supreme Court held that the manner in which impact fees are spent does not affect the constitutionality of the initial demand for fees, which is the focus of the *Koontz* monetary exactions analysis.[102] Thus, because the developers failed to cite any cases that applied a *Nollan/Dolan* analysis to a municipality's expenditure of impact fees, the Utah Supreme Court held that the developers failed to state a takings claim for which relief could be granted.[103]

2.3 THE RELATIONSHIP OF IMPACT FEES TO THE COMPREHENSIVE PLAN

The reasonableness and proper exercise of the police power issue tie-in with the concept of having impact fees based upon and an implementation of the local government's comprehensive plan. In short, it is easier to convince a judge of the reasonableness of an impact fee program if it is based upon and even required by specific comprehensive plan language.

Planning legislation in some states (e.g., Florida) requires all land-use regulations to be consistent with the comprehensive plan. Such a requirement makes impact fee and comprehensive plan consistency a necessity and not just a luxury.

The more specific the language in the comprehensive plan, the easier it is to make the consistency argument. The following language is suggested as the "bare bones" expression of the planning principles upon which impact fees are grounded:

- Land development shall not be permitted unless adequate capital facilities exist or are assured.
- Land development shall bear a proportionate cost of the provision of the new or expanded capital facilities required by such development.
- The imposition of impact fees and dedication requirements are the preferred methods of regulating land development in order to assure that it bears a proportionate share of the cost of capital facilities necessary to accommodate that development.

The third principle listed above is directly related to the capital improvement program (CIP) element of comprehensive plans.[104] Without such an element or planning process and the levels of service for infrastructure items which they should establish, it is difficult, if not impossible, to determine the proportionate share of new development.[105] Impact fee programs lacking a CIP to supplement them are susceptible to attack under the *Nollan/Dolan* rational nexus requirements.[106] Moreover, intergovernmental coordination elements of comprehensive plans are increasingly vital to impact fee programs.[107] For example, the jurisdictional boundaries of impact fees have come under fire in Florida, where considerable controversy has arisen regarding whether Florida municipalities are subject to the impact fee programs enacted by counties in which the municipalities are located.[108] While the framework of the state constitution may determine the conflict's outcome—i.e., whether a county impact fee program extends to the municipalities and

local governments within the county—the absence of intergovernmental coordination can potentially play a pivotal role in the controversy's outcome.

2.3.1 State Authorizing Legislation

The "tests" for impact fee validity discussed above relate primarily to basic land-use control and local government law principles. Many states have statutory provisions authorizing or enabling impact fees.[109] These statutory provisions range from a few short paragraphs, which generally authorize all or certain local governments to adopt impact fee programs (e.g., Arizona) or briefly "solve" a very specific impact fee issue (e.g., Florida), to lengthy and comprehensive impact fee codes that cover most impact fee issues in considerable detail (e.g., Texas, Georgia, and New Mexico).[110] In most states, the relevant statutory provisions not only authorize impact fees but also establish requirements they must meet in order to be valid. Careful attention must therefore be paid to the express statutory language.

2.3.2 Drafting Impact Fees to Pass Judicial Scrutiny

The increasing number of judicial decisions and state statutory provisions authorizing impact fees has resulted in more numerous and more varied impact fee ordinances and comprehensive plan provisions. The attention of planners, judges, attorneys, and local government officials has shifted in many states from the issues of statutory authorization, constitutional validity, tax versus land regulatory charge, and rational nexus to how to draft impact fee ordinances in order to bring them within the parameters for validity established by the courts. Drafting requirements vary according to the jurisdiction in question, but some generally applicable standards can be formulated. At this point, some of the general considerations will be discussed. The following basic list should be considered:

- An impact fee ordinance should expressly cite statutory authority for local government regulation of the substantive area selected.
- A need for service or improvements resulting from new development should be demonstrated.
- The fee charged must not exceed the cost of improvements.
- The improvements funded must adequately benefit the development that is the source of the fee (even if non-residents of the development also benefit).
- In place of a rigid and inflexible formula for calculating the amount of the fee to be imposed on a particular development, a variance procedure should be included so that the local government may consider studies and data submitted by the developer to decrease his/her assessment.
- The expenditure of funds should be localized to the areas from which they were collected.

Cases from various jurisdictions give further indications of judicial requirements that will likely be imposed on impact fee-related ordinances. A decision by the Supreme Court of Arkansas[111] should prove to be a leading case in point. The city required a cash contribution from the plaintiff land developer of $85 per lot, which was to be invested by the city and eventually used for the acquisition and development of parks. The court held for the plaintiff on the basis that the city did not have a sufficiently definite plan for parks and park facilities to justify the contribution, and further noted that no provision was made for refund of the contributions if the area is not developed as expected.

Both of these points would seem to translate into principles that should be followed in formulating and drafting impact fee

ordinances. The easiest with which to comply is the concern that provisions for refunds should be included in the ordinance so that feepayer is entitled to get fees returned if they are not properly spent for the purposes for which they were collected within a reasonable period of time after their collection. The reasonableness of the time period should be tied to the capital funding planning period for the infrastructure in question. If, for example, the jurisdiction works with a five-year capital improvement program, that five-year period plus an extra year for flexibility could be stated as the refund period.

The more important requirement established by the Arkansas court is that money can be collected for capital expenditures only if there is a "reasonably definite" plan for its expenditure. What the court seems to be—and should be—requiring is that impact fees and related ordinances must implement comprehensive plans. Impact fees, it should be remembered, are land-use regulations, and thus their validity should be dependent upon their being an implementation of the local government's plan for capital facilities. If a fee is to be collected from new development for park acquisition or park facilities construction, then the jurisdiction should have a plan for parks as well as a standard for park facilities against which the validity and fairness of the park impact fee can be judged.

Careful earmarking and restriction of funds for expenditure for the benefit of the geographic areas from which they are collected also merit careful attention. Lee County, Florida, has addressed this concern in its Parks Impact Fee Ordinance by requiring that all impact fees will be deposited into a "special trusts fund" to be used "exclusively for capital improvements within or for the benefit of the regional parks impact fee districts from which the funds were created."[112] Lee County's Roads Impact Fee Ordinance[113] similarly creates specific trust funds for the revenues collected from road impact fees. Montgomery County, Maryland, has likewise separated the revenues for its road impact fees. The ordinance directs the County Department of Finance "to establish separate accounts for each impact fee area and … maintain records for each such account so that development impact fee funds collected can be segregated by the impact fee area of origin."[114]

Many state impact fee statutes require that local government impact fee ordinances establish "one or more" benefit districts or service areas. The goal is to ensure that impact fees are spent close enough to the developments that pay them so that the second prong of the dual rational nexus test (i.e., the fees must be spent so as to benefit those who pay them) is respected. Since the statutes generally leave to the local government the decisions as to how many service areas or benefit districts are established, many local governments that are large in area establish only one district. This practice has led to allegations by fee payors that the districts are so large that impact fees can be spent so distantly from the development that generates them that little, if any, benefit is received by them. Litigation has ensued. In *City of Olympia v. Drebick*,[115] for example, the fee payor unsuccessfully sought to have the city's road impact fee invalidated because the city had a single service/benefit area even though the city constituted 17 square miles.

The controversy over size of service areas/ benefit districts led to statutory changes in the impact fee legislation in Georgia and Nevada in 2007. In 2006, the Georgia legislature considered several bills that would have set a maximum area size for service areas, but none were enacted. Instead, Georgia House Bill 232[116] was enacted in 2007 and, in effect, applies only to the City of Atlanta and only to road impact fees. It requires the city, when spending impact fees, to consider the proximity of the improvements to developments that have generated the fees and the improvements that will have the greatest effect on levels of service (LOS) of the development that have paid the fees. Nevada took a more direct approach in 2007 by enacting Nevada Assembly Bill 253,[117] which limits the use of single jurisdiction-wide service areas for cities with fewer than 10,000 residents and counties with fewer than 15,000 residents.

The necessity of a "tie-in" between the plan and the impact fee should be stressed in formulating the impact fee and the ordinance implementing it. The *City of Fayetteville*[118] decision emphasizes the necessity of wedding planning and law in the formulation, adoption, and implementation of impact fees designed to fund capital expenditures for infrastructure to service new development. A decision by the Supreme Court of Utah revisits the absolute necessity for careful and highly competent economic analysis in the impact fee formulation and implementation process. Ostensibly, *Lafferty v. Payson City*[119] simply reiterates the requirement discussed earlier in connection with the decision of the Supreme Court of Florida in *Dunedin*,[120] which states that impact fees monies must be earmarked so they can be spent only for the purpose for which they were collected. More important, however, the Supreme Court of Utah takes the opportunity in *Lafferty* to reemphasize the economic analysis it formulated in *Banberry* to guarantee that impact fees do not treat new residents unfairly "in determining the relative burden already borne and yet to be borne by newly developed properties."[121]

Complex and sophisticated economic analysis is required to assess the considerations deemed crucial by the Utah Court. Nonetheless, courts in other jurisdictions will doubtless turn them into standards that impact fee calculation formulas must meet to be held valid. Even in jurisdictions in which the courts are less demanding, local developers, new residents, taxpayers, and others will doubtless require of their elected officials sound economic analysis to support impact fee programs.

2.3.3 Extending the Applicability of Impact Fees Across the Development Spectrum

Impact fees are currently being used for a wide variety of public services and now represent a common fiscal tool used by local governments in funding public service infrastructure needs. Impact fees are assessed for the provision of water and sewer systems, roads, solid waste facilities, libraries, parks, schools, police and fire facilities, emergency medical facilities, environmental and habitat preservation, public hospitals, and even public cemeteries.[122] The most common use for impact fees is in the funding of capital improvements for potable water and sanitary sewer facilities. Transportation services such as highways and bridges are the next most common type of impact fee.[123]

If impact fees are going to be effective in mitigating the costs of development to the public, not only must the scope of infrastructure be expanded to include "green" and "social" infrastructure in order to correctly assess the true costs and impacts of growth, but the types of development that cause impact and therefore should share in its mitigation must be expanded. For example, it is often the practice to confine developer funding requirements for parks and schools to residential development. This practice places an inequitable burden on residential developers because commercial and industrial developments also "use" school facilities (e.g., hurricane shelter, adult education, recreation, and libraries) and parks (e.g., corporate athletic teams, office picnics, and sports competitions).[124]

2.3.4 Making Impact Fees More Sensitive to Affordable Housing and Other Societal Needs

Impact fees are now a commonplace means of infrastructure finance. By requiring new land development to bear a proportionate cost of providing the new or expanded infrastructure, it will require, and impact fees provide, in part, an answer to the dilemma faced by local governments when searching for sources of funding for capital expenditures. Now that impact fees have been widely accepted by the courts as regulatory measures, rather than unconstitutional taxes; they are widely seen as funding programs that reasonably allow local governments to maintain levels of capital facilities that can keep up with growth.

There are limitations, however, to the traditional use of impact fees. While they respond to the issues of location, availability, and provision of capital infrastructure with regard to new development, they are "largely unresponsive and even insensitive to the issue of the quantity and type of growth that should be allowed to occur."[125] Furthermore, the traditional impact fee fails to respond to other growth and development issues such as housing and employment needs.[126]

Partly in response to these shortcomings associated with the traditional impact fee, and partly because of the success of impact fees in raising funds for many infrastructure items, local governments have begun to explore the possibility of using the impact fee concept to fund "soft" or "social" infrastructure needs such as child care facilities and workforce or affordable housing,[127] art in public places and environmental mitigation programs.[128] Developer funding requirements designed to raise funds for "soft," "social," and now "green" infrastructure items are frequently referred to as "linkage fees,"[129] Linkage fees charge developers a fee to provide for expanded services that are incurred by the community because of the new development.

Underlying every linkage program is the fundamental concept that the new downtown development is directly "linked" to a specific social need. The rationale is fairly simple: Not only does the actual construction of the commercial building create new construction jobs, but the increased office space attracts new businesses and workers to fill new jobs. The new workers need places to live, transit systems, daycare facilities, and the like. From the perspective of linkage proponents, the new commercial development is directly linked to both the new employment opportunities and to increased demand for improved municipal facilities and services.[130]

When first implemented, "linkage" fees were thought to be something distinct from "impact" fees.[131] *Nollan v. California Coastal Commission*[132] dealt the first blow to the perceived difference between linkage and impact fees by holding that a nexus was essential to any condition of development approval requiring a dedication. The Ninth Circuit further diminished any distinction in *Commercial Builders of Northern California v. City of Sacramento*[33] by applying essentially impact fee criteria to what was characterized as an affordable housing "linkage" requirement. The city ordinance conditioned nonresidential building permits upon the payment of a fee for housing to offset expenses associated with the influx of low-income workers for the new project. The developers argued that the ordinance was a taking because it placed the burden of paying for the housing upon the new development without a sufficient showing that nonresidential development contributed to the need for new low-income housing in proportion to that burden.

The court found no taking, however, as the fee was enacted only after a study revealed that the need for low-income housing would rise as a direct result of demand from workers on the new development. The court found that "[t]he burden assessed against the developers thus bears a rational relationship to a public cost closely associated with such development."[134] The court seemingly broadened its holding beyond the imposition of a fee for low-income housing when it stated that "[a] purely financial exaction, then, will not constitute a taking if it is made for the purpose of paying a social cost that is reasonably related to the activity against which the fee is assessed."[135]

Perhaps the most famous linkage case decided thus far is the New Jersey case, *Holmdel Builders' Ass'n v. Township of Holmdel*,[136] which upheld the imposition of fees on commercial and non-inclusionary residential developments for the construction of low-income housing per the local government's responsibilities under the *Mt. Laurel* doctrine.[137]

Not all linkage fee programs have fared as well as those just discussed. In *San Telmo Assoc. v. City of Seattle*,[138] the Supreme Court of Washington had before it a Seattle housing preservation ordinance, which provided that property owners who wished to demolish low-income housing units had to replace a specified percentage of the housing or contribute to the city's low-income housing replacement fund. The court found the requirement to constitute an unauthorized tax.

Today, the weight of opinion is that there are no fundamental differences between "linkage" and "impact" fees, but the convention of labeling soft, social, or green impact payments "linkage" and applying the term "impact fee" to hard infrastructure remains. To the extent that any differences can be identified between linkage and impact, most linkage programs have the primary goal of problem mitigation or abatement rather than payment. Impact fees are almost the reverse, in that the expectation is that payment of the fee will be the primary means of compliance. A linkage program would identify a concern and require that the concern be abated or mitigated, and, if not abated or mitigated, a payment would be made, and the proceeds derived would be used to abate or mitigate the problem. An impact fee program would require the payment of a specified amount, the proceeds of which would be used to construct specified public facilities, unless the individual elects to sufficiently mitigate or abate the problem by construction/dedication of those facilities.

The list of issues raised in regard to the validity of linkage fees is almost identical to the list of issues regarding the validity of impact fees. These include the authority of the local government to enact linkage programs,[139] illegal tax rather than land-use regulation,[140] violation of due process, equal protection or takings provisions of US and state constitutions,[141] and the standard to be applied to govern the reasonableness of the exercise of the police power.

In this last regard, *Holmdel* is of particular interest since it held that linkage programs for low-income housing need not meet the rational nexus test:

We conclude that the rational-nexus test is not apposite in determining the validity of inclusionary zoning devices generally or of affordable housing development fees in particular.*** Inclusionary zoning through the imposition of development fees is permissible because such fees are conducive to the creation of realistic opportunities for the development of affordable housing; development fees are the functional equivalent of mandatory set-asides; and it is fair and reasonable to impose such fee requirements on private developers when they possess, enjoy, and consume land, which constitutes the primary resource for housing.[142]

A similar issue exists in regard to environmental mitigation fees, which are assessments made by local governments against new development to reimburse the community for the new development's proportionate negative impact on the community's environment.[143] Whether these fees will parallel impact fees or linkage programs and become another legally authorized and acceptable aspect of developer funding to offset the impact of development is also an issue of current and considerable importance.

2.4 CONCLUSION

As far as local governments are concerned, there seems to be no doubt that the impact analysis-oriented land regulatory measures referred to as "impact fees," "dedication requirements," and "in-lieu payments" provide at least a partial answer to local governments' capital funding dilemma by providing a means whereby local governments can require new land development to bear a proportionate cost of providing the new or expanded capital facilities required by new development. The judicial acceptance of impact fees and their characterization as land regulation charges have not come easily in many high-growth jurisdictions. Recent court decisions indicate an increasing judicial acceptance of impact fees and their role in land development regulations in general and growth management in particular.

In spite of the increased judicial acceptance of impact fees, their formulation, drafting, and implementation are becoming more complicated, and courts more demanding in their scrutiny of such measures. Nonetheless, an assiduous melding of legal, planning and economic analyses offers hope to local governments pushed to the verge of bankruptcy by the infrastructure demands placed on them by considerable and sometimes rampant growth.

The important role that impact fees can now fill for local governments should, however, not obscure their limitations. They are largely unresponsive and even insensitive to the issue of the quantity and type of growth that should be allowed to occur. They are only responsive to the issue of the location of new development in terms of the availability and provision of capital infrastructure. They are also inadequate for solving socioeconomic issues such as housing and employment needs, which are so closely related to growth. These limitations are indicated by the phenomenon that, even though impact fees are quite new in their political and judicial acceptance, they have already been somewhat relegated to second place in the eyes of many planners and planning attorneys by linkage programs that seek to broaden the responsibility of the private sector for the ramifications of new development. Perhaps the most exciting developments in regard to impact fees in the near future will relate to their interrelationship with linkage programs and other developer funding requirements.

There are currently various approaches available to a local government that wishes to require developer funding of infrastructure. These include required dedications, in-lieu fees, user fees, impact fees, rezoning conditions, and linkage programs. The legal frameworks for these various approaches have developed in different time periods and in different contexts, and they are therefore often subjected to different standards and legal requirements. While treating them differently and in a parallel manner has probably been helpful in obtaining their legal and political acceptability, the time has come to "unify" them for several reasons.

First, from a developer perspective, there is a possibility that, by treating them differently, the developer may be required to make overlapping "contributions," which means that unless proper credit for one against the other is given the developer could end up paying more than once for the same impact. This is usually avoided through credit provision of impact fee programs, which require previously made dedication or payments to be deducted from the impact fees otherwise due. Nonetheless, the coordination is not always clear or totally effective.

Second, in some jurisdictions, the funding required of the development may vary based on the stage in the development process when it is "collected" or required. This is not fair to either the developer (vis-a-vis other developers) or to the local government since, if they are mutually exclusive, the local government may not be able to collect for the total impact the development has on infrastructure needs.

Third, treating them separately may limit the "options" of both the developer and the local government in making the contributions as palatable as possible to the developer and as economically effective as possible for the local government

Finally, from a legal perspective, coordination and assimilation of the various methods should result in clearer and more consistent standards for the various approaches that will increase fairness and efficiency for developers and local governments.[144]

NOTES

1 Major portions of this chapter closely parallel the impact fee law coverage found in the following publications: Juergensmeyer, Roberts, Salkin & Rowberry, LAND USE PLANNNG AND DEVELOPMENT REGULATION LAW Ch 9 (4th ed 2018) and Juergensmeyer & Roberts, LAND USE PLANNNG AND DEVELOPMENT REGULATION LAW Ch 9, West Practitioner Series (3rd ed 2012). Readers seeking more in depth legal coverage and comprehensive citations are directed to those versions.

2 A review of impact fee law for attorneys is found in Chapter 9, Juergensmeyer, and Roberts (2012), and Juergensmeyer, Roberts, Salkin, and Rowberry (2018). See also Nicholas, Nelson, and Juergensmeyer (1991).

3 See Chapter 4 for a list of state enabling statutes; see also www.impactfees.com.

4 Juergensmeyer and Roberts (2012), Section 9.9.

5 For most of the country's history, inflation averaged 2 percent or less, with the periods of war being significant exceptions. Beginning in the 1960s and continuing through the 1980s, inflation existed at hitherto unprecedented rates, peaking at over 18 percent in the late 1970s. See US Department of Labor, Bureau of Labor Statistics. [Accessed January 24, 2008] Available at www.bls.gov.

6 See generally Susskind (1983); Arthur C. Nelson, "And Then There Were Property Taxes: A Primer on Property Taxes, Economic Development, and Public Policy," Urban Land Institute Working Paper Series, Paper 661 (July 1998).

7 Both state governments and the federal government abandoned funding programs for public investments because of a sharp rise in cost. Furthermore, there was a greater burden on the local governments responsible for handling these matters because of required improvements to many infrastructure facilities, such as water pollution control facilities. See, e.g., The Water Pollution Control (Clean Water) Act, 33 U.S.C. Sections 1251 et seq. (1994).

8 See Chapter 1.

9 The water could be turned off or the trash left uncollected.

10 This distinction among types of services, while important in public administration, received little if any judicial recognition. This may explain why the courts had little problem with applying proprietary review criteria to "governmental" functions.

11 The Fort Lauderdale-Hollywood metropolitan area.

12 See *Broward County v. Janis Development Corp.*, 311 So.2d 371 (Fla. 4th DCA 1975)

13 *Contractors and Builders Assn. of Pinellas County v. City of Dunedin*, 329 So.2d 314 (Fla. 1976).

14 The idea of regulation had to be expanded from the concept of simply imposing rules and standards to actually imposing fees not classified as taxes, for public health, safety, and welfare purposes.

15 In *Holmdel Builders' Ass'n v. Township of Holmdel*, 121 N.J. 550, 583 A.2d 277 (1990) the court distinguished taxation from regulatory fees. The court stated that, if the primary purpose was to "reimburse the municipality for services reasonably related to development, it was a permissible regulatory exaction." *Id.*

16 Ira M. Heyman & Thomas K. Gilhool, *The Constitutionality of Imposing Increased Community Costs on New Suburban Residents Through Subdivision Exactions*, 73 Yale L. J. (1964).

17 Juergensmeyer and Roberts (2012).

18 A hybrid form of the two has developed in Virginia where "proffers" combine many aspects of both by requiring developer payment of negotiated fees based on schedules tied to infrastructure provision costs.

19 See Nicholas, Nelson, and Juergensmeyer (1991), at 28–33.

20 Juergensmeyer (1988a), at 96–112.

21 Impact fees are also collected at one or more of the following stages of development: rezoning, platting, development order issuance, building permit issuance, and certificate of occupancy issuance. Collecting them late in the development process is best for the developer since he/she has no (or low) finance charges to pay on the impact fee amount. Local governments prefer collecting the fee as early as possible in the development process so that funds will be available to start construction in time to provide infrastructure when the development is completed. The conflicting preference of payors and payees has been resolved in most jurisdictions by providing for payment at the time a building permit is issued.

22 Juergensmeyer and Roberts (2012), Chapter 7.

23 Juergensmeyer and Blake (1981).

24 Juergensmeyer (1988b), at 51-65.

25 Recent decisions on point include *Mayor and Board of Alderman, City of Ocean Springs v. Homebuilders Ass'n of Mississippi, Inc.*, 932 So.2d 44, 61 (Miss. 2006)(impact fees void because taxes); *Home Builders Association of Greater Des Moines v. City of West Des Moines*, 64 N.W.2d 339 (Iowa 2002) (impact fees taxes not regulatory fees); *HBA of Lincoln v City of Lincoln*, 711 N.W.2d 871 (Neb. 2006) (impact fees "taxes" but city authorized by its charter to collect them); *Durham Land Owners Association v. County of Durham*, 630 S.E.2d 678 (N.C. 2006) (county lacked authority to impose impact fee; no discussion of fee versus tax); *Home Builders Ass'n of Dayton v. City of Beavercreek*, 89 Ohio St.3d 121, 729 N.E.2d 349 (2000) (impact fee valid under city's powers pursuant to Ohio Constitution); *City of Olympia v. Drebick*, 126 P.3d 802 (Wash. 2006), cert. Denied, 127 S.Ct. 436 (2006) (Wash Sup. Ct. held city's transportation impact fee really excise tax and

therefore not subject to dual rational nexus requirements). See Smith and Juergensmeyer (2007); Kristin B. Flood, "Who Should Pay for the Impact of New Development in Iowa: developers or the Preexisting Community? Analysis of Home Builders Association of Greater Des Moines v. City of West Des Moines," 91 *Iowa L.Rev. 751 (2006).*

26 See *Home Builders Association of Greater Des Moines v City of West Des Moines*, 644 N.W.2d 339 (Iowa 2002) (park impact fee found to be a tax; authority to promote the peace, safety, health, welfare, comfort, and convenience of its residents does not bestow broad powers for financing of local government activities).

27 See Nicholas, Nelson, and Juergensmeyer (1991), at 29–30.

28 *Ponderosa One Ltd. v. Salt Lake City Suburban Sanitary District*, 738 P.2d 635; 59 Utah Adv. Rep; 1987 Utah LEXIS 723 citing *Murray City v. Board of Education Murray City*, 16 Utah 2d 115; 396 P.2d 628; 1964 Utah LEXIS 357.

29 22 Ill.2d 375, 176 N.E.2d 799 (1961).

30 *Id.*

31 25 Misc.2d 1004, 209 N.Y.S.2d 729 (1960), affirmed 15 A.D.2d 815, 225 N.Y.S.2d 538 (1962).

32 25 Misc.2d 1004, 209 N.Y.S.2d 729 (1960), affirmed 15 A.D.2d 815, 225 N.Y.S.2d 538 (1962).

33 See Nicholas, Nelson, and Juergensmeyer (1991), at 31.

34 28 Wis.2d 608, 137 N.W.2d 442 (1965), appeal dismissed 385 U.S. 4, 87 S.Ct.36, 17 L.Ed.2d 3 (1966).

35 28 Wis.2d 608, 137 N.W.2d 442 (1965), appeal dismissed 385 U.S. 4, 87 S.Ct.36, 17 L.Ed.2d 3 (1966).

36 *Id.*

37 631 P.2d 899 (Utah 1981).

38 See Nicholas, Nelson, and Juergensmeyer (1991), at 28–33.

39 Maryland Attorney General Opinion 86-018.

40 *Russ Building Partnership v. City and County of San Francisco*, 199 Cal.App.3d 1496, 246 Cal.Rptr. 21 (1987). See also *Northern Ill. Home Builders Ass'n v. County of Du Page*, 251 Ill.App.3d 494, 621 N.E.2d 1012 (Ill.App. 1991) (concluding no equal protection violation from differing fees), aff'd 165 Ill.2d 25, 649 N.E.2d 384 (Ill. 1995).

41 401 F.Supp. 701 (M.D. Fla. 1975).

42 329 So.2d 314 (Fla.1976), on remand 330 So.2d 744 (Fla.App.1976).

43 663.2d 611; 1983 Colo. LEXIS 520 (1983).

44 255 Ga.App. 764, 566S.E.2d 470 (2002), cert. den. Ga.Supreme Court (Feb. 24, 2003).

45 *Id.*

46 *Penn Central Transportation Co. v. New York City*, 438 U.S. 104, 124, 98 S.Ct. 2646, 2659.

47 See Chapter 21, A Rational Nexus Approach to Workforce Housing Land Development Conditions, infra.

48 483 U.S. 825, 107 S.Ct. 3141 (1987)

49 *Dolan v. City of Tigard*, 512 U.S. 374, 114 S.Ct. 2309 (1994).

50 317 Or. 110, 854 P.2d 437 (1993).

51 12 U.S. 377, 114 S.Ct. 2309, 2312, 129 L.Ed.2d 304 (1994).

52 12 U.S. 377, 114 S.Ct. 2309, 2315, 129 L.Ed.2d 304 (1994).

53 *Id.*

54 *Id.* at 2318.

55 512 U.S. 389, 114 S.Ct. 2318.

56 144 Mont. 25, 394 P.2d 182 (1964).

57 18 N.Y.2d 78, 271 N.Y.S.2d 955, 218 N.E.2d 673 (1966). Also see Heyman and Gilhool (1964), 1119, 1146–55. Compare the following cases: *Montgomery v. Crossroads Land Co.*, 355 So.2d 363 (Ala.1978) (in-lieu fee a tax); *Venditti-Saravo, Inc. v. Hollywood*, 39 Fla.Supp. 121 (17th Cir.Ct.1973) (impact fee an invalid property tax); *Haugen v. Gleason*, 226 Or. 99, 103, 359 P.2d 108, 110 (1961) (in-lieu fee borders on tax); *Contractors and Builders Assn. of Pinellas County v. CItu of Dunedin*, 329 So.2d 314 (Fla.1976), on remand 330 So.2d 744 (Fla.App.1976)(impact fee properly earmarked not a tax); *Western Heights Land Corp. v. City of Fort Collins*, 14 Colo. 464, 362 P.2d 155 (1961) (not a tax because not intended to defray general municipal expenses); *Home Builders Ass'n of Greater Salt Lake v. Provo City*, 28 Utah 2d 402, 503 P.2d 451 (1972) (charge for services not a general revenue measure); *Call v. West Jordan*, 606 P.2d 217 (Utah 1979), on rehearing 614 P.2d 1257 (in-lieu fee not a tax but a form of planning).

58 12 U.S. 377, 114 S.Ct. 2309, 2319, 129 L.Ed.2d 304 (1994).

59 22 Ill.2d 375, 176 N.E.2d 799 (1961). Note that the case has been reinterpreted by the Illinois courts in *Northern Ill. Home Builders v. County of Du Page*, 165 Ill.2d 25, 208 Ill.Dec. 328, 649 N.E.2d 384 (1995).

60 Note 33, supra.

61 512 U.S. 374, 391, 114 S.Ct. 2309, 2319-20, 129 L.Ed.2d 304 (1994).

62 512 U.S. 374, 391, 114 S.Ct. 2309, 2319-20, 129 L.Ed.2d 304 (1994).

63 See *McCarthy v. City of Leawood*, 257 Kan. 566, 894 P.2d 836, 845 (1995) and *Clajon Production Corp. v. Petera*, 70 F.3d 1566 (10th Cir.1995), both finding *Dolan* inapplicable to nonphysical conditions. See *Commercial Builders of Northern California v. City of Sacramento*, 941 F.2d 872 (9th Cir. 1991), cert.denied 504 W.S. 931, 112 S.Ct. 1997, 118 L.Ed.2d 738 (Wash.1995) ("Under Dolan, a land use regulation does not effect a taking if the local government shows by individualized determination that its exaction is 'roughly proportional' to the impact of the development."). For discussions of various cases on point, see David Callies, ed., *Takings: Land-Development Conditions and Regulatory Takings after Dolan and Lucas* (Chicago: American Bar Association, 1996); B. Gerry, "Parity Revisited: An Empirical Comparison of State and Lower Federal Court Interpretations of Nollan v. California Coastal Commission," 23 *Harv.J.L & Pub. Pol'y* 233 (1999); R. Faus, "Exactions, Impact Fees and Dedications—Local Government Responses to Nollan/Dolan Takings Law Issues," 29 *Stetson. L.Rev. 675 (2000).*

64 183 Ariz. 243, 902 P.2d 1347, 1352 (1995).

65 P.2d 429-50 (1996).

66 Note 62, supra.

67 187 Ariz. 479, 930 P.2d 993 (1997), cert. Denied 521 U.S. 1120, 117 S.Ct. 2512, 138 L.Ed.2d 1015 (1997).

68 *Id.* at 1000.

69 12 Cal.4th 854, 50 Cal.Rptr.2d 242, 911 P.2d 429 (1996), cert. Denied 519 U.S. 929, 117 S.Ct. 299, 136 L.Ed.2d 218 (1996).

70 12 Cal.4th 854, 50 Cal.Rptr.2d 242, 911 P.2d 429, 433 (1996), cert. Denied 519 U.S. 929, 117 S.Ct. 299, 136 L.Ed.2d 218 (1996).

71 Id *12 Cal. 4th at 860.* We arrive at this conclusion not by reference to the constitutional takings clause alone, but within the statutory framework presented by the Mitigation Fee Act (Gov. Code, Section 66000 et seq.). ... We thus interpret the Act's "reasonable relationship" standard of review formulated by the high court in Nollan and Dolan opinions. ... Applying this standard in this case, we conclude, first, that the city has met its burden of demonstrating the required connection or nexus between the rezoning ... and the imposition of a monetary exaction to be expended in support of recreational purposes as a means of mitigating that loss. We conclude, however, that the record before us is insufficient to sustain the city's determination that plaintiff pay a so-called mitigation fee of $280,00 as a condition for approval of his request that the property be rezoned to permit the construction of a condominium project. Because the city may be able to justify the imposition of some fee under the recently minted standard of Dolan, we follow the Oregon's Supreme Court's disposition in that case and direct that the cause be remanded to the city for additional proceedings in accordance with this opinion.

72 27 Cal.4th 643, 117 Cal.Rptr.2d 269, 41 P.3d 87 (2002).

73 Note 46, supra; note 47, supra.

74 126 P.3d 802 (Wash. 2006), cert. Denied, 127 S.Ct. 436 (2006) (Wsh. Sup. Ct. held city's transportation impact fee really excise tax and therefore not subject to dual rational nexus). For a discussion of the *Drebick* case, see Smith and Juergensmeyer (2007).

75 See *Taking Sides on Takings Issues: Public and Private Perspectives* (Thomas E. Roberts, ed.) (Chicago: American Bar Association, 2002), Chapters 13–15.

76 125 P.3d at 807–08.

77 See F. Bossleman, "Dolan Works, Taking SIdes on Taking Issues" (T. Roberts, ed.) (Chicago: American Bar Association, 2002), Chapter 14 at 353:

> The *Dolan* test is well established: it is logical in its outcome and it seems to work reasonably well for both developers and local governments. Let's not complicate the legal picture unnecessarily by imposing illogical limitations on the type of exactions to which the *Dolan* test applies.

78 See N. Stroud, "A Review of Del Monte Dunes v. City of Monterrey and its Implications for Local Government Exactions," 15 *J. Land Use and Envtl. Law* 195 (1999).

79 See D. Curtin and C. Talbert, "Applying Nollan/Dolan to Impact Fees: A Case for the Ehrlich Approach," in *Taking Sides on Takings Issues* (T. Roberts, ed.) (Chicago: American Bar Association, 2002), Chapter 13.

80 Id. *at 357.* Juergensmeyer and Nicholas (2002).

> No takings analysis of dual rational nexus-based impact fees is appropriate or necessary. If an impact fee is valid, i.e., it satisfies the dual rational nexus test, then it cannot destroy property rights. If an impact violates the nexus test … it is invalid.

81 544 U.S. 528, 125 S.Ct. 2074 (2005).
82 *Agins v. Tiburon,* 447 U.S. 255, 100 S.Ct. 2138 (1980).
83 544 U.S. 528, 125 S.Ct. 2074 (2005) at 2086.
84 544 U.S. 528, 125 S.Ct. 2074 (2005) at 2086.
85 *Loretto v. Teleprompter Manhattan CATV Corp.,* 458 U.S. 419, 102 S.Ct. 3164 (1982).
86 *Koontz v. St. Johns River Management Dist.,* 133 S.Ct. 2586, 186 L. Ed. 2d 697, 76 Env't. Rep. Cas. (BNA) 1649 (2013). For a discussion of the implications of Koontz for local governments, see Nolon, Bargaining for Development Post-Koontz: How the Supreme Court Invaded Local Government, 67 Fla. L. Rev 171 (2015). See also, Zygmunt J. B. Plater and Michael O'Loughlin, Semantic Hygiene for the Law of Regulatory Takings, Due Process, and Unconstitutional Conditions—Making Use of a Muddy Supreme Court Exactions Case, 89 Colorado L.Rev. 741 (2018)
87 *Koontz v. St. Johns River Water Management Dist.,* 133 S.Ct. 2586, 2595, 186 L. Ed. 2d 697, 76 Env't. Rep. Cas. (BNA) 1649 (2013)
88 133 S.Ct. at 2607.
89 133 S.Ct. at 2600.
90 *Cal. Bldg. Industry Assn. v. City of San Jose,* 61 Cal. 4th 435, 189 Cal. Rprt.3d 475, 351 P.3d 974 (2015), cert. denied. *Cal. Bldg. Indus. Ass'n v. City of San Jose,* 136 S. Ct. 928, 928 (2016)
91 The above discussion of the *Lingle* case is taken from Professor Roberts' discussion in Juergensmeyer and Roberts (2007), Section 10.5 (the numerous citations have been omitted).
92 *Dabbs v. Anne Arundel Cty.,* 232 Md. App. 314, 157 A.3d 381, cert. granted sub nom. *Dabbs v. Anne Arundel Co.,* 454 Md. 677, 165 A.3d 473 (2017), and aff'd, 458 Md. 331, 182 A.3d 798 (2018), cert. denied sub nom. *Dabbs v. Anne Arundel Cty.,* Md., 139 S. Ct. 230, 202 L. Ed. 2d 127 (2018).
93 Id.
94 *Dabbs v. Anne Arundel Cty.,* 232 Md. App. 314, 157 A.3d 381, 384, cert. granted sub nom. *Dabbs v. Anne Arundel Co.,* 454 Md. 677, 165 A.3d 473 (2017), and aff'd, 458 Md. 331, 182 A.3d 798 (2018), cert. denied sub nom. *Dabbs v. Anne Arundel Cty.,* Md., 139 S. Ct. 230, 202 L. Ed. 2d 127 (2018).
95 Id. (Additionally, "legislatively prescribed monetary fees"—as distinguished from ad hoc monetary demands by an administrative agency—"that are imposed as a condition of development are not subject to the Nollan-Dolan test"); San Jose, supra, 61 Cal.4th at p. 459, fn. 11, citing San Remo Hotel, supra, 27 Cal.4th at p. 663-71; see Ehrlich v. City of Culver City (1996) 12 Cal.4th 854, 876 [heightened scrutiny appropriate when exactions are imposed on individual and discretionary basis].

96 See *Dabbs v. Anne Arundel Cty.,* 458 Md. 331, 356 cert. denied, 139 S.Ct. 230 (2018); *CBIA,* 61 Cal. 4th at 459 n.11 (citing *San Remo Hotel,* 27 Cal. 4th at 666-69); *Alto Eldorado P'ship v. Cty. Of Santa Fe,* 634 F.3d 1170, 1179 (10th Cir. 2011); *St. Clair Cty. Home Builders Ass'n c. City of Pell City,* 61 So. 3d 992, 1007 (Ala. 2010); *Spinell Homes, Inc. v. Municipality of Anchorage,* 78 P.3d 692, 702 (Alaska 2003); *Krupp v. Breckenridge Sanitation Dist.,* 19 P.3d 687, 696 (Colo. 2001); *Home Builders Ass'n of Cent. Arizona v. City of Scottsdale,* 930 P.2d 993, 996 (Ariz. 1997), cert. denied, 521 U.S. 1120 (1997).
97 See *Town of Flower Mound, Tex. v. Stafford Estates Ltd. P'ship,* 135 S.W.3d 620, 641 (Tex. 2004); *Home Builders Ass'n of Dayton & the Miami Valley v. City of Beavercreek,* 729 N.E.2d 349, 355-56 (Ohio 2000); *Curtis v. Town of South Thomaston,* 708 A.2d 657, 660 (Maine 1998); *City of Portsmouth, N.H. v. Schlesinger,* 57 F.3d 12, 16 (1st Cir. 1995); *Northern Illinois Home Builders Ass'n Inc. v. City of Du Page,* 649 N.E.2d 384, 397 (Ill. 1995); *Manocherian v. Lenox Hill Hosp.,* 643 N.E.2d 479, 483 (N.Y. 1994), cert denied, 514 U.S. 1109 (1995); *Trimen Development Co. v. King Cty.,* 877 P.2d 187, 194 (Wash. 1994).
98 *California Bldg. Indus. Ass'n v. City of San Jose, Calif.,* 136 S. Ct. 928, 194 L. Ed. 2d 239 (2016) (THOMAS, J., dissenting).
99 See *616 Croft Ave., LLC v. City of W. Hollywood,* 138 S.Ct. 377 (2017) (No. 16-1137); *Common Sense All. V. San Juan Cty.,* 137 S.Ct. 58 (2016) (No. 15-1366); *CBIA,* 136 S.Ct. 928 (No. 15-330); *Cherk v. Cty. of Marin,* No. A153579, 2018 WL 6583442 (Cal. Ct. App. Dec. 14, 2018), review denied (Mar. 13, 2019).
100 *Alpine Homes, Inc. v. City of W. Jordan,* 2017 UT 45, 424 P.3d 95
101 Id. at 104-105
102 Id. at 105
103 Id.
104 See § 9:7. Capital improvement programming, Land Use Planning and Development Regulation Law § 9:7 (3rd edn).
105 See Arthur C. Nelson, James C. Nicholas & Julian C. Juergensmeyer, Impact Fees: Principles and Practice of Proportionate Share Development Fees Ch. 7 (2009). See also *City of Fayetteville v. IBI, Inc., 280 Ark. 484, 659 S.W.2d 505 (1983)* (requiring "reasonably definite" plan for expenditure of impact fees).
106 Land Use Planning and Development Regulation Law § 9:7 (3rd edn).
107 Id.
108 Id.; See *City of Ormond Beach v. County of Volusia, 535 So. 2d 302 (Fla. 5th DCA 1988); Seminole County v. City of Casselberry, 541 So. 2d 666 (Fla. 5th DCA 1989).*
109 See Chapter 3 for a listing and detailed analysis of state impact fee legislation.
110 See "2007 Impact Fee Enabling Acts" prepared by Clancy Mullen, AICP, of Duncan Associates of Austin, Texas. Updated material may be obtained from the Duncan Associates website: www.duncanplan.com and www.impactfees.com. See also Nicholas, Nelson, and Juergensmeyer (1991), Chapters 4 and 15; J.Bart Johnson and James van Hemert, *Development Impact*

Fees in the Rocky Mountain Region, 2nd edn (Denver: Rocky Mountain Land Use Institute, University of Denver, 2006); J. Nicholas and D. Davidson, *Impact Fees in Hawaii: Implementing the State Law* (Honolulu: Land Use Research Foundation, 992); Terry D. Morgan, "Recent Developments in the Law of Impact Fees with Special Attention to Legislation," 1990 Institute on Planning, Zoning, and Eminent Domain, Section 4; Terry D. Morgan, "State Impact Fee Legislation: guidelines for Analysis," *Land Use L. & Zoning Dig.* (March 1990 and April 1990); Martin L. Leitner and Susan P. Schoettle, "A Survey of State Impact Fee Enabling Legislation," 25 *Urb. Law.* 491 (1993). See Chapter 5, infra for a comparison of the Florida and Georgia statutory provisions.

111 *City of Fayetteville v. IBI, Inc.*, 659 S.W.2d 505, 507 (Ark. 1983).

112 No. 85-24 (July 31, 1985).

113 No. 85-23 (July 31, 1985).

114 Montgomery County Council Bill No. 17-86, Section 49A-8(c) (July 29, 1986).

115 126 P.3d 802 (Wash. 2006), cert. denied, 127 S.Ct. 436 (2006).

116 Codified as Official Code Georgia Annotated Section 36-71-2, 36-71-4, 36-71-5 and 36-71-8 (2007).

117 Codified as Nevada Statutes Section 278B.100 (2007)

118 *City of Fayetteville v. IBI, Inc.*, 280 Ark. 484, 659 S.W.2d 505 (Ark.1983).

119 642 P.2d 376 (Utah 1982).

120 329 So.2d 314 (Fla.1976), on remand 330 So.2d 744 (Fla.App.1976).

121 Note 36, supra.

122 This list is merely illustrative, not exhaustive. See generally Nicholas, Nelson, and Juergensmeyer (1991), at 2.

123 *Id.*

124 Smith and Juergensmeyer (2007).

125 Nicholas, Nelson, and Juergensmeyer (1991), at 48.

126 Andrews and Merriam (1988). See also Kayden and Pollard (1987), at 127, 128-29.

127 For a discussion of affordable housing as "social" infrastructure, see Marc T. Smith and Ruth L. Steiner, "Affordable Housing as an Adequate Public Facility," 36 *Val. U.L. Rev.* 443 (2002).

128 Juergensmeyer and Roberts (2007), at 442.

129 See generally Andrews and Merriam (1988).

130 Andrews and Merriam (1988), Chapter 19, at 228. See also Kayden and Pollard (1987), at 127.

131 See Connors and High (1987), at 69.

132 Note 71, supra.

133 941 F.2d 872 (9th Cir. 1991), cert. Denied 504 W.S. 931, 112 S.Ct. 1997, 118 L.Ed.2d 593 (1992).

134 *Id.* at 874.

135 *Id.* at 876. The *Commercial Builders* court also rejected the developer's contention that *Nollan* requires a more stringent taking standard, held that

> Nollan does not stand for the proposition that an exaction ordinance will be upheld only where it can be shown that the development is directly responsible for the social ill in question. Rather, Nollan holds that where there is no evidence of a nexus between the development and that problem that the exaction seeks to address, the exaction cannot be upheld.

136 121 N.J. 550, 583 A.2d 277 (1990).

137 67 N.J. 151, 336 A.2d 713 (1975) (Mt. Laurel I), appeal dismissed, cert. Denied 423 U.S. 808, 96 S.Ct. 18, 46 L.Ed.2d 28 (1975).

138 108 Wash.2d 20, 735 P.2d 673 (1987). See also *Sintra, Inc. v. City of Seattle*, 119 Wash.2d 1, 829 P.2d 765 (1992) (ordinance was found to be an illegal tax, and when the city persisted in applying the ordinance to other property, court found behavior which led to Section 1983 damages).

139 See Note 14, supra; *Bonan v. City of Boston*, 398 Mass. 315, 496 N.E.2d 640 (1986) (court did not reach issue of authority that was raised by lower court).

140 *San Telmo Assoc. v. City of Seattle*, 108 Wash.2d 20, 735 P.2d 673 (1987).

141 For a full discussion of due process, equal protection, and taking challenges, see William W. Merrill and Robert K. Lincoln, "Linkage Fees and Fair Share Regulations: Law and Method," 25 *Urb. Law* 223 (1993).

142 Note 120, supra.

143 See Ledman (1993), at 835; Nicholas, Juergensmeyer and Basse (1999), Part I, 7 *Env. Liab.* 27 ("Given the limitations of impact fees and Market-based environmental models, regulators may be able to combine advantages of both ... [in] a new regulatory alternative, the environmental mitigation fee." *Id.* Part II at 71); Nicholas and Juergensmeyer (2003); Nelson, Nicholas, and Marsh (1992), at 1.

144 See "Infrastructure and the Law: Florida's Past, Present and Future" (Juergensmeyer (2008)).

3 STATE IMPACT FEE LEGISLATION

This chapter provides an overview of state impact fee statutes, with summary tables and examples of evolving state statutes. This information is useful to practitioners because state statutes obviously affect local impact fee design. A broader purpose, however, is served by observing patterns in laws enacted by various states. Among other things, the statutes represent legislators' understanding of principles laid down by the courts. An understanding of case law can contribute to an understanding of the intent of the statutes, while the statutes themselves provide interpretations of the meaning of case law.

Impact fees were pioneered by local governments in the absence of explicit state enabling legislation. Consequently, such fees were originally defended as an exercise of local government's broad "police power" to protect the health, safety, and welfare of the community. The courts developed broad guidelines for constitutionally valid impact fees.

State legislatures then began imposing specific regulations. These statutes are often referred to as impact fee "enabling acts," although they are often adopted by states where local governments already had broadly construed police powers that provided sufficient authority to assess impact fees. In such states, the impact fee statutes often took away authority that previously existed, especially by limiting the types of facilities for which impact fees could be assessed.

There is some debate over which state was the first to adopt an impact fee statute. Utility connection fees that can function much like impact fees have long been authorized in most states. It appears that Texas adopted the first general impact fee statute in 1987. There also appears to have been precursors of current statutes in Arizona, California, and New Jersey in 1987, although we have not pinned down dates for those adoptions. Oklahoma became the latest state to adopt an impact fee act in 2011. To date, 29 states have adopted legislation for impact fees for facilities other than water and wastewater, which often already had statutory authorization (see Figure 3.1 and Table 3.1).

In some states that lack broadly construed police power authority or an enabling act, such as Maryland, Tennessee, and North Carolina, impact fees are authorized for individual jurisdictions through special acts of the legislature. A number of Maryland charter counties have been granted the authority to impose school impact fees, making Maryland the state with the fourth-highest number of school impact fees, after California, Florida, and Washington. In Tennessee, cities with mayor-aldermanic charters have the authority to impose impact fees without special authorizing legislation. In North Carolina, no new grants of impact fee authority via special acts have been approved by the legislature for many years.

In addition to road impact fees specifically authorized by statute, Virginia has a formalized system of developer exactions, known as cash proffers, that functions somewhat like impact fees. However, the proffer system does differ significantly in that there is no required nexus study or published fee schedule. Instead, developers "voluntarily" offer land dedications, capital improvements or cash payments as part of their application for rezoning, which may or may not be granted depending in part on whether the local governing body feels that the proffers sufficiently mitigate the project's impacts. In its essential characteristics, Virginia's proffer system is

DOI: 10.4324/9781003336075-4

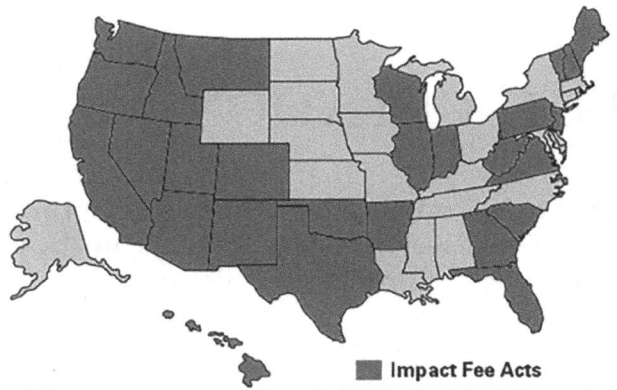

■ **Impact Fee Acts**

FIGURE 3.1 States with impact fee statutes.

closer to the negotiated developer exactions used by many communities across the country than it is to an impact fee system.

3.1 BASIC IMPACT FEE PRINCIPLES

Impact fees were pioneered by local governments in the absence of explicit state enabling legislation. Consequently, such fees were originally defended as an exercise of local government's broad police power to protect the health, safety and welfare of the community.

TABLE 3.1 State Impact Fee Statutes

State	Year	Citation
Arizona	1988	Ariz. Rev. Stat. Ann., § 9-463.05 (cities), § 11-1102 et seq. (counties)
Arkansas	2003	Arkansas Code, § 14-56-103 (cities only)
California	1989	Cal. Gov't Code, § 66000 et seq. (mitigation fee act); § 66477 (Quimby Act for park dedication/fee-in-lieu); § 17620 et. seq. (school fees)
Colorado	2001	Colo. Rev. Stat., § 29-20-104.5; § 29-1-801804 (earmarking requirements); § 22-54-102 (school fee prohibition)
Florida	2006	Florida Stat., § 163.31801
Georgia	1990	Georgia Code Ann., § 36-71-1 et seq.
Hawaii	1992	HIRev. Stat., § 46-142 et seq. (cities); § 264-121 et seq. (co.); § 320 (schools)
Idaho	1992	Idaho Code, § 67-8201 et seq.
Illinois	1987	605 Illinois Comp. Stat. Ann., § 5/5-901 et seq.
Indiana	1991	Indiana Code Ann., § 36-7-4-1300 et seq.
Maine	1988	Maine Rev. State. Ann., Title 30- A, § 4354
Maryland	1992	Maryland Code, Art. 258, § 13D (code home rule counties only)
Montana	2005	Montana Code Annotated, Title 7, Chapter 6, Part 16
Nevada	1989	Nevada Rev. Stat., § 2788
New Hampshire	1991	New Hampshire Rev. Stat. Ann., § 674:21
New Jersey	1989	New Jersey Perm. Stat., § 27:1C-1 et seq.; § 40:550-42
New Mexico	1993	New Mexico Stat. Ann., § 5- 8-1 et seq.
Oklahoma	2011	Oklahoma Statutes, § 62-895
Oregon	1991	Oregon Rev. State, § 223.297 et seq.
Pennsylvania	1990	Pennsylvania Stat. Ann., Title 53, § 10502-A et seq.
Rhode Island	2000	General Laws of Rhode Island, § 45- 22.4
South Carolina	1999	Code of Laws of South Carolina, § 6-1-910 et seq.
Texas	1987	Texas Local Government Code Ann., Title 12, § 395.001 et seq.
Utah	1995	Utah Code, § 11-36-101 et. seq.
Vermont	1989	Vermont Stat. Ann., Title 24, § 5200 et seq.
Virginia	1990	Virginia Code Ann., § 15.2-2317 et seq.
Washington	1991	RCW, § 82.02.050 et seq.
West Virginia	1990	West Virginia Code, § 7-20-1 et seq. (counties)
Wisconsin	1993	Wisconsin Stats., § 66.6017

The courts gradually developed guidelines for constitutionally valid impact fees, based on a "rational nexus" that must exist between the regulatory fee or exaction and the activity that is being regulated. The guiding principles developed in case law have been incorporated into state impact fee enabling acts to some degree. Some state acts have just borrowed terminology from case law, while others elaborate on the guidelines more explicitly.

Almost all of the state enabling acts contain words or phrases that indicate that impact fees should only charge new developments for their fair share of the capital costs they impose on the community. A number of different terms are used to express this sentiment. Arizona's act, for example, states that impact fees "must bear a reasonable relationship to the burden imposed ... to provide additional necessary public services to the development." Georgia's act states that new development cannot be required to pay "more than its proportionate share of the cost of public facilities needed to serve new growth." Many acts use multiple terms. For example, "proportionate share" is often defined as the cost of improvements that "reasonably relates" to the needs created by growth. The majority of state acts use one or more of the terms "proportionate share," "reasonable relationship" (or "reasonably related" or "reasonably attributable") or "necessitated by and attributable to."

While there is virtual unanimity among the state acts that impact fees should only require new development to pay for the cost of improvements that are reasonably related to its impacts, not all of them are clear on what this means. One of the things it should mean is that impact fees should not charge new development for a higher level of service than is provided to existing development. If the fees are based on a higher level of service than is provided to existing development in the community, other funding must be identified to remedy the existing deficiencies. This principle is expressed colloquially in the saying, "impact fees should not be used to pay for the sins of the past." Not all the enabling acts are clear on this point, but a majority state this principle in one way or another, as evidenced by the following examples:

Arizona: "Costs for necessary public services made necessary by new development shall be based on the same level of service provided to existing development in the service area." (Sec. 9-463.05.B.4, Ariz. Rev. Statutes)

California: "A fee shall not include the costs attributable to existing deficiencies in public facilities ..." (Sec. 66001(g), California Government Code)

Colorado: "No impact fee or other similar development charge shall be imposed to remedy any deficiency in capital facilities that exists without regard to the proposed development." (Sec. 29-20-104.5(2), Colo. Rev. Stat.)

Georgia: "Development impact fees shall be calculated on the basis of levels of service for public facilities that are ... applicable to existing development as well as the new growth and development." (Sec. 36-71-4(c), Ga. Code Ann.).

Montana: "New development may not be held to a higher level of service than existing users unless there is a mechanism in place for the existing users to make improvements to the existing system to match the higher level of service." (7-6-1602.5(d), Montana Code Ann.)

Utah: "... the local political subdivision may not impose an impact fee to cure deficiencies in public facilities serving existing development." (11-36-202(4), Utah Code)

A corollary principle is that new development should not have to pay more than its proportionate share when multiple sources of payment are considered. This principle is often expressed informally as "new development should not be charged twice for the same facilities." Virtually all of the state enabling acts require construction credits for developments that make in-kind contributions, such as the dedication of property or construction of improvements. The reduction of impact fees on a case-by-case basis for a particular development to account for such contributions is known as a "construction credit." All but four of the 29 state acts explicitly require that developers be given reimbursements or credits for in-kind contributions for the same type of capital facility costs covered by the impact fee. South Carolina's act words this principle as follows:

A developer required to pay a development impact fee may not be required to pay more than his proportionate share of the costs of the project, including the payment of money or contribution or dedication of land, or to oversize his facilities for use of others outside of the project without fair compensation or reimbursement.

(Sec. 6-1-1000, Code of Laws of S.C.)

Other sources of payment could include future property taxes that will be generated by the new development and used to pay debt service on existing facilities, or sales tax revenues earmarked to remedy existing deficiencies in facilities serving existing development. Since it is generally not possible to charge new development a lower property or sales tax rate than existing development, the solution is to reduce the impact fees by an amount equivalent to the future payments. Such a reduction is referred to as a "revenue credit." A majority of the state enabling acts explicitly require consideration of revenue credits. California stands out as the one state where revenue credits are generally not provided (this may be due to the interpretation of state courts). However, those acts that do mandate consideration of revenue credits often provide little guidance on how this should be accomplished. Georgia's act provides more guidance than most:

Development impact fees shall be calculated on a basis which is net of credits for the present value of revenues that will be generated by new growth and development based on historical funding patterns and that are anticipated to be available to pay for system improvements, including taxes, assessments, user fees, and intergovernmental transfers.

(Sec. 36-71-4(r), Ga. Code Ann.)

Most of the acts require credits only for future revenues that will be generated by the new development in the future. However, six state acts require credits for past revenues generated before the property was developed as well (referred to as "past credits"). In most cases, such credits are limited to property taxes paid by vacant land prior to development.

The basic standards enunciated by the enabling acts for calculating impact fees are summarized in Table 3.2. Florida's act is the only one not to contain any guiding terms or standards, probably because these are well-articulated in that state's case law. Florida aside, it is interesting to note that there is no unanimity among the state acts on clearly spelling out even the most basic impact fee principles.

3.2 ELIGIBLE FACILITIES

One of the most important things that most enabling acts do is restrict the types of facilities for which impact fees may be imposed. The types of facilities that are eligible for impact fees in the various state acts are listed in Table 3.3. It would be more accurate to say that these are the types of impact fees that are not prohibited by the enabling acts.

An exception is water and wastewater impact fees. In most states, with or without impact fee enabling acts, local governments

TABLE 3.2 Basic State Legislative Standards

State	Guiding Terms	No Higher LOS	Constr. Credits	Revenue Credits	Past Credits
Arizona	reasonable relationship	explicit	explicit	explicit	
Arkansas	reasonably attributable				
California	reasonable relationship	explicit	explicit*	explicit*	
Colorado	directly related	explicit	explicit		
Florida	proportional; reasonably connected; rational nexus		explicit		
Georgia	proportionate share; reasonably related	explicit	explicit	explicit	
Hawaii	proportionate share; reasonably attributable	explicit	explicit	explicit	yes
Idaho	proportionate share; reasonably relates	explicit	explicit	explicit	
Illinois	proportionate share; specifically and uniquely attributable	explicit	explicit	explicit	yes
Indiana	proportionate share		explicit	explicit	
Maine	reasonably related		explicit		
Maryland	required to accommodate new construction				
Montana	proportionate share; reasonably relates	explicit	explicit	explicit	
Nevada	necessitated by and attributable to		explicit		
New Hampshire	proportionate share; reasonably related				
New Jersey	fair share; reasonably related	explicit	explicit		
New Mexico	proportionate share; necessitated by and attributable to		explicit		
Oklahoma	proportionate share		explicit	explicit	
Oregon	equitable share		explicit	explicit	
Pennsylvania	necessitated by and attributable to	explicit	explicit	explicit	
Rhode Island	proportionate share; reasonably relates	explicit	explicit		
South Carolina	proportionate share; reasonably relates	explicit	explicit	explicit	
Texas	necessitated by and attributable to	explicit	explicit	explicit	
Utah	prop. share; roughly proportionate; reasonably related	explicit	explicit	explicit	yes
Vermont	proportionate share		explicit		
Virginia	necessitated by and attributable to proportionate share; reasonably related	explicit	explicit	explicit	yes
Washington			explicit	explicit	yes
West Virginia	proportionate share; reasonably attributed	explicit	explicit	explicit	yes
Wisconsin	proportionate share	explicit	explicit		

*Developer credits explicit for road and park in-kind contributions; revenue credits explicit for special district taxes used to finance schools.

have the authority to require payment of a fee at the time of meter purchase or connection to the public utility system. The fact that the general impact fee enabling act in a state does not specifically authorize water and wastewater impact fees does not necessarily mean that such fees are prohibited. In fact, it is likely that such fees are authorized under a separate statute governing public utilities.

3.3 PLANNING AND ANALYSIS REQUIREMENTS

For the most part, state legislation does not establish maximum fees that can be charged. Instead, the state acts require, implicitly or explicitly, that a study or analysis be done to determine how to apply the "proportionate share" or other guiding standard in order to determine the maximum amounts that the local government can charge. The planning and analysis requirements of the various state impact fee enabling acts are summarized in Table 3.4. Note that eight of the 29 acts do not even explicitly require that a written analysis be performed. However, it is hard to imagine how compliance with the general impact fee principles expressed by the acts could be demonstrated without some kind of written report.

Many of the state acts require that the local government identify the "service area" where the impact fees will be collected based on the service provided to new development from a common set of facilities. Most acts require that impact fees collected within a service area must be spent on capital improvements within the same service area. In general, local governments are allowed broad discretion in defining service areas, which can cover the

TABLE 3.3 Facilities Eligible for Impact Fees by State

State	Roads	Water	Sewer	Storm Water	Parks	Fire	Police	Library	Solid Waste	School
Arizona (counties)	X	X	X		X	X	X			
Arkansas (cities)	X	X	X	X	X	X	X	X		
California	X	X	X	X	X	X	X	X	X	X
Colorado	X	X	X	X	X	X	X	X	X	
Florida	X	X	X	X	X	X	X	X	X	X
Georgia	X	X	X	X	X	X	X	X		
Hawaii	X	X	X	X	X	X	X	X	X	X
Idaho	X	X	X	X	X	X	X			
Illinois	X									
Indiana	X	X	X	X	X					
Maine	X	X	X		X	X			X	
Maryland	X	X	X	X	X	X	X	X	X	X
Montana	X	X	X	X	*	X	X	*	*	*
Nevada	X	X	X	X	X	X	X			**
New Hampshire	X	X	X	X	X	X	X	X	X	X
New Jersey	X	X	X	X						
New Mexico	X	X	X	X	X	X	X			
Oklahoma	X	X	X	X	X	X	X		X	
Oregon	X	X	X	X	X					***
Pennsylvania	X									
Rhode Island	X	X	X	X	X	X	X	X	X	X
South Carolina	X	X	X	X	X	X	X	X	X	X
Texas (cities)	X	X	X	X						
Utah	X	X	X	X	X	X	X			
Vermont	X	X	X	X	X	X	X	X	X	X
Virginia****	X									
Washington	X				X	X				X
West Virginia	X	X	X	X	X	X	X			X
Wisconsin (cities)	X	X	X	X	X	X	X	X	X	

* Can be imposed by a super-majority vote of the city council or unanimous vote of the county commission.
** School construction tax up to $1,600 per unit authorized in districts with populations up to 50,000 (NRS 387.331).
*** Development tax of up to $1.00/sq. ft. for residential and $0.50/sq. ft. for nonresidential may be imposed by school districts.
**** Impact fees may be imposed on a by-right residential subdivision of agriculturally zoned parcels for a broad array of facilities under certain circumstances.

TABLE 3.4 State Legislation: Planning Requirements

State	Written Analysis	Service Areas	List of Projects	Growth Projection	LOS Standards
Arizona (cities)	yes	yes	yes	yes	yes
Arizona (counties)	yes		yes		
Arkansas	yes		yes	yes	yes
California	yes		yes		
Colorado					
Florida					
Georgia	yes	yes			yes
Hawaii	yes	yes	yes	yes	yes
Idaho					yes
Illinois	yes	yes	yes	yes	yes
Indiana	yes		yes	yes	yes
Maine					
Maryland					
Montana	yes	yes	yes	yes	yes
Nevada	yes	yes	yes	yes	
New Hampshire	yes		yes	yes	
New Jersey					
New Mexico	yes	yes	yes	yes	
Oklahoma	yes	yes	yes		
Oregon	yes	yes			
Pennsylvania	yes	yes	yes	yes	yes
Rhode Island	yes		yes		yes
South Carolina	yes	yes	yes	yes	yes
Texas	yes	yes	yes	yes	
Utah	yes	yes	yes		
Vermont	yes	yes	yes		yes
Virginia	yes	yes	yes	yes	
Washington		yes			
West Virginia					yes
Wisconsin	yes	yes	yes		

entire jurisdiction, or only a subarea of the city or county. An exception is the Texas act, which limits service areas for transportation impact fees to no more than six miles.

Two-thirds of the state acts require that the impact fees be based on a capital improvement plan. In some state acts, as in the original Texas act, the required "capital improvements plan" is both a list of projects to be funded with the impact fees and the written analysis used to calculate the impact fees. Some of these capital plan requirements simply mandate that a list of projects be developed on which the fees will be spent. The Arkansas act, for example, requires that the municipality adopt a "capital plan," which is defined as:

A description of new public facilities or of new capital improvements to existing public facilities or of previous capital improvements to public facilities that continue to provide capacity available for new development that includes cost estimates and capacity available to serve new development ...

(Sec. 14-56-103(a)(1),
Arkansas Code)

About half the state acts require land use projections that cover the same period as the capital plan. The combination of these two requirements, the capital plan and growth projections, would seem to imply that impact fees in these states must be calculated using a "plan-based" (or "improvements-driven") methodology. Such a methodology determines capital improvements needed to accommodate projected growth over a fixed planning horizon; it then divides the total improvement cost by the projected growth in service units to determine the gross impact fee (i.e., before consideration of revenue credits). Some states with these requirements, such as Texas, even specify that impact fees may not exceed the amount determined by dividing the costs of the capital improvements by the total number of projected service units. Yet, while these requirements do force the impact fee calculations to take the form of a plan-based methodology, in many cases the fees are actually based on a simple, system-wide ratio (e.g., 10 acres of park land per 1,000 residents), for which a plan-based methodology is not required.

One cannot calculate an impact fee without at least an implicit level of service standard. Without such a standard, it would not be possible to determine the impact of a new development on the need for capital facilities. However, only about half of the state acts require that the local government explicitly describe the level of service standards on which the impact fees are based. Some states that do not mandate explicit levels of service prohibit the use of impact fees from being used to remedy existing deficiencies, which in turn implies the use of a level of service standard.

In an ideal world, impact fees would always be based on extensive planning. However, many communities, especially smaller ones, do not have the resources to prepare long-range facility master plans, and it is possible to calculate defensible impact fees in the absence of such planning documents. Intentionally or not, state acts with extensive planning requirements may make it more difficult for communities to adopt impact fees.

3.4 SUBSTANTIVE REQUIREMENTS

A review of the state statutes reveals that, outside of the general principles and planning standards discussed above, there is little agreement about what form state regulation should take. State impact fee statutes impose both substantive and procedural requirements. Selected substantive provisions of the state acts are summarized in Table 3.5. The first column, showing the length of the various acts, illustrates that statutes range from brief grants of authority and statements of general principles (Arkansas, Florida, Maine, Maryland, Vermont, Wisconsin) to the lengthy, detailed and overlapping provisions of California's legislation.

About one-third of the statutes allow impact fees to be collected at any time during the development process. Most of the others provide that impact fees cannot be collected prior to the building permit or certificate of occupancy.

A majority of the state acts explicitly allow local governments to recoup costs incurred prior to the development, provided that the capacity is available to serve the development. It should be noted that recoupment fees are not necessarily prohibited by the state acts that do not explicitly authorize them. Rhode Island's act commonsensically provides that the portion of an impact fee deemed recoupment is exempted from provisions requiring expenditure in eight years (Sec. 45-22.4-5(c)). To the extent that the capital improvement that the fees are paying for has already been paid for, recoupment fees can be returned to the general fund or used for whatever purpose the local government chooses.

Several states, following Texas' early lead, have imposed a recalculation requirement. This provision mandates that the local government recalculate the impact fees after completion of the capital improvements plan, and then refund any excess collected if actual costs were less than projected costs. This provision from the original Texas act was copied almost verbatim in several other acts. Texas has since repealed the provision. The provision is seldom applicable since impact fees are usually updated before the completion of the

TABLE 3.5 State Legislation Substantive Provisions

State	Word Count	When Collected	Recoupment?	Recalc. Required?	Platting Locks in Fee?	Explicit Wavers	Waiver Funding Required?
Arizona (cities)	1,652	bldg. permit	yes	yes	2 years	schools*	yes
Arizona (counties)	887	anytime				schools*	
Arkansas (cities)	1,634	cert. of occ.	yes				
California	22,907	cert. of occ.	yes				
Colorado	3980	anytime				afford hsg*	no
Florida	1,035	anytime				schools/afford hsg	
Georgia	3,757	bldg. permit	yes		180 days	ec.dv./aff.h.	yes
Hawaii	2,017	bldg. permit	yes				
Idaho	7,124	bldg. permit				afford hsg**	yes
Illinois	5,670	bldg. permit					
Indiana	9,705	bldg. permit			3 years	afford hsg	yes
Maine	465	anytime	yes	yes			
Maryland	49	anytime					
Montana	1,809	bldg. permit	yes				
Nevada	4,685	bldg. permit				schools	no
New Hampshire	2,356	cert. of occ.	yes	yes			
New Jersey	8,760	bldg. permit					
New Mexico	6,575	bldg. permit	yes	yes	4 years	afford hsg	unclear
Oklahoma	2,537	bldg. permit	yes			multiple	yes
Oregon	4,111	anytime	yes				
Pennsylvania	6,115	bldg. permit		yes		afford/other	no
Rhode Island	1,942	cert. of occ.	yes			general	no
South Carolina	4,624	bldg. permit				afford hsg	yes
Texas	8,641	bldg. permit	yes		forever	afford hsg	no
Utah	5,553	anytime	yes			afford hsg	yes
Vermont	1,229	anytime	yes	yes		general	no
Virginia	1,893	bldg. permit		yes			
Washington	2,064	anytime	yes			general	yes
West Virginia	3,105	anytime	yes			general	yes
Wisconsin	1,167	bldg. permit				afford hsg	no

Notes:

afford hsg=affordable housing
bldg. permit=building permit
cert. of occ.=certificate of occupancy
ec. dev.=economic development

* Public schools are exempt from all impact fees except for streets and utilities.
** Plus "taxing entities" unless adopting ordinance expressly provides otherwise.

entire capital plan. However, Arizona's statute for cities requires refunds if the actual cost of an individual construction project is more than 10 percent below the estimated cost.

Another type of provision pioneered by the Texas act stipulates that fees are assessed at platting and locked in for a period of time. In the Texas act, the fee schedule in effect at the time of final subdivision approval is the maximum fee that may be charged to the development within the subdivision, regardless of when building construction actually occurs.

Another four states lock in the fee schedule in effect at the time of platting for a fixed period of time.

While about half of the acts are silent on the issue of waivers or exemptions, the other half explicitly authorize local governments to waive impact fees for certain types of projects. Most of them limit waivers to affordable housing or, to a lesser extent, economic development projects. Of the acts that authorize waivers, about half require that the local government reimburse the impact fee fund from some other, non-impact fee revenue source.

3.5 PROCEDURAL REQUIREMENTS

In addition to substantive provisions, many impact fee statutes set forth procedural requirements for impact fee adoption and updating. Some of these procedural provisions are summarized in Table 3.6. Ten states require that an advisory committee be appointed to oversee the development of the impact fee system, although Arizona cities have the option of conducting a certified biennial audit. The committee generally must have significant representation from the development community, most commonly 40 percent.

State acts generally require that impact fees be adopted by ordinance at a duly noticed public hearing. Many of the acts even specify the minimum time period that notice must be published before the public hearing is held. Six state acts specify the time period that must elapse between the adoption of an impact fee ordinance and the imposition of the new or increased impact fee (see the "Fee Phase-In" column in Table 3.6).

A majority of state acts require that impact fee revenues be spent within a specified number of years or be refunded to the fee payer. These requirements range from 5 to 15 years, with 6 years being the most common. In states with refund requirements, local governments must keep records on fee payments to be able to track the payment and expenditure of fees on a "first-in, first-out" basis. In practice, however, refunds due to the failure to spend the money within the required time period are rare. Most acts are silent on how frequently the fees must be updated. Of the less than one-third that require periodic updates, every five years is the most common requirement. Four states, Arizona, California (school impact fees only), Nevada (road impact fees only), and Oregon, have guidelines for indexing fees for inflation between periodic updates.

Several state acts authorize the use of a portion of impact fees collected to defray the cost of administering the impact fee system. Some set limits on the percentage of impact fees that can be used for this purpose, while others require that administrative fees be limited to actual administrative costs. Some limit the use of such fees to paying for the costs of preparing the impact fee study or capital improvements plan.

3.6 FROM A FLURRY TO FINE-TUNING: THE PROGRESSION OF IMPACT FEE STATUTES WITH SPECIAL REFERENCE TO FLORIDA

From 1987 to 1993, there was a flurry of legislative activity as 21 states adopted impact fee statutes. This was an average of three new acts each year. Since then, eight additional states have adopted enabling legislation. There have been no new statutes since Oklahoma's in 2011. A major factor in the initial surge of impact fee acts was the support of builder groups, who wanted impact fees that were being imposed by local governments under their police powers to be regulated. Now that virtually all states with significant growth and impact fee activity have statutes, one might expect builders' and legislators' attention to shift to fine-tuning existing legislation.

Following the 2007 housing market crash and the ensuing economic recession, some

TABLE 3.6 State Legislation: Procedural Provisions

State	Advisory Committee Size	Advisory Committee Dev. Rep.	Hearing Notice	Fee Phase-In	Spending Limit	Update Frequency	Admin. Fee
Arizona (cities)	5+ (1)	50%	60 days	75 days	10 years (2)	5 years	
Arizona (counties)			120 days	90 days			
Arkansas (cities)					7 years		
California			30 days	60 days	5 years		3% (3)
Colorado							
Florida				90 days			actual cost
Georgia	5–10	50%			6 years		3%
Hawaii			15 days		6 years		
Idaho	5+	2+	2 weeks	8 years (4)	5 years		
Illinois	10–20	40%	30 days		5 years	5 years	
Indiana	5–10	40%			6 years	5 years	5%
Maine							
Maryland							
Montana	n/a	A					
Nevada	5+	n/a	20 days		10 years	3 years	study cost
New Hampshire					6 years		
New Jersey							
New Mexico	5+	40%	zoning		7 years	5 years	3%
Oklahoma	planning commission		15 days			annual report	
Oregon			90 days				study cost
Pennsylvania	7–15	40%	2 weeks				
Rhode Island					8 years		
South Carolina			30 days	3 years (5)	5 years (6)		
Texas	5+	40%	30 days		10 years	5 years	study cost
Utah			2 weeks	90 days	6 years		
Vermont					6 years		
Virginia****	5–10	40%			15 years	2 years	
Washington				60 days	6 years		
West Virginia			1 week		7 years		

Notes: dev. rep. means development industry representation. (1) optional, can choose biennial audit; (2) 15 years for water/wastewater; (3) school impact fee only; (4) 11 years if finding of reasonable cause; (5) "An impact fee must be refunded … if: (1) the impact fees have not been expended within three years of the date they were scheduled to be expended"; (6) "review" every 5 years, "update" every 10 years.

state legislatures restricted local governments' impact fee authority. Wisconsin became the first state to withdraw authority to impose impact fees when it repealed the authority of counties to impose fees and prohibited fees for major park improvements and public safety vehicles in 2006. Florida prohibited state courts from using a deferential standard when ruling on legal challenges to impact fees in 2009. Arizona imposed a two-year freeze on new or increased impact fees in 2009, extended the freeze for another year in 2010, and made its statute for municipalities much more restrictive in 2011 by, among other things, prohibiting fees for general government facilities, parks over 30 acres, libraries over 10,000 square feet and library books and equipment, community centers over 3,000 square feet, solid waste facilities, and fire and police administrative and training buildings and aircraft. North Carolina imposed new requirements on water and wastewater development fees, including a provision that the authority to impose system development fees is to be narrowly construed to ensure that the fees do not unduly burden new development in 2017, and the following year repealed the private act allowing Orange County to impose school impact fees after the county significantly raised those fees. Florida passed three impact fee bills in 2019 and 2020 requiring developer credits to be based on full market value, to be transferrable to other projects within the same benefit district, and to be increased by the same percentage by which impact fees are increased.

In addition to legislative actions, court decisions favorable to development interests in Mississippi and North Carolina in 2006 undermined home rule authority for impact fees in those states that lack explicit state authorization.

Not all the impact fee legislative changes in recent years have restricted local governments' impact fee authority. Nevada added authority to impose impact fees for traffic signals, parks, and police and fire stations in 2001. In 2007, Hawaii gave the state school board the authority to designate school impact districts where school impact fees and dedication requirements apply. Oklahoma adopted a new impact fee statute for municipalities in 2011 that authorizes a wide variety of fees, including for public transportation. South Carolina authorized school impact fees in 2016.

While it is difficult to generalize, there does seem to have been a hardening of resistance among development interests and legislators to granting additional impact fee authority or even allowing the existing authority to continue to be available. This may be due, in part, to the increasing level of impact fees being charged, as well as the depressed state of the development industry prior to the last few years. Evidence of this resistance is mounting. The retrenchment of impact fee authority in Wisconsin (2006) and Arizona (2011) are prime examples. Legislation in New Mexico that attempted to retroactively prohibit Albuquerque's "growth tier" impact fee system was narrowly defeated in 2005. The relatively benign Florida act was enacted only after a very restrictive version narrowly failed, and local governments in that state are now conducting annual battles with legislators to preserve their relatively unfettered impact fee authority. Court decisions favorable to development interests in Mississippi and North Carolina in 2006 undermined home rule authority for impact fees in those states. Efforts in the Florida legislature in 2009 to freeze impact fees for three years were narrowly defeated, while similar efforts in 2009 to freeze impact fees for two years succeeded in Arizona (in 2010 this was extended for another year). In sum, future legislative battles seem likely to revolve around preserving, rather than expanding, impact fee authority, at least in the near term.

3.7 SUMMARY

The majority of the states have statutes that authorize and regulate local governments' imposition of impact fees on new development. These statutes vary widely in terms of the types of facilities for which fees are authorized and the content of the regulations. All the statutes use one or more terms that are drawn from case law, such as "proportionate share." The majority endorse in some form the key legal principle enshrined in impact fee case law – that the fee should not exceed the cost to maintain the existing level of service. Most of the statutes also contain provisions relating to impact fee calculation, ordinance, and administration, including planning requirements, substantive regulations, and procedures.

The earliest impact fee ordinances were adopted in states where local governments had relatively broad police power to regulate development so as to protect and preserve the health, safety and welfare of the community.

Now, in most states with widespread local interest in using impact fees as a funding source, the state legislature has preempted local authority in the field. The current phase of this evolution appears to be one of fine-tuning and often further restricting that authority.

4 A TALE OF TWO STATES

Texas and Georgia Impact Fee Legislation Compared

As the review in Chapter 3 of the key features of state impact fee legislation reveals, states have taken very different approaches in regard to impact fee legislation. Some states, Georgia, for example, have striven for a comprehensive and coherent impact fee act that attempts to give legislative direction and answers to as many legal and administrative issues as possible. Others, such as Florida, for example, have left it to courts and local governments to formulate a legal and administrative framework for impact fees. In effect, they have chosen a piecemeal approach to giving legislative input on nitty-gritty issues. This unfortunately catches the attention of lobbyists who aim to convince the state legislature to resolve politically only a short list of sensitive issues and uncertainties usually on a legislative session by legislative session basis. Still other states, Texas, for example, have aimed for the middle and seek to comprehensively cover some aspects of impact fee administration and implementation but leave other aspects without legislative direction. Georgia's and Texas's statutes have served as models for many states regardless of whether they strive for comprehensive legislation or a piecemeal approach.

The outlier among states may be California. While its impact fee statute, AB 1600, was crafted during the same era as Texas and Georgia (1987), it includes many more facilities. And given how broadly worded many of its provisions are, the California Act would seem to provide local governments with the most flexibility in designing and implementing impact fee programs.[1]

In recognition of the popularity of legislative provisions of Texas and Georgia, this chapter analyzes how they approach the same impact fee issues with respect to the following elements:

Life of Capital Improvements
Types of Capital Improvements for Which There Can Be Impact Fees
Forms of Local Governments That May Act
Time for Assessment and Collection
Affordable Housing Exemptions
Service Units and Service Areas
Collection of Impact Fees When Services Are Unavailable
Government Payment of Impact Fees
Refunds
Advisory Committees
Moratoriums
Capital Improvements Plan Requirements
Intergovernmental Agreements
Impact Fee Caps
Credit Provisions
Project Improvements vs. System Improvements
Appeals
Comprehensive Plans
Proportionate-Share Calculation

Impact fee practice in these states is influenced heavily by how each of these elements is addressed by their enabling acts.

4.1 LIFE OF CAPITAL IMPROVEMENTS

The Georgia statute defines capital improvement as an improvement having a useful life of ten years or more, which increases the service capacity of a public facility.[2] The Texas Code section, on the other hand, explains that capital improvement means a facility with

DOI: 10.4324/9781003336075-5

a life expectancy of three or more years and owned and operated by or on behalf of a city or county.[3]

4.1.1 Types of Capital Improvements for Which There Can Be Impact Fees

The list of public facilities that can be funded by impact fees is more extensive in Georgia Development Impact Fee Act ("Georgia Act") than the one in Texas Local Government Code ("Texas Code"). In Georgia, public facilities covered by impact fees include roads, water, stormwater, sewer, parks, fire, police, library, and related services.[4] In Texas, impact fees can only be used to fund roads, water, stormwater, and sewer facilities.[5] Since impact fees provide additional revenue for local governments without having to raise taxes for the construction of capital improvements, local governments in Georgia end up being equipped with more ways to obtain financial resources than their Texas counterparts for covering infrastructure needs associated with the new developments. Governments in Georgia can charge fees to fund parks, recreation areas, and open spaces, all of which promote a cleaner environment, healthier communities, and better quality of life that could otherwise be lost to new developments. Fire, police, and emergency medicine can also be covered without having to create additional tax burdens. In Texas, cities sometimes scramble for money to hire new police officers or to build new fire stations, let alone to fund new parks when a new development comes along. In Georgia, under similar circumstances, impact fees can cover at least some of such costs.

4.1.2 Forms of Local Governments that May Act

In Georgia, both cities and counties may impose impact fees. In Texas, only cities can impose impact fees. Although the Texas impact fee list excludes stormwater, drainage, and flood control, the statute allows Harris County, the home of Houston, and adjacent counties to do so.[6]

4.1.3 Time for Assessment and Collection

The time for assessment and collection of development impact fees is different in Texas and Georgia. In Georgia, impact fees cannot be collected before the issuance of a building permit authorizing construction or site improvement.[7] In Texas, the timing of plat recording is a factor. For land platted before June 20, 1987, cities and counties in Texas can collect impact fees at either the time of recordation of the subdivision plat, at the time the building permit or certificate of occupancy is issued, or at the time of connection to the city/county water or sewer system. For new developments platted after June 20, 1987, the impact fees can be assessed before or after the time of plat recordation, connection to the city/county's water or sewer system, or once the building permit or the certificate of occupancy is issued.[8] We also note that in Texas, once the impact fee ordinance is adopted, platting locks the current fees in place in perpetuity. These provisions can complicate impact fee collection at the time of building permit issuance.

4.1.4 Affordable Housing Exemptions

Texas allows for the possibility of a complete impact fee waiver for affordable housing developments.[9] The Georgia Act also offers an impact fee exemption associated with affordable housing, but under the condition that a revenue source other than development impact fees is secured to fund the anticipated infrastructure needs before the exemption can be granted.[10] While the Texas Code seems to promote a more favorable policy toward affordable housing construction, it does not assure the quality of services provided to the new affordable housing developments. In Georgia, affordable housing exemption is more difficult to get, since another infrastructure funding source has to be secured, but the new affordable development is more likely to enjoy standard roads, water, fire, police, EMS, etc.

4.1.5 Service Units and Service Areas

The service area that benefits from the impact fees collected is more strictly defined in the Texas Code. For example, in the Texas Code, the service area for roadway facilities cannot exceed six miles.[11] The Georgia Act does not provide for such mileage restrictions. Instead, municipalities in Georgia have more discretion than their Texas counterparts as to how to spend the funds collected as impact fees, so long as proximity to developments that have paid the fees and the greatest effect on levels of service on roadways affected by those new developments is considered. Otherwise, transportation impact fees can be spent anywhere within the city limits.[12]

4.1.6 Collection of Impact Fees When Services Are Unavailable

In Texas, except for roadways, impact fees may be assessed but may not be collected where services are currently unavailable, unless an exception applies. One of such exceptions is a credit against the impact fees otherwise due from the new development if the city or county agrees that the owner of the new development may construct or finance the capital improvements. Alternatively, the city can agree to reimburse the owner for such costs from impact fees paid from other new developments that will use such capital improvements.[13] Georgia offers similar credit or reimbursement options.[14] We note that the Texas provision is repeated in several other acts. As a practical matter, this provision may have little effect because impact fees are rarely collected at the platting stage.

4.2 GOVERNMENT PAYMENT OF IMPACT FEES

In Texas, municipalities, counties, and other governmental entities may pay impact fees. School districts in Texas, though, are not required to pay impact fees unless the board of trustees of the school district consents to the payment by entering into a contract with the government that imposes the fees.[15] School districts in Georgia do not enjoy such an exemption.

4.2.1 Refunds

Both the Texas Code and Georgia Act provide for impact fee refunds but impose different conditions. In Georgia, upon impact feepayor's request, a municipality or county has to refund development impact fees if the impact fees have not been encumbered or construction has not begun within six years of the date the fee was collected.[16] The Texas Code gives cities less time: A refund has to be issued upon impact feepayor's request if construction has not begun within two years or services have not been made available within a reasonable time, but "in no event later than five years from the date of payment."[17] However, we observe that this occurs only where fees are collected, and service is not provided within 10 years.[18] Furthermore, whether intentionally or not, the Texas Code does not specify whether the original payor or a successor owner should be refunded if the impact fees are not spent or encumbered in a timely manner. The Georgia Act, on the other hand, does, possibly saving judicial resources by reducing litigation commenced to clarify refund recipients.

4.2.2 Advisory Committees

The Texas statute requires that prior to imposing an impact fee, the political subdivision (a municipality or a county) appoint a capital improvements advisory committee. Such a committee serves in an advisory capacity to, inter alia, review, monitor, and evaluate the capital improvements plan and to advise of the need to update or revise the capital improvements plan, the land use assumptions, and the impact fee.[19] Similarly, prior to the adoption of a development impact fee ordinance, the Georgia statute requires that a municipality or county establish a Development Impact Fee Advisory Committee. The advisory committee in Georgia, like its Texas counterpart, serves in an advisory capacity to assist with regard to the adoption of a development impact fee ordinance.[20]

Yet another albeit small difference between Georgia and Texas impact fee legislative provisions is that the Texas version requires "not less than" 40 percent of the capital improvements advisory committee to be representatives of real estate, development, or building industries,[21] while Georgia's version mandates "at least" 50 percent of the Development Impact Fee Advisory Committee's membership be from building, development, or real estate industries.[22] One of the impact fee criticisms has been that it is a top-down structure, giving governments too much power to interfere with property rights by imposing a fee without meaningful developer input. The Georgia Act rebuts this criticism by clearly mandating that at least half of the Committee is composed of those likely to become feepayors; thus, the developer community is given a fair chance to contribute in an advisory fashion. Texas Code does not provide for such an advisory committee membership balance.

4.2.3 Moratoriums

Texas Code prohibits moratoriums on development while impact fees are being assessed,[23] while the Georgia Act does not. A development moratorium is a tool to help the city plan for the anticipated growth in a calculated and reasonable manner. Local governments in Texas do not have such luxury and are left with responding to growth in a possibly rushed way.

4.2.4 Capital Improvements Plan Requirements

In Georgia, in order to assess an impact fee, local governments must have a comprehensive plan with a "capital improvements element."[24] A "capital improvements element" means a component of a comprehensive plan which sets out projected needs for system improvements during a planning horizon established in the comprehensive plan, a schedule of capital improvements that will meet the anticipated need for system improvements, and a description of anticipated funding sources for each required improvement.[25] Texas has a much more robust capital improvements plan provision that requires a number of specific enumerations.[26]

4.3 INTERGOVERNMENTAL AGREEMENTS

In Georgia, municipalities and counties which are jointly affected by development are authorized to enter into intergovernmental agreements with each other, with authorities, or with the state for the purpose of developing joint plans for capital improvements or for the purpose of agreeing to collect and expend development impact fees for system improvements, or both.[27] The Texas Code is silent on such intergovernmental agreements.

4.3.1 Impact Fee Caps

Differences regarding the calculation and application of impact fees exist between the two states. In Georgia, impact fees are to be a proportionate share of the cost and calculated on the basis of the level of service required for the new area. The fee in Georgia must be based on the actual cost of the improvement or a reasonable estimate. Texas, on the other hand, limits fees to the construction price, surveying and engineering fees, land acquisition costs, and fees for developing plans. Texas also has a provision that sets a maximum fee limit, which is not found in the Georgia Act.

4.3.2 Credit Provisions

Georgia and Texas differ slightly in their credit provisions. Texas has a simple provision that allows any construction of, contributions to, or dedications of off-site roadway facilities agreed to or required by a political subdivision as a condition of development approval to be credited against roadway facilities impact fees otherwise due from the development.[28] Georgia allows for credit to be applied against impact fee credit for the present value of any construction of improvements or contribution or dedication of land or money required or accepted by a municipality or county from a developer or his predecessor in title or interest for system improvements of the category for which the development impact fee is being collected.[29] Georgia does not allow credits to be given for project improvements.[30] Additionally, if a developer in Georgia constructs, funds, or contributes system improvements with a value that is in excess of the impact fee for the project, then the developer may be reimbursed for such excess contribution.[31]

4.4 PROJECT IMPROVEMENTS VS. SYSTEM IMPROVEMENTS

The Georgia code provides a clear distinction between project improvements and system improvements. Project improvements are site improvements and facilities that are planned and designed to provide service for a particular development project and that are necessary for the use and convenience of the occupants or users of the project and are not system improvements.[32] System improvements are capital improvements that are public facilities and are designed to provide service to the community at large.[33]

4.4.1 Appeals

The Texas and Georgia codes also differ in their appeals processes. The Georgia code section on appeals is fairly brief and directs local governments to hear appeals on impact fee determinations for particular projects.[34] The Georgia code section also allows for developers to pay impact fees under protest, which allows for them to obtain any permits or approvals to begin work on the development while preserving their rights to appeal and receive refunds.[35] Georgia also allows local governments to provide that disputes over impact fees be resolved through binding arbitration.[36]

The Texas Code section on appeals gives developers the right to a trial *de novo* if they have exhausted all administrative remedies with the local government.[37] Any lawsuit under this section must be filed in the county where the development is located within 90 days of the establishment of the impact fee.[38] The Texas Code section also entitles developers and owners to specific performance of the services by the local government for which the fee was paid.[39]

4.4.2 Comprehensive Plans

Georgia Act requires that impact fees be calculated based on public facilities adopted in the municipal or county comprehensive plan. The Texas Code does not mention that standards are needed in a comprehensive plan as a necessary component of impact fee calculation. Instead, the Texas Code mandates a capital improvements plan, but such a plan can be made contemporaneously with the impact fee calculations and seems to only cover the area that would benefit from the particular impact fee.

The Georgia Act's requirement for governments to have a comprehensive plan prepared before impact fees could be charged guides more structured and thought-out urban growth management practices. This empowers governments to anticipate growth needs and problems before the growth actually occurs. In Texas, the governments are sometimes left to wait until growth occurs and then to respond to the needs of that unplanned urban expansion.

One concern some may have about linking impact fees to the plan is that it could limit impact fee calculations to only the plan-based approach (see Chapter 15). Smaller communities may find this difficult to do except for roads where consultants are used routinely. Georgia may strike a sensible balance by clearly articulating the basic principles that should guide fee calculations but not try to over-regulate how they are done.

4.4.3 Proportionate-Share Calculation

Last but not least is how each state defines and implicitly applies proportionate-share impact fee calculations. For instance, the Texas statute does not explicitly require that impact fees be proportionate to the impact on facilities associated with new development. Proportionality is implied however through the words "attributable to the new development":

"Impact fee" means a charge or assessment imposed by a political subdivision against new development in order to generate revenue for funding or recouping the costs of capital improvements or facility expansions necessitated by and *attributable to the new development*.[40]

(Emphasis added)

Georgia is clear with these two definitions of key terms:

"Proportionate share" means that portion of the cost of system improvements that is reasonably related to the *service demands and needs of the project* within the defined service area.[41]

(Emphasis added noting that the word "the" is in the singular)

"Project" means *a particular development on an identified parcel of land*.[42]

(Emphasis added noting that the highlighted term is in the singular)

Statutory language would appear to have this apply to the building permit applied for a particular parcel of land, such as an individual lot, since that is when the impact fee as assessed as opposed to the entire development. This is confirmed in:

"Development" means any construction or expansion of *a building, structure, or use*, any change in use of *a building or structure, or any change in the use of land*, any of which creates additional demand and need for public facilities.[43]

(Emphasis added noting the use of the singular)

Taken together, the Georgia Act requires that impact fees are not based on a broad average of a class of land use, such as all single-family homes in one class and all multi-family homes in another, but rather on the nature and extent of the impact of each particular development project within each class on each parcel, such as the size of each particular residential unit on an individual parcel. After all, this is done routinely for all nonresidential land uses in Georgia and elsewhere.

California goes one step further in specifically mandating that impact fees for residential development be based on the square feet of residential space subject to narrow qualifications.[44] A key purpose of this provision is to ensure that smaller and less costly homes, which data show have fewer occupants and thus less impact than larger and more costly homes, at least to a point, pay less than those larger and more costly homes.[45]

4.5 CONCLUDING OBSERVATIONS

Most impact fee legislation *restricts* how impact fees are prepared and in their application to a prescribed list of facilities. Our comparison of Texas and Georgia merely illustrates differences in how this is accomplished. To some extent, we worry that efforts to protect development interests and property rights while assuring open and transparent processes can actually backfire on facilitating development.

Consider schools for which impact fees are not allowed in either Texas or Georgia, or most other states with impact fee legislation.[46] If a residential development proposal requires discretionary approval, such as a rezoning, conditional use, or subdivision approval, and local schools cannot absorb the new demand, local officials may be pressed into denying the application. Yet, if school impact fees are enabled, this reason for denying the proposal may be taken off the table. Indeed, one view is that the more restrictive an impact fee enabling act the less sensitive the state and its communities may be to meeting the needs of growth and development—this applies to both Georgia and Texas.

Although we did not review California in detail, we know that these issues are not as relevant to that state. Its multiple mitigation statutes apply to a much larger list of facilities and is much more flexible administratively than in Texas or Georgia. The application of specific California statutes addressing environmental preservation and schools are illustrated in Chapters 24 and 26, respectively.

While one could hardly argue that impact fee acts have curtailed growth, one might ask "growth for whom" if those acts can be used in ways to advance exclusionary practices, even if inadvertently. Tim Beatley raises the ethics of impact fees in Chapter 14, while Mark Kay Peck Delk and Susan A. Wood in Chapter 15 show how impact fee design that does not account for truly proportionate impacts of development may not be consistent with the social equity provisions of the American Institute of Certified Planners' Code of Ethics. As Dwight Merriam states in the Foreword, impact fees may be exclusionary in effect even if that is not the intent. We address these concerns in Part 3 and offer several innovative approaches to resolving them in Part 4.

We conclude Part 1 with a national survey of impact fees that includes impact fee trends before, during, and after the Great Recession of the late 2000s.

NOTES

1 See Fee Mitigation Act, Gov. Code Section 66000 et seq. For a critique, see Hayley Raetz et al., *Residential Impact Fees in California: Current Practices and Policy Considerations to Improve Implementation of Fees Governed by the Mitigation Fee Act*, Terner Center for Housing Innovation, University of California Berkeley (2019).
2 O.C.G.A § 36-71-2.
3 Tex. Local Gov't Code § 395.001 (1).
4 O.C.G.A § 36-71-1(17).
5 Tex. Local Gov't Code § 395.001.
6 Tex. Local Gov't Code § 395.079
7 O.C.G.A. § 36-71-4(d).
8 Tex. Local Gov't Code § 395.016(a),(b).
9 Tex. Local Gov't Code § 395.016(g).
10 O.C.G.A. § 36-71-4(l).
11 Tex. Local Gov't Code § 395.001(9).
12 O.C.G.A. § 36-71-8(c)(B).
13 Tex. Local Gov't Code § 395.019.
14 O.C.G.A. §36-71-7.
15 Tex. Local Gov't Code § 395.022
16 O.C.G.A. §36-71-9 (1).
17 Tex. Local Gov't Code §395.025 (a).
18 Tex. Local Gov't Code §395.025(c).
19 Tex. Local Gov't Code §395.058.
20 O.C.G.A. § 36-71-5.
21 *see* Tex. Local Gov't Code § 395.058.
22 *see* O.C.G.A. § 36-71-5(b).
23 *see* Tex. Local Gov't Code § 395.076
24 O.C.G.A. § 36-71-3
25 O.C.G.A. § 36-71-2
26 see Tex. Local Gov't Code § 395.014
27 O.C.G.A. § 36-71-11
28 Tex. Local Gov't Code § 395.023
29 O.C.G.A. § 36-71-7
30 Id.
31 Id.
32 O.C.G.A. § 36-71-2(15)
33 O.C.G.A. § 36-71-2(20)
34 O.C.G.A. § 36-71-10
35 O.C.G.A. § 36-71-10
36 Id.
37 Tex. Local Gov't Code § 395.077
38 Id.
39 Tex. Local Gov't Code § 395.077

40 Tex. Local Gov't Code § 395.001(4).

41 O.C.G.A. § 36-71-2(16)

42 O.C.G.A. § 36-71-2(14)

43 O.C.G.A. § 36-71-2(5)

44 Calif. Gov. Code, § 66016.5, subd. (a)(5)(A), effective 2022.

45 See Michael G. Colantuono and Ephraim Margolin, New restrictions on development impact fees on housing, *Public Law Report*, November 29, 2021, retrieved January 29, 2022, from www.californiapubliclaw report.com/2021/11/new-restrictions-on-development-impact-fees-on-housing/

46 California's impact fee act does not allow school impact fees because they are addressed in a separate statute. Calif. Gov. Code Section 65995 authorizes school districts to charge fees for the construction of new school facilities

5 NATIONAL IMPACT FEE SURVEY[1]

Unlike in-kind developer exactions, impact fees are expressed in dollars and have published fee schedules, making it easy to compare fees charged by different jurisdictions. This chapter summarizes the results of a detailed survey conducted in 2019 of impact fees from a sample of jurisdictions across the country, including where impact fees appear to be most common, how much jurisdictions in various states are charging, the types of facilities for which fees are being charged, and how fees vary by land use. The survey was conducted before the pandemic of 2020–2021, so it reflects the nature of impact fees in practice before then. Because this survey has been periodically updated over time, comparisons with surveys from previous years also show how fees have changed over time, and how impact fee increases compare to increases in home values.

5.1 WHAT QUALIFIES AS AN IMPACT FEE?

The multitude of names used to refer to impact fees is one obstacle to developing an accurate survey of such fees. Common terms used to refer to impact fees include "capacity fees," "facility fees," "system development charges," and "capital recovery fees." Their common characteristics are that (1) they are charged only to new development, (2) they are standardized fees as opposed to *ad hoc*, negotiated payments, and (3) they are designed and used to fund capital improvements needed to serve growth.

5.1.1 Utility Connection Fees

Water and wastewater connection fees that are used to fund growth-related capital improvements should be classified as impact fees.

However, connection fees often mix impact fee components with service fees that cover other types of costs, such as the purchase of a water meter, the inspection of the connection, or the administrative cost of establishing a new customer account. In addition, because water and wastewater fees preceded other kinds of impact fees, they are often authorized under separate statutory authority and are often more difficult to find. This presents the researcher with a problem. Counting only clearly labeled water and wastewater impact fees is likely to underrepresent them, but seldom are there sufficient resources to interview local officials to determine what portion of a connection fee is actually an impact fee. For these reasons, it is often useful to look at "non-utility" impact fees separately from total impact fees.

5.1.2 Fees In-Lieu

Fees charged *in-lieu* of land dedication for parks and schools are conceptually very similar to impact fees and should also be counted in an impact fee survey. Essentially, they function much like an impact fee for the land component of the facility. Indeed, some communities use an impact fee for the construction cost component and combine that with a land dedication/fee-*in-lieu* requirement for the land component. In California, park fees *in-lieu* of land dedication are known as "Quimby fees," after the name of the 1966 state act authorizing such fees. Because they are not labeled as impact fees, land dedication fees-*in-lieu* are often overlooked in impact fee surveys.

5.1.3 Development Taxes

Another class of fee that is functionally very similar to an impact fee is the development

DOI: 10.4324/9781003336075-6

tax, which is sometimes also referred to as a development excise tax, privilege tax, or facilities tax. This is a tax that only applies to new development, often on a per square foot basis, and is earmarked for capital improvements. The two can be difficult to distinguish. For example, Boulder, Colorado, hired consultants to conduct a nexus study and adopted an ordinance that had all trappings of an impact fee ordinance, including earmarking of funds for specific types of capital facilities and providing credit against the charges for developer-constructed improvements, but instead of adopting them as impact fees the city adopted them as development taxes. This survey includes development taxes.

5.1.4 Some Caveats

The results of impact fee surveys can be easily misinterpreted. This can be avoided if the reader keeps the following caveats in mind.

5.1.5 Not Exhaustive Samples

Like most impact fee surveys, this survey only includes communities that charge impact fees and excludes those that do not. Thus, an "average impact fee" must be understood as an average fee for those communities that charge impact fees, not as an average for all communities. Although in California state limits on local taxing authority and relatively liberal impact fee enabling legislation have combined to make impact fees virtually universal, in most other parts of the country communities that have impact fees (other than ubiquitous water and wastewater connection fees) tend to be in the minority.

5.1.6 Not Random Samples

Impact fee surveys tend to be opportunistic, and this one is no exception. For the most part, the inclusion of a community is determined by how readily available the information is. Communities that post their fee schedules on their websites are more likely to be included in a survey than communities that do not. In addition, consultants who compile surveys are more likely to include communities that have been clients or that are in the same region with former clients, and this one is no exception. For example, our firm compiled extensive surveys of impact fees in Arizona and Florida for client communities in those states. While we have a national practice, we have not been active on the West Coast, so we make a special effort to include jurisdictions from that part of the country.

5.1.7 Average Total Fee vs. Sum of Average Fees

In this survey, average fees are presented for a variety of capital facilities. These averages exclude communities that are represented in the survey but do not charge impact fees for the particular facility type. One could sum these average fees by facility type, but this "sum of the average fees" does not represent the average fee for communities that charge impact fees. A more meaningful statistic, and the one reported here, is the "average of the total impact fees" charged by all communities represented in the survey.

5.1.8 Only Published Fees

The fact that a community does not charge a particular impact fee does not mean that developers make no contributions to that type of capital facility. This is particularly true in the case of roads because many communities without road impact fees require developers to dedicate right-of-way and make substantial improvements to abutting roadways as conditions of development approval. In communities with road impact fees, developers who are required to make in-kind contributions may receive credit against their impact fees for the value of those contributions. Thus, developers may actually contribute more on average to the cost of major road improvements in communities without road impact fees than in communities with modest road impact fees.

5.2 FEE INCIDENCE BY STATE

As noted earlier, this survey is opportunistic, so the number of jurisdictions represented in the survey is not proportional to the actual incidence of impact fees. Nevertheless, the survey jurisdictions do provide some indication of the states where impact fees are most common. The 2019 survey includes 270 jurisdictions (plus nine Florida counties that have suspended all their fees, and so are excluded from the average fee totals). Not surprisingly, the surveyed jurisdictions are concentrated in the South and West, especially Washington, Oregon, California, Arizona, Utah, Colorado, Georgia, and Florida (see Figure 5.1).

Average impact fees vary significantly by state. As illustrated in Figure 5.2, the average total non-utility fee charged for a

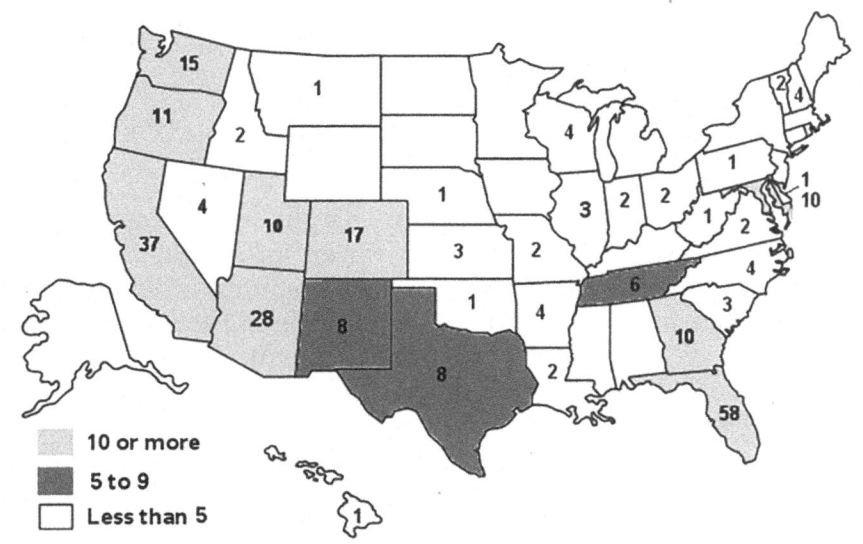

FIGURE 5.1 Survey jurisdictions by state, 2019.

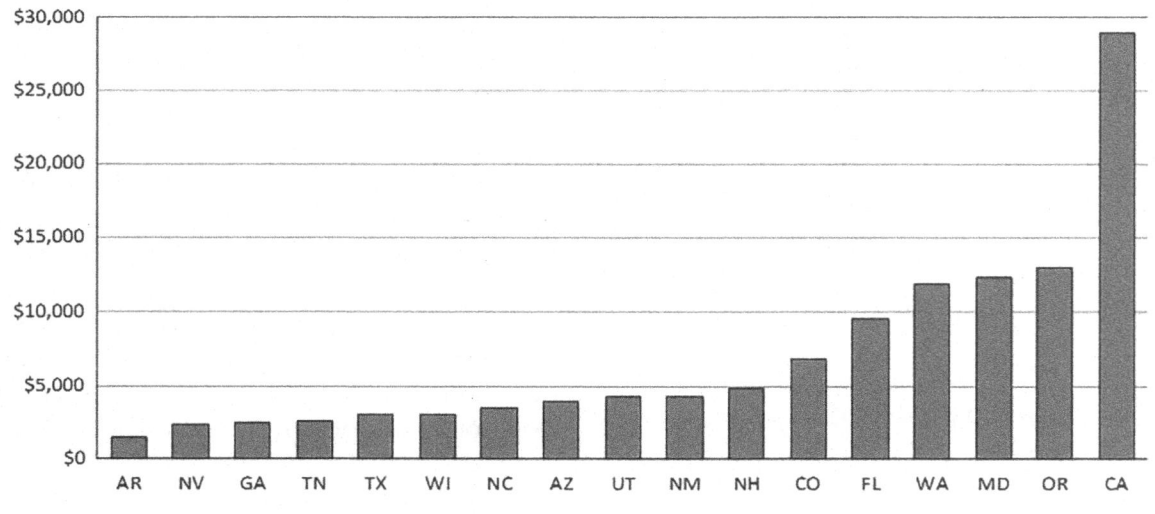

FIGURE 5.2 Average single-family non-utility fees by state, 2019.

single-family detached unit is much higher in California than elsewhere in the country (the chart includes only those states with at least four jurisdictions represented in the survey).

5.2.1 Average Fees by Land Use

Average impact fees by land use and facility type are presented in Table 5.1 and illustrated in Figure 5.3. Except in the few states where school fees are charged,[2] road, park, and utility fees are the primary fees for residential land uses. Other types of fees tend to be small (public safety) or infrequently charged (general government or drainage). For non-residential land uses, road fees are the dominant component of the total fee.

5.2.2 National Impact Fee Trends

The major economic event that occurred in recent years was the housing crisis and the resulting Great Recession, which was the worst economic downturn since the Great Depression. As shown in Table 5.2, new home starts in the United States peaked in 2005 and

fell precipitously over the next four years. The Great Recession lasted from December 2007 to June 2009 in the US and helped trigger a global recession in 2009.

While the housing bubble affected over half of US states, among the most affected were Florida and Arizona. While permits nationally were 40 percent higher in 2005 compared to five years earlier, they were up 96 percent in Florida and 65 percent in Arizona from 2000. California had a much smaller bubble, with housing starts only slightly more than the national average (46 percent), while permits in the rest of the country were up 32 percent compared to five years earlier. In 2018, the US had new home starts that were back up to 71 percent of what they were in 2000.

Figure 5.4 illustrates the change in new home starts for Arizona, California, Florida, all other states combined, and the nation as a whole. The number of permits has been adjusted so that all five areas are shown at approximately the same point on the graph in 2000. The peak year for all areas was 2005, with Florida, Arizona, and California leading the way, with the combined permits for all other states lagging behind the national

TABLE 5.1 Average Fees by Land Use and Facility Type, 2019

Facility Type	Sample Size	Single-Family Unit	Multi-Family Unit	Retail (1,000 sf)	Office (1,000 sf)	Industrial (1,000 sf)
Roads	218	$3,691	$2,493	$5,970	$3,772	$2,143
Water	128	$4,249	$1,680	$654	$854	$889
Wastewater	138	$3,896	$1,986	$853	$1,217	$1,662
Stormwater Drainage	56	$1,622	$852	$1,011	$815	$962
Parks	195	$2,993	$2,283	**	**	**
Library	62	$455	$344	**	**	**
Fire and EMS	130	$484	$370	$523	$503	$359
Police	103	$395	$295	$404	$270	$173
Gen. Government	57	$1,573	$1,197	$665	$649	$388
Schools	114	$5,395	$3,134	**	**	**
Total Non-Utility*	261	$9,887	$6,476	$6,439	$4,640	$2,877
Total*	270	$13,627	$8,034	$6,760	$5,407	$3,942

* Average of total fees charged by jurisdictions, not the sum of average fees by facility type (non-utility fee excludes water and wastewater fees)

** Rarely charged to non-residential land uses, with the exception of school fees in California

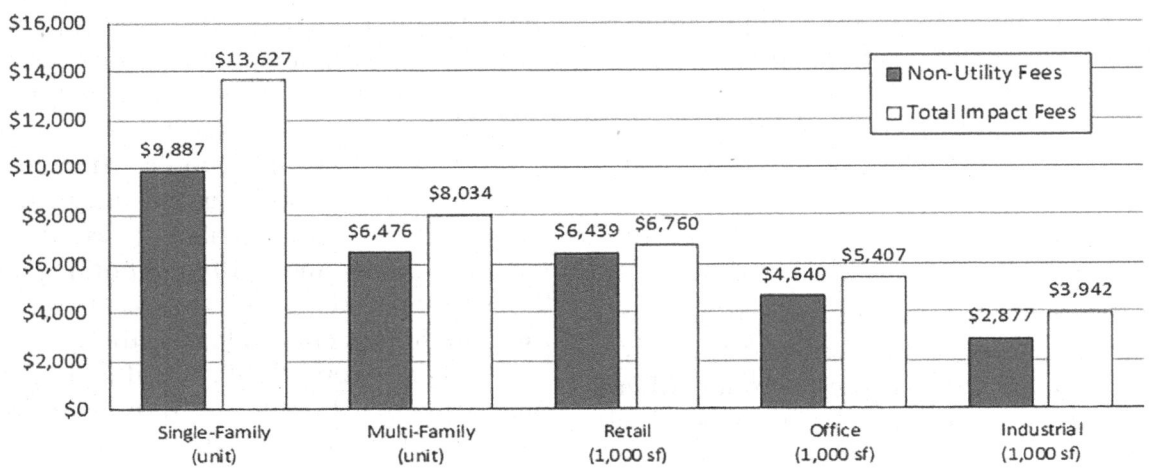

FIGURE 5.3 Average fees by land use, 2019.

TABLE 5.2 Annual Single-Family Detached Building Permits, 2000–2018

Year	Permits for New Single-Family Detached Units					Annual Percent Rate				
	Arizona	California	Florida	Other	Total	AZ	CA	FL	Other	US
2000	48,844	105,018	106,447	937,758	1,198,067	n/a	n/a	n/a	n/a	n/a
2001	51,839	107,361	118,702	957,648	1,235,550	6%	2%	12%	2%	3%
2002	55,798	123,013	128,719	1025090	1,332,620	8%	15%	8%	7%	8%
2003	65,845	139,870	156,852	1,098,320	1,460,887	18%	14%	22%	7%	10%
2004	80,778	151,568	187,643	1193456	1,613,445	23%	8%	20%	9%	10%
2005	80,804	154,703	209,162	1,237,299	1,681,968	0%	2%	11%	4%	4%
2006	55,633	107,714	146,236	1,068,637	1,378,220	−31%	−30%	−30%	−14%	−18%
2007	37,666	68,266	70,030	803,927	979,889	−32%	−37%	−52%	−25%	−29%
2008	19,153	32,432	38,709	485,260	575,554	−49%	−52%	−45%	−40%	−41%
2009	12,826	25,525	26,636	376,161	441148	−33%	−21%	−31%	−22%	−23%
2010	10,755	25,693	30,040	380,823	447,311	−16%	1%	13%	1%	1%
2011	10,306	21,705	31,874	354,613	418,498	−4%	−16%	6%	−7%	−6%
2012	16,189	27,736	42,178	432,592	518,695	57%	28%	32%	22%	24%
2013	16,841	39,220	56,250	522,286	634,597	4%	41%	33%	21%	22%
2014	16,841	39,222	56,259	527,996	640,318	0%	0%	0%	1%	1%
2015	22,311	45,644	67,670	560,373	695,998	32%	16%	20%	6%	9%
2016	24,853	50,311	75,148	600,484	750,796	11%	10%	11%	7%	8%
2017	28,072	57,132	85,267	649,505	819,976	13%	14%	13%	8%	9%
2018	32,127	58,831	97,055	667,309	855,322	14%	3%	14%	3%	4%

Source: US Census Bureau building permit estimates (www2.census.gov/construction/bps/).

average. By 2018, no area was issuing new single-family permits at the level they were in 2000, although Florida was coming the closest at 91 percent.

This survey is relatively little changed in terms of jurisdictions since 2007. In an attempt to quantify trends in impact fees over the last 12 years, a constant sample was compiled from the 2007, 2011, 2015, and 2019 surveys, consisting of 266 jurisdictions that were included in all four surveys and charged at least some non-utility fees. While all the jurisdictions charged at least some fees in 2007, eight had repealed or suspended all their impact fees by 2011, and

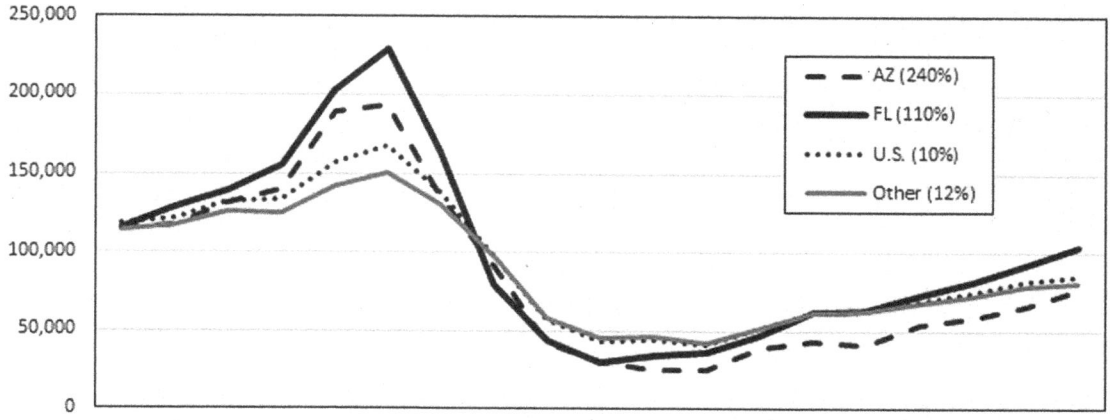

FIGURE 5.4 Change in annual single-family building permits, 2000-2018.
Note: Number of permits adjusted by percentages shown in legend.

TABLE 5.3 Change in Average Fees by Land Use and Facility Type, 2007–2019

Facility Type	Single-Family Unit	Multi-Family Unit	Retail (1,000 sf)	Office (1,000 sf)	Industrial (1,000 sf)
Roads	28.1%	29.2%	15.9%	18.1%	10.7%
Water	29.6%	6.4%	0.4%	39.4%	44.5%
Wastewater	35.8%	20.5%	21.9%	99.2%	139.4%
Stormwater Drainage	18.8%	15.6%	11.2%	13.7%	7.5%
Parks	17.7%	18.3%	**	**	**
Library	21.9%	80.7%	**	**	**
Fire and EMS	16.3%	16.9%	40.9%	58.9%	66.1%
Police	11.9%	11.1%	−21.3%	−11.3%	−15.9%
Gen. Government	38.5%	37.2%	15.1%	19.7%	−30.1%
Schools	22.2%	32.1%	**	**	**
Total Non-Utility*	33.4%	32.7%	11.1%	17.7%	8.4%
Total*	32.3%	27.3%	14.4%	29.4%	32.9%

* Average of total fees charged by jurisdictions, not the sum of average fees by facility type (non-utility excludes water and wastewater).

Source: 2007–2019 constant sample.

nine had done so by 2015 and were continuing not to assess fees in 2019. All nine jurisdictions are in Florida, and most, if not all, of these had originally adopted fees shortly before the housing crash. While they were kept in the sample for later surveys, the fact that they no longer charged fees was not factored into the average fees as a zero. This is consistent with the methodology used in this survey of not including jurisdictions that don't charge fees in computing average fees charged.

Table 5.3 shows the changes in average impact fees by land use and facility type from 2007 to 2019. Total impact fees are up about one-third from 12 years ago for single-family detached units. In general, residential fees have gone up more than non-residential fees. This is primarily due to the fact that road impact fees, which are the major fee paid by non-residential, have gone up much less for non-residential uses. This in turn is the product of changes in trip generation rates.

For example, the number of average daily trip ends for a single-family detached unit declined by 1 percent from 2007 to 2017, while trip rates for shopping centers and general office buildings fell 12 percent, the rate for light industrial fell 29 percent, and the rate for warehousing was down 65 percent.[3]

5.3 STATE IMPACT FEE TRENDS

National average non-utility fees for a single-family unit, as well as average fees for the eight states with the largest sample sizes, are shown in Table 5.4 for 2007, 2011, 2015, and 2019, along with the national averages. Arizona, Florida, and California account for over half the jurisdictions in the survey. Because fees are so much higher in California, national averages without California are also shown.

Total non-utility fees for a single-family unit over the 2007–2019 period are illustrated for the eight states in Figure 5.5. By 2011, impact fees had come down from pre-recession levels in Florida, and were also down on average for states with smaller sample sizes that are not identified separately. But in the other seven major impact fee states, average fees did not

TABLE 5.4 Average Single-Family Non-Utility Fees, 2007–2019

State	Sample	2007	2011	2015	2019
Arizona	27	$5,196	$6,501	$4,707	$4,070
California	37	$18,672	$23,849	$22,795	$28,918
Colorado	17	$5,524	$6,859	$6,917	$6,898
Florida	67	$8,601	$7,862	$7,568	$9,511
Maryland	10	$8,588	$11,248	$11,486	$12,333
Oregon	11	$6,000	$9,102	$104	$13,019
Utah	8	$4,364	$4,745	$4,555	$4,357
Washington	15	$5,403	$7,115	$7,300	$11,849
All Other States	74	$3,163	$2,991	$2,964	$3,293
National Average	266	$7,540	$8,593	$8,237	$10,059
Average Outside CA	229	$5,741	$6,039	$5,754	$6,858

Source: Duncan Associates' surveys, using a constant 2007–2019 sample of 266 jurisdictions.

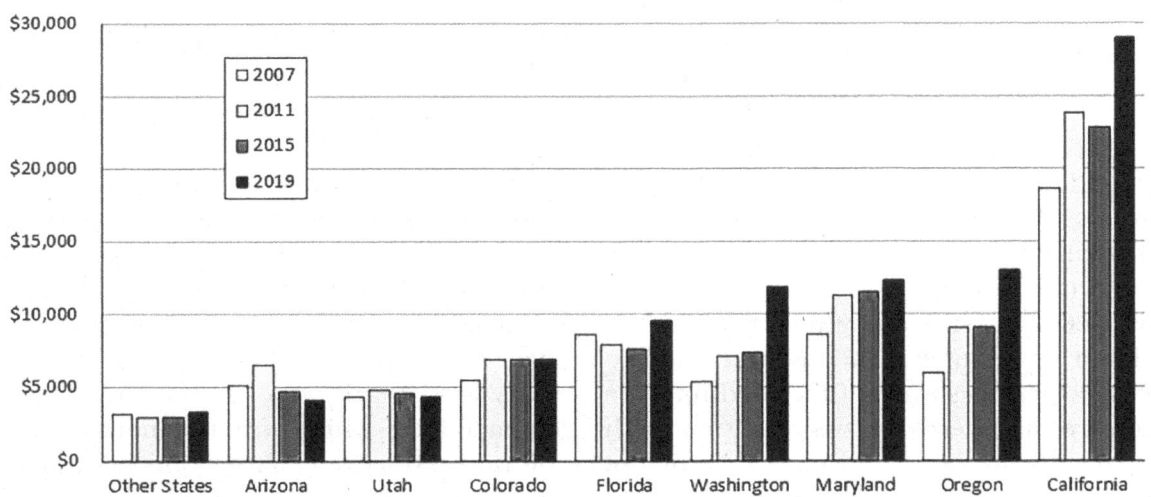

FIGURE 5.5 Average single-family non-utility fees, 2007–2019.

decline until later, if at all. Since 2015, average fees have rebounded in most states.

Unfortunately, the rather robust constant sample for the 2007–2019 period does not reveal how impact fees were changing prior to the recession. For this, we must rely on a much smaller constant sample for 2003 and 2007 (152 vs. 266 jurisdictions). The major difference between the two constant samples is California, which had only six jurisdictions in the 2003–2007 constant sample vs. 37 in the 2007–2019 sample.

While we cannot compare the fees themselves between these two different constant samples, we can compare percentage changes. Table 5.5 below shows percentage changes from 2003–2007 as well as intervals from 2007 through 2019. The four years preceding the recession included the peak of the housing bubble, and average non-utility impact fees went up about 80 percent nationally from 2003–2007. The rate of increase slowed dramatically during 2007–2011 (except in Oregon and Washington), average fees declined from 2011–2015, and they began increasing again over the last four years.

The percentage changes from Table 5.5 above are illustrated graphically in Figure 5.6. Of the eight states for which we have reasonable samples, six had dramatically lower rates of increase in the four years after the recession. Washington and Oregon had bigger increases than before the recession, but those rates fell dramatically over the following four years.

State-specific events may help explain some of these changes. As noted earlier, Arizona and Florida were both epicenters of the housing bubble, but the reactions to the housing crash in terms of impact fees were quite different. In Arizona, the state legislature, in response to the housing crisis, prohibited cities from adopting new impact fees or increasing existing fees from June 30, 2009, to June 30, 2012. Legislation effective January 1, 2012, outlawed some types of impact fees, including general government and solid waste, as well as fees for parks over 30 acres, libraries over 10,000 square feet and public safety training facilities, resulting in some mandatory fee decreases in cities that had not pledged the fees to pay the debt. Cities were also required to comply with a completely new impact fee enabling act that imposed major new requirements by August 1, 2014. Arizona cities did not generally reduce or suspend impact fees except as necessary to comply with these state mandates.

TABLE 5.5 Change in Average Single-Family Non-Utility Fees, 2003–2019

State	2003–2007	2007–2011	2011–2015	2015–2019	2007–2019
Arizona	86%	25%	−28%	−14%	−22%
California	46%	28%	−4%	27%	55%
Colorado	24%	24%	1%	0%	25%
Florida	149%	−9%	−4%	26%	11%
Maryland	75%	31%	2%	7%	44%
Oregon	10%	52%	0%	43%	117%
Utah	103%	9%	−4%	−4%	0%
Washington	24%	32%	3%	62%	119%
All Other States	70%	−5%	−1%	11%	4%
National Average	77%	14%	−4%	22%	33%
Average Outside CA	84%	5%	−5%	19%	19%

Source: Duncan Associates' annual surveys, using the 2003–2007 constant sample of 152 jurisdictions and the 2007–2019 constant sample of 266 jurisdictions.

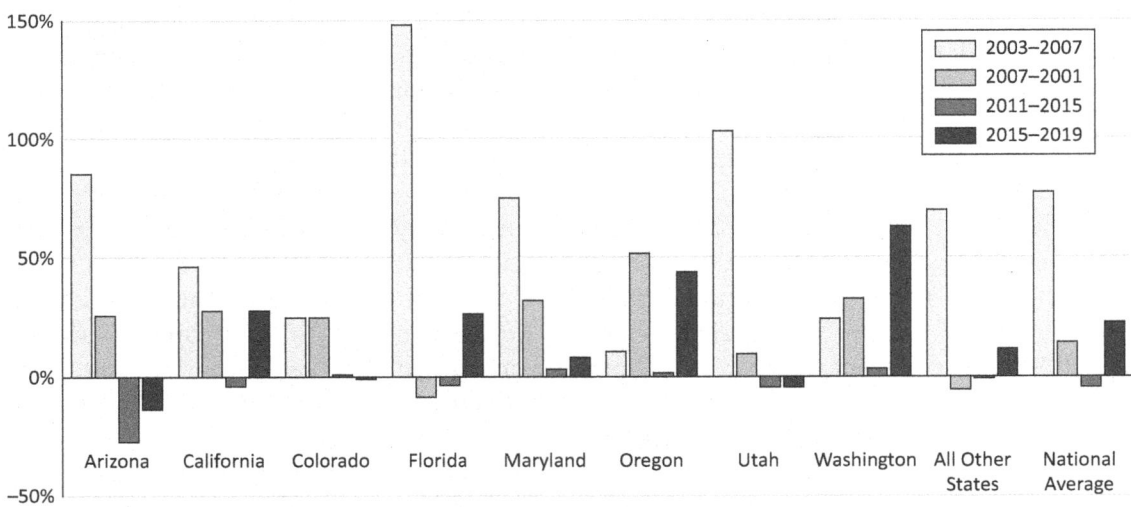

FIGURE 5.6 Percent change, average single-family non-utility fees, 2003–2019. *Source:* Table 5-5

In contrast, the Florida legislature did not take action to reduce impact fees, but a number of jurisdictions took such action independently. Some cities and counties updated studies and lowered fees to reflect reduced land and construction costs, while others reduced or suspended some or all fees based on policy, in the hopes of stimulating new development. It is not clear why the reactions in Arizona and Florida to the housing crisis were so different. It could be that state-wide action in Arizona took the pressure off local governments to come up with their own responses with respect to impact fees. This was not the case in Florida, and jurisdictions tended to look to what others were going through, perhaps leading to a "race to the bottom" in an attempt to be the most attractive place for what little development was still happening. Based on anecdotal information, this response was not confined to Florida, although for the most part it appears to have been relatively absent in Arizona.

5.4 IMPACT FEES AND HOME PRICES

How the change in impact fees since the housing crash compares to the change in the value of new construction is a question that we can partially answer with this small but arguably reasonably representative impact fee survey. Housing value is a reasonable proxy for construction value in general. A commonly used measure of home value over time is a repeat transaction method that tracks resale mortgage values. One of the largest such surveys in the US is government-financed secondary loans made by Federal Home Loan Mortgage Corporation (Freddie Mac) or Federal National Mortgage Association (Fannie Mae). The index based on this database, known as the Freddie Mac House Price Index, uses the average value of single-family detached homes and townhouse units. Nationally, the picture is clear based on the data shown in Table 5.6. Since the Great Recession, the average house price nationally increased 18 percent, while the average impact fee for a single-family detached unit increased 33 percent. Impact fees increased at almost twice the rate of home value appreciation.

The national picture, however, obscures significant regional variations. Home prices in Arizona have increased by only 5 percent, while impact fees have gone down 22 percent. Home prices in Utah have increased 34 percent, with no increase in impact fees.

Three West Coast states, California, Oregon, and Washington, which account

TABLE 5.6 Impact Fee and Home Price Change, 2007–2019

State	House Price Change	Impact Fee Change
Arizona	5%	–22%
California	15%	55%
Colorado	68%	25%
Florida	6%	11%
Maryland	–6%	44%
Oregon	28%	117%
Utah	34%	0%
Washington	35%	119%
National Average	18%	33%

Source: Average impact fee change for a single-family detached unit from Table 5.5; average home price change is the change from June 2007 to June 2019 in the Freddie Mac House Price Index, September 2020 release (www.freddiemac.com/fmac-esources/research/docs/State_and_US_SA.xls).

for almost a quarter of the impact fee survey jurisdictions, had the biggest impact fee increases in percentage terms, and also the biggest changes relative to increases in housing prices. In these three West Coast states, impact fees increased three to four times the rate of housing prices.

Two states that were epicenters of the housing bubble prior to the crash, Arizona and Florida, have not experienced much increase in housing prices, which have only increased 5.6 percent since 2007. The average impact fee in Arizona declined significantly over the 12 years, which may be largely due to much more restrictive impact fee legislation, while Florida's fee increase is one of the lowest of the states for which we have reasonable sample sizes.

5.5 SUMMARY

The data on average impact fee amounts presented here represent a relatively small, non-random sample of jurisdictions across the nation that assess at least some impact fees for other than water and wastewater facilities. They do not represent average fees for all local governments, many of which do not assess any impact fees. Still, they provide some perspective on the amount of fees that are typically charged.

The fact that the same sample of jurisdictions has been tracked over a number of years allows the data to provide a sense of how typical fees have changed during recent years, including the effect of the Great Recession. The national average non-utility fee for a single-family unit fell from 2011–2015, but rose significantly over the next four years. From the early days of the recession in 2007, housing prices had increased 18 percent by 2019, while impact fees had increased 33 percent.

The changes in the national average home fee disguise a lot of regional variation. The two states that were most affected by the housing bubble and the ensuing bust, Arizona and Florida, experienced the biggest subsequent fee reductions and among the slowest increase in home prices since the recession. Local governments in both states lowered impact fees during several years following the recession, but for different reasons. Generally though, local governments appear much more willing to increase impact fees when there is a strong local housing market.

NOTES

1 With assistance from Matt Dixon, graduate research assistant at the University of Arizona, and David Hymel and Stuart Wallace, JD candidates at Georgia State University College of Law.
2 Florida, Washington and Maryland have extensive and significant school impact fees. California's school fees are widespread, but are capped by State law at a relatively modest level.
3 Institute of Transportation Engineers, *Trip Generation Manual,* 7th edition (2007) and 10th edition (2017).

PART 2

Foundations of Planning, Calculation, and Implementation

We turn now to the processes and methods of crafting proportionate share development mitigation tools, such as impact fees, which are the focus of this part. It comprises four chapters, with the first, Chapter 6, making the link to planning. Remember from Chapter 2 that impact fees are regulatory devices that implement comprehensive plans, capital improvement programs, and other planning policies. These plans provide the rational basis for calculating, collecting, and spending impact fees. As we showed in Chapters 3 and 4, the whole concept of using impact fees as a form of impact mitigation is predicated on planning. Chapter 6 goes into considerable detail on what goes into plans generally and how they are used to assess current conditions, project future needs based on adopted level of service standards, and design service areas to assure reasonable benefits are received for impact fees paid proximate to new development, and then craft capital improvement programs to guide expenditures.

Chapter 7 presents numerous methodological issues associated with actually calculating impact fees for each major type of infrastructure, such as water and wastewater, transportation, parks and recreation, and public safety, among others. It also shows several ways in which to apportion impact so that different types of land uses impacting different types of facilities are nonetheless assessed for their impact proportionately. This chapter also addresses to need to give credit for new revenue that new development brings to the community lest it pay twice for its impact on facilities: once for the impact fees it pays and again for the new revenues it generates that are also used to help pay for the same facilities. Although this chapter focuses on the basics, Part 4 offers numerous innovations that use the proportionate share methodology to calculate impact fees and other forms of mitigation fees for a wide range of purposes.

Once a plan is prepared showing the need for facilities to serve new development, and once mitigation measures such as impact fees are calculated, an ordinance is needed to justify implementing the fees. A model impact fee ordinance is offered in Chapter 8.

We conclude this part with Chapter 9, "A Word About Independent Studies, Exemptions, and Waivers." This chapter has two elements. The first discusses the role of independent fee calculations to help assure proportionality in impact mitigation. Independent fee calculations occur either when a particular development activity is not addressed or addressed adequately in the impact fee schedule, or when the feepayer asserts that a different (usually lower) fee should be assessed. We identify issues that are rarely raised but may become sources of future litigation, perhaps drawing the attention of courts for reasons noted in Chapter 2. The second element explores issues relating to exemptions and waivers. We define exemptions as situations where a development activity does not increase its impact on infrastructure, and therefore no

DOI: 10.4324/9781003336075-7

impact fees are due. Rebuilding a home that recently burned down with no increase in size may be an example. Waivers occur when a new development is charged an impact fee, but local policymakers want to eliminate all or a part of it. Elected officials are especially keen to advance their key interests in part by waiving impact fees for such laudable activities as affordable housing and economic development. But who pays for the fees not collected? Waivers can be especially problematic to implement financially.

6 IN ACCORDANCE WITH THE PLAN

We must cultivate in our minds and in the mind of the people the conception of a city plan as a device or piece of ... machinery for preparing, and keeping constantly up to date, a unified forecast and definition of all the important changes, additions, and extensions of the physical equipment and arrangement of the city which a sound judgment holds likely to become desirable and practicable in the course of time, so as to avoid so far as possible both ignorantly wasteful action and ignorantly wasteful inaction in the control of the city's physical growth. It is a means by which those who become at any time responsible for decisions affecting the city's plan may be prevented from acting in ignorance of what their predecessors and their colleagues in other departments of city life have believed to be the reasonable contingencies.

(Frederick Law Olmsted, Jr.,
third National Conference
on City Planning, 1911, from
T. J. Kent 1964: 1)

6.1 OVERVIEW

As the excerpt above shows, the concept of modern planning in the United States dates from the early twentieth century. In this overview, we begin at the beginning of what might be considered the formalization of the modern comprehensive planning outlined by Olmstead: The Standard City Planning Enabling Act—SCPEA (Advisory Commission on City Planning and Zoning 1928). It was prepared by future president Herbert Hoover's Department of Commerce as a model for states to enable planning among their cities, although implicitly all general-purpose local governments. The SCPEA envisions that a planning commission will prepare plans:

Such plan, with the accompanying maps, plats, charts, and descriptive matter shall show the commission's recommendations of said territory, including, among other things, the general location, character and extent of streets, viaducts, subways, bridges, waterways, water fronts, boulevards, parkways, playgrounds, square, parks, aviation fields, and other public ways, grounds and open spaces, the general location of public buildings and other public property, and the general location and extent of public utilities and terminals, whether publicly or privately owned or operated, for water, light, sanitation, transportation, communication, power, and other purposes; also the removal, relocation, widening, narrowing, vacating, abandonment, change of use or extension of any of the foregoing ways, grounds, open spaces, buildings, property, utilities, or terminals; as well as a zoning plan for the control of the height, area, bulk, location, and use or buildings and premises.

(SCPEA 1928: 6–16)[1]

Further, the plan is to be based on:

Careful and comprehensive surveys and studies of present conditions and future growth of the municipality and with due regard to its relation to neighboring territory.

(SCPEA 1928: 16–17)

In reflecting on the role of the comprehensive plan in guiding community development nearly 30 years later, Charles M. Haar (1955a) wrote that the emergence of the comprehensive plan as a local government policy represented a unique shift in local efforts to influence the land market. A key reason was that the rise of modern industrialized society, in which land uses became interdependent,

DOI: 10.4324/9781003336075-8

justified the role of municipal controls over private property. The challenge of comprehensive plans was to have them guide implementing ordinances and give courts a reasonable foundation on which to view regulation as a tool to implement policy reflected in the comprehensive plan.

Haar (1955b) goes on to make the case that a comprehensive plan is an "impermanent constitution." Much as federal and state constitutions establish rights and procedures guiding governance decisions, local government guides land-use decisions through a comprehensive plan. While federal and state constitutions are viewed as permanent,[2] Haar viewed comprehensive plans as impermanent. By their nature, comprehensive plans anticipate changes over 5 to 20 years (rarely longer), so they require periodic remaking to reflect new challenges informed by past plan implementation experience to guide public land-use decision-making over the next planning horizon. He also reports a content analysis of all state statutes that had adopted the SCPEA, finding that (Harr 1955b) plans were often: (1) a source of information about local conditions; (2) a program to remedy shortcomings in the community; (3) projections of the future; (4) identification of community goals; (5) processes for coordinating land-use and development decisions; and (6) a method for advancing the public interest in responsible development (Haar 1955b: 356). These are indeed the basic elements of land-use planning today (see Berke, Godschalk, and Kaiser 2006; Juergensmeyer, Roberts, Salkin, and Rowberry 2018).

To be effective, plans need to be implemented. The institutions of plan implementation—particularly zoning—are outlined in the US Department of Commerce's *A Standard State Zoning Enabling Act*—SZEA (Advisory Committee on Zoning 1926). Its principal purposes are to: (1) protect residential properties from incompatible uses; (2) craft a police-power argument to support zoning; and (3) facilitate a clear delegation of zoning as a police-power function to local governments (Meck 2002). Those and other arguments helped persuade the US Supreme Court in *Village of Euclid, Ohio v. Ambler Realty Co.*, 272 U.S. 365 (1926) to uphold zoning as a constitutional exercise of police power. Haar (1955a) reminds us that the SZEA requires local land-use and development ordinances, and decisions based on the, to be "*in accordance with a comprehensive plan*" (Haar 1955a: 1156, emphasis added). He thus warns that a land-use or development control ordinance, or decision thereon, that is not in accordance with a comprehensive plan, is *ultra vires*—meaning that it is done without the authority of or inconsistent with the comprehensive plan (Haar 1955a: 1156).

We know this today as the "consistency doctrine" in planning. Zoning and other land-use controls must be consistent with the comprehensive plan (DiMento 1980). By implication, development permitted based on zoning, and other land-use controls must also be consistent with the comprehensive plan (Juergensmeyer, Roberts, Salkin, and Rowberry 2018).

Often overlooked is the role of impact fees in implementing the comprehensive plan. In most states, regulations such as zoning and subdivision ordinances need to be consistent with the comprehensive plan, general plan, land-use plan, growth management plan, or other names. These plans also drive capital improvement plans CIPs) which implement the capital improvement elements (CIEs) of the plan. But there is confusion in nomenclature and process among state statutes. In Georgia, for instance, the "short-term work program" functions like a CIP in implementing CIE. In Utah, the impact fee facilities plan (IFFP) is in effect a short-term CIP, but also in that state there is no link between the comprehensive land-use plan, CIE, and implementation of IFFPs through impact fees. Arizona and Texas are similar in that comprehensive plans are not required to provide the legal or logical foundation of CIEs. Those states, however, require long-range land assumptions with associated infrastructure needs and a financing plan to realize those assumptions, including impact fees. In this book generally and this chapter, in particular, we characterize the comprehensive land-use plan as the kind of impermanent constitution advanced by Haar, which provides the logical foundation for plan-making, the role of CIEs in facilitating development in accordance with the plan, implementation through such land-use controls as zoning and subdivision ordinances, the need to create short-term CIPs to implement the CIE, and the role of impact fees as a form of gap financing to make the CIP financially feasible.

We organize this chapter as follows. First, we introduce the role and position of impact fees in the planning process. We then offer a primer on comprehensive plans both as a refresher for those with planning degrees or backgrounds in planning, and for others as an introduction to them. This discussion includes overall perspectives on comprehensive plans, the comprehensive planning process, aspirational goals along with principles guiding infrastructure planning and finance to help achieve those goals, and key elements of the comprehensive plan.

This is followed by a detailed review of the capital improvements element as it relates to impact fees which include such foundational features as establishing current and designing acceptable levels of service (LOS) standards, crafting service areas tailored to the characteristics of each category of infrastructure, projecting infrastructure needs including identifying deficiencies or excess capacity, and creating CIPs to implement CIEs—which is the stage at which impact fees are calculated.

Throughout this chapter we allude to the role of zoning, subdivision controls, and other forms of land-use regulation that help implement the comprehensive. We do not offer a detailed discussion of them, however, preferring to focus on the role of impact fees in the grand scheme of comprehensive planning. We conclude this chapter with an overall perspective on the role of impact fees to help assure that new growth and development occur in accordance with the plan.

6.2 IMPACT FEES AND THE PLANNING PROCESS

In review, this chapter addresses impact fees in the context of planning. Properly construed, impact fees help finance the CIP, which implements the CIE[3] of a comprehensive plan, which is itself designed to meet projected development needs consistent with specific community goals. In effect, impact fees are the last step in the planning and implementation process, as illustrated in Figure 6.1. This section summarizes the key components of the comprehensive planning and implementation process with special reference to impact fees. The planning components include:

Projecting population, households, housing, employment and other sources of demand on land and infrastructure.
Formulating specific community goals.
Crafting a comprehensive, long-range land-use plan that choreographs development needs around community goals.
Creating the long-range CIE addressing infrastructure needs of service areas based on policy-drove LOS standards.

The implementation components include:

Establishing land-use regulation and development controls.
Implementing the CIE through a short-term CIP that in the context of impact fees determines the shortfall in revenues needed to mitigate the impact of growth and apportions that shortfall proportionately to new development.

Appendix 6A offers a simplified overview of the impact cost analysis process. Chapter 7 reviews the details of impact fee design consistent

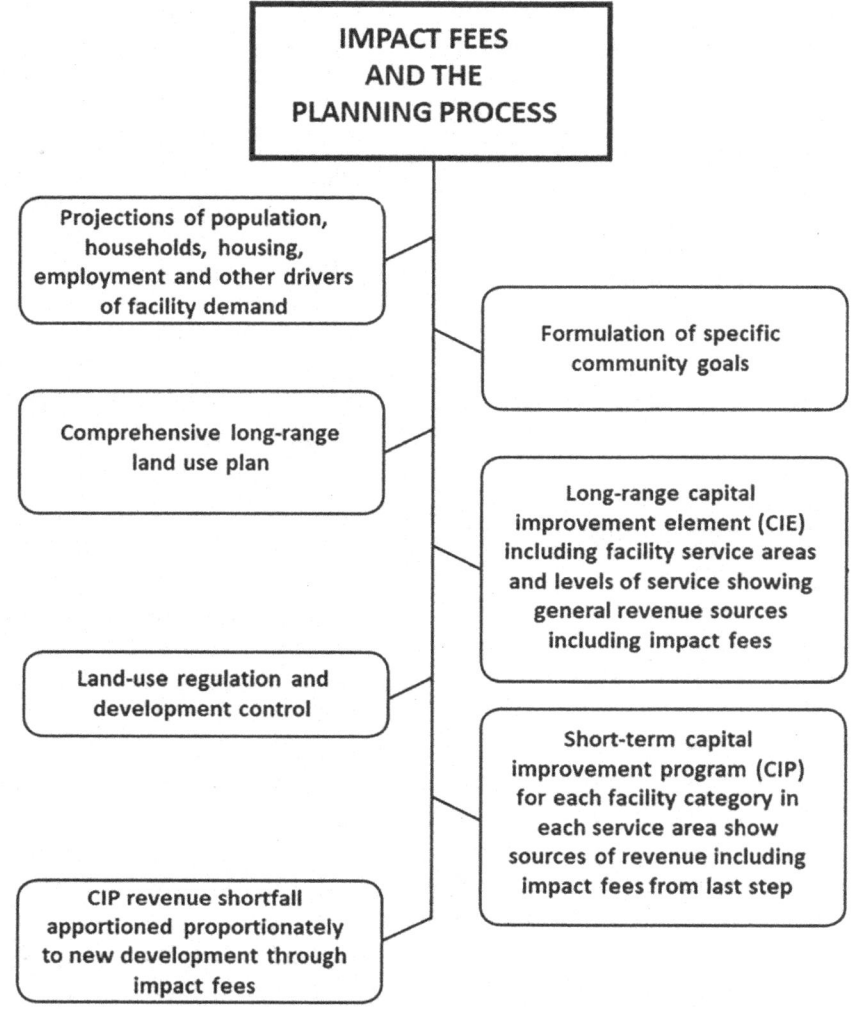

FIGURE 6.1 Impact fees in the context of the comprehensive land-use planning process.

with the principles outlined in this chapter. We review key features of each planning and implementation component next.

6.3 A PRIMER ON THE COMPREHENSIVE LAND-USE PLAN

Because many impact fee professionals may not have planning degrees or in other ways are not familiar with comprehensive plans, we offer a primer here. We recommend several books for more detail on this, especially *Guidelines for Preparing Urban Plans* (Anderson 1995), *Urban Land-Use Planning* (Berke, Godschalk and Kaiser 2006), and *Community Planning* (Kelly 2010). For approaches to generate the data needed by the planning process, we recommend *Planner's Estimating Guide: Projecting Land-use and Facility Needs* (Nelson 2004).

In this section, we start with perspectives on the role of the comprehensive plan in guiding local development decisions toward community goals and then outline the comprehensive planning process. We continue by posing aspirational goals for comprehensive planning. This is followed by a brief review of the common elements of comprehensive plans with special reference to the CIE, which is implemented by the CIP, which itself is implemented in part by impact fees. The CIE–CIP–impact fee link is reviewed in more detail in a later section of this chapter,

6.3.1 Perspectives

A comprehensive plan is an officially adopted policy or set of policies that guide official actions of local government toward long-range community goals. It is "comprehensive" because the plan addresses all geographical parts of the community as well as all functional decision-making that affect physical development. It is "long range" because it frames immediate decisions from the perspective of achieving long-range goals. It should also be designed to achieve at least six purposes in guiding local development decision-making. They are presented in Box 6.1, verbatim from T. J. Kent's pioneering book on crafting comprehensive plans.

One of the over-arching perspectives is that the client of the plan is the local government decision-makers themselves (Kent 1964). This seems contrary to the conventional wisdom that the client of the plan should be the people it serves. Yet, unless elected officials allocate resources to implement the plan, it will just gather dust on a shelf. In contrast, if the plan is embraced by elected officials, even ideally as their platform for election, resources will be allocated to implement it.

We review the comprehensive planning process next.

BOX 6.1 THE SIX PURPOSES OF A GENERAL PLAN

The fundamental purposes which the general-plan process is intended to achieve are as follows:

(1) *To improve the physical environment of the community as a setting for human activities—to make it more functional, beautiful, decent, healthful, interesting, and efficient.* This purpose is in accord with the broad objective of local government to promote the health, safety, morals, order, convenience, prosperity, and general welfare of the community. These phrases are customarily associated with police power; they actually pertain to all acts of government.

(2) *To promote the public interest, the interest of the community at large, rather than the interests of individuals or special groups within the community.* The comprehensive nature of the general plan contributes to this purpose, for it facilitates consideration of the relationship of any question to the overall physical development of the entire community. Because the plan is based on facts and on studies that attempt to be thorough and impartial, it helps to prevent arbitrary, capricious, and biased actions. The contributions of the plan to democratic, responsible government help to safeguard the public interest.

(3) *To facilitate the democratic determination and implementation of community policies on physical development.* The plan is primarily a policy instrument. The plan constitutes a declaration of long-range goals and provides the basis for a program to accomplish the goals. By placing the responsibility for determining policies on the city council and providing an opportunity for citizen participation, the plan facilitates the democratic process.

(4) *To effect political and technical coordination in community development.* Political coordination signifies that a large majority within the community is working toward the same ends. Technical coordination means a logical relationship among the physical elements dealt with in the plan and the most efficient planning and scheduling of actual improvements so as to avoid conflict, duplication, and waste. Effective coordination of such a complex subject requires a unified, integrated plan if the physical elements of the environment are to be managed

without costly conflicts of function and if the political forces of the community are to deal with controversial development issues, including the plan itself, in a constructive manner.

(5) *To inject long-range considerations into the determination of short-range actions.* In effect, this purpose is intended to achieve coordination through time, to attempt to make sure that today's decision will lead toward tomorrow's goal. The extensive use of forecasts and the establishment of long-range goals are significant features of the general plan. The plan represents an effort to add an important time dimension to the decision-making process.

(6) *To bring professional and technical knowledge to bear on the making of political decisions concerning the physical development of the community.* This purpose is intended to promote wiser decision-making, and to achieve informed, constructive government. Through the general plan, the special knowledge of the professional city planner is brought into play in the democratic political process.

—Adapted from T. J. Kent, *The Urban General Plan* (1964, 1990), pp. 25–26.

6.3.2 Comprehensive Planning Process

Here we present key steps in the comprehensive planning process.

Assessing Conditions and Trends Through Data

Assessing current conditions and trends through data provides decision-makers with the context for planning (see Hopkins and Zapata 2007). Census data may be used to understand how the community has changed over time, and where it seems headed. Tens of thousands of suburban communities designed to meet the needs of the Baby Boom generation (those born between 1946 and 1964) now face an aging population with far fewer children, and many are in decline. Economic data can also be used to assess changes in jobs and household income. Federal, state, local, non-profit, and other data can be used to help assess the environment, transportation conditions, social conditions, demands on public services and utilities (more on this for CIEs below), and housing and land-use conditions, among others. These data can then be used to frame future trends, and lead to projections and future housing, economic and infrastructure needs.

A key part of the assessment process is understanding demographic changes and challenges. This should include data and analysis relating to the community's population by age, gender and racial characteristics, total and average household size, as well as households by type and householder age and race/ethnicity, birth and death rates, and migration rates and patterns. It should also include demographic projections through the planning horizon (Jepson and Weitz, 2020).

Finally, and although it should go without saying, plans need to include projections. Especially to support impact fee policies, projections are needed to help calibrate the impact of new growth and development on infrastructure. Unfortunately, too many plans make no projections whatsoever. Even when communities make projections, they are often just of the population as a whole with no details relating to households and types of housing needed, or jobs and the nature of non-residential land-use impact (see Nelson 2004).

Projections are not enough, however. It is important to understand trends. For instance, we have seen some communities assume that if the overall population grows by 20 percent, so will demand for schools. What if the adult population grows while the school-aged population (children) declines? Not only would impact fees for schools be in excess of demand based on demographic trends, but the community may be promising to build new schools that are not needed during the planning horizon. For impact fee purposes, projections should be made for at least the following:

Households (which predict housing demand) by household type (such as with children, two or more adults without children, single person) and householder age (such as under 35, 35–49, 50–64, and over 64).

Housing units both occupied and vacant, by type (such as single-family detached large and small lot, townhome, condominium, apartment, manufactured home) and tenure (owner and renter).

Employment with associated building and land area by such major land-use sectors such as industrial, office/service, institutional, retail, education, arts/culture/ entertainment, and lodging.

Each of these projections would be compared to the current or baseline conditions so that the nature and magnitude of change can be understood and used for the rest of the planning process.

Identifying Issues

While some planners may wish to identify issues first, in our experience, using data to help frame current conditions helps identify and frame issues. These data, together with trends and projections, can be used to engage community stakeholders in coming to a consensus on issues to be addressed by the comprehensive plan.

Establishing Goals

Data and its analysis combined with identifying issues should lead to community goal setting. We offer a set of aspirational goals in the next section. Goal setting is not a trivial exercise, but fortunately there is a wide range of techniques available to facilitate this step. Scenario planning is a particularly useful technique for communities to establish goals.[4]

Preparing the Plan

From the assessment of current conditions to the identification of issues and establishment of goals, the community can prepare a comprehensive plan. This process, however, is often iterative as alternative ways to achieve the same goals are weighed (Berke, Kaiser, and Godschalk 2006; Anderson 1995).

Adopting the Plan

Consistent with the advice of Kent, the community needs to adopt the plan as an official statement of policy that will guide future development decisions of all local government agencies. This is done through resolutions or ordinances, although occasionally it is done as an amendment to the city or county charter (Juergensmeyer, Roberts, Salkin, and Rowberry 2018).

Implementing the Plan

To be effective in guiding development, plans need to be implemented through zoning, subdivision controls, and other land-use control measures. In many states, implementing ordinances and especially decisions based on them must be consistent with the comprehensive plan (Juergensmeyer, Roberts, Salkin, and Rowberry 2018). One of the implementation devices is the CIP which will be discussed in detail in a later section.

Plan Monitoring

As Haar cautioned above, a comprehensive plan is not a permanent document. In communities that change quickly—through either rapid growth or decline, for instance—plans need to be updated every 5 to 10 years. In communities with more moderate change, plans may be updated every 10 to 20 years.

We turn next to what we call aspirational goals.

6.3.3 Aspirational Planning Goals

There are perhaps as many definitions of planning as there are people engaged in it. Here we review some of the key principles of what constitutes "good" planning in our view. These principles are adapted from Nelson, Duncan, Mullen, and Bishop (1995) as well as Nelson, Marshall, Nicholas, and Juergensmeyer (2017). These principles include the following, which are also explained albeit briefly:

- Meet market demand-based needs;
- Preserve public and merit goods;
- Maximize the use of existing infrastructure to minimize costs;
- Minimize adverse land-use interactions and maximize positive ones;
- Equitably distribute the benefits and burdens of change; and
- Elevate quality of life.

6.3.4 Meet Market Demand-Based Needs

At their heart, land-use plans address the needs of growth and change consistent with community goals. This begins with a projection of future development needs for all land uses and development types as well as an inventory of current development to determine the extent to which current development meets future needs (see Nelson 2004), net of replacement development (see Nelson 2013). This technical analysis is followed by allocating land to meet future needs consistent with goals on where development should and should not occur based on environmental and preservation objectives and infrastructure investment commitments.

6.3.5 Preserve Public and Merit Goods

Often a key goal of planning is to preserve what is called public and merit goods such as clean air and working landscapes (farms, ranches, forests). Technically, a public good is something such as air that no one can be excluded from using (how does one charge for the air someone else breathes?) and which is so abundant that there will rarely be too

many users. Because there is no market for these kinds of goods, the public has to provide or preserve them through taxes, regulations, and other means of intervention. A merit good is something for which its future value is worth more than the present, but since the market only pays for the present value, future options may be foreclosed, such as in the case of developing farms. Community goals are needed to identify public and merit goods to be provided. For instance, if the preservation of farms is considered important because of their air-cleansing public good and long-term food production merit values, land-use plans need to prevent their development (see Chapter 13 for an illustration of this).

6.3.6 Maximize the Use of Existing Infrastructure to Minimize Costs

Infrastructure can be very expensive to construct and maintain. As such, one community goal may be to maximize its use to minimize the cost of infrastructure investments. For instance, if a road has the capacity to serve 10,000 homes in an area, zoning to limit homes to half that number means road costs per home are doubled. We also know of situations where the reconstruction of older roads in low-density neighborhoods costs more than all the property taxes generated by the neighborhood it serves for decades into the future. This is one reason why road repairs are delayed because those costs often come out of budgets for public safety, schools, and other taxpayer services (see Nelson, Nicholas, and Juergensmeyer 2022).

6.3.7 Minimize Adverse Land-use Interactions and Maximize Positive Ones

Zoning was invented to separate land uses deemed incompatible with one another. The famous *Euclid v. Ambler* case in which the US Supreme Court determined that zoning was a police-power function dealt in part with the city wanting to separate new subdivisions from noxious industrial uses. Indeed, there is ample evidence showing that certain land uses impose negative externalities on others that drive down real estate values (Nelson 1992). But land uses can also be complementary in ways that modern planning and zoning codes do not appreciate. Many land uses that might seem incompatible have synergistic effects that raise property values collectively. Indeed, because of modern environmental policies, building codes, and design advances, it may be more the case that incompatible land uses are the exceptions.

6.3.8 Equitably Distribute the Benefits and Burdens of Change

Just communities find ways in which to fairly distribute the benefits and burdens equitably among their residents. Although there may be some "losers" in land-use change, just communities will find ways to offset those losses through value-added investments (such as parks) and economic compensation. Indeed, the AICP Code of Ethics requires planners to seek ways in which to do this (see also Chapter 15 and its Coda):

Seek social justice by identifying and working to expand choice and opportunity for all persons, emphasizing our special responsibility to plan with those who have been marginalized or disadvantaged and to promote racial and economic equity. Urge the alteration of policies, institutions, and decisions that do not help meet their needs.[5]

6.3.9 Elevate Quality of Life

Research shows that mixed land uses, higher densities, and improved accessibility elevate measurable elements of quality of life such as personal and public health, economic resilience, and sense of community. Planning goals that advance quality of life would be wise

to encourage more compact and integrated land-use patterns than offered in conventional suburban communities, for instance.

We posit that when achieved collectively, the result is "good" planning, which we discuss in the context of good and bad planning in Chapter 13.

These aspirational goals can be achieved in part through infrastructure planning and financing that is guided by five principles as they apply to impact fees:

Encouraging new development to occur where facilities already exist through an infill/redevelopment strategy that would not charge impact fees where growth could be accommodated with existing infrastructure.

Charging new development the full cost of infrastructure based on differences in service areas and not an average spread across all service areas regardless of differences in costs between them.

Reducing impact fees reflecting lower impact associated with more efficient land uses through master planned and mixed-use development with respect to roads, water, wastewater, drainage and other infrastructure—this would likely be negotiated through development agreements.

Scaling impact to the size of development mostly based on nature (type of land use) and extent (in square feet or other continuous measures) of residential and non-residential development.

Facilitating low-and moderate-income housing as well as target economic development through reduced or waived impact fees but having other local government accounts pay those fees on behalf of such targeted development (see Chapters 8 and 9 for further discussion).

The key objective of this approach is to reduce potential inequities that can occur because of impact fees (see Chapters 14, 15, and 16, as well as the Coda to Chapter 15). It also advances several aspirational goals noted earlier. We next introduce key elements of the comprehensive plan.

6.3.10 Comprehensive Plan Elements

Comprehensive plans will have many, sometimes dozens, of specific community goals as well as numerous objectives and implementing policies, among other features. Keeping the aspirational goals in mind, we review common elements of comprehensive plans, although reserving the CIE to the next section.

Each community will have its own set of plan elements reflecting those that are most important to it. Perhaps without exception, all communities will include land-use, housing, economic development, transportation, environmental/conservation, recreation, and infrastructure elements. Some communities may include coastal, mountain, desert, or other elements unique to their landscapes. Others may have historic or cultural preservation elements, while still others may have resort/tourism elements. An increasing number of communities have energy/solar/wind power elements, as well as an element tied directly to climate change. As Haar noted in his analysis back in 1955, nearly every state that enables planning includes elements required in local plans.

A succinct organization of key plan elements is outlined by Rouse and Piro (2022), grouped into these functional areas:

Natural Systems addressing planning in harmony with nature to create healthy and sustainable communities focusing an integrated ecosystem approach with special reference to climate change.

Built Environment Systems including land use, development patterns, community character facilitated by an infrastructure system that advances efficient use of such facilities as mobility services, water, energy, public safety, education, parks and recreation, cultural and social services, and government,

typically through a capital improvement element (CIE) that will be discussed in detail later.

Social Systems focusing on environmental justice, neighborhoods, social infrastructure, and housing to support people with an emphasis on *planning with an equity lens* (see also Chapter 15) to meet the needs of all members and groups comprising the community.

Economic Systems that aim to achieve economic opportunity for all, economic resilience, and efficient use of resources through such efforts as asset-based economic activity; the green, circular, and sharing economies; disaster preparedness and recovery; and fiscal sustainability that latter of which includes mitigating development impacts on infrastructure.

Healthy Community advancing the role of the comprehensive plan to improve community health and reduce health disparities through proactive efforts in environmental health, improving access to healthy foods, and enhancing public safety.

Regional Connections highlighting the importance of regional governance to that address the intergovernmental role in improving natural, built environment, social and economic systems that transcend jurisdictional boundaries.

We focus next on the role of the capital improvement element and the capital improvement plan that implements it, noting especially the role of impact fees.

6.4 CAPITAL IMPROVEMENT ELEMENT

The CIE is necessary to link impact fees to the overall community comprehensive plan. We will start with the policy framework relating to LOS standards and service areas, continue with an assessment of the capacity of existing facilities to accommodate the demands of new development, and finish with an overall perspective on the role of the CIE in assuring that development occurs in accordance with the comprehensive plan.

But first an overview of what the CIE is and does.[6] One of the authors of this chapter (Nelson) helped train staff of the Georgia Department of Community Affairs about impact fees and then helped draft earlier versions of the materials it used to guide the preparation and implementation of impact fees in Georgia. Many of the principles used by Georgia are applicable to impact fee analysis everywhere.

Local plans should have CIEs otherwise, logically, how can those parts of the plan dependent on infrastructure be implemented? The CIE's timeframe is usually the same as the plan horizon. But they are *not* a CIP that specifies which facilities will be constructed, when and where, and how they will be financed—this is discussed later.

A key role of the CIE is to assure that public infrastructure investments are made in accordance with the plan, as this will help guide development so that it, too, is in accordance with the plan. CIEs should have these elements:

- Inventory of existing facilities.
- Adopted LOS standards for each type of infrastructure.
- Service areas for each type of infrastructure based on its unique service characteristics.
- Projected future infrastructure needs.
- Estimated costs.
- Prospective sources of revenue to finance the needed improvements.

We proceed with a review of each of these elements and their relation to impact fees.

6.4.1 Inventory of Existing Levels of Service

The first step in preparing a CIE is to inventory existing facilities to determine current conditions. This will lead to determining the existing LOS for each facility. The inventory would normally be done for the community as a whole and later for each service area (see below). The inventory to establish the existing LOS should include:

- **An inventory of current levels of service for each category of capital improvements for which impact fees are proposed to be charged. Service levels must be expressed in quantifiable terms or in a manner sufficient to allow future evaluation of progress in meeting capital improvements goals.**

Generally, "level of service" is a measure of the relationship between service capacity and service demand for public facilities in terms of demand to capacity ratios, or the comfort or convenience of use or both. Thus, to define service levels in a CIE, the inventory must develop criteria for measuring and describing service levels. These criteria will be different for different categories of capital facilities but will always be designed to measure capacity against demand.

For example, a CIE might describe the current park service level as two acres of neighborhood park land for every 1,000 people. Or it might assign a five-mile service radius for neighborhood parks as a measure of "convenient" access to such parks. Note that it would be possible, using the criteria described in this example, to calculate that a community with an existing population of 10,000 would need ten more acres of neighborhood park land to maintain the current level of service if it added 5,000 new people over the next decade. Or one could see that some portions of the county fall outside the service radius of existing neighborhood parks and thus pinpoint neighborhoods with a lower standard of convenience than others. Also, it would be possible to calculate that if the community chose to raise its service level for neighborhood parks to three acres per 1,000 residents, it would need 15 acres of park land in addition to the 10 acres calculated above.

- **Determination of whether the existing level and quality of services is adequate to meet current needs and clearly identify major deficiencies or under-utilization of existing facilities within the jurisdiction.**

   This part of the analysis should consider whether the community is satisfied with the level of services currently provided. This will also be part of the formal process to determine the LOS standards that will guide facility planning which is reviewed below. The CIE should determine whether deficiencies in services create significant problems for the community or present obstacles to meeting the community's needs

   Basically, the analysis should ask what it will cost to expand infrastructure or raise service levels, and will the benefits justify the costs?" and "What service levels are the community willing to support?" It should also identify any opportunities for economic development or land development presented by excess infrastructure capacity, if this exists. Are road upgrades needed? Will housing stock in a historic neighborhood deteriorate unless infrastructure investments are made? If a community is experiencing a great deal of new development, capital facilities will need to be expanded or added just to maintain existing service levels. Before proposing to raise service levels, a community should assess what maintaining existing service levels is likely to involve.

- **Description of variations in current service levels throughout the community (i.e., geographic areas that differ with respect to available capacity, distribution systems or quality of service delivery).**

   These data may be inventoried in the local comprehensive plan. If not, it is important to indicate areas within a jurisdiction that lack specific services. Are there development "hot spots" in a community where roads, public utilities, and other services are overburdened? Are roads congested in some areas but almost unused in others? Does part of the county have fire hydrants, while the rest must depend on pumper trucks? Does the jurisdiction contain community improvement districts with higher levels of service than elsewhere? Is a centralized sewer available only in urban centers? Are recreation facilities more plentiful in one part of the county than in another?

- **Identification of parts of the community where the provision of services is, or will be, limited by engineering, economic, or environmental factors.**

   For example, perhaps the topography and drainage patterns make it five times more expensive to provide sewer service in one part of the community relative to other parts. Do inadequately sized water lines make it physically and/or economically infeasible to install fire hydrants in sparsely populated parts of a jurisdiction? Assessing these limitations in the inventory will provide a rational framework to support the decisions reached later in the CIE relating to both formal LOS standards and service area design.

   We move now to address the formal level of service standards.

6.4.2 Establishing LOS Standards

The LOS standard is a term used to describe the quantitative relationship between the nature of development and the amount or scale of facilities needed to serve it. If, for example, roadways are severely congested, the parks are overcrowded, and water rationing is required every summer, one would conclude that the level of service provided by these facilities is low. However, in some cases a community might be willing to tolerate a relatively low level of service. This could be because a low level of service is less expensive to provide, or because it promotes other policy objectives such as encouraging the use of public transit or conserving water. There are several nuances to consider in establishing LOS standards in the CIE to guide impact fees (see also Chapter 7).

Adopted vs. Existing Levels of Service

A distinction should be made between the actual level of service, which can be measured at a given time, and the desired level of service. The desired level of service should be formally adopted in the CIE (or elsewhere in the comprehensive plan). The relationship between the adopted level of service that is used to calculate impact fees for new development, and the actual level of service existing at the time of impact fee adoption, has important implications in the context of an impact fee system. These implications are summarized in Table 6.1 (see also Chapter 7).

If a community establishes a desired level of service that is higher than the existing level, existing facilities will be found to be deficient when compared to the adopted standard. New developments will pay impact fees calculated on the cost to maintain the adopted level of service but will be sharing existing facilities that operate at a lower level of service. As impact fees are spent, facilities will be upgraded, and the level of service will improve for all users. However, new developments would not be receiving the level of service for which they are being charged, and existing users would be benefiting from the improved level of service paid for by new development.

Such a situation would clearly violate the proportionate fair-share impact fee principles. If the community decides to adopt a level of service higher than the existing service level, it must find non-impact fee revenue sources to upgrade existing facilities to the adopted service level. Such revenues should be available based on realistic projections to remedy any deficiencies over a reasonable period.

At the other extreme, the community could adopt a level of service that is below the level currently provided. Such an approach would mean that existing facilities have excess capacity that would be available to serve new development. Impact fees may be used to recoup the cost of constructing this excess capacity.

Recoupment fees are calculated and handled administratively in the same manner as any other impact fee. Since the impact fee itself is collected based on those facilities for which the impact fee is calculated, those fees should be used for capital preservation purposes of those facilities, such as maintenance, repairs, and replacement. They can also be used for new capital improvements of the same type especially if they add capacity. In our view, recoupment fees may not be used enough to help communities increase capacity. For instance, if the existing park level of service (LOS) is 5 acres per 1,000 residents but the adopted LOS is 4 acres per 1,000 residents, the value of the difference can be converted into a recoupment form of impact fee with the proceeds used to add more park land perhaps in target areas within the service area that may be under-served.

TABLE 6.1 Alternative Level of Service Standards

Adopted Level of Service Compared to Existing Level of Service			
Outcome	Below Existing	Same as Existing	Higher than Existing
Amount of Impact Fee	Low	Moderate	High
Future Level of Service	Decline	Maintain	Improve
Existing Deficiencies	None	None	Must Remedy
Excess Capacity	Recoupment	None	None

Like all fee calculation methods, recoupment must respect the general principles of not double-charging and adjusting credits to reflect the time–value of money. The recoupment option therefore requires careful analysis of how and when each applicable capital project was originally financed. Moreover, setting an artificially low level of service for this purpose alone could be short-sighted. While more of the sunk costs of existing facilities would be recaptured, impact fees collected for future system expansion would be limited to the costs of providing the lower level of service. In addition, the lower the level of service that is adopted, the lower the annual amount of impact fee revenues received.

The third option, of course, is to adopt a level of service that is identical to the existing level of service. In many ways this is the simplest and most direct approach. It does not create any existing deficiencies or excess capacity, and simply charges new development the cost to maintain the level of service that existed prior to the development.

Varying Level of Service by Service Areas

Because one size does fit all, LOS standards should vary by service area (discussed below) based on policy objectives, development patterns, environmental conditions, or other factors. For example, the community may be willing to tolerate higher levels of traffic congestion in the downtown area, where alternative transportation options such as public transit are more readily available, than in outlying areas, where the automobile is the primary transportation mode. More permutations of this concept are discussed in the service areas below.

If there is a logical reason for providing more intensive services in a particular part of a jurisdiction, or constraints that prevent extending capital facilities to certain areas, it is best to state the reasons for the decisions a community has made in the comprehensive plan.

Level of Cost Recovery

Another issue that relates to the level of service is the level of cost recovery desired by the community. For a variety of reasons, many communities adopt impact fees at a level that is below the actual cost to serve new development. The impact fee level established in neighboring jurisdictions with which the community considers itself in competition for new development is often a major factor in such considerations.

There are basically two approaches to lowering impact fees. Probably the most common approach is to calculate the full cost to serve new development at the existing level of service standard, but then charge impact fees at a fixed percentage of the calculated cost, such as 75 percent. But this carries risks. As will be seen below and discussed throughout the book, if fees are assessed at below the level needed to fund the CIP, who makes up the difference? After all, impact fees are *per se* the gap financing needed to make up the difference in the first place.

Consider the implications if impact fees are assessed at less than full cost recovery:

- Developers who are promised a suite of facilities benefiting their development may find that many promised facilities are not being built.
- If impact fees are based on maintaining the current LOS, but revenues are insufficient to maintain it, the LOS will erode, thereby reducing community quality of life.
- Over time, growing deficiencies in LOS for lack of revenue to deliver the promised LOS will undermine future impact fee studies. After all, it would be the community at large and not a new development that would need to remedy existing deficiencies—either that or reduce the LOS perhaps below that needed to sustain the community's quality of life.

The CIE is the best place in the comprehensive plan in which to establish level of service standards. They should be clearly identified for each facility, even facilities for which impact fees are not assessed, and for each service area if the LOS standard are to vary by geographic area.

Appendix 6B offers a sample of LOS standards based on surveys of local governments. The list is not intended to be exhaustive but rather to illustrate the range of possibilities.

We turn next to service area design.

6.4.3 Service Areas

Many state impact fee enabling acts require service areas and define them in terms that we consider meaningless since they lack objective criteria. For instance, to paraphrase, the Georgia Development Impact Fee Act requires that service areas be designed based on sound planning and engineering principles. Many state enabling acts have no standards. Some states enable local governments to arbitrarily declare their entirety a single service area regardless of vast differences between geographic areas within them. Yet, there are standards that ought to be used based on features of individual systems. We offer some principles of design in Chapter 7 as well as below.

A key purpose of service areas is to assure that impacts fees of new development are mitigated at a small enough scale to reflect its true cost impacts on a discrete area but large enough to assure that sufficient funds can be collected from and invested into the area. Service area boundaries should also reflect the existing or planned urban form for sub-areas of the local government. For instance, a service area may be created for the downtown and separate ones for first-ring suburbs, new suburban areas, the suburban fringe and rural areas—depending on the size and landscape composition of the local government. We offer the following general guidance in crafting service areas based on mitigating the impacts of new development attributable to the smallest reasonable areas feasible.

First, each facility must have its own service area design because each facility has its own spatially related cost characteristics. For instance, while a stormwater drainage basin usually serves large land areas, a neighborhood park may serve areas within a mile or two in radius. However, service areas may include multiple types of facilities as part of an overall planning process that is aimed at steering development to target to achieve more efficient and less costly development patterns, among other reasons.

Second, costs may vary from one part of a jurisdiction to another because of engineering or environmental factors. If revenues collected from infrastructure—such as an average-cost-based water or sewer hook-up fee—does not reflect the actual cost of providing the service, leapfrog development may be encouraged. Service areas should be designed to reflect the real cost of providing services to it.

Third, while one service area might lend itself to one LOS standard, another might lend itself to a different one. For instance, overlapping service areas for public safety, water, sewer, and transportation might take the form of a set of tiers around a growing city where an intensive array of public services would be appropriate, with the balance of the community considered rural with little or no planned growth thereby requiring a different mix of services. Another example would be a special purpose service serving an industrial corridor that might need special wastewater pretreatment facilities or major road expansions. Service areas tailored to planning objectives can be used to assure that infrastructure costs are attributable to those land-use activities that will benefit from them.

Fourth, while perhaps not necessarily prohibiting development in underserved or environmentally sensitive areas, separate service areas can be used to assure development elsewhere in the community is not forced to subsidize the extra costs of providing services to those underserved service areas.

There may also be key planning purposes to be addressed in designing service areas. These include:

- Steer infrastructure away from areas with severe development constraints;
- Phase or prioritize infrastructure investments in different service areas to advance environmental or land-use policies; and
- Minimize problems associated with making older, built-out areas conform to service levels appropriate for developing suburban areas.

The latter point warrants more discussion. In some cases, bringing all areas of a community up to a desired service level will be physically impractical. For example, if a downtown business district were included in a road service area where a local government proposed to raise the volume-to-capacity ratio of all arterial streets, the city might be forced to condemn some very expensive real estate, remove parking spaces, or narrow sidewalks to an unacceptable width to add the required traffic lanes. Conversely, if a community does wish to raise service areas in previously developed areas, there may be benefits to drawing service area boundaries to link older neighborhoods with vacant land expected to generate plenty of impact fee revenues for new facilities or improvements. For example, a local government building a community park might want to include both developed and undeveloped land in the same service area. In general, service area boundaries should encompass the area where most users of its facilities will live or work. An alternative is to design service areas based on such standardized data collection geographies as census block groups or census tracts and traffic analysis zones.

However, service areas must not be designed based on political representation districts. Instead, they need to be based on an objective analysis of the service characteristics of facilities which often cross political representation. Doing so also may reduce the temptation for some elected officials to reward or punish others for political gain.

Sometimes the LOS for certain facilities will vary because of the location or other characteristics of a jurisdiction. For instance, in sprawling jurisdictions that cannot afford high-quality fire protection service everywhere, one service area close to the center of the city may be designed for a five-minute response time while another much farther away may be designed for a ten-minute response time. Fire insurance ratings will then vary perhaps considerably based on response time. Variations in the level of service can be applied to transportation, parks, and recreation, among other facilities.

Needless to say, decisions about LOS for individual service areas can have important implications for community infrastructure investment, and financial obligations of owners and tenants of new development. In the case of fire station planning, if one service area is designed to have a shorter response time than another, its fire insurance premiums could be lower. This may be troublesome politically, leading to decisions to provide all development with the same response time, regardless of the expense. On the other hand, keeping the same response times throughout the community could guide impact fee analysis to show much higher costs per unit of development in low-density areas compared to higher-density ones, which may influence local government development deliberations.

The rationale for varying the LOS by service area should be included in the plan and then be used to guide the fiscal impact analysis.

Additional service area considerations are presented in Appendix 6C.

6.4.4 Projecting Future Facility Needs

This portion of the CIE projects future facility needs. This is done in two ways: identifying current excess capacity to meet future needs and estimating new or expanded facilities to meet future needs. In general, the projection of future facility needs should include the following:

Identify Excess Service Capacity in
Existing Facilities Based on Adopted
LOS Standards by Service Area
The LOS standards will help guide the determination of existing facilities that have the capacity to serve the needs of at least some of the new development projected to occur in the plan. This analysis needs to be done for each service area to show, for instance, those service areas that have the capacity to accommodate new development over a certain number of years, and those that do not.

Determining Where New Facilities Will Be
Needed to Implement the Comprehensive Plan
The availability of facilities, especially water, wastewater, and road facilities, will affect development patterns. Adding more water and wastewater capacity near highway interchanges may encourage growth and clustering of commercial activities. Areas with poor soils that are not suitable for septic systems may need new wastewater systems along with new water and road facilities. Moreover, if an area already has excess facility capacity, the community plan may wish to target new development in them first. Or, if the community wants to attract industry to locate in certain areas, extending water, wastewater, and road facilities into them may be needed, regardless of excess capacity to serve new development in places that are not appropriate for industrial activities. In sum, this part of the CIE needs to balance existing facility capacity in some parts of the community with the desire shown in the plan to attract certain kinds of development to other parts of the community.

Environmental constraints will also need to be considered. For instance, if the plan calls for protecting wetlands, floodplains, high water tables, steep slopes, and agricultural land among others, facilities will need to steer development away from them even if in some cases excess capacity exists—such as adequate road capacity in and near floodplains. The CIE may determine that centralized wastewater treatment is a high priority in aquifer recharge areas. As it helps implement the plan, the CIE needs to show where facilities should and should not go, by when, and at what scale to meet adopted LOS standards.

Data and Projection Methodologies
Need to Be Consistent with the Plan
The projection used to guide plan-making needs to also be used to guide facility planning. As such, the CIE needs to show how facilities will meet the demands of projected growth and in areas where growth is directed. Put differently, the CIE provides local decision-makers with the ability to say "no" to development proposals requiring new or different scales of facilities needed to implement the plan.

Identification of Facilities Needed to Be
Installed or Upgraded by Service Area
It goes almost without saying that the CIE needs an inventory of the facilities needed to be built or upgraded to meet the needs of new development. This should also include those existing facilities that are currently deficient in meeting the needs of existing development as well as a way in which to remedy the deficiencies from non-impact fee revenues. This will also need to be done by service and showing approximate time frames for investments, such as five-year increments.

Estimating the Costs and Prospective
Sources of Revenue to Finance the CIE
Lastly, the CIE needs to estimate the costs of providing all the facilities needed to accommodate the needs of new development, even those facilities for which impact fees are not

part of their financing. These costs need to be apportioned by service area and time frame, such as five-year increments.

Revenues will need to be identified as well to determine the extent to which all the improvements identified in the CIE to implement the plan can be financed. These may include such revenues as:

- General obligation bonds are financed through the property, sales and other taxes;
- Revenue bonds are financed from fees generated by users, such as water and wastewater rates, hotel occupancy taxes, and other revenues;
- Dedicated taxes and fees for specific purposes such as water and wastewater surcharges, park and recreation levies, and public safety levies, among others;
- Special assessments applied to small areas where revenue is generated from new and existing development in the area to finance facilities serving substantially only that area;
- General fund budgets from the local government themselves are comprised of local tax and fee revenue, intergovernmental transfers (such as state revenue sharing with local government), and all other revenue collected by local governments that are placed into and special local government account to be used for this purpose;
- Grants from all levels of governments, foundations, organizations, individuals and other sources; and
- All other non-impact fee revenue is used to help finance infrastructure that is also financed in part from impact fees.

Funding sources would be identified for all facilities. This same exercise would be applied to all facilities for which impact fees are an allowable source of expenditure. If identified sources of revenue are sufficient to finance those facilities, impact fees would not be needed. But if those revenues leave a gap or shortfall in financing, this is the amount that would be financed from impact fees.

6.4.5 Capital Improvement Plans

As we reviewed in Chapter 2 ("Legal Foundations") and Chapter 12 ("Toward a Supply-Side Theory of Impact Fees"), there are two broad ways in which to mitigate the impact of new growth and development on infrastructure: case by case negotiation leading to development agreements (see also Chapter 16, "The Option of Impact Fees") and scheduled charges such as impact fees. For their part, impact fees are considered a regulatory tool because they are rooted in the police-power function of government to protect public health, safety, and general welfare. Generally, local government has the authority to require that new growth and development mitigate its impact on infrastructure either by making the mitigations directly (such as building a new water treatment plant and perhaps seeking reimbursement from future development) or paying fees to local government proportionate to its impact for the same purpose. Indeed, a better name for them could be *regulatory* impact fees. But their correct role is in implementing the CIE[7] through the CIP, which is reviewed here.

The CIE is implemented by the CIP.[8] It is typically designed to fund capital improvements over periods ranging from one to 10 years though typically about five years, and updated annually. Moreover, there should be a CIP for each service area. CIPs should be comprised of the elements outlined below and illustrated in Table 6.2.[9]

Column 1 Project Description—The row headings will summarize the facility projects that would be funded at least in part with impact fees and either under construction or planned for construction within the CIP period.

TABLE 6.2 Example of Parks and Recreation CIP

Project Description	Service Area	Project Start	Project Completion	Project Cost	Impact Fee Share	Funding Sources
James Park (20 acres)	East	2020	2022	$1,450,000	40%	Park bonds 60%, impact fees 40%
Julian Park (20 acres)	South	2021	2023	$1,440,000	75%	Park bonds 25%, impact fees 75%
Clancy Park (20 acres)	Central	2022	2024	$1,260,000	100%	Impact fees 100%
Arthur Park (20) acres	West	2023	2025	$1,300,000	50%	Development agreement 50%, impact fees 50%

Note: This is for illustration purposes only. Communities will create formats appropriate for their contexts.

Column 2 Service Area—This would apply to CIE and CIPs with more than one service area though in the example shown in Table 6.2, there is only one impact-funded park for each of the four service areas.

Column 3 Project Start—This is the year in which the project is scheduled to start. If the project is delayed, the new start year will be shown in the annual CIP update.

Column 4 Project Completion—This is the year in which the project is scheduled to be finished. As above, if the project is delayed, the new start year would be shown in the annual CIP update.

Column 5 Project Cost—This is the estimated total cost for this project though it may be revised based on new information contained in the updated CIP. ·

Column 6 Impact Fee Share—This is the share of the project cost that is eligible for funding from impact fees. It could also be expressed in dollars.

Column 7 Funding Sources—This is the source of funds allocated to make the improvement. It includes a brief summary of the source and the percentage share in this example, though it can also be the dollar share.

Where there may be a variety of construction and management agencies involved, another column might be added to identify that entity.

The reason projects funded at least in part from impact fees are called out separately is to show that they are qualified for impact fee funds. For instance, some CIP projects may be for repair, maintenance and replacement without adding capacity, such as road resurfacing. Or some CIP projects might increase capacity to remedy a deficiency in current facilities relative to the adopted LOS standard, such as increasing the supply of parks from 4 acres per 5 acres of park land per 1,000 residents to bring the supply current with LOS-driven needs.

Often, the purposes of CIP projects are mixed. There might be a road widening that doubles capacity, but the existing lanes also need resurfacing. Resurfacing the original lanes would not qualify for impact fee funding, but the additional lanes would: the CIP would apportion costs between these two purposes, separating costs that are "deficiency" related and those that are "growth related." Likewise, if 5 acres of a 10-acre park expansion remedies a deficiency, those costs cannot be funded from impact fees, but the other 5 acres would.

There is always the potential that the same improvement services multiple service areas, perhaps as a main thoroughfare extending across three service areas. One solution would be to have one service area for just that thoroughfare. Another might be to simply apportion costs and impact fee revenues across the service areas apportioned to the costs and development demands of each service area.

Mentioned in other chapters but also raised here is the distinction between "project" and "system-wide" improvements. System-wide improvements are facilities designed to accommodate the needs of development throughout the community or its service areas. These do not include improvements made within specific developments pursuant to subdivision or development permitting. They also do not include off-site improvements that are needed to serve just the development itself, such as ingress or egress lanes.

However, there may be some facilities included in the CIP that are designated for private funding, such as "latecomer" assessments. For instance, suppose a major water line extension is needed to serve parcels owned by one or a few entities whose development timing is uncertain, though development seems certain within a few years. The cost for extension may be shown in the CIP, but the source of funding could be noted as from other than public funds, including impact fees. When a parcel is developed, the developer may incur the entire cost, but as other developments occur in the area, they reimburse the lead developer for their proportionate share costs.

These arrangements would be part of a master development agreement.

An important part of the CIP process is tracking the costs actually incurred compared to budgeted costs. This will help gauge progress toward meeting LOS targets as well as follow the cash flow to help identify potential adjustments. An example of this is shown in Table 6.3 for illustration purposes only. The simplified example shows an annual report for two facilities—transportation and public safety—for their respective service areas. The columns and rows are described as follows.[10]

Row 1 Facility Type—This row identifies the facilities funded in part from impact fees. If there are numerous facilities, each having multiple service areas, it may be best to report each facility for each service area separately though the format may be similar.

Row 2 Service Area—This row identifies the service area for each facility. As noted above, if there are multiple facilities with multiple service areas, it may be best to report each facility for each service area separately.

Row 3 Beginning Impact Fee Fund Balance— This is the amount of impact fee funds available to be spent on the respective

TABLE 6.3 Example of Annual CIP Reporting

Facility Service Area	Transportation East	Transportation West	Public Safety North	Public Safety South	Public Safety Central
Beginning Impact Fee Fund Balance	$232,403	$254,303	$157,891	$181,586	$0
Impact Fees Collected	$295,649	$301,649	$108,887	$323,541	$328,945
Accrued Interest	$1,051	$951	$1,482	$1,486	$2,895
Project Expenditures	($4,658)	($4,658)	($8,363)	($13,093)	($8,800)
Administrative Costs	($1,234)	($1,324)	($2,668)	($3,259)	($4,360)
Impact Fee Refunds	$0	$0	$0	$0	$0
Ending Impact Fee Fund Balance	$523,211	$550,921	$257,229	$490,260	$318,680
Impact Fees Spent/ Encumbered	$512,031	$525,351	$250,000	$320,890	$256,650

Note: This is for illustration purposes only. Communities will create formats appropriate for their contexts.

facility within its respective service area at the beginning of the year.

Row 4 Impact Fees Collected—This row reports the impact fees collected during the year for the respective facility in the respective service area.

Row 5 Accrued Interest—This row reports all interest earned on impact fee collections during the last completed fiscal year. Again, this information is broken out for each facility and service area.

Row 6 Project Expenditures—This column reports the expenditures made during the year for the respective facilities and service areas.

Row 7 Administrative Costs—In some states, there is a limit on the costs of administrating impact fee programs, such as three percent. This row shows the cost of administering the impact fee program for respective facilities and their service areas. This may be simply the pro rata share of total impact fee administrative expenses in the community.

Row 8 Impact Fee Refunds—In most states with impact fee enabling acts, impact fees must be expended within a certain number of years or be refunded. Impact fee ordinances may also provide that if construction of a project for which impact fees have been paid has been abandoned, and the permits voided, refunds may be issued.

Row 9 Ending Impact Fee Fund Balance—This is the ending balance of impact fee funds for the current year, which becomes the beginning balance for the next.

Row 10 Impact Fees Encumbered—Many state impact fee enabling acts allow impact fees to be encumbered in one year, albeit not actually spent until a later year. The concept of being encumbered means that the funds are obligated by contract or otherwise committed for use by appropriation or other official acts of the community. In effect, they are deemed to have been expended even though funds remain in the account. As such, this row essentially reports the future obligation of impact fees for respective facilities and their service areas.

6.4.6 Apportioning Revenue Shortfalls to New Development through Proportionate Share Impact Fees

Impact fees are the last step of the planning process; we have sometimes called them the revenue tail that wags the planning dog. Technically, it is during the CIP process, and illustrated in the CIP analysis, that the need for impact fees is established. They are a form of gap financing as they make up the difference between CIP costs—which are based on implementing the CIE, which itself is designed to help implement the plan—and revenues available to finance it.

The gap itself, leading to impact fees, is tempered in two respects. First, impact fees must not require newly developed properties to bear more than their equitable share of the capital cost in relation to the benefits conferred. Second, determining the equitable share of the capital cost to be borne by new development requires that government determine the relative burdens previously borne and yet to be borne by those properties relative to existing development. As such, the impact fee cannot exceed the amount sufficient to equalize the relative burdens of new development in relation to existing development.[11] This final stage of impact fee analysis addresses seven elements of the so-called *Banberry* criteria (see also Chapter 2). In review, these criteria (*with commentary*) are:[12]

(1) The cost of existing capital facilities (*to establish the rational basis for determining the value of excess capacity that may be assigned to development*).
(2) The manner of financing existing capital facilities such as user charges, special assessments, bonded indebtedness,

general taxes, or federal grants *(to establish the extent to which local taxpayers created value in the excess capacity).*

(3) The relative extent to which the newly developed properties and the other properties in the municipality have already contributed to the cost of existing capital facilities by such means as user charges, special assessments, or payment from the proceeds of general taxes *(to estimate the credit or reduction in the impact cost to prevent development from being double charged for the same facilities—once through impact fees again through contributions they make through taxes and other fees that help finance the same facilities).*

(4) The relative extent to which the newly developed properties and the other properties in the municipality will contribute to the cost of existing capital facilities in the future *(to also prevent charging new development twice for the same facilities for the reasons noted in (3)).*

(5) The extent to which the newly developed properties are entitled to a credit because the municipality is requiring their developers or owners by contractual arrangement or otherwise to provide common facilities inside or outside the proposed development that have been provided by the municipality and financed through general taxation or other means apart from user charges in other parts of the municipality *(thereby further preventing double charges for reasons noted in (3) and (4)).*

(6) Extraordinary costs, if any, in servicing the newly developed properties *(to allow consideration for unique circumstances).*

(7) The time–price differential inherent in fair comparisons of amounts paid at different times *(to adjust for the time–value of money both from the perspective of estimating the current value of existing public facilities and the costs of future public facilities, which are then offset by the time–value of money affecting those who pay impact fees).*

We end this chapter where we began, with the role of impact fees in assuring that new development occurs in accordance with the plan.

6.5 IN ACCORDANCE WITH THE PLAN REVISITED

We conclude this chapter by summarizing how the American Planning Association views the role of impact fees in implementing plans, and in mitigating the impacts of development. We paraphrase its policy here.[13]

Taxpayer revolts against higher taxes as well as declining federal and state aid combined with unfunded mandates strains local governments' ability to serve new development. Many local governments see two choices: constrain and even deny new development for lack of facilities or use impact fees to facilitate growth. Communities choosing impact fees thus shift the burden of paying for new or expanded facilities away from taxpayers to new development that creates the demand for those facilities. Impact fees are thus a form of mitigation.

Impact fees need to be based on a comprehensive plan. When used in conjunction with a sound CIEs implemented with an equally sound CIP, impact fees can ensure adequate public facilities are available concurrent with the demand for new development. In this respect, impact fees are a form of land-use and development regulation that protects public health, safety, and general welfare from the adverse effects of development on public facilities. They are thus used in tandem with local planning and land-use regulations such as zoning and subdivision control to advance the local police power. But they are not used to stop growth; rather, they are used to facilitate growth by helping to provide funds for public facilities that are needed to support growth in the first place.

Yet, impact fees can be improperly designed, resulting in lower-cost development and even lower-income households subsidizing higher-cost development and higher-income households, as seen in the case of the school impact fee we note in Chapter 15 and its Coda,[14] which applies proportionate share concepts to efficiency and social equity. As was noted in Chapters 14 and 15, as well as its Coda, we are troubled by community plans that speak to the need to address housing affordability yet design impact fees that perpetuate inefficiencies and social inequities in ways that are inconsistent with proportionate share principles. In these respects, if the local plan wishes to improve housing affordability, *improperly designed impact fees would not be in accordance with the plan.*

We conclude this chapter with three appendixes that offer more details on the impact fee calculation steps and their relation to the plan (Appendix 6A), a survey of the LOS standards (Appendix 6B), and a conceptual service area design to meet efficiency and equity objectives through proportionate share principles (Appendix 6C).

APPENDIX 6A

IMPACT COST CALCULATION STEPS IN RELATION TO THE PLAN

This chapter outlined the general relationship between the comprehensive plan—or in the case of some states, "land-use assumptions"—and impact fees for infrastructure. This appendix goes into more detail about calculating the cost of serving the needs of new development. This is called the *impact cost*, which is not the *impact fee*. For instance, the cost provides new roads in a community might be $100 per trip mile. However, if the community has grants, bonds, and other sources of revenue available to help finance road improvements, the impact cost will be adjusted to the *net impact cost*. How this is calculated is shown in Chapter 7. But the net impact cost is not necessarily the impact fee because local decision-makers may wish to charge only a portion of the net impact cost.

This is addressed in Chapters 8 and 9, along with numerous limitations. The appendix takes a simplified approach by assuming that the current level of service is also the adopted one.

The process entails four basic steps assuming that the level of service is equal to the current ratio of faculty supply to demand. Those steps are:

Step 1—Calculate the current level of service (LOS)

Step 2—Adopt LOS standards and Project Future Infrastructure Demand

Step 3—Calculate the Cost to Meet Projected Demand at the Adopted LOS standard

Step 4—Impact Cost per Impact Unit at Adopted LOS

Each step is described next.

STEP 1—CALCULATE CURRENT LOS

Inventory of Current Infrastructure Supply

÷Current Infrastructure Demand

= Current Level of Service — LOS

The purpose of this step is to determine the community's current LOS. The community can then determine whether the current LOS is too high, too low, or just right.

The first piece of the formula is an inventory of the supply of current facilities. The metric is *infrastructure supply*. This is the numerator in the current LOS formula. Examples are:

Acres of improved parks.[15]

Gallons per day of wastewater treatment capacity.

Square feet of police facility space.

Fire station bays.

Number of workforce housing units, and so forth.

For many kinds of infrastructure, the *infrastructure supply* metric can be divided further. For parks, metrics could include ball parks, miles of trails, picnic benches and so forth. For police facilities metrics could include spare feet of meeting space, interview space, office space, prisoner holding facilities and so forth. For workforce housing, it could be the number of housing units affordable to workers at different income levels. Some communities find it useful to assemble detailed inventories and then package them into prototypes, such as a typical acre of a community park that is comprised of an average of so many ball fields, picnic areas and so forth, or a typical police station that is comprised of an average of the amount of square feet with percentage allocations to key functions. While communities are free to decide the level of detail and how the data are assembled, what is needed nonetheless is an inventory of service supply units it has.

The denominator in the formula is the *infrastructure demand* metric. This is a metric based on people because people are the course of impact to be mitigated. (People can include workers and visitors as shown in Chapter 7). It is used to calculate the *current level of service*. For instance, if there are 50 acres of parks in a community of 10,000 residents, the current LOS is 1 acre of park per 0.005 residents. Because this is a small number, parks metrics are usually converted to acres per 1,000 residents, or 5 acres per 1,000 residents in this case. This would be the current LOS. While the metric seems simple and straightforward, the concept is rife with efficiency and equity implications.

Consider a basic efficiency implication. Park impact fees are often based on people. If the current LOS is 5 acres of parks per 1,000 people and if the average home has 2.5 persons living in it, and if the net impact mitigation cost is $80,000 per developed acre, the impact cost per home is $1,000:

$$(\$80,000/acre \times 5\,acres/1,000\,residents$$

$$\times 2.5\,residents/home) = \$1,.000/home$$

However, this presupposes that only residents use parks and are thus the only sources of impact fees to be mitigated as well as the only beneficiaries. In most communities, this is not correct because non-residents use parks such as visitors and local workers who do not live in the community. Businesses often use parks and recreation facilities for functions. Sometimes, local citizens cannot use their own park infrastructure because they are reserved for businesses that do not pay park impact fees. In effect, the supply of parks is inefficiently low because it is not calibrated to consider all people who use them. One solution is to create an infrastructure demand metric that includes non-residential development. We discuss this later.

The other issue is equity. Although the community may average 2.5 persons per household, this will vary by the size of the residential unit. We discuss this implication in Step 4 below.

STEP 2—ADOPT A LOS STANDARD AND PROJECT FUTURE INFRASTRUCTURE DEMAND

Adopted LOS Standard × Impact Units =

New Infrastructure Demand Units

Once the inventory is conducted and the existing LOS established, the community will need to assess whether current conditions are unacceptably low, acceptable, or in excess of what is needed in accordance with the comprehensive plan. For now, let us assume that the current LOS is acceptable and adopted to guide infrastructure planning. Suppose the current LOS is 5 acres of park per 1,000 residents, and this is adopted. Suppose the community is comprised entirety of residential development and will add 10,000 residents by the end of the planning horizon, thereby sidestepping the efficiency issue noted above. These 10,000 new residents are the *impact units*. For some applications, impact units might be residents, workers, visitors, or a combination of all three. They are not the homes as these new residents are themselves the people who will inhabit the homes. Determining the appropriate impact units is discussed in Chapter 7. In this example, the formula for calculating new infrastructure demand units shows that the community will need to add 50 acres of parks to mitigate the impact of new development.

STEP 3—CALCULATE THE COST TO MEET PROJECTED DEMAND AT ADOPTED LOS STANDARD

New Infrastructure Demand Units

×Cost per Infrastructure Unit

= New Infrastructure Demand Cost

This step projects the total cost of meeting the needs of future development. In this example, new infrastructure demand units are the 50 acres of parks the community needs. Using the $80,000 per acre of improved park noted earlier, the new infrastructure demand cost is $4,000,000:

$$(\$80,000/\text{acre} \times 50\,\text{acres}) = \$4,000,000$$

STEP 4—IMPACT COST PER IMPACT UNIT AT ADOPTED LOS STANDARD

New Infrastructure Demand Cost

÷ Impact Units

= Impact Mitigation Cost per Impact Unit

In this example, the $4,000,000 cost to mitigate the park impact of 10,000 new residents is $400 per person. If there are no adjustments to the impact mitigation cost (see Chapter 7), the impact cost can be used to create a park impact fee schedule. For instance, if the community expects only single-family detached homes of about the same size that average 2.50 persons per unit after adjusting for the *vacancy rate*, the impact fee would be $1,000 per home.

A vacancy adjustment is needed because vacant homes do not generate people who impact parks. Suppose the community had an average household size of 2.60 persons and the local vacancy rate based on the census American Community Survey is 4.00 percent, the overall average number of persons per residential unit, including vacant ones, would be 2.50:

$$\big[2.60\,\text{persons/household} \div$$

$$\big(\text{persons/household} \times$$

$$\big(1.0 - 0.04\,\text{vacancy rate}\big)\big)\big] = 2.50$$

If a vacancy rate adjustment is not made, the community will collect more impact fees than needed the mitigate the impact of 10,000 new residents. This violates proportionate share principles.

We mentioned the concern about equity above and in more detail in Chapter 15. If the community expects detached and attached homes and further if the sizes of those homes are expected to vary in size, such as square feet, impact mitigation will vary accordingly. We explore this and related equity issues in Chapter 15 and its Coda.

APPENDIX 6B

SURVEY OF LOS STANDARDS

This appendix summarizes findings from a detailed content analysis of impact fees from a selection of 67 communities across the nation. The purpose is to illustrate that not one-size-fits-all but rather that when considering local conditions, planning goals and policies, development patterns and the like, the impact fee "solution" used in one community is not necessarily suitable for the next. The methodologies vary considerably by geography and complexity. One thing many have in common is that they were prepared by some of the nation's most prominent impact fee firms.[16]

Jurisdiction Type Breakdown

Urban/Suburban/Rural designation is given based on the jurisdiction location in relation to Census 2000 Metropolitan Statistical Areas (MSAs) or Combined Metropolitan Statistical Areas (CMSAs). If a jurisdiction is the major city of an MSA or one of the major cities constituting a CMSA, it is classified as "urban." If a jurisdiction is or lies within a county that is part of an MSA or CMSA but is not or does not contain a major city of that MSA or CMSA, it is classified as "suburban." If a jurisdiction is not within any MSA or CMSA, it is classified as "rural." If the jurisdiction is a county that does contain a major city of an MSA or CMSA, it is classified as 'mixed', since the county would contain the major city as well as suburban jurisdictions.

APPENDIX 6C

CONCEPTUAL SERVICE AREA DESIGN TO MEET EFFICIENCY AND EQUITY OBJECTIVES

A key purpose of service areas is to enable an analysis of the fiscal impacts of development at a small enough scale to assess the marginal cost impacts of development but large enough to assure that sufficient funds can be collected from and invested into the area.

TABLE 6B.1 Number of Impact Fee Programs Reviewed by Type

Instances of Each Fee Type (263 Total)	
Parks and Recreation and/or Open Space and/or Trails	52
Fire and/or EMS and/or E911 Communications	40
Roads and/or Traffic Signals and/or Transit	37
Police and/or Criminal Justice or Combined Public Safety	35
Libraries	21
Water Infrastructure and/or Water Resources	20
Government Buildings and/or Public Facilities and/or Combined Public Infrastructure	18
Wastewater	15
Schools	12
Stormwater/Drainage	10
Other	3 (Sanitation, Solid Waste, Animal Control)
Jurisdiction Population Breakdown (2000 Census)	
< 50,000	27
50,000–100,000	9
100,000–200,000	13
200,000–500,000	14
> 500,000	4

TABLE 6B.2 Number of Jurisdictions Reviewed by Type

City/Town	44
County	23
Urban	12
Suburban	46
Rural	4
Mixed	5
State Legal Environment	
Specific Enabling Legislation (Dillon's Rule State)	43
Specific Enabling Legislation (Home Rule State)	8
No Specific Enabling Legislation (Home Rule State)	11
No Specific Enabling Legislation (Dillon's Rule State)	5

TABLE 6B.3 Parks and Recreation and/or Open Space and/or Trails (52)

Assessment Distribution	
Residential Only	42
Includes Non-Residential Uses	10
Residential Differentiation	
Differentiation by Residential Type and Size	3
Differentiation by Size Only	1
Differentiation by Type Only	37
No Residential Differentiation	11
<u>*Type Differentiation—Number of Categories*</u>	
Two categories	12
Three categories	20
Four categories	4
Five categories	4
Service Areas	
One Service Area	45
Multiple Service Areas	7
Method	
Cost Recovery/Buy-In	1
Incremental Expansion	26
Plan-Based	8
Combination Buy-In/Incremental	4
Combination Buy-In/Plan-Based	0
Combination Incremental/Plan-Based	4
Combination All Three	0
Indeterminate	9
Level of Service Measure Units (The number of occurrences may not match the total number of fee examples due to multiple LOS standards within a single fee)	
Acres	69
Dollars (replacement cost/expenditure)	47
Square Feet (rec. facilities)	2
Vehicles and Equipment	2
Number of Rec. Facilities	1
Linear Feet (trails)	1
Miles (trails)	1
Residential Demand Unit Cost Unit	
Person/Resident	31
Dwelling Unit	10
Equivalent Dwelling Unit (EDU)/Single-Family Equivalent (SFE)	8
Functional or Seasonal Population	2
Vehicle Miles Traveled	1 (trails fee)

TABLE 6B.4 Fire and/or EMS and/or E911 Communications (40)

Assessment Distribution	
Residential Only	1
Includes Non-Residential Uses	39
Residential Differentiation	
Differentiation by Residential Type and Size	0
Differentiation by Size Only	0
Differentiation by Type Only	29
No Residential Differentiation	11
Type Differentiation—Number of Categories	
Two categories	9
Three categories	13
Four categories	5
Five categories	1
Six categories	1
Service Areas	
One Service Area	39
Multiple Service Areas	1
Method	
Cost Recovery/Buy-In	1
Incremental Expansion	21
Plan-Based	2
Combination Buy-In/Incremental	2
Combination Buy-In/Plan-Based	0
Combination Incremental/Plan-Based	6
Combination All Three	0
Indeterminate	8
Level of Service Measure Units (The number of occurrences may not match the total number of fee examples due to multiple LOS standards within a single fee)	
Dollars (replacement cost/expenditure)	63
Vehicles/Apparatus	14
Square Feet (station/communications buildings)	14
Acres (station sites)	4
Stations	2
Communications Equipment	1
Residential Demand Unit Cost Unit	
Person/Resident	17
Dwelling Unit	10
Service Demand Unit/Service Call/Incident	5
Equivalent Dwelling Unit (EDU)/Single-Family Equivalent (SFE)	4
Functional or Day-Night Population	4

TABLE 6B.5 Roads and/or Traffic Signals and/or Transit (37)

Assessment Distribution	
Residential Only	0
Includes Non-Residential Uses	37
Residential Differentiation	
Differentiation by Residential Type and Size	3
Differentiation by Size Only	0
Differentiation by Type Only	32
No Residential Differentiation	2
Type Differentiation—Number of Categories	
Two categories	12
Three categories	12
Four categories	6
Five categories	4
> 5 categories	1
Service Areas	
One Service Area	31
Multiple Service Areas	6
Method	
Cost Recovery/Buy-In	0
Incremental Expansion	7
Plan-Based	18
Combination Buy-In/Incremental	0
Combination Buy-In/Plan-Based	2
Combination Incremental/Plan-Based	4
Combination All Three	1
Indeterminate	5
Level of Service Measure Units (The number of occurrences may not match the total number of fee examples due to multiple LOS standards within a single fee)	
Dollars (replacement cost/expenditure)	38
Per Trip	23
Per Vehicle Mile Traveled (VMT)	15
Vehicle Miles of Capacity (VMC) (per VMT)	9
Trips (per Lane Mile)	3
Vehicles (per Lane Mile)	1
Traffic Signals (per VMT)	1
Residential Demand Unit Cost Unit	
Trip (includes both peak-hour and average daily)	22
Vehicle Mile Traveled (VMT)	13
Equivalent Dwelling Unit (EDU)/Single-Family Equivalent (SFE)	1
Dwelling Unit	1

TABLE 6B.6 Police and/or Criminal Justice or Combined Public Safety (35)

Assessment Distribution	
Residential Only	0
Includes Non-Residential Uses	35
Residential Differentiation	
Differentiation by Residential Type and Size	0
Differentiation by Size Only	0
Differentiation by Type Only	24
No Residential Differentiation	11
Type Differentiation—Number of Categories	
Two categories	7
Three categories	8
Four categories	7
Five categories	2
Service Areas	
One Service Area	34
Multiple Service Areas	1
Method	
Cost Recovery/Buy-In	0
Incremental Expansion	15
Plan-Based	5
Combination Buy-In/Incremental	4
Combination Buy-In/Plan-Based	0
Combination Incremental/Plan-Based	9
Combination All Three	0
Indeterminate	2
Level of Service Measure Units (The number of occurrences may not match the total number of fee examples due to multiple LOS standards within a single fee)	
Dollars (replacement cost/expenditure)	53
Square Feet (station or justice/corrections facility buildings)	21
Vehicles	6
Acres (station or justice/corrections facility sites)	3
Communications Equipment	1
Residential Demand Unit Cost Unit	
Person/Resident	16
Dwelling Unit	9
Functional or Day-Night Population	7
Service Demand Unit/Service Call/Incident	2
Equivalent Dwelling Unit (EDU)/Single-Family Equivalent (SFE)	1

TABLE 6B.7 Libraries (21)

Assessment Distribution	
Residential Only	21
Includes Non-Residential Uses	0
Residential Differentiation	
Differentiation by Residential Type and Size	0
Differentiation by Size Only	0
Differentiation by Type Only	14
No Residential Differentiation	7
<u>*Type Differentiation—Number of Categories*</u>	
Two categories	5
Three categories	6
Four categories	2
Five categories	1
Service Areas	
One Service Area	21
Multiple Service Areas	0
Method	
Cost Recovery/Buy-In	0
Incremental Expansion	10
Plan-Based	2
Combination Buy-In/Incremental	0
Combination Buy-In/Plan-Based	0
Combination Incremental/Plan-Based	2
Combination All Three	0
Indeterminate	7
Level of Service Measure Units (The number of occurrences may not match the total number of fee examples due to multiple LOS standards within a single fee)	
Square Feet (library buildings)	15
Books/Volumes	15
Dollars (replacement cost/expenditure)	12
Acres (library sites)	3
Support Vehicles	1
Computer Facilities	1
Residential Demand Unit Cost Unit	
Person/Resident	14
Dwelling Unit	5
Equivalent Dwelling Unit (EDU)/Single-Family Equivalent (SFE)	2

TABLE 6B.8 Water Infrastructure and/or Water Resources (20)

Assessment Distribution	
Residential Only	0
Includes Non-Residential Uses	20
Residential Differentiation	
Differentiation by Residential Type and Size	2
Differentiation by Size Only	0
Differentiation by Type Only	4
No Residential Differentiation	14
(13 of the fees are assessed using meter categorizations as opposed to dwelling unit)	
<u>*Type Differentiation—Number of Categories*</u>	
Two categories	3
Three categories	2
Four categories	1
Five categories	0
Service Areas	
One Service Area	19
Multiple Service Areas	1
Method	
Cost Recovery/Buy-In	3
Incremental Expansion	4
Plan-Based	7
Combination Buy-In/Incremental	0
Combination Buy-In/Plan-Based	2
Combination Incremental/Plan-Based	2
Combination All Three	2
Indeterminate	0
Level of Service Measure Units (The number of occurrences may not match the total number of fee examples due to multiple LOS standards within a single fee)	
Gallons per Day	32
Per Equivalent Dwelling Unit (EDU)/Single-Family Equivalent (SFE)	26
Per Customer/Meter	4
Per Other Unit	2
Dollars (replacement cost/expenditure)	11
Per Equivalent Dwelling Unit (EDU)/Single-Family Equivalent (SFE)	6
Per Customer/Meter	2
Per Other Unit	3
Residential Demand Unit Cost Unit	
Equivalent Dwelling Unit (EDU)/Single-Family Equivalent (SFE)	18
Gallon per Day	2

TABLE 6B.9 Wastewater (15)

Assessment Distribution	
Residential Only	0
Includes Non-Residential Uses	15
Residential Differentiation	
Differentiation by Type and Size	2
Differentiation by Size Only	0
Differentiation by Type Only	4
No Residential Differentiation	9
(8 of the fees are assessed using meter categorizations as opposed to dwelling unit)	
<u>*Type Differentiation—Number of Categories*</u>	
Two categories	3
Three categories	2
Four categories	1
Five categories	0
Service Areas	
One Service Area	13
Multiple Service Areas	2
Method	
Cost Recovery/Buy-In	1
Incremental Expansion	3
Plan-Based	5
Combination Buy-In/Incremental	0
Combination Buy-In/Plan-Based	1
Combination Incremental/Plan-Based	3
Combination All Three	1
Indeterminate	1
Level of Service Measure Units (The number of occurrences may not match the total number of fee examples due to multiple LOS standards within a single fee)	
Gallons per Day	18
Per Equivalent Dwelling Unit (EDU)/Single-Family Equivalent (SFE)	12
Per Customer/Meter	2
Per Other Unit	4
Dollars (replacement cost/expenditure)	9
Per Equivalent Dwelling Unit (EDU)/Single-Family Equivalent (SFE)	3
Per Customer/Meter	5
Per Other Unit	1
Residential Demand Unit Cost Unit	
Equivalent Dwelling Unit (EDU)/Single-Family Equivalent (SFE)	12
Gallon per Day	2
Person	1

TABLE 6B.10 Stormwater/Drainage (10)

Assessment Distribution	
Residential Only	0
Includes Non-Residential Uses	10
Residential Differentiation	
Differentiation by Type and Size	1
Differentiation by Size Only	0
Differentiation by Type Only	3
No Residential Differentiation	6
(6 of the fees are assessed per acre of land area as opposed to per dwelling unit)	
<u>*Type Differentiation—Number of Categories*</u>	
Two categories	1
Three categories	3
Four categories	0
Five categories	0
(one methodology calculates each fee separately based on land-use and other factors)	
Service Areas	
One Service Area	7
Multiple Service Areas	3
Method	
Cost Recovery/Buy-In	1
Incremental Expansion	2
Plan-Based	4
Combination Buy-In/Incremental	0
Combination Buy-In/Plan-Based	2
Combination Incremental/Plan-Based	0
Combination All Three	0
Indeterminate	1
Level of Service Measure Units (The number of occurrences may not match the total number of fee examples due to multiple LOS standards within a single fee)	
Dollars	19
Per Acre	13
Per Service Demand Unit (takes into account soil type, etc.)	5
Per Other Unit	1
Residential Demand Unit Cost Unit	
Acre	4
Service Demand Unit	4
Equivalent Dwelling Unit (EDU)/Single-Family Equivalent (SFE)	2

TABLE 6B.11 Government Buildings and/or Public Facilities and/or Combined Public Infrastructure (18)

Assessment Distribution	
Residential Only	2
Includes Non-Residential Uses	16
Residential Differentiation	
Differentiation by Type and Size	0
Differentiation by Size Only	0
Differentiation by Type Only	12
No Residential Differentiation	6
<u>*Type Differentiation—Number of Categories*</u>	
Two categories	2
Three categories	7
Four categories	2
Five categories	1
Service Areas	
One Service Area	17
Multiple Service Areas	1
Method	
Cost Recovery/Buy-In	0
Incremental Expansion	9
Plan-Based	3
Combination Buy-In/Incremental	1
Combination Buy-In/Plan-Based	0
Combination Incremental/Plan-Based	4
Combination All Three	0
Indeterminate	1
Level of Service Measure Units (The number of occurrences may not match the total number of fee examples due to multiple LOS standards within a single fee)	
Dollars (replacement cost/expenditure)	24
Square Feet (buildings)	7
Support Vehicles	3
Acres (building sites)	2
Residential Demand Unit Cost Unit	
Person/Resident	11
Dwelling Unit	3
Acre	2
Equivalent Dwelling Unit (EDU)/Single-Family Equivalent (SFE)	1
Square Foot	1

TABLE 6B.12 Schools (12)

Assessment Distribution (Outside California Only)	
Residential Only	12
Includes Non-Residential Uses	0
Residential Differentiation	
Differentiation by Type and Size	0
Differentiation by Size Only	0
Differentiation by Type Only	12
No Residential Differentiation	0
<u>*Type Differentiation—Number of Categories*</u>	
Two categories	4
Three categories	5
Four categories	2
Five categories	0
Six categories	1
Service Areas	
One Service Area	11
Multiple Service Areas	1
Method	
Cost Recovery/Buy-In	0
Incremental Expansion	11
Plan-Based	0
Combination Buy-In/Incremental	0
Combination Buy-In/Plan-Based	1
Combination Incremental/Plan-Based	0
Combination All Three	0
Indeterminate	0
Level of Service Measure Units (The number of occurrences may not match the total number of fee examples due to multiple LOS standards within a single fee)	
Dollars (replacement cost/expenditure)	36
Square Feet (school and support buildings)	28
Acres (school sites)	23
Relocatable Classrooms	14
Buses	3
Support Vehicles	1
Residential Demand Unit Cost Unit	
Student	11
Equivalent Dwelling Unit (EDU)/Single-Family Equivalent (SFE)	1

Service area boundaries should reflect the existing or planned urban form for subareas of the local government. For instance, a service area may be created for the downtown and separate ones for first-ring suburbs, new suburban areas, the suburban fringe and rural areas—depending on the size and landscape composition of the local government. One approach to designing service areas is to recognize the extent to which existing facilities are sufficient to meet development needs through a tiering analysis.

Consider a common way to create service areas based on tiers, in this case three of them for illustration:

- Fully Served (FS) meaning that excess capacity exists substantially to serve projected development;
- Particularly Service (PS) meaning there is little or no excess capacity in existing facilities to meet the needs of projected development, but there exists a plan to provide such facilities concurrent with the impacts of new development; and
- Not Served (NS) means services are not included in the plan to serve development during the current plan horizon.

These broad designations would be designed for individual types of facilities such as roads, parks and recreation, and public safety. The tiered service area designations can also address different spatial elements of the same facility class. For instance, for roads, a freeway with excess capacity that serves multiple service areas may be designated as FS, while collector roads serving some service areas may be classified as a PS, and local serving streets may be classified as NS, suggesting that development proposals may need to include those streets in its proposals rather than relying on local government to plan and finance them during a plan horizon.

Sometimes the LOS standards for certain facilities should vary because of the location or other characteristics of a jurisdiction. For instance, in sprawling jurisdictions that cannot afford high-quality fire protection service everywhere, one service area close to the center of the city may be designed for a five-minute fire response time while another much farther away may be designed for a ten-minute response time. Likewise, roads closer to the center of a community might have a LOS standard of E (where F is congestion), but in suburban areas the LOS standard may be C (where A is devoid of any delay). Variations in LOS standards can be applied to other facilities.

Tier-based analysis can also include special policies. For instance, in areas with underinvestment but also with excess facility capacity, a policy decision can be made to not assess impact fees there. The rationale could include economic development, encouraging infill and redevelopment, and directing new development to areas where excess capacity already exists, thereby saving taxpayers the cost of building new or expanded infrastructure elsewhere. These reasons should be included in the plan.

Needless to say, decisions about LOS for individual service areas can have important impacts on the community infrastructure costs. This may be troublesome politically, leading to decisions to provide all development with the same response time, for instance, regardless of the expense and inherent inequities as lower-cost areas subsidize higher cost ones. The rationale for varying LOS standards by service area should be included in the plan.

Table 6C.1 illustrates the tiering approach applied to several types of facilities.

A composite example of an actual tier-based analysis is shown in Table 6C.2. The differences are striking. In the central most part of the city, where infill and redevelopment are the most prominent, the total service area cost per unit was only 28 percent of the average for the city as a whole. In the most expensive area, where new facilities are needed to accommodate nearly all new development, costs run about 1.5 times the citywide average.

Consider the issue of average costs. If a community designs its impact fees based on communitywide average costs, the following inefficiencies and inequities may result based on this case study:

- Development in the lowest cost area of the community would pay 3.6 times more than its costs, while development in the highest cost area would pay only 60 percent of its costs.

TABLE 6C.1 Illustrative Fiscal Analysis Zones

Facility Type	Fully Served	Partially Served	Not Served
Public Safety			
East		X	
West		X	
Mesa			X
Drainage			
Northwest		X	
Northwest		X	
Central	X		
Southwest		X	
Southwest		X	
Far West			X
Parks			
Northeast		X	
Central	X		
Foothills		X	
North		X	
Valley		X	
Mesa		X	
Hilltop		X	
Mesa			X
Roads			
Downtown	X		
Northeast		X	
North		X	
East		X	
Central		X	
Northwest		X	
Southwest		X	
Mesa			X

Source: Adapted from analysis by the authors.

TABLE 6C.2 Service Area-Based Impact Fees

Service Area	Service Area Impact Fees, Total	Percent of Aver. (age Cost)	Ratio to Average Cost
Central	$1,366	28%	3.6
Foothills	$1,633	33%	3.0
Northeast	$3,069	63%	1.6
North	$3,911	80%	1.3
Southwest	$5,344	109%	0.9
Northwest	$6,570	134%	0.7
West	$7,071	145%	0.7
Far West	$7,280	149%	0.7
Mesa	$7,775	159%	0.6
Communitywide Average	$4,891		

Source: Authors.

- Because lower-cost development is charged more than its total costs, there would be less of it.
- Because higher-cost development is charged less than its total costs, there would be more of it;
- The effect is that development in lower-cost areas subsidizes development in highest costs areas.
- The potential result is a fiscally unsustainable outcome as inefficiently induced higher-cost development puts increasing stress on local finance.

By designing service areas to reflect substantial differences in costs between them based on location, terrain, density, and other considerations, as well as allowing for differences in LOS standards between them, communities can achieve more efficient development outcomes that are also more equitable.

NOTES

1 Footnotes appearing in the original have been removed.
2 Thomas Jefferson had a different opinion about the "permanence" of constitutions: "Every constitution, then, and every law, naturally expires at the end of

nineteen years. If it be enforced longer, it is an act of force, and not of right." Thomas Jefferson to James Madison, 1789. ME 7:459, Papers 15:396.

3 These terms are somewhat interchangeable. Some states specify the precise terms and the content of the plans and elements while other states mention them and still others are silent yet a plan supporting impact fee analysis, collection and expenditure is needed nonetheless.

4 For a review of techniques and applications, see www.planning.org/knowledgebase/scenarioplanning/ accessed May 31, 2021.

5 See www.planning.org/ethics/ethicscode/.

6 Much of this discussion is adapted from www.dca.state.ga.us/development/planningqualitygrowth/DOCUMENTS/Publications/ImpactFees/Guide.DIFA.pdf retrieved November 20, 2017. One of us (Nelson) helped draft substantial elements of earlier versions of this guide.

7 We remind readers that in some states and communities, the capital improvement element is called a capital improvement plan and is implemented through short term budgeting arrangements that are known by several names.

8 For a summary of the CIP process and elements, see https://opengov.com/article/capital-improvement-plans-101

9 One of the authors (Nelson) advised the Georgia Department of Community Affairs on earlier versions of the general design of CIE and CIP reporting forms (see www.dca.ga.gov/node/2513/documents/10 accessed December 14, 2019). Information provided in that document is adapted here.

10 As noted above, one of the authors (Nelson) advised the Georgia Department of Community Affairs on earlier versions of the general design of CIE and CIP reporting forms (see www.dca.ga.gov/node/2513/documents/10 accessed December 14, 2019). Information provided in that document is adapted here.

11 For elaboration, see https://propertyrights.utah.gov/banberry-development-corporation-v-south-jordan/

12 *Banberry v. South Jordan* 631 P.2d 899 (Utah 1981).

13 See www.planning.org/policy/guides/adopted/impactfees.htm retrieved December 14, 2019.

14 See also Newport Partners and Nelson (2007).

15 Some facilities lend themselves to multiple levels of service for different kinds of applications, especially park and recreation facilities. We have seen LOS standards for these facilities run to 20 or more elements including picnic benches, barbeque pits, all forms of ball fields, and so forth. This can make the actual expenditure of funds inflexible and nonresponsive to needs of particular areas. One solution is to craft proto-typical kinds of parks comprised of a range of features the final selection of which meets localized needs.

16 We are indebted to Darren Smith for this analysis conducted while he was a graduate research assistant at Virginia Tech on a contract for the National Apartment Association. We are also indebted to the NAA for support leading to this analysis.

REFERENCES

Advisory Committee on Zoning. (1926). *A Standard State Zoning Enabling Act*. Washington, DC: US Department of Commerce.

Advisory Committee on Zoning. (1928). *A Standard City Planning Enabling Act*. Washington, DC: US Department of Commerce.

Anderson, L. T. (1995). *Guidelines for Preparing Urban Plans*. Chicago: American Planning Association.

Berke, P., Godschalk, D., & Kaiser, E. (2006). *Urban Land Use Planning* (5th ed.). Chicago: University of Illinois Press.

DiMento, J. (1980). *The Consistency Doctrine and the Limits of Planning*. Concord: Oelgeschlager, Gunn, and Hain.

Haar, C. H. (1955a). The master plan: An impermanent constitution. *Law and Contemporary Problems*, *20*, 353–418, retrieved December 10, 2016, from http://scholarship.law.duke.edu/lcp/vol20/iss3/2.

Harr, C. M. (1955b). In accordance with a comprehensive plan. *Harvard Law Review*, *68*, 1154–1170.

Hopkins, L. D., & Zapata, M. A. (2007). *Engaging the Future: Forecasts, Scenarios, Plans, and Projects*. Cambridge, MA: Lincoln Institute of Land Policy.

Jepson, E. J., Jr., & Weitz, J. (2020). *Fundamentals of Plan Making: Methods and Techniques* (2nd ed.). New York: Routledge.

Juergensmeyer, J. C., Roberts, T., Salkin, P., & Rowberry, R. (2018) *Land Use Planning and Development Regulation Law* (4th ed.). St, Paul: West Academic Publishing.

Kelly, E. D. (2010). *Community Planning*. Washington, DC: Island Press.

Kent, T. J., Jr. (1964). *The Urban General Plan*. Reprinted 1990. Chicago: American Planning Association.

Meck, S. (2002). *Growing Smart Legislative Guidebook: Model Statutes for Planning and the Management of Change*. Chicago: American Planning Association.

Nelson, A. C. (2004). *Planner's Estimating Guide: Projecting Land-use and Facility Needs*. Chicago: American Planning Association.

Nelson, A. C. (2013). *Reshaping Metropolitan America*. Washington, DC: Island Press.

Nelson, A. C., with Genereux, J. (1992). Price effects of landfills on house values. *Land Economics*, *68*(4), 359–367.

Nelson, A. C., Duncan, J. B., Mullen, C., & Bishop, K. R. (1995). *Growth Management Principles and Practices*. Chicago: American Planning Association.

Nelson, A. C., Marshall, J. T., Juergensmeyer, J. C., & Nicholas, J. C. (2017). *Market Demand-Based Planning and Permitting*. Chicago: American Bar Association.

Nelson, A. C., Nicholas, J. C., and Juergemeyer, J. C. (2022). *Guide to Smart Growth Fiscal Analysis with Model Fiscal Impact Analysis Ordinance*. Washington, DC: Smart Growth America.

Newport Partners, & Nelson, A. C. (2007). *Impact Fees and Housing Affordability: A Guidebook for Practitioners*. Washington, DC: US Department of Housing and Urban Development.

Rouse, D., & Piro, R. (2022). *The Comprehensive Plan: Sustainable, Resilient, and Equitable Communities for the 21st Century*. London: Routledge.

7 IMPACT FEE METHODOLOGY

This chapter describes the fundamentals of how impact fees are calculated in accordance with the legal principles discussed in Chapter 2. It discusses each component of the fee calculation and provides examples. It concludes with some observations about the pressures on and biases of consultants who calculate impact fees.

Key components of an impact fee methodology include the following:

- The *set of facilities* for which the impact fees are charged.
- The *geographic area* served by that set of facilities ("service area").
- The *level of service* (ratio of capacity to demand).
- The *capacity* of the facilities.
- The *demand* on the facilities ("service unit").
- The *cost per service unit* to accommodate new development at the appropriate level of service.
- The appropriate *revenue credits*, or amounts by which the cost per service unit is reduced to account for future revenues attributable to new development that will pay for the same facilities or existing deficiencies.
- The *fee schedule*.

While it gets more complicated in its application, the basic impact fee formula is simple. The cost per service unit is reduced by the revenue credit per service unit to determine the net cost per service unit, which is then multiplied by the number of service units generated by a land use per development unit (e.g., dwellings, 1,000 square feet of building area) to determine the proportionate fair-share fee per development unit. The basic formula is summarized in Figure 7.1.

7.1 SET OF FACILITIES

Impact fees are assessed for a defined set of related capital facilities that serve a defined geographic area. Typical facility types authorized in many state impact fee acts include transportation, water, wastewater, stormwater drainage, parks, libraries, fire rescue, emergency medical services (EMS), police/law enforcement, and correctional facilities. Only a limited number of states specifically authorize school impact fees by general or private act (i.e., applying only to a specific jurisdiction). This may be because they tend to be relatively sizable fees that apply only to residential development, combined with the power of homebuilder associations at the state level. A few state acts do not restrict the types of facilities for which impact fees may be adopted, and in those

Fee = Service Units Generated x
Net Cost per Service Unit

where:
Service Units Generated =
Assessment Units x
Service Units per Assessment Unit

Net Cost per Service Unit =
Cost per Service Unit –
Revenue Credit per Service Unit

FIGURE 7.1 Basic impact fee formula.

DOI: 10.4324/9781003336075-9

states one may see fees for general government facilities such as administrative buildings, public works yards, etc.

The set of facilities can be defined broadly or narrowly. Transportation impact fees, for example, can be broken down into functional classification, with separate fees for collector and arterial roads. Similarly, separate fees are sometimes calculated for neighborhood, community, and regional parks. At the narrowest extreme, a service area could be structured around a single proposed improvement, such as a particular road or park. This is rarely done, however. Such a service area structure needs to consider factors like the integrated nature of the road system or the overlapping service areas of individual parks. It only works if the proposed improvement will primarily serve new development in the service area, which would need to be relatively undeveloped to avoid having a large existing deficiency that would offset the cost.

If distinct sets of facilities serve the same service area and have the same land use categories, it is possible to combine them. For example, if city parks and libraries both serve the entire city, and the costs of both types of facilities are attributed solely to residential development, the fees could be combined into a single parks and recreation impact fee, which would give the city greater flexibility to spend the funds on priority improvements in either category. Similarly, fees for police, fire protection and emergency medical services could be combined into a single public safety fee, which seems reasonable because all three often respond to the same emergency incidents. One sees these types of impact fee structures in common use, but it is not clear how far one could take this. School fees are also generally assessed only on new residential development, so in principle school fees could be combined with fees for parks and libraries, but it is not clear that one can simply take the sum of fees for a variety of unrelated facilities and call it a general-purpose impact fee

that can be spent on any of the component facilities.

7.2 SERVICE AREA

A "service area" is a geographic area in which a defined set of public facilities provide service to development within the area. The set of facilities determines at least the outer bounds of the service area, which may be the entire jurisdiction. With or without the use of this term, service areas must be identified in impact fee studies in order to determine the amount of development served by those facilities and thus the level of service in the area.

A particular set of facilities may not provide service to all parts of a city or county's jurisdiction. Wastewater services, for example, may not be available in all areas, with some served by on-site systems or by a private or neighboring jurisdiction's system. Another common example is a county fire department that serves the unincorporated area and some municipalities within the county that lack their own fire departments. In such cases, the service area for the impact fee would be the area where the service is provided.

Integrated or intertwined services may not serve the same area. For example, a county sheriff's office may operate correctional facilities that serve the entire county and provide law enforcement patrol only to development in the unincorporated area. Similarly, a fire/EMS department may provide fire rescue and EMS services to different areas. In these cases, the general approach is to allocate costs between separate fees that apply only in the areas where each service is provided.

For most sets of related facilities, there is a gray area about how the service area(s) should be defined. Many contain facilities that provide more localized and more regional services (neighborhood and regional parks, collector and arterial roads, distribution and transmission lines, elementary vs. high schools, etc.). At the same time, these components tend to be integrated, in the sense that the more localized components rely on more regional facilities (e.g., a water or wastewater treatment plant), or have centralized administrative/ maintenance facilities. Other factors also provide integration: fire stations respond to major incidents far from their initial response zones, school attendance zones can be redrawn, and libraries are connected by inter-library loans.

Most state impact fee acts leave the determination of service areas to the discretion of the local government. Texas is an exception when it comes to road impact fees. Its act limits the size of road impact fee service areas to a maximum of six miles (the statute does not specify whether this is measured as a maximum width or in square miles). One of the few changes made since the original act was adopted in 1987 was to expand the permitted size from three miles to the current six miles.

In general, the tendency is for impact fee service areas to be defined rather broadly. This is due to a number of factors, including the interconnectedness of system facilities, the difficulty of drawing subarea boundaries that accurately reflect the nexus between demand and benefit, and the need to be able to accumulate sufficient funds to make improvements in each area. Smaller municipalities in particular generally employ jurisdiction-wide service areas.

Some impact fee practitioners advocate multiple service areas where appropriate to better reflect differential costs to construct improvements in subareas of a jurisdiction. Parks, for example, are land-intensive facilities, and land costs often vary significantly by subarea. New development in outlying areas tends to have longer trip lengths and put more traffic on the road system, and often necessitate the construction of new roads that will have a lot of excess capacity for an extended period of time. One could argue that these factors tend to be temporary, while impact fees are intended to address long-term impacts. Relatively undeveloped areas will increase in density over time, causing land

prices to rise and trip lengths to approach the system-wide average.

Sometimes an explicit goal of designing multiple service areas is to have new "leapfrog" development pay higher fees, both to recognize the generally higher costs of serving such development and to serve as a disincentive to develop in more remote areas. Contiguous development is much more cost-effective from the perspective of providing public facilities, although limits to developable land imposed by regulations, including urban growth boundaries to mandate contiguous development may tend to push up land costs and make housing less affordable. It is not clear whether higher impact fees in more undeveloped areas are a big enough factor to have any real effect on steering new development into more cost-effective locations, and experience suggests such efforts can be controversial.

A case in point is an impact fee program implemented by the City of Albuquerque in 2004. The basic approach taken in the 2004 impact fee studies[1] was to develop differential impact fees by geographic subareas to reflect actual differences in the cost of providing services. The differential fees were intended to act as incentives to encourage new development in older, more established areas of the city, where the needed infrastructure is already largely in place and where it would be less expensive for the City to provide services. At the same time, higher impact fees in developing areas arguably discourages urban sprawl and the accompanying costly investments in new infrastructure.

While these were laudable goals, on close inspection the fee differentials were largely due to policy choices in how to allocate revenue credits, and only modestly related to documented cost differences. More extensive revenue credits for denser areas than would normally be provided sapped the new fees of some of their revenue potential. The resulting impact fee system was also complex, with different service area configurations for each of the facility types.

The impact fee ordinance further sapped the fees' revenue potential by adding a number of waivers and exemptions. The residential "green path" reductions, in particular, were popular with builders but virtually eliminated impact fee revenue from new single-family housing. The amount of the fee reduction may have exceeded the relatively low cost beyond current code requirements needed to qualify, and the likelihood that many builders would build green in the absence of the exemption to secure a marketing advantage, suggest this exemption may have acted more as a subsidy than an effective incentive. A problem with impact fee waivers is that they are often perceived as not costing the government anything. If energy-efficient housing was a high priority, strengthening code requirements or providing targeted general fund-supported rebates would likely have been more cost-effective approaches. The fundamental rationale for impact fees is to ensure that new development pays close to its fair share of the cost of the initial public infrastructure costs required to serve it. Attempting to structure impact fees to accomplish other socially desirable goals may work against this core objective.

Albuquerque's differential fee structure by service area generated political opposition from residents in the area with the highest proposed fees, who feared they would stifle non-residential development in an area with a dearth of shopping and related opportunities. The opposition grew even stronger after adoption, and bills were even introduced in the New Mexico legislature to essentially ban the use of multiple service areas. The experiment was short-lived, however, as the housing crisis and financial recession of the late 2000s stymied development and led the City to suspend impact fees in 2009. Before reinstating impact fees in 2012, a new study[2] was conducted that recommended city-wide service areas for roads (restricted to arterial streets), fire, and police facilities. Open space and trail fees continued to be city-wide. The number of park service

areas was reduced from seven to four. In sum, the multiple service area approach was essentially abandoned. Much of the criticism was likely unfair. The total fee for a single-family unit ranged from a low of about $1,400 to about $7,300, a maximum spread of $6,000 per home, which seems too small to have had the impact on development attributed to it. Yet the system created regional resentments that proved to be politically toxic.

7.2.1 Benefit Districts

Smaller service areas can strengthen the nexus between need and benefit by ensuring that the fees are used to construct improvements in closer proximity to the fee-paying development. An alternative approach to achieving this end is to have multiple "benefit districts" within a larger service area. Benefit districts, like service areas, restrict funds collected in a geographic area to be spent on improvements located within or primarily serving that area. Unlike service areas, impact fees are not calculated individually for each benefit district. Benefit districts are referenced in the state impact fee act only in Florida, where they are extensively used. They appear to be less used in other parts of the country.

A case in Idaho provides an illustration of how not to structure subarea fee districts. The Ada County Highway District (ACHD), which is responsible for all the roads in the county except state and federal highways, adopted a road impact fee in 1989[3] that had four "assessment" districts. The cost per service unit (vehicle-mile of travel) was calculated county-wide, so the entire county was implicitly the service area. The fees were calculated for each of the assessment districts by using the average trip length for trips to and from development in the subarea, derived from transportation modeling. The assessment districts also served as benefit districts because the fees collected in each subarea was required to be spent in the same area. The fees for a single-family home varied from a low of $837 for the Boise

Metro Area to a high of $1,039 in the Far Rural district, a maximum difference of $202 per home. The differential was small and was not a major issue in the adoption process.

When the study was updated in 1996,[4] the number of assessment districts was expanded from four to eight in order to more accurately reflect differences in average trip lengths by area. The updated fees for a single-family unit ranged from $838 in downtown Boise to $2,347 in the Rural district. The most vocal opposition came from local officials, residents, and builders in the three smaller cities to the west of Boise. The updated fees were adopted but, as in the Albuquerque example discussed above, were short-lived. The western cities threatened legal action, arguing that much of their travel to Boise was made on state roads rather than ACHD roads, something that had not been taken into account in the trip length modeling. They also argued that the funds had to be spent on improvements in their subareas, where right-of-way costs were lower.

The first issue could have been addressed by redoing the modeling to exclude travel-miles on state roads, and the second by separating assessment districts from benefit districts. The benefit districts could have been defined as pie-shaped wedges extending from the county line and converging in Boise, where much of the impacts of development in the suburban cities was being felt. But the real problem was that despite the relatively small fee differentials (an average of $600 per house higher in the western cities than downtown Boise), the higher impact fees were blamed for discouraging development, and this opposition could not be addressed with technical fixes. The District soon decided to switch to a county-wide fee schedule.

7.3 LEVEL OF SERVICE

The most important legal principle for impact fee methodology is related to the concept of "level of service." Level of service (LOS) is critical in the determination of the appropriate cost per service unit and revenue credit per service unit.

Impact fees should not charge new development for a higher LOS than is provided to existing development. This principle recognizes that public infrastructure provides a shared level of service to all development within a service area. Both new and existing development in the service area will have access to any improvement funded with impact fees paid by new development. If impact fees are based on a desired level of service that is higher than is being provided to existing development, new development would bear a disproportionate share of the cost of raising the LOS. If impact fees are the only revenue source used to fund capital improvements, new development would pay impact fees that would be used both to maintain the same LOS paid for by existing development, as well as to raise the LOS, which would benefit existing development as well as new development.

Impact fees can be based on a higher LOS than that existing at the time of the enactment or update of the fees, but another funding source must be identified to remedy the resulting deficiencies. However, it is difficult to identify a revenue source that is only generated by or attributable to the development existing at the time the study is done. Impact fees must be reduced to account for any revenue that new development will generate that is used to remedy the existing deficiencies, in order to avoid double-charging. In order to avoid these complications, the typical practice is to base the fees on a LOS that is equal to or less than the existing actual LOS being provided at the time the impact fee analysis is done.

Generally speaking, level of service is the ratio of the capacity of the facilities to the demand for those facilities. Examples of common levels of service are vehicle-miles of capacity per vehicle-mile of travel, park acres per 1,000 population, and water treatment capacity (gallons per day) per daily gallon of water consumption. However, while level of service is an indispensable concept in impact fee analysis, attempts to quantify it in terms of physical ratios of capacity to demand are not always appropriate.

7.4 CAPACITY

The capacity component of the level-of-service ratio is discussed here, while the next section discusses measures of demand. Specific capacity measures are discussed separately for "hard" and "soft" types of facilities.

7.4.1 Hard Facilities

Capacity can be more precisely determined for so-called "hard" facilities, such as roads, water, wastewater, and drainage infrastructure. Schools, while not normally considered a hard facility, have developed techniques for measuring student capacity. Similarly, the capacity of detention facilities can be quantified in terms of inmate beds.

Physical LOS standards make the most sense for facilities that are reasonably homogenous, have a relatively representative physical capacity measure (such as vehicle trips per day for roads, or gallons per day for water and wastewater), and often have a significant amount of excess capacity. For hard facilities, improvements tend to come in large increments due to economies of scale, resulting in fluctuating capacity that is often beyond some minimum required reserve capacity. It is not feasible, for example, to build half of a two-lane road.

To the extent that existing capacity exceeds the amount required to serve existing development, the cost of that excess capacity should not be included in the cost per service unit calculation. Most commonly, the practice is to assume a one-to-one ratio between capacity and demand as the level of service, likely because this does not require making a qualitative judgment as to what amount of reserve capacity should be maintained over the long term. Examples of such ratios include one daily vehicle-mile of capacity per daily vehicle-mile

of travel, or one gallon of daily water treatment capacity per daily gallon of water demand.

Even for hard facilities, quantifying capacity is not always straightforward. Water and wastewater systems, for example, consist of many interrelated components, such as treatment plants, wells, distribution or collection lines, pumps, and reservoirs. A single capacity measure, such as for treatment facilities, is seldom representative of all other system components. For transportation, using vehicular capacity provides simplicity, but at the expense of ignoring multi-modal improvements that are important components of the transportation system. In addition, road capacity is intimately tied to the quality and safety of the driving experience, with better levels of service associated with fewer cars on the road and therefore less capacity to accommodate vehicle trips.

In some cases, it may be reasonable to use the incremental expansion approach (see Section 7.6) generally used for soft facilities for hard facilities. A recent transportation fee update for Atlanta is a case in point.[5] As a mature city with few opportunities for traditional vehicle capacity improvements, their traditional consumption-based model was a poor fit, and it did not easily accommodate other types of mobility improvements. It was unclear whether Georgia legislation authorizing "road" impact fees gave the City the authority to fund transit improvements, but it would appear to include road-related bike/ped improvements. The study itemized the cost of the City's existing investments in turn lanes, signals, medians, bikeways, and sidewalks, and added that to the cost of vehicle travel lanes. It took the total road capital investment and divided by the cost of a travel lane-mile to get equivalent lane-miles per service unit.

7.4.2 Soft Facilities

For so-called "soft" facilities, such as parks, libraries, fire, police, and emergency medical services, capacity is more difficult to quantify in any meaningful way. For some hard facilities, such as water and wastewater systems, only a specific quantity of capacity is necessary to accommodate a specific quantity of demand – any additional capacity is "excess" capacity that does not improve the quality of service. This is generally not the case with soft facilities, where more capacity generally means a better level of service.

Many impact fee studies for soft facilities try to mimic the approach often used for hard facilities by attempting to express the level of service in terms of physical ratios. For parks and recreation impact fees, a common LOS standard is acres of park land per person. This is most appropriate if the fee is intended to cover land costs only, but it is also often used for more typical park impact fees that are intended to cover park improvements as well. In such cases, the physical LOS variable is a "dummy" variable that has no actual effect on the fee calculation (it essentially involves multiplying and dividing by the same number). This is illustrated in the hypothetical example below. The two bolded variables are all that determine the cost per person.

With Physical LOS:

$$\textbf{2,000 acres} \div \textbf{100,000 population}$$

$$= 0.02 \, \text{acres per person}$$

$$\textbf{\$20,000,000 park capital investment}$$

$$\div \, 2,000 \, \text{acres} = \$10,000 \, \text{per acre}$$

$$0.02 \, \text{acres per person} \times \$10,000 \, \text{per acre}$$

$$= \$200 \, \text{per person}$$

Without Physical LOS:

$$\$20,000,000 \, \text{park capital investment}$$

$$\div \, 100,000 \, \text{population}$$

$$= \$200 \, \text{per person}$$

Inserting a physical LOS standard is probably so widely used because it seeks to mimic the approach used for hard facilities, and perhaps also because it may seem more precise to quantify the level of service (that is, put a number on it that is not a dollar value). This does not cause a problem as long as all parties understand what is really important, which is the capital investment that has been made by existing development. However, misunderstandings can arise about how literally to take such physical ratios.

To continue the park example for fees that cover improvement costs, an acre of land is not a good measure of park capacity because it doesn't take into account the cost of the park facilities on that land. Some analysts have attempted to address this issue by calculating dozens of physical LOS ratios for various types of improvements (tennis courts, swimming pools, ballfields, etc. per person) and preparing forecasts of the number of each of these that would need to be added over the next 5–20 years to accommodate projected growth. This implies the jurisdiction won't add any new types of improvements, and that the current mix will be rigidly maintained in the future. That's a clearly unrealistic scenario and could provide a potential basis for a legal challenge on the grounds that the community is not maintaining all the adopted LOS standards.

For soft facilities, where quantifying capacity is often problematic, the typical practice is to base the fees on the existing LOS. Under this approach, the total replacement cost of existing land, facilities and equipment is divided by the existing service units (with or without an intervening physical LOS ratio) to determine the cost per service unit). This approach is often referred to as the "incremental expansion" methodology. It assumes there is little or no excess capacity, and it assesses new development based on the cost to maintain the existing LOS currently provided to existing development.

Even for soft facilities for which capacity is more difficult to quantify, the issue of excess capacity may arise. For example, a new building may have recently been constructed that will likely be able accommodate future demand for many years. This can be addressed by dividing the cost of that building by anticipated service units in a future year, rather than by existing service units, or by reducing the cost of the building by the percentage that is not currently utilized.

Level of service is an important concept in impact fee law and methodology. However, trying to quantify LOS in terms of physical ratios is not always necessary or appropriate.

7.5 DEMAND

Demand is expressed in terms of a "service unit." A service unit is a common unit of demand applicable to all types of development. For types of facilities for which demand is primarily generated by residential development (parks, libraries, and schools), common service units are persons, residents, and students.

For facilities that provide benefits to both residential and non-residential development, the service unit can be expressed in terms of the demand generated by an average single-family unit, which is typically called an "equivalent dwelling unit" (EDU) or a "single-family equivalent" (SFE). These relative types of service units can be used for any type of facility. Relative measures may technically be service units, but they are not the demand units themselves. They are simply the ratios of the number of demand units for a land use type (or water meter size) to the demand units associated with a typical single-family unit.

Demand units tend to be specific to a particular type of facility, such as gallons per day for water and wastewater, vehicle trips or travel-miles per day or per peak hour for roads, square feet of impervious cover for drainage, and average daily calls-for-service for police and fire protection.

A more generalized demand factor than service calls for police and fire facilities is to allocate costs based on the average number of people present at the land use, based on the common-sense intuition that the demand for service is roughly proportional to the presence of people. These more generalized service units include "persons + jobs" and "functional population." The persons + jobs approach allocates facility costs for the residential population entirely to residential development and employees entirely to non-residential development. Persons and jobs are added together and are treated as having the same impact.

In contrast to the persons + jobs approach, the functional population approach allocates only the average percentage of a person's time spent at home to the residence and attributes the remainder to non-residential development in the form of the time spent on land use by employees, visitors, and shoppers. Employees are weighted more heavily because they spend more time on land use than a typical visitor or shopper. Given that most fire department calls are actually related to their role as first responders to medical and other emergencies, it is understandable that the demand for public safety facilities would be strongly related to the presence of people. This was in fact borne out in a comparison of EDUs by major land use categories based on calls-for-service vs. functional population.[6] They also tend to be more stable over time and can be calculated for types of land uses not captured in a locality's calls-for-service records (if those are even available). Beyond police and fire protection facilities, these types of service units are also used for general government facilities, courts, and correctional facilities.

Commonly used service units for different types of impact fee facilities are summarized in Table 7.1. As noted above, relative service units such as EDUs and SFEs are ratios that must be based on a demand unit.

A demand schedule is a table that identifies the number of service units generated

TABLE 7.1 Commonly Used Service Units by Facility Type

Facility Type	Common Demand Units	Relative Measure
Transportation	Trip, Vehicle- or Person-Mile of Travel	EDU or SFE
Water	Gallon of Water Consumption	EDU or SFE
Wastewater	Gallon of Sewer Generation	EDU or SFE
Stormwater Drainage	Square Feet of Impervious Cover	EDU or SFE
Schools	Student or Student by Grade Level	rarely used
Parks	Person, Resident (Person+Job or Functional Person for Non-residential)	EDU or SFE
Libraries	Person, Resident (Person+Job or Functional Person for Non-residential)	EDU or SFE
Fire/EMS	Service Call, Functional Person, Person/Job	EDU or SFE
Police/Law Enforcement	Service Call, Functional Person, Person/Job	EDU or SFE
Jails/Corrections/Courts	Service Call, Functional Person, Person/Job	EDU or SFE
General Government	Functional Person, Person/Job	EDU or SFE

by different types of development. Different land uses may have different assessment units (dwelling units, bedrooms, square feet), each of which is associated with a different number of service units. A demand schedule is not necessary in rare cases where the service unit and assessment unit are the same. For example, a drainage fee based on the additional square feet of impervious cover constructed on the property and measured from the site plan would not require a demand schedule, because the assessment unit for all land use types is the service unit (square foot of impervious cover). For most impact fees, however, a demand schedule is needed.

Demand schedules tend to differ significantly between utility (water and wastewater) and non-utility facility types. We start with non-utility facilities.

7.5.1 Non-Utility Facilities

For facilities other than water and wastewater, the demand schedule generally includes a list of land use types. For each land use type, a unit of development is specified, such as a dwelling unit, 1,000 square feet of floor area, or other physical characteristic. The number and types of land use categories listed in the

demand and impact fee schedules have important implications for the fees assessed on different land uses and the ease or difficulty of impact fee administration.

An example of a typical demand schedule for a road impact fee is shown in Table 7.2. In this case, the service unit is a daily vehicle-mile of travel (VMT). This is the product of one-half the trip generation rate,[7] the percentage of trips that are new trips (this excludes pass-by trips), and the average length of the trip in miles. This example uses broad land use categories for both residential and non-residential developments.

Residential Land Uses

While non-residential uses are mostly assessed by the square feet of floor area in the building, the traditional approach for residential is to assess a flat-rate fee per dwelling unit by housing types, as in the example road impact fee schedule shown in Table 7.2. In recent years, however, there has been growing interest in taking the size of the dwelling unit into consideration, usually measured in terms of square feet of living area or number of bedrooms.

Let's take the square footage approach first. The relationship between persons to the square footage of occupied dwelling

TABLE 7.2 Example of a Road Impact Fee Demand Schedule

Land Use Type	Assessment Unit	Daily 1-Way Trips	Percent New Trips	Average Trip Length (miles)	Vehicle-Miles of Travel/Unit
Single-Family Detached	Dwelling	4.71	100%	8.76	41.26
Multi-Family	Dwelling	3.37	100%	8.76	29.52
Mobile Home Park	Dwelling	3.56	100%	8.76	31.19
Hotel/Motel	Room	2.83	80%	11.30	25.58
Shopping Center/ Commercial	1,000 sq ft	18.50	44%	7.04	57.31
Office	1,000 sq ft	5.42	75%	6.49	26.38
Institutional/Quasi-Public	1,000 sq ft	3.37	75%	9.77	24.69
Manufacturing/Industrial	1,000 sq ft	1.68	95%	11.30	18.03
Warehouse	1,000 sq ft	0.85	95%	11.30	9.12
Mini-Warehouse	1,000 sq ft	0.72	95%	11.30	7.73

Note: sq ft means square feet.

units are illustrated in Figure 7.2 for both single-family detached and multi-family units (including townhouses and condominiums). The average numbers of residents are consistently higher for single-family units than for multi-family units. In general, larger units, in terms of square footage, tend to have more residents.

There are anomalies at the extremes for single-family on the low end and multi-family on the high end, which may be due to small sample sizes. Having the smallest size single-family category be less than 1,000 square feet and having the largest multi-family category be 2,000 square feet or more eliminates those anomalies.

Impact fee practitioners have generally avoided assessing residential use using a flat rate per square foot, as is typically done for non-residential land use types. To some, it looks too much like a tax. Available national data suggest that such an approach would not be even close to representative of actual demand by unit size. Figure 7.2 illustrates the average number of persons per unit by size category by size category if based on the average number of people per square foot (0.0014) derived from the latest American Housing Survey. It does not display as a straight line

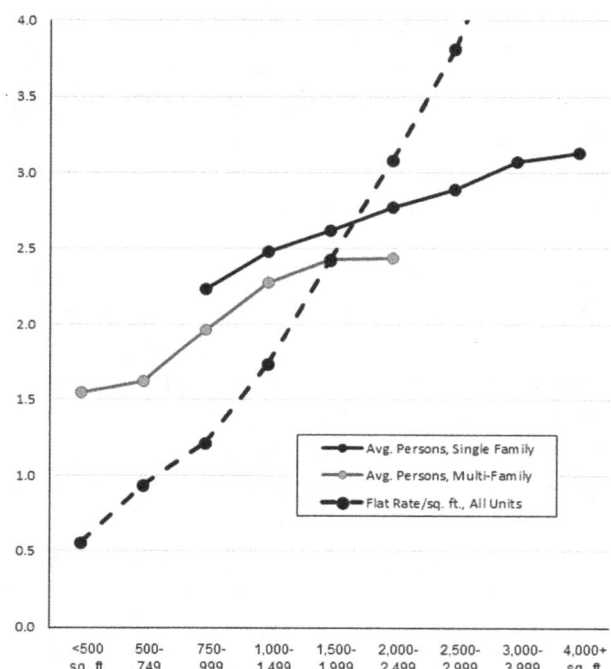

FIGURE 7.2 Average persons by size category and flat rate per square foot, US.
Source: 2019 American Housing Survey.

because the size categories do not represent uniform ranges.

The flat-rate per square foot approach is representative only of the average unit. It indicates that occupied units of less than

750 square feet average less than one person per unit, which is of course impossible. And it would predict that a unit of 4,000 square feet or more would have almost seven residents (not shown on the chart), while the data by housing type indicate it is less than half that. The relationship between unit size and residents or school-age children is clearly not linear. In the face of this data, it would be hard to argue that a flat rate per square foot would be reasonably proportional to the impact of the unit. A flat-rate per square foot assessment is not a recommended practice for residential development.

Another common practice in impact fee demand schedules is to assess residential development by the number of bedrooms. This approach has the advantage that local data on bedrooms and the number of persons are available from the Census Bureau (census data does not include information on unit square footage). While information on the size of units may be available in local property tax records, that data source does not include information on the number of residents in those units. Using bedrooms makes it unnecessary to combine information from different data sources, which can introduce the potential for significant errors.

The most recent American Housing Survey data on average persons and school-age children (6–17 years old) by number of bedrooms for occupied units is illustrated in Figure 7.3. Multi-family units tend to have somewhat more residents and school-age children than single-family homes with the same number of bedrooms. They may be close enough, however, to argue that using the averages for all housing types would be reasonably proportional to impact. Local census data might also show more similarity by housing type.

A drawback of using bedrooms as the residential assessment unit is the additional administrative effort required. It requires an analysis of the floorplan for each unit, and a

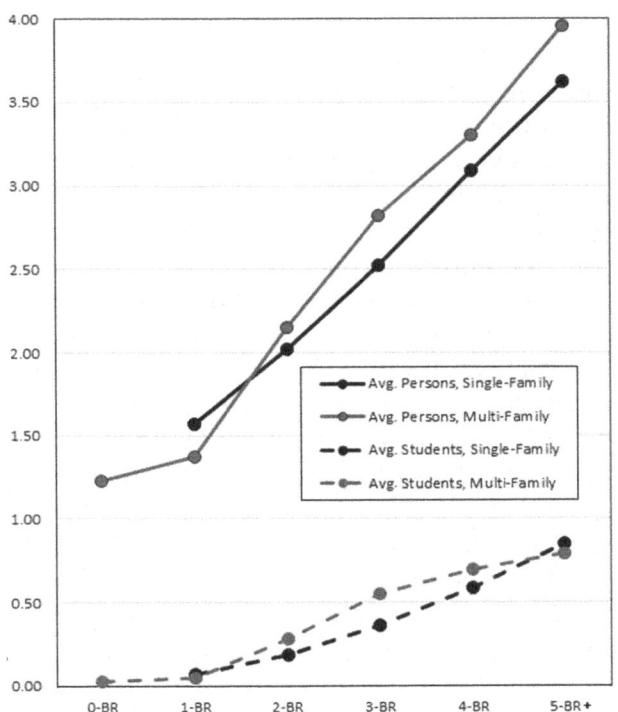

FIGURE 7.3 Average persons and school-age children by bedrooms, US.
Source: 2019 American Housing Survey

determination of which rooms qualify as bedrooms. This issue is likely responsible for the growing interest in using the much more easily identifiable characteristic of unit square footage.

Non-Residential Land Uses
A limited number of broad non-residential categories is typical for many non-utility services, such as police and fire protection, because there is limited data on the demand factors. Transportation demand schedules, however, often contain a much more extensive list of non-residential categories. Published national trip generation data have long been available for hundreds of non-residential use categories, including such specialized categories as bread/bagel/donut shop and trampoline park. Trip rates are inputs into most

transportation fee calculations, and they are also inputs into the functional population demand schedule that can be used for many other types of non-utility fees (see Section 7.6).

However, the fact that trip generation rates are available for so many land uses does not mean all of those uses must be included in the demand schedule for the sake of accuracy. Trip rates for many land uses are based on only a few studies, and they are generally not the only input. Most road impact fees, for example, also consider the percentage of pass-by trips, for which much more limited data are available, and many include the average length of the trips generated, for which data is also limited. The descriptions of land use in the ITE manual are often vague and overlap with other categories. Paradoxically, having more land use categories often makes it more difficult to classify proposed development projects, often requiring building officials to distinguish between related uses, such as whether a new restaurant is a quality restaurant, a high-turnover restaurant, or a fast-casual restaurant.

An alternative approach is to use a smaller number of broader, more generalized non-residential categories. Having learned that attempts to enumerate every possible land use in the fee schedule is both unnecessary and overly complicated, many communities are now moving in this direction.

A policy choice related to broad vs. detailed land use categories is whether fees should be assessed on new development based on the impact of the general long-term use of the development, or on the impacts of the specific initial occupant of the development. Much retail/commercial space can accommodate a wide range of uses and may cycle among them during a building's useful life. As a reflection of the longer-term impact, the general retail/commercial rate may be the most appropriate for these types of developments. Shopping centers include a wide variety of uses. The ITE *Trip Generation Manual* notes that some of the centers in its surveys include "non-merchandising facilities, such as

office buildings, movie theaters, restaurants, post offices, banks, health clubs and recreational facilities." It also notes that some of the centers surveyed include outparcels, which often contain service stations, drive-in banks and fast-food restaurants.

The main argument for assessing fees based on the initial use is that the immediate impacts can be measured more precisely, and if the development changes to a more intensive use in the future, an additional fee can be assessed for the increased impact. Given data constraints for many specialized uses, the accuracy even for the immediate impacts may not be as great as might be imagined. Change-of-use fees are paid by a prospective buyer or tenant and can be a disincentive to the reuse of vacant retail/commercial buildings. There is also an equity issue in that refunds are not provided if the use changes to something less intensive.

One potential issue with broad non-residential land use categories is that some specific retail/commercial uses have daily trip rates that are significantly lower than the shopping center rate (37.01 trip ends per 1,000 square feet). A furniture store, for example, generates an average of 6.30 daily trip ends per 1,000 square feet. Most impact fee ordinances allow applicants to prepare an independent fee calculation study, so a broad retail/commercial category could potentially generate a large number of such requests. In practice, however, such studies can be expensive and are relatively rarely utilized. The equity/proportionality issue can be addressed based on long-term impact. That new furniture store could house a craft brewery ten years down the road. The independent fee calculation provisions could require the study to address the long-term use of the structure, rather than the expected impact from the initial proposed use.

7.5.2 Utility Fees

For water and wastewater utilities, impact fees are most often assessed based on the capacity of the water meter rather than by land use type. Meter-capacity is generally measured in gallons per minute (gpm). The most common approach is to use a relative measure of demand based on the capacity of each meter compared to the capacity associated with the meter size typically used by a single-family unit, which is generally the smallest meter size. In the example below (Table 7.3), the 3/4" meter represents the demand associated with an EDU.

Under the typical "meter-capacity" approach described above, total daily gallons of water consumption is divided by system-wide EDUs to derive average daily gallons per EDU. The cost per gallon, which may be calculated in a variety of ways (see Section 7.6 below) is multiplied by daily gallons per EDU and EDUs per meter to determine the cost per meter.

A variation on this approach is to determine average daily water consumption for the smallest meter size (generally the one used by most current single-family customers) to determine the demand represented by the smallest meter. The demand by meter size for larger meters is calculated by multiplying the capacity of the meter by the capacity of the smallest meter

One might wonder why local consumption data by meter size is not typically used instead of meter-capacity. After all, water utility rates are almost always based on metered consumption, so the utility should have historical data that can be used to compute average water consumption by meter size. In practice, however, this is rare, except perhaps for single-family meters. One analyst[8] researched consumption by meter size to explore this alternative basis. He found from Phoenix's water utility data that there was a lot of variation in average consumption by meter size, especially for larger meters where there is a small sample size. He found anomalies where a larger meter had lower average consumption than a smaller one. These variations may be due to idiosyncratic factors. For example, some industrial, commercial and hospital uses appeared to have meters sized for occasional high-demand episodes. Also, the city phased out new 5/8" × 3/4" meters, but older homes with grass landscaping and inefficient appliances still have them and tend to consume more than newer homes with 3/4" meters.

The use of meter capacity to allocate relative water demand avoids these kinds of issues. The size of meter installed represents, in effect, the purchase of a certain amount of capacity. The new customer makes the choice of the size of meter that it thinks will meet its needs. This is a simple, intuitive approach that has become the standard practice in water impact fee studies. More refined approaches that improve proportionality for residential developments are available, such as illustrated in Chapter 28.

Wastewater impact fees are also commonly based on water meter size, especially by combined water and wastewater utilities. Wastewater flows are seldom metered for other than the largest customers. The general idea

TABLE 7.3 Water Impact Fee Demand Schedule

Meter Size (inches)	Type	Capacity (gpm)	EDU Multiplier
3/4"	Disc	15	1.0
1"	Disc	25	1.7
1-1/2"	Disc	50	3.3
2"	Disc/Turbine	80	5.3
3"	Compound	160	10.7
4"	Compound	250	16.7
6"	Compound	500	33.3
8"	Compound	800	53.3
3"	Turbine	175	11.7
4"	Turbine	300	20.0
6"	Turbine	625	41.7
8"	Turbine	900	60.0
10"	Turbine	1,450	96.7
12"	Turbine	2,150	143.3

Source: Meter capacities in gallons per minute (gpm) represent the recommended maximum rates for continuing operations from the American Water Works Association for disc meters (AWWA C700), compound meters (AWWA C702) and vertical shaft and low-velocity horizontal turbine meters (AWWA C701).

is that the amount of water that is consumed is proportional to the sewage that flows out. The exception of course is irrigation water, which does not enter the sewer system. Many water utilities sell irrigation-only water meters, which are not assessed wastewater impact fees. Developments that are not water customers are assessed fees based on the water meter size determined by the utility to be appropriate for the proposed use. Some large regional wastewater utilities base fees on average sewage generation estimates for various land use categories and require an individual analysis for large industrial uses to take into account the presence of contaminants as well as the volume of the projected wastewater flow.

7.6 COST PER SERVICE UNIT (METHODOLOGY)

Impact fee methodologies are classified based on how the cost per service unit is calculated. Impact fee calculations also require

consideration of possible revenue credits, which are discussed in the next section.

A wide range of methodologies have been developed to calculate impact fees, consistent with the legal requirements and guidelines described above. A relatively typical list of such variations is presented in Table 7.4. These kinds of typologies obscure the essential distinction between them. There are two primary types of methodologies, which can be referred to as "standards-based" and "plan-based." The standards-based methodology is calculated based on a generalized LOS standard. The plan-based approach methodology, as the name implies, is based on a plan and an identified set of improvements.

Of the variants listed in Table 7.4, the first two ("planned facilities" and "incremental cost") are different names for a plan-based methodology. Naming the utility version "incremental cost" is confusing because "incremental expansion" is a term often used to describe the most common variant of the standards-based methodology. There is no

TABLE 7.4 Typical Typology of Impact Fee Methodologies

Method Name	Cost per Service Unit Calculation	Context
Plan-Based	Cost of Planned Projects ÷ New Service Units	Used for planned facilities that will only serve future growth, or one can calculate the growth portion.
Incremental Cost	Cost of Planned Projects ÷ New Service Units	Used when a utility system has little capacity to serve growth and improvements are needed.
Existing Inventory	Current Value of Existing Facilities ÷ Existing Service Units	Used when a long-range plan for new facilities is not available, but improvements are needed to maintain the existing level of service.
System Buy-in	Current Value of Existing Facilities ÷ Existing Service Units	Used when the utility system has existing capacity to serve growth over the long term.
System Plan	(Existing Facility Value + Planned Facility Cost) ÷ (Existing + New Service Units)	Used when jurisdiction cannot delineate which portion of planned facilities will serve future growth.

Source: Adapted from Terner Center for Housing Innovation, the University of California at Berkley, *Improving Impact Fees in California: Rethinking the Nexus Study Requirement*, November 2020, Table 1.

real distinction between them, as indicated by the same description of the basic calculation used.

The next two variants ("existing inventory" and "system buy-in") also share the same calculation and have simply been given different names depending on whether it is used in the context of a utility fee or a non-utility fee. While the basic "system buy-in" calculation in Table 7.4 (total cost of existing facilities divided by total existing demand) is sometimes used, the vast majority of water and wastewater fees use the consumption-based calculation (total cost of existing facilities divided by total system capacity) because there is usually a significant amount of unused excess capacity.

The fifth variant described, the "system plan" approach, divides the combined cost of existing and planned improvements by the anticipated amount of development at the end of the planning horizon. This approach falls outside the proposed basic typology, and for a number of reasons should be used cautiously because it could charge new development for a higher level of service than existing development has paid for. For example, a jurisdiction might decide to create a city fire department to replace the service previously provided by contract with another entity. Existing development has not made any long-term investment in fire protection facilities. The new development would pay impact fees to fund its share of the new system and would also generate some of the additional tax revenues that will be needed to pay for the existing development's share.

It seems that the correct approach would be to calculate the cost to maintain the existing level of service using a standards-based methodology and recommend the result of this methodology only if it results in a lower cost per service unit. This would be an appropriate approach for a community approaching build-out, for example, to ensure that it does not collect more revenue than it will have a need for. But this so-called "hybrid" methodology is not adequate by itself to meet legal principles because it does not identify the existing level of service.

Such attempts to catalog a variety of methodologies that have been used in impact fee studies are not highly informative. Instead, let's focus on the two basic methodology types and the variants within them.

7.6.1 Standards-Based

A standards-based methodology typically uses a generalized level of service standard, such as the number of park acres per 1,000 residents, to determine the costs to accommodate new development. This approach does not require that there be a master plan, or even a list of specific planned projects that will be funded with the impact fees.

Most often, the standards-based approach uses the actual LOS that exists at the time the study is prepared. In its simplest form, the standards-based approach divides the replacement cost of existing facilities by the existing development being served by those facilities to determine the cost per service unit. In essence, the cost to maintain the existing LOS is defined as the existing investment in capital facilities per service unit currently using those facilities. In many cases, physical or quasi-physical LOS ratios are used as intermediary factors, but the resulting fee is the same. The two major variants of the standards-based methodology—"incremental expansion" and "consumption-based"—are described below.

7.6.1.1 Incremental Expansion

When the cost per service unit is based on the existing LOS, this approach is sometimes referred to as "incremental expansion." The basic assumption is that it will be necessary to expand capital facilities proportional to growth. Basing the fees on the existing LOS assumes that there is little or no excess capacity to accommodate future growth. However, a standards-based methodology can also be based on a LOS that is lower or higher than the current existing LOS. When there is a significant amount of excess capacity, a lower-than-existing LOS may be used.

The incremental expansion approach is almost always used for so-called "soft facilities" (parks, libraries, public safety, and general government facilities) for which capacity is difficult to measure. Occasionally an adjustment may be made to account for a recently built facility that clearly has some excess capacity, even though it may be difficult to measure precisely. Suppose a community has recently constructed a new city hall or public safety administration building that is currently only half occupied and clearly has excess capacity to serve future development. This could be addressed by only including half the cost of the building in the total value of the system that is serving existing development. Because of the difficulty of measuring capacity, the plan-based methodology is rarely used for soft facilities and should not be used without also using a standards-based calculation to identify the existing LOS or cost per service unit.

An example of a cost-per-service-unit calculation for a park impact fee is shown in Table 7.5. In this case, the county provides both community parks, which primarily serve the unincorporated area, and regional or specialty parks that serve the entire county. The municipalities provide community parks within their own jurisdictions. The cost of the existing facilities represents the current cost to replace those facilities. The total cost of community park facilities is divided by the total number of park service units in the unincorporated area to determine the community park cost per service unit (equivalent dwelling unit or EDU), while for regional/ specialty parks the cost is divided by county-wide EDUs.

7.6.1.2 Consumption-Based

For hard facilities (transportation, drainage, water, wastewater, and schools), the most common standards-based approach is often referred to as "consumption-based." This approach charges a new development the cost required to replace the capacity it will consume in the system. In essence, instead of dividing the cost of all existing facilities by the existing demand units being served, as is done in the incremental expansion variant, the replacement cost of existing facilities is divided by the total capacity of those facilities. The reason for this difference is that the hard facilities tend to have measurable excess capacity in existing facilities.

The consumption-based approach for transportation impact fees uses travel-miles as the service unit rather than trips. One can't determine the cost of trip capacity without including the distance component. The cost of adding capacity for a trip to a 5-mile road segment will be roughly five-times the cost of adding capacity for one trip on a 1-mile segment. So, the service unit of choice is a mile of travel. This can refer to either vehicle-miles or person-miles. Most transportation impact fee studies continue to be based on vehicle-miles because the data on vehicular trips is so much more robust than it is for bike/ped or other modes of travel.

With a consumption-based methodology, if a development is expected to generate 100 VMT per day, it is charged impact fees based on the average cost to add 100 vehicle-miles of capacity (VMC). Most well-functioning roadway systems have considerably more than one VMC for each VMT, but at least a portion of this surplus represents excess capacity. The level of service is a VMC/VMT ratio of one, although this is seldom stated. The average cost per VMC (and thus per VMT) can be based on the cost divided by the VMC created by a typical set of recent or planned road improvements.

While this is the most common consumption-based approach, some impact fee studies have used a capacity/demand ratio higher

TABLE 7.5 Park Cost per Service Unit—Incremental Expansion

Park Amenity	Unit	Existing Units		Unit Cost	Total Cost	
		Community	Regional/ Special		Community	Regional/ Special
Land	acre	238.68	728.23	n/a	$7,600,984	$31,510,635
Non-Standard Improvements	n/a	n/a	n/a	n/a	$5,968,268	$36,687,960
Baseball Field (lighted)	each	0	4	$1,005,000	$0	$4,020,000
Baseball Field (unlighted)	each	3	15	5,733,000	$2,199,000	$10,995,000
Softball Field (lighted)	each	5	4	5,532,000	$2,660,000	$2,128,000
Softball Field (unlighted)	each	0	1	5,370,000	$0	$370,000
Football Field (lighted)	each	4	0	5,709,000	$2,836,000	$0
Football Field (unlighted)	each	2	3	5,569,000	$1,138,000	$1,707,000
Soccer Field (lighted)	each	0	2	$443,000	$0	$886,000
Soccer Field (unlighted)	each	0	6	5,303,000	$0	$1,818,000
Basketball Court (lighted)	each	2	6	106,000	$212,000	$636,000
Basketball Court (unlighted)	each	7	3	$65,000	$455,000	$195,000
Tennis Court (lighted)	each	12	8	128,500	$1,542,000	$1,028,000
Tennis Court (unlighted)	each	7	3	$83,000	$581,000	$249,000
Playground	each	15	11	5,207,000	$3,105,000	$2,277,000
Restrooms	each	12	17	5,236,000	$2,832,000	$4,012,000
Splash Pad	each	1	2	5,378,000	$378,000	$756,000
Swimming Pool	each	0	3	1123000	$0	$3,369,000
Picnic Pavilion	each	7	14	161000	$1,127,000	$2,254,000
Trail (unpaved)	lin. ft.	4.579	80,503	$27	$123,633	$2,173,581
Total					$32,757,885	$107,072,176
÷ Existing Park Service Units (EDUs)					$88,915	$103,154
Park Cost per Service Unit					$368	$1,038

Note: Service units for community parks in an unincorporated area, regional parks in county-wide service area.

than 1.0, but less than the existing ratio, an approach that has been referred to as a "modified consumption-based" methodology. The higher ratio is intended to address the need to maintain some reserve capacity to accommodate unforeseen events. This modification of the consumption-based approach is seldom used in practice, probably because there is often little guidance on what ratio other than one is appropriate.

An example of a cost-per-service unit calculation for a road impact fee is shown in Table 7.6. The capacity added by a representative set of historical planned improvements is multiplied by the length of the improvement to determine the new VMC. The total cost of the improvements is divided by the total VMC added to calculate the cost per VMC.

School impact fees also typically use the consumption-based approach. They are almost always based on the cost of one permanent student station per student generated by the development.

The standards-based methodology most often used for water and wastewater facilities is most commonly referred to as a "system buy-in" approach. It is basically the same as the consumption-based approach. The implicit level of service is a one-to-one ratio between capacity and demand. In other words, the cost of accommodating one new unit of demand is the cost of constructing one additional unit of capacity.

In sum, there are two major variants of the standards-based methodology, incremental expansion and consumption-based. In general, the variant can be identified by whether

TABLE 7.6 Road Cost per Service Unit—Consumption-Based

Roadway	Lanes	Miles	Average Daily Capacity			New VMC	Total Cost	Cost/VMC
			Before	After	New			
Edgewater Phase 2, Harbor-Midway	2 to 4	1.90	15,824	28,879	13,055	24,805	$29,828,000	$1,203
Midway Blvd, Sharpe-Kings Hwy	2 to 4	2.00	13,154	28,879	15,725	31,450	$30,943,000	$984
Burnst Store, Notre Dame-Zemel	2 to 4	4.20	15,824	35,407	19,583	82,249	$49,467,000	$601
Burnst Store, Zemel-Lee County	2 to 4	2.60	15,824	35,407	19,583	50,916	$29,084,000	$571
CR 771, SR 776-Rotunda Blvd E	2 to 4	2.50	15,824	35,407	19,583	48,958	$22,319,000	$456
Piper Rd N, Henry-US 17	New 4	1.35	0	28,879	28,879	38,987	$14,363,000	$368
Winchester, SR 776-CR 775	New 4	3.00	0	35,407	35,407	106,221	$28,880,000	$272
Total/Weighted Average Cost per VMC		17.55				383,584	$204,884,000	$534

Note: New vehicle-miles of capacity (VMC) is product of new trip capacity and segment miles.

the cost per service unit is per unit of demand or per unit of capacity.

7.6.2 Plan-Based

In contrast to standards-based methodologies, which rely on generalized, system-wide LOS standards, plan-based methodologies rely on a specific list of planned improvements. A plan-based methodology basically divides the total cost of a set of planned improvements over a fixed time period by the anticipated growth in service units over the same time period. The least defensible of these approaches are those based on a short-term capital improvements plan, because there is not necessarily much correlation between short-term planned improvement costs and long-term costs to accommodate new development. Much more defensible are those based on a long-range or build-out master plan.

A plan-based impact fee calculation must address the legal principle that impact fees should not charge new development for a higher LOS than is currently provided for existing development. A planned-based methodology looks at levels of service for individual facilities, rather than the system as a whole. The conception is that aside from a few isolated facilities that need improvement to adequately accommodate existing demand and need to be addressed with other funding, the current system is providing an adequate LOS. Modeling the amount and geographic distribution of anticipated growth allows the identification of the specific improvements that will need to be made to accommodate that growth. A new development is not charged for its consumption of excess capacity in existing facilities, and consequently does not warrant a discount for any excess capacity that the planned improvement might create. In essence, there are lots of individual facility capacity thresholds that when crossed trigger the need for a specific improvement. On the basis of this logic, the total cost of the planned improvements, less the cost of any that are required to remedy an existing deficiency, can be attributed to the anticipated growth.

This ideal form of a plan-based methodology is really only feasible for the traditional "hard" facilities, such as transportation, water, wastewater, and drainage, for which capacities of individual facilities can be readily determined and the effects of growth on the system can be modeled. Even for these facilities, the plans are rarely as rigorous as the ideal suggests. Many transportation master plans, for example, are not based on a transportation demand model, but may simply project recent trends in growth in traffic volumes to identify planned improvements, and rely more heavily on professional judgment than hard data. Multi-modal transportation master plans, where the focus shifts from vehicle trips to person trips, involve even more complexities, alternatives, trade-offs and professional judgment. On the other hand, many transportation plans are fiscally constrained, and for this reason may be less likely to overcharge new development.

An example of a plan-based cost per service unit calculation for a road impact fee is shown in Table 7.7. The cost of the improvements required to accommodate projected growth over a 30-year period is divided by the anticipated new service units to determine the cost per service unit. In this case, the service unit is expressed in terms of an EDU, which represents the travel demand associated with the average single-family detached dwelling unit. More refined analysis would be needed to apportion impacts to different types and sizes of residential units (see Chapter 29 for a case study).

7.6.3 Methodology Summary

The basic types of impact fee methodologies are summarized in Table 7.8. The standards-based methodology has two main variants. The incremental expansion variant is generally used for "soft" facilities, such as parks, libraries, and public safety. The consumption-based variant is typically used for transportation, water, wastewater and schools. This methodology uses a system-wide level of service. The basic formula is to divide the total existing system replacement value by existing demand (in the incremental expansion variant) or existing capacity (in the consumption-based variant)

The plan-based methodology is primarily used only for "hard" facilities, such as transportation, water, wastewater, and stormwater drainage. A long-range master plan determines the improvements that will be required

TABLE 7.7 Road Cost per Service Unit—Plan-Based

Street	Segment Limits	Proposed Improvements	Est. Cost
Sunset Rd	UGB to Nolensville Rd	Widen to a typical three-lane section	$12,780,000
Sam Donald Rd	Split Log Rd to Nolensville Rd	Widen to a typical three-lane section	$15,420,000
Williams Rd	Clovercroft Rd to Nolensville Rd	Widen to a typical three-lane section	$5,870,000
York Rd	Nolensville Rd to Batey Rd	Widen to a typical three-lane section	$8,070,000
Rocky Fork Rd	Nolensville Rd to Rocky Springs Rd	Widen to a typical four-lane section	$15,020,000
Rocky Fork Rd	Rocky Springs Rd to Rutherford Co.	Widen to a typical four-lane section	$11,060,000
Rocky Springs Rd	Rocky Fork Rd to Rutherford Co.	Widen to a typical four-lane median divided section	$7,900,000
Kidd Rd / Battle Rd	Nolensville Rd to Davidson Co.	Widen to a typical three-lane section	$13,210,000
Total Cost			$76,120,000
÷ New Equivalent Dwelling Units (EDUs), 2010-2040			$16,568
Cost per EDU			$4,594

TABLE 7.8 Typology of Basic Impact Fee Methodologies

Methodology/Variant	Level of Service (LOS)	Basic Calculation
Standards-Based	System-Wide LOS	Depends in Variant
Incremental	Existing LOS	Existing System Value ÷
Expansion	(no excess capacity)	Existing System Demand
Consumption-Based	Lower-than-Existing LOS (to account for excess capacity)	Existing System Value ÷ Existing System Capacity
Plan-Based	Facility-Specific LOS	Planned Improvement Cost ÷ New System Demand
Hybrid	Different LOS measures for the two methodologies	Lower of Standards-Based or Plan-Based Cost per Service Unit

to maintain adequate levels of service for all system components while accommodating anticipated growth. The basic formula is to divide the total cost of planned improvements by the anticipated growth in demand.

A hybrid approach is occasionally used for communities approaching build-out. It involves calculating alternative costs per service unit using each of the basic methodologies and basing the fees on the lower of the two. The idea here is to ensure that the cost per service unit of the build-out plan does not exceed the cost to maintain the existing level of service.

7.7 REVENUE CREDITS

A revenue credit is an amount subtracted from the cost per service unit to determine the net cost per service unit. The net cost per service unit is then multiplied by the service units generated by new development to determine the impact fee. When it is necessary to provide such credits, and how they should be calculated, are among the most unsettled areas of impact fee methodology and practice. The key questions are: (a) what are the legal principles involved? and (b) how do we apply those principles to make the necessary distinctions between what's creditable and what's not?

Revenue credits should be provided when needed to comply with key principles

articulated in impact fee case law and codified in most state impact fee acts. One of the most fundamental principles arising out of case law is that impact fees should not charge new development for a higher level of service than is currently being provided to existing development. A related principle is that new development should not have to pay for its share of the cost of growth-related improvements through impact fees, and also pay additional amounts in the future for those same improvements through taxes and other revenue sources.

7.7.1 Existing Deficiencies

An existing deficiency is an existing facility or set of facilities that are not currently providing the minimum acceptable level of service to accommodate the demand generated from existing development. A deficiency credit will be necessary if existing facilities are not providing the same level of service to existing development that new development will be paying for through their impact fees.

In the context of a standards-based methodology, existing deficiencies are generally not an issue. The LOS is measured at the level of the entire system, and if the cost per service unit is based on the existing LOS, there is no existing deficiency. The deficiency issue only arises if the cost per service unit is based on a desired

LOS that is higher than the actual LOS being provided by the system. Under that scenario, the deficiency should be remedied with other funding sources. However, it is difficult to identify funding sources that new developments paying impact fees today will not also contribute. Even though impact fees will not be used to fund the deficiency, the new development would need credit for the present value of its share of other funds that would be used to remedy the existing deficiency. The standard practice with standards-based fees is to base them on the actual existing LOS (or a lower one in the case of the consumption-based variant), which avoids any deficiencies.

Existing deficiencies are harder to avoid with a plan-based methodology, which measures LOS at the level of individual system components. In general, the need for a separate credit calculation is avoided by removing the cost of improvements needed to remedy existing deficiencies from the cost per service unit calculation.

7.7.1.1 Outstanding Debt

Outstanding debt on existing facilities that are included in calculating the cost per service unit will be retired, in part, by revenues generated from new development. Given that new development will pay impact fees to provide the existing LOS for itself, the fact that new development will also be paying taxes to retire debt for the facilities that provide that same LOS for existing development would amount to paying for more than its proportionate share. Consequently, impact fees should be reduced to account for future payments by new development that will retire outstanding debt on existing facilities in the future.

However, if the outstanding debt is attributable to excess capacity that is available to accommodate new development, there is no need to provide a debt credit. In fact, the impact fees could be used to retire that debt instead of funding the construction of new facilities. This is generally not an option under the incremental

expansion variation of the standards-based methodology, unless the cost per service unit is calculated based on a lower-than-existing LOS, but it would be an option under the consumption-based variant. Nor is it an option under a plan-based methodology, which restricts impact fee revenue to new improvements identified in the long-range plan (although the fees could be used to retire bonds issued to fund the planned improvements).

There are a number of ways to calculate a revenue credit for outstanding debt. Regardless of approach, the initial step is to identify the remaining debt attributable to past capacity-expanding improvements. For standards-based fees, the simplest method is to divide the outstanding debt principal by existing service units to determine the credit per service unit. This puts new development on equal footing with existing development in terms of the portion of their cost that is financed with debt. Alternatively, the debt principal could be subtracted from the total cost of existing facilities in the calculation of the cost per service unit with the same resulting net cost, avoiding the need to calculate a separate revenue credit for outstanding debt.

A more complicated approach is to project future service units over the life of the bond, determine the average annual debt service payment (including interest) per service unit, and multiply that by a present value factor to determine the net present value of those future payments per service unit. The result would be the debt credit per service unit. Whether this would result in a lower or higher credit than the simpler approach described above would depend largely on the discount rate embodied in the present value factor and the interest rate for the bond.

7.7.1.2 Other Credits

Revenue credits are clearly required for existing deficiencies and outstanding debt attributable to past improvements that are serving existing development, but the rationale is much less clear-cut when it comes to other types of revenue that may be used to make "capacity" improvements. Capacity improvements are those not related to repair, replacement, or rehabilitation of existing facilities, and are the types of improvements that impact fees are designed to fund. Revenue credits per service unit can be calculated separately and subtracted from the cost per service unit or taken into consideration when determining the cost per service unit. Plan-based fees often reduce the total cost of the plan to account for certain types of anticipated non-impact fee funding before dividing by the growth in service units.

Aside from impact fees, a variety of other revenue sources are also used to fund capacity improvements. These include unrestricted general funds (often consisting of local property or sales taxes), funds that are restricted to supporting certain types of facilities or services (e.g., local gas taxes for transportation, or school or fire district taxes), dedicated funding (such as a portion of the property tax or sales tax earmarked for a planned set of capital improvements), and state and federal grants, to name a few. There is virtually no guidance in case law or state statutes about how to apply the general principle of not double-charging new development to what types of revenues warrant a credit, much less how that credit should be calculated.

In the absence of clear legal guidance, consultants, not to mention lawyers that have a practice defending local governments, have tended to be conservative and provide revenue credits generously. This was especially the case in the early days of impact fees in the 1970s and 1980s, when impact fees relied on the police power of local government as the source of their authority, and impact fee ordinances often triggered lawsuits. In this context, keeping the new fees as low as possible, especially for new homes, also lessened the likelihood of attracting litigation, and generous revenue credits result in lower fees.

The conservative approach to credits became the dominant practice in many states

as local governments modeled their studies on those earlier studies that had withstood legal challenges. While this orthodoxy is not uniform across states, with California being the most notable exception, it is certainly the status quo in Florida (the birthplace of the rational nexus standard) and seems to have become established in many other states. Given that the authority issue is largely settled in most states, and that state acts and case law are extremely vague on this specific issue, it may be a good time to look more carefully at what guidance the more general legal principles that have been articulated by the courts in the arena of impact fees and development exactions can provide for this unsettled area of impact fee methodology.

Discretionary Local Funding

Proponents of the most conservative approach believe credit should be provided for any revenue source that has been used for capacity-expanding improvements in the past, on the assumption that this historical rate of funding will continue into the future. Let's take the extreme case (although a not uncommon one)—a community that has not historically had impact fees. Why should it be assumed that the community will continue this same pattern of spending after it has adopted impact fees? After all, the purpose of impact fees is to shift the capital cost attributable to a new development from the community as a whole to new development. A variant of this approach is to look at the most recent 5–6 year capital improvement program rather than historical capital expenditures, but such plans are based on projections of revenue available from current funding sources.

Faced with this scenario, some who ascribe to this viewpoint have allowed that it may sometimes be permissible not to provide a credit for discretionary local revenue, but only if the governing body makes an explicit statement of its intent not to spend any non-impact fee revenue for capacity improvements of the same type of facilities covered by the impact fee. It is unclear why their intent or subsequent actions should be determinative. This suggests a problem with the most expansive view of the need for credits, as well as the difficulty of defining in any precise way the line to be drawn between non-impact fee revenues that warrant a revenue credit vs. those that do not.

In general, the expenditure of discretionary non-impact fee funds will improve the system-wide LOS, which will provide a benefit to both existing and new development, and both existing and new development will generate their share of the additional general fund revenues. If this is the case, new development is not being overcharged for the improved LOS, and it is hard to identify a rationale for providing a revenue credit. Impact fees cannot be used to raise the LOS, and requiring a revenue credit would make increasing it from its current level more difficult.

Even for facilities where capacity can be more easily quantified, adding capacity with non-impact fee revenue will tend to improve the LOS. For example, more capacity in the road system will reduce congestion and improve traffic flow, and more student stations will reduce class sizes. However, this may not be the case for expanding water and wastewater treatment plants that already have a significant amount of excess capacity—the additional non-impact fee funding will benefit only future customers. In such cases, the additional funding could appropriately be treated as a loan to the impact fee fund to be repaid from future impact fees.

Dedicated Funding

One of the earliest attempts to draw a line between types of local revenues was the distinction between "discretionary" and "dedicated" funding. Dedicated funding is restricted to be spent on capacity improvements or a specific list of projects that includes capacity improvements. Restrictions on how the funds can be spent may be included in a voter-approved proposition or an ordinance adopted by the local government.

Most local revenue sources are not dedicated to funding only capacity improvements or only a list of projects that include capacity improvement. A broader conception of dedicated funding would be to include revenue sources that support the same type of facility to which the impact fee applies, such as a local gasoline tax, water or wastewater utility rate, school district tax, or a fire district tax or assessment. However, these types of revenues are still discretionary in terms of whether they are used for operations and maintenance rather than capacity improvements.

While discretionary vs. dedicated funding sounds like a reasonable distinction, the same observation about discretionary funding also applies to dedicated funding – the additional funding will raise the general level of service and will be paid for and benefit all development. The rationale for a credit is still hard to discern. If there is no equity issue, the credit against the impact fees amounts to an unwarranted subsidy of new development.

Non-Local Funding/Grants

In addition to local funding sources, communities also tend to have access to some non-local funding, such as federal and state grants. Some of these grants will fund capacity improvements. Such non-local funding is not directly generated by developments within the local jurisdiction, but local developments do generate the sources of funding through payments such as gas taxes, state sales taxes, and state and federal income taxes. In this light, it is not unreasonable to attribute such funding to existing and new development in the community.

Grants are often specific to an individual improvement, so the expenditure of the grant money is not at the discretion of the local government. However, many grants must be applied for, and what kinds of grants to apply for introduces some discretion. On balance, it seems reasonable to consider grant funding to be like dedicated local funding. That in itself, however, provides no real rationale for credit, as discussed above.

There are specific circumstances where a stronger case can be made that credit should be provided. An example might be federal/state transportation funding. Of all the types of impact fee facilities, transportation systems tend to be highly integrated between jurisdictions, particularly in the form of the state and federal highway systems. Neither the federal government nor any state government assesses a transportation impact fee (although Louisiana considered the idea[9]), and local governments often contribute to the cost of improving such roads, because matching local funding will make the improvement more attractive to the state transportation department. Many communities include state and federal highways in their transportation impact fee studies because they form an integral part of the local transportation system. However, the local government is not responsible for these roads, which are primarily funded from federal and state revenues. Such funding is clearly outside the discretion of the local government. In this instance, a credit would seem to be warranted.

7.7.1.3 Revenue Credit Summary

In this section, we challenge the conservative orthodoxy in many parts of the country that a revenue credit should be provided for virtually any non-impact fee funding that a local jurisdiction might use to make capacity improvements for the same type of facility for which an impact fee is assessed. Fundamental legal principles seem to clearly require credits for funding existing deficiencies and for outstanding debt attributable to facilities serving existing development. They may also be warranted under specific circumstances, such as state/federal transportation funding. But the litigation-averse strategy of dealing with revenue credits seems outdated now that impact fee authority is largely settled in most states. It's time to develop a more coherent philosophy on this topic. We hope this helps start that process.

7.8 IMPACT FEE SCHEDULE

The impact fee schedule brings the methodology components together to calculate the impact fee. It consists of the land use type and assessment unit (or meter size), the service units associated with that type of development, the net cost per service unit (cost per service unit, net of any revenue credits), and the calculated fee per type of development.

In the example of a typical road impact fee schedule (Table 7.9), there is a detailed list of land uses, assessment units that depend on the land use, the service units generated per assessment unit (vehicle-mile of travel, or VMT), the net cost per service unit, and the calculated road impact fee by land use (product of VMT per unit and net cost per VMT). (Chapter 29 provides an example that varies residential transportation impact fees by the size of residential units to help advance equity objectives discussed in Chapter 12 and its Coda.)

Table 7.10 shows an example of a water impact fee schedule. In this example, residential development is assessed per dwelling unit, while non-residential development is assessed based on the size and type of water meter. (Chapter 28 illustrates how to modify this approach to various residential water impact fees according to the size of residential units to further help with the equity objectives presented in Chapter 15 and its Coda.)

7.9 ART VS. SCIENCE?

It has often been said that impact fee calculation is an art, not a science. One could presumably say the same for all the social sciences. Like economic models, for example,

TABLE 7.9 Road Impact Fee Schedule

Land Use Type	Unit	VMT/ Unit	Net Cost per VMT	Net Cost per Unit
Single-Family, Detached	Dwelling	27.75	$221	$6,133
Multi-Family (1-2 stories)	Dwelling	18.67	$221	$4,126
Multi-Family (3+stories)	Dwelling	13.87	$221	$3,065
Mobile Home/RV Park	Space	11.50	$221	$2,542
Hotel/Motel	Room	4.78	$221	$1,056
General Retail/Comm./Shop. Ctr	1,000 sq ft	33.13	$221	$7,322
New/Used Auto Sales	1,000 sq ft	49.17	$221	$10,867
Tire Superstore	1,000 sq ft	23.82	$221	$5,264
Supermarket	1,000 sq ft	62.07	$221	$13,717
Home Improvement Superstore	1,000 sq ft	23.38	$221	$5,167
Pharmacy/Drug Store	1,000 sq ft	29.98	$221	$6,626
Furniture Store	1,000 sq ft	9.95	$221	$2,199
Bank, Walk-In	1,000 sq ft	33.56	$221	$7,417
Bank, Drive-In	1,000 sq ft	56.59	$221	$12,506
Movie Theater	1,000 sq ft	152.56	$221	$33,716
Quality Restaurant	1,000 sq ft	101.35	$221	$22,398
High-Turnover Restaurant	1,000 sq ft	126.24	$221	$27,899
Fast-Food Rest. w/Drive-Thru	1,000 sq ft	279.97	$221	$61,873
Gasoline/Service Station	1,000 sq ft	139.71	$221	$30,876
Conv. Market w/Gas Pumps	1,000 sq ft	194.50	$221	$42,985
Super Conv. Market (10+ Pumps)	1,000 sq ft	203.70	$221	$45,018
Self-Service Car Wash	Serv. Bay	80.05	$221	$17,691
Marina	Berth	6.35	$221	$1,403
Golf Course	Hole	80.39	$221	$17,766
General Office	1,000 sq ft	23.07	$221	$5,098
Medical Office/Clinic	1,000 sq ft	85.95	$221	$18,995
Industrial Park	1,000 sq ft	8.32	$221	$1,839
Manufacturing	1,000 sq ft	9.65	$221	$2,133
General Light Industrial	1,000 sq ft	12.28	$221	$2,714
Warehousing	1,000 sq ft	4.31	$221	$953
Mini-Warehouse	1,000 sq ft	2.42	$221	$535
Nursing Home	1,000 sq ft	7.65	$221	$1,691
Elementary School (Private)	1,000 sq ft	22.96	$221	$5,074
Middle School (Private)	1,000 sq ft	23.71	$221	$5,240
High School (Private)	1,000 sq ft	18.60	$221	$4,111
University/Junior College	1,000 sq ft	53.56	$221	$11,837
Church	1,000 sq ft	12.21	$221	$2,698
Day Care	1,000 sq ft	35.28	$221	$7,797
Hospital	1,000 sq ft	24.58	$221	$5,432

impact fee methodologies require inputs that require professional judgments, and those choices affect the results. We focus here on the context in which impact fee studies are prepared, and how that can affect the choices made in the study.

Impact fees inherently tend to be politically controversial because they shift infrastructure costs associated with new development from the community at large to new development. Some developers who subdivide large tracts of land may see the virtues of impact fees, especially if they are currently subject to other types of fees, *ad hoc* exactions, or dedication requirements, to create a more uniform and equitable system in which they are not singled

TABLE 7.10 Water Impact Fee Schedule

Housing Unit/Meter Type	EDUs per Unit/Meter	Net Cost per EDU	Net Cost per Unit/Meter
Single-Family Unit	1.000	$3,397	$3,397
Multi-Family Unit	0.377	$3,397	$1,281
Non-residential Meter (inches):			
3/4" Disc	1.500	$3,397	$5,096
1" Disc	2.500	$3,397	$8,493
1 1/2" Disc	5.000	$3,397	$16,985
2" Disc/Turbine	8.000	$3,397	$27,176
3" Compound	16.000	$3,397	$54,352
3" Turbine	17.500	$3,397	$59,448
4" Compound	25.000	$3,397	$84,925
4" Turbine	30.000	$3,397	$101,910
6" Compound	50.000	$3,397	$169,850
6" Turbine	62.500	$3,397	$212,313
8" Compound	80.000	$3,397	$271,760
8" Turbine	90.000	$3,397	$305,730

out. But homebuilder associations, which are dominated by small-scale builders and contractors, almost universally oppose them, and tend to be politically powerful at both the local and state level.

Local governing bodies vary in how they view impact fees, but they are also aware of the risks to their re-election prospects if they support the adoption of new impact fees or significant increases from current fees when the studies are updated. There can also be backlash from voters if they appear to have adopted new or updated fees at low percentages of the maximum fees calculated in the study to appease development interests. Even though governing bodies can adopt fees at a lower percentage than the maximum amounts calculated in the study, this can put some pressure on the impact fee consultant not to calculate fees that are as high as could reasonably be justified. While less common, calculating very low fees can also mobilize opposition, and at the minimum will require explanation if the updated fees are significantly lower than the current fees.

There is also the possibility of attracting litigation, especially in states where the authority to adopt impact fees is unsettled. It may also trigger a backlash from the state legislature.

A recent proposal by one Florida county to increase road fees by 75 percent to respond to voters' backlash to a property tax increase led a local state legislator, who also worked for the county's largest developer, to file a bill to impose a maximum limit on annual percentage increases.[10] That bill subsequently became law.

Some impact fee studies are prepared by local government staff, but most are prepared by independent consultants. The local jurisdiction is the impact fee consultant's client. The consultant works closely with the jurisdiction's staff, and only occasionally interacts directly with the governing body. However, management is usually aware of their governing body's leanings and desires related to the impact fee issue and will often convey that to the consultant. Overt pressure on the consultant for specific outcomes is rare, but the consultant will generally have a sense of the type of outcome the jurisdiction would like to see, such as fee increases being as low or as high as possible. Even if the consultant is not familiar with the locality's politics, experience has taught that the calculation of big fee increases or decreases will often generate controversy that can imperil the adoption of the study.

In addition to political considerations, consultants have their own motivations. Consultants have an interest in having their studies adopted, securing repeat business, and having positive references from clients. Studies that become controversial can require much more time on the consultant's part, who often has a fixed-fee budget. Studies that depart from the standard practice in the region will draw additional scrutiny, leading most to avoid breaking with a dominant conservative orthodoxy in favor of generous revenue credits. There is often limited current local data available required for some of the inputs into the methodology, and where assumptions must be made, the tendency is to be conservative. These factors result in a general bias toward studies that underestimate the full proportionate-share fees needed to accommodate growth.

NOTES

1 Tindale-Oliver & Associates, *2004 Roadway Facilities Impact Cost Study*, August 2004; Integrated Utilities Group, *Drainage Impact Fee Study*, September 2004; James C. Nicholas and Arthur C. Nelson, *Park, Recreation, Trail and Open Space Costs of Accommodating New Development and Recommended Park, Recreation, Trails and Open Space Development Impact Fees*, November 2004; James C. Nicholas, *Public Safety Costs of Accommodating New Development and Recommended Public Safety Development Impact Fees*, August 2004.

2 Duncan Associates, *Impact Fee Land Use Assumptions and Capital Improvements Plan, 2012-2022*, September 2012.

3 James Duncan and Associates, *Road Impact Fee Study, Ada County Highway District*, 1989.

4 James Duncan and Associates, *Road Impact Fee Update, Ada County Highway District*, 1996.

5 Duncan Associates, *Impact Fee Study, City of Atlanta, Georgia*, February 2021.

6 Clancy Mullen, "Fire and Police Demand Multipliers: Calls-for-Service versus Functional Population," paper presented at the National Impact Fee Roundtable, Arlington, VA, October 5, 2006.

7 Trip rates like those reported in the Institute of Transportation Engineers (ITE) *Trip Generation Manual* represent trip ends. Every trip has two trip ends – an origin and a destination. To avoid double-counting, half of the trip is allocated to the origin and the other half to the destination.

8 Doug Frost, former Principal Planner with the City of Phoenix Water Service Department, May 19, 2021 communication.

9 Duncan Associates, *Method for Quantifying the Impact of New Development on the State Highway System*, prepared for the Louisiana Department of Transportation and Development, December 2013.

10 Joe Byrnes, WMFE Radio, "Sumter County Approves 75 percent Increase In Impact Fees To Help Fund Roads Tied To Growth Of The Villages," March 24, 2021.

8 MODEL PROPORTIONATE SHARE IMPACT FEE ORDINANCE

Once the planning foundations for and the calculation of proportionate share impact fees are completed, they need to be implemented. This is done usually through an ordinance or similar locally adopted instrument. This chapter presents a model proportionate share impact fee ordinance. It is comprised of three parts. Principles of ordinance design are reviewed in the first part. In the second, a model ordinance that is adapted from several ordinances prepared by two of the authors (Juergensmeyer and Nicholas) for Florida jurisdictions is offered with commentary throughout, noting key rationale and issues. (Florida does not have comprehensive impact fee legislation.) The third part is an impact fee ordinance for the City of Canton, Georgia (also prepared by Juergensmeyer and Nicholas). It is instructive in comparison with the Florida model because Georgia does have a comprehensive impact fee enabling act and also because Canton was the first city (outside California) to adopt impact fees that vary by size of the structure (including residential) for all fees assessed. The models apply to transportation impact fees but can be adapted to other facilities. Model ordinances for other types of infrastructure are offered by Nelson, Nicholas and Juergensmeyer (2009). We offer a word about policy issues raised by independent fee calculations as well as impact fee waivers and exemptions in Chapter 9.

8.1 PRINCIPLES OF ORDINANCE DESIGN AND DRAFTING

8.1.1 Adoption

Impact fee programs change the rules of the game for developers and communities. There are usually important considerations to be made. Those considerations include the timing of the effective date and the transition period.

Most impact fee ordinances do not become fully effective on the day they are adopted. Those programs that become effective immediately usually require unanimous approval of the governing body under provisions of state emergency declaration statutes. Where an impact fee program results in the lifting of moratoria (initially imposed because there was no money available to build facilities to support new development), there may indeed be a justifiable emergency declaration.

In general, the effective dates of new impact fee ordinances range from about 30 days to three months from the date of enactment, with some effective dates ranging more than a year in advance. Communities may delay the effective dates of impact fees for several reasons.

First, there is the practical consideration of gearing local government agencies up to handle the new program. Impact fees are usually assessed at the time of building permit issuance, so it is usually the building agency that handles the fee determination and collection. But coordination is usually required between planning, to assure that building permit applications are consistent with land use and other plans; revenue or budget agencies, to assure that impact fee collection is properly recorded and allocated; and the various agencies that will use impact fees, including police, fire, libraries, public works, and parks and recreation. The sheer magnitude of setting up a new, complex administrative system takes time. Public officials who

DOI: 10.4324/9781003336075-10

do not give their agencies enough time to fully implement the system face the choice of delaying the effective date at the last minute (which does not look good politically) or risking mismanagement and possible court action.

Second, there is the practical political consideration of giving the development community enough time to adequately respond to a new assessment program. Developers thinking about projects must be forewarned about the magnitude of fees they will likely be assessed for. This allows them time to change project dimensions and negotiate posture to press for lower land prices.

Third, there is the question of how to deal with projects that have already been approved. For those that have had building permits issued, it is usually impractical to assess fees retroactively. If fees are to be collected upon issuance of occupancy permits, then technically those projects for which fees were not assessed at the building permit stage may still be assessed under the new impact fee program. But pragmatism usually requires that projects for which building permits have already been issued would be exempt from impact fees.

For those projects that have been approved but for which building permits have not been issued, impact fee programs can usually collect fees upon issuance of building permits. Here again, however, developers are likely to argue that initial project approval was based on a set of financial assumptions, one of which included government fees. If that assumption is to change dramatically, then the project may be less financially viable. Communities usually grant exemption to those projects that have been approved prior to the adoption date of the program. Projects approved after the adoption date and issued building permits before the effective date are also usually exempted. Projects approved after the adoption date and issued building permits on or after the effective date are usually assessed impact fees.

8.1.2 Assessment

Impact fees should be assessed according to clear schedules and/or formulas. Ideally, a developer should be able to accurately predict the impact fee so that development dimensions and financing can take full account of the fees. But clear direction must be given to the assessing agency on how to deal with unconventional cases. Among the most common unconventional cases are the demolition of a structure and replacement with a like structure; demolition and replacement with an unlike structure; building additions or expansions; additional buildings added to the same site; and construction of facilities whose impact dimensions (trips, park demand, water and sewer demand, etc.) are difficult to determine.

In the case of demolition and replacement with a like structure, no impact fee is usually required. In the case where the structure is larger but of the same use, the impact fee is usually assessed on the incremental change in size. Where the structure is for a different use, either the entire impact fee may be assessed or the fee would be assessed on the incremental change in impact dimensions; some agencies assess the lower of the two fee calculations.

Building additions, expansions, or new buildings should be assessed an impact fee on the incremental change in impact dimensions. Unfortunately, this sounds easier than it often is. Some building additions, expansions or new buildings on the same site result in higher site activity than the sum of the existing and additional space suggests. Nonetheless, as most impact fee formulas are based solely on units (square feet, bedrooms, etc.), it should be a simple matter to determine the incremental change in demand dimensions resulting from such additions to the site.

The more problematic situation arises when a proposed use is not clearly anticipated by impact fee schedules. Road trip generation estimated for land uses, for example, usually do not cover all land uses. Sometimes the proposed use is like other uses on the schedule, and so reasonable approximations can be made. Other times, officials may allow the developer to pay for an independent, professional determination of demand dimensions associated with that land use. Alternatively, officials may estimate a high fee, then evaluate the observed demand for facilities generated by the development at the end of a year, and then either refund the difference between the initial fee paid and the actual amount necessary or assess the additional amount necessary. As the latter situation may be problematic if the developer refuses to pay, communities should try to avoid having to assess fees after a development is built.

8.1.3 Collection

The fundamental issue in collection is: who will collect the fees? Since the objective of assessing impact fees is to provide the community and its various agencies with needed revenues, close collaboration is needed between the assessing agency and the expending agencies. The collection of impact fees should be handled by one agency. Usually, it is the building agency. Sometimes it is the planning agency or a centralized accounting office. In any event, all agencies need to know from the assessing agency (a) what the fee schedule is, (b) how many fees are collected from which developments, and (c) when the building permit was issued and the expected date of development completion. For example, Broward County has used a five-copy receipt that is distributed to the person who pays, the planning office, the accounting office, the public works staff, and the parks staff. In one county that assesses fees for schools, senior centers, childcare, and housing in addition to more traditional uses, copies of receipts are also sent to those agencies.

8.1.4 Accounting

Accounting procedures are needed to assure that the impact fees collected are deposited into earmarked accounts, expenditures from which will benefit contributing development. That is, impact fees collected for schools, parks, and roads must be earmarked for school, park, and road accounts. Furthermore, if the impact fee ordinance requires segregation of revenues geographically (by service area or district), the accounting system should incorporate such a segregation scheme. The accounting system should also be designed to make available to anyone information on where impact fees from individual contributing developments were spent. This allows public officials and developers alike to be assured that impact fees benefit contributing development.

8.1.5 Disbursement

It goes without saying that impact fees must be spent. The manner of expenditure can be complex, however. Issues are raised relating to earmarking, timeliness of disbursement, location of disbursement, and effect on community capital financing policies.

8.1.5.1 Earmarking

While impact fees should be earmarked to accounts in the manner suggested above, care must be taken not to accumulate so many separate accounts that are too small to be useful or restrict the use of money in accounts in a manner that jeopardizes specific capital improvements. Broward County, Florida, faced this very problem with its road impact fees. Impact fees were deposited into hundreds of accounts, each earmarked for a specific road improvement. Few accounts were large enough to pay for the intended improvement. Eventually, the county reduced the number of accounts and changed administrative procedures to allow the pooling of revenue under certain conditions.

San Diego County, California, collects impact fees for specific projects but puts all money into a single master account. That money is used to construct facilities based on a 20-year capital improvement program. Technically, impact fees collected for one improvement not scheduled for construction until several years later are loaned to another project scheduled for improvement in an earlier year. Impact fees collected for improvements that are already constructed repay funds borrowed from other accounts.

8.1.5.2 Timing

Impact fees must be expended within a reasonable amount of time. Most communities attempt to expend them within a 5- to 10-year capital improvement program. There are exceptions, however. In San Diego County, some improvements are not built until nearly two decades after fees are collected. The program includes a master capital improvements program that explicitly shows when those facilities would be built. The county further demonstrated that there would be no need for those facilities until future years. Contributing development is not deprived of benefits since facilities will be built benefiting development as the need arises.

When facilities financed by impact fees are scheduled for construction but must be delayed, impact fees need not be refunded. Among the conditions needed to extend the expenditure of impact fees are under-collection of impact fees due to reduced growth rates and the discovery of extraordinary costs that affect prudent construction of facilities at the time originally planned.

8.1.5.3 Location

Various schemes are used to assure that contributing development benefits from the facilities it helps to finance. In Loveland, Colorado, it is presumed that all facilities financed in part by impact fees benefit all new development. This is an easy presumption since the town is rather small, and it is reasonable to expect that all new development benefits from the construction of all new facilities.

Where impact fees are collected on a countywide basis or in larger cities, however, it is usually customary to devise benefit districts or zones for each facility to be financed by impact fees. For example, the city of Atlanta, Georgia, divides its city into two road benefit zones. Road improvements within each zone are estimated, and impact fees for each zone are determined. New development within each zone pays a different road impact fee.

Unlike the zonal system used by Atlanta, Broward County expends impact fees for local parks within 2.5 miles of contributing development. It spends fees for regional parks within 15 miles of contributing development.

But some counties finance some facilities with impact fees that benefit all new development everywhere, and there is no need to devise benefit districts or zones. For example, Manatee County, Florida, applies the same solid waste disposal impact fee on all development.

Matching the location of contributing development with the location of facilities financed by impact fees depends on the facility. Each facility has its own unique service area: local parks may serve areas within a 2.5-mile radius, while regional parks may serve areas within a 15-mile radius. Expressways may serve an entire county, but certain collector streets serve limited areas. Solid waste sites serve large regions but compacting and transfer stations may serve smaller areas. In general, impact fees must be tailored to the service area of the facility being financed with those fees.

8.1.5.4 Effect on Capital Improvement Policy

Impact fees can, however, influence existing capital improvement policy. For example, suppose that impact fees are assessed for a regional park scheduled for construction in five years. Impact fees pile up, and substantial revenue is on deposit. But after five years it is discovered that park construction prices have risen faster than impact fee collections and account yields. The local public officials face the choice of deferring construction of the park, at risk of political pressure or opposition from developers who contributed money to the park or taking money from other projects and diverting it to the park.

The availability of impact fees that are dedicated to certain facilities may thus place them on a higher priority than other projects. This will happen in those communities that must contribute general funds to projects because credits had to be given to new development for other payments new development made to existing facilities benefiting existing development. The effect, however, is to place at higher priority facilities that may solely benefit new development, and place at lower priority facilities that are long overdue but solely benefit existing development, or that benefit the entire community.

8.1.6 Enforcement

Two factors dominate the consideration of impact fee program enforcement: timely payment of impact fees and consistency of development with permitted activity.

Timely payment is an issue easily resolved when only one community is involved in collecting impact fees. It becomes a more complex issue when one jurisdiction, a county perhaps, must collect fees from developments located in separate jurisdictions, perhaps cities. Such was the case in Broward County. Several cities in Broward County issue their own building permits, but the county collected impact fees to finance facilities benefiting new development inside and outside of cities. Developers received building permits from cities and were required to pay impact fees to the county. But many developers "forgot" to do so. Broward County implemented a system to check the building permits of cities and notify cities when developers failed to pay impact fees. The average monthly impact fee revenue jumped several fold.

Another problem is assuring that developments use the land consistent with that which was approved. The most serious situation occurs when development is approved for and is occupied by one kind of activity, perhaps low employee density activities, and is eventually replaced by higher employee density activities. Roads are more greatly impacted by the development than initial projections and impact fees estimated. Communities thus need to monitor the actual use of developments to assure consistency with initial permitted uses or initial fee payments. This may be accomplished by monitoring business license changes. When a license indicates a different or more intensive use, there may be a land use violation. The remedy may include additional impact fees.

Suffice it to say that this element of impact fee programs is perhaps the least well developed and potentially the most problematic.

8.1.7 Credits

Chapter 7 spells out several situations in which developers would be granted credit against impact fees. Those credits include recoupment of past and future payments the development will make toward the financing of existing facilities benefiting existing development, the time-price differential inherent in the expenditure of money at different times, and installation of facilities of general public benefit.

Communities must clearly describe the nature of these credits. Developers will naturally attempt to claim as many credits as possible. Administrative provisions can clearly specify the conditions under which credit is allowed, credit formulas, credit parameters (number of past and future years to consider, interest or discount rates), and limitations of credit (the particular impact fees that can be reduced).

Communities can limit credit to only the impact fee; to allow more credit than the impact fee is to have communities pay for new development. Communities can also limit credit to like contributions; for example, a credit for past and future property tax payments for parks would be applied only to the park impact fee and no others.

Where a developer installs facilities for which credit will be given, there might be a question on the amount of credit due. That is, a developer may claim more expenses than actually incurred to install the improvements. This is resolved by having public works officials estimate the value of the work to be undertaken by the developer, and then certify satisfactory completion of the work before the credit is given. Perhaps the developer can install the improvement at less than the public estimate, but so long as the improvement is installed satisfactorily there should be no issue.

8.1.8 Waivers

Impact fees can have undesirable effects on the provision of low- or moderate-income housing, and on desirable economic development. At issue is the extent to which impact fees raise the price of housing or raise the price of rent for economic activities. These effects may be offset in two ways.

First, a community could waive the impact fee for qualifying low-and moderate-income housing. But there are problems with this approach. Waiving fees will result in lower revenue, and there is no explicit recoupment mechanism to make up for the loss of impact fees. The more difficult problem is that there is a risk of invalidation of ordinances that include any waivers of impact fees for "desirable" developments that have impacts. There is no apparent way to show equal application or equal protection if the fees will vary while the impact does not. These charges are fees and not taxes. As such, they must be applied equally and fairly. Any community feeling the need to incorporate waivers should seek legislative authority for such waivers. The better

approach, however, would be to follow the option set out below.

The second way entails the community paying the impact fee or a portion of it out of the general fund. Some communities cut the impact fee on low-income housing by half, but contributes the difference out of the general fund. We know of other communities that reduce the impact fee on new industrial activities after one year. That is, the new industrial development pays the fee, but after one year the city rebates the fee out of the general fund in proportion to the number of new jobs created after the first year. Hillsborough County, Florida, will pay the impact fee for developments which attain a public purpose from "other sources" that may include intergovernmental transfers or the general fund. However, this may require consideration of a credit against impact fees to the extent that new development generates new intergovernmental transfer or general fund revenue.

We add an extensive discussion about waivers and exemptions in Chapter 9.

8.2 Independent Fee Calculations

Impact fee programs must include provisions for variance. At issue is the impossibility of knowing exactly the impact fee due for every project. Developers, for example, may claim lower road impact fees for a particular project than indicated or implied on the formal road impact fee schedule. Variance provisions would allow developers to perform their own impact fee analysis and present it to either administrators or the governing body (or its designee, such as the planning commission). Administrative hearings may be conducted where the fee proposed by the developer is up to 25 percent (or so) less than the schedule would assess. Differences of more than that amount could be heard before the governing body. Differences of less than 10 percent may not be subject to hearing, however, as the estimated impact of the community would be close to that estimated by the developer.

The decision to allow all or part of the developer's variance request would probably depend on the community's independent analysis. One hedge is to require a full deposit of the fee with an evaluation of the project's impact after one year (or so). The difference between the actual impact and the impact fees paid based on the community's estimate would be refunded with interest.

In any event, to protect against development delays, the impact fee would be paid in advance of the hearing, but the portion of the impact fee in dispute would be held in a special interest-bearing account. A refund of all or part of the disputed portion would be paid from this account.

We offer additional discussion about independent fee calculations in Chapter 9.

8.2.1 Refunds

Sometimes impact fees collected may not be used as intended. Unlike tax revenue, they cannot be diverted to other purposes. Unspent impact fees may need to be refunded if the facilities they were to finance are canceled and unreasonably delayed. The questions involved here focus on notice and the parties who should be paid.

Start with whom should be paid. Impact fees paid by a developer are recouped by the developer through lower land prices or higher development prices, or a combination of the two. Developers may also take a smaller profit. It is impossible for a community, however, to decide which party in the complex development process paid how much of the impact fee. Instead, communities may simply opt to entitle only current owners of the contributing development under the theory that it is ultimately the owners who absorb most of the impact fee in higher priced, lower quality, and/or higher density development.

Notice may then be given to all owners of contributing development as shown on the local property tax records. Notice should be by registered mail. Owners should be given a reasonable period of time, perhaps three months to one year, to claim the refund. Refund claims should be relatively simple, involving only certification of ownership.

For its part, determining the appropriate impact fee to be refunded involves using the very formulas or schedules used to determine the impact fee when first paid. Refunds should also include interest, probably at the local government borrowing rate.

8.2.2 Data Maintenance

The impact fee program must be continually updated as to assumptions, facility cost estimates, growth patterns and rates, demographic changes, and so on. Impact fee assessments will therefore be kept current and less subject to adverse court review. Three considerations are posed.

First, the community should establish the frequency at which it updates each impact fee schedule or formula. Specific staff should be explicitly assigned this responsibility. Data updating may require establishing formal links between agencies; perhaps an impact fee updating task force comprised of representatives of all affected agencies would meet annually to review changes. Florida, for instance, requires that impact fees be updated frequently based on then-current cost data. Those estimates should be made annually.

Second, the governing body or its designee should establish a formal process by which changes are made. This may include a formal public hearing during which the changes are proposed and adopted. Citizens and developers would also be allowed to propose changes at that hearing. Changes that are adopted should be supported by findings. Such a process should remove the taint of arbitrariness whenever the changes result in higher fees.

Third, the community might decide the conditions under which unscheduled re-evaluation would occur. Changes may include substantially higher or lower than projected growth rates, large formerly unplanned annexations, and major changes in the construction standards of new facilities (for example, federal requirements for vastly improved and more expensive water and wastewater plants).

8.2.3 Administrative Expense

Impact fee programs carry initially high implementation costs (including the costs associated with analysis, planning, and programming). But they can be administered at a relatively low cost. Figures vary and figures reported here are informally gathered, but the cost of administering impact fee programs range from about 2 to about 5 percent of impact fee collections.

If the cost of administration can be determined, it may be recovered by impact fees themselves. This is acceptable practice throughout Florida, for example. The procedure involves reasonably documenting the cost of administering impact fee programs as a percentage of total impact fee receipts (sometimes divided into each impact fee assessed). This cost is then added to impact fees as a proportionate increase covering administrative costs.

We proceed to the model ordinance with commentary. The reader is referred to numerous model ordinances for specific types of infrastructure, including social infrastructure, provided in Nelson, Nicholas, and Juergensmeyer (2009).

8.2.4 MODEL ORDINANCE WITH COMMENTARY

This model ordinance is for transportation facilities, but the basic structure can be applied to all other infrastructure. Commentary is offered in **bold italics**. Although reference is made to a county and its board of commissioners, the model ordinance is applicable to all public and even private governing entities that assess, collect and expend impact fees.

1. ***Legislative Findings. The ordinance should include legislative findings in which the governing body of the local government determines that the impact fee meets the dual rational nexus test. As to the first part of the test, the governing body should determine that there is a reasonable connection between the need for new capital facilities and the new development charged the impact fee. As to the second part, the governing body should determine that there is a reasonable connection between the expenditure of the impact fees collected and the benefits to the new development.***

Section One: Legislative Findings

The Board of County Commissioners of ** County finds, determines, and declares that:

A. ** County must expand its road system in order to maintain current levels of service if new development is to be accommodated without decreasing current levels of service. This must be done in order to promote and protect public health, safety, and welfare;

B. The ** Legislature through the enactment of ** Statutes has sought to encourage ** County to enact impact fees;

C. The imposition of impact fees is one of the preferred methods of ensuring that development bears a proportionate share of the cost of capital facilities necessary to accommodate such development. This must be done in order to promote and protect public health, safety and welfare;

D. Each of the types of land development described in Section Seven hereof, will generate traffic necessitating the acquisition of rights-of-way, road construction, and road improvements.

E. The fees established by Section Seven are derived from, are based upon, and do not exceed the costs of providing additional rights-of-way, road construction, and road improvements necessitated by the new land developments for which the fees are levied.

F. The report entitled "** County, **, Impact Fee Methodology," dated _____, sets forth a reasonable methodology and analysis for the determination of the impact of new development on the need for and costs for additional rights-of-way, road construction and road improvements in ** County.

2. *Short Title, Authority, and Applicability. It is generally recognized as good practice for an ordinance to include a recitation as to the authority upon which it is based. In the case of impact fees, the clause may cite the home rule power of counties, the land use and regulatory powers of counties and the lengthy case law history of impact fees.*

Section Two: Short Title, Authority and Applicability

A. This ordinance shall be known and may be cited as the "** County Road Impact Fee Ordinance."

B. The Board of County Commissioners of ** County has the authority to adopt this ordinance pursuant to Article _____ of the Constitution of the state of **, and Chapter _____ _____ ____ of the ** Statutes.

C. This ordinance shall apply in the unincorporated area of ** County and in the incorporated areas of ** County to the extent permitted by Article _____ of the Constitution of the state of **.

3. *Intent and Purposes. This provision should identify the type of development subject to the fee. For example, an ordinance imposing an educational facilities impact fee will limit the fee to residential development, and a transportation impact fee characteristically applies to all types of development: residential, commercial, and industrial development. The ordinance should indicate the scope of its effect, such as whether it applies to development throughout the entire county or only the unincorporated area or only in a municipality.*

Section Three: Intents and Purposes

A. This ordinance is intended to assist in the implementation of the ** County Comprehensive Plan.

B. The purpose of this ordinance is to regulate the use and development of land so as to assure that new development bears a proportionate share of the cost of capital expenditures necessary to provide roads in ** County.

4. *Rules of Construction. Many ordinances contain rules of construction which facilitate the drafting and understanding of the ordinance.*

Section Four: Rules of Construction

A. The provisions of this ordinance shall be liberally construed so as to effectively carry out its purpose in the interest of public health, safety and welfare.

B. For the purposes of administration and enforcement of this ordinance, unless otherwise stated in this ordinance, the following rules of construction shall apply to the text of this ordinance:

(1) In case of any difference of meaning or implication between the text of this ordinance and any caption, illustration, summary table, or illustrative table, the text shall control.

(2) The word "shall" is always mandatory and not discretionary; the word "may" is permissive.

(3) Words used in the present tense shall include the future; and words used in the singular number shall include the plural, and the plural

the singular, unless the context clearly indicates the contrary.

(4) The phrase "used for" includes "arranged for," "designed for," "maintained for," or "occupied for."

(5) The word "person" includes an individual, a corporation, a partnership, an incorporated association, or any other similar entity.

(6) Unless the context clearly indicates the contrary, where a regulation involves two

(2) or more items, conditions, provisions, or events connected by the conjunction "and," "or," or "either...or," the conjunction shall be interpreted as follows:

(a) "And" indicates that all the connected terms, conditions, provisions, or events shall apply.

(b) "Or" indicates that the connected items, conditions, provisions, or events may apply singly or in any combination.

(c) "Either ... or" indicates that the connected items, conditions, provisions, or events shall apply singly but not in combination.

(7) The word "includes" shall not limit a term to the specific example but is intended to extend its meaning to all other instances or circumstances of like kind or character.

(8) "Administrator" means the Administrator or the county or municipal officials he/she may designate to carry out the administration of this ordinance. Any municipal official so designated shall be approved by the appropriate municipality before exercising duties hereunder.

(9) A road right-of-way used to define road impact fee district boundaries may be considered within any district it bounds.

5. *Definitions. Complex and lengthy ordinances typically include a definitional section for words and phrases used precisely and frequently throughout the ordinance to lessen the complexity of the ordinance and facilitate its understanding.*

Section Five: Definitions

A. A "feepayer" is a person commencing a land development activity which generates traffic and which requires the issuance of a building permit or permit for mobile home installation.

B. A "capital improvement" includes transportation planning, preliminary engineering, engineering design studies, land surveys, right-of-way acquisition, engineering, permitting, and construction of all the necessary features for any road construction project including, but not limited to:

(1) construction of new through lanes,

(2) construction of new turn lanes,

(3) construction of new bridges,

(4) construction of new drainage facilities in conjunction with new roadway construction,

(5) purchase and installation of traffic signalization (including new and upgraded signalization),

(6) construction of curbs, medians, and shoulders, and

(7) relocating utilities to accommodate new roadway construction.

C. "Expansion" of the capacity of a road applies to all road and intersection capacity enhancements and includes but is not limited to extensions, widening, intersection improvements, upgrading signalization, and expansion of bridges.

D. "Land Development Activity Generating Traffic" means any change in land use or any construction of buildings or structures or any change in the use of any structure that attracts or produces vehicular trips.

E. "Road" shall have the same meaning as set forth in Section _____ of the ** Statutes.

F. "Arterial Road" shall have the same meaning as set forth in Section _____ of the ** Statutes.

G. "Collector Road" shall have the same meaning as set forth in Section _____ of the ** Statutes.

H. "Site-related Improvements" are capital improvements and right-of-way dedications for direct access improvements to and/or within the development in question. Direct access improvements include but are not limited to the following:

  (1) access roads leading to the development;

  (2) driveways and roads within the development;

  (3) acceleration and deceleration lanes, and right and left turn lanes leading to those roads and driveways; and

  (4) traffic control measures for those roads and driveways.

I. "Independent Fee Calculation Study" means the documentation prepared by a feepayer to allow the determination of the impact fee other than by the use of the table in Section Seven (A) of this ordinance.

J. "Level of Service" shall have the same meaning as set forth in the Highway Research Board's Highway Capacity Manual (1965).

K. "Development Order" means a regulatory approval by ** County or a municipality therein.

L. "Mandatory or required right-of-way dedications and/or roadway improvements" means such non-compensated dedications and/or roadway improvements required by the County or by a municipality within ** County which has not opted out from the effect of this ordinance.

6. *Imposition of Fee. An impact fee ordinance will impose the impact fee and identify at what point in the development process the impact fee will be due, such as the issuance of a building permit, the platting of the land, the issuance of a certificate of occupancy or some other point.*

Section Six: Imposition of Road Impact Fee

A. Any person who, after the effective date of this ordinance, seeks to develop land within ** County, by applying for: a building permit; an extension of a building permit issued prior to that date; a permit for mobile home installation; or an extension of a permit for mobile home installation issued prior to that date, to make an improvement to land which will generate additional traffic, is hereby required to pay a road impact fee in the manner and amount set forth in this ordinance. The impact fees established by this ordinance shall not be effective within the boundaries of any municipality which issues building permits until such municipality has executed an interlocal agreement with the county to collect such fees. The impact fees established by this ordinance shall not be effective within a municipality which has by municipal ordinance repealed the effect of this ordinance within its boundaries.

B. No new building permit or new permit for mobile home installation for any activity requiring payment of an impact fee pursuant to Section Seven of this ordinance shall be issued unless and until the road impact fee hereby required has been paid.

C. No extension of a building permit or permit for mobile home installation issued prior to the effective date of this ordinance, for any activity requiring payment of an impact fee pursuant to Section Seven of this ordinance shall be granted unless and until the road impact fee hereby required has been paid.

7. *Computation of the Amount of Impact Fee. Impact fee ordinances frequently incorporate and adopt the impact fee study, which provides a factual and legal basis for the fees. The methodology may be actually placed in the ordinance. Fee schedules should be incorporated into the ordinance. It is not unusual for an impact fee ordinance to authorize a developer to submit its own calculation of impact fees and to provide for a determination by staff as to the accuracy and adequacy of the developer impact fee. An appeal process may be specified. The fee schedules outlined below are simple, but they can be very detailed based on the needs of the local government.*

Section Seven: Computation of the Amount of Road Impact Fee

A. At the option of the feepayer, the amount of the road impact fee may be determined by the following fee schedule. The fee schedule includes a credit for future motor fuel tax payments and reflects a discount of __ percent from net cost to encourage use of this schedule in order to avoid the expenditure of administrative time on the processing of independent fee calculation studies.

FEE SCHEDULE

LAND USE TYPE (UNIT)

RESIDENTIAL PER SQUARE FOOT OF HEATED AND COOLED LIVING AREA: SINGLE-FAMILY DETACHED [Insert $ value of fee]

SINGLE-FAMILY ATTACHED [Insert $ value of fee]

MULTI-FAMILY [Insert $ value of fee]

MOBILE HOME EACH UNIT [Insert $ value of fee]

HOTEL/MOTEL ROOM PER ROOM [Insert $ value of fee]

OTHER RESIDENTIAL EACH UNIT [Insert $ value of fee]

INDUSTRIAL AND WAREHOUSE PER 1,000 SQ FT:

INDUSTRIAL BUILDINGS [Insert $ value of fee]

WAREHOUSE BUILDINGS [Insert $ value of fee]

STORAGE BUILDINGS [Insert $ value of fee]

OFFICE AND FINANCIAL PER 1,000 SQ FT:

FINANCIAL OFFICES [Insert $ value of fee]

GENERAL OFFICES [Insert $ value of fee]

RETAIL PER 1,000 SQ FT [Insert $ value of fee]

NOTE: SQ FT means square feet.

(1) If a building permit is requested for mixed uses, then the fee shall be determined by using the applicable schedule by apportioning the space committed to uses specified on the applicable schedule.

(2) For applications for an extension of a building permit or an extension of a permit for mobile home installation, the amount of the fee is the difference between that fee then applicable and any amount already paid pursuant to this ordinance.

(3) If the type of development activity that a building permit is applied for is not specified on the applicable fee schedule, the Administrator shall use the fee applicable to the most nearly comparable type of land use on the fee schedule. The Administrator shall be guided in the selection of a comparable type in the most recent edition of the *Trip Generation Manual* prepared by the Institute of Transportation Engineers. If the Administrator determines that there is no comparable type of land use on the applicable fee schedule then the

Administrator shall determine the fee by:

(a) using traffic generation statistics provided by government transportation agencies or contained in or derived from the *Trip Generation Manual* and;

(b) applying the formula set forth in Section Seven (B) hereof; and

(c) reducing the fee so determined by the appropriate percentage as indicated in Section Seven (A) above.

The Administrator shall determine the fee by applying the formula set forth in Section Seven (B) hereof and reduce the fee so determined by the appropriate percentage as indicated in Section Seven (A) above. (4) In the case of change of use, redevelopment, or expansion or modification of an existing use which requires the issuance of a building permit or permit for mobile home installation, the impact fee shall be based upon the net positive increase in the impact fee for the new use as compared to the previous use. The Administrator shall be guided in this determination by traffic generation statistics provided by public transportation agencies or contained in the *Trip Generation Manual* prepared by the Institute of Transportation Engineers.

B. If a feepayer opts not to have the impact fee determined according to Paragraph (A) of this section, then the feepayer shall prepare and submit to the Administrator an independent fee calculation study for the land development activity for which a building permit or permit for mobile home installation is sought. The independent fee calculation study shall follow the prescribed methodologies and formats for the study established by the Guidelines and Procedures Manual adopted by motion of the Board of County Commissioners of ** County. The traffic engineering and/or economic documentation submitted shall show the basis upon which the independent fee calculation was made, including but not limited to the following:

(1) Traffic Engineering Studies:

i. Documentation of trip generation rates appropriate for the proposed land development activity.

ii. Documentation of trip length appropriate for the proposed land development activity.

iii. Documentation of any other trip data appropriate for the proposed land development activity.

(2) Economic Documentation Studies:

(a) Documentation of the cost per lane per mile for roadway construction appropriate for proposed land development activity.

(b) Documentation of credits attributable to the proposed land development activity, which can be expected to be available to replace the portion of the service volume used by the traffic generated by the proposed land development activity.

(c) Independent fee calculation studies shall be prepared and presented by professionals qualified in their respective fields. The Administrator shall consider the documentation submitted by the feepayer but is not required to accept such documentation as he/she shall reasonably deem to be inaccurate or not reliable and may, in the alternative, require the feepayer to submit additional or different documentation for consideration. If an acceptable independent fee calculation study is not presented, the feepayer shall pay road impact fees based upon the schedules shown in Paragraph (A) of this section. Determinations made by the Administrator pursuant to this paragraph may be appealed to the Board of County Commissioners by filing a written request with the Administrator within ten (10) days of the Administrator's determination.

(d) Upon acceptance of an independent fee calculation study, the following formula shall be used by the Administrator to determine the impact fee per unit of development:

[The actual ordinance should insert formulas used to calculate fees here, if any.]

8. *Payment of Impact Fee. The collection method of impact fees may be provided by ordinance. The ordinance may make the fees payable in a lump sum or it may provide for the payment of the fee on an annual or monthly basis over a period of years. If a county-imposed impact fee is charged to development on a countywide basis, the impact fee ordinance may provide for an interlocal agreement with a municipality to address the administration of the impact fee within the incorporated area, including an administrative fee to the municipality for the cost of collection.*

Section Eight: Payment of Fee

A. The feepayer shall pay the road impact fee required by this ordinance to the Administrator or his designee prior to the issuance of a building permit or a permit for mobile home installation.

B. All funds collected shall be properly identified by the road impact fee district and promptly transferred for deposit in the appropriate Road Impact Fee Trust Fund to be held in separate accounts as determined in Section Ten of this ordinance and used solely for the purposes specified in this ordinance.

9. *Impact Fee Districts. Impact fee districts may be described to draw a tighter nexus between the fee and the benefit to the property.*

Section Nine: Road Impact Fee Districts

There are hereby established _____(__) road impact fee districts as shown in Appendix I attached hereto and incorporated herein by reference. No district shall include any area within a municipality that issues building permits and that has not entered into an interlocal agreement with the county to collect road impact fees or that has by ordinance repealed the effect of this ordinance within its boundaries

10. *Impact Fee Trust Funds Established. The ordinance should establish a separate account so that there is assurance that the impact fees are properly expended in a manner that provides the requisite benefit to the development charged the impact fee.*

Section Ten: Road Impact Fee Trust Funds Established

A. There are hereby established _____(__) separate Road Impact Fee Trust Funds, one for each road impact fee district established by Section Nine of this ordinance.

B. Funds withdrawn from these accounts must be used in accordance with the provisions of Section Eleven of this ordinance.

11. *Use of Funds. A delineation of the type of capacity-adding capital facilities that will be funded with the revenues from the impact fees should be included. Impact fees may be bonded.*

Section Eleven: Use of Funds

A. Funds collected from road impact fees shall be used for the purpose of capital improvements to and expansion of transportation facilities associated with the Arterial and Collector road network as designated by ** County and under the jurisdiction of ** County, any municipality within ** County which has not opted out from the effect of the ordinance, or the state of **.

B. No funds shall be used for periodic or routine maintenance.

C. Funds shall be used exclusively for capital improvements or expansion within the road impact fee district, including district boundary roads, as identified in Appendix I, hereof, from which the funds were collected or for projects in other road impact districts which are of benefit to the road impact district from which the funds were collected. Funds shall be expended in the order in which they are collected.

D. In the event that bonds or similar debt instruments are issued for advanced provision of capital facilities for which road impact fees may be expended, impact fees may be used to pay debt service on such bonds or similar debt instruments to the extent that the facilities provided are of the type described in Paragraph (A) of this section and are located within the appropriate impact fee districts created by Section Nine of this ordinance or as provided in Paragraph (C) of this section.

E. At least once each fiscal period the Administrator shall present to the Board of County Commissioners a proposed capital improvement program for roads, assigning funds, including any accrued interest, from the several Road Impact Fee Trust Funds to specific road improvement projects and related expenses. Monies, including any accrued interest, not assigned in any fiscal period shall be retained in the same Road Impact Fee Trust Funds until the next fiscal period except as provided by the refund provisions of this ordinance.

F. Funds may be used to provide refunds as described in Section Twelve.

G. The collecting governmental entity shall be entitled to retain not more than _____ per cent (__) of the funds collected as compensation for the expense of collecting the fee and administering this ordinance.

12. ***Refund of fees paid. Typically, an impact fee ordinance will provide for refunds to the owner of the property at the time of a refund in the event the impact fees are not expended within a reasonable period of time after collection.***

Section Twelve: Refund of Fees Paid

A. If a building permit or permit for mobile home installation expires without commencement of construction, then the feepayer shall be entitled to a refund, without interest, of the impact fee paid as a condition for its issuance except that the County shall retain _____ percent (__) of the fee to offset a portion of the costs of collection and refund. The feepayer must submit an application for such a refund to _____ within 30 days of the expiration of the permit.

B. Any funds not expended or encumbered by the end of the calendar quarter immediately following six (6) years from the date the road impact fee was paid shall, upon application of the then-current landowner, be returned to such landowner with interest at the rate of _____ percent (__) per annum, provided that the landowner submits an application for a refund to _____ within 180 days of the expiration of the six-year period.

13. *Exemptions and Credits. An impact fee ordinance may provide for an exemption from the fees for housing deemed affordable at specified income levels. The exemption may be a credit against the fee or a refund for fees paid by low-income owners. Credits may be given for the donation of property or improvements to a governmental entity which reduces that development's impact on the infrastructure served by the impact fee. Credits must be incorporated under two conditions. First, taxes or revenues paid by the newly constructed development must be legally available to fund the same infrastructure for which the impact fee is collected. Second, the taxes or revenues must have been applied toward reducing the cost of those infrastructure requirements for the newly constructed development, which pays the impact fee.*

Section Thirteen: Exemptions and Credits

A. The following shall be exempted from payment of the impact fee:

   (1) Alterations or expansion of an existing building where no additional units are created, where the use is not changed, and where no additional vehicular trips will be produced over and above those produced by the existing use.

   (2) The construction of accessory buildings or structures which will not produce additional vehicular trips over and above those produced by the principal building or use of the land.

   (3) The replacement of a destroyed or partially destroyed building or structure with a new building or structure of the same size and use provided that no additional trips will be produced over and above those produced by the original use of the land.

   (4) The installation of a replacement mobile home on a lot or other such site when a road impact fee for such mobile home site has previously been paid pursuant to this ordinance or where a mobile home legally existed on such site on or prior to the effective date of this ordinance.

Any claim of exemption must be made no later than the time of application for a building permit or permit for mobile home installation. Any claim not so made shall be deemed waived.

B. Credits

   (1) No credit shall be given for site-related improvements or right-of-way dedications.

   (2) All mandatory or required right-of-way dedications and/or roadway improvements made by a feepayer, subsequent to the effective date of this ordinance, except for site-related improvements, shall be credited on a pro-rata basis against road impact fees otherwise due or to become due for the development that prompted the County or the municipality to require such dedications or roadway improvements. Such credits shall be determined and provided as set forth in Section Thirteen B (3) (a), (b), (c), and (d).

   (3) A feepayer may obtain credit against all or a portion of road impact fees otherwise due or to become due by offering to dedicate non-site-related right-of-way and/or construct non-site-related roadway improvements. This offer must specifically request or provide for a road impact fee credit. Such construction must be in accordance with county, municipal, or state design standards, whichever is applicable. If the Administrator accepts such an offer, whether the acceptance is

before or after the effective date of this ordinance, the credit shall be determined and provided in the following manner:

(a) Credit for the dedication of non-site-related right-of-way shall be valued at (i) 115 percent of the most recent assessed value by the ** County Property Appraiser, or (ii) by such other appropriate method as the Board of County Commissioners may have accepted prior to the effective date of this ordinance for particular right-of-way dedications and/or roadway improvements, or (iii) at the option of the feepayer, by fair market value established by private appraisers acceptable to the County. Credit for the dedication of right-of-way shall be provided when the property has been conveyed at no charge to, and accepted by, the County in a manner satisfactory to the Board of County Commissioners.

(b) Applicants for credit for construction of non-site-related road improvements shall submit acceptable engineering drawings and specifications, and construction cost estimates to the Administrator. The Administrator shall determine credit for roadway construction based upon either these cost estimates or upon alternative engineering criteria and construction cost estimates if the Administrator determines that such estimates submitted by the applicant are either unreliable or inaccurate. The Administrator shall provide the applicant with a letter or certificate setting forth the dollar amount of the credit, the reason for the credit, and the legal description or other adequate description of the project or development to which the credit may be applied. The applicant must sign and date a duplicate copy of such letter or certificate indicating his agreement to the terms of the letter or certificate and return such signed document to the Administrator before credit will be given. The failure of the applicant to sign, date, and return such document within 60 days shall nullify the credit.

(c) Except as provided in Subparagraph (d), credit against impact fees otherwise due will not be provided until:

(1) the construction is completed and accepted by the County, a municipality within the county which has not opted out from the effect of this ordinance, or the state, whichever is applicable;

(2) a suitable maintenance and warranty bond is received and approved by the Clerk of Courts of ** County, when applicable; and

(3) all design, construction, inspection, testing, bonding, and acceptance procedures are in strict compliance with the then-current County Paving and Drainage Ordinance, when applicable.

(d) Credit may be provided before completion of specified roadway improvements if adequate assurances are given by the applicant that the standards set out in Subparagraph (c) will be met and if the feepayer posts security as provided below for the costs of such construction. Security in the form of a performance bond, irrevocable letter of credit or escrow agreement shall be posted with and approved by the

Clerk of Courts of ** County in an amount determined by the Administrator consistent with the then-current County Paving and Drainage Ordinance. If the road construction project will not be constructed within one (1) year of the acceptance of the offer by the Administrator, the amount of the security shall be increased by ten percent (10%) compounded, for each year of the life of the security. The security shall be reviewed and approved by the Clerk of the Board of County Commissioners prior to acceptance of the security by the Clerk. If the road construction project is not to be completed within 5 years of the date of the feepayer's offer, the Board of County Commissioners must approve the road construction project and its scheduled completion date prior to the acceptance of the offer by the Administrator.

(4) Any claim for credit must be made no later than the time of application for a building permit or permit for mobile home installation. Any claim not so made shall be deemed waived.

(5) Credits shall not be transferable from one project or development to another without the approval of the Board of County Commissioners and may only be transferred to a development in a different impact fee district upon a finding by the Board of County Commissioners that the dedication of right-of-way or road construction for which the credit was given benefits such different impact fee district.

(6) In the event that a municipality within ** County shall pass an ordinance or law that prevents the application of this ordinance within that municipality, there shall be no credit given for right-of-way dedications or roadway construction ordered by that municipality against fees due hereunder because of improvements constructed outside of the boundaries of the municipality.

(7) In the event fee schedules are subsequently changed to reflect increases or decreases in construction costs or other relevant factors, then a feepayer may request a recalculation of credits to fairly reflect such changed circumstances.

(8) Determinations made by the Administrator pursuant to the credit provisions of this section may be appealed to the Board of County Commissioners by filing a written request with the Administrator within ten (10) days of the Administrator's determination.

14. *Review. To assure the continued relevancy of the impact fee charges, the ordinance should provide for a periodic review of the impact fees. The ordinance should provide for the future review and update of the underlying construction costs and demographic data upon which the impact fees are based. An impact fee ordinance may provide for the appointment of an impact fee review task force prior to the periodic review and update of the impact fee as provided for in the ordinance. Some local governments establish such a task force prior to the imposition of a new impact fee.*

Section Fourteen: Review

The fees specified in Section Seven (A) shall be reviewed by the Board of County Commissioners at least once each fiscal biennium.

15. *Penalty Provision. An impact fee ordinance may include a provision that an uncollected*

impact fee operates as a lien against the property until the impact fee is paid.

Section Fifteen: Penalty Provision

A violation of this ordinance shall be prosecuted in the same manner as misdemeanors are prosecuted, and upon conviction the violator shall be punishable according to law; however, in addition to or in lieu of any criminal prosecution ** County shall have the power to sue in civil court to enforce the provisions of this ordinance

16. *Severability. Lengthy ordinances with numerous distinct provisions may provide that in the event a portion of the ordinance is found unlawful, the remainder of it is to be considered valid, and the unlawful portion is to be deemed severed.*

Section Sixteen: Severability

If any section, phrase, sentence, or portion of this ordinance is for any reason held invalid or unconstitutional by any court of competent jurisdiction, such portion shall be deemed a separate, distinct and independent provision, and such holding shall not affect the validity of the remaining portions thereof.

    1   **Effective Date.** An impact fee ordinance typically provides an effective date for the imposition of the fees so that the fees apply to a new development at a date certain in the future.

    2   **Notice Requirements.** Notice requirements are embedded in state laws governing ordinance promulgation for local governments.

ROAD DEVELOPMENT IMPACT FEE ORDINANCE

Section Seventeen: Effective Date

This ordinance shall become effective on
_____.

City of Canton, Georgia, Road Impact Fee Ordinance
AMENDMENT TO THE CITY OF CANTON CODE OF ORDINANCES
    ORDINANCE NO. _____

An amendment to the city of Canton Code of Ordinances regarding road development impact fees; to repeal conflicting ordinances, and for other purposes.

An ordinance relating to the regulation of the use and development of land in the city of Canton, Georgia; imposing a development impact fee on land development in the city of Canton for providing road and related facilities necessitated by such new development; stating the authority for adoption of the ordinance; making legislative findings; providing definitions; providing a short title and applicability; providing intents and purposes; providing rules of construction; providing definitions; providing for the computation of the amount of the road development impact fee; providing for the payment of a road development impact fee; providing for road development impact fee service areas; providing for the establishment of road development impact fee trust funds; providing for the use of funds; providing for the refund of fees paid; providing for exemptions and credits; providing for review of the fee schedule; providing for appeals; providing a penalty provision; providing for severability; providing a repealer; providing an effective date.

Pursuant to the authority conferred by the Constitution of the State of Georgia, Article 9, Section 2, Paragraph III, and pursuant to Section 1-1-9 of the Code of Ordinances of the City of Canton, the City of Canton hereby amends the following Article for the purpose of promoting the health, safety, morals, convenience, order, prosperity, and the general welfare of the City of Canton, Georgia.

That Article _____ of the City of Canton Code of Ordinances, regarding _____, is hereby amended to add Sections _____, to read as follows:

Section One: Legislative Findings

The City Council of the City of Canton has considered the feasibility of imposing development impact fees and finds, determines and declares that:

A. The Georgia Legislature, through the enactment of the Georgia Development Impact Fee Act, Georgia Code Title 36-71-1 through 36-71-13, has authorized the City of Canton to enact development impact fees;

B. The City of Canton established a Development Impact Fee Advisory Committee pursuant to the Georgia Development Impact Fee Act, Georgia Code Title 36-71-5, and that Committee has served in an advisory capacity and assisted and advised the City of Canton with regard to the development and adoption of this development impact fee ordinance.

C. The City of Canton Comprehensive Plan contains within it Land Use Assumptions, a Road Capital Improvement Element, and the establishment of a level of Service for Road Capital Facilities for the planning horizon to 2015; and the City of Canton Comprehensive Plan has been submitted to the Atlanta Regional Commission and certified by that commission so as to qualify the City of Canton as a "Qualified Local Government" pursuant to the State of Georgia Planning Act of 1989.

D. The City of Canton must expand its road system in order to maintain current road standards if new development is to be accommodated without decreasing current standards. This must be done in order to promote and protect the health, safety, morals, convenience, order, prosperity, and the general welfare of the City of Canton, Georgia;

E. The imposition of development impact fees is a preferred method of ensuring the availability of capital facilities necessary to accommodate new development;

F. Each of the types of land development described in Section Seven hereof, will create demand for the acquisition or expansion of roads and the construction of road improvements.

G. The fees established by Section Seven are derived from, are based upon, and do not exceed a proportionate share of the costs of providing additional roads and road improvements necessitated by the new land developments on which the fees are levied.

H. The report entitled "The City of Canton, Georgia, Road Impact Fees," dated _____, sets forth a reasonable methodology and analysis for the determination of the development impact of new development on the need for and costs for additional roads and road improvements in the City of Canton.

I. The report entitled "The City of Canton, Georgia, Impact Fee Service Areas," dated _____ sets forth a reasonable basis for the establishment of service areas for road facilities for the City of Canton.

Section Two: Short Title, Authority and Applicability

A. This ordinance shall be known and may be cited as the "The City of Canton Road Development Impact Fee Ordinance."

B. This ordinance shall apply throughout the incorporated area of the City of Canton.

Section Three: Intents and Purposes

A. This ordinance is intended to assist in the implementation of the City of Canton Comprehensive Plan.

B. The purpose of this ordinance is to regulate the use and development of land so as to assure that new development bears a proportionate share of the cost of capital expenditures necessary to provide roads and road improvements in the City of Canton.

C. This ordinance is intended to comply fully with each and every relevant provision of the Georgia Development Impact Fee Act, Georgia Code Title 36-71-1 through 36-71-13, and shall be interpreted and implemented to so comply.

Section Four: Rules of Construction

A. The provisions of this ordinance shall be liberally construed so as to effectively carry out its purpose to promote and protect the health, safety, morals, convenience, order, prosperity, and the general welfare of the City of Canton, Georgia;

B. For the purposes of administration and enforcement of this ordinance, unless otherwise stated in this ordinance, the following rules of construction shall apply to the text of this ordinance:

1. In case of any difference of meaning or implication between the text of this ordinance and any caption, illustration, summary table, or illustrative table, the text shall control.

2. The word "shall" is always mandatory and not discretionary; the word "may" is permissive.

3. Words used in the present tense shall include the future; and words used in the singular number shall include the plural, and the plural the singular, unless the context clearly indicates the contrary.

4. The phrase "used for" includes "arranged for," "designed for," "maintained for," or "occupied for."

5. The word "person" includes an individual, a corporation, a partnership, an incorporated association, or any other similar entity.

6. Unless the context clearly indicates the contrary, where a regulation involves two (2) or more items, conditions, provisions, or events connected by the conjunction "and," "or," or "either … or," the conjunction shall be interpreted as follows:

a. "And" indicates that all the connected terms, conditions, provisions or events shall apply.

b. "Or" indicates that the connected items, conditions, provisions or events may apply singly or in any combination.

c. "Either … or" indicates that the connected items, conditions, provisions or events shall apply singly but not in combination.

7. The word "includes" shall not limit a term to the specific example but is intended to extend its meaning to all other instances or circumstances of like kind or character.

8. "Impact Fee Administrator" means the municipal official designated by the Mayor to carry out the administration of this ordinance.

Section Five: Definitions

A. "Applicant" is a person applying for the issuance of a building permit.

B. "Building permit" is the approval issued by the City of Canton that authorizes the construction or permanent placement of a building, dwelling or other structure on a site.

C. "Capital equipment" is buildings and other improvements which increase the service capacity of a public facility all with an expected use life of ten years or more.

D. "Capital improvement" includes planning, land acquisition, site improvements, and capital equipment, but excludes maintenance and operation.

E. "Developer" means any person or legal entity undertaking development.

F. "Development" means any construction or expansion of a building, structure, or use, any change in use of a building or structure, or any change in the use of land, any of which creates additional demand and need for roads and road facilities.

G. "Development approval" means any written authorization from the City of Canton which authorizes the commencement of construction.

H. "Development impact fee" means a payment of money imposed upon development as a condition of development approval to pay for a proportionate share of the cost of road system improvements needed to serve new growth and development.

I. "Encumber" means to legally obligate by contract or otherwise commit to use by appropriation or other official act of the City of Canton.

J. "Feepayor" means a person who pays a development impact fee or his/her successor in interest. In the absence of any express transfer or assignment of the right or entitlement to any refund of previously paid development impact fees, the right or entitlement shall be deemed "not to run with the land."

K. "Floor area" shall have the same meaning as in the Building Code of the City of Canton.

L. "Living area" shall have the same meaning as in the Building Code of the City of Canton.

M. "Present value" means the current value of past, present, or future payments, contributions or dedications of goods, services, materials, construction, or money.

N. "Project" means a particular development on an identified parcel of land.

O. "Project improvements" means site improvements and facilities that are planned and designed to provide service for a particular development project and that are necessary for the use and convenience of the occupants or users of the project and are not system improvements. The character of the improvement shall control a determination of whether an improvement is a project improvement or system improvement, and the physical location of the improvement on-site or off-site shall not be considered determinative of whether an improvement is a project improvement or a system improvement. If an improvement or facility provides or will provide more than incidental service or facilities capacity to persons other than users or occupants of a particular project, the improvement or facility is a system improvement and shall not be considered a project improvement. No improvement or facility included in a plan for public facilities approved by the governing body of the municipality or county shall be considered a project improvement.

P. "Proportionate share" means that portion of the cost of system improvements which is reasonably related to the service demands and needs of the project.

Q. "Roads and road facilities" may include roads, streets, and bridges, including rights of way, traffic signals, landscaping, and any local components of state or federal highways; as provided in Georgia Development Impact Fee Act, Georgia Code Title 36-71-2(16)(C)

R. "Service area" means a geographic area defined by the City of Canton in which a defined set of public facilities provide service to development within the area. Service areas shall be designated on the basis of sound planning or engineering principles or both.

S. "System improvement costs" means cost incurred to provide additional public facilities capacity needed to serve growth and development for planning, design and construction, land acquisition, land improvement, design and engineering related thereto, including the cost of constructing or reconstructing system improvements or facility expansions, including but not limited to the construction contract price, surveying and engineering fees, related land acquisition costs (including land purchases, court awards and costs, attorneys' fees, and expert witness fees), and expenses incurred for qualified staff or any qualified engineer, planner, architect, landscape architect, or financial consultant for preparing or updating the capital improvement element, and administrative costs, provided that such administrative costs shall not exceed 3 percent of the total amount of development impact fee receipts. Projected interest charges and other finance costs may be included if the development impact fees are to be used for the payment of principal and interest on bonds, notes, or other financial obligations issued by or on behalf of the municipality or county to finance the capital improvements element but such costs do not include routine and periodic maintenance expenditures, personnel training, and other operating costs.

T. "System improvements" means capital improvements that are public facilities and are designed to provide service to the community at large, in contrast to "project improvements."

Section Six: Imposition of Road Development Impact Fee

A. Any person who, after the effective date of this ordinance, seeks to develop land within the City of Canton, Georgia, by applying for a building permit is hereby required to pay a road development impact fee in the manner and amount set forth in this ordinance.

B. No building permit for any activity requiring payment of a development impact fee pursuant to Section Seven of this ordinance shall be issued unless and until the road development impact fee hereby required has been paid.

Section Seven: Computation of the Amount of Road Development Impact Fee

A. At the option of the applicant, the amount of the road development impact fee may be determined by the following fee schedule.

Insert fee schedule about here

The fees set forth above include a 3 percent charge for administrative expenses.

1. If a building permit is requested for mixed uses, then the fee shall be determined through using the above schedule by apportioning the space committed to uses specified on the schedule.

2. If the type of development activity that a building permit is applied for is not specified on the above fee schedule, the Impact Fee Administrator shall use the fee applicable to the most nearly comparable type of land use on the above fee schedules. The Impact Fee Administrator shall be guided in the selection of a comparable type by the City of Canton Comprehensive Plan, supporting documents of the City of Canton

Comprehensive Plan, and the City of Canton Zoning Ordinance. If the Impact Fee Administrator determines that there is no comparable type of land use on the above fee schedule then the Impact Fee Administrator shall determine the appropriate fee by considering demographic or other documentation which is available from state, local and regional authorities.

3. In the case of change of use, redevelopment, or expansion or modification of an existing use which requires the issuance of a building permit, the development impact fee shall be based upon the net positive increase in the development impact fee for the new use as compared to the previous use. The Impact Fee Administrator shall be guided in this determination by the sources listed in (2) above.

B. If an applicant opts not to have the development impact fee determined according to Paragraph (A) of this section, then the applicant shall prepare and submit to the Impact Fee Administrator an independent fee calculation study for the land development activity for which a building permit is sought. The documentation submitted shall show the basis upon which the independent fee calculation was made. The Impact Fee Administrator shall consider the documentation submitted by the applicant but is not required to accept such documentation as he/she shall reasonably deem to be inaccurate or not reliable and may, in the alternative, require the applicant to submit additional or different documentation for consideration. If an acceptable independent fee calculation study is not presented, the applicant shall pay road development impact fees based upon the schedule shown in Paragraph (A) of this section. If an acceptable independent fee calculation study is presented, the Impact Fee Administrator may adjust the fee to that appropriate to the particular development. Determinations made by the Impact Fee Administrator pursuant to this paragraph may be appealed to the City Council by filing a written request with the city manager within ten (10) days of the Impact Fee Administrator's determination.

C. On the request of an applicant, the Impact Fee Administrator shall certify the road development impact fee schedule or road development impact fees resulting from an individual assessment, whichever is applicable, and said certification shall establish the applicable development impact fee for a period of 180 days from the date thereof.

Section Eight: Payment of Fee

A. The applicant shall pay the road development impact fee required by this ordinance to the Impact Fee Administrator or his/her designee prior to the issuance of a building permit.

B. All funds collected shall be properly identified by Road Development Impact Fee Service Area and promptly transferred for deposit in the appropriate Road Development Impact Fee Trust Fund to be held in separate accounts as determined in Section Ten of this ordinance and used solely for the purposes specified in this ordinance.

Section Nine: Road Development Impact Fee Service Areas

There are hereby established one (1) Road Development Impact Fee Service Areas; which shall cover the entire incorporated area of the City of Canton.

Section Ten: Road Development Impact Fee Trust Funds Established

A. There is hereby established one (1) Road Development Impact Fee Trust Fund for the Road Development Impact Fee Service Area established by Section Nine of this ordinance.

B. Development Impacts fees placed in this fund shall be maintained in an interest-bearing account.

C. All road development impact fees collected shall be promptly deposited in the Road Development Impact Fee Trust Fund and maintained there, including interest thereon, until withdrawn pursuant to this ordinance.

D. Funds withdrawn from these accounts must be used in accordance with the provisions of Section Eleven of this ordinance.

Section Eleven: Use of Funds

A. Funds collected from road development impact fees shall be used solely for the purpose of acquiring and/or making capital improvements to roads under the jurisdiction of the City of Canton, Cherokee County, or the State of Georgia, and shall not be used for maintenance or operations.

B. Funds shall be used exclusively for acquisitions, expansions, or capital improvements within the Road Development Impact Fee Service Area from which the funds were collected.

C. In the event that bonds or similar debt instruments are issued for advanced provision of capital facilities for which road development impact fees may be expended, development impact fees may be used to pay debt service on such bonds or similar debt

instruments to the extent that the facilities provided are of the type described in Paragraphs (A) and (B).

D. In the event a developer enters into an agreement with the city to construct, fund, or contribute system improvements such that the amount of the credit created by such construction, funding or contribution is in excess of the development impact fee otherwise due, the developer shall be reimbursed for such excess construction funding or contribution from development impact fees paid by other development located in the service area which is benefited by such improvements.

E. At least once each fiscal period the Impact Fee Administrator shall present to the City Council a report describing the amount of development impact fees collected, encumbered and used, and a proposed capital improvement program for roads, assigning funds, including any accrued interest, from the several Road Development Impact Fee Trust Funds to specific road improvement projects and related expenses. Monies, including any accrued interest, not assigned in any fiscal period shall be retained in the same Road Development Impact Fee Trust Funds until the next fiscal period except as provided by the refund provisions of this ordinance.

F. Funds may be used to provide refunds as described in Section Twelve.

G. Funds shall be considered expended on a first in, first out basis.

Section Twelve: Refund of Fees Paid

A. If a building permit expires without commencement of construction, and then the feepayor shall be entitled to a refund, without interest, of the development impact fee paid as a condition for its issuance except that the city shall retain 3 percent of the fee to offset a portion of the costs of collection and refund. The feepayor must submit an application for such a refund to the Impact Fee Administrator within 30 days of the expiration of the permit.

B. In the event that development impact fees have not been expended or encumbered by the end of the calendar quarter immediately following six (6) years from the date the development impact fee was paid, the Impact Fee Administrator shall provide written notice of entitlement to a refund to feepayors or their successors in interest.

Funds not expended or encumbered by the end of the calendar quarter immediately following six (6) years from the date road development impact fee was paid shall, upon application of the then-current landowner, they must be returned to such feepayor with interest that is a pro-rata share of the interest earned by the fund, provided that the feepayor submits an application for the refund to the Impact Fee Administrator within one year of the expiration of the six-year period or the publication of the notice of entitlement, whichever is later. Refunds shall be made to the feepayor within 60 days after it is determined that a sufficient proof of claim for a refund has been made.

Section Thirteen: Exemptions and Credits
A. The following shall be exempted from payment of the development impact fee:
1. Alterations or expansion of an existing building where the use and size are not changed.
2. The construction of accessory buildings or structures.

3. The replacement of a building or structure with a new building or structure of the same size and use.

Any claim of exemption must be made no later than the time of application for a building permit. Any claim not so made shall be deemed waived.

B. Credits
1. Road land and/or capital improvements may be offered by the applicant as total or partial payment of the required development impact fee. The applicant must request a road development impact fee credit. If the Impact Fee Administrator accepts such an offer the credit shall be determined and provided in the following manner:
a. Credit for the dedication of land shall be valued at:
i. 115 percent of the most recent assessed value by the Property Appraiser, or
ii. By fair market value established by private appraisers acceptable to the city. Credit for the dedication of road land shall be provided when the property has been conveyed at no charge to, and accepted by, the city in a manner satisfactory to the Impact Fee Administrator.
b. Applicants for credit for the construction of road improvements shall submit acceptable engineering drawings and specifications, and construction cost estimates to the Impact Fee Administrator. The Impact Fee Administrator shall determine credit for construction based upon either these cost estimates or upon alternative engineering criteria and construction cost estimates if the Impact Fee Administrator determines

that such estimates submitted by the applicant are either unreliable or inaccurate. The Impact Fee Administrator shall provide the applicant with a letter or certificate setting forth the dollar amount of the credit, the reason for the credit, and the legal description or other adequate description of the project or development to which the credit may be applied. The applicant must sign and date a duplicate copy of such letter or certificate indicating his/her agreement to the terms of the letter or certificate and return such signed document to the Impact Fee Administrator before credit will be given. The failure of the applicant to sign, date, and return such document within 60 days shall nullify the credit.

c. Except as provided in Subparagraph (d), Credit against development impact fees otherwise due will not be provided until:

i. The construction is completed and accepted by the City, the County, or the State, whichever is applicable; and

ii. A suitable maintenance and warranty bond is received and approved by the Impact Fee Administrator, when applicable.

d. Credit may be provided before completion of specified road improvements if adequate assurances are given by the applicant that the standards set out above will be met and if the applicant posts security as provided below for the costs of such construction. Security in the form of a performance bond, irrevocable letter of credit or escrow agreement shall be posted with and approved by the Impact Fee Administrator in an amount determined by the Impact Fee Administrator. If the road construction project will not be completed within one (1) year of the acceptance of the offer by the Impact Fee Administrator, the amount of the security shall be increased by 10 percent compounded, for each year of the life of the security.

e. The road facility for which credit is sought is consistent with the Road Element of the City of Canton's Comprehensive Plan, and

f. The request complies with the security provisions set forth in (B)(1)(c) of this section.

2. Any claim for credit must be made no later than the time of application for a building permit. Any claim not so made shall be deemed waived.

3. Credits shall not be transferable from one project or development to another unless so provided in a development impact fee credit agreement.

Section Fourteen: Appeals

A. Any Applicant or Feepayor aggrieved by a decision of the Impact Fee Administrator made pursuant to this ordinance shall have the right to appeal to the Mayor and City Council. Prior to any such appeal the aggrieved Applicant or Feepayor shall file a request for reconsideration with the Impact Fee Administrator, who shall act upon such request within 15 days.

B. All appeals shall be taken within 15 days of the Impact Fee Administrator's decision on the request for reconsideration by filing with the Impact Fee Administrator a notice of appeal specifying the grounds therefore. The Impact Fee

Administrator shall forthwith transmit to the Mayor and City Council all papers constituting the record upon which the action appealed from is taken. The Mayor and City Council shall thereafter establish a reasonable date and time for a hearing on the appeal, give due notice thereof, and decide the same within a reasonable period of time following the hearing. Any Applicant or Feepayor taking an appeal shall have the right to appear at the hearing, to present evidence and may be represented by counsel.

C. An Applicant may pay a Road Development Impact Fee under protest to obtain a building permit and by making such payment shall not be estopped from;

1. Exercising the right of appeal provided for in this section or
2. Receiving a refund of any amount deemed to have been illegally collected.

Section Fifteen: Review and Automatic Update of Fee Schedule

A. The fee schedule contained in Section Seven (A) shall be reviewed by the City Council at least once each fiscal biennium.

B. Unless otherwise directed by the City Council, the impact fee schedules shown in Section Seven A above shall be adjusted by the Impact Fee Administrator in May of each calendar year based on the methodology described in Paragraph (C) of this section. Any adjustments to the impact fee schedules, made pursuant to this section, shall be effective the following first day of October.

C. The base for computing any adjustment is the January Highway And Street Construction Cost Index published by the United States Department of Commerce, Bureau of Labor Statistics, Series Identification # PCVBHWY. The percentage change in the impact fee shall be equal to the percentage change in the Highway and Street Construction Cost Index from the base year to the current year. For the purpose of this section the initial index to be referenced is January of the last year, when the impact fees were updated with cost or demographic data.

D. If the index is changed so that the base year is different, the index shall be converted in accordance with the conversion factor published by the United States Department of Labor, Bureau of Labor Statistics. If the Highway and Street Construction Cost Index is discontinued or revised, the Construction Cost Index published by McGraw-Hill or such other index or computation with which it is replaced shall be used in order to obtain substantially the same result as would be obtained if the Highway and Street Construction Cost Index had not been discontinued or revised."

Section Sixteen: Penalty Provision

A violation of this ordinance shall be prosecuted in the same manner as misdemeanors are prosecuted, and upon conviction the violator shall be punishable according to law; however, in addition to or in lieu of any criminal prosecution the City of Canton shall have the power to sue in civil court to enforce the provisions of this ordinance.

Section Seventeen: Severability

If any section, phrase, sentence or portion of this ordinance is for any reason held invalid or unconstitutional by any court of competent jurisdiction, such portion shall be deemed a separate, distinct and independent provision, and such holding shall not affect the validity of the remaining portions thereof.

Section Eighteen: Repealer

Any ordinances covering the subject matter contained in this ordinance are hereby repealed and all ordinances or parts of ordinances inconsistent with the provisions of this ordinance are hereby repealed.

Section Nineteen: Effective Date

This Ordinance shall take effect from and after the _____ day of _____, 20__.

9 A WORD ABOUT INDEPENDENT STUDIES, EXEMPTIONS, AND WAIVERS

Impact-fee programs are implemented through ordinances and usually administrative codes, the key elements of which were introduced in Chapter 2. Models for each are also provided in Chapter 8 as well as in Nelson, Nicholas, and Juergensmeyer (2009). However, not every land use is included in a fee schedule, and not every development activity creates a new impact. Additionally, sometimes local decision-makers decide that not every development should be required to pay impact fees to achieve other policies. This chapter addresses issues related to independent studies, exemptions, and waivers. We conclude with a call for transparency.

9.1 INDEPENDENT STUDY

No impact fee schedule can anticipate all of the various land uses nor the prospective impacts of all developments. Individuals, usually developers, need an opportunity to make the case that their development does not generate the impacts assumed by a fee schedule. This is necessary to preserve due process (see Chapter 2). It is for this reason that feepayors should be extended the opportunity to conduct an independent analysis of their impacts and argue for a different—typically lower—impact fee. We say lower because there is usually no incentive for new developers to argue for higher impact fees, although that could happen if a developer anticipates large amounts of credits based on in-kind contributions, such as providing facilities included in the capital improvements plan that form the basis for impact fees.

Allowing for independent calculations is required in several states' impact fee legislation as well as being best professional practice. Georgia's statutory provision is representative:

A municipal or county development impact fee ordinance shall include a provision permitting individual assessments of development impact fees at the option of applicants for development approval under guidelines established in the ordinance.
(O.C.G.A. § 36-71-4.(g))

Although procedures vary, several features are common among community policies. First of all, feepayers are given the option of paying the scheduled fee or electing to provide an individualized study. If the option of the individualized study is chosen, it needs to be based on a credible analysis using acceptable sources of engineering or planning data, or based on actual, localized information, or other information that the impact fee administration considers acceptable. Usually, these studies need to be conducted by engineering, planning, or other relevant professionals. As these studies can be expensive, the feepayer will need to be sure that reduced fees more than offset the costs of processing the request. The impact fee administrator then needs a certain amount of time to evaluate the study and accept, reject, or conditionally accept the study.

In some cases, the independent analysis may take time to prepare and present, and more time for the community to evaluate and respond. If the developer wishes to proceed before a decision is made, fee payments based on the existing schedule may be paid conditionally until the issues are resolved. The community may also need to conduct its own independent analysis to verify or contradict the analysis submitted.

DOI: 10.4324/9781003336075-11

It can also be that the same issues arise in similar projects. For instance, a community may have just one impact fee for all residential units that could stimulate independent studies from builders of multi-family units. Approval of a reduced impact fee for one type of project may become the basis for all other similar projects to request similar relief. The administrator may have the authority to offer blanket alternative fees for all similar projects, rather than having such issues going to the governing body. The community should consider amending its impact fee ordinance to reflect this policy.

Although one assumes that independent fee studies would be taken seriously by local government, it is our experience that sometimes they are not, at least in our opinion. Two examples come to mind, although we have experience with many more.

In the first, a townhouse development with attached homes on 2,000 square feet lots was assessed for outdoor ("secondary") water impact fees based on 10,000 square foot lots under the assumption that all residential units are on lots of 10,000 square feet, and thus have the same impact on secondary water demand. Moreover, the local government had other policies encouraging reductions in water use, including outdoor irrigation, but they were not linked to impact fees. On appeal, the court sided with the local government in part because the impact fee policy was legislative in nature. (One may wonder why the city even needed an independent study procedure except to comply with the statute.)

In the second, an age-restricted community was charged park impact fees based on the occupancy of the average single-family detached home, which was about twice that of the age-restricted units. Although the applicant used census data and other analyses to show that the impact on parks would be about half that assumed in the impact fee ordinance, the city rejected the independent fee calculation and imposed the full fee. The developer decided not to appeal since legal counsel advised the issue was mostly legislative in nature, and the odds of success would be small.

In some cases, developers have requested impact fee adjustments *after* projects were approved. In such cases local officials argued in part that the developers either knew about the impact fees and did not raise the impact fee issue during the development approval process ("raise it or lose it") or did not disclose fully their project's impact on community infrastructure thereby leading decision-makers to assume impacts would be comparable to other projects. But in other cases, impact fees were implemented after development approval, arguably an attempt to recover from the development that which was not conditioned during the approval process. This leads to the observation that developers may consider including in their development entitlements the parameters around which existing or prospective impact fees would be assessed.

This brings us to an issue raised in Chapter 2. Recall that courts give considerable deference to legislative actions even though in recent years they have also created the *Dolan* two-pronged rough proportionality standard for mitigation as part of discretionary or administrative approvals. In review, the local government must make an individualized determination that the required mitigation is related both in nature and extent to the proposed development's impact. This determination could be made by accepting the independent study submitted by the developer or by some alternative analysis prepared or commissioned by the jurisdiction.

There may be a middle ground through the independent fee calculation process. The key conceptual issue is that once an independent fee calculation proceeding is commenced, the application of legislative actions to a particular development makes the decision administrative and not legislative. After all, the *Dolan* litigation was triggered when otherwise legislative decisions became administrative through the application to specific developments. Let us explore how this approach works.

When legislatively adopted, impact fees are based often on a broad average of a class of land uses for all similar developments. When applied to a particular project, the impact fee becomes an administrative matter. Experience has shown that most developments fall within the parameters of the enacted impact fee. It is only when a particular development falls outside the parameters comprising the impact fee schedule (and the analysis behind it) that the independent fee calculation process would be triggered. The resulting process is administrative in nature and would be expected to fall within the scope of the *Dolan* decision.

We now move on to issues related to exemptions and waivers.

9.2 EXEMPTIONS AND WAIVERS

We turn now to the issues of exemptions and waivers. There is confusion between exemptions and waivers even in state legislation. Notwithstanding statutes and the approaches used in individual communities, we differentiate these concepts as follows:

Exemptions occur when a development, typically a change in land use, *does not create* any new impact. It would follow that if there were no (new) impact, there would be no impact fee due.

Waivers occur when a new development might *create an impact* and would thus be subject to impact fees, but all or part of those fees are waived based on local policy. In some states and jurisdictions, it is required that funds that would mitigate the impact are identified.

We address exemptions first and then waivers.

9.2.1 *Exemptions*

The following are examples of developments where no impact occurs and exemptions would seem to be in order (see Chapter 8 for further discussion):

- Alterations or expansion of an existing building or buildings where no additional units of impact are created, where the use is not changed, and otherwise where there is no additional activity over and above those produced by the existing use.
- The construction of accessory buildings or structures that will not produce additional impacts over and above those produced by the principal building or use of the land.
- The replacement of a destroyed or partially destroyed building or structure with a new building or structure of the same size and use.

The test here is whether the development activity creates new impacts on infrastructure. Communities can be creative with the exemption concept, however, within the limits of state legislation combined with meeting the no-new-impact test noted above. Consider these examples.

To encourage rehabilitation of existing structures and promote redevelopment, some communities may wish to give blanket exemptions if there is no net new space created, or if the resulting uses would arguably be no more intensive than prior uses. Although there is a certain appeal to this for planners, public officials, and especially owners of affected properties, caution is recommended. Suppose older buildings have been vacant for many years while the service area within which they are located has continued to grow. The rehabilitation of these structures could indeed adversely impact infrastructure if there is little or no capacity remaining, given the adopted LOS standards. To help guard against this, some communities limit the rehabilitation/redevelopment exemption to properties that have been vacant for no more than five years, or so, and further limit the exemption to the pre-rehabilitation/redevelopment scale. In the case of residential rehabilitation or redevelopment, residential impact fees based on the number of units would allow the expansion of residences without the need to pay an impact fee as long as no additional dwelling units are created.

There can be interesting nuances to this approach. Consider accessory dwelling units (ADUs) created within the footprint of an existing home. No new area in terms of square feet is added. The community may decide as a matter of policy that ADUs within the footprint of an existing primary unit are considered part of that unit and as such there is no new impact. This may work only where impact fees are assessed on a square foot basis and where the ADU does not add any more space. However, if the impact fee is based on the unit and not size, the ADU is clearly a new unit, so an impact fee may need to be assessed accordingly. Given the rising popularity of ADUs, it may be best for impact fee studies and ordinances to address them specifically in both nexus analysis and fee schedules. Another option is to define "unit" as including any accessory unit provided that the accessory unit does not exceed some magnitude, such as 800 square feet.

We turn next to the thornier issue of waivers.

9.2.2 Waivers

Waivers are different because they involve reducing or eliminating impact fees on new development that would otherwise be assessed. Legislation in many states allows waivers for affordable housing and economic development, but some states also require waived funds to be replaced from sources other than impact fees.

Waivers can be fraught with problems. Consider waivers of impact fees to promote housing affordability. Defining what affordable housing is to be eligible for such waivers can become a thorny political issue, as there will be units just outside of the defined range

of affordability. This can be addressed by a sliding scale of waiver or assistance.

Once waived, how is the impact due from those developments mitigated? After all, if replacement funds are not generated, infrastructure may not be built on time or even built at all, thereby undermining the impact fee nexus. Sources of funds for waivers can include local government affordable housing and economic development funds, Community Development Block Grants, and other federal funds, where allowed, private foundations, and other groups, and, of course, general funds. Several communities in Florida charge impact fees on affordable housing but defer payment for as long as the home meets in intended affordable housing purpose, but then payment is due when its status changes. Chapter 23 reviews some of the innovative ways that Florida communities waive impact fees on affordable housing. Variations of these techniques are used throughout the US.

With respect to economic development in jurisdictions requiring the replacement of waived impact fees, it would seem possible for a community to estimate new revenues generated by such development net of public service and infrastructure needs and use a portion of those net new revenues to retire deferred impact fees. These net new revenues could be put into an account dedicated to waiving such fees. The option always exists to fund waivers from any other revenue source, including the general fund.

9.3 TRANSPARENCY

We end this chapter by noting that from legal, political, and simply public relations perspectives, impact fee programs need to be transparent. One way this is done is through a visible impact fee deliberation process, often assisted by a formal advisory committee. There are other ways that impact fee programs can be transparent. We are guided by insights from the Terner Center (Raetz et al. 2019) in this respect.

Above all, impact fee studies and supporting documentation must be easily available to the public. All too often, citizens, landowners, investors, developers, analysts, and even students need to sift through local government public records or even submit a freedom of information act (FOIA) request to access the studies, sometimes even paying a fee! Communities must clearly post these studies on their websites.

Sometimes impact fee and other development fee schedules are difficult to find and confusing to use by those who will pay them. If an online calculation tool is not available, staff should provide estimates as well as guidance on how to calculate development fees due. In all too many communities, it takes a visit, often with a staff appointment, to estimate the cost of development fees during the due diligence stage of development. Current fee schedules with clear instructions for calculating fees improve transparency for developers, citizens, and even local government officials themselves. Developers especially need this information in a timely fashion, not only because they will pay the fees but they need to negotiate purchase prices with landowners and suppliers that reflect such costs as impact fees. Knowing the amount of fees, including impact fees, that would be assessed and due at the time of development approval is important for developers, bearing in mind that fee schedules can and do change, often annually.

Whether required by state legislation or not, communities should make annual fee reports easily available to the public. These reports need to show the fee schedules, revenues received, specific projects funded by the fees, and other expenditures such as bond or debt payments, administrative costs, and so forth. These reports should be easily available online. All too often, this information is simply not available and even if required by state law are not accessible, sometimes requiring a FOIA request as well as for a fee once granted. In our view, such a lack of transparency needlessly engenders distrust in local government.

REFERENCES

Nelson, A. C., Nicholas, J. C., & Juergensmeyer, J. C. (2009). *Impact Fees: Principles and Practice of Proportionate-Share Development Fees.* Chicago: American Planning Association.

Raetz, H., Garcia, D., Decker, N., Kneebone, E., Reid, C., & Galante, C. (2019). *Residential Impact Fees in California: Current Practices and Policy Considerations to Improve Implementation of Fees Governed by the Mitigation Fee Act.* Berkeley: Terner Center, University of California at Berkeley.

PART 3
Efficiency, Ethical, and Equity Concerns with Policy Options and International Perspectives

Perhaps no method of public facility financing elicits more debate than impact fees. We devote Part 3 to exploring several perspectives that frame the debate. We begin with Chapter 10, "Evaluation of Impact Fees Against Public Finance Criteria," in which Douglass B. Lee assesses impact fees in the context of public finance theory, finding they are mostly a second-best solution compared to general taxes for public safety, education, and parks and recreation although sound choices for water-related and electrical utilities, and transportation. But if the best alternatives are not available such as higher taxes, second best is better than nothing at all.

Chapter 11, "Impacts of Proportionate-Share Development Fees," by Gregory Burge and Trey Dronyk-Trosper, puts some of these concerns into context by showing that outcomes to impact fees can be more efficient and lead to fewer ethical outcomes than one may presuppose otherwise. For instance, impact fees appear to improve economic development outcomes compared to the alternative of less money available for roads, water, sewer and amenities—the very community investments that attract firms to them. They also help expand the supply of multifamily housing perhaps by undermining NIMBY (not-in-my-backyard) opposition that apartments "don't pay their way" because, with impact fees, they do. Impact fees can also steer new development to areas where excess facility capacity exists, thereby leading to more efficient development patterns.

Chapter 12, "Toward a Supply-Side Theory of Development Impact Mitigation," explores the economic implications further by suggesting that when impact fees are truly proportionate to impact based on the size and location of housing, they can actually increase the supply of housing and improve housing affordability. We acknowledge that this is a novel theoretical approach that invites empirical testing and theoretical refinement.

We then explore the role of impact fees in advancing good planning that leads to more benefits than costs, as well as the role of impact fees in capturing part of the value public infrastructure investments make. This is done in Chapter 13, "Good Planning, Value-Added Planning, and Value Capture."

Timothy Beatley raises numerous ethical dilemmas in Chapter 14, "Ethical Issues in the Use of Impact Fees to Finance Community Growth," as when communities decide to shift paying for publicly provided facilities from general taxes paid by all taxpayers to special fees charged on just newcomers. Some of those dilemmas include creating us-vs.-them ("we have ours, so why do we pay for theirs?"), inter-generational (decisions today often foreclose future options), representation (newcomers do not have a say in deciding how facilities are financed), and club membership (only those

DOI: 10.4324/9781003336075-12

who can afford to pay our fees can join our community) outcomes, among many others.

Mary Kay Peck Delk and Susan A. Wood go further in Chapter 15, "The Ethics of Impact Fee Equity," by suggesting circumstances where impact fees may not advance professional planning ethics and how perhaps modest changes in practice can have a large effect on impact fee equity.

Chapter 15 is followed by a Coda that includes Delk and Wood as co-authors with us. It does three things. First, it presents nine principles that establish a core of professional standards of practice that apply an equity lens to the calculation of proportionate share impact fees. We anticipate that principles will be refined and more added over time. Second, it presents a method to calculate impact fees for residential dwelling units on the basis of size regardless of type. This may be the very best way in which to calculate truly proportionate share impact

fees for residential development that help advance social equity as well as housing affordability. The third contribution of the Coda is a detailed checklist of impact fee decision making items that incorporates the equity lens in impact fee design and implementation.

We continue with Chapter 16, "The Option of Impact Fees," which frames the decision process leading to the selection of impact fees over alternative financing approaches.

This part of the book finishes with Chapter 17, "Impact Fees in an International Context: Comparisons and Similar Fiscal Tools," by David Amborski. It offers international perspectives on the role of development charges to facilitate development in a wide range of government structures and institutional fiscal constraints.

Part 4 follows, exploring many proportionate share impact fee and development mitigation innovations.

10 EVALUATION OF IMPACT FEES AGAINST PUBLIC FINANCE CRITERIA

DOUGLASS B. LEE

The differing perspectives that underly discussions of impact fees are so broad that assumptions are frequently only implicit, and the conclusions offered can be hard to reconcile. The hope here is to provide some abstractions from the field of public economics that will fill the gaps between theories of taxation and urban public services, on the one hand, and the need to justify fees and their application, on the other.

The central question to be addressed in this chapter is the purpose of impact fees. The purposes are broken down into two categories: efficiency and equity. Efficiency concerns the realization of maximum net social (public plus private) benefits from the use of scarce resources, whereas equity is concerned with the fairness of the distribution of costs and benefits. To the extent that fees can serve as a price mechanism, fees can serve to improve efficiency. Pricing can sometimes be applied to public infrastructure and the provision of urban services. Alternatively, if fees are like taxes, the criterion for designing them is fairness and the equal treatment of taxpayers in similar circumstances. Social costs to be considered include low-density sprawl, climate change, social inequities, and transportation externalities. Impact fees may have some value in serving these purposes, but they are limited in critical ways. This structure is shown in Figure 10.1.

10.1 ROLE OF IMPACT FEES IN URBAN DEVELOPMENT

The process of converting land from rural to urban use is simple enough in the abstract but messy in the particulars. Because the land is typically in private ownership while the transformation requires public facilities, the actual timing and location are subject to the whims of particular landowners, developers, and government agencies. Developers find potentially available land and acquire contractors to undertake the construction and then market the results. The land, however, needs to have services such as roads, water, and sewers either available or planned; typically these are not provided much in advance of the land development. Thus, the process goes through a period of gestation before the activities proceed, partly in parallel.

Influencing this process are markets that allow participants to anticipate conditions that will allow them to act. Land, of course, because it has a spatial dimension, is never perfectly substitutable, so these markets are inherently imperfectly competitive. The outcomes may be influenced by monopoly or other market imperfections.

10.1.1 The Dynamics of Urban Expansion

An urban area grows because employment and business opportunities attract workers to the area, and firms recognize the trends and move to serve them. Businesses expand that build housing and support urban services, construction workers see hiring patterns trending upward, landowners see taxes increasing and development taking place, agencies observe permit applications and construction activities indicating land development is intended, and schools and utilities

DOI: 10.4324/9781003336075-13

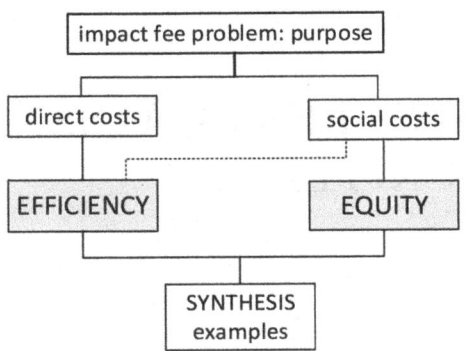

FIGURE 10.1 Economics of impact fee evaluation.

see immigrants arriving and try to provide for them.

Areas in and near the urban fringe can expect new construction in places likely to be developed, and actors make preparations, such as taking options on land, and coordinating with contractors and government agencies. Agencies anticipate the rate of new housing construction and the utilities that will be needed to serve the new housing. Developers talk to landowners about buying/selling land in locations that might be suitable, and about prices and timing. Deals are proposed and encouraged or resisted. Actions are taken to advance some of these activities in a sequence that transforms vacant or farmland into residential or other urban use. These actions occur when parties to a deal arrive at common perceptions about future consequences of these actions, including prices of mutual commitments.

10.1.2 The Price of Housing

The supply of new housing in growing communities has been insufficient to accommodate the increase in population, due to NIMBY (not in my backyard) resistance and other restrictions on development. There is a recent movement to permit ADUs (accessory dwelling units) in areas zoned for single-family housing, but the resistance to increasing

density is strong, and the result is cumulative inflation in the price of housing.

It is possible that impact fees could be used to exacerbate this problem by overcharging for infrastructure that is already covered by other revenue. The rational nexus requirement is intended to prevent such excess charging. Other kinds of regulation, however, still have the effect of suppressing the supply of new housing and increasing its price.

10.1.3 Focus on Off-site Improvements

For infrastructure located on the land being developed, the developer or builder is required to provide the facilities as an in-kind contribution to the stock of public facilities. Where on-site facilities will serve a larger community than the development itself (e.g., a park), the developer may bear only part of the full cost. Off-site facilities, alternatively, are more typically covered by a fee, and the construction is carried out by another entity. On-site infrastructure is thus not the subject of impact fees, but such fees may be applied to off-site requirements.

10.2 BASIC PRINCIPLES

A number of basic ideas are applicable to discussing the idea of impact fees and whether such fees are useful in urban development. These concepts are reviewed briefly further on.

10.2.1 Financing and Funding

The topic of financing public improvements can be broken into two topics: first, where the money comes from, which is funding; and second, the arrangements for matching costs and payments at different points in time, which is financing. Financing involves borrowing, which converts a lump sum into a series of payments over time. When a home is sold, the buyer and seller have agreed upon a price, and the buyer typically commits to a 30-year stream of constant monthly payments. These payments, because of their monthly periodicity, may appear to be similar to a price such as a rental payment, but the mortgage payment is fixed for 30 years, and amounts to a single extended payment. Housing rents, alternatively, can vary depending upon market conditions.

10.2.2 Amortizing Investment

A basic model of infrastructure provision is that a capital improvement is accomplished by an upfront investment that is financed by borrowing, which in turn is recovered by periodic payments over its lifetime. A new renter could start at any time, make payments over the period of use, and thereby pay an appropriate share of the capital costs over the duration of the tenancy. The payments match the depreciation (wearing out) out of the asset. Taxes allow this matching to occur for public assets, so that taxpayers pay for their infrastructure as they use it. The taxpayer buys into this "layaway" plan by purchasing property in the jurisdiction. There is no need to "buy" a stock of capital upon entry into the community and "sell" it when leaving.

10.2.3 The Impact Fee Hypothesis

The idea of an impact fee is that there are some public infrastructure costs of urban fringe development that represent additional costs that have previously been paid for by existing residents, who are now subsidizing the new development. These costs include water and sewer, roads, schools, and perhaps police and fire services. Therefore, new residents should pay a share of the costs previous residents have paid to provide for the accumulation of existing infrastructure.

This concern for unfair economic transfers has some validity, but it depends on the specific circumstances.

10.2.4 Definitions

These terms are in common usage and are familiar in their vernacular form, but they are used here in a technical form that requires more precision in how they are used with respect to public finance. These definitions are intended to be consistent with the usage found in an introductory microeconomics text.

1. Cost: The economic cost of a resource (capital, labor, land) is the opportunity cost of that resource stated in terms of what other things must be foregone in order to obtain the good or service in question. If all resources are "monetized," i.e., their value stated in a common "numeraire," such as dollars, "cost" can be represented as its dollar price, but the principle of the cost being measured in terms of opportunities foregone is important. "Price" is the cost to the consumer, which may or may not be the same as a social cost.

2. Fixed vs. Variable Costs: A resource whose value is not reduced by consuming the output enabled by the resource is a fixed cost with respect to the output. Because an impact fee is a single-time application of a lump sum, it is more likely to be applicable to fixed costs rather than variable, although, to the extent that facilities wear out from usage, that portion of a fixed cost is variable. Also, some operating costs may bear no relationship to usage (grass mowing along the highway), so they are effectively fixed. Because of their means of implementation, impact fees are more likely to be useful for fixed costs. A resource whose value is used up by the consumption of the output is a variable cost, with respect to the market. It is the opposite of a fixed cost. If a fee is expected to serve as a price on a variable cost, it must be able to track with the cost, such as water consumption and traffic.

3. Capital vs. Operating Costs: The purchase of an asset that lasts longer than a year is labeled a "capital" cost as distinct from operating costs. Capital costs are commonly fixed costs in production, but not always; some capital assets are partly variable—such as a street pavement—and can be worn out by usage. An operating cost is purchases of factors of production that have lifetimes of less than a year. In general, operating costs are used up in consumption, and are considered variable costs.

4. Price: The cost of a good or service to the consumer is its price, and may include in-kind costs, such as travel time, and exclude externalities, such as pollution. In an economic market, the function of the price is to reconcile supply and demand. Once producers and consumers agree on a price, exchange can take place. One of the fundamental questions regarding impact fees is whether they can serve as prices. If demand in a market is assumed to be exogenous (autonomously determined), then price is the factor that determines the quantity of the market's output that is taken by consumers. Efficiency in a market is determined by the price, which equilibrates supply and demand.

5. Discounting: Discounting enables the restatement of a resource value at a different point in time than the date at which it is originally stated (e.g., the present value of a bond that pays out $1,000 at a given date in the future). Discounting also allows the value to be projected forward (also known as compounding), and allows lump sum values to be restated as an equivalent stream of payments (annuity), or a stream of payments to be converted into a single sum (capitalization). A popular misconception is that discounting is the reverse of inflation. For purposes of discussion here, inflation is zero, and everything given in dollars or an implied dollar value is stated in constant dollars

of some arbitrary base year. Discounting is still applicable, however, because comparisons across different time periods must account for the opportunity costs of postponing consumption or production. Replacing a sewage treatment plant in 30 years means we don't need to have the revenue right now; hence, the future costs are discounted for current decisions. Future cost and benefit flows (e.g., taxes and schools) could not be capitalized into present worth terms without discounting; otherwise, they would be infinite.

6. Capitalization: The incorporation of a stream of future costs or benefits into the price of an asset, such as a residence, is capitalization. The future stream may be payments (such as property taxes) or benefits (such as property tax savings). An impact fee is normally a lump sum charge, meaning that it occurs once in the lifetime of a dwelling or other building. Other forms of charging are periodic or recurring. If the stream of future charges were known, exactly or even probabilistically, then this stream can be represented as (capitalized into) a single equivalent lump sum. This capitalization depends upon the relative certainty of the amount at the present time (hence, present value); if the future charge depends on a future choice, then the total value of the stream is uncertain, and the stream can only be partially capitalized or not at all. Future property taxes are partly capitalized because the owner can predict the future amount within a reasonable range.

7. Elasticity: Elasticity is the responsiveness of output quantity in a market to a change in price. There are both supply and demand price elasticities, but we will be mostly paying attention to demand price elasticity.

8. Externality: An externality is a defect in an economic market that occurs because either the price paid or the cost accrued is different from the social demand or the

social cost. Most externalities of interest are negative, due to cost exporting (cost not paid by the consumer). Pollution and congestion delay is negative externalities.

9. Related Market: All markets are interrelated in that resources not consumed in one market can be diverted to another. In closely related markets, a change in price in one market shifts the demand curve in the related market. The related market is often a close substitute. A tempting strategy is to compensate for underpricing in one market (say, the highway market) by shifting demand in another (transit market) by offsetting underpricing. The relationship between markets exists, but the effect in the primary market is typically small.

These terms will be used below with these somewhat restricted definitions, although their vernacular meaning is still very similar to their technical meaning.

10.2.5 Prices vs. Taxes

Impact fees act sometimes like user fees, and sometimes like taxes: user fees when the payer is a willing buyer, taxes when a public good is being funded. The question of whether impact fees are prices rather than taxes is partly a technical definition, but is mainly one of intent. Because the purpose of a price is to influence consumer behavior, efficiency is determined by how well the price allocates resources to activities/uses. If all markets are competitive, setting a price equal to the marginal cost of producing the output maximizes efficiency.

When the purpose of taxes is to raise revenues for the government to produce public goods, the criterion for taxation is fairness, admittedly a vague and amorphous standard, but nonetheless one of practical guidance. The effectiveness of taxation is determined by whether the application is non-distorting, meaning whether the tax changes the allocation away from its (market-determined) efficient allocation.

10.2.6 Distinguishing between Equity and Efficiency

Fairness, in turn, has two goals: first, equal treatment of equals (sometimes referred to as horizontal equity), and second reduction in inequality (vertical or distributional equity). Some observers claim that making consumers pay for the costs they create is equitable, which makes a tax look the same as a price, but the distinction remains: is the intent to induce a preferred behavior, or to provide social justice?

If the intent is that residents pay for water and sewer services, then we might look for instruments other than impact fees that would function as appropriate prices. The capital costs of treatment and distribution can be spread out over the lifetimes of the assets, and charged to the resident as the assets depreciate in property taxes. This is amortization.

Impact fees are ambiguous in this regard. If the fees are based, for example, on the number of dwelling units, this would seem to be a price: if the development project cannot cover all its costs, including urban services, from prices paid by willing buyers, then the development will most likely not occur (without subsidy). This is the way prices signal costs in properly functioning markets. Alternatively, if the impact fee is based on the square feet of office space, it is not the intent that users should consume less space, but simply that they pay their fair share of infrastructure costs.

The question of intent is subtle: is it that development should pay its fair share (an equity purpose) or that development should be guided by fees to be better in some way? The latter anticipates that impact fees function as prices to incentivize how much and when. The equity goal implies zero elasticities, and hence no behavior changes; no one is deterred.

10.3 ECONOMIC EFFICIENCY

Given the above overview, the separate topics of efficiency and equity can be expanded into more detail.

The goal of creating the maximum net benefits possible from the resources available is summarized in the term "economic" efficiency. It refers to the total benefits to society (and all its members), minus the total costs of providing the benefits. Efficiency is determined by both production and consumption decisions, which allocate resources to alternative purposes.

Economic efficiency is commonly summarized as the greatest good for the greatest number. Although highly simplified, it at least suggests that efficiency is desirable and very broad. It is sometimes pejoratively labeled "narrow," but conceptually it includes everything (except equity). The criterion for efficiency in a single market assumes that there is a non-zero price elasticity in all markets, and that there are no positive or negative externalities. A question to be addressed here is whether impact fees can improve efficiency in land development (e.g., internalize externalities?), and if so under what conditions? Determining those conditions requires being able to predict the impacts of revenue instruments such as impact fees.

10.3.1 The Price-Equals-Marginal-Cost Criterion

This criterion states that each category of output (each "market") should be expanded until the marginal cost of an additional unit of output (dwelling unit, vehicle mile, gallon of water) equals the marginal benefit. In the diagram shown in Figure 10.2, marginal benefits are represented by the demand curve. This equivalence assumes that all benefit is internalized by the consumer. Society's goal is to produce the right amount of each output, considering that more of one good is less of something else.

Because the area under a marginal curve represents the cumulative value of the output up to that point (e.g., q_1), the area under the demand curve is the total benefit (area ACq_1), and the area under the cost curve is the total cost (BCq_1). The area between the two curves is the net benefit, for the given output (ABC). The area between the curves up to the efficient output ($q1$) is the maximum net benefit; anything less leaves an opportunity for net benefit on the table, and anything more reduces the total. The shaded triangle is the negative net benefits, labeled efficiency loss, and this subtracts

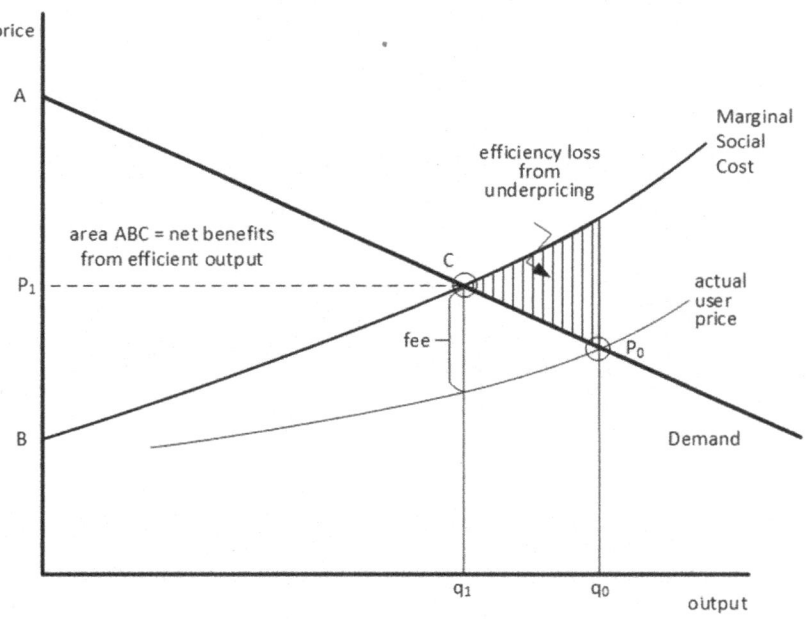

FIGURE 10.2 Optimizing social efficiency.

from total net benefit. The cause, in this example, is underpricing (p_0), which stimulates output (from q_1 to q_0) that is not worth what society has to give up in order to produce it.

If all relevant costs and benefits are internal to producers and consumers making the decisions, then it is possible for competitive markets to tend toward efficiency without further guidance (at price p_1). This has been referred to as the invisible hand. In this example, the market price needs to be augmented by adding an amount equal to the "fee" in order to reach the efficient output. The goal of efficiency is basic; whether it is achieved in actual markets is another matter.

The diagram is generic. If the market is urban land development, the output might be dwelling units, the demand is for homes, price is the purchase price of a home, user cost is the price the buyer would pay, including the developer's price and any other charges in the transaction, and the fee would be impact fees and other charges that are intended to make the buyer's price equal the social marginal cost of producing the dwelling. In this example, the price without the correction is below the marginal cost, but it could be above, depending on the market.

10.3.2 Difficulty of Empirical Estimation

Although we might try to evaluate the efficiency of a given land development market by measuring the prices paid for new housing over a given period of time (representing benefits), and comparing that to cost by measuring all the private and public costs over a comparable time period (allowing for the lag between public investment and sales to willing buyers), the effort would be considerable, and a host of judgmental interpretations would be needed to get even a rough approximation of actual efficiency loss.

In order to address such questions, the effects of each possible factor on price and quantity in each market need to be isolated and quantified, and everything else held constant. An impact implies a difference between one state and another. We don't attempt to actually derive smooth functions such as those shown in Figure 10.2. Instead, we measure increments and small movements along the curves. A question such as "how much of the impact fee was included in sale prices of properties" requires a counterfactual (the basis for comparison) such as "what would the sale price have been if there were no impact fee?" The counterfactual cannot be observed, and knowing what the conditions were *before* some action was taken is not necessarily the same as knowing what they would have been *after* that action *had it not been taken.* What is needed is a "with vs. without" comparison, which is often not answered by a "before vs. after" comparison.

Instead of either whole-scale or incremental analyses, we might simply look for symptoms of inefficiency, such as traffic congestion, sewer moratoria, nuisances like smoke and noise, and evident incompatibilities, that suggest the sorts of market failure that might give rise to such inefficiencies. Typically though, inefficiency seldom manifests itself in such obvious ways.

The most revealing form of analysis may be to focus on the *process* of market decision-making. Do choices seem to acknowledge unit costs/prices, and do the real costs seem to be recognized, or is attention mostly directed at tangential considerations? Because the actual markets do not match the economist's abstraction, are the deviations (distortions, imperfections, failure) close enough to the simplified ideal to identify actual tendencies, or so remote as to be uninformative? Do the possible actions (an impact fee) move the market in the direction of price-equals-marginal-cost, or farther away, or have no relevant effect? If the instrument has no behavioral impact, it does not improve efficiency; if it does shift behavior, it could make it worse (e.g., reduce density).

10.3.3 Imperfect Competition

In the pure microeconomic theory of markets, perfect competition drives the economy toward efficiency. The "pure" theory has no government sector (hence, no public goods), no externalities, no transaction costs, and no monopoly. If any of these "defects" are present, the market is imperfectly competitive. The price may be too high in the market, but the cause may be, for example, either monopoly or insufficient information (a transaction cost). Once imperfect competition is acknowledged, it becomes challenging to predict or explain outcomes, such as whether an impact fee is passed on or not.

10.4 IMPACT FEES AS PRICES

Continuing the focus on efficiency leads to evaluating the opportunities for applying pricing to impact fees. Adjustments to the market price imposed by a government agency are intended to align price to marginal cost. A congestion toll, for example, is an attempt to improve the efficiency of highway operation.

For pricing to be effective, the instrument needs to be aligned with the applicable cost function. A road congestion charge has to apply to each vehicle by time of day, location, and direction of travel, i.e., because the price varies as a result of these factors, the charge must also. An impact fee that is fixed in magnitude and paid only once cannot possibly have an impact on congestion. Even if the fee is equal to the sum of all efficient congestion tolls that would apply to a specific vehicle over a year, the fee will have no effect on congestion unless the bill were itemized for every instance and the amount determined by the vehicle's actual behavior. A lump sum charge can only serve as a price for one transaction at one point in time, although the charge may include downstream effects if known in advance.

Whether the fee has a non-zero price elasticity may sometimes be aided by separating the fee into parts, one of which has a non-zero price elasticity. A water fee might consist of a portion for service within a given zone plus a hookup charge for locations outside the zone. This might encourage some development to be deferred until it can be incorporated into the zone.

Impact fees may potentially alter the efficiency of land development, and also the efficiency of the associated public services. If impact fees function as prices, overcharging new development (intentionally or not) causes too little to occur, while undercharging causes too much. Underinvestment in sewage treatment capacity restricts growth inefficiently, while overcapacity may stimulate unwarranted growth, and waste resources. Low highway user fees encourage sprawl development.

It may sometimes be suitable to consider the price elasticity of location, in that the price effect of a development fee may be to shift the development to another location in the same development, in another development in the same metro area, or to a different city.

10.4.1 Approximation

If demand varies continuously, as in traffic demand at the time of day, price as measured by travel time also varies continuously. A congestion fee that changes in several steps over the peak period is sufficiently accurate to smooth out demand. There may be some distortions that are artifacts of the approximation (e.g., what happens at the price breakpoints), but the approximation is still efficient enough.

On the other hand, if the peak period is treated as part of the daily travel cost and priced as a single lump sum (per day or per year), it is not a valid approximation of congestion. The incentive effect is nil because the amount of peak travel doesn't affect the charge. In fact, there is an elasticity between the peak and the off-peak within a day, and all-day pricing does not utilize that elasticity. Some approximations are not accurate enough to be called prices, with respect to the behavior of interest, namely, peak period travel. An annual charge for peak travel based on historical daily averages is not a peak price; it will have no effect on peak travel, whatever it is called.

10.4.2 Indirect Prices

Because impact fees are one-off lump sum charges, their utility for pricing variable costs of the development (i.e., variable costs rather than fixed) is limited. Traffic, sewage and water consumption, and emissions are variable costs that occur in the future of the development; the control of these impacts offered by the design of a capital facility is small. Direct damage to the environment is controlled in the on-site subdivision design, but off-site damage (storm runoff, emissions) is only weakly controlled or not at all. In general, the more indirect the control, the more tenuous it becomes and the more unsuitable impact fees are as a pricing mechanism.

Charges on fuel consumption, for example, track fairly well with air pollution emissions, although the design of the engine, the climate or weather, and the way the vehicle is operated also have substantial effects on emissions. Taxing fuel is an approximation of an indirect charge for emissions. Charging a tax on fuel is also an indirect charge for vehicle operation, which is affected by location (urban, rural), type of road (street, highway), surface quality (rough, smooth), and driving style (compliant, aggressive) that only roughly approximates public cost for vehicle operation (traffic control, enforcement, administration). The relationship between the price and behavior is too indirect for the charge to serve as a price, but close enough to use for funding as a user tax.

10.4.3 Traffic Impact Fees

A traffic impact fee might be aimed at the additional off-site traffic that would be generated by a development, measured in additional peak lane-miles of road capacity that would leave traffic conditions unchanged (e.g., as in total delay). The fee would be based on the design of the development containing the property(s) on which the fee was levied: if the design reduced auto trip origins or destinations below the default norm, then the fee charged would be lower than the fee for typical development. The baseline fee would assume typical traffic generation patterns. Such fees will still be second-best because the relationship is so indirect.

Improved design might emphasize bicycle access or TOD (transit-oriented design) for commuting or centralized package delivery, but the traffic-reducing alternatives would need to be maintained indefinitely as effective substitutes. The estimates would need to be quantified and tied analytically to the characteristics of the development. Reducing the fee would have to assume that the projected traffic impacts were permanent, at least over the lifetime of the road improvements (e.g., 30 years). Whether the value of this discount would be worth the design features in the land use development is up to the developer. Hence, these features are effectively priced.

10.4.4 Congestion Pricing

Although the theory of MCP (marginal cost pricing) as applied to road pricing is well developed, it is worth reviewing here because its specific features are relevant in evaluating whether impact fees are applicable or not in particular contexts. Figure 10.3 represents the output of a service for which there is a constraining capacity, and variable costs of producing that output are constant until the capacity limitation exerts an effect. For roads, congestion appears in the marginal cost curve as delay, which increases travel time and hence generalized user cost. For other services, such as sewerage and schools, capacity may create congestion-analogous effects, but only roads are suitable for congestion pricing.

Road congestion exhibits the relationship that increasing congestion creates an increasing deviation between the efficient price and the actual user price. At volume v_0 the user price is p_0, which includes all operating costs and user taxes such as fuel excise taxes. To match the user price to marginal cost, a price increment is needed, labeled "toll" in the diagram.

Because demand for trips or VMT (vehicle miles of travel) varies over a period of less than a day, the efficient toll also varies (the demand curve shifts horizontally while the cost curves remain fixed). The user has an incentive to shift the time of the trip to

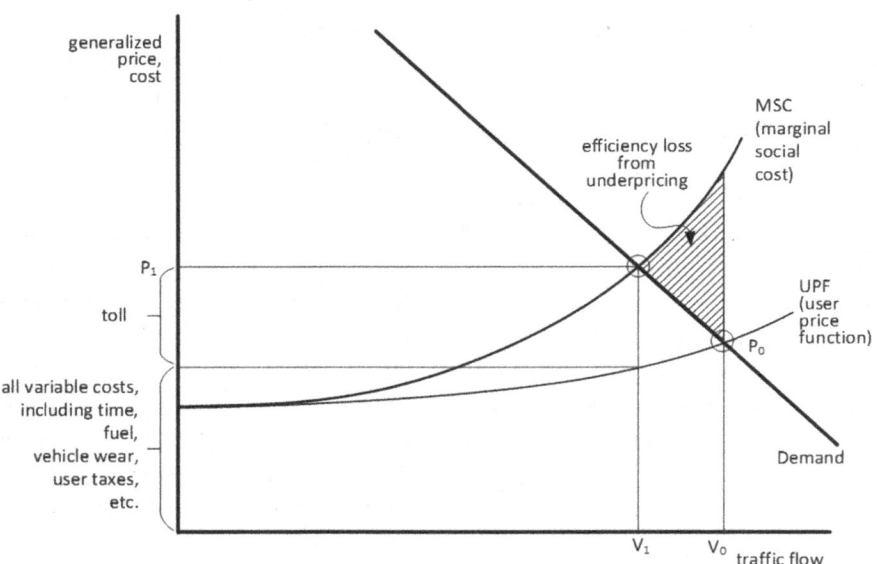

FIGURE 10.3 Marginal cost pricing.

periods when the toll is low, so the efficient fee is determined from one minute to the next by factors affecting demand. A fixed a priori fee cannot match supply and demand over daily periods of demand variation.

For roads, the toll revenues provide a basis for increasing capacity if the incremental capacity costs are exceeded by the surplus of toll revenue over other fixed costs. The tolls also ensure that the available capacity is most efficiently utilized by travelers choosing to use the facility, as well as vehicle occupancy, time of day, and direction of travel. The inefficiency of underpriced roads spills into the land market in the form of inefficiently low density; hence, efficiency in the road market is important in the land development market.

10.4.5 Congestion in Related Markets

Congestion is a symptom of underpricing so that the revealed demand exceeds capacity. Traffic congestion indicates a market failure, but it is one that originates in road management, not land development. There are no indirect ways to price congestion; the pricing must be directly metered on the congested facility at the times of day the congestion occurs and in the direction of travel that is congested. Impact fees on land development cannot provide a remedy to congestion. Impact fees might increase the overall price of highway travel, but they would have a negligible impact on any given road section and a minuscule impact on peak travel. If the objective is to expand access, impact fees can be used to fund road building, and even in specific locations, but they cannot indirectly solve the congestion in the road market.

10.5 EQUITY IMPACTS

Equity can be evaluated by an incremental change, such as that resulting from pricing or regulation, whose impact can be estimated with respect to which subgroups gain and lose by the particular change. Horizontal equity corresponds to the equal treatment of equals, and implies that development candidates that create more cost or "bads" (e.g., environmental damage) should pay more than those that are more benign. Vertical equity refers to the change in the distribution of income or cost relative to the existing shares, and the impacts can be described in terms such as "progressive" vs. "regressive."

Both types of fairness depend on price elasticity. If the demand elasticity is constant and absolute zero, then the price has no efficiency impact. In practice, price elasticities can range from very low (unresponsive, where large changes in price result in little change in expressed demand) to high (small price changes deter many consumers or they shift to substitutes). Taxes are best imposed on inelastic output, which means broadly based measures that are unlikely to change in response to the tax (property, sales, and income).

Alternative mechanisms for affecting behavior include regulation, statutes that prescribe rules for certain activities, such as hooking up to a sewer line or using a septic system, standards that apply to building construction, and training for driving. Pricing is only sometimes the most efficient method.

10.5.1 Price Discrimination

There are good and bad reasons for discrimination. Suspect categories are presumed to be unjustifiable, but many surrogates are less obvious and may need to be scrutinized for deleterious impacts. Voters can abuse the tools of zoning to design instruments that effectively exclude additional people from gaining entrance to a particular community. The community as a whole has an obligation to provide primary education to all young children, but taxpayers without children may try to minimize their tax burdens by zoning out land use categories expected to produce children of school age. It is therefore necessary to ensure that impact fees are not used to serve anti-social motives. If the logic, impacts, and data support the structure and levels of fees (i.e., a rational nexus), then it should be feasible to screen out NIMBY purposes and other malicious applications.

Motives such as collecting more revenue for general or other purposes, enhancing the monopoly value of existing housing, reducing taxes on existing property, excluding school-age children, and excluding less desirable (e.g., lower-income) people are suspect motives. Voters, property owners, and even government agencies may seek to make mischief that is not necessarily in the public interest. Grounds for suspicion are that the persons negatively impacted by impact fees are not currently residents of the taxing jurisdiction and have no political voice there.

10.5.2 Passing Costs On

In general, it is desirable that costs of production be passed on from each stage of production to the next stage. If someone finds a way to reduce those costs, then competitive markets will tend to squeeze out those producers that fail to figure out how to reduce the costs. But if the costs are inherent to the production of the output, then they should be passed on to the final consumer, whether they are directly incurred by the landowner, the developer, the public agency, or the buyer.

Participants within the same market pay the same price for the same good/service if there is no price discrimination. Those that were there first have no claim on a lower price that may have been acceptable when they first arrived. Gentrification, for example, means that the price of land goes up as demand increases, and the existing owners reap a windfall, while those who are only renters or customers face higher prices.

Individuals *not* in the market, however, should not have to pay the price. If payment for a sewer bond issue is required of all properties within the sewer district, although the facilities being funded serve only a portion of the district, this is inequitable (non-beneficiaries are paying the same price as beneficiaries) and inefficient (the price of membership is distorted in favor of the minority benefited). Districts may need to be specially designed to match beneficiaries to taxes in the same watershed or other service area.

If there is uncertainty—about whether the fees will be imposed or how much, or whether land development will actually proceed, or when—the shifting will be partial, either by expected value (weighing the probabilities) or discounted (by the timing), or both. For efficiency, constructing the infrastructure sooner than necessary is a form of welfare loss, and results in long-run costs that are greater than the possible minimum.

If the purpose of the amount charged (price) is to ration service consumption, then the amount charged must be related to the cost of supplying the service. If the purpose of the price is not rationing, then the basis for the charge is equity. If the charge is to pay for a "public" good (for community benefit, such as education, not just the payer), then a general tax instrument will serve to raise government revenues to support public goods. Because public goods are not "used up" by their consumers, there is no relationship between the amount of service consumed and the cost to society of the consumption; the amount that should be paid by any individual consumer is arbitrary. Hence the criterion of charging is left to equity. If the marginal cost of the consumption is zero, the price does not need to have any deterrent effect. An appropriate tax for a public good is a charge scaled to the ability to pay. The intended impact of distributional (vertical) equity is to reduce the disparity of incomes, i.e., to lower the ratio between the highest and lowest incomes.

10.5.3 Types of Instruments

The income tax is the dominant instrument for promoting distributional equity, for the simple reason that it uses income as its base, but even if it were suitable for urban development it is not available because the income of the residents is not known and can't be taxed until they become residents. The cost of the dwelling, however, can be estimated, and can serve as a proxy for income. Thus an *ad valorem* tax can be an equitable development fee for some infrastructure.

Ideally, each cost would be matched to each property that the cost pertained to, for the duration of the time period it was meant to cover. Because the current practice is that the same tax rate is applied to all properties, the equity of the tax is largely controlled by the timing and amount of expenditure and the ways it is financed.

For those specific costs that can be paid as a lump at the beginning of the development's life, before occupancy starts, impact fees can be useful for fine-tuning payments to costs. Other instruments for this purpose are special improvement districts or special assessment districts and negotiated exactions.

10.5.4 Tax Instruments for Equity Goals

A primary conceptual distinction among tax instruments is ability-to-pay vs. benefit-received. The ability to pay obviously does not take into account the amount of the service that the payer consumes or receives. In the real estate development situation, the tax is based on the anticipated value of the residential unit as a surrogate for the owner's income. Benefits received might be reflected in the capitalized value of the service to the property.

Although correction for externalities can be a legitimate basis for imposing charges, there are several drawbacks: first, it is always preferable to correct negative externalities in the relevant market, rather than indirectly in a related market; indirect attempts at compensation are mostly ineffective. Second, land use policy may be to control externalities (nuisances) through zoning (segregation of incompatible land uses), thereby preventing the negative impacts. Common externalities (road delay, emissions, health, noise, danger, and other spillovers) need to be confirmed or metered in some way, and are not well addressed by a fixed lump sum charge.

The burden of an *ad valorem* tax on housing may be regressive (because the tax is a smaller share of income for the wealthy), but an *ad valorem* tax is less regressive than a head tax (like a poll tax) or a fee that acts as a price.

10.6 EXAMPLES OF IMPACT FEE DESIGN

With the above review of public finance principles and a range of normative goals for designing impact fees and other revenue instruments, how can this be carried out in practice? Some practical options are discussed below.

10.6.1 Impact Fee Design Process

The process of calculating an impact fee has many complications, so we will make a host of assumptions in order to simplify the discussion. One requirement is the condition of concurrency: the public services must be available for use when the fee is paid. We assume that this issue of timing has been resolved. Another requirement is that the costs subject to the fee, such as off-site sewerage, are clearly defined as the responsibility of the land development being charged, have been unambiguously measured, and will not be covered by any other public revenue instrument. If the same fee or tax, say, per dwelling unit, is applied to a geographic area that includes multiple properties, it is assumed that all properties are receiving equal or proportionate service. If the revenue collected is directed at a social goal, such as affordable housing, then it is assumed that existing development or land uses are also contributing comparably to that goal. The "nexus" requirement is assumed to be satisfied.

Subject to these assumptions, the calculation of an impact fee involves four steps:

1. Definition and measurement of the total costs to be covered by the fee. The costs may be incremental costs for a given facility or a portion of such costs, and separable from other costs not being charged for. The timing of the costs should be for a specific time period.
2. Prioritization of the goals to be addressed, such as efficiency, pricing, distributional equity, tax equity, or other.
3. Selection of the instrument to be used, such as impact fee, special assessment, *ad valorem* tax, or other.
4. Design a formula that can be applied to the tax base that will allocate the total revenue to be raised to the elements in the tax base. This includes the choice of taxable unit, such as dwelling unit, assessed value, household size, land area, floor area or other.

For example, the costs might be off-site road expansion caused by the development, the goal might be sprawl deterrence, the instrument might be an impact fee, and the formula might increase the fee inversely proportional to the density of the development.

10.6.2 Choosing Which Goals to Emphasize

Often there are multiple goals that would be desirable, but a single charging instrument is unlikely to serve more than one goal at a time. For example, in infill areas, where density is likely to be high without inducement, a tax instrument that favors transit-oriented design may be more productive than a density reward.

A major goal of land use development planning is to reduce or counter urban sprawl, or the tendency to spread out (smaller population on more land), a pattern that has occurred for many decades resulting in lower average density and more VMT. In locations on the fringe where density tends to be low, an inducement for higher density can help establish or enable a more intense pattern in a small or modest-sized area. A long-range plan is desirable for support.

Where physical goals are relatively inelastic to the pricing of services, equity in the distribution of growth costs may be more beneficial. Disincentives to auto dependency and rewards for pedestrian amenities may alternatively guide site design and can be rewarded with lower costs.

Fuel taxes were considered justified for highway funding because they would be paid only by users (non-highway fuel use was exempted), and that was fair. It was not meant to meter highway use, although it was a license to consume. Auto and tire excise taxes, and driver and license fees are also user taxes. As mentioned above, fuel taxes do serve to track miles driven to some extent, and vehicle weight to an even lesser extent, but that was not their purpose, which was an administratively inexpensive means for collecting revenue.

10.6.3 Market Failure and Social Costs

In looking at the patterns of existing urban development, and the possible goals of applying impact fees, it is hard to avoid coming to the conclusion that policy failures have overwhelmed whatever efficiency tendencies were present in the many markets involved in urban expansion. The problems of global warming, sustainability, income inequality, air and water pollution, etc., may not have been primarily caused by urban development, but their solution seems to require considerably more than making some modest adjustments in how development pays for infrastructure.

Congestion pricing, for example, could greatly improve the management of the roads currently in existence, but it will have little impact on the way urban development has spread out over the decades since WWII. Universal shifting to electric cars can help to reduce the consumption of fossil fuels and associated air pollution, but there are other costs to sprawl that are unsustainable.

The implication is that impact fees would need to *reduce* the amount of urbanized land in order to generate a social benefit. There is already too much land for residential and commercial use, and we should be trying to reduce that footprint rather than just making the next increment more dense. This means that, at the least, impact fees should

be graduated according to such attributes as density, auto dependency, and auto generated VMT.

10.6.4 Matching Fees to Service Provision

Ideally, public services would be provided in accordance with what is needed/justified and then fees or taxes set to match, guided by whatever strategy was appropriate to the purpose. In practice, the reverse is more common: taxes or fees are determined so as to raise a given revenue, and a uniform charge is applied to all customers. Thus the service provision is adjusted to match the charge.

At the other end of the spectrum, each property could pay a bundle of fees that were applicable to that particular property. Some of these could be impact fees. Some would be assessments that apply to special districts; some could be general-purpose levies that support a given level of government. If the fees and taxes were designed equitably and were only applied to those jurisdictions that warranted the charge, then the result would be both efficient and equitable.

If the jurisdiction charges the same *ad valorem* tax rate to every property, then it should continuously adjust its expenditures so that benefits to each property are equitable over the long run, if not in the short run. Such taxes would not be considered prices except to the extent that residents and prospective residents evaluate the Tieboutian tax-vs.-services balance of each candidate jurisdiction and choose their residence accordingly.

10.6.5 Short Run vs. Long Run

The theory of MCP is specifically based on short-run marginal cost and does not address the long run because marginal cost only applies to variable costs. Long-run equilibrium depends on efficient investment in capital facilities, which is intended to be guided by benefit–cost analysis, but that is not an explicit part of the government-free abstract model. Benefit–cost evaluation of investment alternatives is analogous to marginal cost pricing (incremental investment), but it is at a lower and less abstract level.

It does reveal, however, a difference in perspective. Short-run decisions may be efficient in the marginal-cost-equals-price sense, but the long-run BCA analysis may be biased. The urban development process may be continuously efficient in the short run, but cumulatively inefficient over the long run. If road expansion has been overinvested and roads continuously underpriced, the long-term effect may be excessive road mileage, and a lack of viable alternative substitutes modes of travel. Under these conditions, impact fees may correctly pass on the incremental costs of public infrastructure, yet perversely reinforce further sprawl that is inefficient in the long run.

Some of the failures and misguided policies that have created this bias are under-priced roads, home loan subsidies biased toward fringe development, tax deductibility for home loan borrowing, white flight from urban minorities, and failure to control urban air and noise pollution. The actions that can compensate for these mistakes will need to reward greater density, equal treatment, reduced emissions, as well as to share infrastructure costs. We might consider developing impact fees based on short-run efficiency and equity measures, and different fees designed to counter long-run distortions. Clearly, the fee structure is limited and can at best address only one goal at a time.

10.6.6 Graduated Impact Fees

Reasoning backward from goal to instrument, what would impact fees have to look like if they were used to induce more compact development? Planners believe that low-density sprawl is incompatible with climate change, economic efficiency, and reducing inequality. If this can be quantified, then impact fees should be higher for low density. The higher the number of dwellings per acre, the lower the impact fee. The costs of land consumption would be measured in externalities, such as road transportation, water and sewer distribution networks, solid waste, and emissions.

A difficulty with this strategy is the fact that it applies to existing development as well as new development. If densification of existing development warrants the same treatment, then impact fees or some comparable instrument(s) would need to be applied, since equal treatment requires that burdens on new developments (e.g., affordable housing) should also be the responsibility of existing developments.

10.6.7 Public Goods Aspects of Urban Services

Many types of revenue instruments can be used to fund urban services, but some are more suitable than others. The most effective instrument to use and the basis for allocating costs depend upon the characteristics of the service being provided. Some pertinent characteristics are described in Table 10.1, in which the definition of the public good is followed by a practical description. These characteristics relate to whether a pricing or user fee instrument is workable, or whether the primary purpose is equity. The characteristics also describe the aspects of the service that justify the local public provision of the service.

These characteristic dimensions or attributes of the services can be roughly scored for each service, as has been done in Table 10.2. Sewage collection and treatment is similar to a private good, but exhibits economies of scale and high upfront costs, suggesting public provision. Storm drainage requires minimizing impervious surfaces, holding runoff on-site in recharge areas, and similar regulatory efforts. Services like fire, police, libraries, and parks follow a pattern of distributed access points and monopolistic provision with

TABLE 10.1 Public Goods Characteristics of Urban Services

Publicness	The degree to which the characteristics of the service conform to a true public good, meaning that the marginal cost of additional consumer is zero and there is no capacity constraint.
Economies of scale	Diminishing marginal cost of additional output; theory says that competition will force producers to price at marginal cost, therefore lose money and be unable to replace their capital, hence public provision or subsidy is required; also natural monopoly.
Demand elasticity	Non-zero price elasticity means that price has an effect on quantity, so a fee per unit of output has an effect on efficiency; pricing at marginal cost may be feasible.
Pricing suitability	Besides sensitivity to price, other considerations may be relevant, such as whether exclusion is feasible and consumption is rival.
Related market	If there is a related market, then indirect pricing (through the related market) may be possible.
Equity priority	For the particular service, progressive redistribution is the primary goal.

TABLE 10.2 Characteristics of Urban Services

Urban Service	Public Good	Economies of Scale	Demand Elasticity	Pricing Suitability	Related Market	Equity Priority
sewerage	low	high	low	mod	water	low
water distribution	low	high	low-mod	mod	sewer	low
drainage	mod	mod	mod	mod	none	mod
trash/recycling	mod	mod	mod	mod	none	mod
fire	mod	low	low	low	none	mod
police	mod	low	low	low	none	mod
park	high	low	mod	low	none	mod
library	high	low	mod	low	none	mod
road network	mod	high	high	high	none	mod
transit	mod	mod	high	mod	none	mod
schools	high	mod	mod	low	none	high
housing affordability	high	low	mod	low	none	high

equitable funding. Pricing is inappropriate because consumption is encouraged. Roads, in contrast, can be user funded. Fixed fees, however, are limited where pricing requires that usage be metered. If the service has a related market, this opens the possibility that indirect fees could affect behavior, but few services have a related market.

The types of improvements that impact fees can be attached to can be grouped into six categories, as shown in Table 10.3.

The first category—water, sewer, and drainage—contains services involving physical things and represents the most common application of impact fees in practice and the category for which impact fees are most suitable. The infrastructure is readily identified with the development requiring the service.

Sewer districts are necessarily constructed in increments. The system can be designed as it will be in build-out, and portions constructed as they are needed, including increased capacity at the treatment facility. The total can be shared equally as of some base year, and then charged as of the year of development. The charges would not depend on the length of the pipe, although location might be a factor if the development were poorly located. It is less costly if the facilities are built as much as possible at the same time, so to the extent a

TABLE 10.3 Considerations in Designing Instruments for Specific Services

Sewer and Water	Sewage Collection and Treatment	Minimize cost of provision, design for scale economies; natural monopoly, external benefit from treatment.
	Water Distribution	Natural monopoly; protect natural sources, minimize cost, maximum quality, equal service, metered.
	Drainage	Disincentivize impervious surface; surface water retention, filtering, recharge, regulatory enforcement.
	Trash/Recycling	Land fill, haz mat disposal, low or no profit private good; external benefit from waste collection and disposal.
Service Areas	Fire	Optimize service area, apportion for equity, low conflagration risk on urban fringes, low elasticity, difficult for private market.
	Police	Optimize effectiveness of provision, response time, benefit received, ad valorem.
	Parks	Open space and active recreation space outside the home, collective good, equitable access.
	Library	Access to references, fiction, internet, and other information and educational resources; support for education, important equity function.
Transportation	Roads	Network properties, natural monopoly, direct charges preferred to indirect, offsite network expansion.
	Public Transit	Option demand, site design important.
Social Goods	Schools	Primary and secondary public education; a major public good is equal opportunity; primary and secondary schools are regarded as public goods, in the belief that everyone benefits from universal education. Not only do we benefit as neighbors and residents, commercial activities and employment relationships are facilitated by universal education. Tax all residents on ability to pay, children or not, residential or other.
	Affordable Housing	Housing for the poor, elderly, or moderate income, subsidized or market; redistributional.
Commercial	Hotel	Infrastructure used by visitors.
	Office	Square footage of floor area.

development lengthens the span of time the system is under construction – by starting prematurely or by delaying build-out, the development can be charged a higher fee.

The second category is fire, police, parks, libraries, and other facilities for which a bounded geographic service area can be defined. Price elasticity is low, and social benefits come from greater consumption rather than less, implying the fees are taxes rather than prices.

Fire and police stations are service centers that can be distributed like market areas, in which response times depend at least partially upon the distance to the station. The number of service locations and the distances between them can be optimized in design, given the resources of the community.

Transportation infrastructure comprises the third category, and impact fees have a significant but limited role in this sector as indirect user charges. Roads ideally should be paid for with user fees or user taxes, with a general charge for off-site road expansion.

Social purposes such as schools and affordable housing form the fourth category, and tax equity is by far the dominant goal. Schools can be funded with fees for new school buildings, graduated by expected income, and not

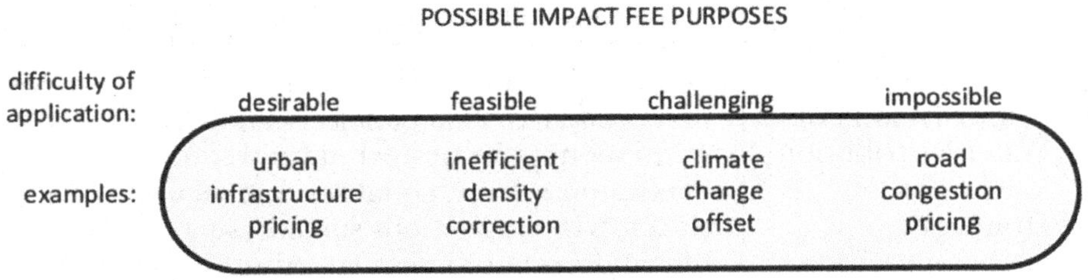

POSSIBLE IMPACT FEE PURPOSES

difficulty of application:	desirable	feasible	challenging	impossible
examples:	urban infrastructure pricing	inefficient density correction	climate change offset	road congestion pricing

FIGURE 10.4 Spectrum of potential purposes for impact fees.

depending upon the number of children. Affordable housing can be supported with linkage fees if sufficient affordable housing is not created on-site.

Finally, fees can also be levied on commercial land uses in proportion to occupancy or square feet of interior space.

10.7 CONCLUSION

The goals of economic efficiency and equity open a wide range of possible purposes for impact fees—within the array of possible charges and taxes that can be used to support urban development—while at the same time constraining what instruments can be used for what purposes and challenging the ways to shape fees to achieve social objectives. Thus some purposes for impact fees are more plausible than others, as illustrated by the examples shown in Figure 10.4.

Charging new developments for the public infrastructure costs they give rise to may not necessarily produce the expected results.

Impact linkages are complex. Affordable housing conflicts with fiscal zoning. Deterring development away from environmentally damaging locations is desirable, and preventing leapfrog sprawl may be only a timing issue. Rewarding compactness and mitigating climate effects require a scale of fees and rewards that create incentives across the spectrum of density.

The ideas proposed above are superficial and underdeveloped. It will take creative talent to apply the abstract principles of public finance to achieve the varied social purposes that are relevant to urban development.

BIBLIOGRAPHY

Freilich, R. H., & Bushek, D. W., Eds. (1995). *Exactions, Impact Fees and Dedications.* Chicago: American Bar Association.

Nicholson, W. (1998). *Microeconomic Theory* (7th ed.). New York: Harcourt Brace.

Tideman, N., Ed. (1994). *Land and Taxation.* London: Shepheard-Walwyn.

11 IMPACTS OF PROPORTIONATE-SHARE DEVELOPMENT FEES

GREGORY BURGE AND TREY DRONYK-TROSPER

11.1 INTRODUCTION

When it comes to paying for the significant costs of growth, local governments throughout the United States play the biggest role. This responsibility is particularly acute in rapidly growing cities/suburbs, as demand for new infrastructure (i.e., roads, schools, sewers, parks and recreation facilities, and public safety) can outstrip the means to pay for it using existing revenue streams. But why is this so important now, when the US has long been an expanding nation?[1] One reason is that raising property taxes to pay for these additional infrastructure costs has become increasingly difficult over the past several decades. During the 1970s, high inflation boosted nominal property values and, in turn, property tax collections, creating substantial taxpayer resentment (Altshuler and Gómez-Ibáñez 1993). This manifested in the property tax revolts of the late 1970s and early 1980s. States responded by passing property tax limitations that limited property tax growth rates. In such an environment, cities have become hesitant to raise property taxes to pay for the additional expenses associated with new development and have instead created ways to "shift" the costs of public improvements away from existing residents.

One of the most innovative and popular of these methods is impact fees. Impact fees are one-time levies, predetermined through a formula adopted by a local government unit, that are assessed on property developers during the permitting process. As of 2019, 29 states have enacted impact fee enabling legislation. In practice, impact fees bridge the gap between the cost of new municipal infrastructure and revenue streams that will help pay for it. They also provide local politicians with ammunition that can be used to appease anti-growth contingencies within the community. Consider the historical lineage of impact fees. Antecedents to impact fees were in-kind exactions, land dedications or build/install requirements for the construction of specific facilities. Impact fees, paid as monetary rather than in-kind contributions, first came into use in the 1970s, providing a more efficient and flexible means of local infrastructure financing than negotiated or *ad hoc* exactions. Since then, they have become more popular as communities have gradually warmed to the idea that impact fees may be a pragmatic means of addressing fiscal shortfalls and adding capacity to public infrastructure systems that badly need it.

Impact fees remain controversial, however. The development community often complains that impact fees inhibit economic development by driving up costs, thereby causing developers to "vote with their feet" by building in communities with no (or lower) impact fees. They argue that impact fees will drive prices up and construction down. A particularly concerning criticism is that impact fees may disproportionately burden low-income groups and have negative effects on housing affordability among smaller units. If true, this means impact fees may lead to higher racial and income-based segregation and lower homeownership rates among Hispanic and African Americans (Baden and Coursey 1999; Braun 2003). Others say that impact fees are

DOI: 10.4324/9781003336075-14

the only feasible means of financing sufficient new infrastructure in a tax-averse political environment and that they may actually have many positive effects on communities, serving more as an efficient user fee than as a tax.

Because so many public discussions over the relative merits of impact fees have been based upon speculation and anecdotal evidence, there is much that can be gained from a better understanding of what the literature has to say about the impacts of these programs on market conditions. This chapter is designed to provide a summary of the various theoretical and empirical investigations of the effects of impact fees over the past three decades. It is designed to synthesize the existing evidence concerning three critical market conditions: 1) residential property values, 2) residential construction rates, and 3) non-residential economic development and job growth. The chapter concludes with a brief summary and some comments on how these findings contribute to the public debate over the use of impact fees.

11.2 HOUSING PRICE EFFECTS

As mentioned above, critics of impact fees often claim that they will lead to higher construction costs and therefore higher housing prices, potentially having adverse effects on housing affordability issues within communities. This section addresses the effect of impact fees on housing prices. Most theoretical and empirical studies have either explicitly or implicitly investigated the price effects that impact fees have under a relatively normal price elasticity of demand; that is, the housing market is relatively competitive.[2] This assumption is reasonable given that patterns of impact fee use reveal they are most likely to be implemented in growing areas, where the vast majority of jurisdictions face competition in the housing market.

11.2.1 Theoretical Evidence

Work by Keith Ihlanfeldt and Tim Shaughnessey (2004) has shed an important

light on the relationship between impact fees and housing prices. They begin by noting there are "old" (heretofore, traditional) and "new" theoretical approaches to addressing this issue. The traditional view, advanced by Altshuler and Gómez-Ibáñez (1993), Delaney and Smith (1989a, 1989b), Downing and McCaleb (1987), Huffman, Smith, Nelson, and Stegman (1988), and Singell and Lillydahl (1990) considers impact fees to be an excise tax on the production of housing. As such, the fee acts just as any other tax in a competitive market and shifts the short-run supply of housing up by the amount of the fee. This leads to a higher price for housing, lower profits for developers, and a reduction in the quantity of new homes built. The share of the fee paid by each participant in the housing market depends upon the relative elasticities of supply and demand for developable lots and constructed residences.[3] Also, to the extent that housing consumers find new and existing housing of equal quality to be close substitutes, there should be an increase in the price of existing housing.

In the long run, developers are assumed to be mobile across jurisdictions and are therefore able to fully avoid the incidence of the fee. The incidence must either be shifted forward to consumers in the form of higher housing prices or backward to the owners of land. Although Huffman et al. (1988) argue that backward shifting is unlikely in many markets because landowners have a reservation price below which they will not sell, some have challenged this conclusion. Ihlanfeldt and Shaughnessy acknowledge that while a reservation price may prevent price concessions in the short run, it does not eliminate the possibility that impact fees will be shifted backward in the longer run. Moreover, they argue that in weak markets occasioned by the business cycle, reservation prices are likely to decline, resulting in backward capitalization of at least part of the fee.

In a groundbreaking 1998 piece, Yinger challenges many conclusions of the traditional view and develops what some have labeled the "new" view. Later, Moody and Nelson (2003), Ihlanfeldt and Shaughnessy (2004), and Burge and Ihlanfeldt (2006a, 2006b) extended the conclusions of the new view. According to this view, impact fees a) reflect the cost of providing valued facilities needed to serve new development and b) may offset property taxes that would otherwise have been assessed, leading to savings in these costs that will be capitalized into home values. Yinger assumes mobility for housing consumers (a stronger assumption than assuming mobility for developers) so that they are protected from the long-run burden of impact fees just as developers are. While impact fees should still lead to higher housing prices, the implication is that price increases come from higher reservation prices consumers are *willing to pay* due to the value of the public infrastructure and the present value of the expected future savings in property taxes that are associated with the impact fee regime. The process by which impact fees lead to higher housing prices under the new view is traced by Ihlanfeldt and Shaughnessy. Initially, it is assumed that local governments rely exclusively on property tax to finance new facilities. Assuming there is no change in the quality of facilities accompanying the financing regime shift, the new view suggests that prices for both new and existing homes will go up.

The increase in prices should equal the capitalized value of the property tax savings that homeowners expect from the reduction in the tax rate. The tax rate declines because the imposition of the impact fee shifts the costs of new infrastructure from existing property owners to developers. *(Burge and Ihlanfeldt 2006a, p. 4)*[4]

Moody and Nelson (2003) extend this approach by arguing that since impact fees enhance the timely provision of public infrastructure, they might predictably expand the supply of easily developable land. This expansion may reduce the equilibrium price of land, but the interpretation is different than was the case under the traditional view. The conjecture of the traditional view is that, since developers pay the impact fee (but receive no benefit), they reduce their demand for land to the extent that they are not able to fully shift the fee forward to consumers. However, if impact fees make more areas developable by adding capacity to existing public infrastructure systems, it may well be that an increase in the supply of developable land also causes lower prices.

Burge and Ihlanfeldt (2006a) also emphasize the possibility that impact fees may increase the supply of developable land, but offer a different explanation. They argue that communities may have exclusionary fiscal motives causing them to zone their undeveloped land in ways that protect themselves from high levels of (affordable) residential development. Because residential development does not generate enough additional tax revenue to cover the costs of providing new public services, the community may adopt exclusionary barriers to the construction of residential property. Under these conditions, developers are more likely to face costly variances/rezonings, which may not even be approved in the end. Therefore, impact fees may cause communities to willingly zone more of their undeveloped land for residential purposes and lower other regulatory barriers. Hence, supply-side price effects may be nuanced. On the one hand, developers have the statutory burden of paying a fee. On the other, they may benefit from savings in non-impact fee-related project approval costs if a fiscal motivation for exclusion exists within communities. As such, the extent to which developers are forced to shift excess costs forward or backward is mitigated by these direct savings.

Their model also builds on the Yinger proposition that impact fees offset property tax revenues. Since consumers under impact fee regimes are willing to pay a higher price for housing to the extent that it is offset by savings in property taxes, they point out that the present value of these savings should vary directly with the value of the home. One prediction of their theoretical model is that increases in the constant quality price of housing across different segments of the market should be proportional to the values of homes in that segment. For example, if a $1,000 per home impact fee reduces property tax rates, the additional willingness to pay for expensive homes may rise by over $1,000, while the increase in the willingness to pay for smaller homes may be much smaller.

While Yinger (1998) asserts that home buyers will value the additional public facilities provided by the impact fees such that they willingly pay higher prices, he takes no stance on the magnitude of this effect. Ihlanfeldt and Shaughnessy (2004) suggest that if the benefits from the new facilities financed from impact fees are valued highly enough by new homebuyers, it is possible that housing prices will increase by a greater amount than the size of the fees. In fact, evidence to support this possibility is found in several studies discussed below. The result that one dollar of impact fee leads to a greater than one dollar price increase for a new home is commonly referred to as "over-shifting." One explanation in support of the over-shifting hypothesis is that impact fee revenues may be used strategically by local governments to secure additional benefits to the community. Note that impact fees rarely cover the full cost of facilities, typically financing less than half the cost. However, because impact fees must be spent to deliver the quality or level of service on which the fee is predicated, often within binding time limits, local governments may attempt to leverage impact fee revenues along with other revenues to provide the facilities.[5] If this conjecture is valid, impact fees may add value to the community that is greater than the fees themselves if they are leveraged to provide facilities of higher value than the fees assessed.

11.2.2 Empirical Evidence

Previous empirical investigations on the price effects of impact fees include studies by Delaney and Smith (1989a and 1989b), Singell

and Lillydahl (1990), Nelson et al. (1992), Skaburskis and Qadeer (1992), Dresch and Sheffrin (1997), Baden and Coursey (1999), Mathur, et al. (2004), Campbell (2004), Ihlanfeldt and Shaughnessy (2004), and Burge and Ihlanfeldt (2006a). There was a great deal of inconsistency across early findings and little consideration as to whether or not observed price increases were due to reductions in supply or increases in demand. Much of the early work also suffered from important methodological weaknesses, often related to a lack of appropriate data. More recent investigations have the benefit of being able to account for the significant developments in our theoretical understanding of the effects of impact fees on house prices and have also used more appropriate data.

In one early investigation, Delaney and Smith examined the effect of a single impact fee adopted by the city of Dunedin, Florida, in 1974. In their first paper, they found that impact fees raised the price of new homes by roughly three times the size of the original impact fee. Their second paper found that impact fees also raised the price of existing housing, but by a much smaller amount. In addition to the implausibly large price effect on new homes, it is difficult to believe the price effects of impact fees are so dissimilar between new and existing homes when other evidence suggests they are such close substitutes. Yinger (1998) points out that their results are based on the assumption that the price of land does not change as a result of the fee (which may or may not hold) and that their failure to control for public infrastructure quality and neighborhood characteristics may be a critical flaw in their empirical models. Singell and Lillydahl (1990) found a very different set of results in their study. Using data from Loveland, Colorado, that spanned a three-year period (1983–1985), they examined the price effects of a $1,182 increase in impact fees that occurred during that time period. Consistent with Delany and Smith, they found an increase in the price of new homes of just over three times the size of the impact fee. However, they also found the fee increased the price of existing homes by $7,000—roughly six times the size of the original fee and a highly implausible result. Troubling aspects of this study include the fact that so few sales were used (429) and that only one impact fee change in a single jurisdiction was analyzed. Because both of these studies analyzed only one impact fee change in a single community, any price effects they observed could be attributed to an omitted time-related factor.

Studies by Nelson et al. (1992) and Skaburskis and Qadeer (1992) are important in that they investigated the relationship between impact fees and the price of undeveloped land within the community. To the extent that price effects on land are directly related to potential price effects on housing, their results belong in a discussion of the effects of impact fees on housing prices. Nelson et al. (1992) found significant positive effects on the price of land, but the effect differs dramatically across selected housing markets. The positive effect on the price of land is consistent with the over-shifting results from previous work. They offered two arguments to support their finding. First, because impact fees establish a contract for development rights, developers may prefer impact fee programs to situations with no fees but fewer certain development rights. They also argue that impact fees may delay the timing of development until housing prices, and in turn land prices, increase enough to offset the fee and any interest charges on the fee amount. Findings from Burge and Ihlanfeldt (2006), to be discussed in Section 11.3, provide evidence in support of the former argument but not the latter. One troubling point is that the effect of impact fees on land prices varies widely across the different areas included in their study—ranging from strong positive effects to sometimes insignificant effects. Skaburskis and Qadeer (1992) also found that the price of land increased with the presence

of an impact fee. Their models describe prices as a function of development costs (including impact fees), location variables, and the expected future growth in housing prices and construction costs. They found that lot prices increased by 1.2 times the amount of the impact fee, again indicating over-shifting. Unfortunately, these studies both suffer from similar data limitations, as did many other early studies. However, they do provide initial evidence that the price effects of impact fees may not be driven entirely by a reduction in supply.

In their 1997 article, Dresch and Sheffrin used data on housing sales in Contra Costa, California, spanning a four-year period. The study was broken down into two areas, Eastern County and Western County. As is still common in California, impact fees were substantial in their case study—over $16,000 and $24,000 in the Eastern and Western County areas, respectively. In Western County, an additional $1 of impact fees was found to significantly increase the price of new homes by $1.88, while in Eastern County, the increase was only $0.25. Although the authors provide a number of explanations for the large difference in magnitudes across areas, their arguments are not consistent with the new view of impact fees, and there is no satisfactory resolution to this troubling issue.

Another attempt to measure the price effects of impact fees was made by Baden and Coursey (1999). They used sales from both new and existing homes in the Chicago area between 1995 and 1997 to regress logged sales prices on a detailed set of structural variables and an impact fee variable. Their results produced an estimated elasticity of impact fees on the full sample of new and existing homes that ranged between 0.011 and 0.013. After multiplying these coefficients by the mean selling price for each of their municipalities, they found significant and positive effects—again larger than the size of the fee itself. They offer an explanation that is contrary to the Nelson et al. (1992) argument that impact fees reduce uncertainty, essentially arguing the reverse—that impact fees *add* additional uncertainties and delay costs into the approval process, forcing developers to more than fully recoup the cost of the fees. Given that the magnitude of their price effect is consistent with other recent estimates that lend support to the over-shifting hypothesis, it is unclear why the authors failed to discuss any potentially positive effects of impact fees (e.g., enhanced infrastructure) or cite earlier findings concerning their potential effects on the price of land. Still, this study produced the first set of estimated price effects that hold up to more current evidence.

Mathur, Waddell, and Blanco (2004) examined the effect of impact fees on the prices of new single-family homes in Kings County, Washington, using sales data from 38 jurisdictions for the years 1991 through 2000. In hedonic models that control for a number of structural, locational, and jurisdictional attributes, they found that $1 of impact fee was correlated with a $1.66 increase in price for a new home selling for $246,000—the mean from their data set. Impact fees were found to have an even larger effect on the selling price of higher quality homes ($3.58 for $1 of fees), while their effect on lower quality new homes was found to be statistically insignificant. This is the first piece of evidence that impact fees may cause different price effects on homes falling into different value ranges, a finding also supported by Burge and Ihlanfeldt (2006a). Mathur et al. speculated that the effect on high-quality home prices was so large because the value of the infrastructure paid for by the fees was greater than the cost of the fee. Their findings were also consistent with the idea that impact fee revenues may reduce future property tax liabilities, thus increasing the demand for housing in the community proportionally to property values. While the authors focus on the fact that their price effect result becomes insignificant when looking at homes falling into the lower quality tier, it is worth noting that their

point estimate is still positive (roughly $0.60) with a *t*-statistic of nearly 1.5. All things considered, this study can be taken as evidence that the *overall* effects of impact fees on the price of housing are positive (with roughly $0.60 cents of over-shifting if we look at the mean in their sample) and that the magnitude of these price effects depends upon the value of the new home.

Ihlanfeldt and Shaughnessy (2004) use time-series data from Dade County, Florida, to investigate the effects of impact fees on the price of both new and existing housing. Their sample included sales of new (39,792) and existing homes (107,376) that transacted during the study period. An improvement to the existing literature was that they used hedonic and repeat sales regression methods to construct monthly constant quality price indexes for new and existing single-family housing as well as undeveloped residential land, which was then used in a second stage that estimated the price effects of impact fees on these measures. They found that $1 of impact fee increased the selling price of new and existing homes by $1.64 and $1.68, respectively. Both were statistically significant, although neither differed significantly from 1. The explanation offered was consistent with the new view that impact fees act to reduce the property tax burden felt by community residents—lowering future property tax rates. In separate regressions, they estimate the present value of these future property tax savings to be about $1.20 for each $1 of additional impact fees- providing one of the most direct pieces of empirical evidence to support the new view to date.

Ihlanfeldt and Shaughnessy interpreted their results as evidence in support of the argument that impact fees add value for consumers that are capitalized into home prices rather than operating merely as an excise tax that may be passed on to consumers given the right market conditions. This finding is important because it gets to the heart of the most important issue regarding impact fees price effects—are price increases primarily driven by reductions in supply or by increases in the demand for housing due to a more favorable ratio between public infrastructure services and levels of property taxation? Been (2005) has recently commented on Ihlanfeldt and Shaughnessy's interpretation of their findings. She argues that because impact fees add amenity value only to new homes, and because any future savings in property taxes should accrue equally to owners of both new and existing homes, we would expect the Ihlanfeldt and Shaughnessy results to show larger price effects for new as opposed to existing homes. However, because enforceable legal standards generally require equitable access to public services across different parts of a community, the conclusion that impact fees generate public facilities valued *exclusively* by owners of new homes is difficult to believe. While rational nexus tests require impact fee dollars be spent in ways that directly affect new construction, it seems a rather strong assumption that these revenues would be spent on projects that are worthless to existing residents. An example involving school impact fees clarifies this point.

Suppose a community is dealing with overcrowding in their existing elementary schools. Also, suppose that impact fee revenues from an existing school impact fee are pooled and used to pay for at least a portion of the capital cost of building a new elementary school—adding capacity to the school system. While new residents may predominately send their children to the new school, it is incorrect to assume this does not also benefit existing residents since the new school alleviates overcrowding at all existing schools. It is reasonable to characterize this situation as providing a higher level of service to all community residents, rather than just households sending their children to the new school. Note also that this situation would easily pass a rational nexus test. A similar argument can be made for road impact fees leading to less congestion on major thoroughfares throughout the community, even when they are used to build or widen a road traversed primarily by newer residents.

Campbell (2004) finds very similar results using a similar methodology. He investigates the effects of impact fees on house and land prices in several jurisdictions located within the Orlando SMSA. Although it is difficult at times to point to one conclusive piece of evidence given that individual price effects models are estimated for each jurisdiction in his sample, the average price effect coefficient of roughly $1.50 (per $1 of impact fee) for new homes falls in line with the Ihlanfeldt and Shaughnessy study as well as the Mathur, Waddell, and Blanco study. He also estimates the average price effect on existing homes to be roughly $1.00.

Burge and Ihlanfeldt (2006a) investigated the price effects of impact fees on the constant quality price of housing as estimated across different segments of the market for single-family homes. While the work was primarily concerned with estimating the construction effects of impact fees, the authors investigated the price effects as well, to further explore the hypothesis that homebuyers find communities more attractive after they pass or increase impact fees. In the first stage of a two-stage process, they estimated constant quality housing price indexes using both new and existing home sales for each of three "tiers" across all Florida counties that had used impact fees, including water and sewer impact fees, during an eleven year time period from 1993–2003. The natural log of the estimated price indexes was used as the dependent variable in the second stage, which regressed two categories of impact fees (water/sewer impact fees and non-water/sewer impact fees) on housing prices, along with various controls, in both fixed effects and random trends price models. Non-water/sewer impact fees (i.e., roads, schools, parks, etc.) were found to have positive effects on prices, generally achieving statistical significance at conventional levels of confidence. At the point of means, estimated coefficients implied that a $1.00 increase in impact fees would increase the price of small, medium, and large-sized homes by $0.39, $0.82, and $1.27, respectively. While all were significant, the difference in magnitudes implies that the absolute change in price is roughly proportionate to the value of the homes- interpreted as evidence that market demand is increasing from a more favorable ratio between public service levels and future property taxes.

Extending this research to one of the inputs into housing prices, land, Burge (2014) documented how the implementation of impact fees impacted the constant quality price of residential and commercially zoned undeveloped land. He used a 16-year panel dataset of the Florida counties to analyze the effect of various types of impact fees on 1.7 million parcels of land. In particular, the paper focused on the fact that different types of impact fees may have heterogeneous effects on land prices, particularly given that residential and commercial development have different requirements and desires. Findings include the fact that water/sewer impact fees have a differentially stronger and negative impact on undeveloped residential properties than on commercial properties. Given that impact fees for other non-school and non-water/sewer services impact have a larger impact on commercially zoned parcels, this provides evidence that the government regulatory environment likely has a significant impact on how impact fees influence market pricing. In addition, Burge notes that school impact fees, which are a substantial portion of impact fees in some Florida counties, are positively associated with commercial land prices, but negatively associated with residential prices.

11.2.3 Summary

Collectively, evidence to date concerning the price effects of impact fees indicates:

1) Impact fees do lead to higher average housing prices. Focusing on several recent studies that use reliable data and methodological approaches, the estimated price effects for new homes have mostly pointed to a range between $1.50 and $1.70 for a $1.00 increase in impact fees. For existing homes, point estimates are somewhat less consistent, starting at $1.00 and ranging as high as $1.68. Collectively, over-shifting is definitely occurring in the market for new homes and may be occurring in the market for existing homes.

2) Demand-driven increases in willingness to pay are, at least in large part, responsible for these price increases. (As opposed to a reduction in supply.) The new view of impact fee incidence accounts for two positive demand-side effects of impact fees, namely that impact fees are expected to offset future property tax liabilities and that they create infrastructure valued by community residents.

3) Impact fees do not cause price increases of similar absolute magnitudes for expensive vs. more affordable homes. Instead, the increase in willingness to pay seems to be approximately proportional to the value of the home.

4) The effects of impact fee programs on the price of undeveloped land depend on the zoning classification of the parcel, and whether or not the specific impact fee program in question levies fees on that particular category of development.

An understanding of the price effects of impact fees is essential for local governments considering their use. Unfortunately, there are many discussions of impact fees that focus mainly on the first point, failing to recognize the others. Public policy concerning impact fees should be mindful of any potential problems low-income housing consumers may face from rising housing prices among the most affordable homes in the community, but should also recognize where the positive pressure on prices seems to be coming from. As such, while concerns over housing affordability should certainly be addressed within the approach a community takes toward implementing impact fees, they should not be used as a barrier to impact fee implementation within communities that are struggling to find ways to pay for badly needed infrastructure expansions.

11.3 HOUSING PRODUCTION EFFECTS

Although related, it is useful to cover housing price effects and housing production effects through separate discussions. One of the chief concerns about impact fees goes beyond whether and to what extent they may increase housing prices, to whether the production of affordable housing is jeopardized. That is to say, in addition to the worry that impact fees may adversely affect affordability issues within a community, critics of impact fees also express concerns that they may stifle the production of new homes (and particularly smaller homes where the fee is a larger percentage of the costs of producing the homes). This section presents the theoretical and empirical evidence concerning the effects of impact fees on residential construction rates.

11.3.1 Theoretical Evidence

As shown in Section 11.2, existing evidence supports the idea that impact fees increase the demand for housing because they a) lower property taxes, the savings of which are capitalized into home values, and b) are used to provide infrastructure of value to both new and existing community residents. It has also been suggested that impact fee revenues may be leveraged with extra-jurisdictional funds to provide greater value in total facilities than the size of the fees themselves- one potential explanation for the over-shifting phenomenon that is found consistently in recent empirical investigations of price effects. But turning to the question of supply effects, the following

discussion considers the effects of impact fees on the supply curve for new homes and, in turn, on the construction of single-family homes. It will demonstrate how the relationship between impact fees and housing production is quite nuanced, with many important dynamics at work. For a more complete discussion of the model, see Burge and Ihlanfeldt (2006a).

First, it is critical to recognize that impact fees may impact both the demand and supply curves for new residential homes in the community. The positive demand shift is discussed in Section 11.2 and will not be reconstructed here but note that the increase in willingness to pay does mean that *ceteris paribus*; we would expect an increase in the production of residential properties. However, all else is not held constant and there are important supply-side effects to consider. In the end, both supply and demand shifts will interact with one another to determine whether impact fees will slow down, speed up, or have no effect upon residential construction rates.

The supply-side effects of impact fees are multifaceted. The development community has largely followed the traditional approach to impact fee incidence and has argued that impact fees are a tax on residential development, which reduces housing construction by causing a backward shift in the housing supply curve equal to the size of the fee.[6] This conclusion is an outgrowth of the traditional approach to impact fee incidence. While there is no question that the fee creates a cost for developers as they go through the permitting process, several offsetting positive effects are at work as well.

To begin, consider what impact fee revenues actually do: they help provide valuable facilities needed to accommodate growth. If, in the absence of impact fees, new facilities cannot be provided to meet the demands of growth, residential development may be slowed if certain areas do not have adequate services. One could take a different approach and assume local governments force existing residents to pay for these facilities through higher taxes so that the demanded facilities will still all be built. In this case, growth will become highly unpopular, and community residents will become resistant over time to further residential development. The homevoter hypothesis, advanced by Fischel (2001), predicts something has to give in this situation—elected officials will not stay in office if they continue to place unpopular tax increases upon existing homeowners to the benefit of future residents. Therefore, it is unlikely that communities will willingly allow high levels of residential development and higher taxes. If elected officials and those who work for them predictably respond to the interests of their constituents, residential development proposals will be more frequently denied, reducing construction. Furthermore, they may employ specific regulatory policies (other than impact fees) that are designed to limit or stop residential growth. Examples include exclusionary zoning policies, minimum lot size requirements, urban growth or containment boundaries, and potentially lengthening the time required to receive approval (or simply making a conscious effort to lower approval rates for residential projects).

All of these reactions to the unwanted fiscal burden of rapid residential development increase developer's compliance costs but create nothing of value to the community. In contrast, because they help provide facilities needed to accommodate growth, impact fees do provide value added to the community in addition to their desired effect of internalizing some of the external fiscal burdens of new residential development. Among other positive effects, impact fees may increase the supply of buildable land in a manner that is more responsive to growth needs. If so, upward pricing pressures that may occur in the absence of buildable land supply may be moderated. In addition to providing infrastructure that increases the supply of buildable land, impact fees may also cause communities to zone a higher percentage of their land for residential

purposes or to allow higher residential densities. Furthermore, impact fees may reduce the presence or stringency of enforcement for the other types of exclusionary barriers outlined above—a point that was first mentioned by Gyourko (1991) in a theoretical piece investigating the relationship between impact fees and optimal density levels for development. This possibility was also picked up on by Altshuler and Gómez-Ibáñez (1993) and Ladd (1998) and is a component of the model developed by Burge and Ihlanfeldt (2006a). Collectively, these factors may generate at least a partial offsetting of the monetary costs of the impact fee itself and lead to higher probabilities of project approval.

Additionally, impact fees may reduce the time needed to review proposals for development. In the absence of impact fees, local governments will need to review development proposals for their full impact on facilities, and this can delay the decision-making process. Another possibility is that local governments may use lengthy review processes and unforeseen time delays as a strategy to slow down the pace of residential development in their community. Because "time is money" these delays can lead to higher housing prices and lower rates of residential construction. Therefore, besides the direct negative effect that impact fees will have on the supply curve, they are also expected to reduce other preexisting monetary and time-related compliance costs. Therefore, *impact fees generate both positive and negative effects on residential construction*, and there is no *a priori* prediction of a positive or negative net effect. This motivates well-designed empirical research that can answer the important question of whether or not impact fees will actually reduce or enhance the number of affordable housing opportunities within communities, the focus of the next section.

It is worth noting that construction effects may vary across different parts of metropolitan areas and across different size ranges of homes. Burge and Ihlanfeldt (2006a) note that the potential for impact fees to lower other regulatory costs is the strongest in suburban areas, where levels of preexisting residential exclusion have been documented to be the most stringent. Also, both monetary and non-monetary compliance costs may be higher for affordable residential developments than for large single-family developments. For a number of reasons, including fiscal budgetary considerations, communities are more likely to try to exclude higher-density residential developments such as starter homes and multi-family structures than they are large single-family subdivisions.[7] All these considerations motivate research that investigates the supply effects of impact fees across different areas and home size ranges.

Prior to the work of Burge and Ihlanfeldt (2006a, 2006b) there were two theoretical studies that investigated the residential construction effects of impact fees. Brueckner (1997) constructed a model that compares an impact fee scheme for infrastructure financing to two alternative types of cost-sharing schemes. His model produced the conclusion that the effect of impact fees on residential construction rates is *a priori* ambiguous, and that the parameters characterizing the housing market would determine whether impact fees actually slowed down or sped up residential development. Turnbull (2004) compared the development patterns that result from impact fees, urban growth boundaries, and an unregulated environment. He found that optimally constructed impact fees lower construction rates in steady state equilibrium and on the equilibrium path, but that this reduction in development reflects a move to the socially optimal level of construction, as opposed to growth boundaries and the unregulated environment, which lead to above optimal growth rates. While Yinger (1998) does not explicitly model the relationship between impact fees and residential construction, one conclusion of his model is that impact fees cause an increase in demand for housing (along with an assumed decrease in

the supply curve by the amount of the impact fee). Thus, his model also does not predict a definitive positive or negative effect on construction rates.

11.3.2 Empirical Evidence

While many studies have analyzed the effects that impact fees have on housing prices, the existing empirical literature on the relationship between impact fees and housing construction is comparatively thin—consisting of studies by Skidmore and Peddle (1998), Mayer and Somerville (2000), and Burge and Ihlanfeldt (2006a, 2006b).

Skidmore and Peddle's data are a panel of 29 cities contained within Dupage County, a suburb of Chicago, covering the years 1977 to 1992. By the end of this period, just over a third of these cities had implemented impact fees. They regressed the number of new single-family homes built in a given city for a given year on a dummy variable indicating whether the city had an impact fee in a year plus year and city dummy variables, resulting in a two-way fixed effects model. Their model included a number of control variables, such as per household property tax revenue and the average assessed valuation of property in a given city and year. Depending on the specific models they employed, Skidmore and Peddle obtained results indicating that a newly imposed impact fee is associated with about a 25 to 30 percent reduction in residential development rates.

Although pioneering, their study suffers from many important shortcomings. Because their impact fee variable simply registers the existence of a fee and not the dollar amount of fees nor the type of services funded by the fee, it is difficult to place much confidence in Skidmore and Peddle's results. Moreover, because new homes are, on average, more expensive than existing homes, their control variables are not exogenous to the number of new homes built. Finally, they made little effort to consider the manner in which impact fees would likely affect the timing of development in a very-short-run increment. It is easily seen that in advance of impact fees being adopted, developers apply for building permits to generate as large an inventory as they can of pre-fee housing units. The most direct evidence to support this idea comes from a yet unpublished study by John Matthews (2002) that analyzed the timing effects of impact fees on residential permitting in metropolitan Atlanta. Matthews collected data on the number of residential building permits issued each month for 18 months before and after the implementation of impact fees in Fulton and Cherokee counties. The author found that for a small number of months leading up to implementation there were extremely high numbers of permits issued, followed by very low counts for a short period of time following implementation. Within six months, permit levels had exceeded pre-fee rates and continued to rise over the rest of the sample.

Mayer and Somerville use quarterly data on 44 metropolitan areas covering the years 1985 to 1996 to regress the log of the number of single-family housing construction permits issued on impact fees, other land use regulatory variables, and a set of control variables. Like Skidmore and Peddle, Mayer and Somerville used a dummy variable as the measure of impact fees. However, Mayer and Somerville's impact fee variable was measured with even greater error than Skidmore and Peddle's. For all quarterly observations coming from a particular MSA, the impact fee dummy variable equals 1 if impact fees were used somewhere within the MSA in 1989. Not surprisingly, this variable was not found to affect the number of single-family construction permits.

Recall that while impact fees may expedite the review process, they also lower non impact fee related monetary costs of regulation, and cause an increase in the demand for housing within the community—they will also directly increase the developer's building permit fees. Therefore, the central question

remains: do impact fees help or hurt the production of low-income housing? To address this question, Burge and Ihlanfeldt (2006a, 2006b) constructed a unique database on impact fee use among Florida counties over an 11-year (1993–2003) period. In both studies, they estimated separate models for central cities, inner and outer suburban areas, and rural areas. Due to the richness of their data, they were able to employ panel data estimation techniques (including fixed effects and random trend models) that were designed to control for factors other than impact fees that may also affect construction rates. Impact fees were broken down into two distinct categories: those that funded services otherwise covered by property taxes (i.e., roads, schools, parks, police, fire, etc., henceforth labeled non-water/sewer impact fees), and those that funded services for which capital expansion costs are otherwise recouped through higher user fees (water/sewer). Their results include several interesting findings.

First, non-water/sewer impact fees were found to increase the construction of smaller homes and multi-family housing built within Florida's inner suburban areas over this time period. This provides the first piece of empirical evidence that, at least within inner suburban areas where a majority of population growth in Florida and where issues of housing affordability have been highlighted as being the most pressing, the positive effects of impact fees seem to outweigh the direct cost of the fee, leading to higher rates of affordable housing construction. On the other hand, this category of fees had no significant effect on construction rates for either type of affordable housing in central city, outer suburban or rural areas. The implication is that in those regions, the benefits are large enough to avoid a negative effect on affordable housing development but are not large enough to cause a positive relationship. Moving to larger single-family homes, their results show a significant positive effect of non-water/sewer impact fees for both inner and outer suburban areas, again, however, with an insignificant effect on construction rates in the central city and rural areas. The finding that this type of fee increases the construction of large homes but not affordable housing opportunities in outer suburban areas may be evidence that exclusion in outer suburban areas is more than just fiscally motivated. They note that, in comparison to inner suburban areas, the outer suburbs are more homogenous with respect to both income and race, and that addressing the fiscal impact of low-income housing may not be enough to overcome exclusionary barriers.

They also show that the effects of impact fees that fund services otherwise covered by user fees, namely water/sewer impact fees, are different. Water/sewer impact fees are found to be an insignificant determinant of construction rates for all size categories of homes and across all parts of the metropolitan area. The implication is that while water/sewer fees do provide enough benefits to avoid lowering construction rates, these benefits are not larger than the fee itself. Additionally, water/sewer impact fees were found to reduce the construction of multi-family housing, an indication that the benefits of this category of fees may not be large enough to offset the direct cost of the fees for developers of multi-family projects. Additional work investigating the reasons why these two classes of impact fees have somewhat different construction effects is merited.

Recently, counties in Florida and some cities in other states have begun implementing zone-based impact fee schemes. In these cases, impact fees are charged based upon the new construction's location within a jurisdiction. Some counties in Florida, for example, have different fire protection impact fee rates depending on how rural the location is and how much fire protection infrastructure is needed to support the new development. These zone-based schemes can theoretically match impact fee source and use data much better than the more standard broad-based schemes, where all impact fees within a given county/jurisdiction are averaged together to get a uniform impact fee rate.

Since zone-based schemes are relatively new, little research has been done exploring their potentially unique impacts. However, in a paper by Burge et al. (2013) the city of Albuquerque's zone-based impact fee scheme was studied to uncover whether these impact fees had differential intra-city impacts on residential construction. They found evidence that both core central city areas, as well as fringe suburban areas, see reduced residential construction with increasing impact fee rates. These effects occur despite the fact that core city impact fees are only one-third the size of fringe city impact fees. However, the interior portions of the city between the core and fringe find no relationship between impact fees and new residential construction. Thus demonstrating that impact fees, even on a dollar-for-dollar basis, have an impact heavily dependent upon where these impact fees are being collected. Importantly, these impacts occur even though the formula for implementing impact fees was similar in all three regions.

11.3.3 Summary

The effects of impact fees on residential construction rates are considerably more complicated than their effect on prices. Also, studies that have directly investigated supply effects are relatively few in comparison to those that focused on price effects. Unsurprisingly then, our understanding of the effects that impact fees have on housing production is somewhat less refined than our understanding of price effects. Still, several important points are worth highlighting:

1) Although early theoretical work predicted impact fees would have an unambiguous negative effect on residential construction rates, more recent investigations conclude that the direction of the relationship is

ambiguous. The eventual effect depends upon the relative magnitudes of several factors, which may partially or fully offset the monetary cost to developers. This motivates the need for well-designed empirical work.

2) The most reliable empirical evidence to date finds that impact fees that are used to provide infrastructure otherwise funded through property tax revenues (i.e., roads, schools, parks, etc.) have a positive effect on residential construction rates in suburban areas and a negligible impact on construction rates in central city and rural areas. For affordable housing opportunities, this effect seems to be limited to inner suburban areas while it applies to all suburban areas for larger homes.

3) Impact fees that fund services otherwise provided for through user fees (i.e., water and sewer) do not seem to have the same positive effect on construction rates. At best, they seem to have a neutral effect and at worst, they may actually inhibit the production of multi-family housing.

4) Zone-based impact fees demonstrate that even when impact fee rates are set according to varied infrastructure needs within a city, each dollar of charged impact fees carries a significant impact on housing construction. In particular, new developments may shift both within cities themselves and between cities, particularly where amenity levels are similar and relatively substitutable.

An understanding of the complex effects of impact fees on residential construction rates is just as important as an understanding of their impact on housing prices. Policymakers are still influenced by the central conclusion of the traditional approach to impact fee incidence, which asserts that they will reduce construction rates. Often the possibility of using impact fees to address growing problems of inadequate public facilities is derailed over the concern that impact fees will stifle residential construction. As such, it is crucial that state and local government officials become familiar with the more recent evidence that impact fees influence residential growth based on impact fee usage and geography, but importantly residential growth is not necessarily reduced in all cases of impact fee usage. All things considered, effectively crafted impact fee programs can be a part of the solution for local governments that are open to growth, but who also want to grow in ways that satisfy the needs of both current and future community residents.

11.4 ECONOMIC DEVELOPMENT EFFECTS

Let us briefly move away from issues of residential development to the effects that impact fees may have on non-residential development and economic growth defined more generally. Even if impact fees do not have adverse effects on housing affordability and availability, there is still the concern that they may stifle economic development and job growth. This is worth investigating because the long-run feasibility of impact fees as a revenue-raising mechanism requires that they not drive away economic development to neighboring communities. This section first reviews some theoretical considerations and then summarizes the results of the one study that directly addresses the connection between impact fees and economic development (as measured by employment growth).

11.4.1 Theoretical Evidence

Two main questions are addressed in this section: What is the role of impact fees in infrastructure provision and land supply, and are impact fees a tax or a user fee? Each question provides important context for understanding the effects of impact fees on employment and economic development defined more broadly.

11.4.1.1 What Is the Role of Impact Fees on Infrastructure and Land Supply?

Often overlooked in debates about impact fees is what they are actually intended to do. The fundamental purpose of impact fees is to generate revenue to build public infrastructure serving new development (Nelson 1988). In the absence of impact fees, local governments may have difficulty raising the revenue necessary to accommodate growth in terms of paying for new infrastructure. In such cases, growth either is stymied through lengthy planning review processes that are preoccupied with the negative impact the proposed development will have on already congested systems (such as roads and schools), stopped or severely restricted through growth moratoria or permit limits, or simply displaced to other communities because developers are wary of locations with inadequate provision of public facilities and services. Therefore, it is worth noting that impact fee revenues generate valuable infrastructure that otherwise would not have been provided or would have been funded through alternative sources that, over time, would almost certainly lead to other forms of opposition to non-residential development.

There is another effect of impact fees that has been long overlooked in the literature: their impact on land supply. Communities that have adequate central facility capacity, such as in water and sewer treatment, may still lack the distribution network to accommodate new development. From an economic development perspective, the ability to plug into key infrastructure systems such as water, sewer, drainage, and roads is perhaps the important ingredient to increasing the supply of land commensurate with development pressures (Blair and Premus 1987). By providing a revenue source for the costs of extending the distribution network to poorly connected areas that may be otherwise ready for economic development opportunities, impact fees may increase the supply of buildable land and markedly facilitate growth in areas that had previously been lacking in basic services.

Finally, some studies have argued that impact fees appear to reduce the uncertainty and risk involved with development (Nelson et al. 1992). This is accomplished by providing developers with a reasonably predictable supply of buildable land. This is important because the eventual success or failure of most commercial developments is highly dependent upon the presence and vitality of *other supporting developments that may not even be in place yet, but should likely follow*. However, the relationship between impact fees and the supply of buildable land has been largely ignored in the literature (with the notable exception of Kaiser and Burby 1998).

11.4.1.2 Are Impact Fees a Tax or a User Fee?

Even though the context here is non-residential development and job growth, in many ways the discussion must revisit the traditional and new views of impact fee incidence that were previously outlined in the context of residential development. The effect of impact fees on development is controversial. The traditional approach considers them to be an *excise tax* on new development. The problem with this approach is that revenues from excise taxes are not generally used in ways that the payer of the tax has a close connection to. Hence, this view of impact fees may lead to some perverse conclusions since it implicitly assumes those who pay the tax receive no benefits from the revenues. If impact fees are simply an excise tax, the predicted impact is clear: they would shift economic development away from otherwise more efficient outcomes and create a deadweight loss to society. Market participants bear the burden of the tax to the extent that the various supply and demand elasticities for land and developed structures dictate. In a competitive market, we would expect the pace of development to slow and the price of buildable land to fall (Downing and McCaleb 1987). Likewise, if impact fees simply act as a tax on capital without creating value in the development process, markets will adjust by shifting the location of development and/or by raising prices, thus reducing consumption and eroding economic efficiency.

On the other hand, impact fees may behave more like a user fee (benefit tax) if the revenues are used to provide sufficient benefits to the payers of the fee. Under this approach, there is the assumption that developers have an underlying demand for public infrastructure services tied to the locations and communities they wish to locate in and are willing to pay for it. Under this approach, it is possible that impact fees may help expand the supply of buildable land, positively impacting the pace and quality of economic development. Under *rational nexus* criteria, impact fees cannot exceed the cost of infrastructure apportioned to the development *net* of other revenues used to finance the same infrastructure. For example, if federal or state funds are available to help finance infrastructure, the impact fee is based on the cost of infrastructure *less* those external revenue sources. In this way, as noted earlier, the impact fee can leverage more infrastructure investments than the development itself pays for through the fee. Also, note that impact fees must be spent according to an agreed-upon plan (Nicholas, Nelson, and Juergensmeyer 1991). This means that developers can reasonably forecast when and where additional infrastructure will be added. The supply of land made available through these infrastructure investments is thus known in advance. Hence, risk and uncertainty are reduced since the supply of buildable land expands in a predictable manner.

Still, it is not clear *a priori* if impact fees generate sufficient benefits to offset their costs to developers, and the question remains: are impact fees a tax that will reduce new commercial development, or a user fee that is a practical and efficient means of investing in needed infrastructure, potentially encouraging non-residential development and economic growth?

11.4.2 *Empirical Evidence*

Turning to the emerging literature investigating the issue of how development impact fee programs influence the overall level of economic activity and job growth, an early study that set this literature in motion comes from Moody and Nelson (2003). They consider the central question:

Between communities that are identical in every respect except for impact fees, are those with impact fees associated with the generation of more jobs at the margin than those without, all things considered?

They used panel data to examine the relationship between local economic development, defined to be the change in jobs at the county level, and aggregate impact fee collections in the 67 counties of Florida during the period 1993 to 1999. Florida's counties vary considerably with respect to size (7,000 to 2.1 million residents), economic growth rates (strongly positive to stagnant or even negative), and demographic characteristics (affluent, minority composition, urban, rural). Their panel followed counties from 1993 to 1999, encompassing various economic cycles and levels of impact fee assessment. Total impact fee revenues collected by counties in their sample rose from about $100 million in 1993 to nearly $200 million by 1997. During the study period, about half the counties had jurisdictions collecting impact fees, and, of those where fees were collected, the variation in aggregate countywide collections was substantial. Thus, they argued there is sufficient variation in the data to evaluate the "boost-or-drag" effects of impact fees on job growth.[8]

Their analysis found a significant positive correlation between impact fees collected per building permit issued in one year and job growth over the next two years. This finding holds even when controlling for base year employment growth, prior decade employment growth, property taxes per capita, the value of local building permit activity, regional, temporal, and other factors. Their finding was consistent with the hypothesis that impact fees spent on infrastructure development are not a drag on local economies with respect to job growth but, instead, can be beneficial to them. This supports the view of impact fees as a user fee rather than an excise tax, again consistent with the new view.

Following a similar approach, Jeong and Feiock (2006) also found evidence for the positive employment effect story using similar data from Florida counties. They moved from using aggregate impact fees as the independent variable of interest to a dummy variable registering whether the county had any impact fee program in place—so their results should be viewed in light of respecting the extensive margin but not the intensive margin. Additionally, since their panel covered Florida counties over the years 1991–2000, and very few counties adopted impact fee programs during that decade, the empirical identification was essentially cross-sectional. Using an expanded set of control variables, they also concluded that the benefits of impact fee programs outweigh the costs for commercial developers—such that impact fee programs lead to higher job growth.

Burge and Ihlanfeldt (2009) also used county panel data from Florida spanning 1990–2005. Using similar OLS models as the previous two studies, they replicated the findings of Jeong and Feiock. Importantly, the positive effects of fees on employment levels fell apart once the models included (two-way) fixed effects. They concluded that commercial impact fees and residential impact fees have countervailing effects on employment levels—with commercial fees deterring jobs but school impact fees attracting jobs.

Another empirical paper that specifically considered the potential effects of impact fees on the number of firms in a jurisdiction comes from Jones (2015). Focusing on 'small-draw' firms (supermarkets, convenience stores, restaurants, dry-cleaners, and liquor stores), and using a binary impact fee variable indicating whether or not an impact fee program was in place, this paper concluded that counties with impact fees have fewer restaurants per capita, but found no significant correlations with the rates of other establishments.

A departure from the typical empirical approach comes from Burge and Ihlanfeldt (2013), who specifically took on the issue of growth sustainability and development impact fee programs in their *Cityscape* piece. They outlined the five major types of externalities associated with new development that plague cities, and explored how development impact fees could be used as an effective tool to mitigate externality problems in each case. The five externalities were, in no particular order: nonconforming land uses, degradation/destruction of open-space amenities, increased congestion, compromised quality of local public infrastructure, and degraded local environmental quality. They noted that impact fees were already being effectively used to address several of these externality problems, and advocated for the expansion of their utilization to address issues related to environmental amenities and open-space preservation.

Finally, a recent working paper published in the Lincoln Institute for Land Policy series, by Burge and Rohlin (2019), explored the issue of development impact fee programs and local business establishments (i.e., economic activity measured through entrepreneurship) using a country "borders approach." The borders approach had been used successfully by Rohlin and other scholars in many recent papers—the idea being to compare outcomes occurring within arbitrarily small distances (typically one mile) on either side of various geographic county "border-pairs." Their results suggested school impact fees, which are only paid by residential developers, increase the level of new business establishments, local employment, and retail sales. These results are consistent across models using countywide measures and cross-border differences. For commercial impact fees, they found positive or insignificant effects in countywide estimations, but negative effects near county borders, highlighting the importance of using methods that properly control for local economic conditions to give cleanly identified causal estimates. The negative effect of commercial impact fees at the borders provided clear evidence that the enhanced provision of public infrastructure played a critical role in offsetting the potentially negative effects of impact fees on economic activity. Their results highlighted the value of public infrastructure to the business community, as well as the potential for efficiency gains from regionally coordinated impact fee programs.

11.4.3 Summary

The relationship between impact fees and economic development is complex. Insightfully, Moody and Nelson (2003) suggested that more rigorous analysis should be undertaken to explore the short and long-run impacts that impact fee programs have on job growth and other measures of economic activity. Since then, several pieces of evidence have surfaced in the literature that suggests the effects of impact fee programs on local economic development depend upon the category of fee and proximity to the public services being provided by the additional funds. A conservative interpretation of the current literature would be that no discernible adverse economic effects from impact fees are present once the benefits of infrastructure are accounted for.

11.5 CONCLUSIONS

Impact fees have become an important facilitator of community growth and development over the past generation. They have become so widespread in many Western (e.g., California, Arizona, New Mexico) and Southern (e.g., Florida, Texas) states that expanding communities *not* using them in these areas are considered unusual. However, the use of impact fees is not without debate, especially since they represent a large shift away from prior public infrastructure financing mechanisms and land use management techniques.

Public debates often reflect a significant lack of understanding of even their most basic effects- perhaps because so much of the convincing empirical evidence concerning their impacts is relatively new. The current debate focuses primarily on the effect of impact fees on housing prices, residential construction rates (and construction patterns in regard to affordable housing opportunities), and non-residential economic development and growth. Let us review several major findings from the literature.

First, political resistance to property tax increases has compromised the conventional approach to paying for infrastructure. The across-the-board property tax increases that are needed to pay for the full array of system and service extensions are unpopular and unlikely to be feasible in the long run. Alternative financing mechanisms such as impact fees are increasingly being recognized as more feasible policies that enable communities to grow in ways that meet the needs of both current and future residents.

Second, unlike excise taxes, impact fees are earmarked for providing facilities that serve new development and may therefore be better characterized as user fees. The evidence suggests this provision is valued by both residential and commercial development. While impact fees generally do not reflect the full marginal cost of infrastructure improvements, they do establish a clear link between those paying for, and those receiving benefits from, new infrastructure. The direct economic benefits include the actual infrastructure investment, such as new roads, new schools, and new water and sewer system extensions. Indirect benefits are also important and may include improved predictability in the marketplace, knowing when and where infrastructure investment will occur, and that all developers are treated more equitably given that they are willing to pay the fees.

Third, in the absence of impact fees, local governments may simply *not be able to generate the revenue necessary to accommodate growth*. They are likely to react in predictable ways—either by severely limiting the supply of buildable land or by enacting other binding restrictions such as exclusionary zoning, service boundaries, explicit or implicit limitations on the number of building permits to be approved, or even outright restrictions on growth such as moratoria. With impact fees, communities can more effectively generate the infrastructure necessary to open areas for development.

Fourth, impact fees have complex effects on housing prices and land prices. A review of recent theoretical and empirical investigations suggests that while impact fees may raise housing prices, this is not because they are simply "passed forward" to home buyers. Instead, housing prices rise because impact fees lower property taxes and provide facilities of value to the community, increasing residents' willingness to pay for housing. Evidence to support this idea comes from the consistent finding that impact fees produce similar *proportional shifts* in price across different segments of the market for single-family homes rather than similar *absolute shifts*. Also, the consistent finding of over-shifting lends support to the conjecture that impact fee revenues may effectively be used to leverage extra-jurisdictional investment.

Fifth, impact fees have dramatically different short vs. long-run impacts on building permit applications. Developers will predictably try to obtain as many approved permits as they can in the months leading up to the implementation or increase of impact fees which is offset by a period of several months following where relatively fewer permits are issued. Once a program is adopted, developers on both sides of the implementation date bear all the same benefits, but only pay the statutory incidence of the fee if they obtain approval after implementation. Why would one wait to receive no extra benefits but incur an extra cost? On the other hand, this very-short-run spike-dip phenomenon is unlikely to have a noticeable impact on housing starts or completion rates. Also, sound empirical approaches account for this short-run phenomenon by using longer time periods to

measure growth and using lagged rather than contemporaneous values of impact fees.

Sixth, the relationship between impact fees and residential construction rates is even more complicated than their impact on prices and may depend upon the type of impact fee being used, the type of residential development under consideration, and the location of the jurisdiction within the greater metropolitan area. Our understanding of this complicated relationship is inhibited by the relative scarcity of empirical research on the issue. Studies by Burge and Ihlanfeldt (2006a, 2006b) provide the most convincing evidence to date. We find that non-water/sewer impact fees are generally able to increase the stock of housing (including affordable housing) in suburban areas but that no significant relationship is found between impact fee levels and construction rates in central city or rural areas. We also find evidence to support the idea that impact fees which replace property taxes (i.e., roads, schools, parks), generate more benefits than impact fees which replace higher user fees (water and sewer).

Seventh, impact fees do not appear to slow job growth or economic development. The direct investigations of this relationship suggest that, at a minimum, impact fees are not a drag on local economies and that it is more likely that they actually enhance commercial activity and economic growth. Only when the negative impacts of paying the fees become isolated from the benefits of improved infrastructure in the implementing community would one see the type of growth deterrent effects that are a common worry.

In the end, impact fees are no panacea. Housing prices, housing production, economic development, and job growth in communities all depend on a myriad of factors. Nonetheless, impact fees can facilitate the provision of infrastructure improvements needed to sustain economic development, meet housing needs, and even potentially generate more affordable housing than may otherwise be produced in inner suburban areas. A perspective that surfaces from spanning the literature on the effects of impact fees is that much of the early work used a partial equilibrium approach. However, impact fee payments are not added to the development process while everything else remains the same. The best framework for public debates and analytical research concerning impact fees and their effects is to recognize what outcomes their implementation is likely to produce *relative to outcomes that occur when methods other than impact fees are exclusively used to handle situations that would typically motivate impact fee use.* Following this approach it is likely that communities in growing regions that have impact fees may enjoy a higher quality of life and fewer negative effects of growth in the long run than communities in those regions choosing not to use impact fees.

NOTES

1 For example, nationwide population growth rates during the 1950s, 1960s, and 1970s far exceed those seen over the past four decades in the US.
2 Empirical investigations often make this assumption implicitly through their choice of data while theoretical investigations generally make the assumption explicitly.
3 See Huffman et al. (1988) for an outline of three specific types of market elasticity conditions and a discussion of the likely distribution of costs in each.
4 Burge and Ihlanfeldt (2006a) point out that under an alternative assumption- that the property tax rate is held constant and instead impact fee revenues are used entirely for *additional* service provision, the result still holds. In either case there is a more favorable ratio of property tax liabilities to public service provision for homeowners that is capitalized into home values.
5 For example, it is a common practice in Florida to use road impact fees to pay for right-of-way acquisition and engineering, which account for about half the costs of road construction, with a majority of the remaining costs subsidized by the state. From anecdotal evidence, it seems possible that impact fees may create value for the community if revenues can be leveraged to secure state or federal funds.
6 See the homepages of the Urban Land Institute (www.uli.org), the National Association of Home Builders (www.nahb.org), and the National Association of Realtors (www.realtor.org) for their positions.
7 See Ihlanfeldt (2004) for a review of the evidence on various forms of exclusionary land use regulation.
8 Also note that Florida is the ideal case study since it has an extensive history of case law that develops and applies the rational nexus test to impact fee programs.

This increases the likelihood that observed correlations reveal a true cause-and-effect relationship between impact fees and market conditions.

REFERENCES

Altshuler, A. A., & Gomez-Ibañez, J. A. (1993). *Regulation for Revenue: The Political Economy of Land Use Exactions.* Washington, DC: Brookings Institution and Cambridge, MA: Lincoln Institute of Land Policy.

Baden, B. M., & Coursey, D. L. (1999). *An Examination of the Effects of Impact Fees on Chicago's Suburbs.* Harris School Working paper 99, 20. Chicago: University of Chicago, Harris Institute.

Been, V. (2005). Impact fees and housing affordability. *Cityscapes, 8,* 139.

Blair, J. P., & Premus, R. (1987). Major factors in industrial location: A review. *Economic Development Quarterly, 1,* 72–85.

Braun, M. E. (2003). Suburban Sprawl in Southeastern Wisconsin: Planning, politics, and the lack of affordable housing. In M.J. Lindstrom & H. Bartling (Eds.), *Suburban Sprawl: Culture, Theory, and Politics.* Lanham, MD: Rowman & Littlefield.

Brueckner, J. K. (1997). Infrastructure financing and urban development: The economics of impact fees. *Journal of Public Economics, 66,* 383–407.

Burge, G. S. (2014). The capitalization effects of school, residential, and commercial impact fees on undeveloped land values. *Regional Science and Urban Economics, 44,* 1–13.

Burge, G. S., & Ihlanfeldt, K. R. (2006a). Impact fees and single-family home construction. *Journal of Urban Economics, 60,* 284–306.

Burge, G.S., & Ihlanfeldt, K. R. (2006b). The effects of impact fees on multi-family housing construction. *Journal of Regional Science, 46,* 5–23.

Burge, G. S., & Ihlanfeldt, K. R. (2009). Development impact fees and employment. *Regional Science and Urban Economics, 39*(1), 54–62.

Burge, G. S., & Ihlanfeldt, K. R. (2013). Promoting sustainable land development patterns through impact fee programs. *Cityscape, 15*(1), 83–105.

Burge, G. S., & Rohlin, S. (2019). *Location-Based Development Impact Fee Programs and New Business Decisions,* Lincoln Institute of Land Policy working paper.

Burge, G. S., Dronyk-Trosper, T., Nelson, A. C., Juergensmeyer, J. C., & Nicholas, J. C. (2013). Can development impact fees help mitigate urban sprawl? *Journal of the American Planning Association, 79*(3), 235–248.

Campbell, D. (2004). *The Incidence of Development Impact Fees* [Dissertation, Georgia State University].

Delaney, C. J., & Smith, M. T. (1989a). Impact fees and the price of new housing: An empirical study. *AREUEA Journal, 17,* 41–54.

Delaney, C. J., & Smith, M. T. (1989b). Pricing implications of development exactions on existing housing stock. *Growth and Change, 20,* 1–12.

Downing, P. B., & McCaleb, T. S. (1987). The economics of development exactions. In J. E. Frank, & R. M. Rhodes (Eds.), *Development Exactions* (pp. 42–69). Washington, DC: Planners Press.

Dresch, M., & Sheffrin, S. M. (1997). *Who Pays for Development Fees and Exactions.* San Francisco: Public Policy Institute of California.

Fischel, W. (2001). *The Homevoter Hypothesis.* London: Harvard University Press.

Gyourko, J. (1991). Impact fees, exclusionary zoning, and the density of new development. *Journal of Urban Economics, 30,* 242–256.

Huffman, F. E., Nelson, A. C., Smith, M. T., & Stegman, M. A. (1988). Who bears the burden of development impact fees? *Journal of the American Planning Association, 54,* 49–55.

Ihlanfeldt, K. R. (2004). Exclusionary land-use regulations within Suburban communities: A review of the evidence and policy prescriptions. *Urban Studies, 41*(2), 261–283.

Ihlanfeldt, K. R., & Shaughnessy, T. M. (2004). An empirical investigation of the effects of impact fees on housing and land markets. *Regional Science and Urban Economics. 34*(6), 639–661.

Jeong, M.-G., & Feiock, R. (2006). Impact fees, growth management, and development: A contractual approach to local policy and governance. *Urban Affairs Review. 41*(6), 749–768.

Jones, A. (2015). Impact fees and employment growth. *Economic Development Quarterly, 29*(4), 341–346.

Kaiser, E.J. and Burby, R.J. (1998). Exactions and managing growth: The land-use planning perspective. In R. Alterman (Ed.), *Private Supply of Public Services: Evaluation of Real Estate Exactions, Linkage, and Alternative Land Policies* (pp. 113–126). New York: New York University Press.

Ladd, H. F. (1998). *Local Government Tax and Land Use Policies in the United States: Understanding the Links.* Cambridge, MA: Lincoln Institute of Land Policy.

Mathur, S., Waddell, P., & Blanco, H. (2004). The effect of impact fees on the price of new single-family housing. *Urban Studies, 41*(7), 1303–1312.

Matthews, J. L. (2002). Across the border? Developers response to impact fee implementation: Case study of metropolitan Atlanta jurisdictions. In Georgia Tech Conference Impact Fee Symposium, Atlanta, GA, April 2002.

Mayer, C. J., & Tsuriel Somerville, C. (2000a). Land use regulation and new construction. *Journal of Urban Economics, 48*(1), 85–109.

Moody, M., & Nelson, A. C. (2003). *Paying for Prosperity: Impact Fees and Job Growth.* Brooking Institution Center on Urban and Metropolitan Policy Paper, 2003.

Nelson, A. C., Ed. (1988). *Development Impact Fees: Policy Rationale, Practice, Theory, and Issues.* Chicago: Planners Press.

Nelson, A. C., Lillydahl, J. H., Frank, J. E., & Nicholas, J. C. (1992). Price effects of road and other impact fees on urban land. *Transportation Research Record, 1305,* 36–41.

Nicholas, J. C., Nelson, A. C., & Juergensmeyer, J. C. (1991). *A Practitioner's Guide to Development Impact Fees.* Chicago: Planners Press.

Singell, L. D., & Lillydahl, J. H. (1990). An empirical examination of the effect of impact fees on the housing market. *Land Economics, 66*(1), 82–92.

Skaburskis, A., & Qadeer, M. (1992). An empirical estimation of the price effects of development impact fees. *Urban Studies, 5,* 653–667.

Skidmore, M., & Peddle, M. (1998). Do development impact fees reduce the rate of residential development? *Growth and Change, 29*(3), 383–400.

Turnbull, G. K. (2004). Urban growth controls: Transitional dynamics of development fees and growth boundaries. *Journal of Urban Economics, 55*: 215–237.

Yinger, J. (1998). The incidence of development fees and special assessments. *National Tax Journal. 51,* 23–41.

12 TOWARD A SUPPLY-SIDE THEORY OF DEVELOPMENT IMPACT MITIGATION

12.1 OVERVIEW

Every land use change has impacts. If the change creates more development serving more people, it will increase demand for such public facilities as water, wastewater, roads, public safety, parks and recreation, and so forth. Who pays for this? Historically, it has been local government and their taxpayers and ratepayers. The problem is that governments are increasingly shifting the burden of paying for mitigating these impacts from taxpayers/ratepayers to the new development itself. Reasons include: declining federal/state aid to local governments; increasing federal and state unfunded mandates; rising service demands as the public wants more and better services; the political ease with which to narrow the funding burden to a smaller base; increasing costs of infrastructure; and sustained taxpayer revolts against new taxes or increases in existing ones.[1]

Chapter 10 evaluated impact fees in the context of public finance theory, finding they are mostly a second-best solution compared to general taxes for public safety, education, and parks and recreation, although sound choices for water-related and electrical utilities, and transportation. While Chapter 10 mostly addresses theory, Chapter 11 synthesizes research into outcomes of impact fees on housing prices and economic development. In this chapter, we present a theory advancing the proposition that impact fees can increase the supply of efficient development, improve equity, and increase the supply of housing that is affordable to more people.

12.2 THE GENERAL SUPPLY-SIDE THEORY OF IMPACT FEES

Impact fees are a form of mitigation and therein lies a source of concern. For some, development brings new demands, changes, and degradation of the community and environment. Those impacts need to be mitigated by new development to remedy its impacts. Does this mean it mitigates all development impacts? If impacts are adverse this may be the case but what if new development brings a higher standard of living to the community or improves its overall quality of life, does it need to undo these benefits? Of course not. Mitigation tends to focus on remedying the negative externalities of new development, leaving the positive externalities alone. To developers and others, the positive externalities need to be weighed against the negative ones with the net difference to be remedied, which could include payments by the community back to the development—a process called concessions.

The balancing of negative and positive impacts can be done through a benefit–cost analysis where net negative externalities are remedied by the development, and net positive ones are payments to the development by the community. But this is not how mitigation works in practice for the vast majority of projects. For one thing, benefit–cost analysis can be expensive and time-consuming, which is why it is limited to mostly large projects, if at all. For another, it requires special sets of skills by analysts, and is prone to litigation which can delay projects for years and sometimes decades. The result may be an inefficient outcome because the process is inefficient. However, by being limited to mitigating the impact on specific facilities, impact fees simplify the analysis of each facility. While being inefficient because not all development impacts are assessed holistically, it is efficient procedurally nonetheless because impact fees

DOI: 10.4324/9781003336075-15

are based on a fee schedule and not ad hoc, case-by-case analysis. Moreover, the development itself can remedy its own impacts if it chooses to do so and will if the cost to mitigate its impacts is less than what it would pay to local government through impact fees. This would be an efficient outcome.

Impact fees are often characterized in the literature as *per se* reducing development because they increase costs. In Chapter 11, Burge and Dronyk-Trosper show that in a competitive real estate market, impact fees are theoretically capitalized backward in the price of land meaning, for instance, that a development projected to pay $100,000 in impact fees will usually result in the price of land to the developer being reduced by $100,000. Much of the literature presupposes this is not the case, however, with the effect being less development after impact fees are implemented than before. Figures 12.1 and 12.2 illustrate this thinking.

Based on the conventional economic theory of development, Figure 12.1 illustrates development conditions before impact fees. The vertical axis is the price of a unit of development

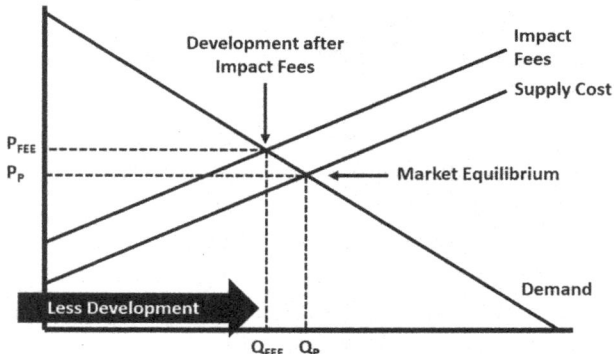

FIGURE 12.2 Standard theory of supply and demand after impact fees. New development can create negative externalities in the form of new demand for facilities. If new revenue from new development is insufficient to finance new facilities it demands, mitigation may be needed in the form of impact fees to do so. Under the conventional theory of land use regulation, impact fees are a cost added to the new development, which increases the price of new facilities. Production of new development falls from Q_P to Q_{FEE}.

(P), while the horizontal axis is the quantity of development produced (Q). The demand (D) for development decreases as costs rise. To the developer, as the price increases, more development can be built, but as the price rises, demand falls. Given developers' cost of production (*Supply Cost*), the equilibrium price is reached at P_P where the quantity of development built is at Q_P. Figure 12.1 provides a base for exploring development outcomes associated with respect to:

Impact fees based on conventional theories of regulation.
Infrastructure investment to facilitate development.
The special supply-side theory of impact fees with respect to housing affordability.

As will be shown, impact fees can facilitate development generally as well as increase the supply of housing that is affordable to more people. We will also show how impact fees can undermine housing affordability.

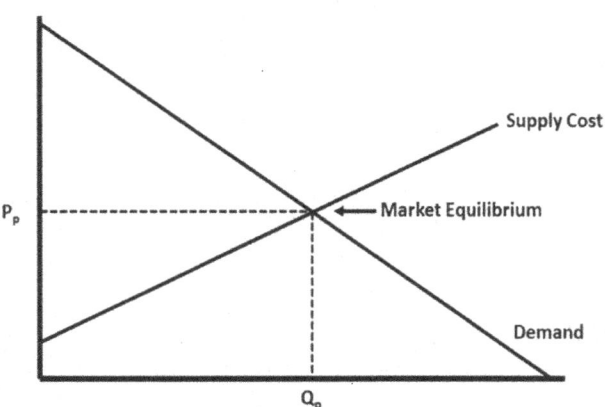

FIGURE 12.1 Development supply and demand before impact fees. As development prices rise, the supply of development will also increase until demand is met at P_P beyond which there is no demand for development at that price, so production is limited to Q_P. This is market equilibrium. Development can include homes, offices, stores and so forth.

12.3 IMPACT FEES BASED ON CONVENTIONAL THEORIES OF REGULATION

Suppose development mitigation is implemented in the form of impact fees. According to the conventional theory of land use regulation,[2] all regulations reduce the supply of development illustrated in Figure 12.2. The reduction can be efficient, however, if mitigation compensates society for the impacts of development or prevents negative externalities from occurring. Assuming no backward capitalization of impact fees, impact fees are a cost added to new development, as seen in the *Impact Mitigation Fee* line. Prices rise to offset the costs, thereby shifting the equilibrium from Q_P to Q_{FEE}, meaning that less development occurs because of mitigation, even if efficiency gains are made because negative externalities are internalized.

As discussed in Chapter 11, backward capitalization of impact fees can offset supply reduction effects when land cost is reduced by the impact fee amount. This occurs in the short run when the market attempts to work impact fees into the price of development. There are two potential limitations, either of which can affect development supply in the long run. First, owners of developable land may have a reservation price below which they will not sell—even if their decision is inefficient because they may gain higher long-term returns by reinvesting sales proceeds into new ventures. Second, such owners may be speculators with a long-term perspective. Institutional investors can have multigenerational time frames meaning that immediate returns from the sale of their land may not fit into their long-term scheme. In both cases—reservation prices and long-term speculation—owners may keep their land off the market in the short-term, thus driving prices up.

We turn next to an oft-forgotten purpose of impact fees: increase the supply of infrastructure to make more development possible and perhaps even help drive down the price of new development compared to an infrastructure-constrained scenario.

12.4 IMPACT FEES AS THE GREASE TO FACILITATE DEVELOPMENT

Unlike other forms of mitigation, the sole purpose of impact fees is to expand the supply of infrastructure. They are thus a growth facilitation tool as opposed to a growth control one. In fact, anti-growth, slow-growth, growth control, and NIMBY groups often oppose impact fees for that reason.

If we think of the basic supply/demand diagram shown in the figures above, new entrants into the local housing market where marginal infrastructure costs exceed marginal revenue from new development, then we should expect the demand curve to shift to the left over time for two reasons:

First, there may be a reduction in consumer preferences for lower levels and quality of service and quality of service and,

Second, the relative price of housing locally would increase compared to other areas in the region because a lower quantity of infrastructure restricts supply.

These impacts would result in a reduction in the total quantity of homes provided.

Implementing an impact fee could stabilize marginal infrastructure costs to equal or even be less than marginal revenue from new development. Thus, even if the fee would still result in a lowering of Q as expected normally, it could restore the demand side back to the market equilibrium, pushing Q back upward.[3] If there are other potential positives, as we will note later, this could lead to a high enough shift in demand to result in a Q greater than the initial market equilibrium.

Consider Figure 12.3. In the absence of impact fees and lacking other revenue to

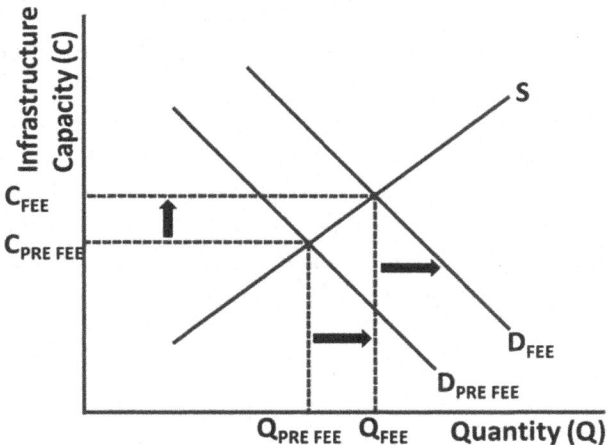

FIGURE 12.3 Development after impact fees expand infrastructure investment. In this figure, the Y-axis is infrastructure capacity (measured in any number of metrics), while the X-axis is the quantity of development. In the absence of impact fees and for lack of funds to expand infrastructure capacity, the line $C_{PRE-FEE}$ shows how this constrains the supply of buildable land (either in volume or capacity of existing sites to be developed), resulting in $Q_{PRR-FEE}$ quantity of development. The market demand that might be attracted to the community is displaced to elsewhere in the region or simply not met, but that may also increase the local cost of housing if local demand exceeds local supply. With impact fees, infrastructure capacity is increased to C_{FEE}. Because more of the market demand can be absorbed by the community, the demand line shifts to D_{FEE}. This allows development to increase to Q_{FEE}.

expand infrastructure commensurate with demand, the supply of development, S, is constrained to the infrastructure capacity at $I_{PRE-FEE}$, where the quantity of development is at $Q_{PRE-FEE}$. This will happen when the supply of buildable land is constrained for a lack of infrastructure capacity. The demand for development in the community is thus constrained at $D_{PRE-FEE}$. In effect, an insufficient infrastructure capacity is a form of growth control in that only some of the regional market demand for development can be accommodated locally. Indeed, this is one of the objectives of anti- or slow- growth control

advocates. What is not shown are price effects when land supply is constrained because of infrastructure constraints. One would normally expect that housing prices would rise.

Consider what happens when infrastructure investment increases, such as increasing water or wastewater capacity, road capacity, school capacity, and so forth. Impact fees increase infrastructure capacity from $I_{PRE-FEE}$ to I_{FEE}. The community can accommodate a larger share of the regional market demand for development, shown in a shift of the demand line from $D_{PRE-FEE}$ to D_{FEE}. This allows more development to occur, illustrated as the difference between $Q_{PRE-FEE}$ and Q_{FEE}.

But impact fees are more than just a direct transfer of mitigation payments by new development for infrastructure. They convey to fee-payers a commitment by the local government to invest in infrastructure. This has four outcomes benefiting development.

First, pursuant to most state enabling acts and in states where home rule and other authority is used, impact fees must be spent for the purposes for which they were collected. In many states, impact fees need to help finance a capital improvement plan comprised of specific facilities and a time frame for improvements (see Chapters 3 and 6). This provides *certainty* in the use of funds.

Second, impact fees must to be spent *timely*. In many states, they must be spent or encumbered within five to ten years of collection, or the funds need to be returned. This ensures timeliness of benefits received based on payments made.

Third, impact fees must be spent reasonably close to development paying those fees (such as through service areas) to ensure a nexus between the impact of new development on infrastructure and benefits received.[4]

Fourth, because of the implied promise to provide facilities for which impact fees were collected, local governments may need to give *priority* to funding impact fee projects over others.

These are important advantages developers enjoy through impact fee programs. They can also put local governments into a bind unwittingly if other needs arise, especially those advanced by citizens, if impact fee projects have higher priority.

We acknowledge that this "development grease" theory of impact fees is in need of formal treatment and testing. One way to approach it would be to model the market for infrastructure in the community and the market for housing separately. The linkage between the two would be the capacity constraint as outlined above. Each could have its own equilibrium price where the price of housing is the key focal point for the housing affordability connection. A key modeling feature would be to allow local public finance officials to bond new infrastructure expansion projects if they have the impact fee program in place, which guarantees the impact fee revenue concurrent with the new housing construction. This is the essence of impact fees "greasing the wheel" of development.[5]

There is yet another, often overlooked but very robust advantage of impact fees: Their ability to *leverage* external funds. For instance, in some states, state investment in highways can be accelerated if a local government acquires rights-of-way and provides the engineering drawings, which might account for about a quarter of total road costs. In this example, one dollar of local impact fee is leveraged into three dollars of external funding. Leveraging can occur to varying degrees for many facilities.

There is also a market capitalization implication. Research has shown that backward capitalization of impact fees occurs in relatively competitive markets. That is, sellers of land will absorb impact fee costs incurred by developers.[6] That does not mean housing prices are reduced because the lower land price is simply offset by impact fees used to provide the infrastructure needed to support new development. Where impact fees are used to leverage more investment, the market will capitalize those incremental benefits into higher sales prices of homes. In this respect, impact feres can *appear* to increase the price of homes when in fact all the market is doing is capitalizing the value of infrastructure leveraged by impact fees.

12.6 THE SPECIAL SUPPLY-SIDE THEORY OF IMPACT FEES WITH RESPECT TO HOUSING AFFORDABILITY

With apologies to Einstein for his special theory of relativity, we pose a special theory of impact fees and housing affordability. We address a nuance of impact fee calculation that is common but that we will show is not consistent with proportionate share principles but does not advance housing affordability. We start by presenting Census information showing that on average larger homes are occupied by more people than smaller homes and thus have more impact on infrastructure.

The concern is that residential impact fees tend to be applied on the basis of the whole unit or sometimes categories of residential units such as single-family detached and multi-family attached (which can include apartments, condominiums, and townhouses, among others). But size matters, as federal data show. In Table 12.1, using the *American Housing Survey* for 2019,[7] we show the persons per unit considering all units residential units by type and size for single-family detached, single-family attached (townhouse) and all other attached units.[8]

We point out four statistically important distinctions within and between these categories of residential development:

TABLE 12.1 Persons per Unit for Occupied and Total Units for Single-Family Detached, Townhouse and All Other Attached Units, 2019

Metric	Square Footage of Persons per Unit based on Unit Size									
	Total	Less than 500	500 to 749	750 to 999	1,000 to 1,499	1,500 to 1,999	2,000 to 2,499	2,500 to 2,999	3,000 to 3,999	4,000 or more
Single-Family Detached										
Persons per Occupied Unit	2.54									
Vacancy Rate	4.78%									
Persons per Unit, all Units	2.42	1.62	1.91	2.14	2.35	2.49	2.63	2.75	2.92	2.96
Single-Family Attached (Townhouse)										
Persons per Occupied Unit	2.36									
Vacancy Rate	5.50%									
Persons per Unit, all Units	2.23	na	1.42	1.88	2.28	2.42	2.18	2.21	na	na
All Other Attached										
Persons per Occupied Unit	1.97									
Vacancy Rate	10.90%									
Persons per Unit	1.76	1.22	1.53	1.87	2.19	1.91	2.03	na	na	na

Note: "na" means small sample size.

Source: Compiled from the American Housing Survey for 2019. See www.census.gov/programs-surveys/ahs.html.

- Single-family detached units range from 1.62 persons per unit less than 500 square feet[9] to 2.96 persons per unit of 4,000 square feet or more. The larger detached homes average 1.8 more persons and therefore nearly twice the impact on facilities as the smaller home.
- Townhouses range from 1.42 persons in units of 500 to 749 square feet to 2.21 persons in units of 2,500 to 2,999 square feet. The larger townhouses average nearly 1.6 more persons and therefore more than half again the impact on facilities as the smaller townhouse.
- All other attached units range from 1.22 persons in units of less than 500 square feet to 2.03 persons in units of 2,500 to 2,999 square feet. All other attached units average nearly 1.7 more persons and therefore

more than half again the impact on facilities as the smaller townhouse.
- The largest discrepancy is between large single-family detached and all other small attached units. Many impact fees are based on an implicit one-size-fits-all assumption that all residential units have the same impact on infrastructure, based on just the average. At the extreme, Table 12.1 shows vast disproportionalities. For instance, at 2.96 persons per unit, single-family homes over 4,000 square feet have 2.4 times the impact on infrastructure as multi-family homes under 500 square feet, which average 1.22 persons per unit.

Vacancy rates are also important, which is why Table 12.1 reports persons per unit based on unit size and type, considering all units, not just vacant ones. (Because of data limits, we use the overall vacancy rate for each type.) For instance, many park impact fee programs charge residential units as though they were fully occupied all the time. The result will be more money is collected than needed to meet the needs of residents occupying homes in the community. This logic applies to educational, library, and other infrastructure as well.

There are efficiency and equity outcomes with a one-size-fits-all residential impact fee. If impact fees are disproportionately higher on smaller, more affordable homes, fewer of those homes will be built. In contrast, if impact fees are disproportionately lower on larger, less affordable homes, more of those homes will be built. Not only do disproportionalities create inequitable outcomes, they also create inefficient outcomes. If impact fees are disproportionately lower on larger homes with more people living in them, the economic outcome would be more larger homes being built than anticipated, thereby creating more demands on infrastructure but with less money to pay for the impacts.

How can analysts generate these kinds of community-specific data for use in impact fee analysis? The 2020 Census will be a convenient way in which to do this over the next several years, if not to the 2030 Census. The 2020 Census will report the number of persons living in units based on the "units in structure," such as single-family detached, single-family attached (townhouse), and all other attached residential units. It will also report vacancy rates for each type of unit. Local property tax assessment records for 2020 can then be used to calculate the total square feet of each residential category. For instance, if there is 2,000,000 square feet of single-family detached space in the community and if there are 5,000 people living in single-family detached units based on the 2020 Census, there is an average of 800 square feet per person. The local impact fee could be scaled based on this combination of federal Census data and local assessor data. The impact fee could be scaled on the basis of the size of the home in square feet. In this way, larger homes that average more people in them and have more impact on facilities than smaller homes would pay proportionately higher impact fees. We apply this principle in the Coda to Chapter 15.

Let us now apply these principles to the special theory of impact fees and housing affordability. Consider a county that charges the same school facility impact fee for all residential units regardless of the number of school children generated by residential units based on their size and type. (We are using figures from a county's actual study.) Table 12.2 shows how the county calculates school impact fees. The county's consultants calculated the fee based on the type of residential unit. However, the county decided to assess school impact fees based on the

TABLE 12.2 County School Facility Impact Cost by Residential Type

Residential Type	Single-Family	Multi-family	Average
Students per Unit[a]	0.273	0.127	0.225
Impact Fee	$2,942	$2,942	$2,942
Proportionate Share Calculation*	$3,573	$1,658	
Impact Fee (Under)-Over Relative to Proportionate Share Calculation	($632)	$1,284	
Ratio of Proportionate Share Calculation to Actual Impact Fee	0.8	1.8	
Multi-Family to Single-Family Multiplier		2.2	

* Proportionate share calculation is:

overall average. The result is that multi-family units are charged about 1.8 times more than their proportionate share of their impact on school facility costs. While single-family units pay about 0.8 times (or about 20 percent less than) their proportionate share, multi-family units pay more than double (about 2.2 times) than single-family units to mitigate its proportionate share impact on schools. This is both inefficient and inequitable.

[The formula is: (Students per Unit for each Type)/(Weighted Mean) x (Weighted Mean Actual Impact Fee)]

We note that this particular county is concerned about dwindling housing affordability. During the years when its average cost-based school impact fees were implemented, the number of permits for townhouse and condominium units fell to zero, while apartments accounted for only six percent of new permits, with single-family detached homes comprising 94 percent. Although circumstantial, one of the outcomes of impact fees that are not proportionate to the size and type of residential units is that the market

shifts away from housing that is more affordable to housing that is less. This is illustrated in Figure 12.4.

In Figure 12.4, the effect of average cost-based impact fees is to increase the cost of smaller, more affordable homes (that have fewer residents and thus lower impacts than larger homes) disproportionately to their impact. In Chapter 13, we show that as impact fees generate benefits for new development—such as increased roads, parks, and sewers—they create more value than the fee itself. But if impact fees are higher than the costs of mitigation, benefits will be lower as total costs rise (see Figure 12.4 for an expanded discussion of this). This is shown in the shift of the cost curve from the *Supply Cost* to the *Impact Fees* line. The effect on housing affordability is to decrease supply from Q_p to Q_{FEE}. The reason is that smaller and usually less expensive homes are paying higher impact fees than are proportionate to their impact. This need not be the case, as we show in Figure 12.5.

Let us suppose that residential impact fees are proportionate to their impact based on

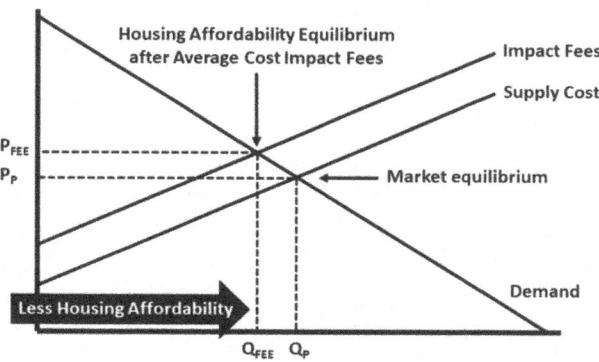

FIGURE 12.4 Supply of housing that is affordable after impact fees with constant impact fees regardless of impact. To help finance infrastructure, impact fees are imposed on all new homes at the same amount (average cost), meaning smaller homes with smaller impacts pay the same as larger homes with larger impacts. For the submarket of homes affordable to lower-income households, the effect of impact fees is to increase supply prices from P_p to P_{FEE} but also to reduce the supply of those homes from Q_p to Q_{FEE}.

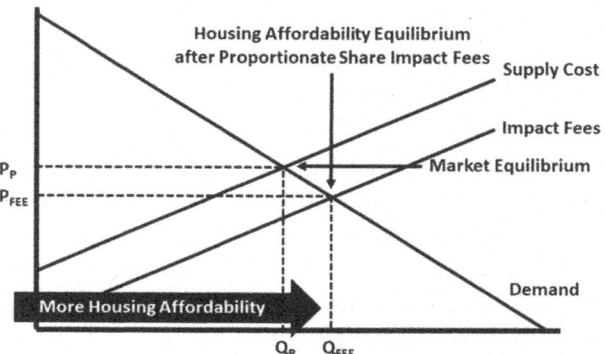

FIGURE 12.5 Supply of housing that is affordable after impact fees are proportionate to impact. Combined with other benefits associated with impact fee policy (see text), if impact fees are scaled to the impact of homes based on size and type, the cost of smaller, more affordable homes falls from the *Supply Cost* line to the *Impact Fee* line. More homes meeting market affordability are produced between Q_p to Q_{FEE}.

house size and type. This is illustrated in Figure 12.5. The *Impact Fee* line shows total costs, including impact fees, and falls below the *Supply Cost* line. Without impact fees, the *Supply Cost* line includes development costs in the absence of impact fees. These can include such things as development approval permitting delay. One feature of impact fees is that a fee schedule replaces ad hoc, case-by-case negotiation leading to off-site mitigations that can be more costly than impact fees and sometimes unconstitutional. Another is that NIMBY (not-in-my-backyard) opposition to affordable housing is mollified since it "pays its own way" through impact fees. This reduces permitting delays as well as costs associated with ad hoc negotiations. Reducing delay and generating more certainly in what is needed for mitigations can reduce development costs relative to the alternative. Moreover, because impact fees can leverage additional funds, benefits can exceed impact fee costs. But these benefits can be swamped if the impact fees themselves are higher than proportionate share costs, which can dampen the supply of housing affordability, as shown in Figure 12.4. If impact fees are proportionate to costs and all the other benefits are present, there can be an increase in housing affordability, illustrated by the shift from Q_P to Q_{FEE}.

Impact fees that are designed to mitigate the costs of a particular development, especially housing, can have a stimulative effect by generating more lower-cost housing. While counter-intuitive to many because any cost added to housing may reduce its supply, the practical effect of no impact fees may be no increase in the supply of infrastructure needed to meet the market demand for lower-cost housing. Yet, if impact fees are higher than the impacts of lower-cost housing, fewer lower-cost housing units will be built. This is the economic outcome of impact fees when they are the same on all housing units regardless of size,

type, and location, as seen in Table 12.2 and illustrated in Figure 12.4. On the other hand, if impact fees are lower than the mitigation cost on higher-cost housing, more of that housing will be built. The outcome is classically inefficient as more high-cost and less low-cost development occurs. This will drive communities to raise new revenues to offset the revenue shortfall associated with under-pricing infrastructure.

In the next chapter, we will extend the economic foundations to good planning and value capture.

NOTES

1 See Arthur C. Nelson, *Development Impact Fees: The Next Generation*, 26 The Urban Lawyer, 541 (1994); Alan A. Altshuler and Jose A. Gomez-Ibanez, Regulation for Revenue: The Political Economic of Land Use Exactions 25-26 (1993); and Alan C. Weinstein, *The Ohio Supreme Court's Perverse Stance on Development Impact Fees and What to Do About It*, 60 Clev. St. L. Rev. 655 (2012).

2 For a review, see Joseph Gyourko and Raven Molloy (2014), *Regulation and Housing Cost*, Working Paper 20536, National Bureau of Economic Research, retrieved April 15, 2021 from www.nber.org/papers/w20536.

3 We are indebted to Trey Dronyk-Trosper for insights from the second paragraph to the discussion of Figure 12.3.

4 A notable exception is Utah where its enabling act allows local governments to declare their entire jurisdiction as one service area. This has the effect of new development paying impact fees for infrastructure investments upwards of 50 or more miles away.

5 We are indebted to Greg Burge for outlining the next steps in theory building and testing.

6 This is often done through a land purchase option agreement where the purchase price is reduced by impact fees and other factors.

7 The American Housing Survey (AHS) is sponsored by the Department of Housing and Urban Development (HUD) and conducted by the US Census Bureau. It has been the most comprehensive national housing survey in the United States since its inception in 1973, providing information on the size, composition, and quality of the nation's housing, measuring changes in housing stock as it ages, and the characteristics of people who live in these homes. The AHS is a longitudinal housing unit survey conducted biennially in odd-numbered years for the national and as well as eight-year cycles for about 40 metropolitan areas. See www.census.gov/programs-surveys/ahs/about.html.

8 We exclude manufactured homes because they are a very small share of total housing and we cannot distinguish between those on individual lots which would make them single family detached units, and those in mobile home parks. Historical AHS data show that the number of manufactured homes in mobile home parks has declined in recent decades.

9 These can include "tiny homes" (see https://thetinylife.com/what-is-the-tiny-house-movement/) as well as "cottage homes" in the US (see www.theplancollection.com/house-plan-related-articles/cottage-style-meets-modern-lifestyle).

13 GOOD PLANNING, VALUE-ADDED PLANNING, AND VALUE CAPTURE

13.1 OVERVIEW

In this chapter, we characterize the economic features of "good" planning and value-added planning, and show how a share of value-added planning can be captured and reinvested in the community to create even more community value. We begin by establishing what we mean by good planning, and then also what constitutes "bad" planning. We then present the concept of value-added planning, which, as the term implies, is planning that creates value for the community. We then review an approach to assigning shares of value added to different sets of decision makers, focusing on the share of value attributable to planning generally and public infrastructure investments in particular. A theory of value capture attributable to planning value added is outlined, which is based loosely on "betterment" and "planning gain" concepts of the United Kingdom. We conclude by outlining methods of value capture used in the US, focusing on "value increment" and "value recoupment" approaches with special reference to impact fees.

13.2 GOOD PLANNING

We start with a conceptual framework for what constitutes "good" planning and proceed with the role of mitigation to advance it.

There are perhaps as many definitions of planning as there are people engaged in it. Here we review some of the key principles of what constitutes "good" planning in our view. These principles are adapted from Nelson, Duncan, Mullen, and Bishop (1995) as well as Nelson, Marshall, Nicholas, and Juergensmeyer

(2017). These principles are summarized and discussed below, albeit briefly:

- Meet market demand-based needs.
- Preserve public and merit goods.
- Maximize the use of existing infrastructure to minimize costs.
- Minimize adverse land use interactions and maximize positive ones;
- Equitably distribute the benefits and burdens of change.
- Elevate quality of life.

We reviewed key features of these aspirational goals in Chapter 6, to which we refer the reader. We posit that good planning is successful when all these principles are achieved.

13.3 BAD PLANNING = INEFFICIENT LAND USE PATTERNS

Bad planning can take many forms, especially in the land use context by allocating more land than needed for development or less land than needed, thereby displacing development of other communities. It can also take the form of over-allocating land for just one kind of land use, such as large single-family detached homes on large lots, thereby forcing everyone to buy only those homes even if they do not want them. The result is often called "urban sprawl," but this can mean different things to different people. We offer our own economic perspective, which defines sprawl as an inefficient allocation of land. This is illustrated in Figure 13.1. For simplicity, the lines are straight, though in reality they are likely curves if not based on power functions such as logarithmic transformations.

DOI: 10.4324/9781003336075-16

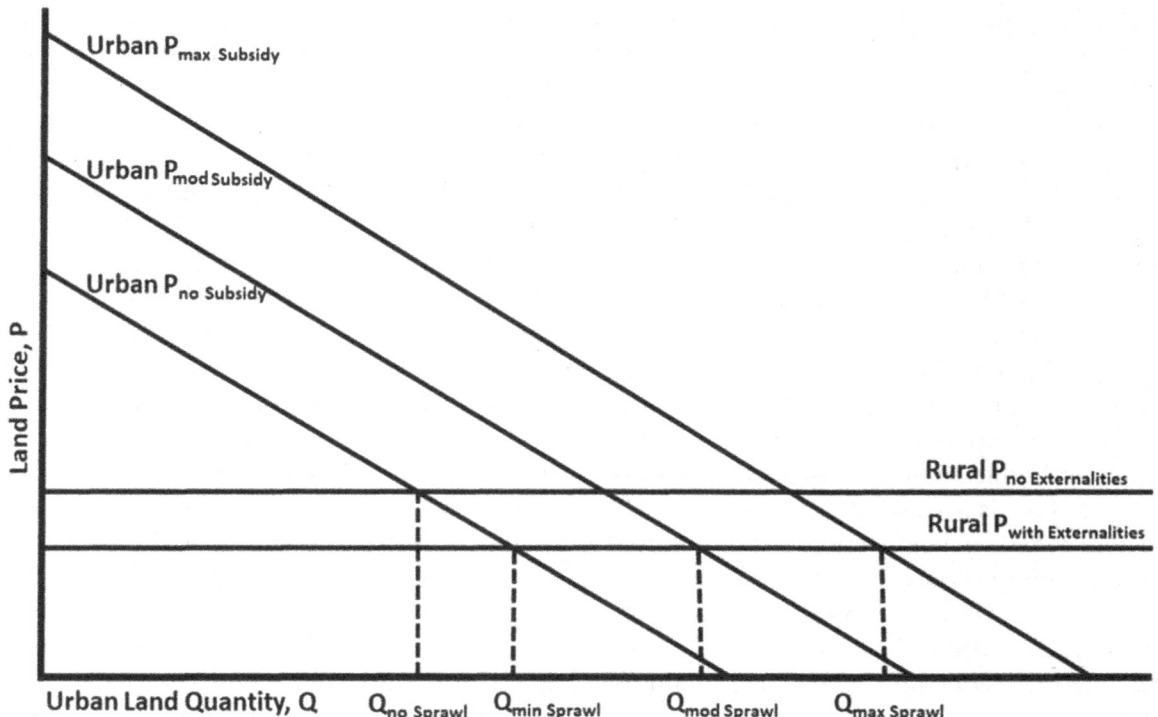

FIGURE 13.1 Urban sprawl as the interaction between negative externalities on rural land and positive subsidies on urban land. The market value of rural land exclusive of negative externalities is shown as *Rural P*$_{no\ Externalities}$. The market value of urban land exclusive of development subsidies is shown as *Urban P*$_{no\ Subsidy}$. The intersection of *Rural P*$_{no\ Externalities}$ and *Urban P*$_{no\ Subsidy}$ is the urban—rural boundary established by the market, *Q*$_{no\ Sprawl}$. Land to the left of it is more valuable for urban uses while land to the right of it is more valuable for rural uses. This is the simplest definition of *efficient distribution of land use* where sprawl does not exist in an economic framework even though it may appear sprawling to observers. However, even in the absence of subsidies for urban development, nearby urban development often imposes negative externalities on rural land (see text). These externalities push the urban-rural boundary to *Q*$_{min\ Sprawl}$ ("min" means minimum). The usual result, however, is where urban development is pushed to one of the two worse sprawl outcomes, *Q*$_{mod\ Sprawl}$ ("mod" means moderate) or *Q*$_{max\ Sprawl}$ ("max" means maximum) where the urban—rural boundary extends much farther out than is efficient. The first outcome occurs when mortgage subsidies and homeowner property tax benefits combined with underpriced water, sewer, highway, and other services among other influences push the value of land for urban uses up to *Urban P*$_{mod\ Subsidy}$. The combined effect of *Rural P*$_{with\ Externalities}$ and *Urban P*$_{mod\ Subsidy}$ is the inefficient use of land for urban development to *Q*$_{mod\ Sprawl}$. Worse is where low urban density zoning at the fringe that requires even more subsidies, *Urban P*$_{max\ Subsidy}$, combined with externalities, *Rural P*$_{with\ Externalities}$, push the inefficient use of land for urban development to *Q*$_{max\ Sprawl}$. Development mitigation aims to reduce sprawl inducing effects of subsidies and negative externalities. Proportionate share impact fees as a form of mitigation can reduce sprawl effects to *Q*$_{mod\ Sprawl}$. However, if impact fees themselves are charged inefficiently (see text), they can have the perverse effect of pushing sprawl toward *Q*$_{max\ Sprawl}$.

In our simplistic scheme, there are two kinds of land: urban and rural. *Urban* land is where most of the people and nonfarm jobs are. *Rural* land is where there are farms, ranches, forests and other forms of "working landscapes" as well as open spaces generally. The price, *P*, for land is set by the market. In a simplistic region, the urban center is on the left of Figure 13.1 while rural landscapes are to the right. In the absence of negative externalities and subsidies, the value of land for urban uses falls with respect to distance from the center, *Urban P* $_{no\,Subsidy}$. Although the value of land for rural uses also falls from the center (left) to rural landscapes (right), we use straight lines to simplify the point. The upper line, *Rural P* $_{no\,Externalities}$, reflects the value of rural land devoid of subsidies for urban development and externalities imposed on it by nearby urban land uses. The efficient allocation of land occurs at the intersection of *Urban P* $_{no\,Subsidy}$ and *Rural P* $_{no\,Externalities}$ which occurs at $Q_{no\,Sprawl}$. Land to the left of this point is more valuable for urban uses and is thus developed, while land to the right of it is more valuable for rural uses and thus not developed. This is a simplistic definition of *efficient land use patterns* where sprawl does not exist from an economic perspective, even though it may appear sprawling to observers. It is also a naïve characterization because there may be sprawl when considering social costs, which we address later.

The value of land for rural uses, however, is impacted adversely by urban externalities. Even in the absence of subsidies for urban land development discussed below, nearby urban development imposes such negative externalities on rural land uses as limitations on activities (hours of operation, the use of fertilizers and pesticides, soil management, to note a few), trespass by urban residents as they help themselves to farm products, and neighborhood dogs and cats disturbing it not killing livestock among others. For their part, anticipating a time when growing homes is more profitable than growing strawberries, rural landowners disinvest in their operations, leading to the "impermanence syndrome" (see Nelson et al., 1995). The value of land for strictly rural uses is therefore reduced to *Rural P* $_{with\,Externalities}$. In the absence of urban subsidies, discussed next, the urban–rural boundary is pushed to $Q_{min\,Sprawl}$. That is to say, more land is brought into urban development because of negative externalities imposed on rural land than would occur otherwise. This leads to an inefficient allocation of land for urban uses.

We consider next the value of land for urban uses. It is influenced by several factors that increase its value above what the market would support. For instance, the mortgage interest deduction induces people to buy larger homes on larger parcels of land than they would without that tax benefit. Based on standard land value theory, the value of this subsidy is internalized in the land market, thereby increasing its price. Another example is where most states reduce property taxes on owner-occupied homes, which are usually larger homes on larger lots. Yet other land uses, especially rental housing, help underwrite the homeowner subsidy leading to social inequities. Yet another example is the subsidy given to roads. Literature shows that in the absence of paying for the full cost of the use of roads, people use roads more than they would otherwise. Underpriced roads are also capitalized in the land market, meaning the value of land for urban uses is artificially high. Then there are subsidies associated with water, wastewater and stormwater systems in that user fees are based on average cost pricing, meaning that more costly development pays less than it costs while less costly development pays more—with the overall effect over time that more high-cost development occurs because it is subsidized while less low-cost development occurs because it is overcharged. The effect of all these and other influences is that the value of land for urban uses is made artificially higher, shown by the line *Urban P* $_{mod\,Subsidy}$. The combination of subsidies for urban development and negative externalities imposed on rural land is that the urban–rural boundary is pushed toward $Q_{mod\,Sprawl}$. Worse is where low urban density zoning occurs at the fringe. Serving low density development requires even more subsidies. The result is high subsidies, *Urban P* $_{high\,Subsidy}$, combined with externalities imposed on rural land, *Rural P* $_{with\,Externalities}$, pushes the inefficient use of land for urban development to $Q_{max\,Sprawl}$.

Many of the factors leading to urban sprawl, as we characterize here, are not easily overcome through planning. For one thing, federal and state laws create subsidies for urban development while doing little to offset negative externalities impacting rural land. For another, utility, highway and other policymakers find it easier to engage in average cost pricing even if the result is that more expensive development is subsidized by lower-cost development, which leads to more high-cost and less low-cost development. The irony is that more money needs to be raised to cover higher costs. Planners, unfortunately, have very few tools to correct for inefficient land use patterns driven by policies over which they have very little control. But there are some tools.

To reduce negative externalities on rural land, zoning is often used to limit land uses to working landscapes or open spaces but with limited success (see Nelson et al., 1995) unless the rural lots are very large. An effective way to reduce although not eliminate urban sprawl is through urban services limits, urban growth boundaries and such that restrict the extension of urban services to a line aiming to clearly separate urban and rural land uses. Other methods include extraterritorial control over new development occurring within a certain distance from city limits, as well as a heightened review of larger projects. These can include developments of regional impact used extensively in Florida and Georgia, municipal utility districts in Texas, and planned unit developments used in most if not all other states. These tools can lead to mitigation measures that have those developments internalize many of their externalities. While the goal may be to eliminate sprawl, a more realistic objective may be to reduce the subsidy effect to the line shown as *Urban P*$_{mod\ Subsidy}$. This would move the urban-rural boundary to $Q_{mod\ Sprawl}$, where a moderate amount of sprawl would still remain.

Impact fees as a form of development mitigation can also reduce sprawl. Recall that a key purpose of impact fees is to charge new development for a share of the cost of new or expanded facilities. Chapters 1, 15, and its Coda, address the need to calibrate impact fees based on several factors such as differences in costs between land use type, location, density, and other factors. Chapter 15 reports a case study where impact fees in high-cost "service area" were many times higher than those in low-cost service areas. Although proportionate share impact fees are usually a small share of total infrastructure costs and their effect on land use patterns may be small, they are not trivial and help lead to improved efficiency in land use allocation, moving the urban–rural boundary toward $Q_{mod\ Sprawl}$ although probably not much more. However, if impact fees themselves are based on average costs applied to each dwelling unit equally regardless of size or type, they can have the perverse effect of inducing sprawl, pushing the urban–rural boundary to $Q_{max\ Sprawl}$. This means that if a plan aims to reduce urban sprawl, its impact fee program will need to be designed in such a way that it is in accordance with the efficiency and equity goals of the plan (see Chapter 6). This has additional efficiency, ethical and equity concerns which are touched on next and discussed in much more detail in Chapters 14 and 15, and the Coda to Chapter 15.

At this point, one might worry that good planning is expensive not only in engaging in the kind of planning needed to maximize good outcomes, but in making infrastructure investments needed to: facilitate desired, market-based development patterns; fairly compensate those who incur harm when desired change creates losers; acquire land that ought not to be developed, or its development rights; and related efforts to minimize inefficient development patterns. Good planning, however, will generate the economic resources to cover these costs through value capture approaches presented below.

13.4 VALUE-ADDED PLANNING

Good planning creates value. This section shows how. At its heart, planning aims to increase the value of a community, broadly speaking. These include not only real estate values but improved environmental and social values in ways that cannot be measured precisely. Indeed, much of planning surrounds the creation of non-economic value, although the creation of economic value may be needed to leverage other values, such as acquiring land for parks and improving it for public use, which then elevates the non-economic value of the community. We thus reveal our planning bias: Planning needs to create economic value broadly speaking, which communities can use to leverage new investments that elevate other values, including non-monetary ones. In this section, we create a framework in which to conceptualize the differences in outcomes between good and bad planning. We call this *value-added planning*. Methods of leveraging planning value added will be described later in the chapter.

Value-added planning can occur at many stages. A key stage is of course when land is designated for certain kinds of development, thereby signaling to the market where future investments of the community will be directed. The most direct ways in which planning value added is achieved, however, is through infrastructure investments that make development possible and then the permitting of development itself. These are not free market decisions where one person or entity decides where the community will make its infrastructure investments and then what will be built, where, and when. These are rather collaborative decisions. For one thing, it is the community's financial capacity that is often used to make infrastructure investments that the private sector cannot make. Those investments are often recovered in part from new revenues generated by new development. In effect, the difference between the value of the land before planning and infrastructure investment and the value afterward is planning value added. As planning value added occurs through a collaborative process, all the key decision makers in the process have a tranche or slice of it, as will be shown in the next section. For now, we will sketch out how planning value added is created through good planning. To do so, we adapt the scheme advanced by Christine Whitehead (2016). We apply the scheme to housing where needed for illustration.

First of all, planning, whether good or bad, establishes the supply of land to be developed by allocating or designating areas for development. The allocation process also establishes the volume of land to be developed, such as acres of land, as well as its intensity, such as homes per acre of land. Timing may also be a

factor in the allocation process, such as limiting development to a certain time frame or conditioning it on such events such as the extension of services. The supply of land for development may also be affected by other factors that may not be known until the entitlement process begins, such as the need to preserve wetlands, habitats, archeologically significant areas, and so forth. The allocation of land by itself does not necessarily affect development demand or price, which is discussed below.

Second, planning affects the nature of demand. For instance, while the supply of land may be substantial, limiting it to large homes on large lots can mean that the supply of land for such homes exceeds demand while the demand for smaller homes on smaller lots or attached homes is not met. In a regional context, a community with an excess supply of land for large homes on large lots can push down land prices and lure part of the regional demand for those homes to the community. The demand for smaller homes on smaller lots might be displaced to other communities. The regional allocation of land for housing becomes inefficient as one community has more larger homes on larger lots but fewer smaller homes on smaller lots or attached homes than needed to meet market demands.

The third thing planning does to affect the price of land is establish the parameters of development. The combination of these influences is illustrated in Figure 13.2. The market price of land, *P*, is on the vertical axis. There are three types of prices revealed in the market: private which is revealed in the absence of planning; misallocation which is revealed when planning under- or over-supplies the market relative to demand; and value-added when planning meets market needs while also arranging land uses and infrastructure to minimize costs where those savings and other benefits are capitalized. The quantity of development, *Q*, homes in this case, is on the horizontal access. As for Price, *P*, there are three outcomes associated with private, misallocation, and value-added planning. There are three supply lines. The first represents conventional private sector planning,

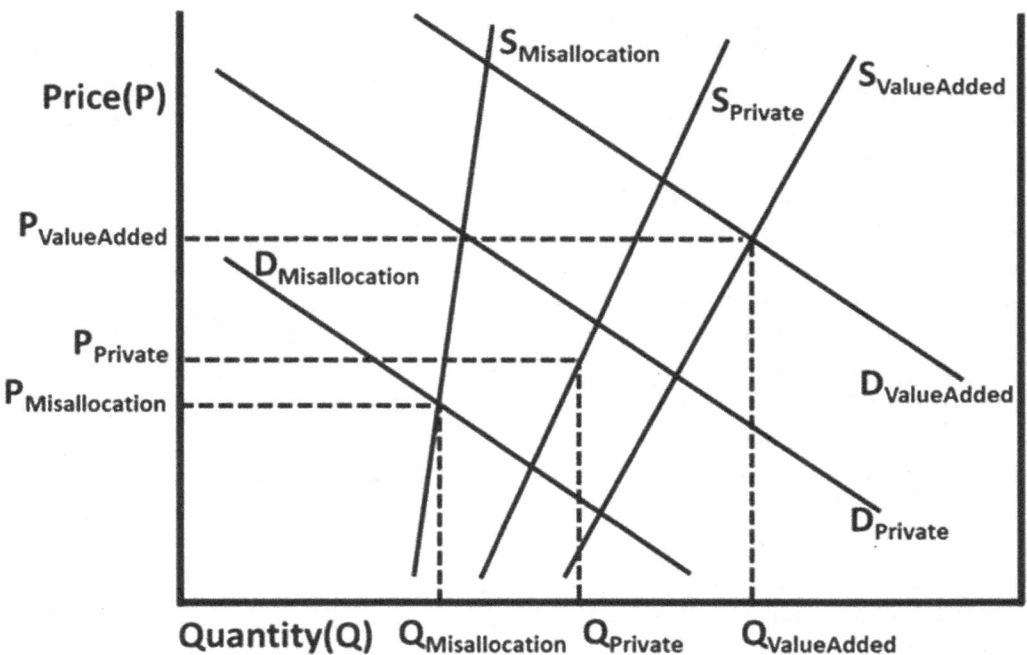

FIGURE 13.2 The effect of private planning, misallocation planning, and value-added planning on quantity of development. Often, more land is allocated to some land uses in excess of demand but to others less than needed to meet demand. The result can be that the aggregate price of land falls from $P_{Private}$ to $P_{Misallocation}$ while production falls from $Q_{Private}$ to $Q_{Misallocation}$. In the context of residential needs, not enough homes are built to meet the demand for all segments of the market. Value-added planning aims to meet the demand for all market segments as well as account for externalities. The aggregate price of land rises from $P_{Private}$ to $P_{Value-Added}$ which intersects with $S_{Value-Added}$, resulting in more total housing, $Q_{Value-Added}$. The difference in price, $P_{Private}$ to $P_{Value-Added}$ multiplied by the increased production, $Q_{Private}$ to $Q_{Value-Added}$ is the economic value added as well as social equity value.

$S_{Private}$. The second represents misallocation, $S_{Misallocation}$. The third represents value-added collaborative public and private sector planning, $S_{Value-Added}$. Value-added planning includes internalizing social and environmental externalities in addition to meeting market demand for all development. (That is to say, development that itself meets market needs after internalizing its externalities on the community.)

Suppose the community decides that it will have only large homes on large lots regardless of market demand. Because of over-allocation relative to market demand, the price of land, $P_{Misallocation}$, intersects with $S_{Misallocation}$ resulting in housing production, $Q_{Misallocation}$. In this case, which is typical, unfortunately, more land is allocated to some land uses in excess of demand but allocations for other land uses are insufficient to meet demand. In the case of housing in our

example, not enough homes are built to meet the demand for all segments of the market.

Value-added planning, however, aims to meet the demand for all market segments as well as account for externalities. The aggregate price of land rises to $P_{Value-Added}$ which intersects with $S_{Value-Added}$ resulting in more total housing, $Q_{Value\ Added}$. The difference in price, $P_{Private}$ to $P_{Value-Added}$ multiplied by the increased production, $Q_{Private}$ to $Q_{Value-Added}$ is the economic and societal value added.

Does this happen? We pose Oregon's statewide land use planning system as mostly an exercise in value-added planning. It requires urban growth boundaries (UGBs) around all urban areas. It also preserves farms, forests and other working landscapes from low density and leapfrog urban sprawl that research shows would reduce productivity (see Figure 13.1). At first blush, limiting the aggregate supply of land means there may not be enough land to meet development demand. However, since its inception in the 1970s, the residential density of new development in Oregon's major metropolitan areas has doubled. One reason is that planning is based substantially on market studies showing the demand for housing by location, type, configuration, and so forth with an eye to changing demographics. For another, Oregon has implemented a suite of tools to expedite development decision-making and effectively reduce, though not eliminate NIMBYism (not-in-my-backyard). So, while the number of acres of land available for development is constrained in Oregon, what is actually built on the limited supply of acres is much more now than in the 1970s. Moreover, we know from studies that higher density development leads to economic resilience, stable neighborhoods, and by some accounts a measurably higher quality of life. Furthermore, while the price of land for development inside the UGBs of Oregon's metropolitan areas, its pace of increase lags that of major metropolitan areas in California and Washington, while housing production has tracked demand better (Nelson 2023). In addition, by protecting working landscapes from low density and leapfrog urban sprawl, its productivity has not only been sustained but has increased in constant dollar terms (Nelson 2023). One might consider the Oregon approach to be an example of value-added planning.

13.5 VALUE CAPTURE CONCEPTUALLY

Value-added planning increases development, especially housing production. It does so in part by adding value to land (see Figure 13.2), which can occur in the form of new or expanded infrastructure investments. In our view, good planning ought to capture a share of value-added planning decisions and reinvest the proceeds back into the community, creating a virtuous cycle of public investment, value capture, reinvestment and new value-added that may be captured and reinvested. This section starts with an overview of what value capture is conceptually and why it is of such interest to policymakers. It then offers a theory of value capture. This is followed by a review of ad hoc and formal value capture approaches, essentially contrasting the UK's "planning gain" system with formalized US-style techniques, especially since *Koontz* (see Chapter 2). The final section concludes the chapter with a broadened perspective of the role of impact fees in shaping development patterns.

13.5.1 What Is Value Capture?

Real estate value is gained through factors such as markets forces, planning decisions that increase development opportunities, and infrastructure investments that make more development possible. The latter two sources of value are created by government decisions, while the last one is conferred by local taxpayers and ratepayers to the benefit of new development.

Land value capture policy aims to recover that part of the incremental value created by public decisions and investment. In turn, recovered value is reinvested into new or expanded infrastructure to support future growth. The heart of value capture is the perspective that public decisions that increase private welfare should generate public benefits in return.

Value capture is not a form of impact mitigation *per se*. It is rather recovering a share of the value added by public decisions and investments that can be over and above the cost of mitigating adverse impacts. For instance, mitigation fees may be used to offset adverse social impacts, such as when development raises the price of housing beyond which can be afforded by the workforce upon which development depends (see Chapter 22). In contrast, value capture is aimed at having development return a share of value added attributable to public decisions and investments for the public sector to use in ways not necessarily related to impact mitigation. In this respect, value capture is akin to the public sector being a partner in the success of private development (Nelson, 2014). The following discussion provides an overview of value capture theory which is followed by a section on value capture tools.

In the context of planning, value capture is predicated on the concepts of externalities, betterment, planning gain, and the mitigation of development externalities. These concepts will be presented next, followed by the role and rationale of value capture.

13.5.2 What Are Externalities?

A basic tenet of economics is that the internalization of externalities will lead to more efficient decisions. In planning, "externalities" often refer to the negative effect of development on the community—the better label should be "negative externalities." If they are caused by developers, they should be mitigated by them. For instance, if new development creates a need for new or expanded infrastructure that is more costly than the new revenues it brings in, either everyone in the community pays higher taxes or fees to subsidize the new development, or the new development is called upon to mitigate its negative externalities on the community. One form of mitigation would be where new development installs the needed infrastructure itself. Another would be where new development pays fees to local government proportionate to its impact, such as through impact fees. There are hybrid approaches as well.

Externalities can also be positive such as when a development attracts new high-end jobs and wages to the community with the total effect of generating more benefits on excess of costs. Sometimes these forms of "positive externalities" are rewarded by government agencies through such concessions as tax abatement, special permitting processes, grants and preferential loans, and even reduced or eliminated impact fees (see Chapter 9). This is not an issue if the community wants these investments. But it can be an issue if the community cannot afford supporting new development's collateral impacts—such as meeting affordable housing needs—without raising taxes and fees.

13.5.3 What Is Betterment?

When the public acts in ways that increase the value of real estate through no particular effort by the owners, "betterment" has occurred in the form of expanded infrastructure capacity, the cost of which is incurred by the public. It is an unearned increment in the value of real estate. Although similar conceptually to a windfall, a windfall does not necessarily trigger public action to recoup a share of it. In the case of betterment, the public may seek a share of the value-added from its investment benefiting new development. In theory, up to all the value of betterment may be recouped to recover its investments as well as mitigate adverse impacts of public decisions on other property owners and people.

What Is Planning Gain?

Suppose a parcel of land has its use changed from five-acre homesites to ten units per acre. The value of the land rises appreciably because of the change in planning designation, over and above the value added through betterment. This windfall accruing to the landowner that is known in the United Kingdom and many Commonwealth countries as a "planning gain." While sometimes the landowner works hard to get the change in designation, perhaps nearby landowners do nothing and still see their values rise.

Recouping Betterment and Leveraging Planning Gain to Mitigate Externalities

The presence of betterment and planning gain leads to discussions about development impact mitigation. Many planners, economists, and public officials share sentiments of the United Nations (1976) that "the beneficiaries of the public investments or the public decisions that increase their land values should partly cover public investment costs or return their benefit to the public." Conceptually, there are four approaches for land value capture (adapted from Grant 1992).

First, gains can be kept by those who received them regardless of the extent to which they were responsible for creating them.

Second, gains can be subject to capital gains taxes applied to land as opposed to the entire real estate investment. In effect, it could be a form of windfall tax capturing up to 100 percent of all the gain not attributable to the investor or developer.

Third, real estate would be differentiated between land and improvements. For instance, infrastructure investments are seen as improving land value mostly because it influences what can be built on the land.

Fourth, recapture of betterment attributable to specific decisions (such as development agreements) and investments (such as infrastructure) can be accomplished through such mechanisms as special service districts and impact fees, among others reviewed below.

It is important to note that impact fees are but one, and even a small, part of value capture schemes. For one thing, value capture schemes are often applied on an ad hoc, case-by-case basis where individualized analysis identifies impacts directly related to new development.

What arises conceptually is this progression of value added.

Infrastructure investments add value through *betterment.*

Planning permission adds value through *planning gain.*

Good planning (see Figure 13.1) adds more value by elevating community quality of life through *planning value added.*

We apply these concepts to the design of value capture policy in the next section and conclude with a survey of value capture techniques of which impact fees are just one.

13.6 VALUE CAPTURE POLICY

Public policy can be designed to recoup the public's costs of betterment (such as infrastructure expansion) as well as gain a share of the planning decisions that increased value through no particular effort by the property owner. The concept dates to David Ricardo (1821) and Henry George (1879). Value capture is based on the principle that property value is reflected in a series of tranches, or slices, illustrated in Figure 13.3, being:

• The intrinsic value of land.
• Value created by private investment.
• Value created by increasing demand for a location through population and economic growth.
• Valued added by public-sector decisions such as changes in land use regulations, infrastructure investments, and the provision of services.

This scheme necessitates an ad hoc process leading to development agreements between the developer and public agencies. An exemplar of the ad hoc approach comes not from the US but from the UK (Crook, Henneberry, and Whitehead, 2016). Let us walk through these stages using the lens of the UK's Town and Country Planning Act of 1947, starting with context. The chief consequence of that Act was that all development values became vested in the state from 1948 forward.

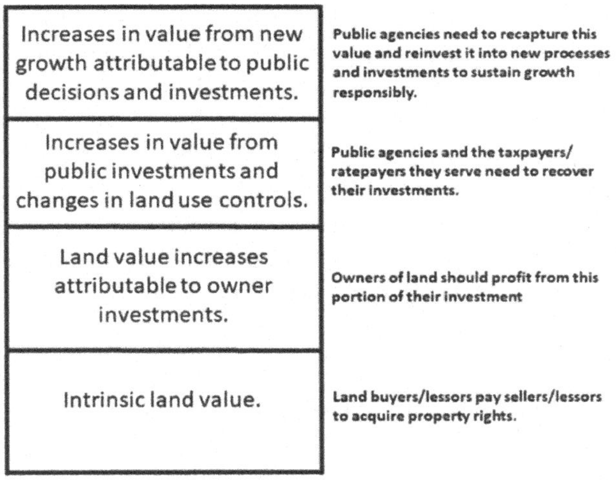

Increases in value from new growth attributable to public decisions and investments.	Public agencies need to recapture this value and reinvest it into new processes and investments to sustain growth responsibly.
Increases in value from public investments and changes in land use controls.	Public agencies and the taxpayers/ratepayers they serve need to recover their investments.
Land value increases attributable to owner investments.	Owners of land should profit from this portion of their investment
Intrinsic land value.	Land buyers/lessors pay sellers/lessors to acquire property rights.

FIGURE 13.3 Components of betterment and value capture. *Source*: Adapted from Hong and Brubaker (2010).

Thereafter, "permission" was needed for anyone to do nearly anything with their property.[1] The Act provided for £300 million—equivalent to about $20 billion in 2022—to compensate landowners for transferring their rights to the national government. The new process worked as follows. A developer would purchase land at its then-existing value based on the underlying vested rights—this is the intrinsic value of land. After permission to develop was acquired, the developer would then install improvements that created new value—the second step of the process. Additional value may be created if the development induces higher market demand by stimulating population and employment growth. The public would also add value through its permission for land use changes leading to development, and its own investments in infrastructure and other services. The latter two value-added elements become part of the calculus for development charges, which can be as high as 100 percent of the difference between the purchase price plus developer improvements and the final value of the land. This would be a negotiated agreement that also allowed permitting authorities to add environmental, social, and other forms of mitigation costs.

In theory, up to 100 percent of all the planning gain can be taxed and used to mitigate impacts broadly defined.[2] In practice, the tax on planning gain often ranges from less than a tenth to about a third, although there is considerable variation, including zero percent in areas needing economic development. Moreover, developers who are more adept than others pay less.[3]

The UK's planning gain system has evolved considerably since 1947.[4] Whereas initially there were few parameters guiding government development permission negotiations, as of this writing, three mitigation tests must be met:[5]

1. Necessary to make the development acceptable in planning terms.
2. Directly related to the development.
3. Fairly and reasonably related in scale and kind to the development.

Let us compare these standards with those in the US.[6] The first standard is similar to the implicit requirement in the US that impact fees help finance a capital improvements program that helps implement the community comprehensive plan (see Chapters 2 and 7). The second point is similar to the "specifically and uniquely attributable test"[7] applied to parkland dedication requirements as a condition of subdivision approval (see Chapter 2). This 1961 case was supplanted in 1965 by the more lenient "reasonable relationship" test, whereby a local government needs to show there is a reasonable relationship between the mitigation required of new development and its impact on the community.[8] Not being experts in British planning jurisprudence, we surmise what is meant is that the mitigation analysis is limited to the development itself and not induced or collateral development. The third point is eerily similar to the "rough proportionality" mitigation standard advanced by *Dolan v. Tigard*, whereby the local government must make an "individualized determination that the required dedication is related both in nature and extent to the proposed development's impact."[9] This test is applied to individual projects much like the UK's current planning gain regime.

The UK's planning gain system has further evolved into impact fee-like "community infrastructure investments" (CILs) fee schedules that replaced prior mitigation approaches in 2010.[10] The rationale is that:

The Community Infrastructure Levy is fairer, faster and more certain and transparent than the system of planning obligations which causes delays as a result of lengthy negotiations.[11]

Like impact fees in many states (see Chapter 3), CILs are limited mostly to roads, flood control, schools, hospitals and other health and social care facilities, park improvements, and green spaces and recreation facilities. Indeed, because of the narrower scope of mitigations allows allowed by the CILs relative to earlier years, some have quipped the planning gain system has not so much evolved as devolved.

What has been the effect of the UK's planning gain system in recent years? Recall from Chapters 10 and 11 that, in competitive markets, impact fees are capitalized into land resulting in lower prices, often on a dollar-for-dollar basis. This is an efficient market response. In contrast, in the absence of such things as clear and objective fee schedules, the unknown magnitude of required mitigations can lead to delay, uncertainty, and broadly the inability of development to meet market needs. Although there is debate in the UK over efficiency and equity outcomes, Dame Kate Barker, a former member of the UK's Monetary Policy Committee, in commenting on the UK's current planning gain system, observes that the "tidy-minded economist" might find it unsatisfactory that planning gain seeks to mitigate development impacts through the planning permission process though it is effective both pragmatically and theoretically.[12] She goes on to observe that economic studies show it is

landowners who incur a backward shifting of pricing, which is consistent with theory (see Chapter 11)[13] (Crook et al. 2016: xv).

We turn next to a review of several, although not all, leading ways in which US local governments can capture the value of betterment and public value-enhancement decisions to (a) recoup public investment and (b) mitigate adverse development impacts.

13.7 LEADING VALUE CAPTURE TECHNIQUES

In the US, a suite of value capture techniques has been developed. In all cases, they capture a portion of the value added to development—such as new transit stations, or savings resulting from publicly funded infrastructure—such as reduced flood control costs in flood-prone areas. Value capture can take the form of one-time fees (including impact fees and their variants), special assessments, specialized taxes, public–private partnerships, and development agreements between government and development interests. Nonetheless, these approaches usually depend on strong real estate markets. We review key techniques here.

13.7.1 Special Districts

Also known as local improvement districts, benefit assessment districts, and business improvement districts, among others, they are formed to help finance infrastructure, promotional activities, and sometimes housing within specific geographic boundaries. From an economic perspective, by financing infrastructure that mitigates its impact on the larger community, special districts internalize development externalities. Capital costs incurred to provide infrastructure are typically financed through debt retired from special assessments based on a variety of formulas. In some countries, these are known as betterment investments and are financed from betterment levies.

13.7.2 Tax Increment Financing (TIF)

Based on a planning, market analysis, and financial analysis, a TIF district is created within which land is assembled, land improvements made (including environmental remediation), infrastructure installed, and other investments made to facilitate development and redevelopment (Nelson 2014). Long-term bonds are financed from the increment in property or sales taxes (the pre-TIF tax base is frozen, which continues to generate tax revenue for local agencies). Once the bonds are retired, all the incremental property and sales tax revenues flow to local agencies.

13.7.3 Joint Venture/Public–Private Partnerships (JV/PPP)

These ventures include public, private, and occasionally nonprofit organizations that pool their unique resources to make development possible. Examples include transit stations, parking garages, and even workforce housing. Each entity benefits differently, with private partners generating higher rents and returns, public partners generating more long-term tax and fee revenue, and nonprofit ones gaining revenue to provide specialized services such as daycare, museums, parks and workforce housing. These efforts usually include long-term debt for capital financing and special revenue streams to provide certain services.

13.7.4 Land Readjustment

Land readjustment occurs when multiple landowners pool their assets into a kind of joint venture to create and implement a redevelopment master plan approved by the local government. Infrastructure investments are financed by the pooled landowners though sometimes involving the retirement of bonds backed by the local government (see TIF above). If this means allocating land for the investment, each landowner receives a smaller parcel on which to develop.[14] This process can create larger, more efficient parcels of land for development, especially in older, underdeveloped areas.

13.7.5 Transfer of Development Rights (TDR)[15]

TDR programs result in landowners forfeiting development rights in areas targeted for preservation ("sending areas") in exchange for selling those rights to buyers (usually developers) who transfer them to "receiving areas" for higher density development (Nelson, Pruetz, and Woodruff, 2011). These programs are especially useful to preserve farmland, wetland, coastal and other landscapes to implement resilience policies but are also used for historic preservation and workforce housing.

13.7.6 Impact Fees

Impact fees are clearly a value capture tool. For instance, if a community expands the capacity of roads, water, wastewater, schools and other facilities for the benefit of new development, it can use impact fees to recoup the cost of new capacity and recover the cost of the excess capacity.

13.7.7 Summary

Except for public–private partnerships, none of these techniques generates more revenue than needed to cover costs. In other words, private development usually reaps all value added above its land and improvement costs and charges such as special assessments and impact fees. An argument can be made that under the right circumstances, local governments should elevate their engagement in JVs/PPPs. In this way, as a partner, they may be able to generate revenues in excess of costs and use those revenues to truly elevate the local quality of life. This is clearly an area in need of theoretical development and demonstration projects.

13.8 THE ROLE OF IMPACT FEES IN SHAPING DEVELOPMENT PATTERNS THROUGH VALUE CAPTURE

There are three ways in which impact fees can be viewed as a value capture technique, but only one of them is usually recognized in the literature—generating new revenue to help finance new or expanded infrastructure. Inasmuch as only that development which benefits from such expansion of infrastructure and can afford to pay for them through the value created by them, impact fees for new or expanded infrastructure is certainly the most obvious form of value capture.

The second form of value capture is unlocking the value of excess capacity in existing infrastructure to recoup prior community investments. This is called "excess capacity value capture." Suppose a community had road capacity to accommodate 10,000 homes but had only 5,000 homes now. Suppose the current replacement value of the capacity—defined as the replacement cost less depreciation—is $100 million. This comes to $10,000 per home. Assuming the community does not already do this, and we believe most do not, an impact fee of $10,000 could be assessed on each new home until a total of 10,000 homes is reached. In other words, the next 5,000 homes can generate $50 million in value capture. This is a classic case of using impact fees as value capture. The current replacement value should be based on the share of the original cost paid by the community from its own funds as opposed to federal, state or other funds. This assures proportionality of benefit to the feepayers in relation to the costs incurred by the community (see also Chapter 6).

The $50 million in the value of excess capacity captured can be used in several different ways. It could be used to build new roads or expand existing ones. It could be used to pay for road impact fees in targeted infill and redevelopment areas or pay the road impact fees for housing meeting the needs of target populations, or the road impact fees for targeted economic development, among others. However, to sustain the connection between the kind of infrastructure from which the value of excess capacity is captured, these fees should be used for the same type of infrastructure.

There is a final way in which impact fees add value that can also be captured: leveraging infrastructure investment. As we show in Chapter 6, impact fees are essentially a form of gap financing. Once the total cost of infrastructure is determined, available funds are determined, with the difference being what is needed from impact fees. Indeed, but for impact fees, some infrastructure might not be built. Impact fees become the grease to make new infrastructure investments happen and thus attract new development. In turn, that new development adds to the property tax, sales tax, and other revenue bases of the community. The value of leveraged infrastructure investments is thus recaptured in part through these net new revenue streams after accounting for the incremental costs of serving new development.

This leads us to Chapter 14, which frames impact fees in the context of equity.

NOTES

1 Given the limitations of space, we refer readers to Malcolm Grant, *Urban Planning Law*, Sweet and Maxwell (1982) for details about the policy and the process.

2 The process is described in Section 106 of the Town and Country Planning Act 1990 (see www.legislation.gov.uk/ukpga/1990/8/section/106). They are commonly known as s106 agreements and are used to make a development proposal acceptable. While focused on infrastructure and housing, s106 agreements can: (1) restrict the development or use of the land in any specified way; (2) require specified operations or activities to be carried out in, on, under or over the land; (3) require the land to be used in any specified way; or (4) require a sum or sums to be paid to the authority on a specified date or dates or periodically.

3 For insights into the extent to which some developers negotiate favorable planning gain conditions see www.theguardian.com/cities/2014/sep/17/truth-property-developers-builders-exploit-planning-cities retrieved April 25, 2021.

4 Through correspondence and lengthy discussions, we are indebted to insights from Malcolm Grant relating to the evolution of the UKs planning gain from its inception to the early 2020s. We are responsible for errors or omissions.

5 Op cit., s106.

6 We are being very broad here as every state has its own nuances.

7 *Pioneer Trust & Savings Bank v. Village of Mount Prospect*, 22 Ill.2d 375, 176 N.E.2d 799 (1961).

8 The leading case guiding is *Jordan* v. *Menomonee Falls*, 28 Wis. 2d 608, 137 N. W. 2d 442 (1965).

9 *Dolan v. City of Tigard*, 512 US 374 (1994) at 375.

10 See www.gov.uk/guidance/community-infrastructure -levy.

11 Department for Communities and Local Government, *Community Infrastructure Levy: An overview* (2010), p. 4, retrieved October 20, 2021, from www.gov.uk/guid-ance/community-infrastructure-levy.

12 We again regret that the publisher, Routledge, requires us to paraphrase passages not in the public domain, which we consider silly because doing to distracts from the wonderful precision of the author(s) on whom we use to build a body of knowledge. We recommend that readers engage in the tedious and time-consuming process of tracking down the original language for precision. We regret this significant inconvenience. We will remind readers of this concern periodically throughout the book

13 This is consistent with the incidence theory of impact fees under conditions of relatively competitive markets noted by Burge and Dronyk-Trosper in Chapter 11.

14 We have adapted this characterization from Germán and Bernstein, *Land Value Capture*, and Gregory K. Ingram and Yu-Hung Hong, eds., *Value Capture and Land Policies*, Lincoln Institute of Land Policy (2012), 290–291.

15 Much of this discussion is based on Nelson et al. (2011).

REFERENCES

Crook, T., Henneberry, J., & Whitehead, C., Eds. (2016). *Planning Gain: Providing Infrastructure and Affordable Housing*. Chichester, UK: John Wiley and Sons Ltd.

Grant, M. (1982). *Urban Planning Law*. London: Sweet and Maxwell.

Grant, M. (1992). The planning balance in the 1990s: Betterment again? *Journal of Planning and Environmental Law, 18,* 67–83.

George, H. (1879). *Progress and Poverty: An Inquiry into the Cause of Industrial Depressions and of Increase of Want with Increase of Wealth: The Remedy.* Garden City: Doubleday.

Hagman, D. G, & Misczynski, D. J., Eds. (1978). *Windfalls for Wipeouts: Land Value Capture and Compensation.* London: Routledge.

Hong, Y.-H., & Brubaker, D. (2010). Integrating the proposed property tax with the public leasehold system. In J. Y. Man & Y.-H. Hong (Eds.), *China's Local Public Finance in Transition* (pp. 165–190). Cambridge, MA: Lincoln Institute of Land Policy.

Lourdes, G., & Bernstein, A. E. (2012). In land value capture. In G. K. Ingram & Y.-H. Hong (Eds.), *Value Capture and Land Policies* (pp. 290–291). Cambridge, MA: Lincoln Institute of Land Policy.

Nelson, Arthur C. (2023). Foreword. In Megan Horst, ed., *Towards Oregon 2050*. Corvallis, OR: Oregon State University Press.

Nelson, A. C. (2014). *Foundations of Real Estate Development Financing: A Guide to Public-Private Partnerships.* Washington, DC: Island Press.

Nelson, A. C., Duncan, J. B., Mullen, C., & Bishop, K. R. (1995). *Growth Management Principles and Practices.* Chicago, IL: American Planning Association.

Nelson, A. C., Marshall, J. T., Nicholas, J. C., & Juergensmeyer, J. C. (2017). *Market Demand-Based Planning and Permitting.* Chicago, IL: American Bar Association.

Nelson, A. C., Pruetz, R., & Woodruff, D. (2011). *The TDR Handbook: Designing and Implementing Transfer of Development Rights Programs.* Washington, DC: Island Press.

Ricardo, D. (1821). *On the Principles of Political Economy and Taxation* (3rd ed.). London: John Murray.

Whitehead, C. (2016). The Economics of Development Value and Planning Gain. In T. Crook, J. Henneberry, & C. Whitehead (Eds.), *Planning Gain: Providing Infrastructure and Affordable Housing* (pp 20-36). West Sussex: Wiley Blackwell.

14 ETHICAL ISSUES IN THE USE OF IMPACT FEES TO FINANCE COMMUNITY GROWTH

TIMOTHY BEATLEY

14.1 INTRODUCTION

Many communities and states have recently embraced the practice of imposing impact fees as a way to fund the costs associated with new growth. There is little dispute that this financing technique is increasingly popular and that many other states and localities are on the verge of adopting it. Thus, it is an opportune and appropriate time to examine a number of political, moral, and ethical implications that may stem from this trend. Much of the recent work in the impact fee area has focused either on the programmatic descriptions of such techniques or on the legal issues involved in their use. Little analysis of the broader value questions has been conducted. This chapter will identify at least the major ethical dilemmas raised by the increasing use of impact fees. The outcome of this analysis is necessarily uncertain and necessarily mixed. Impact-fee systems will neither be wholly assailed nor wholly embraced—rather, a number of precautions are identified. Where possible, suggestions are tendered for mitigating possible inappropriate and unethical outcomes. This ethical analysis leads to my own position about the responsible use of impact fees. Yet even for readers who do not agree with those conclusions, the chapter at least will provide a greater understanding of the ethical assumptions and issues that arise and must be considered. And while I draw from the experiences of specific impact fee programs at a number of points, the chapter is intended to address the broader trend of using impact fees. The problems of intertemporal fairness; factors that may influence the ethical seriousness of those problems; the more general question of what constitutes a fair allocation of the costs of new growth and development; several key questions having a bearing on that determination; the broad issues of political representation, social exclusivity, and sense of community and the implications that the use of impact fees holds for advancing or undermining those values; and several ethical issues that arise during the actual administration of an impact fee system are examined here.

14.2 ALLOCATION OF THE BENEFITS AND COSTS OF GROWTH

14.2.1 Problems of Intertemporal Fairness

The basic philosophical concepts behind impact fees are not new. Subdivision exactions (either in the form of dedicated land or fees in lieu of dedication for such created needs as parklands and schools) have been imposed for many years (Juergensmeyer and Blake, 1981). What is different is both the mechanisms through which this accounting for created needs occurs and the extent or proportion of the costs of growth being shouldered in many communities by new development. The linkage programs implemented in San Francisco, Boston, and other places are also certainly variations on the impact fee concept and are considered at a conceptual level in this chapter. Despite basic similarities between contemporary impact fees and more traditional subdivision and exactions requirements, it is relatively clear that new growth

DOI: 10.4324/9781003336075-17

and development are being required to pay an increasingly greater share of the costs associated with growth. Such a trend raises a number of questions concerning the equity with which these costs are distributed in the community. One obvious equity quandary is what I refer to as the problem of intertemporal fairness.[1] That is, under impact fee arrangements, new growth may be required to assume a greater share of the initial costs of growth compared with existing and older development. Do new residents and developers have a legitimate claim that such a practice is inequitable?

Is it reasonable for a new resident or a developer encountering an impact fee to ask the community on what basis the rules are being changed? Why should new residents be treated differently than the existing residents? A number of replies could be offered; many would not satisfy the new resident. It might be argued, for instance, that building and land development always have taken place within a politically and economically dynamic environment. The rules are, in a sense, always changing, and while it is perhaps unlucky that newer residents are caught in this political period where greater contributions for growth generated public facilities are required, it is certainly not unfair. It also might be argued by established residents that these are not coercive policies, because new residents have the freedom to locate in other communities and regions of the country where such practices may not be common. Thus, the freedom to exit reduces the seriousness of these differences in intertemporal treatment (see Hayek 1960). A related reply is that if the market can sustain these higher contributions, then they must in fact be acceptable to new residents. There are undoubtedly many desirable qualities about the community that counterbalance impact fee contributions, established residents might argue. Moreover, the established residents might contend that it has been their many years of tax contributions, civic activities, and so forth that have created many of the qualities that attract new residents in the

first place. It is only fair, so the argument goes, that new residents be required to provide greater upfront contributions. Intertemporal differences also may be defended by references to broader changes in the patterns of public finance and legal decisions that support those practices, which indicate that the use of impact fees is not restricted to that particular locality. Indeed, in some places, such as Florida, localities are being strongly encouraged to use such techniques (Bosselman and Stroud 1985). New residents and developers of new projects naturally should have adjusted their expectations in accordance with these changing patterns (Beatley 1985). Such a policy also raises serious questions concerning political representation; these are addressed in a later section.

The nature of this possible intertemporal equity problem would seem to depend to some extent on the history of growth and development in a particular community or region. It may be important to determine the extent to which preimpact fee practices assessed new development for its impacts, such as through subdivision exactions or other means. Where the assessment of new development has been a predominant, historically prevalent practice, and where the demands of such practices have been consistently and stringently imposed, it may be more difficult to argue that the development rules have in fact dramatically been changed. The age and historical progression of development in a community or region also may be an important variable. In many areas, impact fees, or substantial subdivision exactions, have essentially accompanied the emergence of these areas, especially in high-growth, new areas of the country—e.g., Sunbelt jurisdictions where fairly recent community growth has doubled, tripled or perhaps quadrupled the size of small jurisdictions (both in terms of geography and population size). In contrast, perhaps, would be changing the rules in such established urban areas as Buffalo or Boston. The distinction between new and old rules in the former case would seem, then, to be less dramatic and thus perhaps less inequitable.

While the policy significance we give the intertemporal problem will depend on answers to a number of questions addressed below, one solution would be to split the difference between the contributions made by new residents and established residents. An attractive theoretical position would be to approximate the upfront contributions that would be made by all residents if one rule were applied throughout the growth and development of a locality. Such a hypothetical contribution would be used to determine the share new development should pay for new facilities and the share that should be funded through general tax revenues. The accounting methodology necessary to compute such hypothetical values would, of course, be quite complex.

It can be argued that the significance of these intertemporal inequities also will depend on the size of the impact fees assessed and whether they gradually are introduced. The intertemporal inequity created by changing the ground rules of development may be substantially greater where the amount of the fees is very large. It is, of course, difficult in ethical analysis to separate this question from the questions of who ultimately bears the brunt of the new costs and for what purposes such fees are exacted. That is, it seems entirely reasonable that we may want to balance the intertemporal inequity of changing the rules in a dramatic way with the fact that such fees ultimately and primarily are borne by land speculators and owners of raw land who otherwise unfairly would reap socially created wealth.

The intertemporal fairness question aside, how much of the costs of growth should new development be required to pay? This I will refer to as the fair allocation question. To properly answer this question requires that we first consider and address several important subsidiary questions. It requires us to consider the distributive effects of impact fees in relation to the social and economic positions and circumstances of those affected. The categories of questions that follow are important in determining the ethics of using impact fees. It is important to note that some of the concerns address the use of impact fees (or other similar forms of exactions) under any circumstances, while other questions raise issues about the use of impact fees in a particular community context or under particular social, political, and economic circumstances.

14.2.2 Who Benefits from Growth?

Implicit in much of the support for impact fees is that those who benefit directly from public services and facilities ought to bear the costs and, moreover, ought to bear them in proportion to the level of benefits received. In the public finance literature, this is typically referred to as the benefit standard (Beatley and Kaiser, 1983; Snyder and Stegman 1986). Yet, while intuitively appealing on one level, it can be argued that impact fees that impose most of the costs of new development directly on it ignore the many broader ways in which the beneficiaries of such growth extend to the larger community. For example, consider a case in which a new industry locates in the community. As a result of this new primary industry, a ripple of economic activity is created, and it generally can be expected that income and employment levels will increase in response. Let us assume that heavy impact fees for capital improvements are imposed both on the industry itself and on the accompanying building and new residential growth stimulated by the industry. While at a narrow level it is certainly true that the industry and its associated residential and other growth are the direct beneficiaries of the new roads, sewer and water service, and so on, the many economic ripples created by this new growth suggest that the indirect beneficiaries are much more widespread. The more extensive and widespread these ripple effects are, the less defensible high impact fees would seem to be.

As a further example, consider the impacts of new residential development without the assumption of an accompanying industry. Does such a beneficiary argument still hold? Perhaps not. However, if the community in question were a major retail or commercial center, this new development may do much to stimulate economic ripples similar to the previous industrial case. Under different assumptions, of course, these community-wide benefits may be much more difficult to envision. Take, for instance, a proposed industrial development project in a suburban community where no major commercial or industrial uses exist and thus where no immediate economic ripple effects can be detected. In this case, indirect beneficiaries of new roads, sewers, and so forth may be located primarily in other adjoining or nearby localities. A local impact fee may make much more sense from the point of view of the benefit standard, although regional taxation devices, such as tax base sharing, ideally would seem to be required here (e.g., Plosila 1976). In any event, it can be argued that impact fees are less justifiable under the benefit standard because of these broader patterns of community-wide benefits.

A related question is the extent to which landowners in high-growth, high-demand areas have benefited or are benefiting from growth. Impact fees may in many situations be supported ethically because they constitute a tax on this windfall. The extent to which the costs of impact fees actually are capitalized into the value of undeveloped land will, of course, depend on many factors, including the price elasticity of demand for this land (see Duncan, Morgan, and Standerfer 1986). Where an impact fee largely reduces the value of otherwise highly priced land it may be more morally defensible. Here, it can be argued that the fee is doing nothing more than simply taking away an undeserved gain. That is, it is the public and other investments of the community at large that primarily are responsible for this value increase and thus in this sense nothing truly deserved or earned is being taken away

(Hagman 1975). There has, of course, been a long and controversial debate concerning the merits of this argument and the use of impact fees falls squarely within this debate (Hagman and Misczynski 1978).

Taxing away the speculative increase in land values appears consistent with intuitive notions of merit and desert. While there are many ways in which desert or merit can be defined, Americans historically have attributed a high value to work and effort and the fairness of rewarding those attributes (Feinberg 1970; Weale 1983). Windfall gains fly in the face of a notion of deserved compensation based upon labor, effort, productivity, or individual contribution. Moreover, for society to permit individuals to become millionaires simply because the public and private sectors make certain investments in certain locations (e.g., highways and shopping centers) would seem to undermine this fair return to labor ethic.

Extracting the full costs of growth and development from landowners with appreciating land values involves several ethical dilemmas, however. First is the objection of the landowners that to impose such an impact fee is to unfairly thwart legitimately formed expectations about the use of land and the expected profits to be obtained therefrom (e.g., see Beatley 1985). Here problems of differential treatment similar to those mentioned earlier are encountered. Moreover, the landowner might contend that such an imposition is unfair because property taxes for years have been paid based on the market value of such land. Many current landowners could contend, and legitimately so, that previous landowners have largely been the beneficiaries of social growth and the attendant high property values (i.e., they have already sold out) and that newer owners of such land actually have not been the major recipients of such windfalls (i.e., because they had to pay high fair market land prices). The legitimacy of landowner claims that windfall extraction is unfair will depend on several factors. Perhaps the most obvious is the extent to which the entire windfall is extracted. In most or many situations, the impact fee imposed will not be large enough to cause the elimination of the entire windfall but rather will only reduce its size. An additional variable is the extent to which landowners have indicated an intention to develop. Legal rulings concerning estoppel and determinations of investment-backed expectations become important. From a practical point of view, it may be difficult to determine whether the intent to develop is present. It does seem intuitively fair, however, that where land has been put to a continuous, economically viable use (e.g., agriculture) that expectations about its developability would be given less weight.

An additional factor is the historical pattern of property taxation evident in the community. As noted, the imposition of impact fees can lead to substantially lower raw land values, which in turn implies that the previous property taxes paid on this land, based on pre-impact fee market values, were too high, given the changing market conditions. Landowners subject to the capitalization effects of new impact fees could argue, and legitimately so that they are deserving of some form of tax rebate to compensate for this effect. Again, however, it can be replied that such outcomes are unavoidable risks in a dynamic political and economic environment, and that these taxes were reasonable in light of the development rules in place at the time (Beatley 1994). In many cases, these lands historically have been taxed at their use value rather than at their market or potential development value, and in these cases such a concern is not as relevant (e.g., see Keene et al. 1976).

Of course, the imposition of impact fees actually may do little to correct such inequitable windfalls. The problem is that in highly desirable areas the fee will simply be passed along to homeowners in the form of higher prices or lower quality (Snyder and Stegman 1986). Furthermore, if new home prices rise, so will prices of competitive existing homes.

The price increase becomes a windfall to existing residents, and impact fees in some situations may not reduce but rather increase undeserved windfalls.

Thus, many individuals benefit from new growth—indeed, many established residents benefit. The construction of new roads and the building of shopping centers, parks, and recreational facilities lead in important and tangible ways to economic and other benefits. Rapid increases in existing land values are a common result. Many benefits may be less quantifiable and socially broader; perhaps the benefits obtained from the amenities that can be supported through larger population bases (e.g., opera, art museums, specialty shopping areas) as well as the cultural and social diversity that urban growth may provide.

A key question is the extent to which the benefits of those creating the new growth pressures (e.g., builders, landowners, new residents) can be distinguished from the benefits experienced by the larger community. Distinguishing among those benefits, at least in any precise way, is difficult. However, where the benefits are assumed to be more widespread, a policy of imposing the full costs of growth seems unjustifiable. Under the benefit standard, the important task is to determine the appropriate relationship between benefits unique to new development and larger community-wide benefits.

An important question in addition to who benefits from growth is who should benefit from growth. This ultimately depends on beliefs about the appropriate role of government and the principles and concepts of social justice it should advance or protect. These issues are addressed more specifically in a later section on the potential exclusivity effects of impact fees.

14.2.3 Who Can Afford to Pay for Growth?

While it appears that impact fees are intended largely to respond to the benefit standard, perhaps a more appropriate criterion is ability to pay (see Snyder and Stegman1986). Impact-fee systems usually are not designed to be responsive to this standard, nor are they usually defended on those grounds.

To defend the use of impact fees on the basis of ability to pay (i.e., over general jurisdiction-wide revenue raising) is to suggest that newer residents (or builders, developers, landowners) are in some sense better situated financially to pay for the costs of growth. It may be, for instance, that the existing community is made up primarily of lower income and working-class citizens, while new development is occurring in the outer, more exclusive areas and is primarily upper income. Impact fees might be supported by elected officials as a way of more equitably paying for requisite services and facilities. Elected officials might even acknowledge that the broader community does benefit from this growth and that if the city were better situated financially (i.e., if the existing community were not so poor) it would assume a larger share of these costs.

An ability-to-pay standard also implies that impact fees may be deemed appropriate in some situations and not so in others. Where the fee is applied, for instance, to homes that are valued at $500,000, the impact fee may be a highly desirable way of funding the costs associated with growth. Where the ability of new homeowners to pay such a tax is substantially lower—for instance, where homes are more modestly priced, say $80,000—it would appear to make more sense to fund the costs of new growth through other means, perhaps through a community-wide property tax. In those situations, impact fees are regressive in their effects.

Thus, the ethical defensibility of an impact fee would be greater in the former case than in the latter.

Impact fee systems that result in lower raw land prices and thus reduce the large speculative gains on such land would appear to be more responsive to the ability to pay. Speculative gains are, of course, unrealized or potential gains, and as such it can be argued

that the impacts of that loss will never truly be felt by landowners. But this argument may not be universally true. There are numerous examples to the contrary, for instance, the case of the long-term farmer who depends on the occasional sale of a lot to keep his or her agricultural operation financially afloat. I would argue that, generally speaking, owners of raw speculative land are in a better financial position to assume the costs of impact fees than are the potential consumers of most new housing (at least moderate and low-income housing).

How might an impact fee system be more responsive to the ability to pay? One approach would be to distinguish in the application of impact fees between those who can and cannot best afford to pay for the costs of growth. In the same ways that circuit breaker programs have been used to reduce the burden of property taxes, so also could such a system be developed for impact fees. For instance, impact fees might be waived for projects oriented to low and moderate-income residents. Similar} impact fees might be tied to a sliding scale so that the proportion of the costs of growth-related facilities (e.g., roads and sewers) assumed by new development directly is proportional to the ability to pay. Those prospective residents most capable of paying might be required to assume the full costs of their growth. Projects involving low or moderate-income housing might have the majority of these costs assumed by the general public. In some communities, such as Loveland, Colorado, impact fees have been structured so as to make them less regressive.

14.2.4 Who Generates the Costs of Growth?

An additional ethical vantage point is obtained by asking who generates or is responsible for the costs associated with growth. This might be described as the culpability standard and conceptually is different from asking who benefits. Conventional thinking suggests that new developments should be required to pay for the costs and disamenities caused or created by it (Jacobson and Redding 1977). The issue is more complicated than this, however, and a number of important questions emerge here.

One question relates to the fairness with which different classes or types of growth are assessed for the costs. Is it equitable to impose an impact fee on new commercial or industrial development to pay for such things as new schools? As the editors of *Nova Law Journal* reported, "Certainly no factory or store ever increased the number of children in the public school system."[2] It seems, however, that in important ways this may not be true. Perhaps the direct cause of the community cost is the presence of new families with children, yet often the indirect cause is the location or presence of new commercial and industrial growth, which attracts or requires families to follow close behind. Such determinations of how the costs of growth actually are generated will have implications for the fairness with which different groups and individuals in the community are treated.

It is perhaps important to note here that the ways in which the costs of growth are perceived and defined may differ substantially among individuals. For instance, while the increased traffic congestion that results from new development may be viewed with great disdain by established residents who remember the community when requisite travel times were not as great, newer residents may not view it as a problem. For those moving to the community from, say, New York or Los Angeles, such levels of congestion may not be viewed as bad at all, perhaps even a marked improvement. In this light, new residents may not view excessive exactions to provide for traffic improvements as important or legitimate. As a further example, some people believe that new park areas should be provided at a high number of acres per resident, while others may see little need for any such facilities (e.g., they may value regular trips to nearby state and federal recreational areas). In a sense it might be argued by those builders, developers, and homeowners unhappy about being forced to pay such fees that people should be allowed to vote with their feet; that is, to make choices about combinations of amenities that are most valuable to them (e.g., see Neenan and Ethridge 1984). Developers may argue that if X acres per person of parkland is desired by new housing consumers, then there are plenty of projects and communities in which they could live where amenities at such levels could be found. Other things being equal, the argument goes, developers and builders should be left to do as they please.

A culpability standard, then, seems to suggest that those groups and individuals directly involved in creating growth-related impacts, that is, builders, developers, and homeowners, should be the ones to incur and pay for those costs. In contrast, it can be argued that the owners of raw land actually have little to do with the direct generation of those impacts and consequently should not be forced to pay for them. They are simply the fortunate beneficiaries of growth and development patterns they have done nothing to directly cause or bring about. Consequently, under a culpability standard, impact fees would appear more ethically defensible where the market conditions are such that these fees will be borne primarily by new homeowners, and not capitalized in the form of lower raw land prices. The application of a strict culpability standard here, however, seems intuitively unacceptable from an ethical point of view precisely because it ignores the benefits and expects the immediate growth catalyst (e.g., the builder, developer) to shoulder the entire burden. Certainly, culpability justifies imposing impact fees on those individuals, but it seems that where benefits accrue to other individuals in the community, such as owners of underdeveloped land, they should share in the costs of growth as well.

By way of clarification, consider a situation where a culpability standard alone might apply. A developer might be required to pay an impact fee to cover the costs of installing certain public drainage or flood control improvements, without which preexisting homeowners would be negatively affected (i.e., by new flooding created by the development). While the new development certainly benefits in a sense from those improvements (without them, the project would not have been permitted), the main justification stems from culpability -the new development is being held responsible for the potential damages and environmental impacts it forces onto others in the community.

14.2.5 Exactions as Quid Pro Quo Trading

An additional ethical perspective is to view the imposition of impact fees and other forms of exactions as the fair outcomes of a kind of quid pro quo trading. The public is willing to permit development to occur in particular ways and at particular intensities in exchange for certain contributions made by the developer. This is the theoretical basis for many of the early subdivision exactions, viewing public approval and acknowledgment of the subdivision of land as a privilege and not a right. The contemporary use of this theory supposes that the public gives up something in exchange for something—certain rights and benefits it holds—in exchange for something else of equal or greater value. While typically this exchange will have a direct relationship to costs created by development, this relationship need not in theory be exact or precise. A developer may be asked to contribute to the conservation of a sensitive and important regional environmental resource in exchange for development approval. This may be a regional need that is not directly or immediately created by the proposed development nor a resource from which the development would directly or immediately benefit. The growing interest in linkage programs reflects this public perspective (Keating 1986).

The quid pro quo theory has its greatest appeal where the public is being asked to grant rights or benefits that are in some sense extra or beyond those given under the existing planning rules or framework. Some exactions are imposed as a condition of rezoning, say from an agricultural or low-intensity use to a high-density residential or commercial use. A question arises as to whether this case presents a unique ethical situation when compared to the case where a landowner just wants to develop his or her land at the designated uses and levels of intensity. Here perhaps one could argue that the exaction is warranted regardless of the extra facility demands that may result because it in a sense serves as compensation to the community—it serves to balance the otherwise inappropriateness of this use as defined in advance by a comprehensive and long-term land-use plan (see *Nova Law Journal*1980). The logic here may be the same as that used to justify the provision of additional density under a bonus/incentive zoning or transferable development rights program (e.g., see Marcus 1980). The trade or exchange may be justified from the public's point of view by reference to the costs generated by a proposed project or the benefits received from it. In this way, the concepts discussed above become relevant as well. It seems that there are other legitimate arguments that also further justify the types of exaction required, for instance, under linkage programs (i.e., improvements and expenditures for broader social needs that may extend beyond a particular new project or development). A strong argument for requiring substantial contributions rather than community-wide taxation to pay for such things as low-income housing or health care is that these exactions are tapping into a process of wealth generation to which the public is a consenting p(even where no zoning changes or regulatory concessions are given). It does not seem unreasonable for the public to lay claim to a portion of the profits generated from, for instance, a proposed office-commercial complex. An additional argument is one from political practicality. While some would argue that many of the broader social goods and services provided through exactions should be financed by the larger public (e.g., through a higher property tax rate), exactions may be the only politically feasible way to finance such needs.

The quid pro quo trade raises the ire of builders and developers who view impact fees and other forms of exactions as a kind of extortion. Yet, from the public's point of view, this is unfair because little coercion is actually involved. Developers and other actors involved in the process of land development are free to choose other localities and regional markets in which to practice their trade if the basic ground rules are unacceptable (e.g., Hayek 1960).

Quid pro quo arrangements that involve public zoning concessions raise serious ethical questions concerning how fairly the resulting public costs are distributed. Often it is the residents of particular neighborhoods who must live with the traffic congestion, air pollution, noise, crime, and other impacts of the increased density that the public permits in exchange for exactions. While the quid pro quo bargain may be efficient from the perspective of the broader public (i.e., it produces net public benefits), particular residents and neighborhoods may believe they are unfairly bearing the brunt of the costs associated with such trades. Adding to this sense of inequity may be the unexpected nature of the density/intensity changes permitted. Landowners and neighborhood residents may legitimately point to the community's plan and land-use regulations as the source of certain expectations that such more intense uses would not be permitted to occur. The ability of developers to bargain in this way for desired zoning changes may cast doubt on the stability and efficacy of a community's entire planning and land-use program.

An interesting question is the extent to which a particular bargain or trade is ethical. Assuming that zoning and land-use concessions are not to be given lightly, at what level of return is the public willing to endure the negative consequences of such concessions (i.e., the consequences of modifying a carefully developed community plan)? A strict utilitarian criterion would suggest that it is sufficient to determine that the benefits from the monetary and other concessions made by the developer exceed the negative consequences of diverging from the community's planned pattern of growth. These negative consequences, and the ways in which they manifest themselves (e.g., highly borne by surrounding residents), suggest perhaps that a trade should be acceptable only from the public's point of view when the benefits are far in excess of these costs, perhaps at least 2 to 1, or 3 to 1, or even 5 to 1. Such a trade would also be more acceptable ethically where the concessions made by the developer are used in some way to compensate affected residents and neighborhoods (e.g., through the financing of certain neighborhood amenities) or used to finance improvements that at least partially mitigate these negative effects (e.g., improvements to deal with new transportation problems). An additional dimension to the ethics of this kind of public–private trading is the amount of profit or benefit the private developer or property owner reaps from the transaction. Even though it may be determined that the public will receive an acceptable return from a proposed trade, the transaction still could be viewed as unethical because the amount of profit reaped by the developer is obscenely high. Because these are public rights being traded away, and because negative social consequences are attached to such trades, the concessions asked for and given by the developer should bear a direct relationship to these profits. To do otherwise would amount to a sort of fire sale at the public's expense.

A parallel might be drawn between the imposition of impact fees under equal quid pro quo trading and the use of equity sharing in public–private partnerships (Fosler and Berger 1982). Equity sharing involves a similar public–private bargain-the public provides certain financial contributions or backing, typically in exchange for a percentage or share of the profits generated by the project.

This suggests that precedent exists for this normative perspective and that experience with public–private partnerships may provide some practical guidance in determining what constitutes a fair trade.

14.3 POLITICAL REPRESENTATION, SOCIAL EXCLUSIVITY, AND SENSE OF COMMUNITY

Heavy reliance on the use of impact fees and other exactions on new development raises several additionally and potentially serious ethical quandaries. One involves the concept of political representation and the extent to which such fiscal tools circumvent or undermine this prized American value. Indeed, this country initiated its struggle for independence in response to the perceived inequity of being taxed without meaningful representation. Similar criticisms can be leveled at impact fees. It is one thing for a locality and its duly elected representatives to decide to tax itself for some desired public service or facility but perhaps another thing entirely to place heavy financial burdens on future individuals who have had no opportunity to participate in the decision or to influence it in any way. Butler and Myers (1984, p. 437) echo similar concerns about the use of independent taxing districts in Texas (municipal utility districts):

Unrepresented in the development negotiations are the interests of the future housing consumer. The development industry argues that it serves those interests by seeking to provide an adequate supply of housing. The city also claims to represent the interests of future consumers. Nevertheless, the outcome of MUD negotiations typically burdens future consumers with financial exactions. The costs of growth are being shifted to the future residents of MUDs through surcharges that will be attached to monthly utility bills in those districts, even after the city annexes the property. Once these future consumers are in place and able to vote, one wonders, will future city councils sustain the long-term commitments to levy special surcharges set by the present city council?

Ceteris paribus, individuals who are assessed such fees, particularly when they are high fees, ought to have a hand in the political decision-making through which they are imposed. Yet, proponents of impact fees can argue that this is not as significant an ethical problem as perhaps initially supposed. First, while future or prospective residents may not have had the opportunity to influence directly past decisions, the possibility of their addition to the local voting and political bloc surely would dictate that current elected officials consider their interests and views. Politicians and elected officials often act prospectively—that is, in accordance with how they believe voters and constituents will react at some point in the future. They will not run the risk of new residents helping to "throw the rascals out of office." There are, of course, problems with this argument, including the very real possibility that elected officials can ignore with impunity this prospective dissatisfaction. Current representatives may in fact be able to gain off-setting political support from existing residents by shifting tax burdens away from this group.

It is also possible that in a high-growth community, the discontent of new residents will lead to a sort of chain reaction in which they become highly supportive of placing similar fees on even newer residents. They've paid theirs, they might argue, and now it's time for new residents to pay their fair share. This may or may not be a healthy attitude to promote a sort of bash the newest resident attitude.

Another view is that the interests of future constituents are already being voiced by surrogate representatives with similar concerns and interests. Builders, developers, and landowners are typically vocal in their opposition to high impact fees and voice concerns about their inequity. They can thus be supposed to represent many of the interests of future residents. While this is undoubtedly true to some extent, it is obvious that (a) the interests of these surrogate groups and future constituents may be substantially divergent (e.g., developers may not be as adamant in their opposition to impact fees if they know that they can pass much of the cost along in the form of higher housing prices), and (b) these surrogate groups may be considerably less effective and hold considerably less credibility in the eyes of elected officials than would members of the general population (e.g., developers are perceived by many to have a biased, one-sided view of the world). Other arguments also can be employed in debunking the political representation concerns. One possible retort is that these impositions, particularly where the fees are not excessive, do not interfere with any fundamental liberties. Individual housing consumers, for instance, have the choice of avoiding the fees simply by locating in some other community or by purchasing a home in an already developed area of town. There are, consequently, ways of escaping these impositions, at least in theory. In many specific situations, such consumers may, in fact, have considerably less freedom than proponents of impact fees may suggest because of geographical limitations (e.g., location with respect to employment), time constraints, and so on.

Current representatives may argue that it is entirely appropriate for them to set the standards by which they will permit the entrance of new development and new constituents into the community. This is almost a proprietary view of the community and its expansion and resembles in some respects the quid pro quo bargaining concept discussed earlier. Another, more theoretical perspective that might be embraced is the idea that new residents would in fact consent to the fees if they were actually participating in the political process. The basis of the consent could involve a number of things from a sense of fairness (e.g., "Yes, because as new residents we are creating these problems we ought to pay for them") to political expediency (e.g., "While as new residents

we don't like the high fees we realize they are necessary to get the project built").

A final reply to this concern is that in some situations, many of the new homes in a developing area may be purchased by those who are already residents of the community. Snyder and Stegman (1986) report that surveys of new home buyers have found this to be partially true. Where the percentage of new constituents made up of old constituents is fairly high, it can be argued that these individuals in fact have had an opportunity to influence policy. Concerns about the lack of political representation are, in these cases, less serious.

It is difficult to resolve the problem of political representation in any ethically definitive way. Arguments for political representation are convincing enough to dictate caution and moderation on the part of elected officials when encumbering future constituents with such financial obligations. On the other hand, local officials typically make numerous decisions that affect future residents in important and fundamental ways and in which such future constituents have little say. These decisions range from the siting of public investments such as roads and hospitals to the regulation of permissible private development (e.g., the permissible height of buildings). The ways in which impact fees encumber future residents may not be very different from these more conventional encumbrances. Yet, planners and public officials must acknowledge the lack of political representation as a real and legitimate ethical concern, and it may suggest that ultimately this negative dimension must be balanced against the other more positive aspects of using impact fees.

The proliferation of impact fees as an approach to financing the costs of new growth raises interesting ethical questions about the larger sense of public or community that exists in a locality. Under a conventional community-wide revenue-raising device, such as a property tax, funds are in theory at least collected and distributed according to the broader community-wide goals and objectives. Taxpayers contribute in taxes and elected officials distribute the funds to those community-wide demands of greatest importance or priority.

A movement toward impact fees as a public finance tool segments or separates the collection and distribution procedures of government. That is, a traffic impact fee is collected and then must be used to address traffic control problems. While the extensive use of impact fees certainly does not preclude the collection of general-revenue/community-wide forms of taxation, it does reduce their political viability. Newer residents in the community are not likely to support both the imposition of extensive impact fees and substantial increases in general-revenue raising (e.g., property taxes). As Stegman (1986, p. 2) notes,

Residents who must pay for their own schools may not continue to support the use of their tax dollars to finance school replacements, and as such residents become more numerous in a community, political support for general-revenue financing is likely to diminish.

What may develop over time is a sort of narrow compartmentalizing attitude—i.e., where the only legitimate public expenditure pattern is one where a user is identified and taxed, and where the proceeds of this tax are used to benefit the user. What could in theory result is a movement away from a larger notion of the public interest. It is interesting that the impact-fee movement comes at a time when notions of broader public civics or public interest appear on the decline (Bellah et al. 1985).

Another somewhat different dimension to this possible effect is the proprietary perspective that might be taken by those who pay high impact fees. That is, residents who have paid large fees for the construction of a new road or the expansion of a park system may become resentful when members of the broader public use those facilities. While their resentment may be legitimate, again the consequences are

that it may be much more difficult to create and maintain a broader sense of community.

The increasing use of impact fees also raises serious questions about the effects of such a system in increasing the exclusivity of communities—that is, if the costs associated with moving to a community are increased, is the ultimate effect that certain classes of individuals are excluded from the community? As noted earlier, the extent to which the costs of impact fees are borne by the new housing consumer (as opposed to, say, the landowner) will depend on a number of factors. In many locations, however, it is clear that serious price impacts will result and that under an impact-fee system, lower and moderate-income residents will find it increasingly difficult to locate there (Dowall 1984). And high impact fees can serve as a tool to discriminate against and exclude (as so much of the history of US land-use policy shows; e.g., Rothstein 2017) individuals and families of color, and if so by either intent or effect, the result in inequitable and unjust.

It has been theorized by some, using the theory of clubs, that imposing certain restrictions on the entrance of new residents into a community may be rational from the point of view of existing residents; that is, necessary to prevent the overcrowding of certain "club goods," "such as streets, schools, and environmental quality" (Blewett, 1983).

The fundamental ethical issue here is the extent to which cities must be accessible to all income and social classes, and the extent to which they should adopt taxing, regulatory, and other policies that enhance accessibility (or at least do not lead to its reduction). The late Paul Davidoff frequently stated his belief that cities are not country clubs (e.g., Davidoff, 1975). Yet an impact fee can act like a membership fee. As noted above, there is substantial evidence that impact fees in many situations will serve to increase considerably the cost of new housing. Moreover, as Snyder and Stegman (1986, p. 97) observe, these effects are particularly evident in "highly desirable communities whose environmental features and amenities are distinct enough to make them much more attractive places to live than other nearby locations." What this perhaps foreshadows is a further exaggeration of the spatial differences between the haves and have-nots. The use of impact fees also may lead to a general community-wide escalation in housing prices, making it difficult for new residents to purchase even existing, older housing in the community (Snyder and Stegman 1986, p. 98).

Leaving aside the empirical question of whether the price of new housing is increased through the use of impact fees, to what extent are cities to be viewed differently than private clubs? I would argue that cities (and towns, counties, etc.) are significantly different from an ethical point of view for a number of important reasons. Among these:

1. Cities are political entities in which individuals have the opportunity to use the most basic of political franchises (i.e., voting, participating, voicing their opinions). Here political equality, not economic or social position, must dictate; as such, cities must strive to be as open and inclusive as possible.
2. Cities as governmental units possess powers that have the potential to affect human lives in numerous and widespread ways; the potential effects of being deprived of "membership" are much greater.
3. Cities are a part of a broader social and governmental network (part of a region, state, nation) and as such are linked economically, socially, and constitutionally to other jurisdictional units. Cities have an obligation to acknowledge and adhere to extra local constitutional and ethical standards (e.g., an obligation to provide for a certain regional fair share of low and moderate-income housing).

Given that public communities are fundamentally different from private clubs, they are subject to broader principles of social justice and governmental conduct. Whether one views exclusivity effects as a problem depends to a large degree on what one believes the obligations of government in fact are, and the appropriate principles of social justice it should recognize and pursue. Some of these, particularly those which relate to public finance, have been identified and discussed above. I have argued elsewhere that a primary principle of government in guiding growth and development is ensuring conditions in which the benefits and opportunities of the least advantaged are maximized first, before those of other social or economic groups and the public at large (specifically Rawls's difference principle; see Rawls, 1971; Beatley, 1984, 1994). Exclusivity as a result of local fiscal and land-use decisions is a concern because it tends to reduce the range of social and economic opportunities available to individuals and tends to solidify existing economic conditions and positions. Impact fees that induce a land-use pattern of clublike communities may be substantially counter to such fundamental notions of social justice.[3] Again, it will depend on the exact configuration of such programs and their actual empirical effects.

The Rawlsian difference principle suggests that social justice will not permit government policies that maximize welfare for the entire community at the expense of the least advantaged. This is a strong principle and one that is no doubt unacceptable to many planners and politicians. We need not invoke such a stringent principle, however, to raise serious questions about the ethics of impact fees and other growth-related policies. I would suggest that the concept of equality of opportunity, with its strong roots in American political and social history, is sufficient to question the legitimacy of impact fees that lead to exclusivity effects, or at least to ensure greater care in their use (Rae 1981).[4] Inequalities of opportunity might be said to exist where, irrespective of their natural talents and abilities of individuals, they are disadvantaged in terms of their social starting points-i.e., in terms of the instruments and means by which to advance in society. Clearly, spatial patterns of social exclusivity affect the nature and quality of these instruments and means in numerous ways (e.g., decent housing, education, health care, development of personal self-esteem, and so on).

Equality of opportunity supports the need to keep social and economic exclusivity to a minimum. It lends support for exactions programs that seek to require contributions for the provision of basic goods and services that advance fundamental equality of opportunity while questioning exactions programs that may reduce the availability of such goods, including but not limited to affordable housing.

We must also be concerned with the broader spatial implications of impact fee use. Situations may arise where some localities in a region or state are using impact fees while others are not. Again, where the fees involved are quite high, impact fees may constitute a sort of membership or admittance fee, in turn creating or exacerbating the social and economic differences between communities. One set of communities may emerge as the "best" clubs, while others emerge as the least desirable clubs, i.e., places to live. Such a system creates or reinforces a spatial pattern of social and economic inequality. While such patterns are not new, and often not primarily the result of impact fees, an impact fee system can serve to increase these intercommunity effects. At the very least, such a finance system does not serve (at least on its face) to mitigate or reduce those social effects.

We must face up to the possibility that impact fees may be used to intentionally exclude certain groups, communities of color in particular, much in the way that zoning has been used in the past. We must confront the possibility that many localities will embrace the impact fee approach not primarily for its fiscal attractiveness, but rather precisely because it does have exclusionary effects, and

serves to further entrench and exacerbate systemic racism and racial inequality. There is growing evidence that many discriminatory land-use practices (e.g. redlining, use of racial covenants) have had long-lasting and pernicious effects, leading to dramatically lower living conditions and quality of life (e.g. systemically lower tree canopy over in neighborhoods of color; e.g. see Hoffman, Shandas, and Pendleton 2020; McDonald et al. 2021).

Intent is a difficult thing to identify in practice, but certainly impact fees will be supported by some precisely because of these kinds of effects. And these discriminatory effects, whether intended or not, lead to unethical and unjust outcomes.

The exclusionary issue aside, some may support impact fees because they view them as additional roadblocks to any type of future growth and development, helping to slow growth and perhaps to displace it to other areas where impact fees are not in use. This raises additional ethical concerns.

In some communities, it may be argued that to forego employing a fiscal revenue-raising device like an impact fee would lead to restrictions on urban growth that would in fact end up being more restrictive. That is, a situation may ensue where the locality refuses or is politically stifled in attempts to keep pace with the public facility demands of local growth. This was found to be an objective of impact fees used in Florida (see *Nova Law Journal* 1980, p. 143). Without impact fees or other similar forms of capital facilities financing, local growth may progress at a snaillike speed, with the attendant results of exclusivity and social inaccessibility. It can be countered again, however, that where the growth being facilitated is primarily upper class or upper income, the results may be no better.

This raises the broader question of the extent to which impact fees, through their ability to get certain facilities financed more quickly and easily, are responding to other important values that often must be included in the equation. Take, for example, a situation where, because of the imposition of an impact fee, a long-needed sewer treatment plant that would not have been feasible before is constructed (e.g., suppose that current residents refused to pass several bond referenda to fund such improvements). As a result, the town is able to move away from heavy reliance on on-site septic tank disposal that threatens to contaminate a highly productive groundwater aquifer. The aquifer, it might be further assumed, is the primary source of drinking water in the region. Even though the imposition of impact fees may raise the cost of new housing and thus make the community more exclusive, it is perhaps reasonable to argue that this is an acceptable outcome when weighed against the health risks and economic impacts of contaminating a regional aquifer. Equally true, the use of a sizable impact fee that results in infrastructural investments or improvements that may help to correct existing inequities or historic injustices—for instance, that might replace harmful lead pipes in neighborhoods of color—would be more ethically defensible.

These kinds of benefits arising from the use of impact fees necessarily must be balanced against the exclusionary and other negative effects that may result.

The extent to which impact fees will cause exclusionary results will, for instance, depend on how the revenues from such fees are actually used and the actual modifications to public expenditure patterns that result. A possible and interesting position is that impact fees will do much to advance social equity because they free general community funds that can then be used for such things as public daycare or housing assistance. This argument seems particularly plausible in this era of fiscal constraint and declining federal assistance for social services and programs (e.g., Juergensmeyer and Blake 1981). It can be expected that in such a period the squeaky-wheel phenomenon prevails (i.e., money will go to fill the potholes, build the freeway exchange, correct the traffic congestion) and less visible social needs will get shortchanged. Impact fees may not

contribute anything directly to assisting the least advantaged groups in the community, yet they may prevent a drain on the public purse that would harm the interests of such groups. Of course, to argue this position requires certain assumptions about the political leadership in a particular locality; that is, there certainly is no guarantee that once such funds are made available they will be used to address such important social needs. Rather, impact fees may simply free local funds that can now be used to finance an additional golf course.

It also might be argued that impact fees can be used as a pricing system to allocate scarce community resources such as classroom space or sewage treatment capacity-and thus will serve to increase allocative efficiency. In theory, impact fees would be assessed in areas where capacity would be exceeded but not assessed in areas where substantial excess capacity existed. The result is, again, a freeing of public revenues to advance other public objectives and goals.

The freeing up of funds argument also raises interesting questions of whether and to what extent a locality should afford priority to the needs and interests of the least advantaged who are already residents of the community, rather than focusing on efforts to alleviate the burdens imposed on the new or prospective disadvantaged (e.g., by keeping the cost of new housing as low as possible). A locality may be able to free funds that can be used for low and moderate-income social programs by imposing high impact fees on new development. In exchange, the imposition of the fees may tend to make the community more economically and socially exclusive. Conversely, a locality might opt to finance a greater share of the costs of new growth through general-revenue funds, perhaps leaving fewer funds available for social programs, yet containing the costs of new housing and in turn. Reducing the community's level of social exclusivity. I would argue that public officials must assess the particular circumstances at hand and undertake those mixtures of financing strategies that have the greatest impact on promoting equality of opportunity. This will, of course, depend on numerous causal and empirical assumptions. If reducing or eliminating the use of impact fees will not have a significant effect on enhancing the availability of low- and moderate-income housing, then it probably makes sense to use impact fees to free other public funds that could be used to provide such goods and services. On the other hand, if the funds freed through impact fees are likely to be used primarily to purchase additional luxury goods (e.g., golf courses) it may make little sense to sacrifice any level of increased housing prices to free funds.

Important ethical issues also arise from intercommunity differences in the use of impact fees, again raising basic questions about the uniformity with which similarly situated individuals are treated. Consider two similar, perhaps adjacent, localities. Assume that one has decided to employ an impact fee while the other has not. The second community believes it has an obligation to fund a major portion of the costs of new growth on a community-wide basis. In the first community, several classes of individuals subject to impact fees may feel that they are unfairly treated compared to the individuals in the second adjoining locality. The owner of undeveloped land in the impact fee community feels that the somewhat lower price he or she must settle for is unfair. The new home buyer wanting to locate in that community views the somewhat higher purchase price that must be paid as unfair. Even certain residents in the nonimpact fee community will feel unfairly treated. For instance, established homeowners, in theory, either will be required to pay higher property taxes (or other taxes) than would be the case in the impact fee locality or pay the same taxes but receive a smaller, less extensive package of community services.

It can be argued again that these types of regional spatial inequities are mitigated to some extent by the fact that (1) individuals are somewhat mobile and can exit a community if they want, and (2) such taxing and financing decisions are arrived at through a democratic representative process (one which at least incorporates the preferences and desires of the existing population) (see Hayek, 1960, pp. 340–350). Each of these mitigating assumptions of course can be challenged. Mobility does the landowner no good whatsoever because he is not able to transport his land and place it in a locality that does not employ an impact fee. While it can be argued that prospective residents can choose to locate where impact fees are not used or are less costly, often individuals have little flexibility in where they reside, for employment, transportation, or other reasons.

14.4 ETHICAL ISSUES IN IMPLEMENTING THE FEE SYSTEM

Assuming that a jurisdiction has overcome many of the initial questions about the use of impact fees in general, there are of course many ethical questions concerning how impact fees are calculated and, more generally, how impact fee requirements are administered (Porter, 1986). Several of the more important of these are identified here, but this certainly does not provide an exhaustive review. Moreover, many of these questions have been identified in the impact fee literature, although they have not been dealt with in any very thorough or systematic fashion. Many of these issues, and their potential resolution, already have been foreshadowed in previous sections. Indeed, many of the broader ethical questions raised in earlier sections must be answered before these administrative and programmatic issues can be resolved.

One dilemma identified in much of the impact fee literature is the threshold problem. That is, which developments should be considered large enough to be required to pay impact fees? It is a complaint of many developers of large projects that they are unfairly assessed while numerous smaller developments escape the fees. Any ethically defensible impact fee system must apply uniformly to all sizes of growth and development-operational equity requires the imposition and collection of fees for small developments, even where the administrative costs of doing so are very high. A second type of threshold problem involves when a proposed project is likely to create public demand or need for some service or facility. In Broward County, Florida, for instance, projects are assessed impact fees only if they will lead to traffic demands that exceed existing capacity. This can result in a situation where a proposed development approved on day 1 is permitted without the imposition of impact fees, while a similar development approved on day 2 is required to pay substantial traffic improvement fees. An equitable impact fee system would seem to dictate that all development be assessed for demand created-even for those projects where existing capacity is sufficient.

As noted earlier, questions also arise concerning the types of uses to which impact fees should apply. Should fees to cover such facility needs as schools and libraries be applied to commercial and industrial as well as residential projects, for instance? In most cases, in the absence of compelling arguments to the contrary, impact fees should be assessed broadly for all such uses. This will ensure a wider and more equitable distribution of the costs of growth (e.g., with costs perhaps even assessed to the ultimate consumers of commercial and industrial goods).

Numerous operational questions also arise in the calculation of the impact fees. Should they be assessed on a square footage basis, according to the number of bedrooms, and so on? Conventional wisdom, and legal decisions, suggest that where possible this calculation process should be logically related to the impacts generated. Assessments on the basis of the number of bedrooms may be an appropriate method, for instance, because it is a reasonably good proxy for the number of new school-aged children who will be added to the community.

Yet, this will depend on which ethical criteria are embraced. Calculating the fee based on the number of bedrooms may be defended on the basis of the benefit principle or culpability but may not at all be responsive to the ability to pay.

As we have seen, an interesting pricing approach would be to create a graduated fee system responsive to the ability to pay. While such a calculation procedure would not completely ignore costs created or benefits received, it might permit the shifting of some of the costs of this growth onto those higher income uses better able to afford them.

An additional programmatic issue is when the impact fee should be imposed. Is it fair to ask developers to make the contributions on project approval or is it more equitable to require the fees to be paid closer to the time at which the impacts actually occur, benefits are received, etc.? Shouldn't fees be paid in a phased or sequenced fashion so that contributions are not made prematurely (e.g., so that the developer or homeowner is not required to pay for a road or park far in advance of their ability to use these facilities)? Again, the ethical criteria will have an influence. While it may seem appropriate to impose an impact fee at the time of project approval under the concept of quid pro quo trading (i.e., because the bargain or exchange is then in a sense consummated), under a benefit or culpability standard this may not be deemed as appropriate. These are but a few of the ethical questions that emerge from the consideration of practical operational issues. A full discussion of these operational issues is beyond the scope of this chapter, yet the preceding analysis of the broad ethical and value dimensions of the issue should be useful to planners and program administrators in developing and implementing impact fee systems.

14.5 CONCLUSIONS

This chapter has identified several of the primary ethical issues that arise from the use of impact fees. As with most discussions of ethical issues, it will raise more questions than it will answer. Indeed, answers in the usual sense are extremely elusive in this type of analysis. I have argued several primary ethical points, however. First, the initial imposition of a system of impact fees raises serious questions of intertemporal fairness and equity, both within the community and within the broader regional network of communities. The seriousness of these inequities depends on the particular historical patterns of private and public investment financing, and the goals and objectives development exactions, including impact fees, are intended to serve.

Second, the ethical defensibility of impact fees will depend both on the ethical standards embraced by communities and the actual empirical effects of such fees. A number of possible evaluative positions have been identified and examined, including the benefit principle, ability to pay, culpability, and the theory of quid pro quo trading. I have argued that, in situations where the costs are borne primarily or to a large degree through lower raw land prices, the imposition of impact fees is, *certeris paribus*, more justifiable. I have suggested that this outcome is responsive to the benefit standard and the ability-to-pay standard as well as fundamental notions of merit and desert. I have argued strongly for the notion of equality of opportunity and the importance of protecting and advancing this concept through public finance policy. Where impact fees, either because of their magnitude or the conditions under which they are imposed, serve to raise the costs of new housing for low- and moderate-income families, and thus increase the exclusivity of these communities, they are less ethically defensible. While impact fees may often in a narrow sense respond to a benefit standard, they may serve to thrust the costs of growth on those groups least able to afford them (i.e., by essentially pricing many individuals out of the market). They may also have the effect (intended or not) of discriminating against individuals of color and further reinforcing racial inequality.

Another major conclusion is that the defensibility of impact fees will depend on their effect on the broader spending decisions and land-use patterns that result in the community. For instance, while impact fees may raise the cost of new housing, they may be more acceptable from the point of view of advancing community accessibility and equality of opportunity if their use serves to free funds to be used to advance those ends (e.g., through whatever means, rehabilitation of existing homes, construction of low-income housing, provision of social services, etc.). As a further example, such fees may be justified because without them community growth and development would be stifled-growth that would provide substantial benefits (e.g., employment, transportation, shopping, etc.) to several of the most disadvantaged neighborhoods in the community. The negative effects of impact fees on the price of housing may have to be balanced against other important values advanced by their use (e.g., the protection of regional water quality).

These conclusions hold implications for how impact fees are used. It is usually not simply a question of whether or not to use them, but in what ways and to what degree they should be used. Impact fees are more ethically defensible where their proceeds are used to finance in part or in toto programs that serve to enhance the community's overall accessibility and equality of opportunity (e.g., by financing the construction of low- and moderate-income housing, job training programs, daycare facilities, mass transit, etc.). Impact fees, as with any public finance tool, must be judged against these broader social and economic goals.

The question of political representation is difficult to resolve. On the one hand, it seems unfair to impose impact fees on an element of the constituency that has no direct representation of their opinions or interests. Yet, many political decisions are made in this way, and prospective residents are not coerced in any fundamental way into paying the fees.

Planners and public officials should be sensitive to this issue and ultimately may need to balance this negative aspect against the positive features of an impact fee system.

NOTES

1 Snyder and Stegman (1986) refer to this as the problem of intergenerational equity.

2 The editors acknowledge in their note the inadequacies of this statement: "It can be argued that commercial and industrial properties don't directly add children to the school system but their employees do add children to the school district. Commercial and industrial properties pay school ad valorem taxes and presumably, impact fees would be assessed on the same theory." *Nova Law Journal*, 1980, p. 180.

3 There is, of course, considerably more to Rawls's theory of justice than the difference principle. Rawls derives his Two Principles of Justice, of which the difference principle is the essence of the second, through hypothesizing about which standards would be agreed upon under certain idealized social decision-making conditions. Rawls refers to this hypothetical construct as the Original Position and specifies a number of important conditions that would prevail there, including the Veil of Ignorance that would prevent individuals from knowing, among other things, information about their own personal life circumstances. See Daniels,1975; Barry, 1973; and Nozick, 1974.

4 A requirement similar to equality of opportunity actually is included by Rawls as a constraint on the workings of the difference principle. Specifically, Rawls requires that all social inequalities be subject to the doctrine of "fair equality of opportunity. "This is a far-reaching stipulation requiring society to provide necessary minimum levels of education, job training, etc., to ensure that all individuals of similar talents and abilities will have a fair chance to secure social and economic positions. This is very close to the definition have in mind here and is obviously quite different from the more narrow, formal sense in which equality of opportunity is often used in this country (e.g., individuals should not be discriminated against because of race or sex). Rae (1981) distinguishes between prospect-regarding and means-regarding forms of equality of opportunity. While local exclusionary policies certainly will have an influence on both types, I am primarily arguing here for a means-regarding definition.

REFERENCES

Barry, B. (1973). *The Liberal Theory of Justice*. Oxford: Clarendon Press.

Beatley, T. (1984). Applying moral principles to growth management. *Journal of the American Planning Association, 50*(4), 459–469.

———. (1985). Paternalism and land use planning: Ethical bases and practical applications. In T. Attig , D. Callen, & J. Gray (Eds.), *The Restraint of Liberty*. Bowling Green, OH: Department of Philosophy, Bowling Green State University.

———. (1994). *Ethical Land Use: Principles of Policy and Planning*. Baltimore: Johns Hopkins University Press.

———, & Kaiser, E. (1983). *Financing Community Infrastructure: An Exploratory Review and Assessment of Alternative Approaches*. Raleigh: North Carolina Board of Science and Technology.

Bellah, R., et al. (1985). *Habits of the Heart: Individualism and Commitment in American Life*. New York: Harper and Row.

Blewett, R. A. (1983). Fiscal externalities and residential growth controls: A theory-of-clubs perspective. *Public Finance Quarterly, 11*(1), 3–20.

Bosselman, F. P., & Stroud, N. E. (1985). Pariah to paragon: Developer exactions in Florida, 1975–85. *Florida State Law Review, 14*, 527–563.

Butler, K. S., & Myers, D. (1984). Boom time in Austin, Texas: Negotiated growth management. *Journal of the American Planning Association, 50*(4), 447–458.

Daniels, N., ed. (1975). *Reading Rawls: Critical Studies of a Theory of Justice*. New York: Basic Books.

Davidoff, P. (1975). Working Toward Redistributive Justice. *Journal of the American Institute of Planners 41*(5), 317–318.

Dowall, D. (1984). *The Suburban Land Squeeze: Land Conversion and Regulation in the San Francisco Bay Area*. Berkeley: University of California Press.

Duncan, J. B., Morgan, T. D., & Standerfer, N. R. *Drafting Impact Fee Ordinances*. Austin: City of Austin.

Feinberg, J. (1970). *Doing and Deserving*. Princeton: Princeton University Press.

Fosler, R. S., & Berger, R. A., Eds. (1982). *Public Private Partnership in American Cities*. Lexington: Heath and Co.

Hagman, D. (1975). A new deal: Trading windfalls for wipeouts. In B. F. Bobo (Ed.), *No Land is an Island* (pp. 169–186). San Francisco: Institute for Contemporary Studies.

———, & Misczynski, D. (1978). *Wind foils for Wipeouts*. Chicago: ASPO Press.

Hayek, F. A. (1960). *The Constitution of Liberty*. Chicago: University of Chicago Press.

Hoffman, J., Shandas, V., & Pendleton, N. (2020). "The effects of historical housing policies on resident exposure to intra-urban heat: A study of 108 US urban areas," *Climate, 8,* 12.

Jacobsen, F., & Redding, J. (1977). Impact taxes: Making development pay its way. *North Carolina Law Review, 55,* 407–420.

Juergensmeyer, J. C., & Blake, R. M. (1981). Impact fees: An answer to local governments capital funding dilemma. *Florida State University Law Review, 9*(3), 415.

Keating, W. D. (1986). Linking downtown development to broader community goals: An analysis of linkage policy in three cities. *Journal of the American Planning Association, 52*(2), 133–141.

Keene, J. et al. (1976). *Untaxing Open Space.* Washington, DC: Council on Environmental Quality.

Maxcus, N. (1980). A comparative look at TOR, subdivision exactions, and zoning as environmental preservation panaceas: The search for Dr. Jekyll without Mr. Hyde. *Urban Law Annual, 20,* 3–73.

McDonald, R. et al. (2021). "The tree cover and temperature disparity in US urbanized areas: Quantifying the association with income across 5723 communities," *PLOS One,* April 28.

Neenan, W. B., & Ethridge, M. E. (1984). Competition and cooperation among localities. In R.D. Bingham & J. P. Blair (Eds.), *Urban Economic Development.* Beverly Hills: SAGE Publications.

Nova Law Journal. (1980). Note on impact fees: National perspectives to Florida practice: A review of mandatory land dedications and impact fees that affect land developments. *Nova Law Journal, 4,* 137–186.

Nozick, R. (1974). *Anarchy, State and Utopia.* New York: Basic Books.

Plosila, W. H. (1976). Metropolitan Tax Base Sharing: Its Potential and Limitations. *Public Finance Quarterly, 4,* 2.

Porter, D. (1986). The rights and wrongs of impact fees. *Urban Land,* May.

Rae, D. (1981). *Equalities.* Cambridge, MA: Harvard University Press.

Rawls, J. (1971). *A Theory of Justice.* Cambridge, MA: Harvard University Press.

Rothstein, R. (2017). *The Color of Law: A Forgotten History of How Our Government Segregated America.* Washington, DC: Economic Policy Institute.

Snyder, T. P., & Stegman, M. A. (1986). *Paying for Growth: Using Development Fees to Finance Infrastructure.* Washington, DC: Urban Land Institute.

Stegman, M. A. (1986). Development Fees for Infrastructure. *Urban Land,* May 2–5.

Weale, A. (1983). *Political Theory and Social Policy.* London: MacMillan Press Notes.

15 THE ETHICS OF IMPACT FEE EQUITY

MARY KAY PECK DELK, ARTHUR C. NELSON, AND SUSAN A. WOOD

15.1 INTRODUCTION

For all disciplines, there is a link between equity and ethics. McCandless and Ronquillo (2020) reviewed professional codes, exploring how social equity is addressed by such professional organizations as the American Society for Public Administration, International City/County Managers Association, and the American Planning Association through its American Institute of Certified Planners (AICP). In all cases, advancing social equity is a professional priority. For planners, this is expressed in the AICP Code of Ethics and Professional Conduct.[1] In the Code, equity is most directly dealt with in Section A: Principles to Which We Aspire. An update to the Code of Ethics was adopted by the AICP Commission in November 2021. This chapter reflects the updated Code of Ethics. One of the main goals of the update is to reorganize the Aspirational Principles to highlight the planner's role in serving the public interest, including the role planners play in social justice and racial equity and the responsibility to eliminate historic patterns of inequity where past planning decisions have played a role.

This chapter addresses the equity of impact fees. In it, we first define equity in the planning field and later apply that definition to impact fees. We discuss the importance of cultivating an equity lens and describe how to use an equity lens. The accepted use of impact fees and how the equity of impact fees has been interpreted over time is detailed. Through the use of four case studies, we apply an equity lens and show how impact fees often are inequitable, even though the fees are equal. We

conclude with specific questions to use when applying an equity lens.

A Coda follows this chapter. It creates a framework to apply the ethics of impact fee equity lens for practitioners.

15.2 DEFINING EQUITY IN PLANNING

In the realm of social justice, equity has been defined by many, including the definition used by the American Planning Association (APA) in the Planning for Equity Policy Guide,[2] adopted in 2019, which established equity policies for APA and its members. This definition, penned by Policy Link, reads: "just and fair inclusion into a society in which all can participate, prosper, and reach their full potential. Unlocking the promise of the nation by unleashing the promise in us all." At the heart of this definition, as with other definitions of equity, is "fairness." In the AICP Code of Ethics, a call for fairness is the underpinning for the Aspirational Principles presented in Section A, which are commitments to stated ideals. As originally stated, these include being conscious of the rights of others; providing clear information to all affected parties; acting on opportunity for meaningful impact; planning for the needs of the disadvantaged and promoting racial and economic integration; and dealing fairly and evenhandedly with participants in the planning process.

As recently reframed, the Aspirational Principles, and the focus on serving the public interest, have not changed but now include expanded commitments that call out the need for effective communication, respect, and compassion for all communities, particularly those

DOI: 10.4324/9781003336075-18

who have been historically underserved or marginalized.[3] Further, the Aspirational Principles require those who participate in the planning process to include an equity focus in planning practice and plan implementation; to utilize measures that will help overcome historic impediments; to use integrity, particularly in engagement with community members; and to work to achieve social justice and racial equity.

The equity policies adopted by APA and the ethical requirements to act in the public interest center the need for planners to use an equity lens, or an equity in all policies approach, in all areas of planning practice and in all planning efforts, including structuring, assessing, and exacting impact fees.

It should be noted that equity and equality are not the same. Sometimes, more is needed to provide equal access to opportunity. It all depends on the starting point.

15.2.1 Applying the Equity Lens

As presented in the Planning for Equity Policy Guide, two key attributes of inequity are disproportionality, described as "when the outcomes of a project or plan create or amplify disparities in only part of a community, the disproportionate impacts can lead to further social and economic impairment of some groups," and institutionalized, which refers to the systemic policies and processes that are embedded in practice and can result in negative outcomes, especially disproportionate impacts.

The APA Planning for Equity Policy Guide presents an equity lens applicable to all policies, which is a holistic approach that considers the complex factors influencing the practice of planning. Without consideration of potential effects on communities and all community members, the impacts, both positive and negative, cannot factor into decision-making and implementation, thus ignoring the potential for unfair outcomes.

To combat inequities, both current and potential, it is essential to use an equity lens, which means to focus our efforts on equity by considering fairness, the full breadth of those who are affected, and the range of effects of our actions, both short and long term. Only by doing so can we begin to address the inequities that are pervasive in our society, some of which resulted from historic practices that occurred, perhaps not at the will of planners, but by using the tools of planners, such as exclusionary zoning and covenants, and the tools of development, such as redlining, discriminatory low-interest mortgage programs, and urban renewal. These practices, many of which became prevalent post-WWII, have served to create and exacerbate wealth disparity and disproportionate impact. Using an equity lens to foresee the potential for disproportionate impact in all aspects of planning practice, including the assessment of impact fees, will initiate a move toward more equitable communities.

15.2.2 Using an Equity Lens in Cross-Cutting Areas

Three cross-cutting areas (gentrification, environmental justice, and community engagement and empowerment) were identified in the APA Planning for Equity Policy Guide as ones that cut across topical areas and areas of planning practice, including the structure or assessment of impact fees. The Policy Guide presents a broad, encompassing approach to addressing inequities through the practice of planning, including broad, rather than specific, policies that are applicable to the assessment of impact fees. This chapter goes into an in-depth analysis of the equity of impact fees, using the definition of equity from the Policy Guide and the concept of using an equity lens. We include the three focus areas of the Policy Guide as examples of applying an equity lens and as a basis for applying an equity lens to impact fees.

Taking an equity approach when considering these areas is necessary to avoid potential disproportionate impact or inequitable results.

15.2.2.1 Gentrification

The term "gentrification" was first coined by Ruth Glass in *London: Aspects of Change* (1964) to describe the transformation of underserved, or poor, areas of a city that occurs when more affluent groups purchase these properties and improve, or invest in, them.[4]

Gentrification occurs when the real estate and development market sees opportunity in investing in neglected areas for the purpose of achieving a net increase in value. This directly contributes to the magnitude of the increase of profit margin, the eventual bottom line. In short, those properties that have greater room for increase in value are those that are most ripe for gentrification. These are typically areas that are characterized as underserved, where investments in infrastructure and aesthetics have not kept pace with more affluent areas. While investment in long-neglected areas is needed, often the result is that property values rise, property taxes rise, and social factors come into play, resulting in displacement of the original residents. Investment in areas that are most in need is desirable; however, means to proactively address and/or mitigate the negative impact of displacement must be scrutinized using an equity lens.

For most, home ownership has presented the greatest opportunity for personal and intergenerational wealth-building. Investment in neighborhoods increases property values and personal wealth for the homeowner. However, gentrification and increased value brings with it increased costs, such as property tax, insurance, and others. When the homeowner can no longer afford their investment, displacement occurs, and along with it, the opportunity for wealth-building.

15.2.2.2 Environmental Justice

Fairness, which is at the heart of equity, is echoed in the Environmental Protection Agency (EPA) definition of environmental justice, which is "fair treatment and meaningful involvement of all people regardless of race, color, national origin, or income, with respect to the development, implementation, and enforcement of environmental laws, regulations, and policies."[5] As it relates to planning, applying principles of environmental justice greatly resembles using an equity lens. For federally funded infrastructure projects, a requirement to exercise environmental justice was codified by President Bill Clinton in 1994, via Executive Order 12898, which required, prior to construction, conducting an analysis to determine the potential for disproportionate impact on underserved communities. If the potential for disproportionate impact exists, avoidance or mitigation is required. Again, using the principles of environmental justice, or an equity lens, in all aspects of planning, including the use of development impact fees, provides the opportunity to foresee and avoid negative consequences of development.

15.2.2.3 Community Engagement and Empowerment

Meaningful community engagement offers the opportunity for empowerment or for community members to play a role in decision-making. As with the two previous cross-cutting areas, to address current and potential inequities in our communities, those who live there must have a say in planning processes, including comprehensive plan preparation, development approval processes, determination of fee structures, fee assessment, and more, in order to be empowered and to be full-functioning community members.

15.3 IMPACT FEES AS A PLANNING TOOL

Impact fees have been a valuable part of the planning tool kit since they were introduced in the late 1970s. In addition, the planning community has generally considered impact fees to be a fair and equitable way of relegating the cost of development to those who benefit most from it, namely, new residents. Rather than have all residents of a community finance infrastructure improvements for new development through the use of property or other tax increases, impact fees are viewed as a politically acceptable way to pass infrastructure costs along to the new residents who create demand for increased services. For example, impact fees are frequently used to finance school expansion and park construction.

There are a number of reasons why the planning community has supported the assumption that impact fees are fair and equitable.

- Impact fees are based on studies that are unique to each community and reflect that community's *individual* costs, growth rates, and demographics.
- Impact fees have withstood a large body of judicial review that includes the rational nexus principle, which requires that there be a verifiable link between the demand created by new development and the level of impact fee charged.
- Impact fee revenues are earmarked for projects that are a direct result of new development and cannot be used for other purposes.
- Impact fees are generally politically acceptable, as they are paid by future community residents who don't yet have a voice.

Past planning practice established and defended the fairness of applying impact fee structures equally and evenly to all affected parties; however, as discussed in the case studies that follow, equal, though seemingly fair at face value, is not always equitable. Therefore, without careful forethought, a fee structure based on equal assessment has the ability to result in unfairness, or disproportionate impact, thus creating the inequities we seek to avoid. Without question, an equal fee structure is simple and easily applied, while a structure based on equity is likely to be more complex. Still, impact fee structures created using an equity lens can serve to avoid, and potentially to address, prior disproportionate impact.

To be fair, we should note that the concept of equity has evolved over time and that impact fee practitioners and members of the planning profession were using the values that prevailed

at the time. An examination of unintended consequences and changing values have led to a sharper look at the equity of impact fees.

The following two excerpts illustrate how the discussion of the equity of impact fees has evolved.

Impact fees have been criticized as being an inequitable means to finance public facilities. By requiring new development to pay for new facilities without benefiting from existing facility capacity, local governments may be bypassing the traditional practice of intergenerational contribution toward public facilities. Some commentators have argued that, when set at high levels, impact fees may also tend to be regressive. Certain public facilities may be considered "public goods" that should be financed by the entire community, such as general government, police, or schools. *To the extent that impact fees are paid by those who are most likely to benefit from the public facilities provided therefrom, however, impact fees are equitable*[6] (emphasis added).

The preceding excerpt is from the APA Policy Guide on Impact Fees, which was adopted in 1997 and remains the organization's official statement on impact fees. Because impact fees would be paid by those who benefit most from them, they were considered equitable.

By 2008, the discussion of the equity of impact fees had made substantial progress.

Local-level debates concerning impact fees can address different types of equity. Intergenerational equity may be of concern because impact fees assessed on new homes may adversely affect the ability of the children of current residents of the community to buy homes where they grew up. Representational equity may be of concern because to the extent that impact fees are assessed on new homes bought by new residents of the community, these new residents had no say in the adoption of the policy. Equity in endowments may be of concern to the extent that impact fees are considered a form of "initiation" fee into a community, much as country clubs charge high initiation fees affordable only to the affluent. While these concepts of equity are important, the focus of this book is how to address proportionate share equity—that is, the extent to which the fee reflects the actual impact different housing units have on community facilities. A critical aspect of proportionality is the extent to which impact fees are based on the impact of new development on facilities. Many impact fee programs assume that each residential unit has the same impact on facilities regardless of size, type, density, location, or other factors. Hence, the impact fee for a large single-family detached home is the same as for a small efficiency apartment, despite the fact that census figures clearly show substantial differences in occupancy rates. These impact fees are described as "flat rate" fees and are inherently unfair.

The result is that flat rate impact fees have a "regressive" effect; that is, they fall disproportionately on those with lower incomes rather than those with higher ones. This book focuses on methodologies for calculating impact fees to ensure that the regressive effect is reduced, if not eliminated. Through taking an approach that more correctly allocates the proportionate share, the resulting fees are far less regressive.[7]

As we show in the later section on best practices, the discussion today would be very different. Through the use of case studies and the application of an equity lens in this chapter, we push this discussion to a new level in its constant evolution.

15.4 CASE STUDIES

Earlier in this chapter, we provided a definition of equity, explained how to apply an equity lens to impact fees, and posited that impact fees aren't always equitable. We will now use the case study approach to illustrate how to apply an equity lens and point out the potential inequities of impact fees. In our case study analysis, we will use the definition of equity and other relevant points from the APA Planning for Equity Policy Guide, the EPA definition of environmental justice, and Section A3.2 of the AICP Code of Ethics, as, when taken together, these components provide an equity lens.

The Aspirational Principle applied to these case studies is:

- Seek social justice by identifying and working to expand choice and opportunity for all persons, emphasizing our special responsibility to plan for those who have been marginalized or disadvantaged and to promote racial and economic equity. Urge the alteration of policies, institutions, and decisions that do not meet their needs.[8]

There are six assumptions that apply to the following case studies. Assumptions 2–5 are based on census data.

1. Impact fees have generally been regarded as inherently fair because of the way they are developed. This notion is challenged, as the reader will see.
2. Detached single-family homes larger than 3,000 square feet generate about twice as many students as detached single-family homes smaller than 1,000 square feet.
3. Studio and one-bedroom multi-family units generate almost no students.
4. Comparing the occupants of with the occupants of multi-family homes, single-family home occupants have higher incomes, and single-family homes are less likely to be occupied by persons of color than multi-family homes.
5. When determining impact fees, nonresidential development is generally not charged for parks and recreation, schools, and libraries even when practitioners acknowledge nonresidential development impacts those facilities; the difficulty is data availability.
6. Costs vary by geographic areas. While service areas can apportion costs based on geography (see Chapters 6 and 7), many practitioners and their clients seem to prefer simplicity with one or very few service areas to complexity even if that leads to lower-cost and often lower-income areas subsidizing higher-cost and often higher-income areas.

Some of the case studies are based on real-life situations. In those instances, the names and details have been altered to keep the communities and participants from being identified. Others are composites or adaptations of studies.

15.4.1 Case Study 1: Impact Fees and Housing Affordability

The first case study takes place in the fictional county of Nirvana, the fastest-growing county in the state and one of the fastest-growing counties in the entire country. The fast growth has produced political pressure to adopt impact fees.

The Nirvana Board of County Commissioners contracted with Schoolmarm Consultants, LLC, to prepare a school impact fee. After adjusting for credits (see Chapter 7), the consultants calculated the following net school impact cost by residential unit type and overall weighted average (see Table 15.1).

Based on the information provided by Schoolmarm Consultants, the County Commission has two choices. The Commission can adopt either variable impact fees that are based on the type of residential unit or impact fees that are an average of all unit types.

If the variable fees are chosen, they will range from $1,500 to $5,250 depending on the type of unit. If the average fees are chosen, each unit will be charged $3,915.

Concerned that the County Commissioners will adopt impact fees based on the average of $3,915 per unit, a local affordable housing group, let's call it CasaEquity, advocates for school impact fees based on the column titled Net Impact Cost Per Unit. It produces a table showing the differences in fees between the residential types compared with the weighted average, something the consultants did not do (see Table 15.2).

TABLE 15.1 Nirvana County Net School Impact Cost by Residential Unit Type and Average

Residential Unit Type	Student Generation Rate per Unit	Net Impact Cost per Student	Net Impact Cost per Unit
Single-Family Detached	0.350	$15,000	$5,250
Townhouse	0.150	$15,000	$2,250
Multi-family	0.120	$15,000	$1,800
Average, Total	0.261	$15,000	$3,915

Source: Arthur C. Nelson, adapted from actual consulting report analysis.

TABLE 15.2 Variation in Net Impact Cost between Residential Unit Types

Residential Unit Type	Net Impact Cost per Unit	Difference from Mean	Proportionality from Mean
Single-Family Detached	$5,250	$1,335	–25%
Townhouse	$2,250	($1,665)	74%
Multi-family	$1,800	($2,115)	118%
Weighted Average, Total	$3,915		

Source: Arthur C. Nelson, adapted from consulting report analysis.

Arguing that it has discretion to set impact fees at the average, the County Commission adopts the average net impact cost as the impact fee for all units, with the following reasoning:

The (school facilities) impact fee is based upon the ***average student generation rate per dwelling*** and does not exceed the costs of providing for the acquisition of new school sites, the expansion and equipping of existing educational facilities, and the construction and equipping of new educational facilities necessitated by new land development for which the impact fee is imposed.

(Actual text with the local government's name redacted and emphasis added)

Because each dwelling unit is charged the same impact fee, one could argue that all residential units are being treated equally. Equal treatment, however, doesn't mean equitable treatment, as we discuss next.

15.4.1.1 Applying an Equity Lens

We begin this analysis by applying an equity lens and by asking the question: Is the action of the Nirvana County Commission equitable?

By examining the analysis presented by CasaEquity, we find that the "average" impact fees that were adopted resulted in single-family homes paying 25 percent less than their proportionate share, while townhouse and multi-family units (including condominiums and apartments) pay 74 percent and 118 percent more than their proportionate share, respectively. This first step of applying an equity lens shows clearly the inequity between the discount given to single-family homes and the over-payment charged to townhouses and multi-family units.

Applying an equity lens means digging deeper and taking the analysis a step further.

Per census data, occupants of single-family homes are more likely to be occupied by white people than people of color and by people who have a higher income than people of color. Conversely, the occupants of multi-family homes and townhouses will pay far more (118 percent for multi-family homes and 74 percent for townhouses) than their fair share of their calculated financial impact and are subsidizing single-family homes. Thus, the average impact fee adopted by the County Commission imposes a disproportionate impact on potential residents of color and in effect, makes it more expensive for people of color to live in Nirvana. The fees fall disproportionately on those with lower incomes.

One might conclude that varying school impact fees by type of unit would have been the more equitable policy. However, to move closer to producing an equitable recommendation, the consultants could have also produced data and analysis showing the student generation by size of unit within each type. For instance, census data indicate that detached homes larger than 3,000 square feet generate about twice the number of students as homes under 1,000 square feet, while studio and one-bedroom multi-family units generate almost no students. This type of analysis would have produced more equitable impact fees.

Follow up. Over the several years since these impact fees were adopted, census data show that 94 percent of all new home construction was for single-family detached units, 6 percent was for townhouses, and no multi-family units were built in Nirvana County. In the meantime, the same Board of County Commissioners routinely expressed concern about the lack of housing affordability.

A possible but by no means only cause of the construction trends in Nirvana County is the inequitable impact fees. The impact fees imposed on single-family homes are a bargain, particularly if viewed from the home builders' point of view of maximizing profit and when examined in terms of percentage of housing prices. For example, a single-family home priced at $300,000 would pay $3,915 or 1.3 percent of its total cost. A townhouse priced at $200,000 would also pay $3,915 or

2 percent of its total cost. However, a $100,000 condominium paying the standard impact fee would pay 3.9 percent of its total cost. The inequity of the impact fees may well have contributed to the lack of interest in building townhouses and multi-family units.

15.4.2 Case Study 2: Residential and Nonresidential Impact Fees in the City of Happiness

The following case is based on a real situation. The numbers have been rounded and circumstances made anonymous to illustrate an impact fee equity concern.

The City of Happiness City Council commissioned Impact Associates, Inc. (IAI) to prepare its public safety impact fees, which would be imposed on both residential and nonresidential properties. IAI used different methods to calculate impact fees for residential and nonresidential property.

To determine residential impact fees, IAI used the census bureau's American Community Survey five-year sample and found that there were 5,000 people living in 2,000 occupied units for an average of 2.5 persons per occupied unit. IAI uses this figure for the residential impact fee part of the fee schedule and recommends $1,000 per person or $2,500 per residential unit regardless of the type or size of the residential unit. It also assumes a 0 percent vacancy rate, since the fee is based on the average number of persons per unit, which is applied to all new residential units permitted.

When we apply an equity lens, we need to dig deeper, look at the demographic data, and ask probing questions, such as: Is this fair treatment? Are we promoting racial integration? Does this policy help residents reach their full potential?

That deeper dig of the same census data shows an average of 3.0 persons per unit for all single-family units, including vacant ones, and 2.0 persons per unit for all multi-family

units, also including vacant ones. At $1,000 per person, the impact fees for single-family units should be $3,000 per unit, while impact fees for multi-family units should be $2,000 per unit. The adopted impact fees show a disparity between how much residents should pay if the fees were equitable and how much they actually pay.

Single-family impact fees, as in case study 1, are subsidized by multi-family impact fees. Single-family units pay $500 less than the population data support; multi-family units pay $500 more than the population data support. Moreover, in Happiness, as perhaps in nearly all communities across the nation, occupants of single-family homes have higher incomes and are less likely to be occupied by persons of color than multi-family homes.

When we apply the equity lens to the Happiness residential impact fees, the results show that people of color are not being treated equitably. The data shows that people of color are more apt to live in multi-family housing and are in fact subsidizing the impact fees for single-family homes, which are more likely to be occupied by white people. Happiness is not an equitable community.

IAI then considers nonresidential land uses and applies the Institute of Transportation Engineers' (ITE) *Trip Generation Manual* schedule of land uses to create more than 100 categories of nonresidential land uses. Using ITE data, the impact fee schedule for nonresidential land uses is based on the number of workers per 1,000 square feet for most categories (such as office, warehouse, retail, industrial, and so forth) and workers per other units of measure (such as restaurant seats, golf course holes, gasoline station pumps, and so forth). The multiplier is $1,000 per worker for these 100+ categories of nonresidential land uses. For instance, a nonresidential land use that averages two workers per 1,000 square feet pays an impact fee of $2,000 per 1,000 square feet, meaning that a 10,000 square foot building pays a public safety impact fee of $20,000. On the other hand, another nonresidential land use that averages 0.50 workers per 1,000 square feet pays an impact fee of $5,000 for a 10,000 square foot building. Moreover, the ITE data includes vacant properties, so a vacancy rate is built into the fee schedule.

When comparing the residential and nonresidential impact fee methodologies in Scenario 2, the nonresidential impact fee methodology is much finer grained. Using more categories and data to develop impact fees produces fees that are more proportionate to the use and thus, more equitable. In this scenario, which is played out all across the country, nonresidential impact fees are more proportionate to impact based on the size and type of unit than residential impact fees and are thus, more equitable than residential impact fees.

15.4.3 Case Study 3: Some Areas Are More Equal Than Others

The following case is adapted from a real situation. The numbers have been rounded and circumstances made anonymous to illustrate an ethics of impact fee equity concern.

George Orwell's allegory about Soviet communism, *Animal Farm*, has four-legged farm animals overthrowing the human farmers to create a totally equal society of farm animals. It ends with a pig standing on two legs declaring: "All animals are equal but some animals are more equal than others." Unfortunately, the design of service areas (see Chapters 6 and 7) can sometimes seem like *Animal Farm* in their inequitable outcomes.

Consider the Rocky Hill Sewer District (RHSD), which provides sewer services to all the cities in the county. Because the state impact fee enabling act allows jurisdictions to declare the entire jurisdiction a single service area, the RHSD does so. It reasons that doing so makes the analysis simple, and besides, what is more fair than having everyone pay the same impact fee for sewer connection everywhere? But, costs vary by location, oftentimes dramatically and inequitably. Table 15.3 applies an equity analysis to the RHSD. The column headed by "Geographically Equitable Sewer Impact Fee" shows the fee that is charged per new single-family detached connection, $2,563, as well as what the fee would be based on differences in flow among the cities. The variations in costs are attributable to:

- Differences in average persons per dwelling unit, where larger homes on average have more people living in them than smaller homes.

TABLE 15.3 Variation in Average Cost Sewer Impact Fees by City

City	Geographically Equitable Sewer Impact Fee	Impact Fee Variance from Mean	Impact Fee Variance from Highest
American River	$4,000	$1,000	20%
Pleasanton	$6,400	($1,400)	–28%
Lower River	$5,800	($800)	–16%
Crestview	$4,800	$200	4%
Lowland	$3,500	$1,500	30%
Maple Hills	$4,800	$200	4%
Rocky Springs	$4,500	$500	10%
Rocky Slope	$4,000	$1,000	20%
Hightown	$8,000	($3,000)	60%
Rocky Hill Sewer District Average	$5,000		

Source: Arthur C. Nelson, adapted from consulting report analysis.

- Lower-density areas often have more inflow/infiltration (I/I) per home flowing into sewer lines (often from stormwater) than higher-density areas.
- Some areas require more expensive installations, such as pumps, longer pipe runs, and associated engineering, than others.

This table shows that impact fees for Hightown (highlighted) are $3,000 or 60 percent less than their geographically equitable share, while fees for Lowland (also highlighted) are $1,500 or 30 percent more.

We note that impact fees are calculated without respect to such social equity metrics as incomes and house values. The reason is that impact fees mitigate the impact of new development on infrastructure that is based only on cost. Thus, there may be occasions where high-cost areas are also where lower-income households live, but this is likely the exception. In the present example, indeed, house values vary as shown in Table 15.3. The table also shows the variation in impact fees as a percentage of house values. For fees based on the overall district average, the range in impact fees as a percentage of home values is

from 1.2 percent in Hightown, which has the highest incomes, to 2.7 percent in Lowland, which also has the lowest home values. While 2.7 percent may not seem high on the base of a home of $185,000, it is not trivial, as it is 2.3 times higher as a share of home value than the highest-value city despite having smaller impacts (see column for "Incidence Ratios with Average Impact Fee Compared with Highest Home Value" in Table 15.4).

Looking at Table 15.4 through an equity lens, it is clear that those who live in the lowest-value homes are carrying a disproportionate financial burden over those who live in the highest-value homes. It may be safe to assume that those who live in lower-value homes also have a lower household income. In that case, there is another inequity. That question could be answered definitively by preparing map overlays that show household income and household value.

15.4.4 Case Study 4: Nonresidential Free Riders Impact Residential Development Inequitably

The town of Bottom Land has spent two decades on improving its quality of life. It is

TABLE 15.4 Variation in Geographically Equitable Sewer Impact Fees by City

City	Mean Value of Single-Family Detached Homes	Average Impact Fee as Percentage of Home Value	Incidence Ratios with Average Impact Fee Compared with Highest Home Value	Geographically Variable Impact Fee as Percentage of Home Value	Incidence Ratios with Geographically Variable Impact Fee Compared with Highest Home Value
American River	$224,000	2.2%	1.9	1.8%	0.9
Pleasanton	$275,000	1.8%	1.5	2.3%	1.2
Lower River	$250,000	2%	1.7	2.3%	1.2
Crestview	$295,000	1.7%	1.4	1.6%	0.9
Lowland	*$185,000*	*2.7%*	*2.3*	1.9%	1
Maple Hills	$315,000	1.6%	1.3	1.5%	0.8
Rocky Springs	$251,000	2%	1.7	1.8%	1
Rocky Slope	$193,000	2.6%	2.2	2.1%	1.1
Hightown	$425,000	1.2%	1	1.9%	1
Rocky Hill Sewer District Average	$275,000	1.8%	1.5	1.8%	1

Source: Arthur C. Nelson, adapted from consulting report analysis.

only 65 percent developed and thus, has a considerable amount of land available for future development. It has used impact fees for building state of the art schools and for acquiring and developing parks, open space, and an interconnected trail system, which is a regional draw. People come from neighboring communities to use Bottom Land's parks, trails, and libraries.

A key element of Bottom Land's economic development strategy is to tout quality of life as a reason for businesses to locate in the community. Quality of life factors include parks, open space, libraries, and schools, all items that are subject to residential impact fees but not to nonresidential impact fees.

In economics, there is a term for those who do not pay the costs they impose on a community: They are called "free riders." They force everyone else in the community to subsidize their costs. In large measure, impact fees address the free rider issue when it comes to new development. But, this is not always successful. For example, suppose a community built a large, expensive park using its tax dollars and impact fees, but the park was then used by people in nearby communities who had not paid for it. It is difficult to capture money from free riders.

But, what if some of those free riders are in the community itself? For instance, it is common practice that only residential development is charged impact fees for parks and recreation, libraries, and schools. Nonresidential development is not charged impact fees for those kinds of infrastructure. The rationale is that nonresidential development does not impact those types of infrastructure, nor does it benefit from them. This may not be true.

Consider that much of a community's population growth occurs because of new nonresidential development, which creates the very jobs that attract people to it. Indeed, many communities use their libraries, parks and recreation facilities, and schools as tools to attract economic development, thereby creating new jobs that bring new households, people, and children to the community. Consider

one community, which specifically cited in its Parks Master Plan that:

The expansion of the City's park system, along with the protection of green space and cultural landscapes and the implementation of city/regional gateways and portals will create … the character of the City and promote opportunities for both active destinations and experiences within nature. This will, in turn, **attract new businesses and industries** that value having the ability to live, work and play all within the same city.

(Anonymous community Parks Master Plan, emphasis added.)

In turn, new businesses increase demand for parks, libraries, and schools through direct effects, such as by attracting households. As businesses attract new households, they in turn attract new businesses to support them.

Moreover, for the most part, planners, consultants, and others assume that only residential developments use such infrastructure as libraries, schools, and parks and recreation, among other types of infrastructure. Businesses, for example, use parks and recreation facilities through organized activities (business sports leagues, social gatherings, and the like) as well as library services for business support activities. Businesses often use schools for training as well as supporting their workers as they gain new skills through professional and continuing education.

Having just residential land uses shoulder the entire impact fee burden for these and related facilities results in disproportionately higher costs borne by these uses relative to the benefits received by nonresidential land uses. The Coda to this chapter outlines ways in which the impact fee burden can be spread across land uses more equitably.

15.5 APPLYING THE AICP CODE OF ETHICS TO THE CASE STUDIES

In determining the ethical obligation of certified planners, we apply Aspirational Principle

A.3.2, as this principle, of all AICP Code provisions, explicitly addresses equity, which we repeat from earlier.

Seek social justice by identifying and working to expand choice and opportunity for all persons, emphasizing our special responsibility to plan for those who have been marginalized or disadvantaged and to promote racial and economic equity. Urge the alteration of policies, institutions, and decisions that do not help meet their needs.[9]

One issue is common to all four case studies. The way that impact fees are currently calculated is often inequitable, based on our case study approach. Impact fees result in disproportionate impacts on persons of color and low-income persons.

The AICP principle cited here is aspirational, one of the standards that planners try to reach. In that spirit, it is planners' responsibility to call for a change in the way impact fees are formulated so that inequities aren't perpetuated. Impact fees are not inherently inequitable and neither are the practitioners who create them; it is the methodology blind to the equity lens that causes inequities.

15.6 SUMMARY

Development impact fees serve as a means to pay for infrastructure and other costs of development. They have long been applied with the intent to have those who will benefit from development pay for it. However, when the focus and emphasis are placed on equity, it becomes apparent that is it important to use an equity lens when structuring and/or assessing impact fees.

The case studies illustrate the following conclusions:

- Nonresidential impact fees are more proportionate to impacts based on the size and type of unit than residential impact fees.
- Requiring the same impact fee for everyone is inconsistent with advancing social equity.

- Impact fees are not calculated using social equity metrics such as incomes and house values, which means there will be some measure of social inequity even if residential impact fees are crafted otherwise through an equity lens.
- Impact fees can have implications for housing affordability that can be addressed in part through impact fees designed consistent with an equity lens.

In summary, equal is not always equitable. It is apparent that in the absence of applying an equity lens when structuring and/or assessing impact fees, the potential for unfairness and disproportionate impacts, or inequities (new or exacerbated), exists.

We conclude this chapter with an approach to apply AICP equity principles to impact fee professional practice.

15.7 THE EQUITY APPROACH IN PRACTICE

Beyond the often-applied practice of fee exemption or reduction of school impact fees for new affordable residential units and facilities for the elderly or disabled, impact fee assessment is not typically done with an equity lens.

The first step in considering equity when structuring or assessing impact fees is to include equity in baseline studies. To do this, planners must ask and answer questions that will determine the likelihood that a fee structure under consideration will have equitable or inequitable results. Evaluation of the information gained from this approach will serve as an equity analysis that can be included in a baseline impact fee study.

These questions, which assist planners in addressing the wealth disparity, or gap, that will continue to widen without intentional interventions, include:

1. Who is affected?
   a. What are the demographics?

b. Are there areas of Environmental Justice populations, defined by EPA as those who are vulnerable, low-income, minority, tribal, and indigenous communities who are already overburdened?[10]

2. How are community members affected?
   a. What groups would be priced out of the market?
   b. Is the proposed application of fees fair?
   c. Would the application of impact fees impose a greater financial burden on those least able to afford it by virtue of a formula that does not consider who pays and how much based on proportionate share impact analysis?

3. Having determined who is affected and how, can the formula for fee assessment be adjusted to result in a more equitable distribution of responsibility in a manner consistent with proportionate share principles? The Coda to this chapter explores many approaches in detail.

15.8 THINKING AHEAD

The case studies and approaches described in this chapter provide the basis and means to apply an equity approach when using development impact fees to fund infrastructure needed for new development in order to avoid disproportionate impact. A further path to investigate is the potential to assess impact fees to mitigate negative impacts that may occur as a result of new development. This methodology could go far in addressing displacement, which is by far the most negative potential outcome of gentrification. Certainly, investments made in a community should result in benefit to all current, not just future, residents. Perhaps, innovations in the design and application of proportionate share development mitigation methodologies could result in funds available to assist current residents with remaining in place or securing new housing. Several examples of innovations are offered in Part 4. By keeping fairness first and foremost, the potential for innovative practices that address equity will continue to grow.

NOTES

1 AICP Code of Ethics and Professional Conduct, APA, Revised November 2021.
2 Planning for Equity Policy Guide, APA, 2019.
3 APA, www.planning.org/ethics/update/.
4 Glass, Ruth. *London: Aspects of Change.* Centre for Urban Studies, editor. MacGibbon & Kee, London. 1964.
5 Environmental Protection Agency, www.epa.gov/environmentaljustice.
6 Retrieved from APA website, 6/8/21, *APA Policy Guide on Impact Fees*, Ratified by Board of Directors, April 1997.
7 IMPACT FEES AND HOUSING AFFORDABILITY A Guidebook for Practitioners Prepared for: U.S. Department of Housing and Urban Development Washington, DC by: Newport Partners, LLC Davidsonville, MD and Virginia Polytechnic Institute and State University Alexandria, VA Authors: Liza K Bowles and Arthur C. Nelson, 2008. Retrieved from internet 6/8/21.
8 Retrieved from American Planning Association Website, July 19, 2022, AICP Code of Ethics and Conduct.
9 Retrieved from American Planning Association Website, July 19, 2022, AICP Code of Ethics and Conduct.
10 EPA: www.epa.gov/environmentaljustice.

REFERENCE

McCandless, S., & Ronquillo, J. C. (2020). Social equity in professional codes of ethics. *Public Integrity, 22*(5), 470–484. https://doi.org/10.1080/10999922.2019.1619442

CODA TO CHAPTER 15

A Standard of Professional Practice for Proportionate Share Impact Fees and Development Mitigation

ARTHUR C. NELSON, MARY KAY PECK DELK, JULIAN CONRAD JUERGENSMEYER, CLANCY MULLEN, JAMES C. NICHOLAS, AND SUSAN A. WOOD

The purpose of proportionate share mitigation is to ensure that new development pays no more than its proportionate share to mitigate its impact on communities. This should not be a novel idea, especially in the context of equity and its ethical implications presented in Chapters 14 and 15. For context, it is important to know that equity is different from equality; achieving equity is not typically as straightforward. There is equity when benefits and impacts are fairly aligned, though the starting point for all those affected may not be the same and hence, not equal. For example, in most instances when impact fees are assessed in a purportedly equal manner, such as through a "one size fits all" approach, equity will not be realized. Put differently, an impact fee that treats all residential land uses equally despite differences in impact based on type or size fails to meet proportionate share standards.

In this Coda to Chapter 15, we provide a framework for planners as a standard of practice for proportionate share impact fees and development mitigation. A key objective is to create an even playing field between land uses and especially among residential ones. We start with our own personal experience of encountering local impact fees or other forms of mitigation that were not proportionate to the impact of new development on infrastructure. We then outline elements of a standard of professional practice for preparing such proportionate share mitigation tools as impact fees.

One of us (Nelson) recalls a client in the 1970s who received approval for a 50-unit subdivision on which he wanted to build smaller homes for lower- to middle-income households. The morning after the approval, the city raised its sewer tap-on fee tenfold, from $250 to $2,500 per home, wiping out the client's profit margin and forcing him to build larger homes for middle-income households.

Of course, not all builders aim for proportionality when it comes to lower-income households. Three of us (Nelson, Nicholas, and Juergensmeyer) helped design impact fees for a western city based on the nature and extent of residential development. The program also paid special attention to the extent to which existing infrastructure in particular locations—"service areas"—served new development or whether new, expensive infrastructure had to be built. The result was exceptionally low impact fees for lower-cost housing in infill and redevelopment areas but high impact fees for larger homes on larger lots in low-density areas needing new infrastructure.

Local builders of larger homes convinced the city council to provide them relief, resulting in equal impact fees for all homes regardless of their size, location, or need for new or expanded infrastructure. Fees for lower-cost housing serving lower-income (mostly minority) households thus became higher than the proportionate share of their impact on infrastructure, while the impact fees for higher-cost housing serving higher-income (mostly white) households was lower than the proportionate share of their impact on infrastructure.

DOI: 10.4324/9781003336075-19

While one could argue that charging each home the same is "fair," since everyone is treated equally, we contend that such schemes: (a) violate proportionate share principles, because not all homes are equal in impact if they vary by type, size, and location; (b) impose inequitable burdens on classes of households based on their income, race, and ethnicity; and (c) are inconsistent with the ethical standards of the planning profession as they apply to advancing social equity (see Chapter 15).

We proceed with outlining a framework of a standard of professional practice for preparing proportionate share impact fees. Concepts introduced in Chapters 1, 2, 6, 11, 12, and 15 are applied to this framework. The focus is limited to impact fees for residential land uses, although there are occasional comparisons with other land uses. Additionally, consideration is given to the unfortunate reality that all too often, impact fees are not assessed on all land uses that impact infrastructure and thus fall disproportionately on residential land uses. The nine "standard of practice principles" are merely a foundation on which principles will be added. Following those principles, we outline a methodology that practitioners can use that will help ensure calculation of proportionate share impact fees for residential land uses that advance social equity as well as housing affordability. We conclude this Coda with a checklist to assist in its implementation.

Standard of Practice Principle 1:

APPORTIONING IMPACT TO ALL DEVELOPMENT

Are impact fees assessed on all land uses? If only residential impact fees are charged for some facilities, the burden of affected facilities falls on only those land uses and not others that also create impact. For instance, oftentimes, impact fees for schools, parks, and libraries are charged only to residential land uses. The argument goes that it is only homes send children to schools, or that only residents of homes use parks or libraries. While limiting impact fees for these facilities

to residential land uses alone is expedient, in our view it is fundamentally facile, because to varying degrees, all land uses impact all facilities. Besides, just because apportioning burden to only residential land uses is easy, this does not make it consistent with proportionate share principles and therefore, consistent with professional ethics as applied to equity. Let us consider why, note key limitations, and then suggest an approach to ensuring that residential land uses are not assessed for impact fees disproportionately.

First of all, why are schools, parks, and libraries among other community land uses needed? The quick answer is that new residential units house people who demand those services. But, what attracted population growth? Usually, jobs drive population growth, but not exclusively. For instance, new firms may attract growth, but that growth then attracts grocery store and personal service jobs. Those jobs in turn may attract more growth. Assigning the complete school, park, library, and related burdens solely to residential land uses arguing that only new homes cause the need for those new facilities is wrong theoretically, because much of the demand for them is traced to new jobs created by new nonresidential development.

As Chapter 25 shows for school impact fees, data and methodologies are available to fairly apportion the burden nonresidential development imposes on these and related facilities, in that particular case for schools. Indeed, the authors of this book have prepared parks and recreation and library impact fees that apply to nonresidential uses where data are available to apportion impact between residential and nonresidential land uses. The "functional population" technique described in Chapter 7 can be used to apportion impact between residential and nonresidential land uses. Conceptually, each resident, worker, and visitor is weighted based on the time they spend in the community, and then, the burden is apportioned based on the shares of functional population attributable to different land uses. There are many ways to calculate the functional population, and doing so is necessary to apportion burden proportionately among the different land uses where data support its use.

As the field of proportionate share impact mitigation matures, there may come a time when failure to apportion impact to all land uses may lead to disproportionately high impact fees on residential land uses in a manner that is inconsistent with proportionate share impact mitigation principles. But why wait?

Standard of Practice Principle 2:

VARIATION IN SIZE OF DWELLING UNIT

Census data show that attached dwelling units have fewer people living in them on average than single-family detached units. American Housing Survey (AHS) data also reveal that smaller units of both types have fewer people living in them than larger units. We showed this in Chapter 12. This applies to school children as well. In Chapter 15, we reported the case of school impact fees being the same for studio apartments, where student generation rates are statistically zero, as for large homes, which have many times more students than smaller ones.

Some impact fee analysts may argue that given the limitations of census data, especially for smaller areas, they are justified in taking an overall average. By embracing that approach, professionals would be rationalizing an easy solution and not the one that advances proportionate share mitigation, or for matter housing affordability and social equity. Professionals in impact mitigation have an obligation to have or acquire the skills needed to use and best available data to apportion impact based on differences in the occupancy of homes based on dwelling unit size.

Below we present statistical justification for varying impact fees based on the size of dwelling units, showing that as size increases so does the number of people living in dwelling units and thus the impact the dwelling unit has on local facilities. We use this information to craft an impact fee schedule that is based on the size of the dwelling unit.

Standard of Practice Principle 3:

ACCOUNTING FOR VACANCY

Residential impact fees are often calculated based on average household size—the number of persons living in occupied units—and applied to all new residential units. There are two errors to this approach. First, it assumes that all future dwelling unit types will be like the present which is unlikely in most communities. Second, it incorrectly assumes that all units will be occupied all the time. The recent average vacancy rate is around 6 percent for rental housing and about 2 percent for owner-occupied housing.[1] About 5 percent own second homes, another factor to be considered.[2] The assumption of full occupancy, full time, overstates the burden on infrastructure by maybe as much as 5–10 percent based on these statistics. The factually incorrect assumption of full-time full occupancy results in impact fees that are disproportionately higher than needed to mitigate impact. Below we offer approaches to calculate impact fees based on the size of dwelling units, because there is a direct relationship between size and people living in the dwelling, and vacancy.

Standard of Practice Principle 4:

AGE-RESTRICTED HOUSING

The federal Housing for Older Persons Act (HOPA) allows qualifying communities to restrict occupants to those 55 years of age and older. HOPA requires that these communities maintain a minimum of 80% of the occupied units to those where at least one person is 55 years of age or older. If the number falls below 80%, however, the community may lose its age-restricted status permanently.

Because of its unique, legal status, age restricted communities have fewer persons per dwelling unit than for non-age restricted homes. A reasonable relationship for this difference is shown in Table 15C.1 which compares average persons per single-family and multi-family dwelling unit between the nation and The Villages, Florida, the nation's largest age

TABLE 15C.1 Comparing Persons per Unit between Age Restricted and
Non-Age Restricted Dwelling Units

Dwelling Unit Category	National Average per Dwelling Unit	The Villages (Age Restricted) per Dwelling Unit*	Ratio of Age Restricted to National
Single-Family (detached and townhouse)	2.54	1.49	0.59
Multi-Family	1.85	1.15	0.62
Overall	2.35	1.40	0.60

*The overall average persons per dwelling unit for The Villages is weighted to the national distribution of single-family and multi-family units.

Source: American Community Survey, 5-year samples for 2019.

restricted community and one for which census data are available. This tables shows that age restricted single-family (including detached and townhouse) dwelling units average 41% fewer persons per single-family unit than the nation while age restricted multi-family dwelling units average 38% fewer persons per multi-family unit. Given the small difference, a reasonable conclusion is that age restricted communities average about 40% fewer residents per dwelling unit (including vacant ones) than non-age restricted communities.

In addition, residents of age restricted communities have smaller impacts on parks and recreation facilities than the community as a whole. For instance, research reported in the *First National Study of Neighborhood Parks* (Cohen at el. 2017) shows that seniors use parks at a rate that is about 20% of the average per person for their communities. To ensure consistency with proportionate share principles, these findings need to be included in impact fee calculations. The extent to which age restricted communities have lower, or higher, impacts on particular facilities is not fully known and worthy future research by analysts.

Standard of Practice Principle 5:

AVOIDING THE FALLACY OF
ASSUMING THE PRESENT
IS THE FUTURE

Sometimes, an impact fee consultant will take the easy route in calculating future residential

impact by using past census figures without recognizing trends. Consider an example that is simplified considerably for presentation here. In this case, which is regrettably similar to others, the consultant, who admitted was not an impact fee expert, used the most recent 5-year sample of the American Community Survey (ACS) to calculate the average household size for all occupied dwelling units in the community, of which about 90% were single family detached. This became the basis for calculating impact fees that were applicable to every new dwelling unit regardless of type or size. The consultant assumed that all new dwelling units would thus average 2.70 occupants and would always be occupied with none of those units ever being vacant, even when ACS data are available to estimate the vacancy rate. This calculation alone results in impact fees being more than the proportionate share of the impact of new homes on community facilities.

Yet during the planning horizon, the consultant knew that about half of all new dwelling units in the community would be age restricted (see above) and a quarter would be townhouses, all being within the same master planned community. Instead of seeking the developer's expectations of household sizes for the age-restricted and townhouse units based on the developer's experience, or seeking other data, the consultant calculated impact fees based on the current mix of residential units. Needless to say, those impact fees exceed the proportionate share of the cost of facilities needed to serve new development, falling disproportionately on age restricted and townhouse dwelling units. A collateral implication is that the community would build and maintain more facilities than needed to mitigate the impact of new development. Local taxpayers would thus pay higher taxes to maintain overbuilt facilities.

Below, we present methods to avoid these pitfalls in ways that are consistent with proportionate share principles while also advancing housing affordability and social equity.

Standard of Practice Principle 6:

THE SPECIAL CASE OF TRANSPORTATION IMPACT MITIGATION

Nearly all transportation impact fees use the Institute of Transportation Engineers' (ITE) *Trip Generation Manual* to calculate impact fees. However, reliance on this source often results in infill and redevelopment, and development in master planned communities, being overcharged. Among many reasons noted in Chapter 18 is that the ITE uses old studies from mostly low-density suburban locations where driving long distances is usually the only mobility option. Knowledgeable consultants can use the insights offered in Chapters 18 and 19 to make necessary adjustments.

More problematic is that consultants often do not differentiate trip generation by the size of residential unit. The reason may be the mistaken assumption that the *Trip Generation Manual* does not do so. Indeed, trip generation rates for the several hundred other land uses are based on the unit of development, such as restaurant seats, gasoline station pumps, and units of 1,000 square feet of office, retail, industrial, and other land uses. The result is that consultants often do not adjust for differences in the size of residential unit, such that smaller units with fewer persons and vehicles per unit than larger ones pay fees disproportionately higher than their impact, while larger units with more vehicles per home pay less. However, knowledgeable consultants can apply data from the National Household Transportation Survey of the United States Department of Transportation[3] or data on trips per person from the *Trip General Manual*[4] to local conditions, and other data, so that impact fees are tailored to the type and size of residential units. Chapter 29 also provides a method to address this.

Standard of Practice Principle 7:

THE SPECIAL CASE OF WATER AND WASTEWATER IMPACT MITIGATION

Perhaps most fees for water and wastewater facilities are based on the meter size, typically a three-quarter inch pipe coming into the detached home. Yet as explored in Chapter 15, smaller homes on smaller lots have less impact on water and wastewater facilities than larger homes on larger lots. Adjustments should be made based on the size of the dwelling unit for water and wastewater impact fees, as well as size of the irrigated yard for water impact fees. Failure to do so means that smaller homes on smaller lots, typically occupied by lower-income and minority households, would be paying disproportionately more than their proportionate share impact on those facilities, while larger homes on larger lots, typically occupied by higher-income and larger households, would pay less. Chapter 28 provides a method to address this issue.

Standard of Practice Principle 8:

SERVICE AREA DESIGN

Different areas within the same jurisdiction may have different cost characteristics. A key element of impact fees is to calibrate fees based on "service areas," which would be reasonably homogeneous areas based on terrain, density, location, and cost characteristics. As noted in Chapter 2, one purpose of service areas is to ensure that a new development paying fees receives a reasonable benefit for the fees they pay. That reasonable benefit requires that fees be expended within a reasonable distance from the new development (see also Chapters 6 and 7). The objective in planning is to craft service areas that are roughly proportionate to the costs of serving them. If service areas are too large, such as entire jurisdictions (counties or very large cities), the nexus between the fees paid and the benefits received may be weak. This happens in communities where fees collected from low-cost areas, paid by developers of lower-cost infill and redevelopment housing, are expended in newly developing areas farther away at the suburban fringe. On the other hand, service areas cannot be too small, because the impact fee revenues received may be insufficient to pay for improvements. Nonetheless, the larger concern is with large service areas that have the pernicious effect of transferring funds generated from low-cost, lower-income areas to high-cost areas, higher-income areas. The social justice implications should be obvious.

Standard of Practice Principle 9:

THE ETHICS OF IMPACT
FEE EQUITY REQUIRES
PROFESSIONAL DUE DILIGENCE

Because so much is at stake in fulfilling ethical obligations to ensure equity, communities and their impact fee professionals must use due diligence in their proportionate share analysis to properly apportion mitigation. In many cases, impact fees and the capital improvement elements, along with capital improvement programs they help implement (see Chapter 6), require an exceptional level of professional, technical, financial, and legal engagement. The Georgia Department of Community Affairs' (GDCA) *How to Address Georgia's Impact Fee Requirements* (2008) offers this advice:

Carried out properly, [impact fees require] exacting tasks that should be approached carefully by local governments and will probably require assistance from legal, fiscal and technical experts.
(GDCA 2008: 2–3)

For instance, we have seen situations where, lacking local census data on persons per townhouse or multi-family home, the consultant defaulted to the persons per unit for detached homes and applied that figure to all new townhouses and multi-family homes. The reasoning was that census data were not available for those land uses in the subject community. Due diligence would entail using a larger, reasonable census geographic scale that would generate those data, likely showing fewer persons per townhouse and multi-family home than for detached homes. Unfortunately, we also know of situations where consultants decided to use the easiest approach to calculate impact fees—as in many examples illustrated in Chapter 15. Sometimes, achieving equity consistent with proportionate share principles is not easy even though it is necessary.

The bottom line is that if due diligence is not pursued in proportionate share mitigation analysis, communities may impose disproportionate burdens on some land uses that are inconsistent with the ethics of planning equity.

In the next section, we present two methods that can ensure consistency with the AICP Code of Ethics as well as those of other professions. Doing so will also advance housing affordability.

A METHOD TO ADVANCE
PROPORTIONATE SHARE IMPACT
FEES FOR RESIDENTIAL LAND USES

Here we present a method to ensure that impact fees are reasonably related to the service demands and needs of the residential development project thereby achieving proportionate share assessments of impact fees for residential land uses. Doing so would also help advance housing affordability and social equity.

Residential impact fees are often in one of two ways:

- **Binary** impact fee that is assessed on all residential land uses regardless of their type or size (where binary indicates whether a development is residential or not) such that the same fee applies to an efficiency apartment with no bedrooms averaging about one person per unit and a mansion averaging more than three persons per unit.

- **Categorical** impact fee that is assessed on types of residential land uses, such as single family detached, townhouse, multi-family unit or projects, mobile homes, and so forth but without respect to size thereby suffering from the size-based limitation noted above especially among detached homes.

Neither are consistent with proportionate share principles for reasons presented in Chapter 15 relating to advancing social equity.

While some communities assess residential impact fees based on the number of bedrooms—which can advance proportionality—this has proven difficult in practice. One reason is that builders may claim a home has one or more dens that would not qualify as bedrooms thereby escaping impact fee assessment because they lacked doors. Once the certificate of occupancy or its equivalent was issued, the builder would hang the missing doors turning one or more dens into one or more bedrooms. While enforcement could recover fees, this is problematic administratively.

To overcome shortcomings of the binary and categorical approaches, and overcome the limitations of using bedrooms as the metric for impact fees, some impact fees are designed with **bands** based on the size of residential units. In these cases, residential impact fees are based on categories of size such as the first 1,000 square feet with increments of 1,000 square feet to 4,000 or so. At first blush this is an improvement over the first two methods because impact fees are based on house sizes grouped into categories. However, banded impact fees often result in excessive charges just above the band breaks.

For instance, suppose an impact fee is $1,000 for the first 1,000 square feet of a home and then increases by $1,000 for the next 1,000 square feet. While a home of 1,000 square feet pays $1,000, a home of just one more square foot—to 1,001 square feet—pays $1,000 more for essentially one additional square foot. While this may seem to be an exaggeration to make the point, we have seen impact fee bands where the next square foot indeed increases fees by several hundred dollars.

To overcome these limitations, some communities, especially in California, charge **continuous** impact fees based on the size of residential units in square feet. This is common practice for school impact fees because of special legislation enabling the practice (see Chapter 26). It is not common practice outside California, however.

Here we present two methods that establishes the reasonable relationship between the size of dwelling units and the number of people living in them. We reason that calibrating impact fees with respect to the size of the dwelling unit best advances proportionate share and in some states may be the only way in which to comply strictly with proportionate share requirements and advance AICP Code of Ethics principles. Doing so also advances housing affordability because impact fees on smaller homes averaging fewer occupants than larger homes averaging more occupants would pay lower impact fees. Why isn't this done routinely? One reason may be that doing so can add complexity to administrative processes, yet those processes already assess impact fees for nonresidential land uses on the basis of square feet, seats, beds, and other continuous measures of size. We suspect that the chief reason for not doing so is the lack of a published rational nexus between the size of residential structures and persons occupying them. We help close this gap as follows.

We first establish the reasonable relationship between the size of residential units and the number of people occupying them. We begin with data from the American Housing Survey for 2019.[5] From these data, we create a table based on "Rooms, Size, and Amenities" applied to "Square Footage". This generates mean house size for each of several house size categories as shown in Table 15C.2. This is followed by adding persons per occupied unit based on "Household Demographics" also applied to "Square Footage". Together, we calculate persons per occupied unit for the house size categories reported in Table 15C.2. The figures are not weighted; that is, it does not matter how many homes are included in each category but the expected number of persons occupying any given unit within each category.

We apply an ordinary least squares regression to these data to establish the linear "goodness of fit" relationship between house size and persons per home. Results are reported below. Table 15C.2 shows that the coefficient of determination ("R-squared") of the model explains about 87% (0.874) of the variation in house size with respect to the number of persons occupying homes. This is a high level of association. The coefficient for the change in house square feet per person indicates that each additional person above the mean of

TABLE 15C.2 Mean House Size and Persons per Home by House Size Category with Regression Results Based on the American Housing Survey for 2019

House Size Category in Square Feet	Mean House Size in Square Feet[a]	Persons per Occupied Unit[b]
Less than 500	315	1.61
500 to 999	780	1.94
1,000 to 1,499	1,201	2.40
1,500 to 1,999	1,694	2.59
2,000 to 2,499	2,175	2.73
2,500 to 2,999	2,679	2.87
3,000 or more	3,306	3.04
Regression Metric		**Results**
R-squared, adjusted		0.874
Standard Error		709.266
Coefficient, Change in Square Feet per Person		753.440
Error of Coefficient		107.225
T-score		7.072
F-ratio		49.375
Mean Dwelling Unit Size, square feet in national sample		1,736
Mean persons per House in national sample		2.45
Mean Square Feet per Occupant, national sample		709

[a] From https://www.census.gov/programs-surveys/ahs/data/interactive/ahstablecreator.html?s_areas=00000&s_year=2019&s_tablename=TABLE8A&s_bygroup1=6&s_bygroup2=1&s_filtergroup1=1&s_filtergroup2=1. The category for 500 to 999 square feet is derived by combining reported categories reported in the AHS for 500 to 749 and 750 to 999 square feet. The same procedure is done to combine categories of 3,000 to 3,999 and 4,000 or more square feet.

[b] From https://www.census.gov/programs-surveys/ahs/data/interactive/ahstablecreator.html?s_areas=00000&s_year=2019&s_tablename=TABLE2&s_bygroup1=6&s_bygroup2=1&s_filtergroup1=1&s_filtergroup2=1. . The category for 500 to 999 square feet is derived by combining reported categories reported in the AHS for 500 to 749 and 750 to 999 square feet. The same procedure is done to combine categories of 3,000 to 3,999 and 4,000 or more square feet.

Source: American Housing Survey, 2019 national sample excluding mobile homes, boats, recreational vehicles, other. For details about the AHS and its methodology, see https://www.census.gov/programs-surveys/ahs.html/

TABLE 15C.3 Ratio of Change in Persons per Occupied Unit between House Size
Categories, American Housing Survey for 2019

House Size Category in Square Feet (mean)	Persons per Occupied Unit	Ratio of Change in Occupants between Groups	Equivalent Occupants per 1,000 Square Feet
Less than 500 (315)	1.61		5.11
500 to 999 (780)	1.94	1.20	2.49
1,000 to 1,499 (1,201)	2.40	1.24	2.00
1,500 to 1,999 (1,694)	2.59	1.08	1.53
2,000 to 2,499 (2,175)	2.73	1.05	1.26
2,500 to 2,999 (2,679)	2.87	1.05	1.07
3,000 or more (3,306)	3.04	1.06	0.92

Source: American Housing Survey, 2019.

2.45 persons per house is associated with an increase in house size of about 753 square feet above the mean, which is 1,736 square feet. The T-score of 7.072 indicates that the odds of direction of this association being incorrect is lower than one in one thousand.

Table 15C.3 shows an important nuance in the association between house size and the number of occupants. The smallest category of house size, that being less than 500 square feet with a mean of 315 square feet per dwelling, is associated with 1.61 occupants which is the equivalent of 5.11 persons per 1,000 square feet. The next two size categories—500 to 999 square feet and 1,000 to 1,499 square feet—are associated with 2.03- and 2.46 persons occupying homes with a mean of 780 and 1,201 square feet or the equivalent of 2.49 and 2.00 persons per 1,000 square feet, respectively. And so on through the largest house size which is associated with the largest number of occupants per house but the smallest equivalent per 1,000 square feet. This leads to the general conclusion that as house size increases so does the number of persons per house while the density in terms of persons per 1,000 square feet falls. These relationships need to be considered in crafting proportionate share impact fees for residential land uses.

Maybe we are just proving the obvious to everyone that the larger the house is the more occupants it has on average but also the more

square feet per occupant, though it is useful to have proven it, nonetheless.

More to the point: This information gives analysts the statistical confidence that they need to apply national relationships to local measures of residential square feet per person to establish a reasonable relationship between house size and occupancy. What follows are two methods for doing so: the "assessor" method and the "census" method. While we prefer the assessor method because it is the most localized, both ensure consistency with proportionate share principles in ways that the binary, categorical, or banded residential impact fees do not for reasons noted above.

ASSESSOR METHOD TO CALCULATE RESIDENTIAL IMPACT FEES BASED ON DWELLING UNIT SIZE

To ensure consistency with proportionate share principles and advance equity principles embedded in the AICP Code of Ethics, suppose Paradise County wishes to vary impact fees continuously based on the size of the residential unit. It starts by calculating the square feet of residential space per resident. To do this, the analyst starts with local property assessor data, assuming they are available and of reasonably reliable quality. (If this is not the case or assessor data are not available, the "census" method may be used.) The analyst can sum the ventilated (heated or cooled) square footage of all residential property for all residential codes. This usually includes adding commercial codes that include residential property such as apartments. It does not matter whether the residential property is occupied because a key element of impact fee analysis is including all residential property in an analysis, not just occupied units. Suppose the analyst determines that for the calendar year ending 2020, there was a total of 168,761,209 square feet of residential space.

Next, the analyst needs to identify the number of people living in residential units, excluding those living in such group facilities as prisons, jails, dormitories, and so forth. The census's 1-year sample of the American Community Survey (ACS) for the county can be used for this purpose.[6] Because the census reports population as of July 1 of each year, the analyst may need to take the average of the two years covering calendar year 2020 which would be 2020 and 2021. Suppose the result is 231,190 people living in residential units averaged over those two years. Table 15C.4 shows that on average, each resident living in residential units in is associated with 730 square feet.

Tables 15C.2 and 15C.3 are used to create a series of residential impact fee brackets in Table 15C.5 that are based on categories of houses by size considering the number of occupants per house and allowing for vacancy. The top part repeats data on occupants per house base on house size categories from Table 15C.2. The "Local Adjustment" part includes these steps:

The derived figure of 709 square feet per person for occupied houses in Table 15C.2 is divided by 94.89% which is the national average vacancy rate derived from data reported in the AHS. This results in 747 total residential square feet per person in the nation which is then divided into the local square feet of residential space per resident (not in group quarters) of 730 creating a local adjustment ratio of 0.9772.

This local adjustment ratio is multiplied by the persons per occupied house from the national AHS sample to derive local persons per house for each house size category. These figures become the impact fee multipliers for each of the brackets based on house size category.

Table 15C.6 pulls everything together in an impact fee schedule that allows fees to vary by size of house between house-size brackets and continuously within each bracket. This ensures proportionality based on size of house with is reasonably related to the number of people living in homes within each bracket. It also avoids the limitations of impact fee bands noted earlier. It is constructed as follows.

The first three numerical columns establish the minimum and maximum square foot ranges for each house size category, and then the difference. The exception is the first row which is the base. It is set at one (1.0) person living in the dwelling unit.

The next two columns report the multipliers for each bracket from Table 15C.5 and the maximum impact fee for that bracket, in this case assuming the fee is $1,000 per person.

TABLE 15C.4 Assessor Method Average Residential Square Feet per Person in Residential Units

Analysis Step	Figure
Assessor Residential Square Feet as of December 31, 2020	168,761,209
Population in Residential Units, Census ACS 2020 & 2021 Average	231,190
Average Square Feet per Resident (rounded to the nearest two decimals)	730

TABLE 15C.5 Assessor Method Square Feet per Person Based on House Size Category

House Size Category in Square Feet	National Persons per Dwelling Unit	
0, Base	1.00	Minimum persons per occupied unit
Less than 500	1.61	
500 to 999	1.94	
1,000 to 1,499	2.40	
1,500 to 1,999	2.59	
2,000 to 2,499	2.73	
2,500 to 2,999	2.87	
3,000 or more	3.04	
Local Adjustment		
Local Sq. Ft/ Person	730	From County Assessor analysis (see Table 15C.4).
Square Feet per Person	709	From American Housing Survey regression analysis (see Table 15C.2).
Occupancy Rate	94.89%	Derived from American Housing Survey for 2019 (based on 124,135 occupied units divided by 130,825 total units being the sum of occupied, for rent, for sale, and rented or sold but vacant)
Adjusted Square Feet per Person	747	National average square feet per occupant divided by national occupancy rate
Local Multiplier	0.9772	Ratio of local to national square feet per person. This is the local multiplier to be multiplied by persons per house size category for local adjustment.
0, Base	0.9772	Local multiplier times national persons per house in respective house size category
1 to 499	1.5734	Local multiplier times national persons per house in respective house size category.
500 to 999	1.8959	Local multiplier times national persons per house in respective house size category.
1,000 to 1,499	2.3454	Local multiplier times national persons per house in respective house size category.
1,500 to 1,999	2.5311	Local multiplier times national persons per house in respective house size category.
2,000 to 2,499	2.6679	Local multiplier times national persons per house in respective house size category.
2,500 to 2,999	2.8047	Local multiplier times national persons per house in respective house size category.
3,000 or more	2.9708	Local multiplier times national persons per house in respective house size category.

Note: Persons per house rounded to four decimal places. This helps reduce cascading effects of unlimited decimal places in future multiplications.

Absent assessor data, we turn next to the Census method.

TABLE 15C.6 Assessor Method Calculating Residential Impact Fee

Impact Fee/Person $1,000, for illustration only.

House Size Category in Square Feet	Bracket Square Feet Minimum	Bracket Square Feet Maximum	Bracket Range	Persons per Dwelling Unit	Bracket Maximum Impact Fee	Incremental Bracket Impact Fee Change	Incremental Bracket Impact Fee Change per Square Foot	Project Square Feet***	Bracket Increment (Project Square Feet Less Bracket Minimum)	Incremental Bracket Impact Fee (Bracket Increment times Impact Fee per Square Foot)	Incremental Impact Fee + Previous Bracket Impact Fee
Base at 0*	0	na	na	0.9772	$977	na	na	na	na	na	$977
1 to 499	1	499	498	1.5734	$1,573	$596	$1.20	400	399	$479	$1,456
500 to 999	500	999	499	1.8959	$1,896	$323	$0.65	800	300	$195	$1,768
1,000 to 1,499	1,000	1,499	499	2.3454	$2,345	$449	$0.90	1,200	200	$180	$2,076
1,500 to 1,999	1,500	1,999	499	2.5311	$2,531	$186	$0.37	1,600	100	$37	$2,382
2,000 to 2,499	2,000	2,499	499	2.6679	$2,668	$137	$0.27	2,250	250	$68	$2,599
2,500 to 2,999	2,500	2,999	499	2.8047	$2,805	$137	$0.27	2,750	250	$68	$2,736
3,000 or more**	3,000	4,000	1,000	2.9708	$2,971	$166	$0.17	3,500	500	$85	$2,890

*The base needs to be one (1.0) person for the entire bracket.

**In this format, impact fees would be capped at 4,000 square feet. The cap can be modified locally.

***The figures shown are illustrative for each category. The fee would be applied to only individual units within the appropriate category. Excel workbooks can easily program rules to assign an individual project to the appropriate category. The published fee schedule should show fees per square foot between categories as shown.

TABLE 15C.7 Assessor Method Residential Impact Fee Schedule

Dwelling Unit Size Category in Square Feet	Bracket Maximum Impact Fee	Impact Fee per Square Foot between Brackets	
0, Base	$977	$0.00	
1 to 499	$1,573	$1.20	per square foot between 1 and 499 square feet
500 to 999	$1,896	$0.65	per square foot between 500 and 999 square feet
1,000 to 1,499	$2,345	$0.90	per square foot between 1,000 and 1,499 square feet
1,500 to 1,999	$2,531	$0.37	per square foot between 1,500 and 1,999 square feet
2,000 to 2,499	$2,668	$0.27	per square foot between 2,000 and 2,499 square feet
2,500 to 2,999	$2,805	$0.27	per square foot between 2,500 and 2,999 square feet
3,000 to 4,000	$2,971	$0.17	per square foot above 3,000 square feet
More than 4,000	$2,971		

fee schedule.

This is followed by columns showing the difference in minimum and maximum impact fees within each house size category which is then converted into incremental impact fee per square foot (calculated as the incremental bracket impact fee range divided by bracket range square feet).

The column with bold figures shows the size of the actual residential project for which an impact fee would be assessed. Although examples are shown for each house size category, mechanically only one cell would be populated with the number associated with the house size category. The exception would be for homes within the Base range which would pay the minimum impact fee. The next column shows the incremental square feet above the minimum for each house size category followed by the incremental fee. It is calculated as the incremental bracket impact fee per square foot times the bracket square feet for the project.

The last column reports the actual impact fee for the project. It is calculated as the incremental bracket impact fee for the project plus the maximum impact fee for the previous (smaller house size category) bracket.

Table 15C.7 distills the methodology table into an impact fee schedule. Some may recognize this table as akin to Internal Revenue Service income tax tables. In our opinion, this method is consistent with proportionate share impact fee principles while advancing the AICP Code of Ethics as well as housing affordability.

CENSUS METHOD TO CALCULATE RESIDENTIAL IMPACT FEES BASED ON DWELLING UNIT SIZE

For the Census Method, the analyst can use national AHS and census data to establish a reasonable relationship between house size and people per house, and therefore establish a nexus between these metrics. While some may worry about applying national numbers to local communities, we remind them that national numbers are used almost exclusively for transportation impact fees not to mention other facilities and often for water and waste-water impact fees not to mention other facilities. Level of service standards are also often based on national data, frequently for parks and recreation, libraries, and public safety impact fees. Moreover, our objective is merely to establish a reasonable relationship between house size and occupants, not a precise one. Finally, we remind readers that the statistical relationship between size and occupancy noted above is very strong.

Because the above analysis was based on occupied homes while impact fees are based on all homes whether occupied or vacant, we adjust for vacancy for each house size category in Table 15C.8. This generates a national average number of persons per dwelling unit by house size category based on local occupancies from the ACS. For jurisdictions of 65,000 persons or more, we would use the 1-year ACS sample. For smaller jurisdictions, we would use the ACS 5-year sample. We would also use the ACS year that best matches the AHS year, in this case 2019.

The first numerical column shows the national persons per dwelling unit from earlier tables. The second column reports the occupancy rates for dwelling unit size categories from the local ACS. Notice there are two figures, one for dwelling units in size categories of less than 1,000 square feet and the other for all other dwelling unit size categories. For the smaller size categories, we use the ACS occupancy rate for multifamily structures of 2 or more units in the structure. We note from the national AHS that more than 80% of all units less than 750 square feet are in attached structures while two-thirds of units between 750 and less than 1,000 square feet are in attached structures. In contrast, two-thirds of all dwelling units between 1,000 and 1,499 square feet are single family detached or townhouse while nearly all dwelling units in larger size categories are single family. We thus find it reasonable to assume that nearly all dwelling units of less than 1,000 square feet can be considered multi-family for purposes of occupancy rate

TABLE 15C.8 Census Method Adjustments to Persons per Dwelling Unit

Dwelling Unit Size Category in Square Feet	National AHS Persons per Occupied Dwelling Unit*	Local ACS Occupancy Rate**	Local Persons per Dwelling Unit
0, Base***	1.00	93.10%	0.93
1 to 499	1.61	93.10%	1.50
500 to 999	1.94	93.10%	1.81
1,000 to 1,499	2.40	96.74%	2.32
1,500 to 1,999	2.59	96.74%	2.51
2,000 to 2,499	2.73	96.74%	2.64
2,500 to 2,999	2.87	96.74%	2.78
3,000 or more	3.04	96.74%	2.47

*Occupied units plus vacant for rent, vacant for sale, and vacant rented and sold. Derived from https://www.census.gov/programs-surveys/ahs/data/interactive/ahstablecreator.html?s_areas=00000&s_year=2019&s_tablename=TABLE8A&s_bygroup1=6&s_bygroup2=1&s_filtergroup1=1&s_filtergroup2=1

**From ACS 2019, the same year as AHS 2019. If the jurisdiction is more than 65,000 residents, use the 1-year sample but if less use the 5-year sample. For dwelling units less than 1,000 square feet, use the occupancy rate for multi-family (2 or more units). For units more than 1,000 square feet. use the occupancy rate for single family.

***Base occupancy at 1.0 persons per occupied unit. Vacancy rate for 1 to 499 square feet is used for base vacancy rate.

analysis while dwelling units in larger categories can be considered single family. The third column is the product of persons per dwelling unit by size category and the respective occupancy rate.

This process establishes a reasonable relationship between dwelling unit size and persons per dwelling unit for local impact fee purposes. We believe this approach is reasonable for application everywhere except perhaps very complex markets (New York City or Los Angeles come to mind). Local analysts will need to exercise judgment on how to use this approach in those situations. (We note that the AHS runs metropolitan level surveys for some of the largest metropolitan areas such as New York City and Los Angeles.)

We also believe the approach we use, based on the 2019 AHS, is reasonable to apply through the 2020s, though we recommend that analysts apply our methodology to the most recent AHS and ACS data that are available.

Table 15C.9 uses this information to craft residential impact fees based on dwelling unit size and persons per dwelling unit consistent with proportionate share principles. The calculation steps are the same as for Table 15C.6. Table 15C.10 distills this analysis into a residential impact.

Both methods can be modified for such specialized residential developments as age-restricted communities formed pursuant to HOPA or other regulations. It can also be used to refine impact fees for water, wastewater, electrical, and other impact fees based on meter size.

Both methods will need to be adjusted to account for seasonal housing in those communities where this is prevalent. These require localized analysis.

TABLE 15C.9 Census Method to Calculate Residential Impact Fees
$1,000.00 *impact fee per person illustration*

Dwelling Unit Size Category in Square Feet	Bracket Square Feet Minimum	Bracket Square Feet Maximum	Bracket Range	Persons per Dwelling Unit	Bracket Maximum Impact Fee	Incremental Bracket Impact Fee Change	Impact Fee per Square Foot between Brackets
0, Base*	0	0	na	0.93	$931	na	na
1 to 499	1	499	498	1.50	$1,499	$568	$1.14
500 to 999	500	999	499	1.81	$1,806	$307	$0.62
1,000 to 1,499	1,000	1,499	499	2.32	$2,322	$516	$1.03
1,500 to 1,999	1,500	1,999	499	2.51	$2,506	$184	$0.37
2,000 to 2,499	2,000	2,499	499	2.64	$2,641	$135	$0.27
2,500 to 2,999	2,500	2,999	499	2.78	$2,776	$135	$0.27
3,000 or more**	3,000	4,000	1,000	2.94	$2,941	$165	$0.17

*The base needs to be one (1.0) person for the entire bracket.

**In this format, impact fees would be capped at 4,000 square feet. The cap can be modified locally.

***The figures shown are illustrative for each category, The fee would be applied to only individual units within the appropriate category. Excel workbooks can easily program rules to assign an individual project to the appropriate category. The published fee schedule should show fees per square foot between categories as shown.

TABLE 15C.10 Census Method Residential Impact Fee Schedule

Dwelling Unit Size Category in Square Feet	Bracket Maximum Impact Fee	Impact Fee per Square Foot between Brackets	Calculation process
0, Base	$931	$0.00	
1 to 499	$1,499	$1.14	per square foot between 1 and 499 square feet
500 to 999	$1,806	$0.62	per square foot between 500 and 999 square feet
1,000 to 1,499	$2,322	$1.03	per square foot between 1,000 and 1,499 square feet
1,500 to 1,999	$2,506	$0.37	per square foot between 1,500 and 1,999 square feet
2,000 to 2,499	$2,641	$0.27	per square foot between 2,000 and 2,499 square feet
2,500 to 2,999	$2,776	$0.27	per square foot between 2,500 and 2,999 square feet
3,000 to 4,000	$2,941	$0.17	per square foot above 3,000 square feet
More than 4,000	$2,941		

The examples given in both methods have been applied to the same moderately growing community of more than 200,000 residents planning to reach more than 300,000 residents by 2040. That results from both methods are very close, especially for impact fees on dwelling units of more than 1,000 square feet, is coincidental. We expect divergence in outcomes between them, even though both establish a reasonable relationship between dwelling unit size and impact based on occupancy differences between dwelling unit size categories.

We proceed with summary observations.

SUMMARY OBSERVATIONS

The field of impact mitigation is evolving. From the privilege theory to proportionality, there have been continuing refinements in how to calculate the mitigation of the impact of new developments. The next step in this evolutionary process is to ensure that impact mitigation is based truly on proportionate share principles framed in Chapters 1 and 2, as well as throughout Part 3. Doing so will advance professional ethics as they increasingly apply to equity.

To aid practitioners, we offer a "Due Diligence Checklist: Impact Fee Standard for Professional Practice for Proportionate Share Impact Fees and Development Mitigation Fees with Special Reference to Consistency with the Ethics of Equity, version 1.0" as shown in Table 15C.11.[7] It includes the basic impact fee design elements presented in Chapters 6 and 7, as well as the ethics of equity considerations reviewed in Chapter 15 and this Coda. It is adapted loosely from several statutes (see Chapter 3) as well as professional experience. It is also noted as "version 1.0" intentionally, as it is intended to evolve. For purposes of Chapter 15 and the Coda, it makes special reference to the ethics of impact fee equity.

In the next chapter, we entertain options for other than impact fees. This is intended to help decision makers determine whether the impact fee option is best for their community.

TABLE 15C.11 Due Diligence Checklist: Impact Fee Standard for Professional Practice for Proportionate Share Impact Fees and Development Mitigation with Special Reference to Consistency with the Ethics of Equity, Version 1.0

Policy Elements	Commentary
Projections *POPULATION &* *HOUSEHOLDS*	Communities need to know whom they serve now and are likely to serve in the future. Society is changing, and in most communities, the demand for homes serving the needs of seniors will be the largest share of all market segments. Projections of population and households need to be consistent with state, regional, or other official projections, unless there are policy reasons for engaging in planning that is inconsistent with them. This inconsistency can make communities more exclusionary.
What are the historical trends and projections of population by race/ethnicity, age, and other features?	America's white population is falling, while multi-racial persons are among the fastest growing. What are the local patterns, trends, and implications?
What are the historical trends and projections of households by type (with and without children, single person)?	The days when most households had children living in them are long gone. In the future, only a quarter to a third of all households will have children living in them. This affects demand for housing by type and location, as well as the nature of services needed.
What are the historical trends and projections of households by age (such as <25, 25–39, 40–64, 65+)?	Society is changing, and in most communities, the demand for homes serving the needs of seniors will be the largest share of all market segments.
What are the historical trends and projections of housing tenure (owner, renter) by income?	In many communities, the future demand for rental housing will be higher than the current share of rental housing. In some communities, most new demand will be for rental housing.
What are the implications of change in population and household mix over the planning horizon?	Many communities are unaware that the largest share of future housing needs is different than current conditions. If a community assumes the current mix of housing and households for the future, its planning and impact fees may not reflect future needs. For example, if 90 percent of homes are detached now, but half of all new homes will be attached with fewer residents per home, the community will be planning for more facilities than it needs, and its impact fees will be higher than proportionate.
What are the projections of population, households, jobs, and visitors in terms that can be applied to impact fees?	All development impacts all facilities, although some more directly than others. Projections of demand for facilities should reflect the totality of development, such as through functional population methods (see Chapters 7 and 15).
Is there an analysis of excess capacity in existing housing stock?	Millions of homes have fewer people living in them now than when they were built. To what extent can this excess capacity be tapped into to meet population needs without adding more homes or infrastructure?

(Continued)

TABLE 15C.11 Continued

Policy Elements	Commentary
Employment & Nonresidential Land Uses	Communities should find ways in which to facilitate reinvestment opportunities among existing structures to rejuvenate local economies at no or very little infrastructure cost.
What are the historical trends and projections of jobs by type, income, education/ training?	Communities need to know how their economic mix may change. For instance, a key emerging change is the rise of first/last-mile distribution centers, data centers, and other employment centers that do not generate sales taxes and may have very low employment density.
What is the nature of the nonresidential built stock in terms of age, floor area ratio (FAR), and obsolescence?	The existing nonresidential stock of many communities is or will be ripe for conversion to higher and better uses within a decade. (An indicator of conversion ripeness is when land value exceeds depreciated structure value presently, within ten years, or within the planning horizon.)
What are the opportunities for retrofitting existing built stock for different or mixed uses?	Related to the above, many existing structures are suitable for conversion, which can reduce demand for new infrastructure and can regenerate local economies.
What local planning, development, and mitigation regulations (such as impact fees) reduce opportunities to retrofit existing structures and rejuvenate older areas?	Small changes to local codes can unlock considerable potential for reinvestment. This can be helped if impact fee ordinances encourage reinvestment by assessing fees on only the net new impacts considering the historical use of existing structures.
Local Fiscal Structure	
To what extent is the local fiscal structure dependent on new development being permitted without regard to long-term operation and maintenance (O&M) needs?	In many communities, local planning and building offices depend on permit revenue for operations, meaning there is little incentive to assess the long-term effects of development on the community's fiscal sustainability.
Is there a plan to provide for the financial sustainability of existing infrastructure to avoid deferred maintenance?	This is unlikely, but it is also not difficult. In many communities, the cost of repaving residential streets exceeds all the local discretionary property tax generated by low-density residential property tax for decades. The bottom line is that local governments must have the ability to maintain the infrastructure for which they charge impact fees. Some communities are now evaluating the long-term impact of new development on operations and maintenance, and replacement. Where allowed by state statutes, impact mitigation can include these assessments.

(Continued)

TABLE 15C.11 Continued

Policy Elements	Commentary
Planning	
Service Areas	Impact fees require service areas based on sound engineering and planning principles, or both. They need to be large enough to ensure that revenues collected are sufficient to finance facilities. But, they cannot be so large as to undermine efficiency and equity principles.
Are service areas designed based on high- and low-cost areas?	A single service area for a jurisdiction, or very large ones, can result in impact fees being higher than proportionate to needs in low-cost areas but lower in high-cost areas. The result can be inefficient, as more development occurs in high-cost areas because it is subsidized by development in low-cost areas, where less development occurs because of higher than proportionate costs. This can lead to fiscal stress. Results can also be inconsistent with the ethics of impact fee equity.
Are service areas tiered to correspond to different spatial areas of need?	Some facilities have different scales of need. A central water plant may serve a large area, but terrain and land use patterns may result in some local areas costing much more than others to be served by mains, lift stations, decentralized treatment, and so forth. Tiered service areas account for costs of the central plant and different costs associated with differences in features in local areas.
Are service areas designed with different levels of service (LOS) standards?	Communities may want different service areas to have different LOS standards to help achieve efficiency, equity, environmental protection, and historical and cultural preservation. Subject to findings and policy, it may be reasonable for some local areas to be outside service areas, or being subject to LOS standards resulting in no or very low impact fees, to help advance housing affordability, revitalization, and related policy objectives.
Level Of Service Standards	Impact fees require formally adopted LOS standards to guide facility planning and financing.
Are the LOS standards based on current conditions that can be sustained?	Communities often adopt current conditions as the LOS for impact fee purposes. But sometimes, the current LOS cannot be sustained even with impact fees. Or although new facilities may be added, the community may not be able to afford staff and O&M to operate facilities. Communities need to assess emerging trends, changing preferences to ensure that their LOS standard can be sustained.
Are the LOS standards based on higher than current conditions?	If the adopted LOS standard is higher than current conditions, a deficiency exists between what new development is expected to support and current conditions. The community will need a plan to expand the current supply of facilities based on the adopted LOS standards, and that plan cannot be financed in part from new development.
Are the LOS standards lower than current conditions?	If this is the case, there is excess capacity. One option would be not to charge impact fees in the service area, at least until the time comes when excess capacity is adopted. Or, impact fees could be used to recoup past community investments, and that revenue may be used to expand or preserve similar facilities in the service area.

(Continued)

TABLE 15C.11 Continued

Policy Elements	Commentary
Do the LOS standards apply broadly to all development?	To varying degrees, all development impacts on facilities (see Part 4 for several examples of this). LOS standards need to allow analysts to apportion facility demand to all development based on proportionate share principles.
CAPITAL IMPROVEMENT ELEMENT (CIE)	Impact fees are a form of regulation intended to implement such plans as the capital improvement element (CIE). In some states, these are known as the impact fee facilities plan (IFFP), impact fee CIE, infrastructure improvement plan (IIP), and related.
Does the CIE include an inventory of existing facilities, condition of those facilities (such as remaining useful life), current LOS, and other features characterizing them, by service area?	This analysis is needed to establish the LOS. However, many communities fail to address the extent to which existing facilities are aging and will need to be rehabilitated or replaced from funds other than impact fees. Communities and their taxpayers/ratepayers may be surprised when the cost of maintaining the current LOS becomes very costly and an unexpected burden.
Is the need to mitigate the impact of new development on selected infrastructure identified?	Impact fees are justified as a form of mitigation needed to ensure that new development does not impact adversely on the community with respect to specific facilities identified in statutes or other legal guides.
Using projections applied to LOS standards, is the need for new facilities net of excess capacities identified by service area?	This is required in many state statutes, although not in others. Inasmuch as impact fees implement plans that include CIE or similar elements, this analysis is clearly part of due diligence.
Is there a schedule of when improvements will be installed?	CIEs tend to be longer term, so improvements may be in multi-year increments.
Is there a financially feasible plan to implement the CIE, which shows the role of impact fees in providing gap financing?	Due diligence requires that funds needed to implement the CIE be identified and quantified. The cost of facilities needed to meet the LOS standard needs to be balanced against reasonably known revenues, with impact fees being the gap needed to make the CIE financially feasible. But, there are nuances. Impact fees cannot provide the gap in revenues needed to raise the LOS, because they cover only the cost that new development should pay. Moreover, if there is no new development, there is no gap for new development to fill. If there is a gap between what existing development enjoys in the existing LOS and the desired LOS, then impact fees are not used to fill that gap.
Capital Improvement Plan (CIP)	The CIP is the short-term (annual to multi-year) tool to implement the CIE.
Is there a schedule of when improvements will be installed?	CIPs are short-term tools that must show when and where projects will be built.
Is the CIP financially feasible?	Due diligence requires that CIPs must show the cost of facilities and that identified revenues equal costs; otherwise, the CIP is not financially feasible and projects funded in part from impact fees may not be built or may be delayed, in which case refunds may be due.

(Continued)

TABLE 15C.11 Continued

Policy Elements	Commentary
CIP projects are eligible for impact fee financing.	It should go without saying that projects built in part from impact fees must be allowed by relevant statutes, rules, and other legal guides.
Impact Fee Analysis	The actual calculation of impact fees is the last step of the planning and regulatory process. See Part 4 for different approaches to calculating impact fees for a wide range of infrastructure types.
Apportionment of impact fees to all new development.	Efficiency combined with the ethics of impact fee equity requires that impact fees be applied to all development. There are many ways to do this, such as functional population; apportionment of demand across all land uses; apportionment within land uses by nature (size) and extent (FAR, density, configuration, other factors affecting facility impact); and so forth. Chapter 7 and Part 4 offer techniques for this. However, there must be a reasonable foundation in data to do so.
Revenue Credits or Offsets	New development cannot be double charged through impact fees and new revenues it generates for the same type of facilities, such as parks. The reason is that new development brings new resources to the community. If it is not credited fully for those resources that benefit all community parks while also paying for its own parks through impact fees, the community gains a financial windfall from new development, so proportionate share impact mitigation is not achieved. (This is the "privilege theory" issue.)
Credit or offset for the extent to which new development has already paid for similar facilities.	Sometimes, new development occurs on real estate that has paid property and other taxes in the past that have been used to finance the same type of facilities also financed from impact fees. One approach among others is to reduce the impact fee by the percentage of the assessed value that is attributable to vacant property.
Credit or offset for the extent to which new development will pay for similar facilities in the future.	If new development adds to the debt service payments of the same or similar facilities, it must be credited for its proportionate share of payments it makes to that debt service. A similar credit is needed if the community has a pattern or history of using budgets to which new development contributes to finance the same or similar facilities.

The authors acknowledge the assistance of Craig M. Call for insights and editing.

NOTES

1 U.S. Census, Third Quarter 2021. www.census.gov/housing/hvs/files/currenthvspress.pdf.

2 www.statista.com/statistics/228894/people-living-in-households-that-own-a-second-home-usa/.

3 See https://nhts.ornl.gov/. Downloadable data can be used to calculate national average trips by household size by type of residential unit. Combined with census data and local data on the size of housing units by type, often from local property tax assessor offices, trips by type and size of residential unit can be inferred by knowledgeable consultants.

4 Trips per person are provided for many residential land uses. As noted in the previous footnote, combined with census data and local data on the size of housing units by type, often from local property tax assessor offices, trips by type and size of residential unit can be inferred by knowledgeable consultants.

5 Retrieved from https://www.census.gov/programs-surveys/ahs/data.html.

6 The census' ACS 1-year samples are produced for geographic areas of 65,000 residents or more. If the geographic area is smaller, the 5-year sample is needed which is crudely the five-year average of the area. The

5-year ACS for 2022 for instance is the average of census figures for each year from 2018 through 2022. However, this complicates the use of assessor data. One solution may be to sort assessor data for parcels built in or before 2018 plus parcels built in or before 2019 and so forth to the fifth year, 2022, then divide the sum of all years by five. We would not recommend using the middle year, 2020 in this case, as it would not be calculated similarly to the census. Accounting for census fiscal year and assessor calendar year reporting will also need to be considered.

7   We are indebted to Craig M. Call for helping us refine the checklist table.

REFERENCES

Cohen, Deborah A., Bing Han, Catherine Nagel, Peter Harnik, Thomas L. McKenzie, Kelly R. Evenson, Terry Marsh, Stephanie Williamson, Christine Vaughan, and Sweatha Katta. (2017). The first national study of neighborhood parks. *American Journal of Preventive Medicine,* 51(4): 419–426. https://doi.org/10.1016/j.amepre.2016.03.021.

Georgia Department of Community Affairs. (2008). *How to Address Georgia's Impact Fee Requirements.* Atlanta: Georgia Department of Community Affairs. Retrieved November 26, 2021, from www.dca.ga.gov/sites/default/files/guide.difa_.pdf

16 THE OPTION OF IMPACT FEES

16.1 OVERVIEW

There are many ways in which to mitigate the impact of new development on community infrastructure. Unless allowed outright and if there is otherwise no discretion, one option is simply to deny permits for new development, perhaps without establishing any conditions for what would be needed for approval, which is one lesson from *Koontz*, reviewed in Chapter 2. Short of raising taxes, what options do local governments have to mitigate the impact of new growth and development on infrastructure? And which of those are politically feasible?

This chapter starts by identifying the three broad categories of options available to local government as it attempts to mitigate the impact of development on its infrastructure. Specific options within each category will be summarized. Readers will see that impact fees are just one of many options in just one of the three broad categories. The next section identifies and applies criteria decision makers may use to evaluate the options. We include implications for housing affordability as one of these criteria. We also offer "decision charts" to help visualize whether impact fees are an important option to consider. We conclude the chapter with an admonition that for all the efficiencies and benefits gained by impact fees, they also establish community infrastructure planning and financing priorities that could foreclose other policy options.

16.2 DEVELOPMENT INFRASTRUCTURE IMPACT MITIGATION OPTIONS

Infrastructure is delivered in three ways: is delivered in three ways: capital to build the initial system; operations and maintenance to run the system; and rehabilitation and replacement to sustain the system. We will focus on the initial impact to be mitigated by new growth and development: investment in the construction or expansion of infrastructure to serve new development. Options to mitigate this impact of new development fall into three broad categories:

Negotiated mitigation
Special assessment districts
Impact assessments, of which impact fees are an option

These broad categories have numerous options within them, which are summarized in this section.

16.2.1 Developer Mitigation

Developer mitigation is generally defined as the private provision of land or facilities to serve public infrastructure needs created by new development; they are made as a condition of development approval. In some states, private contributions must be "volunteered" (often not truly voluntarily) by the developer and are referred to as "proffers." A reminder on terms. We have noted throughout the book that we prefer the term "mitigation" to "exaction" (or "extortion") because it best reflects modern development review jurisprudence and practice.

In most communities, developers are already required to construct at their own expense and dedicate to the local government all public improvements within a subdivision that are designed to serve only that subdivision. These internal improvements, which must be constructed to standards set by the local government, typically include local streets, sidewalks, water distribution lines, wastewater collection mains, and storm sewers.

DOI: 10.4324/9781003336075-20

Clearly, however, the improvements within a subdivision are only a part of the total public improvements that are needed or affected by a new subdivision. Off-site facilities such as schools and parks typically serve residents of a number of different subdivisions. Streets in new subdivisions will always connect to a network of collector and arterial roads outside the subdivision. Similarly, most subdivisions tie into larger networks of water, wastewater, and stormwater systems.

Typical mitigation includes the dedication of park land, school sites, and road rights-of-way. In addition to the dedication of land, developers may be required to construct public facilities, such as widening the portion of a substandard street on which the development has frontage or installing a traffic signal at a nearby congested intersection. Finally, mitigation may take the form of monetary contributions, such as fees in lieu of dedication, or developer participation in a pro rata share of the cost of installing a traffic signal.

Monetary mitigation is superficially similar to impact fees. Indeed, fees in lieu of dedication are a direct precursor of impact fees. The distinction lies in the manner in which the fee is assessed and the purposes of the fee. In-lieu fees are usually based on land costs only and are ill suited to public services not requiring extensive amounts of land. Impact fees, on the other hand, are designed to cover a proportionate share of the capital facility costs and may be applied to a wider variety of services. Monetary or in-kind mitigation other than land are typically site specific and often negotiated on a case-by-case basis, whereas impact fees are based on a general formula that applies equally to all developments.

In general, mitigation falls into two broad categories: mandatory land dedication requirements and negotiated mitigation. A major limitation common to both types of mitigation is that they tend to address only those public improvements that are either on site or in close proximity to the development. Such needs as roadway systems to relieve congestion or treatment plants to relieve the overloaded are generally beyond the power of an individual developer to address through the mitigation process.

16.2.1.1 Mandatory Dedication Requirements

Mandatory park or school dedication requirements with in-lieu fee provisions typically apply only to residential subdivisions and are based on the number of dwelling units proposed. Requirements based on a percentage of site area have been overturned by the courts, since they do not recognize the differing service demands created by low- and high-density developments. Land dedication usually is required at the subdivision stage of the development process.

Land-dedication mitigation has the advantage of being closely related to on-site needs created by new development. It has a long history of use and is generally accepted as legitimate exercises of local police power. A key feature is that they treat all residential subdivisions similarly and are relatively simple to administer.

A major drawback, however, is that land dedication only covers the cost of land and makes no contribution toward the cost of new capital improvements required by new development. In addition, since they are generally administered through the subdivision ordinance, developments not requiring land subdivision, such as apartments or previously platted land, are often exempted from the requirements.

16.2.1.2 Negotiated Mitigation

Monetary or in-kind mitigation is generally the result of open-ended negotiations between the developer and the local government rather than from the application of a previously defined methodology. They may be imposed at any stage of the development process, particularly during requests for regulatory approvals such as zoning, special permits, or planned unit developments, where the local governing body has broad discretionary authority. Such mitigation typically involves public improvements in close proximity to the development.

While negotiated mitigation is standard procedure in many communities, they are tightly regulated in some states. In North Carolina and Virginia, for example, the state governments have authorized two kinds of zoning districts: general-use districts and conditional-use districts. Local governments cannot require developer contributions as a condition of granting general-use zoning and can accept proffers only when conditional-use zoning is requested. In Virginia, jurisdictions outside Northern Virginia and the Eastern Shore that have not been expressly granted conditional zoning authority are severely limited by the types of proffers that may legally be accepted.

In comparison with land-dedication requirements, negotiated mitigation may cover the capital cost of public facilities in addition to land costs. Since such mitigation is based on the specifics of an individual development proposal, they can address public-facility improvement needs, such as turning lanes, that are directly related to the development.

Another drawback of negotiated mitigation is that it lacks the attributes of predictability and equity that gained park dedications their early and wide acceptance. The amount of the mitigation may depend on accidents of geography, such as the amount of land owned by a developer that happens to coincide with right-of-way needs, or on the political or bargaining skill of the applicant. Small developments, although they may cumulatively result in the need for significant capital improvements, often escape such mitigation requirements because individually, they are not capable of making significant contributions. Negotiations are often time consuming and expensive for both the developer and the local permitting authority. Roadway mitigation, for example, may be based on a traffic

impact study required for each major development project.

16.2.1.3 Development Agreements

A variant of both of these approaches is the development agreement that is negotiated between the developer and the local government. Unlike mandatory dedications and negotiated mitigation, development agreements cover a broad range of facilities (and other issues), provide for timing, phasing, and financing schedules, establish obligations of both parties, and help to settle issues that might otherwise emerge in the future. Once in place, development agreements provide certainty to both the developer and local government on what to expect as the project builds out. Development agreements are widely used throughout the nation.

16.2.1.4 Special Assessment Districts

While developer mitigation may be gaining in popularity, they do have their limitations. Mitigation is often limited to one-time exchanges, usually dedicated to capital improvements. As such, for smaller projects, developer mitigation has little relationship to maintenance and operating expenses, and they do not aid in the process of getting existing development to contribute its proportionate share of capital improvements. Special assessment techniques reviewed here help solve this problem. Many local governments will use both developer mitigation and special assessment programs.

"Special assessment districts" is the broad title that includes local improvement districts, municipal utility districts, and other sub-jurisdictional entities whose purpose is to finance and often maintain capital facilities to accommodate growth and development. They are commonly characterized as geographic areas within which fees or taxes are collected (in addition to jurisdiction-wide general taxes) to fund capital investments or special services that clearly benefit properties within the district. The distinctive feature of special assessment districts is the very close and visible tie between the facility constructed or maintained and those who benefit from and pay for it. Unlike other financing options that target new development to pay for a share of community-wide improvements, special assessment districts assess all properties in a defined area for the range of facilities being provided. Assessments can finance debt service needed to provide the initial capital facilities and subsequently finance operations and maintenance costs. It is perhaps for this reason that they are among the fastest-growing segments of American government.

Special assessment districts are attractive for several reasons. They shift the burden of infrastructure finance from the general public to properties receiving direct benefit, while avoiding the short-term time horizon of purely private infrastructure provision. Property owners are assured that their additional taxes or fees will be spent in a manner that will benefit them, with a more single-minded focus than is characteristic of general-purpose government activities. Most states permit the creation of local improvement districts with the approval of the majority of property owners within the district. In many states, the developer can unilaterally impose a local improvement district on all development subject to approval by the governing body. In Texas, "municipal improvement districts" serve the same function and are often tied to eventual annexation to a nearby city if the development is outside the city limits. In most cases, once the district is created, participation is mandatory for all property owners. An exception is Colorado, which permits the creation of special districts with voluntary participation of property owners within the district.

Assessments within special assessment districts are based on attributes of property—such as property value, parcel size, street frontage, or use—assumed to be directly proportional to benefits accruing to property

owners. However, the basis and level of assessments may vary within the district. For water and wastewater, utility assessments can reflect use. For drainage, stormwater assessments can be based on impervious surface area. For roads, assessments are often based on road frontage. For all other facilities, assessments can be based on value.

Special assessment districts have the ability to assess both existing development and vacant land to help pay for capital improvements. Particularly in local improvement districts with a considerable amount of existing development, revenue streams are more predictable than those of impact fees, development taxes, and developer mitigation, which are dependent on development cycles. One concrete advantage resulting from the greater predictability of the revenue stream is that bonds can be issued by pledging to levy assessments necessary to repay the bonds.

Once established to provide infrastructure services, special assessment districts often operate outside the public spotlight that is focused, in most communities, on elected general governments. The proliferation of special assessment districts can weaken the authority of general governments to deal effectively with growth and to govern in the comprehensive way that they should. Widespread use of such districts can create a confusing hodge-podge of overlapping, independent taxing and assessment jurisdictions that lack the visibility and accountability, as well as the ability to coordinate different activities, that characterize general-purpose governmental entities.

16.2.1.5 Tax Increment Financing

A variant of special assessment districts are tax increment financing (TIF) districts. They differ from other special financing districts in that no special fees are assessed in addition to jurisdiction-wide taxes. District revenues consist of a diversion of that portion of revenues attributable to new development within the district. District revenues are used to retire bonds that finance the initial improvements that stimulated the new development. It is this internal financing, or bootstrap redevelopment, approach that accounts for much of the popularity of the TIF technique.

TIF is particularly attractive to cities because other taxing authorities, such as counties and school districts, may be required to contribute to the redevelopment fund, and that fund is ordinarily under the control of the city or its redevelopment agency. In theory, the other jurisdictions do not lose revenue, because there would be no growth in the TIF district's tax base without the stimulating public investment. Even if this were true, however, the development attracted to the TIF district might have otherwise occurred elsewhere in the region.

16.2.1.6 Impact Assessments

Impact assessments are scheduled charges made against new development for the purpose of financing public facilities. Impact fees are obviously included in this category, but so are impact taxes and dedicated real estate transfer taxes.

16.2.1.6.1 IMPACT TAXES

A development impact tax, also called an improvement tax, is a tax on new construction, usually assessed at the time of application for a building permit. Impact taxes are generally based on the value of new improvements and tend to be more popular than other kinds of taxes because they are levied on new construction rather than existing development. However, re-roofing, remodeling, and alterations to existing structures are also subject to such a tax. Even in a high-growth community like San Jose, California, over one-third of total building permit valuation is for such remodeling activities.

Unlike impact fees, impact taxes need not be based on the cost of facilities needed to serve the development, and the special studies required to justify impact fees are not required. In addition, revenues from such taxes may be spent in any way the local jurisdiction sees fit, subject to the provisions of state enabling legislation.

Impact taxes are not widely used. One exception is California; since the passage of Proposition 13 in 1978, which limited local government revenue substantially, many California communities have resorted to impact taxes as a way to finance public facilities. The legislature also enabled impact taxes for schools affecting all new development, not just residential. California is not alone. Oregon enables local governments to impose a transportation impact tax, and Tennessee enables an "adequate public facilities" tax, as needed, to match infrastructure to new development demands.

16.2.1.6.2 REAL ESTATE TRANSFER TAXES

Real estate transfer taxes are levied on real estate transactions. While impact taxes are generally based only on the value of new improvements, real estate transfer taxes are assessed on sales price, which includes the value of both land and improvements. As with all taxes, real estate transfer taxes cannot be adopted by local governments without state enabling legislation. Real estate transfer taxes are not dependent on new development but rather, on an active real estate market. Transfer tax revenues are more predictable than revenues from impact fees or mitigation and hence, more suitable for bond financing. However, to solve infrastructure problems, there must be an explicit dedication of such taxes to infrastructure. In addition, if the real estate transfer tax is applied to all transactions, including resales of existing homes, it will have a markedly different incidence than a program of developer exactions or impact fees.

16.2.1.6.3 IMPACT FEES

Impact fees (also known as development impact fees, system development charges, and connection charges) are charges levied on new development to pay for the construction of off-site capital improvements that benefit the contributing development. Impact fees are typically assessed using a fee schedule that sets forth the charge per dwelling unit or per 1,000 square feet of nonresidential floor space. Impact fees are one-time, up-front charges, with the payment usually made at the time of building permit approval, although some jurisdictions allow extended payments over a period of years.

Impact fees are a political response to the notion that development should pay its own way. In some communities, impact fees are actually considered a pro-growth tool because of their ability to defuse rising no-growth sentiments, ensure facility adequacy, and facilitate development approval. In addition, because they are typically used as a replacement for negotiated mitigation, impact fees add speed and predictability to the development process. Impact fees are also more equitable than informal systems of negotiated mitigation and are likely to generate considerably more revenue.

Impact fees can be used to fund a wider variety of services and types of facilities than is often possible with mitigation or special districts. Unlike dedication requirements that cover only land costs, impact fees can be used to cover the full capital cost of new facilities. Impact fees can also be structured to require new development to buy into service delivery systems with existing excess capacity, thus recouping prior public investments made in anticipation of growth demands. Recoupment of prior investments is generally not possible with other types of mitigation.

The requirement that impact fees be spent to benefit the fee-paying development is typically met by earmarking revenues for expenditure in the service area in which they are collected. The requirement that impact fee revenues be spent within a reasonable period of time following fee payment imposes an additional constraint. However, proper design of service area, provisions for pooling revenues from adjacent zones, and supplementing impact fee revenues with funds from other sources can overcome obstacles to successful fee implementation.

Sometimes, impact fee revenue is pledged to support bonded debt service incurred to provide facilities needed to accommodate growth. In these cases, bond covenants may call for using impact fee revenue first for this purpose, but to ensure timely and adequate payment of debt service, the fiscal base of the community is the underlying basis for the pledge.

The primary strengths of impact fees include applicability to a wide range of public services, ability to promote efficient development patterns, predictability for public and private sectors, acceptability due to a clear linkage with the needs of new development, and some ability to help with bonded debt service. Their limitations and weaknesses include inability to fund operating costs, lack of expenditure flexibility, dependence on construction cycles and state restrictions through enabling legislation (see Chapters 2, 3, and 4).

16.3 DECISION CRITERIA

Each mitigation option presents its own opportunities and constraints. In this section, we offer six criteria to help decision makers decide which options are most suitable to their communities, with special reference to housing affordability:

Revenue potential
Proportionality
Geographic equity
Administrative ease
Public acceptance
Effect on housing affordability

We provide a summary matrix that applies these criteria to a selection of infrastructure financing options. We conclude the section with a set of decision charts to illustrate key questions decision makers may address in deciding whether to pursue the option of impact fees.

16.3.1 Revenue Potential

Any financing scheme must generate sufficient revenue to meet needs. In this context, however, revenue potential means the ability to generate revenue roughly concurrent with the development as well as the ability to use the revenue as supplemental security for general obligation and revenue bonds and for certificates of participation that are used to finance large-scale improvements meeting present and future needs. Finally, revenue potential means the ability to have all development contribute revenues, not just certain development under certain conditions.

The chief limitation of *developer mitigation* is that only development triggering these actions pays, and payment is usually limited to what is negotiated. For example, *mandatory dedications* address only a limited range of facilities, usually school and park land, and affect only new subdivisions and often, only those exceeding a certain size. Although in-lieu fees for land dedication are common, our research indicates that in-lieu revenues are insufficient to provide land of suitable quality at other locations. *Negotiated mitigation* and *development agreements* can address a broader range of facilities, including funds for them. Developer mitigation as a class is poorly to moderately able to generate the revenue needed.

Impact assessments may be better able to generate the revenue needed because the base includes all new development. Here, however, *development taxes* are not widely used and are usually limited to a small range of facilities. On a practical level, *real estate transfer taxes* will not solve infrastructure financing problems unless they are dedicated to that purpose, because otherwise, they will quickly be spent on other needs, and the infrastructure financing problems will remain. *Impact fees* are seen as having the broadest base of dedicated revenue for new facilities of the three alternatives, but even here, state statutes can limit impact fees to a small range of facilities. New Mexico, for example, does not allow impact fees to be assessed for schools, libraries, and community centers, and Georgia does not allow impact fees for schools or transit.

Local improvement districts have potentially the greatest power of all financing mechanisms to generate revenue to finance capital expansion needed to accommodate development, but they often cannot finance off-site facilities impacted by the development they serve.

16.3.2 Proportionality

This is the connection between the demand for facilities created by new development, the cost of meeting those demands, and the extent to which the alternative apportions those costs to new development. Proportionality can also mean geographic equity and housing affordability if costs vary appropriately, but these two issues are separately discussed later.

Proportionality relates to equity, but equity comes in two broad forms: horizontal and vertical. Horizontal equity means essentially that similarly situated people will be treated similarly. Impact fees have survived challenge on this charge because at their simplest, they meet this equity principle. Vertical equity considers differences within the same class based on objective measures or criteria. The trouble is that impact fees can be horizontally equitable but vertically inequitable (see Chapters 14 and 15 and the Coda to Chapter 15). For example, under horizontal equity, all dwellings would be assessed the same impact fee for parks. If dwelling units differ by the number of people living in them based on type or size of dwelling, then vertical equity is not achieved. As seen in Chapter 15 and its Coda, charging each dwellng unit the same impact fee regardless of its size means that the smaller dwelling unit over-pays with respect to its occupancy level, while the larger unit under-pays.

In reviewing the options that are available against the criterion of proportionality, *developer mitigation* is a poor way to ensure proportionality. There exists some potential to achieve this in *development agreements* and to some extent, in *negotiated mitigation*, but our collective experience is that proportionality is a secondary concern to primarily mitigating impacts of new development. Moreover, not all development is subject to developer mitigation. Among the *impact assessment* mechanisms, *impact taxes* and *real estate transfer taxes* are not required by law to be proportionate, but this is the very underpinning of *impact fees*. *Local improvement districts* are probably proportionate, since all costs are internalized and apportioned usually based on some formula, but since they do not usually address off-site impacts, proportionality overall is not likely achieved.

16.3.3 Geographic Equity

This issue results from the fact that some areas are more costly to serve than others. This is one area where marginal cost pricing can become an element of policy-making even where the political will to charge prices based on marginal cost may not otherwise be present. An element of geographic equity is infill and redevelopment, since we often find that older areas have excess infrastructure capacity (such as under-utilized schools). Even where the infrastructure needs to be upgraded, the cost can be lower per unit of development if infill and redevelopment is encouraged.

It is difficult to presume that any *developer mitigation* alternative by its design attempts to achieve geographic equity. The same can be said for *local improvement districts*. Neither *impact taxes* nor *real estate transfer taxes* are sensitive to geographic equity. Only *impact fees*

have this potential, and while not widely used to achieve this form of equity, they are becoming more common across the country.

16.3.4 Administrative Ease

This factor refers to whether an alternative can be administered efficiently, and whether compliance can be achieved at reasonable cost.

Developer mitigation can be costly on local governments in two respects: first, because such mitigation typically engages local government and attorneys on all cases involving mitigation; and, second, because revenue generated (or its in-kind value from dedications) comes only from contributing development. Moreover, development mitigation often does not cover the cost of processing the agreement.

Impact assessments and *local improvement districts* are quite efficient in achieving their purposes. *Impact taxes*, *real estate transfer taxes*, and *impact fees* are assessed and collected easily through standard government processes. *Local improvement districts* are like developer mitigation in that they involve usually extensive negotiations between the parties, but the result is a stream of revenue, some of which may be used to offset the local government cost, and the continuing revenue supports development-specific infrastructure.

16.3.5 Public Acceptance

Above all, the alternative policy must have the potential for receiving broad public acceptance. In our view, this means that current taxpayers/ratepayers will not face higher taxes or rates for the benefit of new development in either the near or the long term.

Most of these alternatives enjoy broad public acceptance. The *real estate transfer tax* may not enjoy a broader base of support, since anyone selling property has to pay it, and almost everyone sells some property in their life. *Developer mitigation* may allow citizens a chance to seek concessions in excess of needed mitigation, but only on the most visible proposals. *Impact taxes* and *impact fees* probably have broad public appeal, but because impact taxes are not as widely used (perhaps because of the word "tax"), impact fees by default are probably more widely accepted.

One concern is that public acceptance can be a two-edged sword and interact in a negative way with housing affordability. When the cost of providing new infrastructure is charged directly to new construction, it means that existing constituents have little incentive to ask for more development standards, which makes it difficult to build lower-priced housing. This is an issue generally with mitigation.[1]

16.3.6 Housing Affordability

This criterion relates to the ability of any alternative to be created or calibrated to reflect differences in facility cost by size and type of housing unit (proportionality), as well as the ability to offset costs for certain housing based on ability to pay.

None of the *developer mitigation* alternatives are explicitly sensitive to housing affordability. *Development agreements* may include housing affordability features, but only on a case-by-case basis. Except for assessing residential development based on type and size of unit, *local improvement districts* are not explicitly sensitive to housing affordability. *Impact taxes* are usually based on house size, so they appear to address housing affordability indirectly; similarly, *real estate transfer taxes* based on property value only address affordability implicitly. *Impact fees* have the greatest potential for being designed to minimize effects on housing affordability and can include provisions to waive fees altogether, as most impact fee enabling statutes provide. Unfortunately, as we discuss in the Coda to Chapter 15, in practice, a large share and perhaps most residential impact fees are not consistent with proportionate share principles. They also to not advance social equity

or housing affordability. The Chapter 15 Coda presents an approach to resolve these concerns.

Table 16.1 summarizes these alternative financing mechanisms in terms of these criteria.

16.3.7 Alternative Funding Decision Charts to Assess the Option of Impact Fees

For a variety of political, legal, and pragmatic reasons, impact fees are often seen as the most flexible option to address facility financing needs, even though for the most part, other funding alternatives may be superior. Nonetheless, it is important to consider alternatives first to be sure that the impact fee choice is the best available option.

Four decision charts are offered for public safety (Figure 16.1), water-based utilities (Figure 16.2), public amenity facilities such as parks and libraries (Figure 16.3), and transportation facilities (Figure 16.4). They are designed to help practitioners make rational decisions on potential funding mechanisms and consider whether impact fees meet their needs. They may be used as a guide in the decision-making process.

16.4 EFFECT OF IMPACT FEES ON COMMUNITY PRIORITIES

We conclude this chapter with the observation that impact fees can sometimes be the tail wagging the local government dog. First of all, impact fee programs explicitly commit local governments to achieve and maintain a certain standard of infrastructure quality across the community, implicitly in perpetuity.

While this assures citizens that a certain quality of services will be delivered over time, it can also foreclose options by elected officials to change priorities because secondly, impact fees commit local governments to a spending program. As we show in Chapter 6, impact fees are a form of gap financing that bridges the difference between what the

TABLE 16.1 Summary of Decision Criteria Applied to Selected Infrastructure Financing Methods with Special Reference to Impact Fees

Mechanism	Revenue Potential	Proportionality	Geographic Equity	Administrative Ease	Public Acceptance	Potential to Reflect Housing Impact Differences
Mandatory Dedications	Low—Usually applies to subdivisions.	Low—Often based on how much can be mitigated in ad hoc negotiations.	Low—Mitigation does not vary by geographic need.	Moderate—Features of actual dedications (such as location of park dedication land) can be disputed.	High—Affects only new development.	Low—Essentially a flat fee type of mitigation.
Development Agreements	High—Can internalize project costs and fund off-site externalities.	Low—Often based on how much can be mitigated in ad hoc negotiations.	High—Can take account of geographic variations.	Low—Often requires complex and expensive negotiations.	High—Affects only new development and can lead to more concessions than other mitigations.	Low—Based only on ad hoc negotiation
Impact Taxes	Moderate—Usually based on statutory limits.	Low—Based usually on statutory limits.	Low—Assessed without respect to geographic variations.	High—Usually based on simple assessment and collection procedures.	Moderate—Existing residents may pay when they buy a new home.	Low to Moderate—Usually based on value or a flat fee per unit.
IMPACT FEES	Moderate—Only based on difference between available revenue and revenue needed.	High—Legal standards require it.	High—Based on service area design, which varies based on geographic differences.	High—Usually based on simple assessment and collection procedures.	Moderate—Existing residents may pay when they buy a new home.	Moderate to High—Can be designed to reflect differences in impact based on house occupancy characteristics.

Real Estate Transfer Taxes	Moderate—Limited to real estate sales and subject to statutory limits.	Low—Based on value but not on proportionality of impact.	Low—Assessed without respect to geographic variations.	High—Usually based on simple assessment and collection procedures.	Low to Moderate—Existing residents may pay when they buy and sell homes.	Moderate—Based on value, which can reflect house impact differences.
Local Improvement Districts	Low—Limited usually to project and does not include development outside districts.	Moderate—Can be designed reflecting proportionate impacts and benefits but often not.	High—Can take account of geographic variations.	High—Usually based on simple assessment and collection procedures.	High—Affects only new development.	Low—Not usually designed to reflect differences in impact based on house occupancy characteristics.

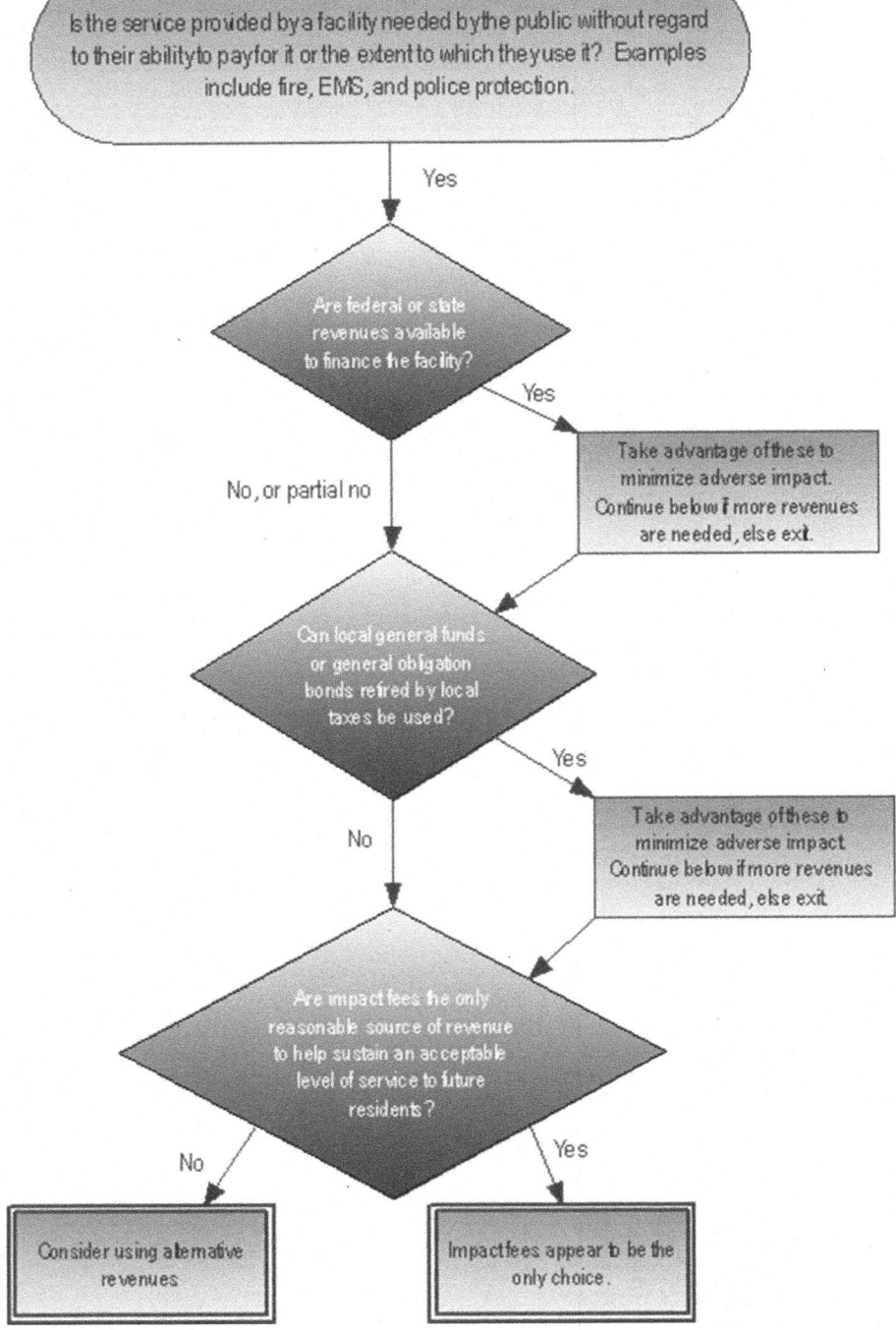

Is the service provided by a facility needed by the public without regard to their ability to pay for it or the extent to which they use it? Examples include fire, EMS, and police protection.

Yes

Are federal or state revenues available to finance the facility?

Yes

Take advantage of these to minimize adverse impact. Continue below if more revenues are needed, else exit.

No, or partial no

Can local general funds or general obligation bonds retired by local taxes be used?

Yes

Take advantage of these to minimize adverse impact. Continue below if more revenues are needed, else exit.

No

Are impact fees the only reasonable source of revenue to help sustain an acceptable level of service to future residents?

No

Consider using alternative revenues

Yes

Impact fees appear to be the only choice.

FIGURE 16.1 Public safety facilities.

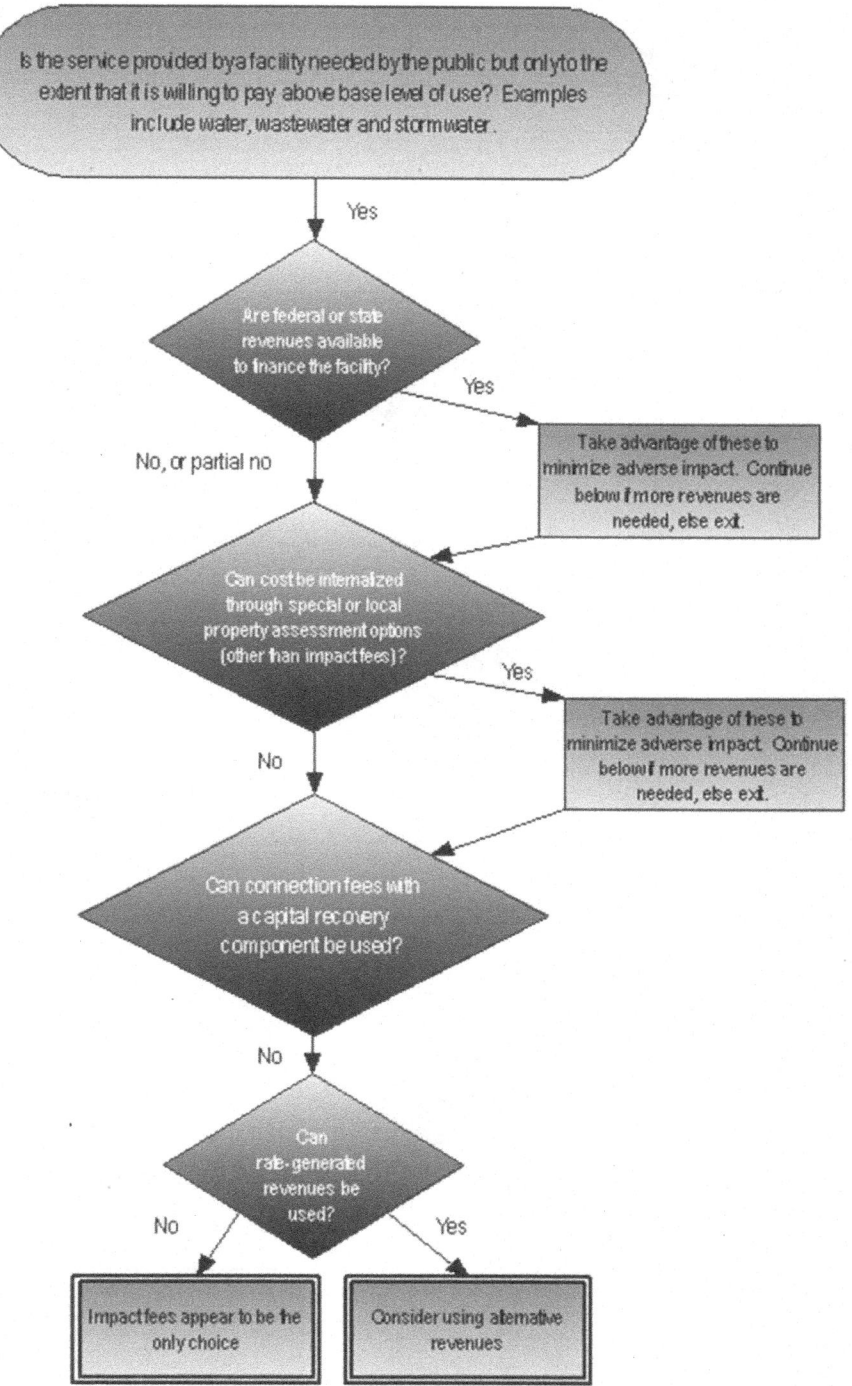

FIGURE 16.2 Water-based utilities.

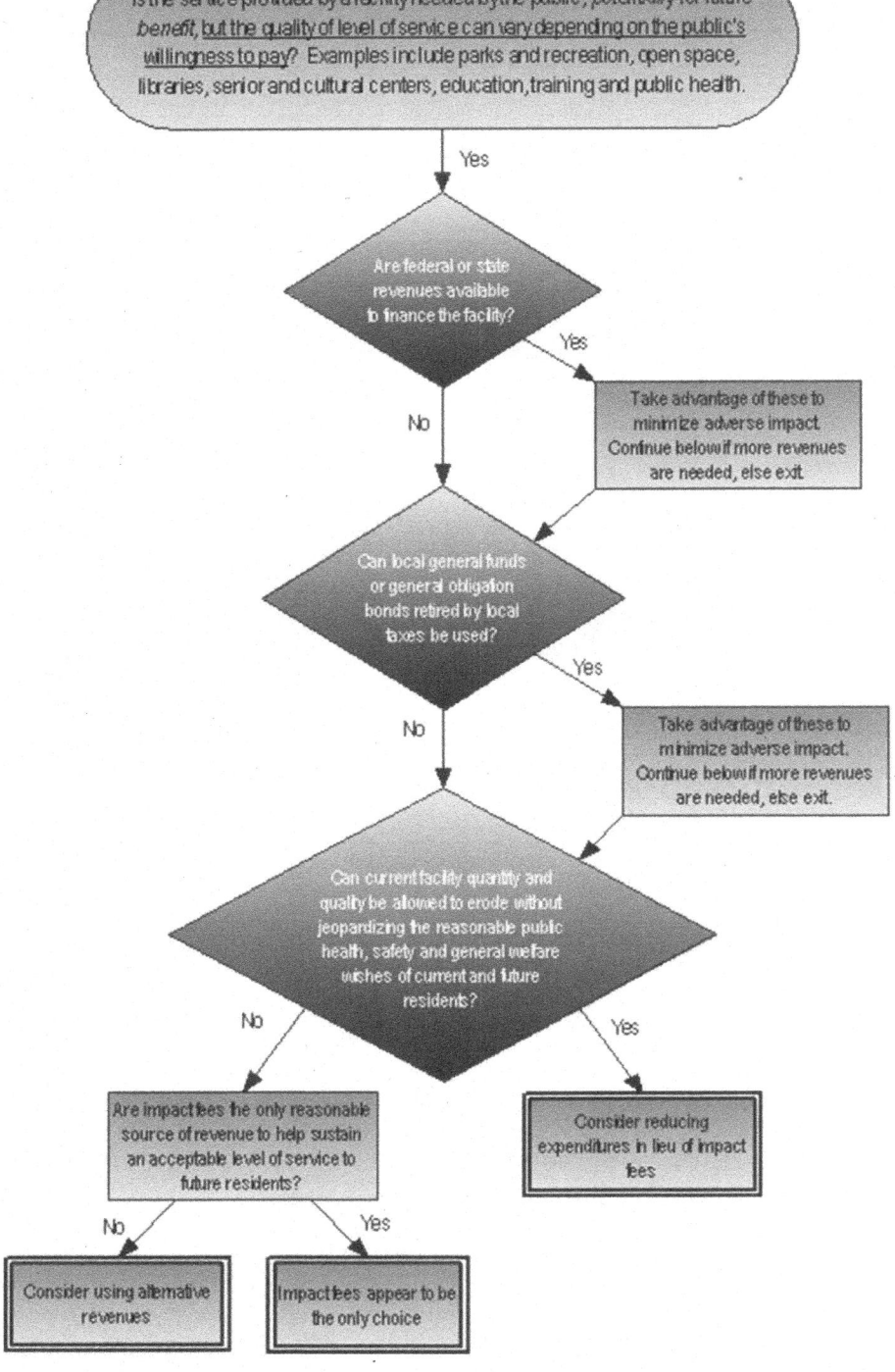

FIGURE 16.3 Public amenity facilities.

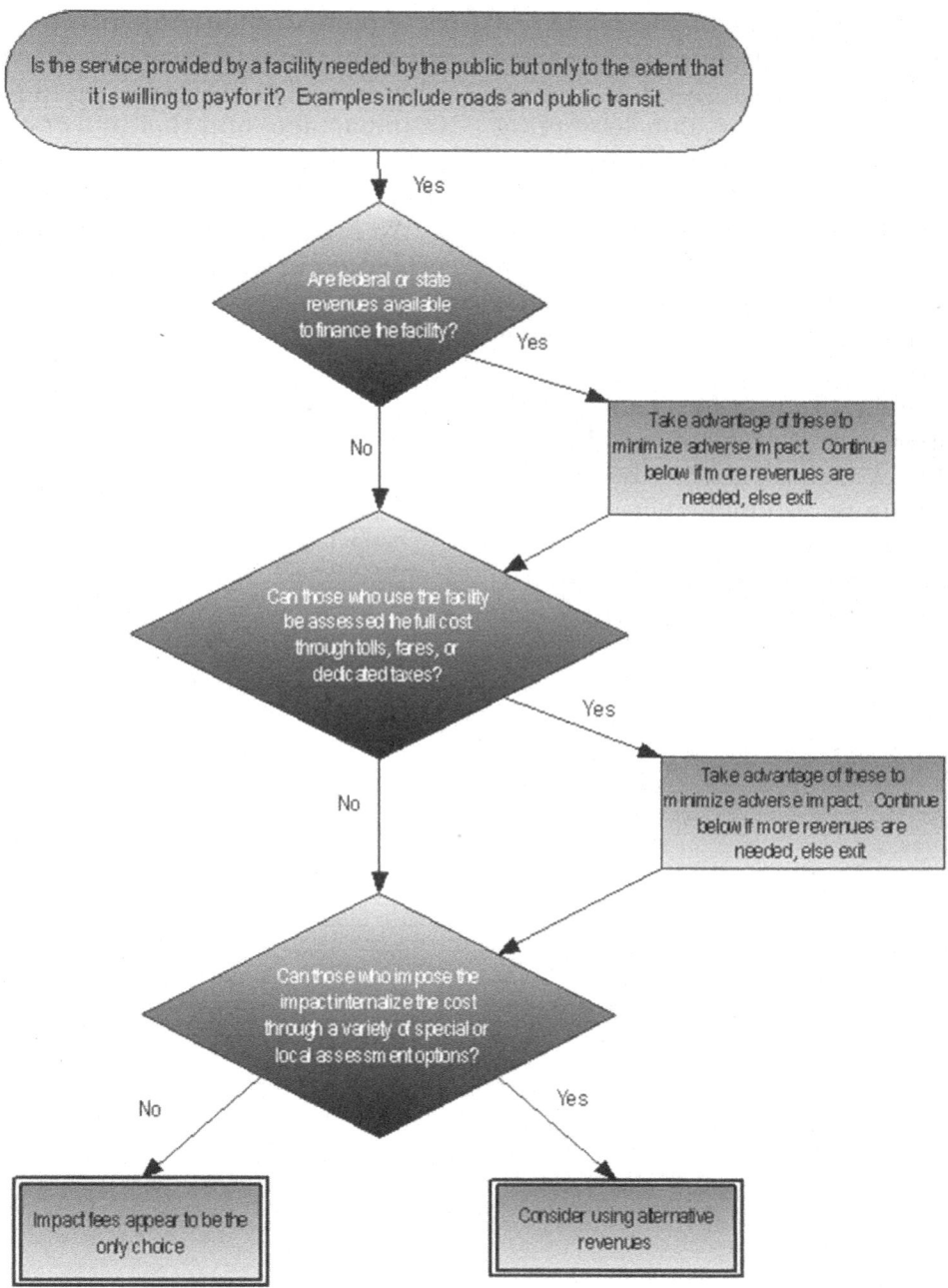

FIGURE 16.4 Transportation.

community wants, in terms of the quality of infrastructure and its costs, and the revenues available to make it happen. In effect, impact fees leverage other revenues. But, leveraging can foreclose options. If highways are being financed from impact fees, for instance, and a share of the total revenues for local highways comes from the state, what happens when state revenues fall? Do the promised roads not get built? Perhaps, but then this could trigger claims for impact fee refunds.

Finally, by design, impact fees benefit principally new growth and development. Indeed, they are not supposed to directly benefit the existing community although that would be a desirable coincidence. The concern is that impact fee programs may force local government to spend more money supporting new development than on addressing other, more pressing community needs. As Aesop admonishes in one of his Fables, put into the context of impact fees and their effect on community priorities: Be careful what you wish for, lest it come true!

We turn next to international perspectives presented in Chapter 17.

NOTE

1 There is also the concern that although this level of facility standard may not change, the nature of new facilities may be quite different. For example, the authors have learned recently a California community that includes large spaces for recreation in new fire stations serving resident fire officials that existing fire stations do not have and they wish to cover part of the cost through impact fees.

17 IMPACT FEES IN AN INTERNATIONAL CONTEXT

Comparisons and Similar Fiscal Tools

DAVID AMBORSKI

17.1 INTRODUCTION

The purpose of this chapter is to provide an international perspective on the use of "impact fee" tools in other countries around the world. Literature on this topic has been well developed over the last 40 plus years in the United States. However, American scholars and researchers may not be as well versed about the use of these tools in other jurisdictions. There have been some attempts previously to look at this issue from an international context even as early as the 1980s, including a compilation edited by Arthur C. Nelson to which I contributed a chapter on the early evolution and use of development charges in the province of Ontario, Canada (Nelson, 1988) However, that chapter was written prior to the specific provincial legislation that was put in place to regulate the application of development charges (Development Charges Act, 1989).

This objective of this chapter is to provide insights into three areas: first, to provide some insights into the range of these types of impact fees across a number of countries; second, to provide a more detailed and updated perspective on the application of development charges in Canada, especially in the province of Ontario; and finally, it aims to expand on the understanding of these fees in the context of the land value capture literature.

In terms of analyzing the international application of these types of fees and the associated literature on their use, it is important to consider the context of the larger literature analyzing land-based financing and/or land value capture tools. This point is illustrated by a study currently being undertaken by the Organisation for Economic Co-operation and Development (OECD). The application of "impact fee" tools made up an entire section of a recent questionnaire administered by the OECD for a compendium on the use of land value capture tools. This questionnaire has been used as part of the basis for the gathering of information for the comparisons in this chapter.

17.2 INTERNATIONAL COMPARISONS

In undertaking an international comparison of the use of "impact fee" tools, it is necessary to understand the source of legislation used to regulate the activities of local governments. This necessitates an understanding of whether the enabling legislation regulating the use of "impact fee" tools is enacted by the country's central government or by a subnational government, as is the case with the US and Canada, where control over land use planning is controlled by state and provincial governments, respectively. This provides a perspective on whether the application is only used in high growth areas or across the country, and who has jurisdiction to amend or enhance the current application.

I requested that OECD share with me information from their preliminary analysis

DOI: 10.4324/9781003336075-21

of their research compendium in order to obtain international perspectives on the application of these types of charges.[1] One of the sections of the survey, for instance, included questions on the use of infrastructure finance, which includes "impact fee" tools. I therefore requested a list of the countries, for which the response to these questions was positive, and the contact information of the country expert who had completed the survey. I then developed a short survey to assess whether and how their country applies "impact fee" tools.

OECD provided me with information on the 40 countries whose respondents indicated that they currently applied "impact fee" tools to help finance growth-related capital costs. However, given the nature in which the survey questions were structured, this did not necessarily indicate that all of these countries applied these types of fees. Consequently, I subsequently sent a request to the contact person for each of these countries to obtain information about their individual applications and received responses from 22 country experts. When the responses were reviewed, not all of the countries responding actually have tools that are comparable to impact fees. The following information is divided into two groups: The first group includes countries/applications that are closely comparable to US impact fee applications, and the second is a group that appears to have some aspects of impact fee type application. Canada is not included, as it is discussed later in the chapter.

In addition to Canada, there are a number of countries that have an established English-language literature and documentation on the application of these types of charges, which provided an opportunity for more detailed insights into current applications. These countries, which comprise the first group, include Great Britain/England, Australia, New Zealand, and South Africa.

These examples illustrate that the use of these "impact fees" is widespread across a number of countries worldwide. There are potentially any number of rationales for the policies in these counties as they were initially developed: whether it was to contribute to the capital costs of the growth-related services; reflected a user charge rationale approach; or was based on a land value capture objective. The application of the last objective, land value capture, would indicate that public action or expenditure led to the increased value of the land, a portion of which should then be captured for some public-benefitting expenditure.

Scholars who study the use of land value capture tools recognize that the primary objective of all land value capture tools is to redirect some portion of unearned increment for the public benefit. In some cases, tools that may capture land value increases are used for other objectives as well. This may be the case where jurisdictions enact impact fee policies. The primary objective of impact fees may be to have growth pay for the capital costs of growth as a form of user fee type application. In other cases, the primary objective may be to capture the unearned increments for the use of the public benefit, such as is the case with the use of betterment taxation or planning gain applications.

17.2.2 Group One

Regarding the four case studies outlined in this subsection, the application of "impact fee" tools in the context of Australia, New Zealand, and South Africa is similar to those in the US and Canada as the use of a user charge to finance the capital costs incurred, while the UK approach draws on a more historical land value capture tradition. It is important to note that the four countries discussed in the following, along with Canada, are part of the Commonwealth of Nations, use English as one of their working languages, and have had their land use planning influenced by British planning traditions.

17.2.2.1 United Kingdom/England

England has a long history of using land-based financing to provide revenue. This revenue may, but is not required to, be used to finance infrastructure. The application of this policy has gone through a number of variations in its application, as at first, it was more related to land value capture objectives rather than focusing on "impact fee" tools. It was only in 2008, with the introduction of the Community Infrastructure Levy, that the approach in England came to more closely reflect an impact fee type of application.

However, the idea of charging a tax on the "betterment" of property land values can be traced back to 1909 with the passing of the Town and Country Act, which gave local authorities the option of imposing a "betterment" charge up to 50% of the increase in the value of the land. In 1932, this was increased to allow a potential charge of up to 75%, though this legislation was repealed entirely in 1948. It was reintroduced in 1967 by the Land Commission Act, which allowed a "betterment" charge of 40%, but these charges were then abolished in 1970.

In 1990, the Town and Country Planning Act, Section 106, introduced a charge on what they referred to as "Planning Gain." The charge was based on the premise that when planning permission is granted, there is a resulting increase in property value that can then be captured in part by the local authority. The funds generated are to be used for the public good, such as investments in community infrastructure, affordable housing, and environmental protection. The contributions from these "planning gains" are to be negotiated, and the intention is not to have a negative impact on the viability of the project. Similar legislation was later passed in 1997 in Scotland in their Town and Country Planning Act, Section 75.

In 2008, the British government introduced proposals to amend and strengthen Section 106 of the Town and Country Act by introducing the use of the Community Infrastructure Levy, which took effect in 2010 in England and Wales. The intent of the levy is to provide revenue to fund infrastructure that is required as a result of the development and which has been identified by local authorities. The infrastructure eligible to be funded by the levy is identified in the Planning Act and includes roads, park improvements, schools, hospitals, community centers, the enactment of flood control measures, and the provision of health and social care facilities. The levy specifically prohibits the use of these funds for affordable housing, however. Levy rates are set upfront rather than negotiated in order to provide more transparency and certainty to the developer. In addition, accountability is ensured by authorities being required to prepare and submit annual reports on the use of the revenues collected.

Authorities must also determine a schedule for the imposition of the levy, taking into account the fact that the revenue is intended to fill the infrastructure gap between the costs incurred and revenue from other sources, such as grants from the central government. An independent examiner must approve the charging schedule and has the authority to approve, reject, or amend the schedule (Department of Communities and Local Government, 2011). The charging schedule must also allow for public consultation on the scheduled rates. The rates themselves may vary by area, are charged on a per square meter basis, and can be made in cash, land, or "in kind" contributions.

It is interesting to note that Great Britain has one of the longest histories of using land-based financing to raise revenue, beginning with the use of "betterment charges" in 1909. In addition to this century-long practice, Great Britain has also approved a funding policy that is similar to what is used for impact fees for revenue to be directly targeted to growth-related infrastructure.

17.2.2.2 Australia

Australia has six states and two territories, each of which has its own legislation and planning system, and each of which enacts its own regulations regarding developer contributions for growth-related infrastructure. A number of these jurisdictions have limited or no contribution requirements, while the states of New South Wales, Queensland, and Victoria have legislation that regulates contribution plans regarding the collection and expenditure of contributions, often referred to as "development charges."

This approach can be illustrated by looking at New South Wales. The enabling legislation, the Environmental Planning and Assessment Act of 1979, sets out the process for planning approvals and the infrastructure contributions that may be levied upon new/approved development. Contributions may be made in cash, in land, or via" in kind" contributions. It provides two options by which municipalities may collect revenue to finance growth-related infrastructure. Section 7.11 of the Act clarifies the process for infrastructure contributions, while Section 7.12 provides for an alternative method of collection, referred to as "levies." Once there is a clear link between the development and the required infrastructure to be funded, contribution plans are prepared to estimate the cost of the infrastructure. Appropriate charges will then be set, developed on a per dwelling or per square meter basis. As the ministry sets thresholds on the amount that can be charged, municipalities desiring to exceed the threshold must obtain approval. The alternative approach, which can be pursued under Section 7.12 of the Act, is to impose a contribution based on the estimated cost of the development. The maximum allowable levy in most areas is 1% of the value of the development, though in some areas, a higher percentage is permitted. This reflects more of a land development tax approach as compared with the first option, which utilizes a user charge for the capital cost of infrastructure.

These contribution plans aim to provide the basis for funding roads, parks, and community facilities. The items included in the plan must have a demonstrable nexus in terms of both location and timing and must be included in the municipality's capital works plan. There have been questions about the ability of municipalities to include affordable housing in their plans. In addition, in 2005, amendments to the legislation permitted municipalities to assess "voluntary contributions," where the proposed development does not meet the current planning regulations, and changes must be made by council to accommodate the development. This would appear to be a type of density or incentive zoning approach for additional contributions.

As has been the case in other countries, the question of developer contributions to finance infrastructure has come under review in Australia. In 2016, the Auditor General in Victoria prepared a report that recommended changes to the existing legislation. And in 2020, the New South Wales Productivity Commissioner issued a report that included 29 recommendations for reforming the system. These were accepted in March 2021 by the government, which prepared a "roadmap" to implement the reforms.

17.2.2.3 New Zealand

New Zealand has used some form of "impact fee" tools for development contributions for growth-related infrastructure dating back to the 1954 Municipal Corporations Act and the 1956 Counties Act. This was consolidated into the Local Government Act in 1974, wherein levies could be collected based on the cost of construction or of upgrading infrastructure for a range of growth-related hard/property-related services.

New Zealand's current regulation of development contribution tools falls under the Local Government Act, 2002. In addition, the Interior Ministry reviewed the legislation and its current applications in 2013. This review reinforced what is referred to as the "causal nexus approach" to charging for services, a policy affirmed by the New Zealand High

Court in 2008. As with reviews of "impact fee" regulations in other countries, the range of topics addressed includes the impact on affordability, equity, and fairness; the nature of costs to be included; the method of calculation; and the process for dispute resolution.

These regulations are applied across the country's 45 jurisdictions and are meant to contribute to the costs of various types of growth-related capital improvements. Not all jurisdictions apply these charges for the same range of services. A current illustration can be provided by looking at the application of these charges in Auckland, one of New Zealand's largest cities.

The application of these polices in Auckland contains many of the elements of the use of "impact fee" tools as seen in North America. The range of services for which charges may be imposed include property-related services such as transportation infrastructure (roads) and planning for the diversion of storm water. (In Auckland's case, though, water supply and wastewater are not included, as they are provided by a third-party organization. Other local governments have responsibility for the provision of this service and may charge accordingly.) In addition, the services for which "impact fees" may apply refers to the provision of "community infrastructure," such as the costs incurred by the construction of sports grounds, libraries, community halls, and recreation centers. The structure of these charges varies by city district and by type of development. The charge also varies by the type of housing being built (Auckland Council, 2019).

This is consistent with other countries, where it is the larger cities that tend to have the most growth and therefore, tend to have the most developed "impact fee" process.

17.2.2.4 South Africa

The application of "development charges," as they are known in South Africa, goes back to the 1980s. This system replaced the previous legislation enacted by the subnational levels of government or "provinces." The "development charges" in South Africa empower the local authorities to impose conditions when approving a land-use change application, which can include a payment for the cost of growth-related infrastructure. These can be made in cash, in land, or "in kind" through the provision of infrastructure.

Developers have had success in challenging these mandatory contributions for infrastructure, however, which has led to uncertainty for local governments that rely on this revenue source.

The legal basis for municipalities to apply this approach is the Municipal Systems Act. However, in 2013, the federal government enacted the Spatial Planning and Land Use Planning Management Act (SPLUMA). SPLUMA has two important sections to support the application of a comprehensive system for the application of development charges. Section 49 of SPLUMA states that developers are responsible for the installation of internal engineering services, while the municipality is responsible for the external services. In addition, Section 10 (1) of SPLUMA specifically provides for the "imposition of development charges." Despite this, a lack of clarity in drafting the sections and uncertainties about how provincial legislation falls under the Act has led to problems in the application of a development charge system. To address these issues, the National Treasury plans to draft new development charge legislation as part of a proposed Municipal Fiscal Powers and Functions Act (Graham and Berrisford, 2015).

The new legislation will need to address broad issues in the land use system, such as equity and fairness, predictability, spatial and economic neutrality, and administrative ease and uniformity. In addition, it will need to look at specific application issues, similar to those faced in North America. There has in fact been a comparison of development charges in Cape Town to those in Georgia in the US (Crawford and Juergensmeyer, 2017).

There are ongoing challenges to the development charges system in South Africa, due in part to strong negative pushback by the development industry and also to the lack of clarity in the overarching SPLUMA legislation. However, there has been some use of a calculator by municipalities in South Africa in an attempt to provide some transparency for developers looking to assess their potential contributions under the development charges system.

17.2.3 Group Two

In addition to the more comprehensive approach to financing growth-related capital costs that are closely related to the type of application that exists with impact fees and infrastructure, a number of jurisdictions have reported elements of this approach or have attempted a partial approach along these lines. In some cases, the application of the tool is not well designed, or it is in the formulative stages. In some cases, the legislation isn't clear and/or comprehensive enough to permit the application. As with the better-established impact fee applications, there was a learning curve and a tweaking of the process and legislation to improve the performance of the application.

There follows a brief summary of the applications in various counties that fall into the category identified here. As most of the information provided was obtained by the short survey of those participants who responded to the OECD compendium survey, there is no significant detail about most of the applications. Rather, the summary provides a status of application, and researchers interested in specific applications/countries would need to undertake further research to better understand the current applications. In some cases, language may be a barrier to obtaining easy access to the legislation, existing studies, and government reports and in some cases, academic commentary/literature.

17.2.3.1 The Netherlands

As mentioned earlier, the counties identified in this session have some elements of what might be considered an impact fee type of application. In the Netherlands, municipalities may charge a betterment tax where public infrastructure is constructed that directly benefits specific properties. This is related to site-specific, on-site infrastructure. In these applications, all benefitting properties must pay their fair share. The presumption is that the provision of this infrastructure has increased the value of their property. The enabling legislation for this and related applications is the 2008 Physical Planning Act.

This legislation also permits the charging of developer obligations where there are to be changes in the planning regulations, such as rezoning, that will lead to increased development potential on land where the necessary infrastructure has not yet been provided. In this case, if the municipality prepares a development contribution plan in addition to the land use regulation decision, they can charge for the cost of on-site public infrastructure. They also can require some limited contributions for major off-site public infrastructure (Munoz Gielen, 2019).

As indicated, the approach in the Netherlands has some limited aspects of impact fee applications. In some cases, this could lead to further extensions to the application. However, due to the presence of an existing betterment tax, this may not be considered as a necessary approach.

17.2.3.2 Portugal

In 1984, due to the pressures for growth and the fiscal pressures on local government, legislation was passed that redefined developers' contributions when new subdivisions were approved. Previously, there were some obligations dating back to 1964 legislation. However, now, for the first time, developers were required to pay a one-time charge known as *Taxa Municipal de Urbanizacao*. It is necessary to pay the fee in order to obtain the development permit. A national legal framework provides guidance to municipalities regarding how to structure and collect the fee. It is necessary that there is a nexus between the public infrastructure provided and the fee charged to the development.

In the early days, the 1980s, it was argued that the contributions were too low. In the 1990s, the contributions were increased. However, with this expansion, the financing went beyond the capital of infrastructure and was used to finance maintenance and renewal. The focus still remained on financing the capital cost of hard infrastructure. The expectation is that other soft infrastructure, such as social and affordable housing, could be financed via other land value capture tools.

Over the history of its application, the nexus of some payments has been challenged, and this has been a point of contention. This is especially true because the revenues from these payments are not "earmarked," as earmarking is not permitted under Portuguese constitutional law (Morais de Sa and Vasconelos Dias Correia, 2019).

17.2.3.3 Poland

Poland does not have a comprehensive approach or legislation to imposing an impact fee type of application, but it does have several specific cases where developers may be required to make growth-related infrastructure contributions. There are several pieces of legislation that enable these applications rather than the more traditional comprehensive legislation. The legislation includes the Spatial Planning and Development Act, 2003, the Public Roads Act, 1985, and a Special Act on Residential Development, 2018. The first case based on the 2003 Act plus a 2015 Revitalization Act requires contributions for affordable housing, but it only applies in identified revitalization zones. The second application under the same legislation may require the "in kind" provision of on-site

basic services, if they don't exist, as a requirement for obtaining a building permit. The third application under the Public Roads Act may require the developer to finance the costs of improvements to a road network resulting from the proposed new development. This tends not to apply to small-scale but only to larger-scale developments.

It is the last, most recent application that is most interesting relative to impact fee type applications. In cases where proposed residential development deviates from a current municipal land use plan, the developer can be required to contribute to public infrastructure such as schools, access to public transit, etc. as a condition of their approval. As this is based on legislation that was only passed in 2018, there has not been much experience or feedback on the application of this policy.

17.2.3.4 Taiwan

Taiwan has a National Urban Planning Law that designates the requirements for urban planning activities undertaken throughout the country. There appear to be different sets of regulations for developer obligations in urban and nonurban areas. For the urban areas, the focus of the contribution is in the form of land, while in the nonurban areas, which are governed by the Regulation of Land Uses in Non-Urbanized areas, there is a requirement for a contribution via impact fees. The requirements are authorized under the Regional Plan Act. This Act clearly specifies that proponents of new development must submit a plan and that they "shall pay the development impact fees to the municipal or county government for the purpose of improving or increasing public facilities." This is required when a development proposal causes changes in the nature of land use in these areas and will impact on the service levels in the proposed and adjacent areas. The types of services for which contributions may be required include roads, schools (for residential development), parks, fire stations, and for some uses, parking lots.

There is an Ordinance of Levy of Development Impact Fee, which also specifies the way in which the fees for each service should be calculated. A number of the input variables are identified in the ordinance, while others are discretionary, leaving some uncertainty about the approach. In addition to the impact fee, there is also a feedback fee based on the Agricultural Development Act. This fee is unlike the impact fee in that it is based on the value of the land and the land use to which the land is being converted (Lin and Ding, 2019).

17.2.3.5 Colombia

Colombia is included in the discussion because it has a long history of using land-based funding to meet its infrastructure needs. Furthermore, it is a South American country, and South America is the only continent without a country included in the preceding examples. The lack of South American examples may reflect the fact that Colombia and other South American countries have employed other successful land value capture tools to help fund infrastructure. This may have led countries to consider those tools that have been successful in the political and social culture of South America (Smolka, 2013).

Colombia uses a variety of value capture instruments. It has used two land value capture tools going back 100 years. *Contribution por valorization* has been used to finance public infrastructure dating back to 1921. This tool is the closest to impact fees, as it requires a contribution in cash or land in order to obtain approval for a development. It has been the focus of numerous judicial reviews. However, it has been deemed to be legal, as it is considered a charge rather than a tax.

A second major tool is *Participation en Plusvalias*. With this tool, there is an attempt to capture increased urbanization values as cities prepare plans, increase densities, and bring property into the urban envelope. Legislation requires cities to capture 30–50%

of the increased value. This has been very successful in a number of cities. It has been estimated that over a 20-year period, 1993–2013, in Bogota, approximately $1 billion of infrastructure was funded from this policy application (Smolka, 2013).

The rationale for the Colombian example is to demonstrate that impact fees may be considered part of the range of land value capture tools that governments may consider for financing infrastructure. In some jurisdictions and political and cultural contexts, there are other land value capture tools that have been proven to be successful to finance infrastructure.

These summaries are limited in that they only provide a high-level rather than an in-depth comparison of these applications, as the purpose is to highlight the existence of these types of charges in many international jurisdictions. The rationale for imposing them may be based on different principles in various countries, including the need to pay for growth-related capital costs, the principle that growth should pay for growth, the application of land value capture tools, political expediency, or other local context principles. This chapter does not drill down to undertake an in-depth analysis of these principles, as my survey responses did not provide access to this type of detailed information. We can look forward to this type of information being included in the OECD compendium.

17.3 CANADA: UNDERSTANDING THE CONTEXT AND UPDATE

17.3.1 Understanding the Context

As previously mentioned, in 1988, I wrote a chapter on the history of development charges in the province of Ontario, Canada. This was written prior to the enactment of the Development Charge Act at a time when the enabling legislation was a vague component of the Provincial Planning Act (Amborski, 1988). More recently, I co-authored a chapter that provides an update of current practice in Ontario along with some additional insights on how development charges are applied in other Canadian provinces, including British Columbia, Alberta, and Nova Scotia. This may prove of interest to those studying the American context, as Canada is its neighbor and has several large and rapidly growing cities, including Toronto and Vancouver (Kaplinsky and Amborski, 2019).

My interest in the practice of using "impact fees" in Ontario, here referred to as "development charges" (originally known as "lot levies" and "municipal imposts"), stems from an interest in municipal finance and the application of user charges. Looking at how these charges have been used in Ontario as municipal finance tools, I also considered Paul Downing's work on user charges, specifically an article in a book on the topic published by the University of British Columbia (Downing, 1975). I found that the use of these charges was not only consistent with economic principles in funding local government infrastructure costs but also had potential as a pricing tool to influence urban planning outcomes.

During my discussions with Paul Downing in the 1980s, it appeared that local American governments had failed to embrace the application of these charges as a broad tool to finance infrastructure for new residential growth. In contrast, I found that contributions for off-site growth-related capital costs had been required to some extent going back to the 1960s in Ontario (Ontario Committee on Taxation, 1968). My early research on these tools addressed the question of whether the application currently used in the Toronto region was based on a user charge (for capital costs)/service pricing approach or was more an application of a form of land development (betterment) tax, which reflected a form of land value capture. I began to consider how these contributions fit into and reflected a form of land value capture tool. This question formed in large part my early research on this

topic, funded by the Lincoln Institute of Land Policy.

The basic mechanism behind the understanding of this process as a land value capture tool reflects the fact that both the provision of servicing to raw land and the provision of planning permissions via subdivision approvals and zoning create an increase the value of the land. As this increase in value is created by public investments, it represents a prime opportunity to apply land value capture principles. Consequently, regardless of which land value capture tool is used to help finance the infrastructure (i.e., a service pricing or land value/betterment tax application), the exaction on the property does capture land value increases.

The use of these types of exactions for off-site infrastructure costs has led to them being considered as a valuable tool for land value capture in many jurisdictions. Consequently, these tools have been included in the research compendium currently being undertaken by OECD, which is attempting to assess the application of various land value capture tools internationally. OECD then identified experts on land value capture mechanisms to complete the questionnaire for their country. One of the sections of the survey, for instance, included questions on the use of infrastructure finance and "impact fee" tools. Consequently, there is a link between impact fee and land value capture policies, as they are alternative approaches that can be used to finance growth-related infrastructure needs. The choice of tool and the details of how it will be applied are dependent on legislation as well as political and social contexts.

17.3.2 Update on the Canadian Application of Development Charges

In the article I published in 1988, I focused on the history and legal basis for the application of what are known as "development charges." As with "impact fees" used by American jurisdictions, development charges are charges that are used to pay for some or all of the growth-related capital costs of off-site infrastructure, thus ensuring that the developer provides all services integral to new (subdivision) development at municipal standards. In the Canadian context, enabling legislation for municipal governance, including development charges, is the responsibility of the provincial governments. Consequently, as with state governments in the US, each province may decide whether or not to permit local governments to impose these types of charges. They also decide the nature of the method and approach that may be used to calculate, collect, and expend the revenue.

In addition to the long-standing application of development charges in the province of Ontario, they are also currently applied in British Columbia, Alberta, and Nova Scotia (Kaplinsky and Amborski, 2019).

My earlier article examining the history and legal basis of development charges in Ontario (1988) was undertaken prior to the passage of the specific Development Charges Act in 1989, which replaced the earlier legislative basis in the form of a few sentences embedded in the Ontario Planning Act. The importance of the Development Charges Act in 1989 was the clarification for a number of the applications that had previously been challenged at the Ontario Municipal Board and in divisional courts. Most importantly, it identified the range of services that could be included in development charges and the method by which these charges could be calculated. In addition to the approved charges being imposed by local and regional governments for the growth-related capital costs, the Act also gave school boards the power to impose development charges to help finance the capital cost of new schools.

The Ontario legislation has had several amendments added since 1989, but it retains substantially the same framework. It spells out the requirements for governments to pass a development charge by-law to collect development charges with a five-year time horizon, and also requires each new by-law to be accompanied by a new development charge study to justify the quantum of the charge. The by-law can also be appealed by property owners after it is approved.

The other provinces examined, British Columbia, Alberta, and most recently Nova Scotia, also have enabling legislation that firmly establishes the legal basis for the application of development charges that may be applied by local governments to help finance growth-related capital costs. In Ontario, these charges were first used in the Toronto region, while the British Columbia provincial government first applied them in the Vancouver region. The province of Alberta has applied them for the most part in Edmonton and Calgary, while most recently, Nova Scotia has used them in the Halifax area. As expected, these represent the areas of each province that have seen the most growth and development (Kaplinsky and Amborski, 2019).

In Canada, it is the Toronto region where local governments have made the greatest use of the development charges applications and revenue. It has become a significant source of financing growth-related capital costs in what is one of the fastest-growing regions in North America. The region has what are probably the highest development charges among all Canadian jurisdictions that currently apply some form of this charge. According to the most recent development charge survey, in several Toronto-area municipalities, the contribution required when building a single-family residential unit, once all the local, regional, and school board charges are accounted for, is in excess of $100,000 Canadian dollars (BILD, 2020).

17.4 CONCLUSION

The objective of this chapter is to provide some international context to the application of impact fee type charges applied to paying for growth-related capital costs. It also aims to place the discussion of the history of these charges in the context of the growing interest in the application of land value capture tools. Finally, it looks to provide a brief update to a much earlier discussion of the application of development charges in the Canadian/Ontario context.

The recent interest in the history of the application of development charges and the development of a compendium of land value capture tools in a broad range of countries has provided the opportunity to gather information on the application of these types of tools in several jurisdictions worldwide. Although the use of impact fees in the US has been well established in a number of high-growth jurisdictions, there is also a history of the application of similar tools in a number of other international jurisdictions.

Canada, a neighbor of the US, for example, has had a long history of using these fees, perhaps, as in the case of Ontario, a history that is even longer than that of most American jurisdictions that have imposed impact fees. In some cases, it has also resulted in higher contribution levels from new development and provides an important contribution for growth-related capital costs.

The jurisdictions most likely to use impact fee type tools are the Commonwealth countries such as Canada, Australia, New Zealand, and South Africa, where English is a common language, and there is some connectivity to British planning traditions.

In some jurisdictions, where there has been a long history of using land value capture tools, the historical tools may be adequate to provide the financing that is required. In other jurisdictions, such as the UK and Poland, there have been some recent attempts to use impact fee type tools.

Countries are increasingly recognizing how the application of these types of charges can be used as part of the application of land value capture tool to help finance growth-related capital costs. These revenues are proving to be important in supporting the fiscal capacity of local governments to meet local needs by having growth paying for growth and in putting less fiscal pressure on local residents to pay for growth-related capital costs.

NOTE

1 The Compendium is a joint initiative of OECD and the Lincoln Institute of Land Policy. I was part of the team who helped to structure the questions for the survey and am thus knowledgeable as to how it was designed. In addition, I completed the survey as the Canadian expert. The instrument was administered in 2020.

REFERENCES AND SELECTED BIBLIOGRAPHY

Alterman, R. (2011). Land use regulations and property values: The windfalls capture idea revisited. In N. Brooks, K. Donaghy, & G. J. Knaap (Eds.), *The Oxford Handbook of Urban Economics and Planning*. Oxford: Oxford University Press.

Amborski, D. (1988). Impact fees Canadian style: The use of development charges in Ontario. In A. C. Nelson (Ed.), *Development Impact Fees*. Chicago: APA Press.

Amborski, D. (2016). Using land value capture tools in Canadian municipalities. *Plan Canada*, Summer.

Auckland Council (2019). *Contributions Policy 2019*. Auckland, New Zealand: City of Auckland.

Berrisford, S., & Graham, N. (2015). *Development Charges in South Africa: Current Thinking and Areas of Contestation*. South Africa: Berrisford Consulting.

BILD (2020). *Summary of Development Charges in the Greater Toronto Area*. Toronto: BILD.

Bryant, L. (2015, January 18-21). Infrastructure charges and residential land prices in Brisbane, Australia, Queensland University of Technology (2007) development contributions guidelines version: 5.9 release date: 16 June 2003 – as amended March 2007, Queensland. In 21st Annual Pacific-Rim Real Estate Society Conference, Kuala Lumpur, Malaysia.

City Forum Consulting (2017). *Amenity Contribution System Phase I Review*, October. http://sirepub.edmonton.ca/sirepub/view.aspx?cabinet=published_meetings&fileid=687104.

City of Cape Town (28 November 2014). *City of Cape Town Development Charges: An Implementation Guide to the Development Charges, Policy for*

Engineering Services for the City of Cape Town. Cape Town, South Africa: City of Cape Town.

City of Edmonton (2017). *Developer Contributed Public Amenities in Direct Control Zoning,* 29 November. Urban Form and Corporate Strategic Development CR_4814. http://sirepub .edmonton.ca/sirepub/view.aspx?cabinet =published_meetings&fileid=687103.

City of Sydney (2016). *City of Sydney Development Contributions Plan: 2015 City of Sydney Town Hall.* Sydney, NSW: City of Sydney.

Correia, P. V. D., & Morais de sá, A. (2019). Developers' obligations in Portugal: The imperfect equation for value capture. In D. M. Gielen & E. van der Krabben (Eds.), *Public Infrastructure, Private Finance: Developer Obligations and Responsibilities* (pp. 134–142). London: Routledge.

Crawford, C, & Jurgensmeyer, J. C. (2017). A comparative consideration of development charges in Cape Town. *Journal of Comparative Urban Law and Policy, 1*(1), Article 4. https:// readingroom.law.gsu.edu/jculp/vol1/iss1/4

Department for Communities and Local Government (May 2011). *Community Infrastructure Levy: An Overview.* England: Department for Communities and Local Government.

Department of Internal Affairs, Policy Group (2013). *Development Contributions Review: Discussion Paper.* New Zealand: Department of Internal Affairs, Policy Group.

Downing, P. B. (1973). User charges and the development of urban land. *National Tax Journal, 26*(4), 631–637.

Downing, P. B. (Ed.) (1975). *Local Service Pricing and Urban Spatial Structure.* Vancouver: UBC Press.

Downing, P. B., & McCaleb, T. S. (1987). The economics of development exactions. In J. E. Frank & R. M. Rhodes (Eds.), *Development Exactions* (pp. 42–58). Washington, DC: Planners Press, American Planning Association.

Gielen, D. M. (2019). The Netherlands developer obligations towards cost recovery. In D. M. Gielen & E. van der Krabben (Eds.), *Public Infrastructure, Private Finance: Developer Obligations and Responsibilities* (pp. 91–99). London: Routledge.

Gilbert, C., Gurran, N., & Searle, G. (2019). Developer obligations under the New South Wales, Australia, planning system. In D. M. Gielen & E. van der Krabben (Eds.), *Public Infrastructure, Private Finance: Developer Obligations and Responsibilities* (pp. 203–210). London: Routledge.

Hagman, D. G. & Misczynski, D. J. (1977). *Windfalls for Wipe Outs: Land Value Capture.* Chicago, IL: American Planning Association.

Halifax Regional Municipality (2000). *Infrastructure Best Practices Guide a Capital Cost Contribution Policy.* Halifax, NS: Halifax Regional Municipality.

Halifax Regional Municipality (2016). *Density Bonusing for Affordable Private Rental Housing.*

Hsiu-Yin, D., & Tzu-Chin, L. (2019). Developers' obligations in relation to land value capture in Taiwan. In D. M. Gielen & E. van der Krabben (Eds.), *Public Infrastructure, Private Finance: Developer Obligations and Responsibilities* (pp. 185–193). London: Routledge.

Kaplinsky, E. S. (2006). *From Farms to Suburbs: Controlling Land Subdivision* [SJD Thesis, University of Toronto, unpublished].

Kaplinsky, E. S., & Amborski, D. (2019). Development obligations in Canada: The experience in four provinces. In D. M. Gielen & E. van der Krabben (Eds.), *Public Infrastructure, Private Finance: Developer Obligations and Responsibilities* (pp. 24–36). London: Routledge.

Lin, T.-C., & Ding, H.-Y. (2019). Developer Obligations in Relation to Land Value Capture in Taiwan. In D. M. Gielen & E. Van Der Krabben (Eds.), *Public Infrastructure, Private Finance: Developer Obligations and Responsibilities.* London: Routledge.

Ontario Committee on Taxation. (1968). *Report Volume II.* Toronto: The Queen's Printer.

Province of Ontario. (1989). *Development Charges Act.* Toronto: Queens Printer.

Smolka, M. (2013). *Implementing Land Value Capture in Latin America: Policies and Tools for Urban Development.* Cambridge, MA: Lincoln Institute of Land Policy.

PART 4

Innovations in Practice

Part 4 presents numerous innovations in proportionate share impact fee and development mitigation practice. The first four chapters (18 through 21) address transportation. Transportation impact fees tend to be among the highest of all infrastructure types (see Chapter 5). The next two chapters (22 and 23) address workforce housing and housing affordability issues, followed by a chapter (24) on calculating environmental and habitat mitigation fees. The next chapter (25) gives an example of an innovative way in which to solve problems through proportionate share mitigation approaches. Four chapters (26 through 29) show how impact fees can be designed as if equity matters by extending impact fees to nonresidential development in the case of schools (Chapter 26) and parks and recreation (Chapter 27)—and by methodological extension to other facilities, and scaling impact fees to the size of residential development for water (Chapter 28) and transportation (Chapter 29) facilities, and by extension similar facilities. The last chapter (30) introduces a novel way in which to engage the public in addressing the role and limitations of mitigating the impacts of development on community infrastructure.

The suite of chapters focusing on transportation starts with Chapter 18, "A Framework for Estimating Multimodal Transportation Impacts for Sustainable Development" by Kristina M. Currans and Kelly J. Clifton. The authors take a look ahead to how transportation mitigation must change and is changing. Through pioneering research, they show the foibles of relying solely on the Institute of Transportation Engineers' *Trip Generation Manual* with its limited multi-mobility and suburban-focus lens. A new approach to measuring transportation impacts based on multi-mobility is shown through a case study of Portland, Oregon.

Jonathan Paul extends this concept to on-the-ground applications of mobility fees in Chapter 19, "Mobility Fees." Using examples mostly from Florida but with logical applications nationally, Paul explains the rationale for broadening transportation mitigation to include all forms of mobility as well as how to craft mobility infrastructure mitigation fees. This is a fast-moving field, in a manner of speaking.

Chapter 20, "Operations and Maintenance Mitigation Fees, and Transportation Utility Fees with Implications for Improving Impact Mitigation," presents two important advances in transportation mitigation, and their logic can be extended to *all* infrastructure everywhere. The first is mitigating the long-term impact of new development on transportation facility operations and maintenance (O&M) costs. A large literature shows that once completed, new development does not pay for its long-term impacts on O&M. One solution is to mitigate this cost through O&M mitigation fees that are invested into an endowment. Eventually, the endowment is large enough to generate new revenues sufficient to cover long-term O&M costs attributable to new development. The second is even more sweeping. In the context of transportation, a utility fee approach can be used to generate O&M and conceivably, all initial and long-term capital expansion and preservation costs. By

DOI: 10.4324/9781003336075-22

extension, both approaches can be applied to all community infrastructure.

Sometimes, development regulations call for more parking downtown than is needed. In Chapter 21, "Parking In-Lieu Fee Incentivizes Development in Downtown Oxnard, California," Alison Bouley shows how that city leveraged its parking surplus to incentivize development in downtown through a parking in-lieu fee. It allows developers to pay into a public fund rather than provide on-site parking, which intensifies downtown land use with more vertical and denser development options. The fund is used to enhance the downtown, making it more valuable to downtown real estate owners.

Two chapters address important housing issues. Chapter 22, "A Rational Nexus Approach Supporting Development Mitigation to Increase Workforce Housing Supply," summarizes a method pioneered by two of us (Nicholas and Juergensmeyer), among others, to increase the supply of workforce housing in a resort-dominated community: Jackson City and Teton County, Wyoming. Among many innovations is local policy stating that workforce housing is a form of community infrastructure, but its provision is a project improvement as opposed to a system improvement (see Chapters 2, 4, and 6 for distinctions). In effect, new development must mitigate its impact on the supply of workforce housing by providing it directly or paying in-lieu fees into a fund for the same purpose.

The second housing chapter, 23, addresses "Innovations in Impact Fee Adjustments to Advance Housing Affordability." The concern of many public officials is that impact fees make housing less affordable, and so, various waivers or offsets are entertained to reduce impact fees on certain kinds of housing. Yet, as we show in Chapter 12, it is not that impact fees increase the price of housing beyond that which is affordable, but for many kinds of housing, impact fees are higher than needed to mitigate its proportionate share impact on infrastructure. Merely fixing fee

schedules accordingly could obviate much of the concern. Nonetheless, based on a survey of Florida communities, which is the only one of its kind, this chapter explores numerous ways in which communities may adjust impact fees to advance housing affordability consistently with proportionate share principles.

In Chapter 24, "Western Placer County, California: Habitat Conservation Fee," Robert Spencer walks us through the planning, environmental, and economic analysis process leading to a suite of development mitigation fees, including land conversion fees for over-arching uses; special habitat fees to help preserve marshes, riparian woodlands, and seasonal wetlands, including vernal pools; temporary effect fees, which apply to a disturbed area as it recovers or is restored within one year; and open space and fire hazard management fees. Many of these fees are in response to the federal Endangered Species Act as it applies to western Placer County.

Alison Bouley gives us an encore innovation in Chapter 25, "Flexible Development Funding for Large-Scale Development." This is a case study of the City of Tracy, California, and the developer of 4,700 homes along with nonresidential uses. Starting before the Great Recession of the late 2000s, both the developer and the City needed to restructure agreements reflecting financial and market realities. Among other elements, the agreement called for the developer to install certain public facilities upfront for the City but received credits against future impact fees.

Chapters 26 through 29 address **impact fees as if equity matters**. J. Richard Recht starts this line of thinking in Chapter 26, "Residential and Nonresidential School Impact Fee Nexus: Case Study of Fremont High School District, California." The logic used by Recht is that because nonresidential development creates the jobs that bring families and their children to the community who need school services, nonresidential development must share in the mitigation of school facility impacts.

Carson Bise offers three chapters that continue this theme of designing impact fees as if equity mattered. In Chapter 27, "Parks and Recreation Impact Fees for Residential and Nonresidential Development," which is a case study of Tucson, Arizona, Bise uses similar reasoning to that offered by Recht to extend parks and recreation impact fees to nonresidential development.

In our view, too many impact fees are not scaled to the size of residential units, even though census and other data show clearly that smaller homes have smaller impacts on facilities than larger ones. For instance, impact fees for water and wastewater facilities are often based on just the size of the meter connecting the home to the system without any consideration of the actual load or demand homes impose on those systems with respect to house and lot size (density). In Chapter 28, Bise addresses this through "Water Impact Fees for Residential Development Based on House Size: Case Study of Bozeman, Montana," showing how water impact fees can be scaled by the size of the residential unit. The logic can be applied to wastewater facilities as well. (As an aside, we note that stormwater facility impact fees are often, though not always, based on impervious surface area.)

Another area of concern is the crude way in which transportation impact fees are often calculated. All too often, the same impact fee is applied to all residential development regardless of the size and type of development. Modest improvement occurs when fees vary by type of residential unit. Nonetheless, transportation data combined with census data show clearly that larger homes average more occupants, who impact roads more than smaller homes. Current transportation impact fee practices overcharge smaller units and undercharge larger ones. As we show in Chapters 10, 11, and 12, this is inefficient. We also know from Chapters 14 and 15, as well as the Coda to Chapter 15, that this is inconsistent with the ethics of equity.

Bise addresses our concern with the last of his trilogy of chapters, Chapter 29, "Transportation Impact Fees Scaled to Residential Unit Size in Tucson Arizona." Bise presents a methodology that apportions transportation impacts fairly between residential and nonresidential land uses and then, scales impact fees for residential land uses based on size. After all, impact fees for nonresidential development are scaled for size, so not doing so for residential development becomes an internally inconsistent calculation flaw and is inconsistent with the ethics of impact fee equity (see Chapter 15 and its Coda).

All four of these case studies show practitioners how equity can be advanced by (a) broadening the base of impact mitigation analysis and (b) scaling impact fees to the size of residential units. Not doing so leads to an inefficient outcome, because economic logic holds that over-charging smaller homes means that fewer will be built, but under-charging larger homes means that more will be built, which can eventually create local fiscal stress.

Missing in much of the discussion about development mitigation policies is the role of public engagement. As Chapter 3 shows, many states with impact fee legislation require the participation of an impact fee advisory committee comprised variously of representatives from development and citizen groups. While the assumption is that these committees represent their constituencies, what seems missing is formal community engagement. This is where Kevin Burnett's Chapter 30, "Impact Fee Focus Groups: Case Study of Town of Queen Creek, Arizona," offers important contributions to the process. In this case, there were eight focus group meetings, lasting two hours each. While the overall cost to development classes increased from an earlier study, the Home Builders Association spoke favorably of the engagement process because of the transparency it provided and stated that it allowed their voices to be heard.

18 A FRAMEWORK FOR ESTIMATING MULTIMODAL TRANSPORTATION IMPACTS FOR SUSTAINABLE DEVELOPMENT

KRISTINA M. CURRANS AND KELLY J. CLIFTON

18.1 INTRODUCTION: WHY IS THERE A NEED FOR A MULTIMODAL FRAMEWORK?

Mitigating the impact of new development on transportation systems is a field that at once evolves and does not evolve fast enough to keep up with advances in measuring transportation impacts. This chapter presents a framework for doing so.

Conventional methods for estimating transportation impacts of land use development have often been criticized for overestimating vehicle demand in urban areas; lacking sensitivity across urban contexts, the built environment, and socio-demographic markets; and ignoring non-automobile demand and infrastructure needs. Originating in the 1960s and 1970s, the traditional approaches were developed specifically for mitigating infrastructure to accommodating and increasing the mobility of automobiles, but multiple recent studies have transformed and reshaped the way transportation impacts are estimated for land development in urbanized areas. The response? Start with people.

By transitioning to person trip behavior, studies can present a holistic picture of activity at land uses, which allows a better basis for understanding demand impacts as well as evaluating future demand, across multiple modes. By collecting new data and working to understand variation in activity behavior (not automobile demand), analysts determine the distribution of person trip activity across modes based on current and/or planned conditions. These data can support new multimodal planning tools, linking development-level transportation impact evaluations across other scales of analysis (e.g., neighborhood or regional). Ultimately, this direction in research and practice reflects an increasing desire to plan for the places that communities desire and not to reproduce past trends and patterns of development.

While some of these new lessons and data have been incorporated into other realms of evaluation of transportation impacts, such as transportation impact analyses or studies, the application of these revised approaches has had limited permeation in the field of impact fees and system development charges. This chapter has three sections: (1) an overview and introduction to these new data and methods; (2) a framework for adopting the state-of-the-art research into practice; and (3) strategies and considerations for advancing local fee schedules. This framework was largely inspired by an initial review of the City of Portland's process through a travel behavior lens, and the results from the review were incorporated into the City's 2017 Transportation System Development Charges schedule update. It seems pertinent that this chapter ends with a case study exploring how the bones of this proposed framework were developed for one city: Portland, Oregon.

DOI: 10.4324/9781003336075-23

18.2 AN OVERVIEW TO THESE NEW DATA AND STANDARDS

The majority of transportation impact fees, utility fees, or system development charges depend heavily on the industry standards: the Institute of Transportation Engineers' (ITE) third edition *Trip Generation Handbook* (Institute of Transportation Engineers 2014) and tenth edition *Trip Generation Manual* (Institute of Transportation Engineers 2017). These two resources provide the methods and data, respectively, that practitioners often use to quantify the transportation impacts of development in terms of the number of trips coming and going from a size as a ratio to the size of the development—often called the "trip end rate" or "trip rate." For more than 60 years, the process for estimating the transportation impacts of new land use development has remained largely unchanged. However, in the last decade, we have seen substantial investment in sponsored research projects—both academic and practitioner-led—to address broad criticisms of the conventional recommended guidelines.

The flaws in ITE's *Handbook* (second edition) are now well documented in the literature. The vehicle trip data were insensitive to urban contexts and did not account for multimodal travel behavior (Clifton et al. 2013; De Gruyter 2019), despite ample evidence that vehicle demand decreases with increases in activity densities or accessibilities (Ewing and Cervero 2010). Several studies found ITE's estimates to overestimate vehicle trip rates for certain land uses across both urban and suburban contexts (Clifton et al. 2012; Schneider et al. 2015; Texas A&M Transportation Institute 2016). The data in the *Handbook* were largely defined as being collected in "baseline contexts" including mostly single-use developments with little to no transit access that were generally not bikeable or walkable and had free and unconstrained parking. Following this, the lack of transparency about where (and when) individual observations were collected corresponds with issues in evaluating the applicability of the data in different local contexts—likely leading to broad application in areas that were not representative of "baseline contexts" (Currans 2017b). The age of the data proved to be another issue, with one study finding that older data had significantly higher rates, likely an artifact of the types of locations collected in studies in the 1960s versus today (Currans 2017a).

Driven by an interest to link decades of travel behavior theory and research with practice, recent studies have explored the variation in vehicular and multimodal demand across urban contexts and new land uses (like affordable housing developments and residential developments with bottom-floor retail). These studies have provided a great deal of insight into the ways in which we collect and quantify multimodal transportation impacts and how they are then applied in practice. But, they have also provided substantial new resources, including new raw data and tools to adjust ITE's rates using originally collected data; see Table 18.1 for relevant studies and reviews by Currans (Currans 2017b) and de Gruyter (2019) for more detailed analysis.

Responding to these criticisms and the growing wealth of new data and methods, ITE developed a panel of experts to consider and incorporate new research in their third edition, including two topics: person trip activity and multimodal behavior. By shifting the focus of impacts from a vehicle-first perspective to a person-based perspective, we can improve the representation of overall impacts of development. A vehicle-first perspective leaves the estimation of the impacts of alternative modes (namely, biking, walking, or transit) for adjustments and assumptions—all of which tend to underestimate the number of biking, walking, or transit trips made. Person-based data collections can then be coupled with intercept surveys and/or models built from household travel surveys to then quantify trip counts by mode (and vehicle occupancy) at a site level

TABLE 18.1 A Sample of Major Studies and Studies That Evolved Transportation Impact Data and Analysis

Study	Data Collected			Developed Methods for Estimation			Land Use Types Collected			Single-Use (SUD) or Mixed-Use (MXD) Developments[a]
	Original Data Collection	Includes Multimodal Data	Collected in Urban Contexts	Adjusts ITE Rates	Directly Estimates Vehicle Trips	Directly Estimates Multimodal Trips	Retail/ Service	Residential/ Lodging	Office	
Contextual Influences on Trip Generation (Clifton et al. 2012) *Portland, Oregon*	X	X	X	X			X			SUD
Urban Context Adjustment (Currans and Clifton 2015) *United States*	X	X	X	X			X	X	X	SUD
Smart Growth Trip Generation, Phase I and II (Schneider et al. 2013, 2015; Texas A&M Transportation Institute 2016) *California*	X	X	X	X			X	X	X	SUD
NCHRP Enhancing Internal Capture for Mixed-Use Developments (Bochner et al. 2011) *United States*	X	X	X	X	X		X	X	X	MXD

(Continued)

TABLE 18.1 Continued

Study	Data Collected			Developed Methods for Estimation			Land Use Types Collected			Single-Use (SUD) or Mixed-Use (MXD) Developments[a]
	Original Data Collection	Includes Multimodal Data	Collected in Urban Contexts	Adjusts ITE Rates	Directly Estimates Vehicle Trips	Directly Estimates Multimodal Trips	Retail/ Service	Residential/ Lodging	Office	
Traffic Generated by Mixed-Use Developments[b] (Ewing et al. 2011) *United States*		X		X			X	X	X	MXD
DDOT Trip Generation Data Collection and Analysis (Ewing et al. 2011; Westom et al. 2017) *Washington, DC*	X	X	X		X	X		X		SUD & MXD
Los Angeles Affordable Housing Trip Generation Study (LADOT 2020) *Los Angeles, CA*	X		X					X		SUD
Affordable Housing Trip Generation Rates and Strategies (Clifton et al. 2018) *San Francisco & Los Angeles, CA*	X	X	X					X		SUD

Notes:

For more context and discussion of these recent changes, refer to the following recent review articles (4, 11).

[a] Mixed-use developments require the estimation of "internal capture" to segments any trips that may occur within the development from those that impact adjacent public facilities. While some of these SUD methods could be modified for application to MXD approaches, the MXD methods identified here were specifically calibrated for this use.

[b] The number of regions has increased to above 30. Variations of this tool use data and information from the DDOT study and the National Cooperative Highway Research Program (NCHRP) to calibrate the tool for single-building mixed-use developments as well as larger mixed-use developments.

Source: Authors.

to estimate vehicle trips and person trips by vehicle, transit, biking, or walking.

Currently, available person trip generation and multimodal travel information data is largely constrained to those larger studies (as seen in Table 18.1); however, the commitment of ITE's new approach moves the desire for access to more people-focused data. In the next section, we consider these new improvements in practice and establish the framework for incorporating a person-driven approach into updated impact fee schedules.

18.3 FRAMEWORK FOR ADOPTING STATE-OF-THE-ART RESEARCH INTO PRACTICE

This framework builds on existing methods for impact estimation, meeting rational nexus requirements between the fee structure and activity at individual development, and providing a sound basis for evaluating a range of impacts across multiple modes and urban contexts. The proposed framework here has two main components: (1) estimating person trip activity; and (2) estimating mode share adjustments.

18.3.1 Let's Think about People: Estimating Person Trip Activity

Across all land use categories, person trip generation rates—the number of people entering or exiting the development during the study period as a ratio of the size of the development (e.g., dwelling units, square footage)—are collected in a very similar way to the conventionally used vehicle trip generation rates, as defined by ITE. The primary recommended approach is to use the person trip generation rates as collected by original data collections—such as those described in Table 18.1—either directly from or similar to local contexts. However, this limited, but growing, pool of data may not provide large enough sample sizes for all land uses in fees schedules.

To incorporate smaller samples of observations, one can opt to aggregate land use categories to derive larger samples. In a study exploring ITE's land use taxonomy, we found that the 67 service and retail land use categories could largely be simplified into a three-tier category (heavy goods; convenience goods and services; and everything else) with little to no loss of explanatory power (Currans and Clifton 2018) The decision to aggregate land use categories may also improve the ease of application of the schedule in practice.

Another option is to consider the time period of data collection. The collection of existing person trip generation data was largely driven by transportation impact analyses, which quantify impacts on the safety and/or operations of adjacent facilities (e.g., level-of-service performance measures, signals, turning bays, sometimes street widenings). As such, the existing person trip generation data is mainly focused on the PM peak hour (generally 4:00 p.m. to 6:00 p.m. or 7:00 p.m.), while many fee schedules are dependent on daily trip generation rates (e.g., 12:00 a.m. to 11:59 p.m.). To accommodate this limitation, agencies may choose to modify the time period of "impacts" assessed in their schedule until more "daily" data become available.

The third option for accommodating limited sample sizes of person trip generation data is to approximate the person trip generation rates using conventional vehicle trip generation rates for your time period of choice. This approximation relies on some assumptions about where ITE's "baseline" vehicle data were collected. The *Handbook* broadly defines "baseline" developments as being single-use sites, with little to no access to transit or active mode infrastructure, and with free and unconstrained parking—in other words, highly suburban. The recommended adjustment approach can be estimated following (IT 2014):

APPROXIMATE PERSON TRIPS PER UNIT-SIZE

= ITE VEHICLE TRIPS PER UNIT-SIZE

*BASELINE VEHICLE OCCUPANCY

/ BASELINE VEHICLE MODE SHARE

Where,

APPROXIMATE PERSON TRIPS PER UNIT-SIZE = The approximated average person trip generation rate (trips per unit-size) converted from existing vehicle trip generation data, for your time period of choice.

ITE VEHICLE TRIPS PER UNIT-SIZE = The average vehicle trip generation rates (trips per unit-size) provided in the ITE *Handbook* and *Manual*, for your time period of choice.

BASELINE VEHICLE OCCUPANCY and MODE SHARE = The average baseline vehicle occupancy and mode share rates may come from intercept survey data collected at ITE's typical "baseline" (highly suburban) sites, or they may be estimated using external data and/or assumptions about these contexts.

Either approach—using person trip rate data directly or approximating person trip rate information using vehicle trip rate data—results in "person trips per unit-size" information to be estimated for each land use category. Following the estimation of the person activity for specific land uses, the value per trip rate can be calculated. The value per trip rate is often compiled using the value estimation of proposed transportation projects or public improvements (less any existing infrastructure value) and divided by the total trips expected to use the new facilities estimated using regional travel demand models and processes. In this new framework, the denominator would replace "total vehicle trips" with "total person trips." This process is calculated for all trips regardless of land use type.

VALUE PER TRIP = VALUE OF PROPOSED SYSTEM

/FACILITIES / TOTAL PERSON TRIPS

Where,

VALUE PER TRIP = the dollar value of each person trip using the new system or infrastructure.

VALUE OF PROPOSED SYSTEM/ FACILITIES = the value or costs estimated for all proposed system facilities or infrastructure, less any existing infrastructure value.

TOTAL PERSON TRIPS = the total person trip ends expected to use the new infrastructure in the development area, less any travel that may pass through the system or any trips that may not occur at land uses in the development area. These data are often estimated through a regional or city-wide transportation demand model.

The person-based fee schedule can then be estimated using the person trip generation rate (either directly estimated or approximated from vehicle trip data) and the value per trip rate:

VALUE PER UNIT-SIZE

= PERSON TRIPS PER UNIT-SIZE

*VALUE PER TRIP

Where,

VALUE PER UNIT-SIZE = The impact fee or charge per unit of development size (e.g., dwelling units, square footage) for each land use category.

PERSON TRIPS PER UNIT-SIZE = The average number of people coming or going for the specific time period (e.g., p.m. peak hour, daily) per unit of development size for each land use category. This may be directly estimated from original data, approximated using vehicle trip generation data, or a combination of both.

VALUE PER TRIP = the dollar value of each person trip using the new system or infrastructure.

18.3.2 Not All Person Trips Have the Same Impact: Mode Share Adjustments

At this point in the framework, the person-based impact fee schedules are set so that every new person trip made in the system contributes in an equal way to the overall cost of infrastructure. But, not all person trips use the system or specific infrastructure in the same way. The second piece of the framework involves adjusting the estimated person trip impact schedule based on mode shares. Mode choices for different trips vary based on the density or destination accessibility of the area and access to mode-specific infrastructure and options (e.g., transit availability and quality, sidewalks and walkability, bike infrastructure) (Ewing and Cervero 2010).

In areas with plans and policies that aim to support multimodal behaviors—including mixed-use zoning at higher densities and multimodal infrastructure capacity or quality improvements—the vehicular impacts of specific types of development (e.g., residential, retail/service, commercial) could end up being far lower than the regional average or national vehicle transportation impact rates. A multimodal adjustment in the impact fee schedule may take two main forms, described in the following: direct mode share adjustment; and planned versus current mode share adjustment. Both of these approaches are applied categorically at a district level to ease the application of the fee schedule—where "districts" may be defined as census tracts/block groups, zoned districts, overlay areas, centers and corridors, or neighborhoods, depending on the needs of the agency (and their current related planning documents). And, both approaches rely on simply allocating the PERSON TRIPS PER UNIT-SIZE estimate from the last section (approximated or directly estimated) into mode-specific trips, which can then be weighted according to the relative impact (as formulated in the following). The decision on which mode share adjustment is needed is context specific and dependent on the local data availability; the disaggregation of explicit mode share goals to a district or neighborhood level; and the desired level of ease for administering area-specific reductions. The general form of the adjustment is:

ADJUSTED PERSON TRIPS PER UNIT-SIZE

= MODE WEIGHTS *

(PERSON TRIPS PER UNIT-SIZE)

Where,

ADJUSTED PERSON TRIPS PER UNIT-SIZE = the reduced person trip rate with mode-specific adjustments, ideally by both land use and district.

PERSON TRIPS PER UNIT-SIZE = derived from the previous person trip analysis by land use.

It is in the modal weights that these two approaches vary. In the **direct mode share adjustment**, the modal weights could be developed based on any number of performance metrics or data, but ideally, they would be calculated for modes by both land use and district area, if data are available and it is agreeable to the administration of the schedule.

MODE WEIGHTS = a vector of weights for each transportation mode (e.g., vehicle, transit, bike, walk) considered, examples of which could include typical trip lengths, vehicle occupancies, the area of facilities consumed by each mode (square feet), and locally relevant mode share data collected for the specific land use.

See the case study at the end of the chapter outlined in Box 18.1 for one such example.

The **planned versus current mode share adjustment** considers both current available data describing district travel behavior information, as well as district-level multimodal goals made in conjunction with both land use and transportation facility planning. In this approach, the planned mode share could be taken as a ratio of the district's or region's mode share, indicating a reduction provided as policy, allowing specific developments that locate within the district to receive a benefit because they take part in moving the area towards planned outcomes.

MODE WEIGHTS = PLANNED MODE SHARE / CURRENT MODE SHARE

A vector of weights that represents the ratio of the planned mode share (e.g., vehicle, transit, bike, walk) to current mode shares. Ideally, this is segmented by district and land use type as well as mode.

PLANNED MODE SHARE = Mode shares for districts by land use estimated as part of a comprehensive planning process and regional forecasting exercise.

CURRENT MODE SHARE = Mode shares for districts by land use estimated as part of a regional modeling or data analysis exercise (i.e., household travel survey summaries, regional modeling outcomes for base-year estimates, pre-package site-level multimodal estimation products such as ET+ or MXD+).

BOX 18.1 CASE STUDY: PORTLAND, OREGON

We apply these insights to a Portland, Oregon case study using this study:

Report: Transportation System Development Charge Update (October 2017). Prepared for: Portland Bureau of Transportation. City of Portland, Oregon.

Prepared by: Fehr & Peers; ECONorthwest; Galardi Rothstein Group; JLA Public Involvement

Case Study Contributing Authors: Kendra Breiland & Don Samdahl

---

In 2017, the Portland Bureau of Transportation (PBOT) in the City of Portland, Oregon updated its Transportation System Development Charge (TSDC) schedule and incorporated a version of this chapter's proposed framework for a person-based, multimodal approach.

While they decided to move to a person-based estimation, they recognized that the limited pool of new available data would require an approximation of person trip rates for most of the land uses from ITE's vehicle trip generation rates. Wherever available, they used person trip generation data. As part of this process, the agency and analyst team also decided to shift trip generation time periods from "daily" to "p.m. peak period" to incorporate larger sample sizes, with a plan to reevaluate during future updates when additional data become available.

A mode share adjustment was applied as a function of the proportion of space each mode consumes per person trip (based on square footage) relative to the most space-consuming mode, "drive alone" (see Table 18.2).

To simplify future applications of any mode share reductions, they opted to aggregate their districts into three categories: central city; centers; and everywhere else—distinguished in the 2035 Comprehensive Plans and parcels within 1000 feet of light rail (excluding single-family, open space, heavy industrial, and general industrial). Similarly, they decided to apply reductions for each of these districts consistently across land uses—leaving one percentage reduction to apply to the fee schedule for each of their defined district types.

AVERAGE WEIGHTED SQUARE FOOTAGE

= MODE SHARE * SQUARE FOOTAGE

Where,

AVERAGE WEIGHTED SQUARE FOOTAGE = The weighted area in square footage that all modes consume "per trip" for each district type.

TABLE 18.2 Area Consumed by Each Mode in Square Footage and the Relative Proportion of That Space to the Larger Consumer

Mode	Square Footage (SQFT)	Percentage of "Drive Alone"
Drive Alone	180	100%
Carpools	108	60%
Bicyclists	22.5	12.5%
Walking	16.2	9%
Transit	5.4	3%

Source: PBOT TSDC Documentation.

MODE SHARE = The mode shares for each type of district estimated for "current" conditions—using the most recent household travel survey, the 2011–2012 Oregon Household Activity Survey—and "future" conditions—based on the 2035 Comprehensive Plan Travel Model (2016).

SQUARE FOOTAGE = Typical area in square feet each type of mode consumes (see Table 18.2)

The future "planned" average weighted square footage for each district was then taken as a percentage of the weighted square footage estimated for "all other areas." For the central city, a 33% reduction of impacts was estimated for future conditions compared with other locations; and for centers, an 8% reduction was estimated compared with all other locations. Developments in these areas that are consistent with planned development (e.g., mixed-use retail or entertainment, multifamily, senior housing, hotel) are eligible for these reductions in these districts.

Moreover, PBOT has identified funds that allow continued improvements to the schedule. Current work is underway to develop tiered rates for different-sized single-family residential dwellings—since the size of the housing is often correlated with the number of people and the corresponding impacts—and to collect local multifamily data—in conjunction departments aimed at improving Transportation Impact Study guidance and transportation demand management strategies. The framework developed by this team of practitioners allows PBOT to continue updating and adopting new research and data as it becomes available, potentially on an annual basis.

18.3.3 Strategies and Considerations for Advancing Local Fee Schedules

While the adjustments suggested in this framework are simple ratios and formulas, there are a number of considerations for agencies and practitioners to discuss to accommodate this shift in industry practice in the application of impact fees. This section discusses strategies that provide stop-gap approaches for transitioning into this new industry to allow agencies and practitioners growing room to make the shift. With a limited, but growing, pool of data, the application of people-based metrics of evaluation is becoming more feasible.

Person trip rates for new development can be approximated by using ITE's vehicle trip rate data, but by assuming that these rates are analogous to person trip rates with a simple adjustment, we are also assuming that person trip rates in ITE's contexts (suburban, vehicle-oriented, single use, little to no transit, no bike/pedestrian facilities) will be approximately the same as in very urban areas, like central business districts or retail/service corridors. In other words, why would restaurants, for example, care about where they located if this did not impact the number of customers they would expect? The variation in person trip rate across contexts should be controlled for, although this is not yet available. As more data are collected, it is possible that some land uses (such as retail and/or service) may see large increases in person trip rate estimates from those approximated ITE rates in more urban contexts; however, these locations should also have observed greater mode share reductions due to better multimodal infrastructure and accessibility. Care is needed as new data are incorporated into rate schedules to ensure that the impacts of any one land use type across districts reflect relative levels of impact.

Ideally, these adjustments are applied at a level where the "districts" and "land uses" are at the most disaggregate levels allowable for reasonable application in practice. However, it is most likely undesirable for agencies to apply a different reduction for land use type and every district or neighborhood in their jurisdiction. To simplify, reducing districts to "district types" and land use types to "broad land use categories" (e.g., residential/lodging, retail/service, commercial) would allow analysts the ability to capture major variations in contexts and agencies the ease of applying a handful of reductions. Similarly, advances in technologies that allow agencies to present more complex, spatially dependent fee schedules may ease the ability to capture more degrees of variation in transportation impacts within the city.

It is worth noting that differences in the urban environment will have more impact than mode choice, as this framework for the adjustment describes. Other influential travel indicators correlated with the urban environment—and relevant to the estimation of transportation impacts—include, but are not limited to, trip length, trip chaining, trip frequency, carpooling, and the temporal pattern of trips throughout the day and week. This largely means that the most accurate (but also most complex) transportation impact estimate process may take into account some combination of all of these outcomes by district and land use type. While one could easily see how complicated this form of analysis or schedule may become, for some land uses, locating in specific urban districts may drastically improve their transportation impacts below regional estimates for all land uses. Analysts are advised to compare mode shares (and other travel metrics) for different land use types, trip purposes, or activities to assess whether there are outlier land uses and districts in the region that have disproportionately higher or lower impacts compared with elsewhere. Additionally, the transportation impacts of transportation demand management (TDM) strategies—such as (un)bundled parking, free or discounted transit passes for residents or employees—are also likely to change behaviors, although more studies are needed to quantify these impacts at a development level.

There are several technologies with emerging applications that could further improve the sensitivity of impact fee schedules to changes in the built environment and therefore, travel behavior. For example, mobile phone signaling data ("pings") have been used to general local residential person trip generation rates (Shi and Zhu 2019). Automated person counting technologies (pressure pad sensors, video detection) may decrease the costs associated with development-level data collection to allow larger sample sizes to be collected or more frequent collection in local contexts. Agencies interested in incorporating this framework or these new methods into their fee schedules should explore the availability of funds in their programs for annual improvement of the schedule, including, but not limited to, partnerships with agency counterparts involved in the guidance for transportation impact studies or TDM programs.

REFERENCES

Bochner, B. S., Hooper, K., Sperry, B., & Dunphy, R. (2011). *Enhancing Internal Capture Estimation for Mixed Use Developments*. Publication NCHRP Report 684. Washington, DC: National Cooperative Highway Research Program: Transportation Research Board of the National Academies.

Clifton, K. J., Currans, K. M., & Muhs, C. D. (2012). *Contextual Influences on Trip Generation*. Publication OTREC-RR-12-13. Portland: Oregon Transportation Research and Education Consortium.

Clifton, K. J., Currans, K. M., & Muhs, C. D. (2013). Evolving the institute of transportation engineers' trip generation handbook: A proposal for collecting multi-modal, multi-context, establishment-level data. *Transportation Research Record: Journal of the Transportation Research Board, 2344*(1), 107–117.

Clifton, K. J., Currans, K. M., Schneider, R., Handy, S., Howell, A., Abou-Zeid, G., Bertini Ruas, E., Roan, S., & Gehrke, S. R. (2018). *Caltrans Affordable Housing Trip Generation Final Report v20180914.pdf*. California Department of Transportation (Caltrans).

Currans, K. M. (2017a). Issues in trip generation methods for transportation impact estimation of land use development: A review and discussion of the state-of-the-art approaches. *Journal of Planning Literature, 2017*, 1–11.

Currans, K. M. (2017b). *Issues in Urban Trip Generation* [Dissertation., Portland State University, Portland].

Currans, K. M., & Clifton, K. J. (2015). Using household travel surveys to adjust ITE trip generation rates. *Journal of Transport and Land Use, 8*(1), 85–119. https://doi.org/10.5198/jtlu .2015.470.

Currans, K. M., & Clifton, K. J. (2018). Exploring ITE's trip generation manual: Assessing age of data and land-use taxonomy in vehicle trip generation for transportation impact analyses. *Transportation Research Part A: Policy and Practice, 118*, 387–398. https://doi.org/10.1016/j.tra.2018 .09.007

De Gruyter, C. (2019). Multimodal trip generation from land use developments: International synthesis and future directions. *Transportation Research Record: Journal of the Transportation Research Board, 2019*, 036119811983396. https:// doi.org/10.1177/0361198119833967.

Ewing, R., & Cervero, R. (2010). Travel and the built environment: A meta-analysis. *Journal of the American Planning Association, 76*(3), 265–294.

Ewing R., Greenwald, M., Ming, Z., Jerry, W., Mark, F., Robert, C., Lawrence, F., & John, T. (2011). Traffic generated by mixed-use developments: Six-region study using consistent built environmental measures. *Journal of Urban Planning and Development, 137*(3), 248–261. https://doi.org/10.1061/(ASCE) UP.1943-5444.0000068

Fehr & Peers, ECONorthwest, Galardi Rothstein Group, & JLA Public Involvement (October 2017). *Transportation System Development Charge Update. Prepared for: Portland Bureau of Transportation*. Portland: City of Portland. Available online and accessed on Oct. 21, 2021 at: www.portland.gov/sites/default/files /2020-08/citywide-rate-study-october-2017.pdf

Institute of Transportation Engineers (2014). *Institute of Transportation Engineers' Trip Generation Handbook*. Washington, DC: Institute of Transportation Engineers.

Institute of Transportation Engineers (2017). *Institute of Transportation Engineers' Trip Generation Manual*. Washington, DC: Institute of Transportation Engineers.

Los Angeles Department of Transportation (LADOT) (July 2020). *LADOT Transportation Assessment Guidelines*, Table 3.3-2. Available online and accessed on Oct. 21, 2021 at: https:// ladot.lacity.org/sites/default/files/2020-07 /ta_guidelines_all-sections_2020.07.04_ attachments.pdf

Schneider, R. J., Shafizadeh, K., Sperry, B. R., & Handy, S. L. (2013). Methodology to gather multimodal trip generation data in smart-growth areas. *Transportation Research Record: Journal of the Transportation Research Board, 2354*(1), 68–85. https://doi.org/10.3141/2354-08.

Schneider, R. J., Shafizadeh, K., & Handy, S. L. (2015). Method to adjust institute of transportation engineers vehicle trip-generation estimates in smart-growth areas. *Journal of Transport and Land Use, 8*(1), 69–83.

Shi, F., & Zhu, L. (2019). Analysis of trip generation rates in residential commuting based on mobile phone signaling data. *Journal of Transport and Land Use, 12*(1). https://doi.org/10.5198/jtlu .2019.1431.

Texas A&M Transportation Institute (2016). *Caltrans Project P59, Trip Generation Rates for*

Transportation Impact Analyses of Smart Growth Land Use Projects DRAFT. College Station: The Texas A&M University System.

Westrom, R., Dock, S., Henson, J., Watten, M., Bakhru, A., Ridgway, M., Ziebarth, J., Prabhakar, R., Ferdous, N., Kilim, G. R., & Paradkar, R. (2017). A multimodal trip generation model to assess travel impacts of urban developments in district of Columbia. Presented at the 96th Annual Meeting of the Transportation Research Board of the National Academies, Washington, DC.

19 MOBILITY FEES

JONATHAN PAUL

19.1 OVERVIEW

Mobility fees are a funding tool that allow local governments to repurpose revenues away from funding road capacity toward funding multimodal projects adopted as part of a mobility plan. A mobility plan is a forward-looking and progressive approach to integrate land use, transportation mobility, parking, and funding. A holistic mobility plan assists in the development of a multimodal network that provides people options, such as: walking, bicycling, accessing transit, driving, or using new mobility technology safely and conveniently. An effective mobility plan identifies multimodal transportation projects, such as sidewalks, trails, bike lanes, and trolley circulators that connect neighborhoods with places where people want to go, e.g., stores, schools, and parks. Mobility plans may also be used to reduce congestion by creating park-once environments through mobility hubs and curbside management, adding turn lanes at busy intersections, improving traffic signals, and identifying strategic road and transit improvements.

For the greater half of the past century, the general assumption has been that population and employment growth, along with associated increases in development, will result in increased traffic and the need for new road capacity (Figure 19.1). Transportation planning, along with the development regulations that support it, such as transportation mitigation systems (e.g., adequate public facility ordinances, transportation concurrency, proportionate fair share) and roadway impact fees, emphasizes widening existing roads and building new roads in order to address travel demand from new growth. Many communities have found that any new road capacity is quickly consumed through what is known as induced demand (build it and they will come).

Growing communities across the country are realizing it is increasingly difficult and expensive to strike a balance between reducing congestion and accommodating new development by adding road capacity, while also preserving the quality of life in their community, minimizing impacts to existing residential neighborhoods, and protecting environmentally sensitive areas. Communities are also struggling as the rate of both crashes and fatalities involving people walking and bicycling continues to increase, with the last four years being the deadliest in three decades.[1]

Sunbelt states, in particular Florida, consistently rank as some of the most dangerous states in the United States for people to walk and bicycle. Cities and metropolitan areas in Florida annually top the list with the highest per capita rate of fatalities from people walking and bicycling.[2] State Departments of Transportation (DOTs), counties, cities, and organizations like the National Association of City Transportation Officials (NACTO) and Smart Growth America are developing and promoting complete streets and enacting transportation mobility plans that emphasize the safe, comfortable, and convenient movement of all people using the transportation system to move toward Vision Zero.[3]

Realizing that it's increasingly difficult to "build their way out of congestion," communities are looking toward mobility plans to identify innovative ways to address congestion, the

DOI: 10.4324/9781003336075-24

FIGURE 19.1 The development-demand-capacity cycle. (From Jonathan Paul, AICP.)

public's travel options, future travel demands, and increased street safety. Many local governments, especially in Florida, are also considering if a community has limitations in financially providing future road capacity, or if elected officials and residents no longer desire to provide road capacity to meet future travel demand, there is still a rational nexus to charge a road impact fee to fund road capacity that is not planned. Increasingly, urbanized areas and coastal communities across the US are looking for new tools, such as mobility fees, to fund and provide mobility by means other than adding road capacity.

This chapter outlines the role of mobility fees in helping to manage the transportation impacts of new development. Many of the examples come from Florida, where the combination of rapid urbanization, scarce land, and some of the most restrictive state and local fiscal laws creates the perfect storm for innovation. The chapter starts with a mobility plan, which is implemented in part by mobility fees. It then compares road impact fees with mobility fees. Most of the chapter is devoted to the mobility fee calculation steps.

The chapter concludes with observations about the future of mobility fees.

19.2 MOBILITY PLANS

In recognition that new and wider roads are not the only means by which to address travel demand and provide mobility, local governments are adopting mobility plans to serve as a foundation to transition from a transportation planning and funding process primarily focused on moving cars to a multimodal system that emphasizes personal mobility and provides people the choice to walk, bike, ride transit, drive a car, or make use of new mobility technology (Figure 19.2). Mobility plans can be developed to focus on: (1) building walkable trails that connect neighborhoods with stores and businesses, (2) providing more visible and safer bicycle infrastructure and crosswalks, (3) planning for enhanced access to existing and future transit service, (4) creating park-once environments through mobility hubs and shared mobility programs, and (5) designing streets to achieve slower speeds and safer crossings at intersections and mid-block locations.

Mobility plans are intended to serve as the basis for the development of a mobility fee, which is intended to replace transportation mitigation systems and roadway impact fees paid by new development. Mobility fees are intended to be used to fund the multimodal projects adopted as part of a mobility plan (Figure 19.3). Mobility fees provide local governments with an additional funding source to transition away from primarily funding road capacity toward funding a wider range of multimodal projects that encourage walking, jogging, bicycling, riding transit, and using new mobility technologies. Mobility fees can also be used to add turn lanes at intersections, improve traffic signals, fund roundabouts, and add road capacity through new roads and the widening of existing roads to the extent

FIGURE 19.2 Multimodal mobility options considered in mobility plans. (From Jonathan Paul, AICP.)

FIGURE 19.3 Role of mobility fees in financing the mobility plan. (From Jonathan Paul, AICP.)

that such projects are included as part of a mobility plan.

Mobility fees were established by the Florida legislature through Florida Statute 163.3180 with the intent to provide an alternative transportation mobility funding system and replace transportation mitigation systems and roadway impact fees. Mobility fees were intended to be a simplified and streamlined process that allowed new development to mitigate its transportation impact through a one-time payment to a local government to fund multimodal transportation projects established in an adopted mobility plan. Mobility fees are only assessed on new development and redevelopment that results in an increase in travel demand over and above the existing use of a parcel of land. Local governments that have adopted a mobility plan and mobility fee have also replaced traffic impact analysis, studies that focus on road capacity, with site impact assessments or studies that focus on access to the development, traffic control devices, multimodal connectivity, cross-access, and implementing the mobility plan.

19.3 ROAD IMPACT FEE AND MOBILITY FEE COMPARED

The primary difference between traditional roadway impact fees and mobility fees is that road impact fees principally pay for the cost associated with adding new road capacity for motor vehicles, while mobility fees are intended to pay for the cost associated with adding new multimodal capacity for people. Roadway impact fees are typically based on the number of vehicle trips, vehicle miles of travel (VMT), and the cost to add road capacity such as the construction of new roads, the widening of existing roads, and the addition or extension of turn lanes at intersections. Mobility fees are based on person trips, person miles of travel (PMT), and the cost to add multimodal capacity. While mobility fees can be used for road and intersection capacity projects, they can also be used to fund sidewalks, trails, bike lanes, protected bike lanes, flex lanes, streetscapes, landscapes, high-visibility crosswalks, dedicated transit lanes, transit stops, transit circulators, mobility hubs, shared-use mobility programs, complete and low-speed shared streets, and new mobility technology, as long as the mobility projects are adopted as part of an adopted mobility plan.

In contrast to "Dillon Rule" states where constitutions grant local governments no powers unless explicitly authorized by the legislature, most state constitutions give "home rule" power to local governments (Richardson, Gough and Puentes 2003). In those states, local governments have broad authority to establish special assessments, create impact fees and mobility fees, implement franchise fees, and assess user fees or other forms of charges on development. Payment of impact fees or mobility fees is one of the primary means through which local governments can require new development, along with redevelopment or expansion of existing land uses that generates additional transportation demand, to mitigate its impact on the transportation system. While road impact fees and mobility fees are both intended to be means by which a development can mitigate its transportation impact, the following highlights major differences between the two.

Road Impact Fees

- Principally pay for the cost associated with adding new road capacity to move people driving motor vehicles

- Partially or fully fund road capacity improvements, including new roads, the widening of existing roads, and the addition or extension of turn lanes at intersections
- Are based on increases in vehicle miles of capacity from road improvements and the projected vehicle miles of travel from new development
- May be based on either an adopted level of service (LOS) standard (aka standards or consumption-based fee) or on future road improvements (aka plan or improvements-based fee)

Mobility Fees

- Pay for the cost associated with adding new multimodal capacity to move people walking, bicycling, scooting, riding transit, driving vehicles, or using shared mobility technology
- Partially or fully fund multimodal projects, including sidewalks, paths, trails, bike lanes, streetscapes and landscapes, complete and low-speed streets, micromobility devices (i.e., electric bikes, electric scooters), programs, and services, microtransit circulators (i.e., golf carts, neighborhood electric vehicles, autonomous transit shuttles, trolleys), services and vehicles, new roads, the widening of existing roads, turn lanes, signals, and Americans with Disabilities Act (ADA) upgrades at intersections
- Are based on increases in person miles of capacity (PMC) from multimodal projects and the projected person travel demand (PTD) from new development
- May include all or portions of a municipality or county as assessment areas, and may vary based on geographic location (e.g., downtown) or type of development (e.g., mixed-use)
- Must be based on future multimodal projects adopted as part of a mobility plan and incorporated or referenced in the local government's Comprehensive Plan

The divergence between road impact fees and mobility fees will only increase with the multiple ways to move people. In most communities, the mode share for people walking, bicycling, and using transit is limited due to lack of safe, convenient, and interconnected multimodal facilities. Mobility plans in communities throughout the US are moving beyond sidewalks and bike lanes and looking at buffered and protected multimodal flex lanes, paths, and trails with high levels of landscape and streetscape amenities, transit services provided on dedicated lanes, and even reimagining and repurposing existing road right-of-ways to create low-speed play streets and shared streets. These multimodal projects are enabling cities and counties to lay the foundation for the use of new micromobility devices (i.e., electric pedal assist bikes (e-bikes), electric scooters (e-scooters)) and microtransit vehicles (i.e., autonomous transit shuttles and golf carts), while also expanding the use of car sharing and ride hailing services provided by transportation network companies (TNCs) such as Uber and Lyft (Figure 19.4).

The methodologies for quantifying road capacity and calculating road impact fees are fairly well accepted. The methodologies quantifying person capacity and calculating a mobility fee, or a multimodal fee, are relatively new in comparison. An often overlooked component of Dolan v. City of Tigard is the recognition that while multimodal facilities may offset traffic congestion, there is a need to demonstrate or quantify how the dedication of a pedestrian/bicycle pathway would offset the traffic demand generated, per the following excerpt from the opinion of the Court delivered by Chief Justice Rehnquist:

As Justice Peterson of the Supreme Court of Oregon explained in his dissenting opinion, however, "[t]he findings of fact that the bicycle pathway system could offset some of the traffic demand is a far cry from a finding that the bicycle pathway system will, or is likely to, offset some of the traffic demand."[4] No precise mathematical calculation is required, but the city must make some effort to quantify its findings in support of the dedication for the pedestrian/bicycle pathway beyond the conclusory statement that it could offset some of the traffic demand generated.[5]

The development of a mobility plan and mobility fee documents and quantifies the potential for multimodal projects to offset traffic demand, meet future PTD, and meet the dual rational nexus and rough proportionality test.

FIGURE 19.4 Comparative design features of different forms of mobility based on travel speed. (From Jonathan Paul, AICP.)

19.4 MOBILITY FEE CALCULATION STEPS

A key distinction between impact fees and mobility fees is that impact fees help improve travel conditions for motor vehicles, while mobility fees help improve travel conditions of people. Mobility fees are thus generally calculated based on the following steps (see also Figure 19.5):

Step 1: Land Use Evaluation

Beyond the development of a mobility plan that integrates land use, transportation, and parking, mobility fees are a means to implement a community's mobility plan, promote economic development, and advance land use goals such as reducing barriers to attainable housing and encouraging mixed use. Mobility fees are a means to move away from one-size-fits-all road impact fees by establishing assessment areas recognizing that new development within established urban areas or mixed-use neighborhoods makes efficient use of existing infrastructure, provides increased opportunities for people to bicycle and walk, and supports shorter overall trip lengths, compared with new suburban development that typically requires additional road capacity and complete streets. A land use evaluation reviews existing development patterns and zoning, future land use plans, and special area plans to develop a mobility fee schedule of uses that incorporates different assessment areas and takes into consideration community desires and goals related to attainable workforce housing and employment-generating uses that promote economic development.

Step 2: Data Collection

Roadway impact fees and mobility fees both require data collection related to demographics, existing traffic, and roadway infrastructure. Mobility fees also require the collection of data related to existing multi-modal facilities, mode share, person trips, person trip lengths (PTLs), person miles or travel, and vehicle occupancy. The National Household Travel Survey (NHTS), last updated in 2017, is one of the best resources for data related to both vehicle and person travel. Big data is also starting to be incorporated into mobility plans and mobility fees to evaluate origins and destinations, travel lengths, and season travel. As the cost of big data becomes more affordable and attainable, the ability to quantify real-time multimodal PTLs and travel demand will provide more accurate, localized, and recent data to be used in developing mobility fees. The Institute of Transportation Engineers (ITE) incorporated person trips and trips based on dense urban areas and proximity to rail in the 10th and the just recently released 11th edition of the ITE *Trip Generation Manual*. Shared mobility operators also collect a significant amount of data for ride, bike, and scooter share programs and services, with many local governments requiring micromobility providers to provide ridership data to the public. Transit agencies are also a key resource for information on transit frequency and ridership. Data collection is a significant component of developing a mobility fee, and it is important to plan accordingly for the increase in data needed for a mobility plan–based mobility fee versus a consumption-based roadway impact fee.

Step 3: Existing Conditions Evaluation

Case law and Florida Statute prohibit local governments from charging new development for overcapacity or "backlogged" roadways

DEVELOPING A
MOBILITY PLAN & MOBILITY FEE

© 2021 NUE Urban Concepts, LLC. All Rights Reserved.
www.nueurbanconcepts.com

1 LAND USE EVALUATION
Review existing development patterns, future Land Use Plans, Special Area Plans, & Zoning Districts

2 DATA COLLECTION
Existing traffic & travel characteristics, demographics, mode share, & multimodal infrastructure

3 EXISTING CONDITIONS EVALUATION
Identify existing system-level traffic backlog & deficiency

(Function: Demonstrates that new growth is not paying for existing backlog & deficiency)

4 FUTURE GROWTH EVALUATION
Calculate Projected Growth in population, employment, & Vehicle & Person Miles of Travel (VMT & PMT). Alternatives: Calculate VMT & PMT based on future land use for defined area or establish future mode share goals

(Function: The first component of the dual rational nexus test is to demonstrate need)

5 PREPARE MULTIMODAL PROJECT COST
Develop Planning Level Cost Estimates for Mobility Plan projects

6 ESTABLISH SERVICE STANDARDS
Develop Areawide Road Level of Service (LOS) & Multimodal Quality of Service (QOS) Standards for Mobility Plan projects

7 ESTABLISH MULTIMODAL CAPACITIES
Develop Multimodal Capacities for Mobility Plan projects based on LOS & QOS Standards

8 IDENTIFY AVAILABLE FUNDING
Existing and Projected Funding Sources

(Function: Ensures new development not paying twice for the same mobility projects by recognizing reasonable anticipated funding of mobility plan projects)

9 CONDUCT NEW GROWTH EVALUATION
Establish the share of Mobility Plan projects assignable & attributable to New Growth

(Function: Demonstrates new growth not responsible for more than its fair share of mobility plan projects)

10 CALCULATE PERSON MILES OF CAPACITY (PMC) OR TRAVEL RATE (PMT)
Based on Steps 3 to 8 develop a PMC or PMT Mobility Fee Rate attributable to New Growth

(Function: Demonstrates new growth is not being charged for existing deficiencies and is being assessed more than its fair share of the cost of mobility plan projects)

11 ESTABLISH ASSESSMENT AREAS
Defined Areas for Mobility Fee assessment & collection

Function: Reflects localized differences in existing infrastructure, the need for mobility plan projects, & PMT

12 ESTABLISH MOBILITY FEE SCHEDULE OF USES
Develop a Schedule of Uses based on Land Use evaluation & established Assessment Areas

13 CALCULATE PERSON TRAVEL DEMAND PER USE
Based on Trip Generation, % of new trips, Person Trip Conversion factors, Person Trip length, Assessment Areas, Limited Access Travel, & Origin & Destination adjustments

(Function: Used to demonstrate that the mobility fee is roughly proportional to the impact of new growth)

14 CALCULATE MOBILITY FEE PER USE
Establish a Mobility Fee per Specific Use & Assessment Area based on Steps 12, 14, & 15

(Function: Calculation of mobility fees to be paid by new development to fund assignable and attributable mobility plan projects)

15 ESTABLISH BENEFIT DISTRICTS
Define Benefit Districts for expenditure of Mobility Fee to fund Mobility Plan projects

(Function: The second component of the dual rational nexus test is to demonstrate benefit)

16 DEVELOP MOBILITY FEE TECHNICAL REPORT
Document Data Sources and Methodology

Function: Demonstrates that the data & methodology used to calculate the mobility fee is legally & statutorily compliant. Provides documentation used to develop or update mobility fee implementing ordinance)

FIGURE 19.5 Steps to develop a mobility fee. (From Jonathan Paul, AICP.)

based on adopted roadway LOS standards. An evaluation of the transportation system-wide capacity is conducted to ensure that new development is not being charged for existing deficiencies. The existing conditions evaluation (ECE) is achieved by dividing the existing transportation system vehicle miles of capacity (VMC) by the existing vehicle miles of travel as illustrated in Box 19.1.

BOX 19.1 EXISTING CONDITIONS EVALUATION FACTOR CALCULATION. (FROM JONATHAN PAUL, AICP.)

Existing Conditions Evaluation factor (ECEf)

$TVMC = \Sigma$ (LENac $\times$ CAPac) + Σ (LENla $\times$ CAPla)

$TVMT = \Sigma$ (LENac $\times$ AADTac) + Σ (LENla $\times$ AADTla)

$ECEf = (TVMC / TVMT)$

Where

LENac = Length of Arterial and Collector Roads

CAPac = Capacity of Arterial and Collector Roads

LENla = Length of Limited Access facilities

CAPla = Capacity of Limited Access facilities

ECEf = Exisiting Conditions Evaluation factor

TVMC = Total Vehicle Miles of Capacity

TVMT = Total Vehicle Miles of Capacity

Source: NUE Urban Concepts, LLC

A VMC/VMT greater than 1.00 indicates that there is currently adequate system capacity to accommodate existing daily traffic. A VMC/VMT lower than 1.00 indicates that there are system deficiencies for which new development should not be assessed. Table 19.1 is

an example of an ECE for Sarasota County using daily traffic for 2022 (mobility fee base year). The evaluation resulted in a VMC/VMT ratio for collector and arterial roads of 1.67 and a system-wide VMC/VMT ratio of 1.36. The evaluation indicated that Interstate 75 was over capacity, with a VMC/VMT ratio of 0.74 (Table 19.1). However, limited access facility improvements and travel on limited access facilities, such as Interstate 75, are excluded from mobility fee calculations, since they are primarily funded through federal and state fuel tax revenues and priority funding through Florida's Strategic Intermodal System (SIS). The major road system within the county provides adequate VMC to accommodate the projected VMT in 2022. Thus, there is no system-wide backlog for which new development would be assessed. For the purposes of calculation of the mobility fee rate, the existing conditions evaluation factor (ECEf) would be set to 1.00. A factor below 1.00 would result in a reduction in the cost of the mobility plan attributable to new development, resulting in a lower mobility fee rate.

The intent of a mobility plan and a mobility fee is to provide a distinct alternative to transportation mitigation through only adding road capacity. One way to make a clean break from transportation concurrency and overcapacity or "backlogged" roads is to replace roadway LOS standards with street quality of service (QOS) standards based on the posted speed limit (Figure 19.6). Florida Statute requires the transportation element of all local government comprehensive plans to contain measurable standards for its transportation system. To move beyond road LOS and still be consistent with State Statute, the City of St. Augustine was the first local government in Florida to eliminate road LOS and replace it with street QOS standards to move toward safer streets for all users of the transportation system.

TABLE 19.1 Existing Conditions Evaluation (ECE)

	Vehicle Miles of Capacity (VMC)	Vehicle Miles of Travel (VMT)	VMC/VMT Ratio
Arterial and Collector Roads	10,539,691	6,316,995	1.67
Interstate 75	2,362,515	3,174,051	0.74
System-Wide Network	12,902,206	9,491,046	1.36

Source: The existing conditions evaluation is based on collected traffic characteristics data for the major transportation network. The VMC and VMT evaluation was prepared by NUE Urban Concepts as of October 2021. The AADT used to calculate VMT was grown to 2022 conditions based on the annual growth rates from the regional travel demand model.

FIGURE 19.6 City of St. Augustine street quality of service standards (QOS). (From Jonathan Paul, AICP.)

An existing conditions QOS evaluation for arterials and collectors within and adjacent to the City of St. Augustine was conducted based on the street QOS standards (Table 19.2). The ECE is intended to establish a baseline QOS analysis and will serve as a performance measure that will allow the city to quantify the change in QOS between mobility plan updates. The existing conditions street QOS evaluation replaces the "backlog" evaluation based on roadway LOS that would typically be conducted as part of a mobility fee analysis. The net result is that there are no system-wide deficiencies, as roadway LOS is no longer calculated, and the mobility plan emphasizes capacity for people, not motor vehicles.

Step 4: Future Person Travel Demand

The first component of the dual rational nexus test requires the demonstration of need. The demonstration of need is based on projected growth in population, employment, VMT, and PMT. Historically, road impact fee studies have referenced growth in population, and sometimes include employment, as the basis to

TABLE 19.2 Existing Street Quality of Service (QOS) Evaluation

Location	QOS A	QOS B	QOS C	QOS D	QOS E
Miles	0	3.74	6.36	2.03	14.59
Percentage of the Network	0%	14%	23.8%	7.6%	54.6%

Source: Street Quality of Service based on existing posted speed limits and total miles of arterial and collector streets within and adjacent to the City St. Augustine past on data collected by NUE Urban Concepts as of June 2021.

demonstrate the need for road capacity. This methodology has sufficed for most moderately to fast-growing communities over the last 40 years, assuming the community's transportation plans or capital improvement programs included improvements to add road capacity. However, the assumption that growth in population equals the need for road capacity is no longer a viable assumption in communities where there are no longer plans to add road capacity. There are numerous communities in Florida with no road capacity projects identified in either a long-range transportation plan or a capital improvements program. Thus, if there is not a need to add road capacity, there is no way to demonstrate how a road impact fee would meet the dual rational nexus test. The lack of need, or desire in some communities, to add road capacity is one of the principal reasons why many local governments are migrating toward mobility fees.

The majority of mobility fees utilize data from the extensive regional travel demand models developed by the Florida Department of Transportation (FDOT) and use elements in their respective comprehensive plans localized to each local government. The following is an example of projected growth in population and employment for the City of St. Augustine and St. Johns County based on traffic analysis zones (TAZs) from the Northeast Regional Planning Model (NERPM). The intent of the analysis is to demonstrate that by 2040 the projected growth in population and employment within and around the city will result in increased PTD (Table 19.3).

The growth in population and employment demonstrates an increase in PTF. The evaluation of the growth in vehicle and PMT is intended to demonstrate that the growth in PTD will result in an increase in PMT and the "need" for person capacity to accommodate that travel demand. There are several ways to project future VMT. Existing traffic counts can be projected to the horizon year of the mobility plan based on historic growth in traffic rates. Those projected counts would then be multiplied by the length of the roadway on which the counts are based to project future VMT. Another way to project growth would be to use future land use plans or development approvals for a specific area and then calculate trip generation (TG) for all development in that area. Trip length would be based on using either the radius of the area evaluated or the radius of the area where impact is to be mitigated or obtaining trip length data from sources such as the NHTS. The radius, versus diameter, of the area would represent average trip lengths. The area-wide TG would then be multiplied by trip length to obtain projected VMT. Under this option, some reduction should be applied based on either internal capture or community capture to reflect the interaction of travel within the area. The third and most common option is to use a regional travel demand model to calculate future VMT.

With each of these options, data from the 2017 NHTS can be used to convert vehicle trips to person trips and VMT to PMT for use in mobility fee calculations. The use of regional travel demand models will be further detailed later.

TABLE 19.3 Projected Growth

Year	City of St. Augustine		St. Johns County	
	Population	Employment	Population	Employment
2018/2020	15,306	19,366	261,900	78,139
2040	28,678	29,062	387,771	155,412
Increase	13,372	9,696	125,871	77,273

Source: 2020 Population data based on Florida Estimates of Population, 2020 prepared by Bureau of Economic and Business Research (BEBR), College of Liberal Arts & Science, University of Florida, Gainesville, FL. The 2018 Employment Data provided by the US Census Bureau OnTheMap. 2040 Population and Employment based on the Northeast Regional Planning Model (NERPM) developed by the North Florida Transportation Planning Organization (TPO) 2040 Long-Range Transportation Plan (LRTP). The City of St. Augustine projections for 2040 may vary from other projections, since the TAZ data includes areas adjacent to and within the City.

One unique option, which requires significant mobility planning, is to base future need on mode share goals. The mobility fee developed for the City of Miami Beach is the only one in Florida based on the mode share goals established in its transportation mobility plan. Ultimately, this would be an ideal scenario to develop mobility plans and calculate mobility fees based on mode share goals, PTLs by mode of travel, and PMT by trip purpose. However, few communities in the US feature both the existing levels of walking, bicycling, and riding transit in Miami Beach and the physical geographic limitations that preclude adding road capacity. The Miami Beach mobility fee was data intensive and benefited at the time from the 2009 NHTS, which included an extensive add-on survey for the State of Florida at the census block level that provided numerous surveys for person trips and PTLs by mode and trip purpose. The 2017 NHTS has similar data, and several states funded add-on surveys at the census block level, but the State of Florida did not, resulting in fewer localized surveys. It was an intensive effort, and an entire chapter could be devoted to just illustrating all the steps and the data needed to develop a mobility plan and mobility fee based on mode share goals.

The projected growth in VMT is used both to develop the mobility plan and to calculate mobility fees. The following is an example from the City of Port St. Lucie, which utilized the Treasure Coast Regional Planning Model (TCRPM) to determine the VMT growth within and around the city between 2020 and 2045 (Table 19.4).

Due to differences in development patterns and future growth, the analyses evaluated the regional model network for the following areas: (1) east of the St. Lucie River; (2) between the St. Lucie River and Interstate 95; and (3) west of Interstate 95 (Table 19.5). The growth in travel on the Florida Turnpike and Interstate 95 was excluded from the mobility fee calculations due to the fact that they are limited access facilities.

The evaluation of future PMT is an integral component in the development of a mobility plan and mobility fee. To calculate PMT and to account for person trips made by walking, biking, riding transit, and vehicle occupancy in a multimodal travel environment, VMT demand is converted into PMT demand based on data obtained from the 2017 NHTS. The increase in PMT calculation used for the City of Port St. Lucie went one step further and calculated the PMT increase for two assessment

TABLE 19.4 Growth in Vehicle Miles of Travel (VMT)

Year	Arterial and Collector Roads	Florida Turnpike and Interstate 95	Total
2015 (Model base year)	2,916,635	1,472,535	4,389,169
2020 (Mobility Plan base year)	3,199,390	1,605,044	4,804,435
2045 (Model and plan future year)	5,220,444	2,469,417	7,689,861
VMT increase (2020 to 2045)	2,021,054	864,372	2,885,427

Source: Projected growth in VMT prepared by NUE Urban Concepts, LLC. The 2015 base year and 2045 future year VMT were extracted using the Treasure Coast Regional Planning Model (TCRPM) Version 5 (May 2021). The model files were obtained from the St. Lucie County TPO. The 2020 mobility plan base year VMT was interpolated based on an annual growth rate of travel on arterial and collector roads of 1.30% east of the river, 1.83% between the river and I-95, 4.37% west of I-95, and 1.74% for the Florida Turnpike and Interstate 95 (Table 19.5). The VMT increase is based on the difference between 2020 and 2045. The model network includes unincorporated enclave areas within the city and portions of the regional road network that extend outside of the incorporated limits of the city.

TABLE 19.5 Growth in Vehicle Miles of Travel (VMT) by Area

Area (Location)	2015	2020	2045	Increase	% Growth
East of St. Lucie River	969,221	1,034,069	1,429,497	395,428	1.3%
Between St. Lucie River and I-95	1,713,910	1,876,185	2,949,264	1,073,079	1.83%
West of I-95	233,503	289,136	841,683	552,547	4.37%
Turnpike and I-95	1,472,535	1,605,044	2,469,417	864,372	1.74%
Total	4,389,169	4,804,435	7,689,861	2,885,427	1.89%

Source: See Table 19.4 as the source information is the same.

areas: (1) east of the St. Lucie River (more urbanized) and (3) west of the St. Lucie River (Box 19.2). The two assessment areas localized mobility fees by accounting for differences in person travel, need for mobility plan projects, mixture of land uses, and future growth rates, resulting in different mobility fees for each assessment area (i.e., lower fees east of the St. Lucie River).

BOX 19.2 CALCULATION FOR PERSON MILES OF TRAVEL (PMT) INCREASE. (FROM JONATHAN PAUL, AICP.)

Increase in Person Miles of Travel (PMTi)

$PMTfe = 1 + (\Sigma PMT10 - \Sigma VMT10) / \Sigma VMT10$

$PMTfw = 1 + (\Sigma PMT15 - \Sigma VMT15) / \Sigma VMT15$

2020 $PMTe = (2020\ VMTe \times PMTfe)$

2020 $PMTw = (2020\ VMTw \times PMTfw)$

2020 $PMT = (2020\ PMTe + 2020\ PMTw)$

2045 $PMTe = (2045\ VMTe \times PMTfe)$

2045 $PMTw = (2045\ VMTw \times PMTfw)$

2045 $PMT = (2045\ PMTe + 2045\ PMTw)$

$PMTi = (2045\ PMT - 2020\ PMT)$

Where

PMT = Person Miles of Travel

VMT = Vehicle Miles of Travel

PMT10 = PMT based on 2017 NHTS for trips 10 miles or less in length

VMT10 = VMT based on 2017 NHTS for trips 10 miles or less in length

PMT15 = PMT based on 2017 NHTS for trips 15 miles or less in length

VMT15 = PMT based on 2017 NHTS for trips 15 miles or less in length e = East of St Lucie River (EOR) Assessment Area

w = West of St Lucie River (WOR) Assessment Area

PMTfe = Person Miles of Travel factor of 1.87 (EOR)

PMTfw = Person Miles of Travel factor of 1.83 (WOR)

PMTi =Person Miles of Travel increase

Source: NUE Urban Concepts, LLC

The data from the NHTS provides vehicle and person trip characteristics by region of the country, by state, by core based statistical areas (CBSAs), by size of metropolitan statistical area, and for urban, suburban, and rural areas. Vehicle and person trips, trip length, and miles of travel by trip purpose can be obtained from the NHTS. The survey data is not provided in readily useable formats that can easily be queried. The data is provided per survey. It took over 120 hours to develop a robust database for Florida that can be used for multiple communities based on trip length, area type, size of metropolitan statistical area, and whether the data was collected within one of the five CBSAs within Florida.

The calculated PMT increase was used to demonstrate the increase of 3,714,346 PMT

between 2020 and 2045 within and around the city (Table 19.6). This increase in PMT was used to identify mobility plan projects "needed" to serve the increase in demand from new growth. The PMT increase can be used in calculations to ensure that new growth is not paying more than its share of the cost of multimodal projects identified in a mobility plan. The PMT increase can also be used to calculate a mobility fee rate per person mile of travel.

Step 5: Prepare Multimodal Project Cost

Some local governments have adopted multimodal impact fees, while others have stated that multimodal improvements can be funded with roadway impact fees. Local governments that have used impact fees for multimodal improvements have typically done so if the multimodal improvements are done in conjunction with adding road capacity and not as stand-alone projects. Increasingly, there are local governments charging road impact fees based on the construction cost and capacity of roads and stating that they can be used to fund stand-alone multimodal improvements because they are offsetting traffic impact.

To date, this approach has not yet been legally challenged, as most local governments

TABLE 19.6 Increase in Person Miles of Travel (PMT)

2020 Vehicle Miles of Travel (VMTe)	1,034,069
2020 Person Miles of Travel (PMTe)	1,933,710
2020 Vehicle Miles of Travel (VMTw)	2,165,321
2020 Person Miles of Travel (PMTw)	3,962,537
2020 Person Miles of Travel (1,933,710 + 3,962,537) = 5,896,247	
2045 Future Year Vehicle Miles of Travel (VMTe)	1,429,497
2045 Future Year Person Miles of Travel (PMTe)	2,673,160
2045 Future Year Vehicle Miles of Travel (VMTw)	3,790,947
2045 Future Year Person Miles of Travel (PMTw)	6,937,433
2045 Person Miles of Travel (2,673,160 + 6,937,433) = 9,610,593	
Increase in Person Miles of Travel (PMTi) between 2020 and 2045	
Increase in Person Miles of Travel (9,610,593 – 5,896,247) = 3,714,346	

Source: Base and future year VMT data from Table 19.5. PMT for EOR are obtained by multiplying VMT by 1.87. PMT for WOR are obtained by multiplying VMT by 1.83. The calculation for the increase in person miles of travel is illustrated in Figure 19.8.

are still somewhat cautious about funding multimodal improvements with road impact fees, especially stand-alone projects. One of the reasons why this approach has not yet been challenged is that until recently, the costs to construct roadways have only included additional cost for paved shoulders or a 4- or 5-foot wide sidewalk on one side of the road. However, as the cost of multimodal improvements increases, and as local governments look at more significant multimodal improvements such as protected bike lanes or separated trails with enhanced landscaping buffers along adjacent roads, it will become more difficult to just include these types of multimodal improvements as part of the overall cost of a road capacity project and not recognize the capacity benefit of multimodal improvements.

For example, a local government had a comprehensive plan policy that required the addition of 5-foot wide bike lanes when a rural arterial or collector road was to be resurfaced. The existing roads often featured 10-foot wide lanes, and the local government found itself spending roughly $1 million a mile to resurface the road and another $1 million a mile to add the bike lanes, not including any additional cost for stormwater facilities or relocation of utilities. After a few projects were completed, the policy was revisited due to the backlog of roads that needed to be resurfaced, the cost associated with providing bike lanes, and the need for bicycle lanes in more urbanized areas.

The overall cost of multimodal facilities is comprising a larger overall percentage of the cost to construct new roads and to widen existing roads as complete street design requirements continue to evolve. The per mile construction cost of a new two-lane urban cross-section road ranges from $4 million to $6.5 million, depending on location and the type of complete street design, based on several completed projects in communities across Florida. Of that cost, roughly $150,000 to $250,000 is to provide

a 5-foot wide 6-inch thick concrete sidewalk, $275,000 to $350,000 is to provide a 12-foot wide multi-use trail, and $750,000 to $1,000,000 to provide 5-foot wide on-street bicycle lanes with green pavement markings approaching intersections. Depending on the local government, design requirements for roads with signal spacing of 1 mile or more are looking at adding protected mid-block crossings with rectangular rapid reflecting beacons (RRFBs) at the cost of $135,000 to $175,000 each. These mid-block crossings are frequently located around schools, parks, retail centers, community destinations, and at transit stops. For roads with transit service, ADA-compliant transit stops with free-standing covered stops and basic amenities such as benches and trash receptacles are between $15,000 and $20,000 each. Assuming the minimum value, $1,405,000 is the construction cost to add these multimodal improvements, plus one mid-block crossing and a transit stop on either side of the road.

Roadways and multimodal facilities must be designed, right-of-way must be acquired, stormwater management facilities provided, utilities relocated, improvements inspected, and landscape and streetscape incorporated into the overall project cost. These additional costs can add anywhere from 20% to 200% of overall cost based on location, complete street design requirements, and adopted QOS standards. These costs do not even account for Project Development & Environment (PD&E) studies, which are equaling 50% to 100% of total construction cost on federal and state projects. For a new two-lane road, the cost of multimodal improvements could be anywhere from 20% to 50% of the overall cost of the roadway, depending on the types of multimodal improvements.

The following is an example of planning-level cost estimates provided for the City of Palm Beach Gardens mobility plan and mobility fee (Table 19.7). The cost estimates for multimodal improvements are provided as stand-alone projects. The new two-lane

TABLE 19.7 Multimodal Improvement Cost

Facility Type	Construction Cost	Additional Cost	Total Cost
Sidewalk (5′)	$153,869	$200,029	$353,898
Multimodal Path (8′)	$190,351	$247,457	$437,808
Multimodal Path (10′)	$237,938	$309,320	$547,258
Multimodal Trail (12′)	$285,526	$371,184	$656,710
15 MPH Flex Lane (7′)	$591,152	$118,230	$709,382
Bicycle Boulevard	$75,000	$15,000	$90,000
Bicycle Lane (4′)	$313,680	$62,736	$376,416
Bicycle Lane (5′)	$391,600	$78,320	$469,920
Green Bicycle Lane (6′)	$539,440	$107,888	$647,328
Protected Bicycle Lanes (10′)	$1,000,000	$200,000	$1,200,000
High-Visibility Mid-Block Crossing	$158,271	$66,636	$224,907
Mobility Hub	$225,000	$292,500	$517,500
Two-Lane Road	$4,981,800	$5,479,980	$10,461,780
Widen Two-Lane to Four-Lane Road	$5,456,415	$6,002,057	$11,458,472

Source: All costs, except for high-visibility mid-block crossings and mobility hubs, are shown on a per mile basis. Construction cost based on city and FDOT cost estimates. Sidewalks, paths, trails, and mobility hubs include the cost for design and engineering (PE), construction, engineering, and inspection (CEI), utility relocation (UR), and stormwater management facilities (SMF), and high-visibility driveway and intersection crosswalk markings (CW) were each estimated at 10% of construction cost; combined, these cost factors were equivalent to 50% of construction cost. Due to the higher land values in Palm Beach Gardens, right-of-way and easement acquisition was estimated at 40% of construction cost for sidewalks, paths, trails, and mobility hubs. To achieve the QOS standards in the mobility plan for sidewalks, paths, trails, and mobility hubs, a high level of street trees and landscape (LS) is required to provide shade and buffers from motor vehicles and is estimated at 20% of construction cost based upon the local cost of street trees, landscape, and installation. To achieve the QOS standards in the mobility plan for sidewalks, paths, trails, and mobility hubs, a high level of streetscape (SS) is required and includes person-scale lighting, benches, waste receptacles, hardscape, and architectural features to create a comfortable experience at an estimated 20% of construction cost based upon the cost of these items from local suppliers. The total additional cost for sidewalks, paths, trails, and mobility hubs equaled 130% of construction cost. The construction cost for high-visibility mid-block crossings includes rectangular rapid flashing beacons (RRFB). Additional cost for high-visibility mid-block crossings includes PE, CEI, UR, SMF, and CW at 42% of construction cost based on city expenditures. Additional cost for bicycle facilities equals PE and CEI, each at 10% of construction cost. Roads include the cost of PE, CEI, UR, SMF, and CW at 10% each; combined, these cost factors were equivalent to 50% of construction cost. The cost of roads includes right-of-way (ROW) at 40% and LS at 20%; combined, these cost factors were equivalent to 60% of construction cost. The total additional cost for roads equaled 110% of construction cost.

road and the widening of a road from two to four lanes includes the cost of 5-foot wide bike lanes and sidewalks on both sides of the roadway. Construction cost and additional cost vary between jurisdictions, counties, and states. When developing a roadway impact fee or mobility fee, construction cost and additional cost should be, to the maximum extent feasible, based on localized cost of constriction and the additional factors.

Step 6: Establish Service Standards

Roadway LOS standards are adopted by local governments across the US and serve as the basis for establishing maximum service volumes (road capacity), planning for road improvements to meet adopted standards, and the review of the transportation impact of new development. The LOS for roadways is typically measured on an individual segment or facility basis. Mobility fees utilize an area-wide or system-wide approach detailed in the ECE (Step 3) to measure roadway LOS that recognizes the ability of a network of roads to accommodate motor vehicle travel. The area-wide approach to roadway LOS emphasizes the vehicle capacity provided by multiple roadways, this allowing for planning and prioritizing road capacity projects on a parallel road where the addition of vehicle capacity may not be possible for a given roadway due to physical constraints or environmental or neighborhood impact. Further, area-wide LOS provides local governments the opportunity to evaluate and prioritize planning for all modes of travel, whether choosing to bicycle, walk, ride transit, use new technology, or drive, as opposed to focusing on adding capacity for a given segment of roadway that may not meet the adopted roadway LOS standard.

The establishment of street QOS standards based on the posted speed limit is both an alternative and a complement to area-wide roadway LOS standards (see Figure 19.6). While area-wide roadway LOS standards are based on road capacity to move cars, street QOS standards are intended to enhance mobility and safety for all users of the transportation system by prioritizing slower speeds for cars. Speed of travel is one of the most important factors in determining the design of a street. Street QOS standards are the inverse of roadway LOS standards in that as speed limits go down, the QOS for streets goes up, whereas as speed limits go down, the LOS of roadways also goes down. Street QOS standards that promote slower speeds provide planners and engineers with greater flexibility to implement innovative street designs, such as low-speed and complete streets, narrower travel lanes, and locating buildings and trees closer to travel lanes.

The establishment of multimodal QOS standards for people walking, bicycling, riding transit, and using new mobility technology is one of the significant differences between roadway impact fees and mobility fees. Multimodal QOS standards are used to establish multimodal capacities for use in the mobility fee calculations and can also be used for establishing performance measures, planning for multimodal improvements, complete street design standards, and prioritizing multimodal projects. Multimodal QOS standards are based on: (1) the width of the facility (i.e., bike lane, path, sidewalk); (2) the type of physical separation between multimodal facilities and travel lanes for cars, SUVs, trucks, and other motor vehicles; and (3) posted speed limits. Multimodal QOS standards for people bicycling and walking are focused on accommodating non-motorized travel demand on greenways, shared-use paths, sidewalks, and multi-use trails (Figure 19.7). The multimodal QOS standards for people bicycling and riding micromobility devices (e.g., e-bikes, e-scooters) are focused on accommodating pedal-powered and multimodal motorized travel demand on bike lanes, multimodal lanes, and multimodal ways (Figure 19.8).

The multimodal QOS standards for transit are based upon frequency of service and type of transit service provided. The multimodal transit QOS standards are only for corridors with existing or future transit service. Generally, the transit QOS for rail and buses is established by rail authorities, and buses are generally operated at a county or regional level. Municipalities have greater ability to establish microtransit and trolley circulators and establish corresponding QOS standards (Figure 19.9).

Step 7: Establish Multimodal Capacities

The establishment of multimodal person capacities enables the calculation of a mobility fee and allows for a shift away from predominately focusing on motor vehicle mobility toward focusing on the movement of people. To demonstrate that the multimodal projects identified in a mobility plan provide the person capacity needed to accommodate future

MOVING TOWARDS VISION ZERO

MULTIMODAL QUALITY OF SERVICE STANDARDS

CITY OF BOYNTON BEACH

MULTIMODAL QUALITY OF SERVICE (QOS) STANDARDS FOR BICYCLING AND WALKING

	TYPES OF SEPARATION FROM TRAVEL LANES				
FACILITY TYPE	LIMITED SEPARATION	STREET TREES	ON-STREET PARKING	LANDSCAPE BUFFER	SPEED LIMIT 25 MPH OR <
TRAIL 12' +	B	A	A	A	A
PATH 10'	C	B	B	B	B
PATH 8'	D	C	C	C	C
SIDEWALK 7' OR LESS	E	D	D	D	D

SOURCE: QOS STANDARDS ESTABLISHED BY NUE URBAN CONCEPTS, LLC
NOTES: THE PRESENCE OF TWO OR MORE PHYSICAL SEPARATION FEATURES, SUCH AS ON-STREET PARKING AND STREET TREES WOULD RESULT IN AN INCREASE IN ONE ADDITIONAL LETTER GRADE. FOR EXAMPLE, A TEN (10) FOOT WIDE PATH WITH STREET TREES AND ON-STREET PARKING WOULD ACHIEVE A QUALITY OF SERVICE OF "A", A FIVE (5) FOOT WIDE SIDEWALK WITH STREET TREES AND A LANDSCAPE BUFFER WOULD ACHIEVE A QUALITY OF SERVICE OF "C"

NUE URBAN CONCEPTS
LAND USE • MOBILITY • PARKING • FEES
REPUBLIC DESIGN
© 2021 NUE Urban Concepts, LLC All Rights Reserved
www.nueurbanconcepts.com

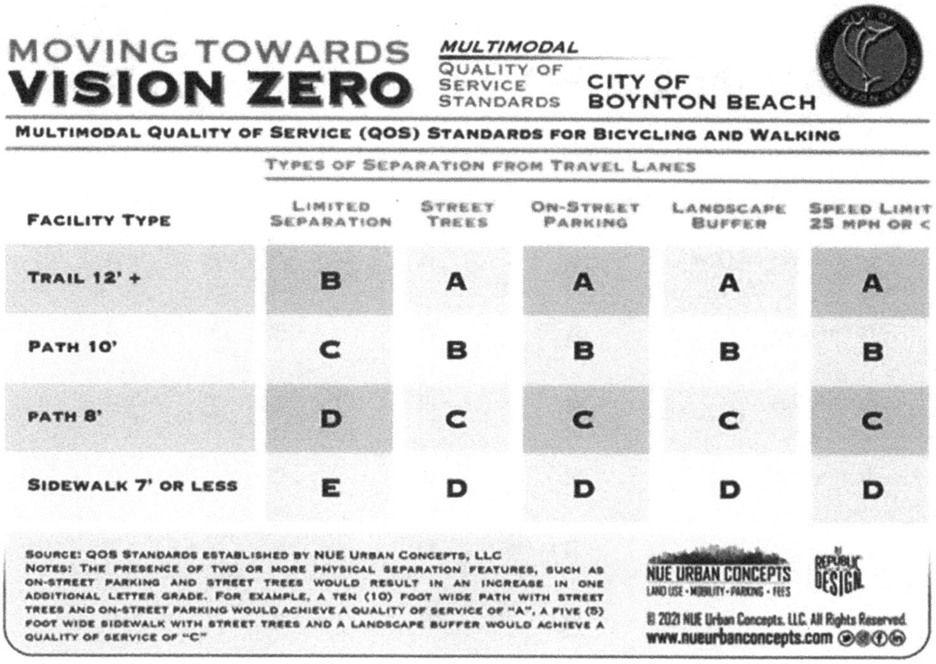

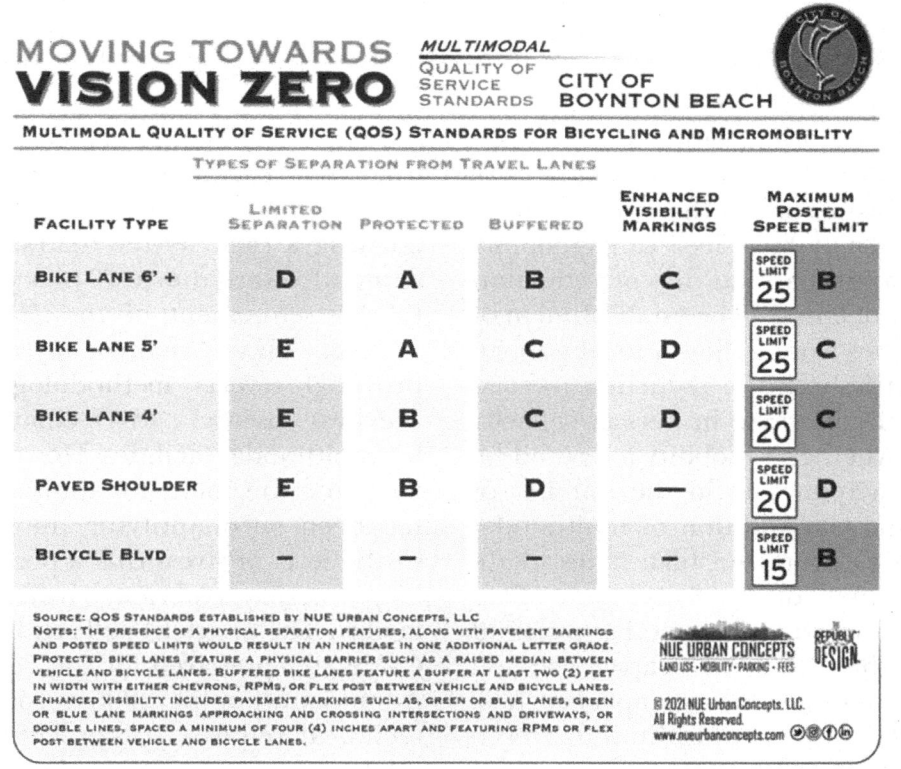

FIGURE 19.7 Multimodal QOS standards for bicycling and walking. (From Jonathan Paul, AICP.)

MOVING TOWARDS VISION ZERO

MULTIMODAL QUALITY OF SERVICE STANDARDS

CITY OF BOYNTON BEACH

MULTIMODAL QUALITY OF SERVICE (QOS) STANDARDS FOR BICYCLING AND MICROMOBILITY

	TYPES OF SEPARATION FROM TRAVEL LANES				
FACILITY TYPE	LIMITED SEPARATION	PROTECTED	BUFFERED	ENHANCED VISIBILITY MARKINGS	MAXIMUM POSTED SPEED LIMIT
BIKE LANE 6' +	D	A	B	C	SPEED LIMIT 25 B
BIKE LANE 5'	E	A	C	D	SPEED LIMIT 25 C
BIKE LANE 4'	E	B	C	D	SPEED LIMIT 20 C
PAVED SHOULDER	E	B	D	—	SPEED LIMIT 20 D
BICYCLE BLVD	–	–	–	–	SPEED LIMIT 15 B

SOURCE: QOS STANDARDS ESTABLISHED BY NUE URBAN CONCEPTS, LLC
NOTES: THE PRESENCE OF A PHYSICAL SEPARATION FEATURES, ALONG WITH PAVEMENT MARKINGS AND POSTED SPEED LIMITS WOULD RESULT IN AN INCREASE IN ONE ADDITIONAL LETTER GRADE. PROTECTED BIKE LANES FEATURE A PHYSICAL BARRIER SUCH AS A RAISED MEDIAN BETWEEN VEHICLE AND BICYCLE LANES. BUFFERED BIKE LANES FEATURE A BUFFER AT LEAST TWO (2) FEET IN WIDTH WITH EITHER CHEVRONS, RPMS, OR FLEX POST BETWEEN VEHICLE AND BICYCLE LANES. ENHANCED VISIBILITY INCLUDES PAVEMENT MARKINGS SUCH AS, GREEN OR BLUE LANES, GREEN OR BLUE LANE MARKINGS APPROACHING AND CROSSING INTERSECTIONS AND DRIVEWAYS, OR DOUBLE LINES, SPACED A MINIMUM OF FOUR (4) INCHES APART AND FEATURING RPMS OR FLEX POST BETWEEN VEHICLE AND BICYCLE LANES.

NUE URBAN CONCEPTS
LAND USE • MOBILITY • PARKING • FEES
REPUBLIC DESIGN
© 2021 NUE Urban Concepts, LLC. All Rights Reserved.
www.nueurbanconcepts.com

FIGURE 19.8 Multimodal QOS standards for bicycling and micromobility. (From Jonathan Paul, AICP.)

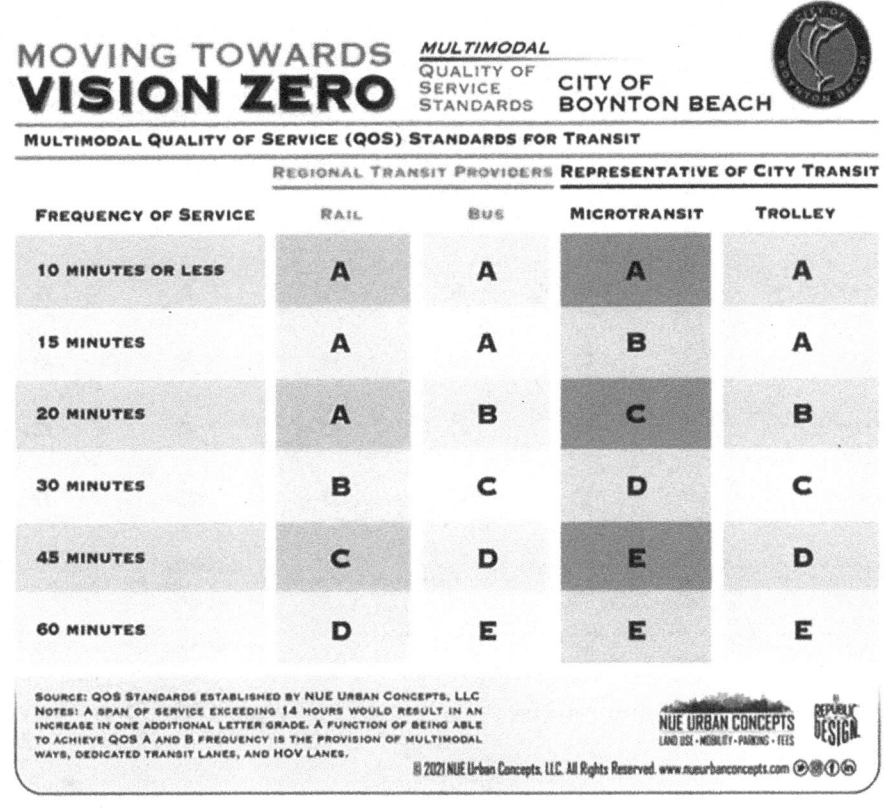

FIGURE 19.9 Multimodal QOS standards for transit. (From Jonathan Paul, AICP.)

PTD requires the establishment of capacities for all modes of travel. This is especially important to answer one of the most common questions about a mobility fee: "can a mobility fee be used to fund a road diet or reduction in the number of lanes?" The establishment of person capacities would allow a local government to quantify both the reduction in road capacity and the increase in person capacity to determine whether a mobility fee could be used to fund a reduction in the number of travel lanes and the addition of multimodal facilities such as protected bike lanes, dedicated transit lanes, or the conversion of an existing street to a shared street. Figure 19.10 demonstrates that the person capacity added exceeds the reduction in road capacity; thus, mobility fees could be used to fund the reimagination of streets to serve multiple modes of travel and the repurposing of existing right-of-way to add multimodal improvements.

Under a mobility fee system, a person capacity is calculated for both roadways and multimodal facilities. The process for calculating a capacity for roadways is relatively straightforward due to 70 plus years dedicated to the refinement of the *Highway Capacity Manual*. The *Highway Capacity Manual* has provided several methodologies, based on previous research, to calculate the capacity for multimodal facilities. However, for the last 20 years, the focus for multimodal facilities has been on quantifying the QOS provided or the level of stress that a person walking or bicycling may experience using a multimodal facility. The Shared-Use Path Level of Service Calculator prepared for the Federal Highway Administration in 2006 is one of the few technical reports that provide useful methodologies for quantifying the capacity of multimodal facilities. The *Transit and Quality of Service Manual* provides several methodologies

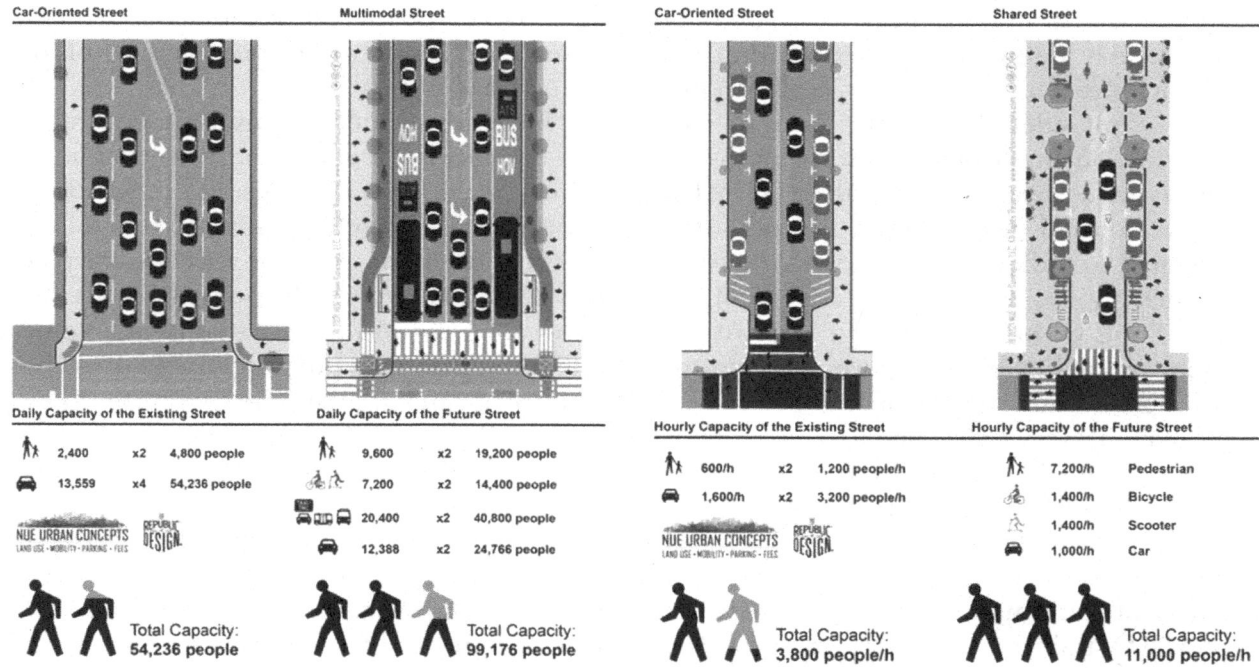

FIGURE 19.10 Reimagining streets and repurposing right-of-way. (From Jonathan Paul, AICP.)

to calculate the capacity of a transit vehicle based on factors such as frequency of service, transit vehicle capacity, and hours of operation (also known as span of service).

NACTO has prepared a frequently referenced multimodal capacity graphic that illustrates hourly multimodal capacities of over 9,000 people walking for sidewalks, 7,500 people bicycling on a bi-directional two-way protected bicycle lane, and 10,000 to 25,000 people riding transit on a dedicated lane or fixed guideway. This graphic illustrates the capacity for roads ranging from 600 to 1,600 vehicles per hour and from 1,000 to 2,800 people per hour with buses in mixed traffic. Those with a background in calculating road capacity will know that the capacity for roads is based on interrupted flow facilities (i.e., traffic signals with g/C ratios between 0.35 and 0.45), whereas the capacities for multimodal facilities are based on uninterrupted flow facilities (i.e., no delay due to traffic signals or transit stops). The multimodal capacities are also based on optimal conditions and volumes that would likely only be achieved in Manhattan and maybe downtown Boston, Chicago, or San Francisco for walking and transit. The capacity for bicycles occurs in places like Amsterdam and Copenhagen.

The calculation of person capacity for multimodal facilities is both an art and a science. The methodology for calculating the maximum capacity for a sidewalk and bicycle lane can be quantified. The maximum number of people walking or bicycling across a specific point over a 1-hour period is a simplified capacity calculation. Using the NACTO example of 9,000 people an hour using a sidewalk breaks down to 2.5 people per second walking across a single point (2.5 × 60 seconds = 150; 150 × 60 minutes = 9,000). Similarly, the 7,500 people an hour bicycling on a two-way protected bicycle lane breaks down to roughly 1.04 people per second bicycling across a single point (1.0417 × 60 seconds = 62.5; 62.5 × 60 minutes = 3,750; 3,750 × 2 = 7,500). Sidewalks in Times Square in Manhattan may achieve that kind of volume for people walking, and protected bicycle lanes in Copenhagen may achieve that kind of volume for people bicycling.

In the US, if a community achieves 1,800 people a day walking or bicycling, that is a major achievement. This is due in part to providing 5-foot sidewalks on the back of curb and 4-foot on-street bike lanes on multi-lane arterials with speeds greater than 45 MPH, not the optimal environment for encouraging people to walk or bicycle unless they have no other choice. To achieve 1,800 people a day walking or bicycling would require one person walking or bicycling every 20 seconds during peak hours (three people per minute [one person every 20 seconds]) × 60 minutes = 180 people; divide 180 by a peak-to-daily ratio of 1.0 [10% of travel during peak hours] = 1,800 people a day).

The difference between the maximum capacity of multimodal facilities represented by NACTO and what occurs in most communities is due to the inverse relationship that exists between the LOS and the QOS for people walking, bicycling, and scooting. An LOS of "A" typically denotes that few people are using a sidewalk or bike lane, and there is ample room for people to freely walk or bicycle. An LOS of "D" typically denotes more people using a sidewalk or bike lane and indicates that movements are more restricted, as when a road becomes more congested. A QOS of "D" typically denotes an environment where there is minimal separation between people walking and bicycling and cars being driven, and denotes that there is a lack of landscape, shade, streetscape, or protections from adjacent traffic. In environments that feature a QOS of "A", there are wider sidewalks or trails, with street trees and/or on-street parking and a landscape buffer, separating people walking and bicycling from cars. For people bicycling on-street, the presence of a protected barrier, a painted buffer, or a green pavement lane marking results in a higher QOS. In most communities, facilities for people walking, bicycling, and scooting feature a LOS of "A" and a QOS of "D" or "E," meaning that few, if any, people use facilities to walk or bicycle. Table 19.8 is an example from West

Palm Beach of the varying person capacities based on QOS standards and the type of multimodal facility.

The establishment of multimodal capacities for moving people requires that motor vehicle occupancy be considered, which is a departure from roadway impact fees focused on the movement of motor vehicles. Based on the 2017 NHTS, vehicle occupancy averages between 1.25 and 2.35 persons per vehicle depending on trip purpose. Table 19.9 is an example from West Palm Beach for the conversion of VMC to PMC based on capacities from the FDOT Generalized Tables and a vehicle occupancy factor of 1.84 from 2017 NHTS.

To obtain a better understanding of the difference between a roadway impact fee based on VMC and a mobility fee based on PMC, and the impact of the cost of including multimodal facilities as part of a roadway impact fee without providing a multimodal capacity benefit, the following calculations will illustrate the difference based **on a new two-lane road with 5-foot sidewalks and bike lanes** based on cost from Table 19.7, road capacity from Table 19.9, and multimodal capacity from Table 19.8:

$$\text{VMC rate} = \$10{,}461{,}780 \,/\, 15{,}600 = \$670.63$$

$$\text{PMC rate} = \$10{,}461{,}780 \,/\, \big(28{,}700 + (2{,}400 \times 2)$$
$$+ (2{,}400 \times 2)\big) = \$273.15$$

Step 8: Identify Available Funding

The availability of funding for mobility plan projects is likely to come from a variety of funding sources. Most road impact fees have provided a formula that provides a credit for gas taxes based on vehicle fuel efficiency and the various gas taxes collected and then, calculates a net present value. Gas taxes have been declining locally, state-wide, and nationally as vehicles have become more fuel efficient and the percentage of electric vehicles and hybrid vehicles increases. The federal government and

TABLE 19.8 Multimodal Capacities

Facility Type	Unit of Measure	Daily Person Capacity
Sidewalks (QOS D)	5' to 7' wide	2,400
Sidewalks (QOS B)	5' to 7' wide	3,600
Sidewalks (QOS D)	8' to 9' wide	3,600
Sidewalks (QOS B)	8' to 9' wide	7,200
Sidewalks (QOS C)	10' wide	4,800
Sidewalks (QOS A)	10' wide	9,600
Sidewalks (QOS C)	12' or wider	6,000
Sidewalks (QOS A)	12' or wider	12,000
Bicycle Boulevard (QOS D)	Street 20 MPH or Less	2,400
Bicycle Lane (QOS D)	4' to 5' wide	2,400
Green Bicycle Lane (QOS C)	4' to 5' wide	3,600
Buffered Bicycle Lane (QOS B)	6' to 7' wide	4,800
One-Way Protected Bike Lane (QOS A)	6' to 8' wide	7,200
Two-Way Protected Bike Lane (QOS A)	10' to 14' wide	14,400
Trail (QOS A)	12' wide	12,000
Dedicated Transit/High Occupancy Vehicle Lane	10' to 12' wide	20,040
Trolley Circulator	per vehicle	2,420
Shared Street	40' ROW	34,320
Shared Street	50' ROW	39,120
Shared Street	60' ROW	43,920

Source: The capacity for sidewalks with a QOS of "C" or "D" is based on an LOS "B" capacity. The capacity for sidewalks with a QOS of "A" or "B" is based on an LOS "C" capacity. The capacity for bike boulevard and bike lane with a QOS of "D" is based on an LOS "A" capacity. The capacity for green bike lanes with a QOS of "C" is based on an LOS "B" capacity. The capacity for buffered bike lanes with a QOS of "B" is based on an LOS "C" capacity. The capacity for protected bike lanes and trails with a QOS of "A" is based on an LOS "D" capacity. Capacity methodologies for sidewalks, trails, and bicycle facilities are based on methodologies established in Transportation Research Record 1636 Paper No. 98-0066, the 2006 Shared-Use Path Level of Service Calculator-A User's Guide developed for the Federal Highway Administration, and the 2010 *Highway Capacity Manual*. The capacity of dedicated transit lanes and high-occupancy vehicle lanes is based on 4 trolleys and buses an hour, with capacities of 36 and 60 persons, respectively, 10 microtransit vehicles an hour, with a capacity of 12 persons, and 600 car/ride share and taxis, with an occupancy of 2.5 persons. The transit circulator capacity is based on a capacity of 36 persons per vehicle, operating at a span of service of 12 hours over a 5.6-mile route (36 × 12 = 432 × 5.6 = 2,420). Shared Streets in a 40' ROW capacity is based on 7,440 vehicles, 2,880 trolley riders, 4,800 scooters and bikes, and 14,400 people walking (8' sidewalks). Shared Streets in a 50' ROW capacity is based on 7,440 vehicles, 2,880 trolley riders, 4,800 scooters and bikes, and 19,200 people walking (10' sidewalks). Shared Streets in a 60' ROW capacity is based on 7,440 vehicles, 2,880 trolley riders, 4,800 scooters and bikes, and 24,000 people walking (12' sidewalks).

most states have not raised gas taxes since the 1990s. The continued use of gas tax as a revenue credit for roadway impact fees or mobility fee does reflect that the gas taxes that are available are largely earmarked for maintenance and operations of the existing transportation network, not adding road or person capacity. There has been some discussion of a VMT tax to replace the gas tax at the federal and state level. Currently, several states are testing pilot projects for a VMT tax. Given the current political climate, a VMT tax is unlikely to pass anytime soon. However, as a greater number of electric vehicles and autonomous vehicles come online, there may be renewed interest in replacing the gas tax with a VMT fee.

TABLE 19.9 Roadway Capacities

Lane Type and Number	Vehicle Capacity	Person Capacity	Per Lane Person Capacity	Turn Lane Person Capacity
Two-Lane Undivided (Class II)	15,600	28,700	14,350	720
Four-Lane Divided (Class II)	33,800	62,190	15,550	780

Source: Florida Department of Transportation, *Quality/Level of Service (LOS) Handbook*, Generalized Annual Average Daily Volumes for Florida's Urbanized Areas. Capacities are based on an LOS "E" standard. The daily person capacity is based on a vehicle occupancy factor of 1.84 per the 2017 NHTS Data for Florida. Turn lane person capacity is derived by multiplying the daily person capacity by 0.5% per the FDOT Generalized Service Volume Tables. Person capacity, per lane person capacity, and turn lane person capacity are rounded to the nearest tenth.

Infrastructure surtaxes (sales tax) provide the broadest opportunity to have available funds to contribute toward mobility plan projects. Infrastructure surtax initiatives require voter approval of a referendum to collect the surtax. Long-Range Transportation Plans (LRTPs) are a source of federal and state funds that typically include multiple funding programs for motor vehicles and multimodal transportation. A large portion of federal and state funds tends to be allocated to the Interstate Highway System and to US and State roadways. To the extent that funding is available or identified in an LRTP, funding offsets should be provided. While not a common source of revenue, property taxes or revenues levied through special assessment districts on properties are a revenue source that is sometimes available. To the extent that roadway impact fee studies provide credit for revenues other than gas tax, they are typically converted into a credit per VMT based on a net present value analysis. Since mobility fees are based on mobility plans, funding offsets are typically provided on a whole dollar basis rather than converted to a credit or offset per a unit of measure. Table 19.10 is an example from the City of Port St. Lucie, which includes existing funded projects, projected intersection funding from federal and state sources, existing impact fees that have not yet been expended, existing and projected state and local including the remaining portion of an infrastructure sale, and a projected future extension of the infrastructure surtax.

TABLE 19.10 Anticipated Available Funding

Mobility Plan Cost	$993,397,192
Currently Funded Corridor Improvements	$97,398,204
Projected Intersection Funding	$87,350,000
Anticipated Available Funding (2026 to 2045)	$156,800,000
Total Anticipated Funding	$341,548,204
Unfunded Mobility Plan Cost	$651,848,988

Source: Anticipated available funding based on $33.4 million in county road impact fees collected by the city on behalf of the county, $11.4 million from various revenue sources between 2026 and 2028, and $112 million in infrastructure sales tax and other revenue sources between 2029 and 2045. The unfunded Mobility Plan cost was obtained by subtracting the total anticipated funding sources from the total Phase One Mobility Plan cost.

Step 9: Conduct New Growth Evaluation

To ensure that new growth is not paying for more than its fair share of the cost of the multimodal projects identified in the mobility plan, as required by case law, a new growth evaluation has been conducted. The new growth evaluation is based on the projected increase in PMT and the projected increase in PMC from the mobility projects. A PMT/PMC ratio lower than 1.00 means that more multimodal capacity is being provided than is needed to accommodate future travel demand and would require a reduction in the overall cost of capacity projects attributable to new growth. A PMT/PMC ratio greater than 1.00 means that new development is not being charged more than its fair share of the cost of multimodal projects, and no additional adjustments would be needed. The calculation for the new growth evaluation factor (NGEf) is illustrated in Box 19.3.

TABLE 19.11 New Growth Evaluation (NGE)

Increase in Person Miles of Travel (PMT)	398,116
Increase in Person Miles of Capacity (PMC)	428,842
New Growth Evaluation (NGE) factor	0.928

Source: The increase in person miles of travel and person miles of capacity is based on Figure 19.8. The new growth evaluation calculation is based on the formula in Figure 19.13.

BOX 19.3 NEW GROWTH EVALUATION. (FROM JONATHAN PAUL, AICP.)

New Growth Evaluation factor (NGEf)

$PMCi = \Sigma$ (LENmp × CAPmpc)

NGEf = (PMTi / PMCi)

Where

LENmpc = Length of Mobility Plan Projects

CAPmpc = Person Capacity of Mobility Plan Projects

NGEf = New Growth Evaluation factor

PMTi = Person Miles of Travel increase

PMCi = Person Miles of Capacity increase

Source: NUE Urban Concepts, LLC

In the following example, the projected increase in PMT and PMC was calculated for the City of Boynton Beach based on the formula provided in Figure 19.8. The projected PMTi/PMCi ratio is 0.928, which is less than 1.0 (Table 19.11). Thus, new growth would be charged more than its attributable share of the cost of projects in the mobility plan. For purposes of calculating the mobility fee, the NGEf is set to 0.928 to ensure new growth is not charged more than its fair share.

Step 10: Conduct Person Miles of Capacity Rate

The unfunded cost of mobility plan projects based on Table 19.10, the ECE factor in Table 19.1, the NGEf in Table 19.11, and the increase in person miles of capacity in Table 19.6

are used in the formula to calculate the person miles of capacity rate (PMCr). The unfunded cost of the mobility plan projects is multiplied by the existing conditions evaluation factor (ECEf) and the NGEf to obtain a final cost of mobility plan projects. The final cost of mobility plan projects is then divided by the increase in PMC to determine the PMCr (Box 19.4).

BOX 19.4 PERSON MILES OF CAPACITY RATE. (FROM JONATHAN PAUL, AICP.)

Person Miles of Capacity Rate (PMCr)

NCSTmi Formula = (GCSTmi – FUNmi) × ECEf

FCSTmi Formula = (NCSTmi × NGEf)

PMCr Formula = (FCSTmi / PMCi)

Where

GCSTmp = Gross Cost of mobility plan projects

FUNmi = Total Anticipated Funding for mobility plan projects

ECEf = Existing Conditions Evaluation factor of 1.00

NCSTmi = Net Cost of mobility plan projects

NGEf = New Growth Evaluation factor of 0.984

FCSTmi = Final Cost of mobility plan projects

PMCi = Person Miles of Capacity Increase

PMCr = Person Miles of Capacity Rate

Source: NUE Urban Concepts, LLC

TABLE 19.12 Person Miles of Capacity Rate (PMCr)

Unfunded Mobility Plan Project Cost	$1,282,691,878
Existing Conditions Evaluation Factor (ECEf)	1.00
New Growth Evaluation Factor (NGEf)	0.984
Final Mobility Plan Project Cost	$1,262,168,808
Person Miles of Capacity Increase (PMCi)	6,628,766
Person Miles of Capacity Rate (PMCr)	$190.41

Source: The unfunded cost of multimodal improvements is obtained from Table 19.10. The existing conditions evaluation factor is obtained from Table 19.1. The new growth evaluation factor is obtained from Table 19.11. The increase in person miles of capacity (PMC) is obtained from Table 19.6. The person miles of capacity rate (PMCr) are determined per the calculation in Figure 19.14.

An example from Sarasota County (Table 19.12) is provided in the following numerical calculation:

$$\left((\$1{,}282{,}691{,}878 \times 1.00) \times 0.984 \right)$$

$$= \$1{,}262{,}168{,}808 \, / \, 6{,}628{,}766 = \$190.41$$

There are limited instances when a local government may elect to utilize the increase in PMT versus PMC. The primary instance would be in communities where projected growth in VMT exceeded the PMC from mobility plan projects by more than 10%. A larger delta would result in a lower mobility fee rate. Another instance would be where per mile cost in urban areas or constrained areas is high compared with the PMC provided by the mobility plan project. An example would be where existing urban cross-sections would be widened to add a protected bicycle lane or flex lanes that resulted in relocating underground stormwater infrastructure or placing above-ground utilities below the road surface, compared with reducing travel lane widths, removing on-street parking, or widening into a raised median or the outside lane of a rural (open drainage) cross-section. Both protected bicycle lanes would provide the same capacity, yet the project where existing drainage or utilities are relocated could cost two to three times as much as other options. The third would be where there are a significant number of mobility plan projects that do not, in and of themselves, add person capacity, such as high-visibility mid-block crossings, way finding systems, special area studies or plans, transit stops, or mobility hubs. Likely, these projects would result in a higher QOS that would result in higher multimodal capacities. The fourth would be a policy decision to have a lower mobility fee rate across all uses based on a technical analysis versus an arbitrary reduction in mobility fees, which may impact uses differently. The reverse of a larger capacity does not have the same impact, as person capacity is correlated with the cost of mobility plan projects, so they tend to go up and down in tandem. There can always be some unique instance where a larger capacity would result in a lower PMC rate, but in general, if it occurs, it is likely to entail a larger increase in PMT.

Step 11: Establish Assessment Areas

Assessment areas are based on either a physical location, such as a downtown or a community redevelopment area, or a type of development pattern, such as a mixed-use or traditional neighborhood development (TND). The intent of assessment areas is to localize mobility fees and recognize that new growth in certain locations, or as part of certain development patterns, will result in lower mobility fees. In instances where multiple assessment areas are established, new development would only pay the mobility fee rate applicable to the assessment area in which the new development is located. The land use evaluation is utilized to establish assessment areas, and the finalization of the mobility plan projects is used to make any adjustments to assessment areas to ensure the areas reflect the need for mobility plan projects attributable to new growth within the area.

An example of a local government with multiple assessment areas is the City of Altamonte Springs, where the following three assessment areas were established: (1) Transit Oriented Development (TOD); (2) Activity Centers; and (3) outside of Activity Centers (Figure 19.11). Development within the TOD receives a 15% reduction for internal capture and 15% mode share capture based on its proximity to SunRail. Development within Activity Centers receives a 15% reduction for internal capture within the activity center limits. For areas outside of Activity Centers and future annexations, no community capture reduction is recognized, and the full mobility is assessed within this area.

The need to evaluate the establishment of multiple assessment areas was reinforced in a recent ruling by the Florida First District Court of Appeal in Board of County Commissioners, Santa Rosa County v. Home Builders Association of West Florida, where the Court referenced Florida Statute requirements that fees be based on the most recent and localized data, as it relates to the failure of the county's school impact fee to account for differences between the northern and southern parts of the county and the differences

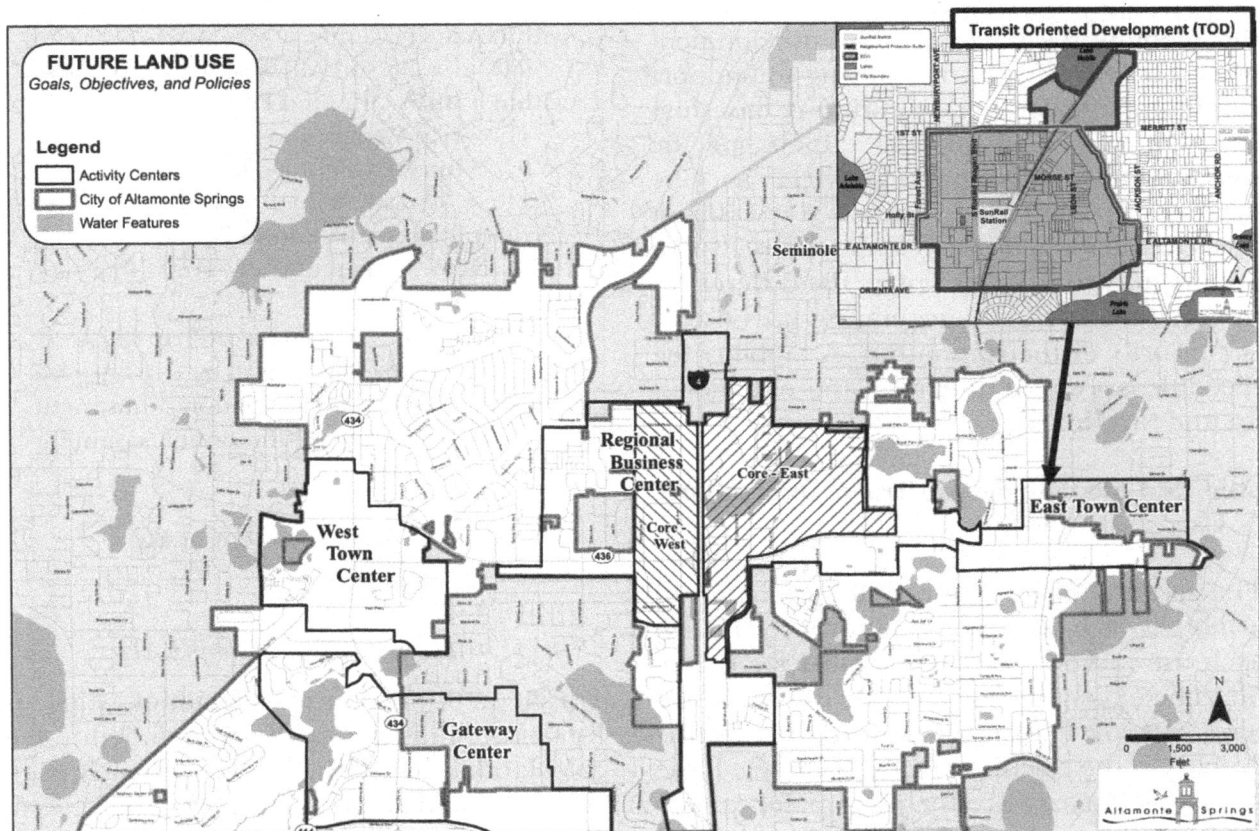

FIGURE 19.11 City of Altamonte Springs TOD and Activity Center. (From Jonathan Paul, AICP.)

in growth and its impact on need. Not all communities will warrant the need for multiple assessment areas, but it is something that should be evaluated as part of the development of mobility fees.

Step 12: Establish Mobility Fee Schedule of Uses

There are multiple options related to the establishment of a mobility fee schedule of uses. One approach is to do what many roadway impact fees do and just use the most common land uses from the ITE *Trip Generation Manual*. The land use evaluation is an important component in developing a schedule of uses that is applicable to the community for which the mobility fee is being developed. While there are many similarities between land uses amongst communities, there are often also times where a community will feature specific uses that should be reflected in the mobility fee schedule. The development of the schedule is also a means to support community goals such as workforce housing, economic development that targets specific uses, and encouraging new growth in specific locations through the inclusion of assessment areas in the mobility fee schedule. It is also an opportunity to fully recognize the differences in impact of high trip-generating uses if that is a priority of the community. A mobility fee schedule is a way to integrate land use, mobility, and funding.

Step 13: Calculate Person Travel Demand per Use

The second component in the calculation of a mobility fee is the calculation of PTD for each use included on the mobility fee schedule. The example from the City of Altamonte Springs (Box 19.5) illustrates that the factors utilized in the calculation of PTD for each use by assessment area are the principal means to achieve the "rough proportionately" test established by the courts and Florida Statute.

BOX 19.5 PERSON TRAVEL DEMAND. (FROM JONATHAN PAUL, AICP.)

Person Travel Demand (PTD) per Use

$Tvmt = (\Sigma \, ACvmt + \Sigma \, LAvmt)$

$LAEf = 1 - (\Sigma \, LAvmt \, / \, Tvmt)$

$PTDu = ((((TG \times \% \, NEW) \times PTf) \times (PTL \times LAEf)) \times ODAf)$

$PTDac = (((((TG \times (1 - ICr)) \times \% \, NEW) \times PTf) \times (PTL \times LAEf)) \times ODAf)$

$PTDtd = ((((((TG \times (1 - (ICr + TRr))) \times \% \, NEW) \times PTf) \times (PTL \times LAEf)) \times ODAf)$

Where

ACvmt = 2022 projected VMT for arterials and collectors

LAvmt = 2022 projected VMT for Interstate 4

Tvmt = Total vehicle miles of travel (VMT)

LAEf = Limited Access Adjustment factor of 0.60 to account for travel using Interstate 4

PTDu = Person Miles of Travel per Use

PTDac = Person Miles of Travel per Use within Activity Center

PTDtd = Person Miles of Travel per Use within Transit Oriented Development

TG = Trip Generation

ICr = Internal Capture Rate of 0.15

TRr = Transit Reduction Rate of 0.15 to account for trips via SunRail

% NEW = Percent of Trips that are Primary Trips

PTf = Person Trip factor by Trip Purpose

PTL = Person Trip Length by Trip Purpose

ODAf = Origin & Destination Adjustment factor of 0.50 to avoid the double-counting of trips

Source: NUE Urban Concepts, LLC

19.4.1 Limited Access Evaluation (LAE)

Travel on limited access facilities, such as Interstate 4, is excluded from mobility fee calculations, as the Interstate system is principally funded and maintained by the Federal Government in coordination with FDOT and funded through the gas tax trust fund.

TABLE 19.13 Limited Access Evaluation (LAE)

Facility	VMT
Collector and Arterial Roads VMT	869,255
Interstate 4 VMT	634,275
Total VMT	1,503,500
Limited Access Evaluation factor (LAEf)	0.67

Source: The 2022 VMT data was obtained using traffic characteristics data. The limited access evaluation factor is calculated per Figure 19.16 and rounded to the nearest hundredth.

To ensure new growth that generates PTD is not charged for travel on facilities such as Interstate 4, a limited access evaluation factor has been developed. The example limited access evaluation factor (LAEf) of 0.60, based on existing travel demand within the City of Altamonte Springs on Interstate 4, is applied to PTLs to account for the 40% of travel occurring on Interstate 4 (Table 19.13).

19.4.2 Trip Generation

Trip generation (TG) rates are based on daily trip information published in the latest edition of the ITE *Trip Generation Manual*.

19.4.3 Internal Capture

The percentage of internal capture (IC) reflects the reduced impact on the overall transportation system by compact, mixed-use, interconnected developments due to a reduction in the number of trips on external roadways and an increase in trips made by walking, bicycling, and riding transit. IC rates are based on the various data, studies, and analyses provided in ITE's *Trip Generation Handbook*, 3rd edition and studies conducted throughout Florida. The policies in the City of Altamonte Springs 2030 City Plan provide for a mixture of residential, commercial, office, and civic uses within a single master development plan for Activity Centers and the TOD.

An IC rate of 15% has been used to account for the IC of vehicular trips and the increase in pedestrian, bicycle, and transit trips that occurs when there is a mixture of land uses and an interconnected local street network within Activity Centers and the TOD.

19.4.4 Transit Reduction

The percentage of transit reduction (TR) reflects the reduced impact on the overall transportation system by land uses near a frequent transit service, such as that currently provided by SunRail. Based upon guidance in the 3rd edition of the ITE *Handbook*, a 15% reduction factor was applied to TG rates for land uses proposed within the TOD due to the proximity of frequent rail transit service.

19.4.5 Percentage of New Trips

The percentage of new trips (% New) is based on a combination of the various pass-by analyses provided in ITE's *Trip Generation Handbook*, 3rd edition and various traffic studies conducted throughout Florida. The percentage of new trips differs slightly from the commonly used pass-by trip term, as it is the percentage difference in trips after pass-by trips are deducted. The concept is better understood based on the following example: 10 trips × (100% – 30% pass-by rate) = 7 trips or 70% new trips. A pass-by trip is a trip that is traveling and stops at another land use between an origin point (commonly a dwelling) and a destination point (e.g., place of employment, shops, gas).

19.4.6 Person Trip Factor

The person trip factor (PTf) is used to convert vehicle trips to person trips based on the recently released 2017 NHTS. To obtain the most recent and localized data, the travel survey was evaluated specifically for Florida. The

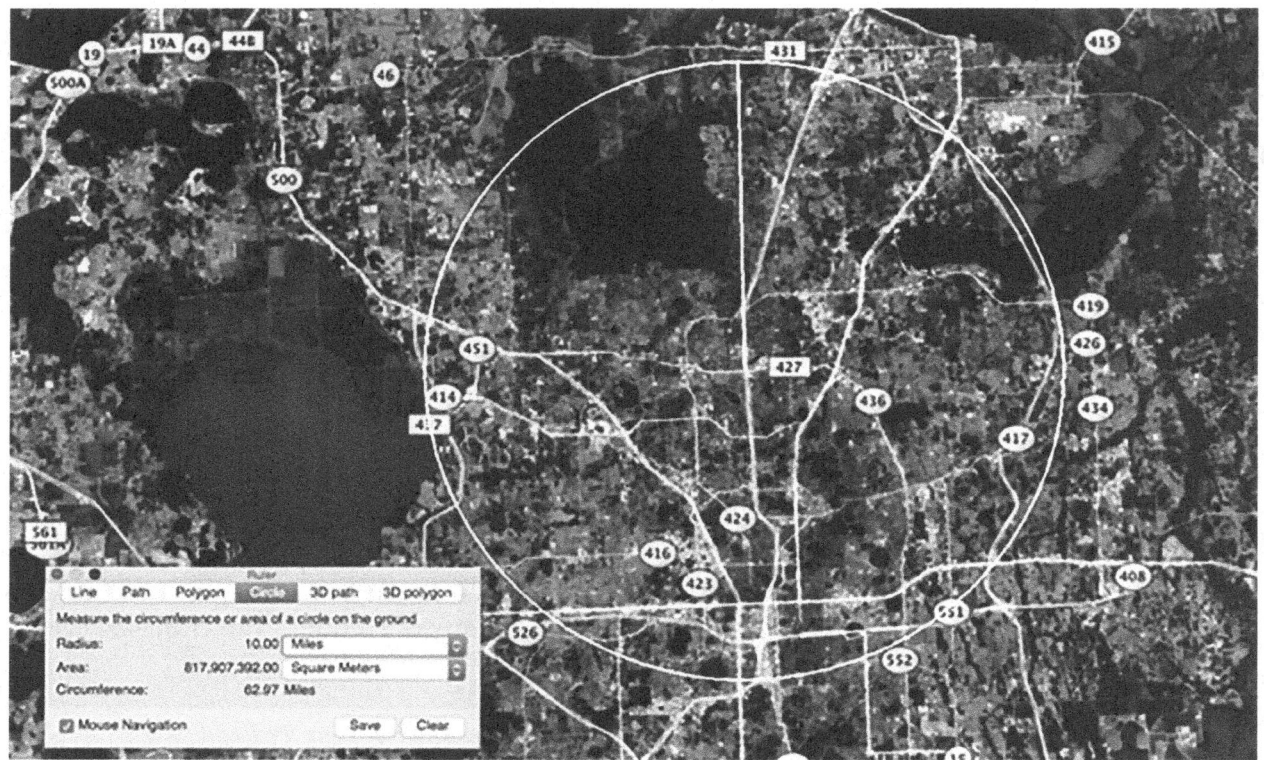

FIGURE 19.12 Ten-mile radius from center of City of Altamonte Springs. (From Jonathan Paul, AICP.)

PTfs vary by trip purpose. The survey data is based on over 5,200 unique survey data points.

south, and out to Apopka and Orange County to the west (Figure 19.12).

19.4.7 Person Trip Length

The PTL is based on the recently released 2017 NHTS. To obtain the most recent and localized data, the travel survey was evaluated specifically for Florida. The PTLs vary by trip purpose. The travel survey data points selected were those for trips that were 10 miles or less in length, which represent over 5,200 unique survey data points. Using the City of Altamonte Springs, travel over 10 miles in length typically makes use of either Interstate 4 or the various toll roads within Central Florida, or occurs outside the limits of Seminole County. A 10-mile radius measured from the Interstate 4 and SR 436 Interchange (approximate center of the city) takes you almost to the Volusia County Line to the north, past SR 417 to the east, past Downtown Orlando and Orange County to the

19.4.8 Origin and Destination Adjustment (ODA)

TG rates represent trip ends at the site of a land use. Thus, a single-origin trip from home to work counts as one trip end for the residence and from work to the residence as one trip end, for a total of two trip ends. To avoid double counting of trips, the net person trips are multiplied by the origin and destination adjustment factor (ODAf) of 50%. This distributes the impact of travel equally between the origin and the destination of the trip and eliminates double charging for trips.

19.4.9 Person Travel Demand (PTD) per Use

The result of multiplying TG rates, IC, TR, the percentage of new trips, the PTf, PTL, the limited access factor, and the origin and destination factor is the establishment of a PTD per use within each assessment area. The PTD reflects the average daily weekday trips generated by the various uses in the mobility fee schedule. The mobility fee schedule includes the unit of measure that will be used to calculate the mobility fee for a given use. The calculated PTD for each use represents the full PTD impact of that use on the multimodal network.

Step 14: Calculate Mobility Fee per Use

To ensure the rough proportionately test is addressed, the PTD of individual uses is evaluated through the development of a mobility fee schedule. The calculations of mobility fees are based on the PTD for each use and each assessment area listed on the mobility fee schedule multiplied by the person miles of capacity rate (PMCr) as illustrated in Box 19.6.

> **BOX 19.6 MOBILITY FEE CALCULATION PER USE. (FROM JONATHAN PAUL, AICP.)**
>
> **Mobility Fee (MF) per use**
>
> $MFu = PTDu \times PMCr$
> $MFac = PTDac \times PMCr$
> $MFtd = PTDtd \times PMCr$
> Where
> u = areas of the City outside Activity Centers
> ac = areas of the City within Activity Centers
> td = areas of the City within the Transit Oriented Development
> PTDu = Person Travel Demand per use outside Activity Centers
> PTDac = Person Travel Demand per use inside Activity Centers
> PTDtd = Person Travel Demand per use within the TOD
> PMCr = Person Miles of Capacity rate
>
> MFu = Mobility Fee per use outside Activity Centers
> MFac = Mobility Fee per use inside Activity Centers
> MFtd = Mobility Fee per use within within the TOD
>
> Source: NUE Urban Concepts, LLC

Step 15: Establish Benefit District

The establishment of benefit districts (aka areas or zones) is done to ensure that mobility fees paid by new development are expended within a district that provides a benefit to those who have paid the fee as required by the benefit test of the dual rational nexus. Mobility fee benefit districts are generally established to reflect travel patterns within a defined area, and the boundaries are frequently formed by county boundaries, municipal limits, limited access facilities, principal arterial roads, conservation or environmentally protected areas, or water bodies. For municipalities that collect mobility fees that mitigate impacts to local, municipal, county, and state roads, the boundaries of a benefit district should include enclaves and extend to logical termini outside of municipal limits to address extra-jurisdictional impact. For counties that establish mobility fees and have interlocal agreements whereby a municipality collects mobility fees from new development of behalf of the county, benefit district should reflect municipal limits, with some extension of those districts to reasonable termini outside municipal limits. Implementing ordinances should establish procedures and require a written finding of benefit provided, in keeping with requirements of the dual rational nexus, for instances where mobility fees could be spent outside a defined mobility fee district for multimodal projects that provide a mobility benefit to the new development that paid the fee. The written finding provides for added transparency that mobility fee funds are expended in a manner that is consistent with legal precedent and applicable statutory requirements.

Step 16: Develop Technical Report

The final step is the development of a technical report (aka analysis or study) that documents the data, methodology, and sources used to development or update a mobility plan and mobility fee. The technical report should reference applicable legal precedent and statutory requirements specific to the local government for which the mobility plan and mobility fee is being developed. The technical report should also provide the information necessary to develop or update an implementing mobility fee ordinance.

19.5 THE FUTURE OF MOBILITY FEES

One of the most significant issues in the development of mobility fees is disagreements between municipalities seeking to develop a mobility fee to replace roadway impact fees and traffic mitigation requirements and counties requiring new development within municipalities to collect roadway impact fees on behalf of counties to add capacity to county and state-owned roads. The momentum behind mobility fees is driven in part by municipalities having needs to improve mobility and accessibility in their community by adding sidewalks, bike lanes, trails, and transit circulators, not by adding road capacity. There are legitimate concerns raised by municipalities that road impact fees are being collected from new development where road capacity is already in place and being expended to widen roads to serve new development in unincorporated areas to facilitate more people driving into municipalities that are attempting to improve multimodal transportation, not encourage additional motor vehicle travel.

There are legitimate concerns raised by counties that they have responsibilities to serve and fund county-level travel and that trips are not just confined to municipal limits. Both concerns are legitimate. The benefit of a mobility fee based on identifiable mobility plan projects is that there are ways to quantify impact and travel on municipal, county, and state roads and to determine the share of the future mobility plan project. There is an ongoing legal challenge between Palm Beach County and the City of Palm Beach Gardens over this very issue, which had concluded the first phase of trial as of the writing of this chapter. There are also ongoing Florida Statute 164 mediation proceedings occurring between St. Lucie County and the City of Port St. Lucie over this issue as of the writing of this chapter. In full disclosure, NUE Urban Concepts prepared the mobility plan and mobility fee for both Palm Beach Gardens and Port St. Lucie. Future chapters could be written to address this issue based on quantifiable data and analysis.

Data, and more specifically, big data obtained through Bluetooth and smartphone tracking, will become increasingly important in the development of mobility plans and mobility fees. Streetlight data was used to measure origin and destination trips and seasonal variations in the development of the Walton County (home to Seaside, the birthplace of New Urbanism) mobility plan to develop a park-once environment to capture day trips and visitor trips at strategically located mobility hubs and encourage use of modes of travel other than driving to reach beach front and community destinations. Census and Household Travel Survey data, which are collected every 10 and 8 years, respectively, have historically been the best data available for travel to develop roadway impact fees and mobility fees. As big data becomes more readily available, and as cost eventually comes down (data is expensive and time consuming to evaluate), there will be opportunities to provide greater levels of accuracy as it relates to vehicle and person travel and trip characteristics. Data for motor vehicle travel is readily available in most communities, as funding and planning systems have spent the last 70 plus years focused on motor vehicle travel. Data for person trips and person travel is not as easy to come by and still relies on conversions between vehicle and person travel. There are additional transportation mobility data sources for person travel that are available in varying capacities through online mapping applications by Apple and Google, shared micromobility (e.g., e-bikes, e-scooters) providers, rideshare providers (e.g., Lyft, Uber), transit providers, and third-party vendors like Streetlight and emerging Mobility as a Service (MaaS). Ongoing advancements in data collection will provide for more localized and recent person travel data.

Mode share has typically been measured by the home to work trip. However, the share of travel to and from work has been declining as a share of overall trips for the past 30 years and now represents fewer than 20% of all daily trips in most communities throughout the US. The home to work trip is one of the harder trips to make by means other than driving, as there are time-certain meetings or firm times to show up at work. As work trends continue to migrate to a more mobile workforce, and work from home continues to accelerate (Covid 19 vastly expedited these trends), the reliance on mode share data for home to work trips becomes less relevant. An overriding goal of most transportation mobility plans is to increase mode share by means other than driving a single-occupant motor vehicle. Ideally, mobility fees would be designed to be a tool to strive toward meeting mode share goals. The data and the multimodal network needed to achieve mode share at any level approaching those seen in Europe is going to require concentrated planning efforts and funding to move toward a viable multimodal environment.

Mobility plans are an opportunity to integrate land use, transportation mobility, and parking, and mobility fees are one of the funding sources to plan, design, and implement mobility plan projects. St. Augustine, America's oldest continuously occupied city (Santa Fe, NM is the oldest state capital), is a leader in transforming its transportation system to make its streets safer for all users and addressing the impacts of climate change by reimagining the function of its multimodal network. The first step was beginning to reconstruct streets in its historic district into low-speed curbless and shared streets. The second was putting in place the land use, transportation, parking, and funding policies to develop a park-once environment. The third is planning to repurpose existing right-of-way to focus on the movement of people. The fourth is using its mobility plan to secure federal and state funding and to serve as the basis for its mobility fee to fund mobility plan projects.

The final graphic Figure 19.13 illustrates how mobility plans and fees come together as a way for local governments to transform their transportation system from a focus on moving motor vehicles toward one emphasizing the movement of people. The illustration shows a mobility plan project for San Marco Avenue right-of-way being repurposed from on-street parking to multimodal flex lanes for micromobility and microtransit and the increase in person capacity from the multimodal changes. Microtransit service will connect the historic district to a peripheral parking garage, parking has been decoupled from land use by removing parking minimums to encourage infill and redevelopment, and multimodal transportation projects will replace on-street parking accommodated in the parking garage and served by frequent microtransit service and micromobility devices.

Looking ahead, mobility fees, partially to be paid from new infill and redevelopment, will be one of the funding sources to fund the planning, design, and construction of the multimodal flex lanes, and funding for microtransit service will come from dynamic pricing of parking near the historic district and parking

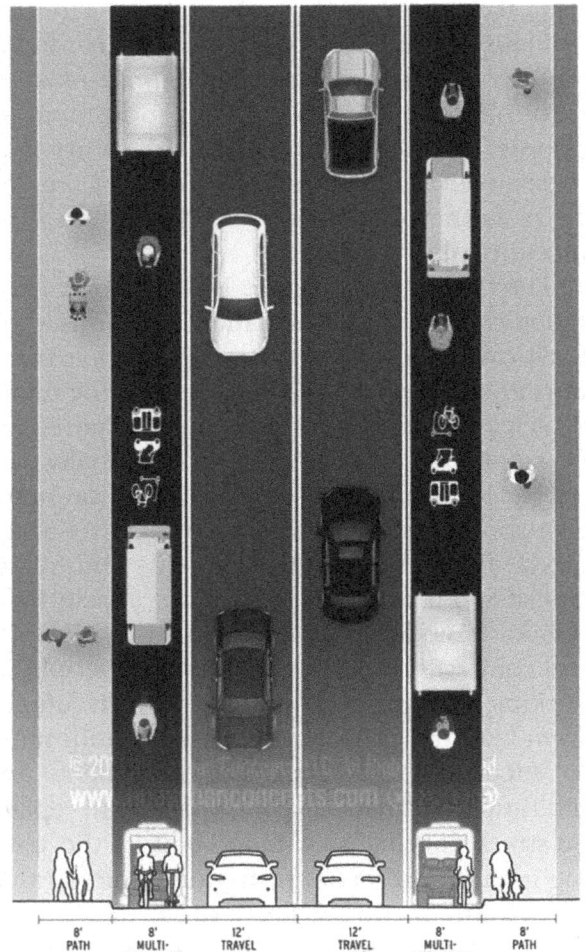

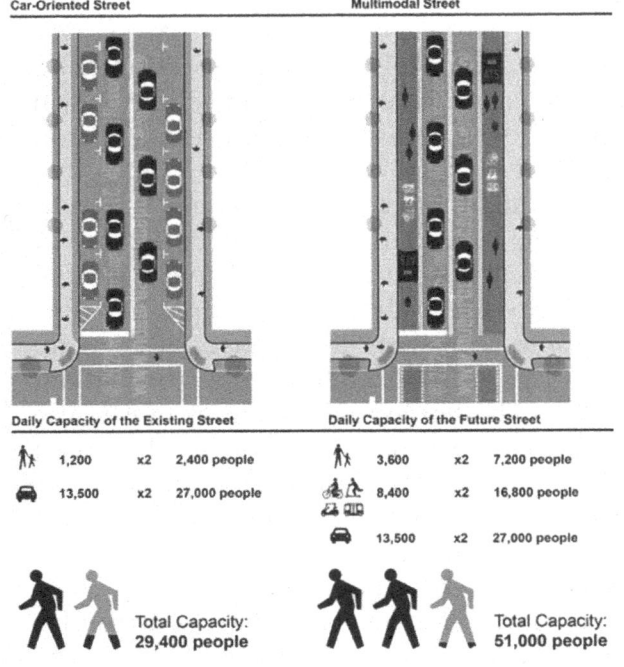

© 2021 NUE Urban Concepts. LLC. All Rights Reserved.
www.nueurbanconcepts.com

FIGURE 19.13 The potential of mobility plans and mobility fees. (From Jonathan Paul, AICP.)

revenues from the garage, offset, if needed, by the increase in property values from land being repurposed from surface parking to infill and redevelopment. Beyond funding gaps in a sidewalk network, a forward-looking mobility plan and mobility fee can be among the tools used by local governments to enhance their community.

NOTES

1 Source: https://smartgrowthamerica.org/dangerous-by-design/.
2 Ibid.
3 Vision Zero is the Swedish approach to road safety thinking where no loss of life is acceptable. Source: http://www.visionzeroinitiative.com/.
4 317 Ore., at 127, 854 P. 2d, at 447 (emphasis in original).
5 Dolan v. City of Tigard, 512 U.S. 687 (1994).

REFERENCE

Richardson, J. J. Jr., Zimmerman Gough, M., & Puentes, R. (2003). *Is Home Rule the Answer? Clarifying The Influence of Dillon's Rule On Growth Management.* Washington, DC: Brookings Institution.

20 OPERATIONS AND MAINTENANCE MITIGATION FEES AND TRANSPORTATION UTILITY FEES WITH IMPLICATIONS FOR IMPROVING IMPACT MITIGATION

20.1 OVERVIEW

Local governments are increasingly stressed financially to pay for infrastructure. The typical sources of revenue, especially local property and sales taxes, face limits usually imposed by state legislatures. Local governments thus search for ways to have users pay for such services as local streets, sidewalks, and associated infrastructure. And why not? It is often more efficient and equitable for many kinds of services to be financed based on use characteristics: Those land uses that impose larger burdens on facilities should pay proportionately more than those that impose smaller burdens. If all land uses pay the same despite their impacts on facilities, those land uses that pay less than their proportionate share are induced to expand, while those that pay more than their proportionate share are discouraged. The net result is that more high-cost development occurs at the expense of less low-cost development. Equity implications also arise if lower-cost, more affordable land uses pay more than their proportionate share.

This chapter does two things. First, it describes how proportionate-share impact mitigation can extend to operations and maintenance (O&M). Second, it presents the concept of transportation utility fees (TUFs) as a way in which all transportation costs—O&M, initial construction and long-term repair, rehabilitation, and replacement—can be internalized to that development which imposes transportation demands. Although the lens is transportation facilities, the techniques can apply to all types of community infrastructure.

20.2 OPERATIONS AND MAINTENANCE (O&M) IMPACT FEE

New development impacts on facilities in more ways than requiring new or expanded facilities to serve it. It may create new demands for O&M than it generates in new revenues to cover (see Nelson et al. 2022). We present two case studies using the impact fee methodology to mitigate the O&M costs new development imposes on transit systems: San Francisco transit (briefly) and Aventura, Florida (in more detail). Both differ widely in scale, but they use the same methodological approaches, as will be seen.

20.2.1 San Francisco Transit O&M Impact Development Fee

In 1981, the San Francisco Board of Supervisors enacted the transit fee in 1981 to recover the capital and operating costs of increased peak-period transit service resulting from new office construction in downtown San Francisco. The transit impact development fee (TIDF) applies to all projects in the downtown area—akin to a service area. The fee varies among land uses but ranged about $12 per square in 2022. It generates several million dollars annually.

DOI: 10.4324/9781003336075-25

Authority for the fee is based essentially on home rule (as opposed to explicit state enabling legislation) and is found in Chapter 38 of the San Francisco Administrative Code. The relevant code section provides:

The demand for public transit service from downtown area office uses imposes a unique burden on the Municipal Railway, qualitatively different from the burden imposed by other uses of property in San Francisco. The need for that level of service provided by the Municipal Railway during peak periods can be attributed in substantial part to office uses of property in the downtown area.

The fee is intended to capture all costs incurred by the Municipal Railway in meeting peak-period public transit service demands created by office uses in each new development subject to the fee, including the expansion of service capacity through the purchase of new rolling stock, the installation of new lines, the addition of existing lines, and the long-term operation, maintenance, repair, and replacement of those expanded facilities.

The overall fee thus includes capital in addition to O&M.

The O&M element of the fee itself is calculated based on a proportionate share of the impact new downtown development has on transit facilities in relation to the new O&M revenue it generates plus reasonable consideration of nonlocal revenues (such as from federal and state agencies). In its original form, the O&M element of the fee was calculated as shown in Table 20.1.

The analysis was extended over 40 years or roughly the useful life of transit facilities. The net present values were estimated using long-term assumptions of inflation (about 2.6 percent), as were long-term revenues. The analytic approach can perhaps be applied to all facilities.

The TIDF was challenged in California courts,[1] which upheld the fee, and the US Supreme Court denied review, indicating at least that the concept was not ripe for review from a Constitutional perspective. As of this writing, San Francisco's TIDF may be the only US example of this application of proportionate-share development fees.

20.2.2 Aventura, Florida Transportation O&M Mitigation Fee

We apply the foregoing principles to an in-depth case study of a pioneer outside California: Aventura, Florida. As background, in the late 2000s, Aventura considered the option to support its Transportation Concurrency Exception Area (TCEA), which is part of the Aventura Comprehensive Plan. The City of Aventura is largely built out, with few if any opportunities to construct new roads or to expand existing roads. While the opportunities to construct expanded roadways are limited, there is a continuing need for additional mobility within Aventura to meet the needs of residential and business developments in this city.

The City of Aventura had developed and provides a system of transit known as the Aventura Express. This is a system of bus routes that is provided to residents and nonresidents alike without charge. The objective of the Aventura Express is to provide mobility by means of buses and thus avoid the need to expand roadways or to suffer increased traffic congestion in the absence of such roadway expansion.

Florida law requires that new developments achieve and maintain adequate levels of transportation service as a prerequisite for development. This is commonly referred to

TABLE 20.1 Original San Francisco Transit Operations Linkage Fee

Net present value of O&M costs per square foot of office	$12.97
Net present value of O&M revenue per square foot of office	$9.46
Net present value of difference in O&M costs and revenues per square foot of office	$3.54

as "transportation concurrency." It is known as "adequate public facilities" in other states. When this law was passed, it was recognized that such a policy would not be sensible in all situations. Aventura is one of those situations. Accordingly, the entirety of the City of Aventura has been designated a TCEA.

The law requires local governments with TCEAs to develop means to support the TCEAs that will promote public transit. The net effect is to allow developers to contribute to public transit, and thus proceed with development, when achieving transportation concurrency by traditional means is not possible or is impractical. Such a program is presented herein. This analysis shows how Aventura may accommodate the mobility needs of new developments by the expansion of the Aventura Express with the payment of a transportation mitigation fee. The amounts of the fees for various land uses are shown in Table 20.2.

These mitigation fees were found to represent a proportionate share of the city's costs to extend additional mobility to new development by means of the Aventura Express. What follows is how the mitigation fee was designed and its relationship to impact fee calculation principles. (We note that although this methodology was pioneered in the 2000s, the city merely updates the fees based on most recent data.)

The objective of an Aventura Transportation Mitigation Program is to support and fund the city's Circulator System so that the Circulator System can satisfy the need for enhanced mobility over time as the city continues to grow.

New residential and non-residential developments within Aventura will contribute to the need for increased mobility. New residences will bring additional people who will live, shop, recreate, and work in or around the city. Each of these activities will require mobility. Additionally, new non-residential developments will attract additional shoppers, employees, customers, and recreators to and within Aventura. Both types of developments will cause a need for enhanced mobility.

A mitigation program will involve the payment of a fee that offsets the costs of accommodating the mobility impacts of new residential and non-residential developments with the Circulator System of the City of Aventura. The first step in developing a mitigation fee is to quantitatively define the Circulator Service. Table 20.3 provides the first part of this definition. At the time of the analysis, the Circulator System comprises 354,860 passenger seats per year. These seats are provided within five routes, running ten times per day on weekdays and 13 times on weekends, illustrated in Table 20.3.

The Circulator System serves the residents of and visitors to Aventura. Our convention in the United States is to define a population of a place, such as Aventura, as the number of people who reside within the borders of that place. This definition is fine for purposes of

TABLE 20.2 Transportation Mitigation per Unit, City of Aventura, Florida

Land Use and Unit	Persons per Unit	Cost per Unit
Residence per Dwelling	0.972	$1,320.70
Office per 1,000 ft²	1.557	$2,115.94
Retail per 1,000 ft²	2.203	$2,993.95
Industrial per 1,000 ft²	1.324	$1,799.30
Institutional & Other per 1,000 ft²	2.396	$3,255.14

Source: James C. Nicholas for the City of Aventura, Florida.

TABLE 20.3 Circulator Service, City of Aventura

	Routes	Runs	Seats	Seats per Day	Seats per Year
Weekday	5	10	22	1,100	280,500
Weekend	5	13	22	1,430	74,360
TOTAL				2,530	354,860

Source: City of Aventura.

voting, but it is not acceptable for purposes of defining a population of people served by services such as police and fire protection, or Aventura's Circulator System. The population served by the Circulator System is the number of people within Aventura, no matter if they are permanent residents, seasonal residents, employees of businesses, or patrons of those businesses within Aventura. The population served is the functional population. These people are served by the Circulator even if they do not ride it. They are served by diverting those who do ride the buses out of their cars and away from the streets, thereby creating capacity for those who prefer driving to bus riding. Additionally, businesses are served even if the owners of the businesses do not ride the buses, because the buses bring their employees and customers to and from those places of business.

The functional population of an area is the number of people who can be expected to be present at businesses, residences, schools, parks, churches, or the myriad of other places where people go or congregate. The number of people within Aventura's functional population is shown in Table 20.4. These are the people served by the City of Aventura.

Table 20.5 shows the derivation of the functional population. These calculations use Miami-Dade County as the base for the calculations. Counties are used because employment data is not reported for geographic areas smaller than counties. Vehicular trip generation rates[2] are used to identify the total number of people present at a site. Employment data are used to identify how many of those persons present are

TABLE 20.4 Service Area Population, City of Aventura

	Resident	Functional
Residential Population	28,207	14,104
Peak Population	40,336	7,277
Visitors to:		
Offices		2,892
Retail		15,134
Industrial		532
Institutional		1,849
TOTAL		41,788

Sources: Census of the Population and functional population analysis.

employees, with the remainder being visitors. The ratios of persons per 1,000 feet of floor area for Miami-Dade County are applied to non-residential floor area within Aventura to estimate Aventura's functional population in non-residential areas. Because many of the people present at and assigned to non-residential areas of Aventura are the occupants of residences within Aventura, it is necessary to adjust the population assigned to residences to avoid double counting those persons. This is done on a time allocation basis.

Table 20.6 shows the Miami-Dade County and Aventura allocations, resulting in a functional population of 41,788 for Aventura. It also shows the functional population of Aventura in terms of persons per unit of land use: 1,000 square feet of floor area for non-residential developments and the dwelling unit for residential development. Recall that many of the residents of Aventura are also employees and patrons of the businesses within Aventura; hence, the relatively low functional population assigned to residences.

TABLE 20.5 Functional Population, City of Aventura

Land Use	Aventura		Miami/Dade	
	Floor Area	Persons at Site	Floor Area	Persons at Site
Non-Residential				
Office	1,857,080	2,892	91,889,361	143,096
Retail	6,868,173	15,134	185,691,556	409,164
Industrial	401,883	532	182,695,376	241,930
Institutional & Other	771,833	1,849	124,193,781	297,529
Full time Residences		14,104		1,189,909
Seasonal Residences		7,277		98,191
TOTALS	9,898,969	41,788	584,470,074	2,379,819

Source: Office of Demographic & Economic Research, Miami/Dade County Property Appraiser and Florida Agency for Workforce Innovation, Labor Market Statistics, Quarterly Census of Employment and Earnings.

TABLE 20.6 Functional Population per Unit, City of Aventura

Land Use	Persons at Site	Units	Population per Unit
Office—1,000 ft²	2,892	1,857,080	1.557
Retail 1,000 ft²	15,134	6,868,173	2.203
Industrial 1,000 ft²	532	401,883	1.324
Institutional & Other—1,000 ft²	1,849	771,833	2.396
Residences—Dwelling	21,381	20,782	0.972
TOTAL	41,788		

Source: James C. Nicholas, City of Aventura, FL.

The annual cost per seat for Circulator Service is shown in Table 20.7. This cost is used to calculate a per capita cost, using functional population, of the Circulator System for the present year and as a present value of future costs.

The level of service provided or expected to be provided in the future is 0.0276 seats per capita per year. The costs shown in Table 20.8 are the costs of continuing this level of service as the city continues to develop,

The basic annual cost of $6,552 per seat is reduced by 51 percent to reflect the allocation of funds to Aventura's Circulator System from Miami-Dade County's Transit System Surtax. The net cost to the city is $3,231 per seat. At a level of service of 0.0276 seats per capita, the cost per capita is $89.29 per year. This is a recurring cost to be borne by the city. The

TABLE 20.7 Circulator Cost per Seat, City of Aventura

	Day	Year
Bus Hours per	53	16,380
Cost per Hour	44	$44
Cost per	$2,332	$720,720

Source: City of Aventura.

TABLE 20.8 Circulator Level of Service, City of Aventura

Population Served	41,788
Seats per Capita per Day	0.0276

Source: James C. Nicholas, City of Aventura, FL.

essence of a mitigation payment is that the developer would pay to the city an amount that reflects the future costs to the city of providing the Circulator Service. This future cost is expressed as a present value of $89.29 per capita per year for the next 25 years with a discount rate of $4.5 percent. This present value is $1,359, as shown in Table 20.9.

The Circulator System mitigation cost per unit of development is shown in Table 20.10. These costs, assessed as an alternative to transportation concurrency, should recoup the City of Aventura's costs of meeting the need for mobility with the City's Circulator System. The total costs to the city have been adjusted for the availability of other funds to pay this cost. As such, the amounts shown represent a proportionate share of the City of Aventura's costs of meeting the needs of additional residential and non-residential development by means of the City's Circulator System.

In review, it should be recognized that the city is requiring developers to make a

TABLE 20.9 Circulator Cost per Capita, City of Aventura

Cost per Route	$144,144
Seats per Route	22
Cost per Seat	$6,552
Paid by County Transit System Surtax	51%
Net Cost to City per Seat	$3,231
Level of Service	0.0276
Cost per Capita	$89.29
Years	25
Discount Rate	4.25%
Present Value	$1,359

Source: James C. Nicholas, City of Aventura, FL

TABLE 20.10 Transportation Mitigation Fee per Unit, City of Aventura

	Persons per Unit	*Cost per Unit*
Residence per Dwelling	0.972	$1,320.70
Office per 1,000 ft²	1.557	$2,115.94
Retail per 1,000 ft²	2.203	$2,993.95
Industrial per 1,000 ft²	1.324	$1,799.30
Institutional & Other per 1,000 ft²	2.396	$3,255.14

Source: James C. Nicholas, City of Aventura, FL.

present payment to cover future costs of providing the Circulator Service. The preferred way of implementing such a program would be for the city to deposit all mitigation fees collected into a trust fund and then annually appropriate the earnings from this fund to the Circulator System. In this way, there is consistency between the assumptions of the fee calculations and the use of the funds. The appendix to this chapter presents an approach to implementing this program through an ordinance. While crafted for specific application to Aventura, the general features of the ordnance may be broadly applicable.

20.3 TRANSPORTATION UTILITY FEE (TUF)

We continue with the full application of a TUF that includes both O&M and capital costs (see Seggerman et al. 2010).[3] Conceptually, a TUF would be assessed on all property within a community based on its estimated burdens on streets and associated infrastructure such as sidewalks and drainage and including all O&M. It would be a recurring fee such as an annual assessment attached to the property tax statement. In addition to being differentiated by land use, ideally, TUF assessments would vary by service area, so that not only are more costly land uses assessed more, but more costly areas are assessed more as well.

Many kinds of facilities are financed through user fees, especially water and wastewater services. These are often called "enterprise funds" because they are self-funded and usually do not rely on local taxes. In this sense, they are a "closed system" in that system costs and revenues are accounted for fully within the enterprise itself. By analogy in the context of water and wastewater systems, utility fees are usually composed of three elements:

Capital facilities such as central treatment facilities and distribution systems. Central treatment includes water and wastewater treatment plants, storage, treatment, and administration. Generally, central facilities serve all users proportionately in that the cost per gallon of treatment is usually the same among different land uses. However, distribution networks are different because they include the lines, pumps, and other facilities that connect users to the central treatment facilities. The per unit cost of distributing facilities can vary by density, terrain, and distance from central facilities, among other factors. Capital facilities costs also include long-term financing, usually through debt such as bonds and pay-as-you go financing from user-based cash flow.

Operations and Maintenance (O&M) includes operations and routine repairs of all capital facilities. While the cost of maintaining and repairing central systems can be assigned to all users proportionately to their use, distribution network costs can vary by location, distance, and density, as noted earlier.

Administrative costs are often considered system-wide financing obligations, but this is incorrect, because maintenance of the distribution networks will vary.

Utility rates are established to recover all three cost components. Usually, this is nothing more than adding up all the costs and establishing average cost assessment methods, which leads to inefficient and inequitable outcomes.

The utility enterprise funding model is gradually being applied to finance transportation systems. TUFs have a significant advantage over property taxes in financing road systems because they are fees dedicated to roads and cannot be used for any other purpose (Ewing 1994). They also allow the local government to off-load all or part of the road maintenance costs from property taxes to the TUF assessment, thereby freeing up property tax revenue for other purposes including reducing them.

What follows are conceptual calculations of TUFs only. We present the general framework first and then applications varying by service area. The basic formula follows:

Unit Demand = number of dwelling units, square feet, or hotel rooms on a particular parcel

Trip Generation Factor = Total Average Daily Trips

Base Rate = Average Yearly Costs based on Total Average Daily Trips

An example application of this formula is shown in Table 20.11. Within this framework, one can imagine the following refinements to improve efficiency and equity in outcomes:

- Residential land uses would be calibrated to the size of the residential unit and broadened to include more of them.
- Instead of daily trips, trip miles could be used, especially if service areas are used to more efficiently and equitably apportion the burden.
- Service areas could be added based on location, terrain, density, and other factors to encourage more efficient land uses as well as help advance equity.

TUFs are used in several states, including, but likely not limited to, Colorado, Florida, Idaho, Missouri, Montana, Oregon, Texas, Utah, and Washington. As fiscal stresses mount, it seems likely that other states will follow.

An important element of TUFs is that they may be a supplement to transportation impact fees. For instance, while impact fees may be used to finance new or expanded capacity, the TUF can be used to finance the repair, rehabilitation, and replacement of existing capital stock.

TABLE 20.11 Transportation Utility Fee Illustration

Trip Application Land Use	Daily Trips[a]	Cost @ $4/ Trip/Year
Single family	10	$40
Multifamily	6	$24
Hotel room	9	$36
1,000 SF office	10	$40
1,000 SF commercial	70	$280
1,000 SF industrial	6	$24

[a]Net yearly costs include O&M and all capital costs including debt service net of other revenues such as dedicated taxes and fees. Net costs would exclude that portion of transportation facilities financed from impact fees, if any.

20.3.1 Trip Calculation

Net Average Yearly Costs* @ $10,000,000 = $4/annual trip
Total Average Daily Trips @ 2,500,000

20.4 SUMMARY OBSERVATIONS

Proportionate-share concepts can be applied broadly, and perhaps outside specific impact fee enabling legislation, where home rule and related powers provide discretion or opportunities and where rational-nexus relationships can be established. Indeed, O&M mitigation fees and more broadly, TUFs are very important advances in transportation mitigation, and their logic can be extended to *all* infrastructure everywhere.

NOTES

1 1. 199 Cal. App. 3d 1496; 246 Cal. Rptr. 21.

2 As reported by the Institute for Transportation Engineers, *Trip Generation*, 7th Edition, 2003.

3 For a detailed analysis of the design and policy features of TUFs, see Voulgaris (2016).

REFERENCES

Ewing, R. (1994). Characteristics, causes, and effects of sprawl: A literature review. *Urban Studies*, 21(2), 1–15.

Nelson, A. C., Nicholas, J. C., & Juergensmeyer, J. C. (2022). *Model Fiscal Impact Ordinance*. Washington, DC: Smart Growth America.

Seggerman, K. E., Nelson, A. C., Nicholas, J. C., Williams, K. M., Lin, P.-S., & Fabregas, A. (2010). *The Transportation Utility Fee*. Tampa: Center for Urban Transportation Research, University of South Florida. Retrieved May 4, 2021 from www.researchgate.net/publication/283707889_The_Transportation_Utility_Fee

Voulgaris, C. T. (2016). A TUF sell: Transportation utility fees as user fees for local roads and streets. *Public Works Management & Policy*, 21(4): 305–323.

21 PARKING IN-LIEU FEE INCENTIVIZES DEVELOPMENT IN DOWNTOWN OXNARD, CALIFORNIA

ALISON BOULEY

21.1 OVERVIEW

This case study shows how the City of Oxnard, California, leveraged its parking surplus to incentivize development in downtown through a parking in-lieu fee.

Home to nearly 210,000 residents in the 2020s, the City of Oxnard is the largest city in Ventura County. Oxnard was founded in 1903 around a sugar beet processing factory built inland from the shipping harbor of Port Hueneme. The City's agricultural roots run deep, but it has evolved to comprise a mix of industries, housing, and commercial entities, including two military bases and a full-service deepwater port. Over the past 20 years, Oxnard has welcomed nearly 40,000 new residents and is projected to grow by nearly 13,000 residents by 2030.

Oxnard's 2030 General Plan seeks to grow and diversify further by advancing the City's business-friendly reputation. Oxnard, like many cities in coastal California, does not have the land for continued geographic expansion and needs to increase density for continued growth. Central to this goal is a downtown corridor redevelopment effort aimed at increasing density, making housing affordable, and creating a more livable, workable community.

The forward-looking initiative envisions a less car-centric live/work space, accounting for emerging trends in transportation like rideshares, mass transit, and biking. Currently, parking is abundant in Oxnard, and the City owns a parking garage. Officials leveraged this surplus of parking to incentivize development by downsizing the City's parking requirements—recognizing the cost-prohibitive nature of garages costing upwards of $40,000 per space.

With the help of the advisors and impact fee specialists at Harris & Associates, Oxnard's leaders are in the process of adopting a parking in-lieu fee. This in-lieu fee enables developers to pay into a public fund rather than provide on-site parking, which can intensify land use with more vertical and denser development options. The City will invest the parking in-lieu funds in new vehicle-reducing infrastructure and pay off the debt associated with the existing parking garage.

The new infrastructure will feature enhanced micromobility solutions that reduce reliance on automobiles—such as new bike routes and bike and scooter share programs—as well as expanded busing options and greater accessibility for the City's Amtrak and Metrolink station. These transit services allow commuters options for car-free travel to neighboring communities from Santa Barbara to Burbank in around an hour.

21.2 POLICY FRAMEWORK

In 1996, the City enacted its first downtown code, allowing types of development that aren't allowed in other areas of the City. Since its initial adoption, the code has been revised several times, most recently in July 2019. The revisions have allowed more intense land uses with higher densities, lower setbacks, and modified parking requirements. The revised

DOI: 10.4324/9781003336075-26

code is also designed to create a more livable and walkable community, transitioning from the urban sprawl that has dominated southern California for the past several decades.

The City's goal is to increase density and create more affordable housing as it grows. The revised development code raises height restrictions, increases allowable densities, decouples on-site parking, and lowers parking requirements. Along with the update to the downtown code, the City adopted a parking in-lieu fee in the fall of 2019. Figure 21.1 shows Oxnard's downtown zoning districts.

21.3 THE GOAL OF IN-LIEU FEES

While impact fees are generally designed for new development to pay a proportionate share of the cost of new or existing infrastructure, in-lieu fees offer developers an opportunity to provide mitigation to a requirement by paying a fee rather than directly meeting the requirement. This allows cities to create large-scale mitigation programs and provides a tool for them to meet community goals—social, economic, and environmental.

The goal of the parking in-lieu fee is to incentivize downtown growth while creating more affordable housing and implementing innovative, sustainable development projects. Traditional parking requirements—where each business and residence mitigates its full parking impact on-site—create underused parking spaces that often sit vacant much of the time.

The legal requirements of an in-lieu fee are less rigorous than those of fees created under the Mitigation Fee Act. Developers are not required to pay in-lieu fees. Offered as an option to meet development requirements, in-lieu fees require a reasonable relationship between the fee and the project's impact.[1]

21.4 TECHNICAL ANALYSIS

In July 2018, the City completed a parking study to understand the quantity and availability of parking in downtown Oxnard. The analysis is straightforward. The study showed that the City currently has a total parking supply consisting of both city-owned on-street and off-street parking, as well as privately owned parking, as shown in Table 21.1

After completion of the parking survey, the City worked with Harris & Associates to create a land-use analysis and projected parking demand for 2030 development under the new parking requirements. The current development in the parking district includes more than one million square feet of non-residential space and 225 residential dwelling units. By 2030, the City expects an additional 225,000 square feet of non-residential space (26% growth) and an additional 771 residential units, as shown in Table 21.2.

The former parking code required one space for every 500 square feet of non-residential development and 1.65 parking spaces per residential unit, which would have required adding 1,723 spaces to the parking district. Under the updated downtown code, the City required one space per 1,000 square feet for non-residential and only one space per unit for residential. The updated parking code will drop the on-site parking requirement to one space per 1,000 square feet of non-residential development with up to 100% of the parking being provided via the in-lieu fee. The residential requirement will drop to one space per residential unit with up to 50% of the parking being provided via the in-lieu fee, as shown in Table 21.3.

The next step is assessing the parking spots needed at buildout of downtown under the old requirements and the new requirements. This leads to Table 21.4 which compares the required parking under the former downtown development code and the updated code.

At buildout, it is expected that several of the existing parking lots will be developed, leaving the City with 2,512 parking spaces. Given the new requirements, and assuming that the developers take the maximum in-lieu option,

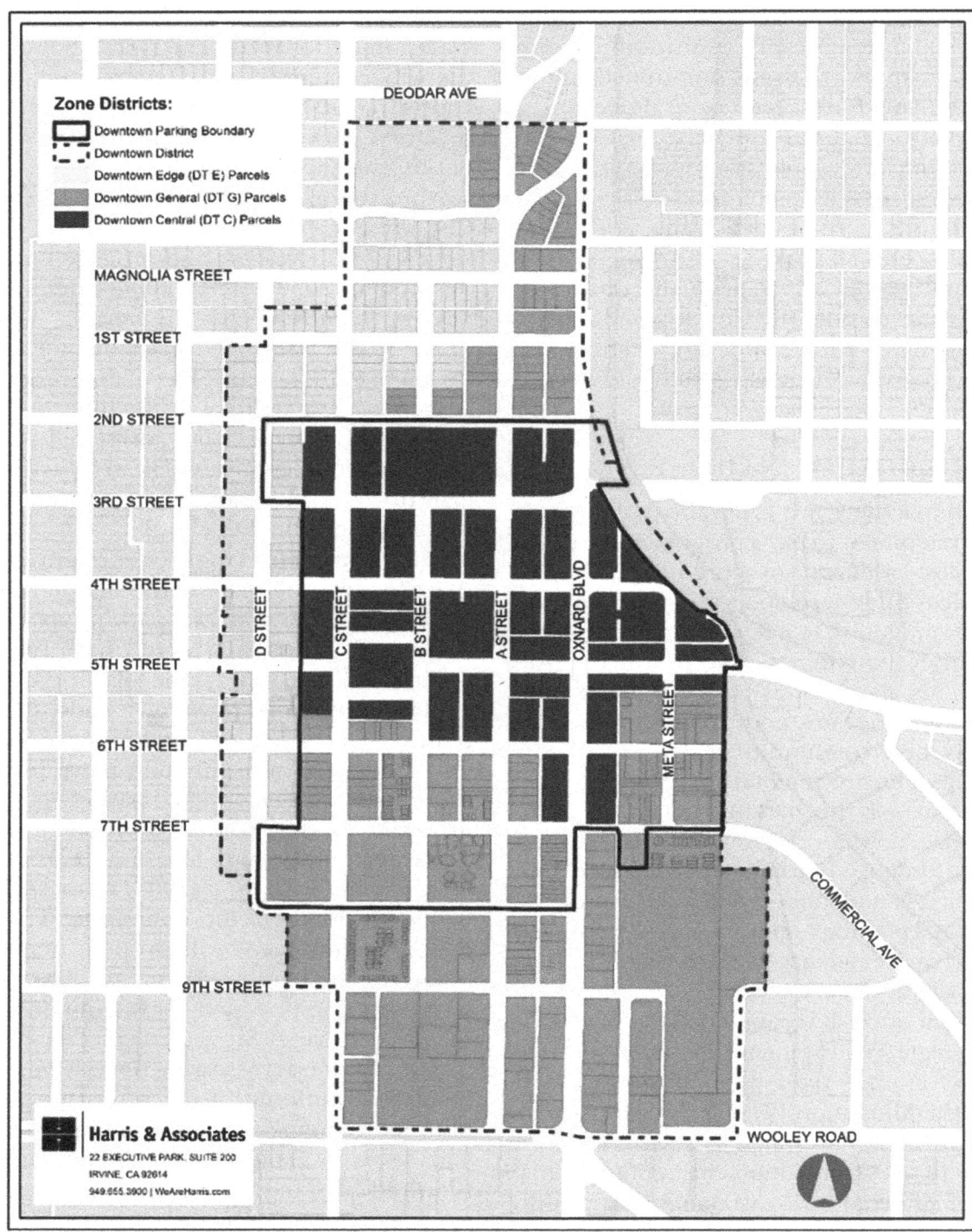

FIGURE 21.1 Zoning districts in downtown Oxnard, California.

TABLE 21.1 Baseline Publicly Owned Parking Supply

Publicly Owned Parking Supply		Privately Owned Parking	Total Parking Supply
On-Street Parking	Off-Street Parking		
1,020 spaces	1,682 spaces	942 spaces	3,644 spaces

TABLE 21.2 Projected Development

Analytic Step	Non-residential Square Footage	Residential Units
Development of Vacant Parcels	19,210	19
AAHOP Sites[a]	–	300
City Revitalization Sites	100,000	430
10% Growth to Existing Development	106,400	22
Projected 2030 Development	**225,610**	**771**

[a]All Affordable Housing Opportunity Program—specific sites identified in the housing element allowed to develop at higher densities than allowed by zoning if the project is deed-restricted as affordable.

TABLE 21.3 Comparison between Former and Updated Parking Requirements

Land Use	Former Required Parking	Updated Parking Requirements	In-Lieu Options
Non-residential	1 space per 500 square feet	1 space per 1,000 square feet	Up to 100% in-lieu
Residential	1.65 spaces per unit	1 space per unit	Up to 50% in-lieu

TABLE 21.4 New Off-Street Parking Needs

Land Use	Square Feet/ Units	Old Requirement Parking	New Required Off-Site Parking (Maximum In-Lieu)
Existing Non-residential Demand	1,064,171	2,129	1,065
New Non-residential	225,610	452	226
New Residential[a]	771	1,273	385
Total		**3,854**	**1.676**

[a]New residential will require 50% of the parking to be provided on-site; 385 is the off-site/in-lieu demand.

the City will have an excess parking capacity of 836 spaces, as shown in Table 21.5.

In order to make a recommendation on the parking-in-lieu fee amount, a survey of recently constructed garages was completed. The cost of a parking spot within a garage averages $44,000 per space, as shown in Table 21.6. In effect, the City could set the in-lieu fee as high as $44,000 per mitigated spot based on the anticipated construction costs of a new garage. Based on the analysis, the City is anticipated to have an excess of 836 spaces at buildout, making the construction of additional parking an unnecessary cost for developers to bear.

The City plans to use the parking in-lieu fees to retire the debt associated with the existing B Street parking garage and pay for projects

TABLE 21.5 Projected Excess Parking Supply

Analytic Step	Figure
2030 On-Street Parking Supply	1,020
2030 Off-Street Parking Supply	1,492
Total 2030 Parking Supply	2,512
Estimated 2030 Maximum Parking Demand	1,676
Excess 2030 Parking Supply	**836**

TABLE 21.6 Parking Garage Construction Cost Survey

City	Garage Size	Cost per Space	Year Completed	Adjusted Cost per Space
Oxnard, CA	440	$24,000[a]	2011	$29,900[a]
Santa Clarita, CA	372	42,000	2018	42,700
LAX, Los Angeles, CA	4,700	44,500	Estimated 2021	44,500
San Diego Airport, CA	4,700	44,200	2018	44,950
Average				**$44,050**

[a]Oxnard parking garage costs did not include land purchase costs and were excluded from the average.

TABLE 21.7 Comparative Parking In-Lieu Fees

City	Parking In-Lieu Fee	Year Adopted
Ventura	$29,484	2017
Huntington Beach	27,350	2014
Carlsbad	11,240	2017
San Luis Obispo	18,641	2015
Dana Point	15,000	2014

that will lower overall parking demand while increasing walkability/alternative transportation options. In order to determine the in-lieu fee in other cities, a survey of surrounding agencies was completed, as summarized in Table 21.7.

City staff proposed a fee of $10,000 to stakeholders. This fee is below the cost to construct garage parking and is designed to spur growth. The City has no projected need to construct an additional garage and is anticipated to still have an excess parking supply in 2030. Under the prior downtown code, building on-site parking would have added $66,000 per residential unit to the construction cost for non-surface lot parking.

Under the new parking code, the cost of parking could be as low as $27,000 per unit (0.5 spaces provided on-site with 0.5 spaces provided via the in-lieu fee). The proposed fee provides parking at a below-market rate that will incentivize growth and balance parking supply and demand. Harris will meet with the Planning Commission, the local development community, and City Council before finalizing the study.

The City estimates nearly all new commercial parking to be mitigated via the in-lieu fee but is uncertain whether residential projects will take advantage of this option. Table 21.8 shows the potential revenues the in-lieu fee could generate for the City.

The City has also discussed establishing a funding mechanism for long-term maintenance of the garage, street parking, and the cost of transportation alternatives through the formation of a downtown parking district. This will help the City reach its goal of

TABLE 21.8 Projected Parking In-Lieu Fee Revenue

Analytic Step	Non-Residential Projections	Residential Projections	Total Potential In-Lieu Revenues
In-lieu Spaces Provided	226	385	611
Revenue per Space	$10,000	$10,000	$10,000
Total Revenue	**$2,260,000**	**$3,850,000**	**$6,110,000**

revenue neutrality for all parking and alternative transportation projects in the parking district.

21.5 CONCLUSION

The City of Oxnard has leveraged its surplus parking supply to incentivize development in downtown by downsizing the City's parking requirements and adopting a parking in-lieu fee. This in-lieu fee enables developers to pay into a public fund rather than provide on-site parking, which intensifies land use with more vertical and denser development options. The City will invest the parking-in-lieu funds in new vehicle-reducing infrastructure and pay off the debt associated with the existing parking garage. The revised parking requirements and in-lieu fees will help the community meet their social, economic, and environmental goals.

NOTE

1 This process was a result of *Building Industry Association of Central California v. City of Patterson*, 171 Cal.App.4th 886 (2009).

22 A RATIONAL NEXUS APPROACH SUPPORTING DEVELOPMENT MITIGATION TO INCREASE WORKFORCE HOUSING SUPPLY[1]

22.1 OVERVIEW

Housing for economically active households, which has come to be known as workforce housing, has become an increasingly vexing problem that is especially acute in resort-type areas where housing is extraordinarily expensive. The unavailability has been a constraint on economic development due to a lack of labor, as well as a concern for community viability if only the wealthy can be housed. Workforce housing is a subset of affordable housing. It is housing occupied by or to be occupied by members of the workforce who are employed but are unable to afford market housing at their levels of earned income. In some communities, workforce housing is being sought so that locally employed households can have adequate housing and the need for labor can be met. In addition, many communities are concerned about the social and cultural problems resulting from excluding a large segment of the population from the community.

Does mitigation to increase workforce housing supply meet judicial standards? Is it possible in states with impact fee legislation? We direct readers to James C. Nicholas and Julian Conrad Juergensmeyer (2019) for the legal rationale buttressing the rational nexus basis for using development mitigation to increase workforce housing supply. In doing so, they address certain admonitions raised by David L. Callies (2019: 769). Callies is concerned that local government must first establish the rational nexus between the market price of housing and the need to require developers to set aside some of their units for affordable housing set-asides before considering imposing mitigation. Moreover, local government needs to first prove that certain new development creates a need for affordable housing and then establish the proportionate number of units that need to be set.

In this respect, Nicholas and Juergensmeyer use data and analysis to show that indeed, Jackson/Teton has demonstrated a "clear rational and proportional nexus between market price and the imposition of below-market cost housing set-asides." Although this chapter reviews the planning-based analysis, readers are advised to review Nicholas and Juergensmeyer (2019) for the legal rationale used to address Callies' concerns.

Having established the legal rationale supporting development mitigation to increase workforce housing supply, Nicholas and Juergensmeyer address potential concerns in states with impact fee legislation. In those states, would workforce housing be considered a form of communitywide infrastructure akin to what are called "system" improvements in some state impact statutes—such as a wastewater treatment plant serving an entire service area—and thus subject to statutory constraints, if not prohibitions? Or, would it be a "project" improvement akin to onsite stormwater detention/retention to mitigate adverse offsite stormwater impacts? If mitigation to increase workforce housing supply based on the methodology presented in this chapter is considered a project improvement—that is, unless the project mitigates its impact on workforce housing either by providing it onsite (or elsewhere) or by paying mitigation fees in-lieu for local government to provide it—limitations of state impact fee legislation may not apply. Readers are again

DOI: 10.4324/9781003336075-27

advised to review Nicholas and Juergensmeyer (2019) for their legal assessment.

This chapter presents a case study of City of Jackson and Teton County (Jackson/Teton), Wyoming in its effort to mitigate the impact of new development on workforce housing supply. It begins with a summary of the background and policy rationale used by Jackson/Teton supporting its mitigation program. It continues with the context and need for intervention to provide workforce housing in Jackson/Teton. This is followed by a review of the steps used to establish a rational nexus approach supporting development mitigation to increase workforce housing supply based on proportionality principles. The chapter concludes with the proposition that workforce housing (and similar forms of mitigation) may be considered project (as opposed to system) improvements because they are obligations of new development to mitigate its proportionate impact on workforce housing in the community.

22.3 BACKGROUND AND POLICY RATIONALE

For background, Craig Richardson, Esq., of Clarion and Associates, together with James C. Nicholas, has prepared developer provisions of workforce housing programs ("the Clarion programs") for local governments in Colorado, Florida, and Wyoming (Clarion Associates 2018). The Clarion programs present a breakthrough method to determine the amount of workforce housing that residential and non-residential developers must provide to attain an adequate supply of affordable workforce housing. The method measures the employee generation of the proposed development and then ascertains the percentage of those employees who will need affordable housing.

The Clarion programs are nexus based, proportionate, and used to internalize the costs associated with new development rather than pass them on to local governments and their taxpayers. They are best labeled as "proportionate share mitigation requirements" in that

developers are being required to mitigate the costs imposed on the jurisdiction. The Clarion programs do not follow the common approach of many local governments that seek to obtain workforce and affordable housing through set-asides required or incentivized through so-called "inclusionary zoning" or "inclusionary housing programs." Unlike the Clarion approach, most inclusionary housing programs require residential unit developers to set aside a certain percentage—often between 10 percent and 20 percent of units—for affordable housing, based on the income of the people who buy or rent them. Many such programs also require non-residential developments, such as office buildings or office parks, to build or fund affordable or workforce housing units. Often, rent restrictions are imposed as part of such programs. One of the problems presented by this usual approach is the basis—nexus and proportionality—for whatever percentage is required.

Instead, the Clarion programs are grounded in the required dedications approach, which was formulated during the heyday of subdivision regulation that evolved to include various mitigation requirements and the policy of allowing developers to pay in-lieu of constructing whatever is needed for mitigation. In most states from the beginning—and now everywhere—these required dedications and mitigations had to meet reasonable standards to satisfy their validity pursuant to the police power. These standards are best encapsulated in the "Dual Rational Nexus Test" (see Chapter 2), which holds that such requirements must have a reasonable or rational nexus with the actual needs created by the development and that such requirements must be reasonably proportionate to the impact of development.

Several communities have established workforce housing programs employing the nexus and proportionality requirements. Perhaps best known are the City of Aspen and Pitkin County, Colorado, Islamorada, Florida, and more recently the City of Jackson and Teton County, Wyoming, which is the case study presented here.

22.4 THE CONTEXT FOR INTERVENTION

When designing a mitigation program, it is important to identify the problem and generate findings that can be used to frame the rational basis of the effort. In this case, housing in the City of Jackson and Teton County (Jackson/Teton) is expensive and results in a serious housing affordability problem for the workforce. This is largely due to influences and factors outside Teton County. The county is a beautiful place, attractive to many affluent second-home buyers and permanent residents. Also, developable land in the county is limited. Consider the findings over the 32-year period from 1986 through 2018 shown, in Table 22.1.

In 1986, housing was affordable to median income earners, since median income was 30 percent of sales prices. The affordability gap grew throughout the period except

during the Great Recession. Incomes were growing, but the housing prices were ballooning at twice the rate of incomes. Figure 22.1 illustrates these trends.

Table 22.2 reports data for sales of homes from 2003 to 2017 by type of housing and sales price. It accounts for the range that housing prices fall into. The bottom of Table 22.2 displays the aggregate conclusion that during 2003–2017, 12.6 percent of houses sold at or below the affordable limit (333 percent of median household income), the vast majority of which were multifamily (condominiums). More recently, between 2013 and 2017, only 6 percent of sales were at or below affordable levels, again mostly multifamily (condominium). Collectively, Tables 22.1 and 22.2 demonstrate the serious housing affordability problem in the City of Jackson/Teton County for the workforce.

After identifying the need for intervention, the next step is to determine the employee households that could not reasonably afford housing. This is done by first determining the cost to build a modest dwelling unit for an employee (a "prototypical unit") and then determining whether the employee could reasonably afford to pay for or rent the unit. Housing costs are based on actual construction and land costs incurred by the Jackson/Teton County Housing Authority ("Housing Authority") to acquire land and construct

TABLE 22.1 Change in Income, Housing Prices, and Income to Price Ratio, 1986–2018

Metric	Change	Annual Rate
Median Household Income	262%	4.1%
Median Selling Prices	1,281%	8.5%

Note: Median family income as a percentage of price fell from 30.2% to 7.4%.

Source: Clarion Associates, 2018.

Household Income and SF Selling Prices
Teton County 1986-2018

FIGURE 22.1 Median household income, affordable housing prices, and median sales prices, Teton County, 1986–2018. (From Clarion Associates, 2018.)

TABLE 22.2 Individual Sales by Type of Housing and Sales Price, Teton County, 2003–2017

Year	Median HH Income	Affordable Price at 333% of Income	Sales at or below Affordable			Total Units Sold			Total Units Sold	Affordable Price Units as % of Annual Sales
			SFD	SFA	Condo	SFD	SFA	Condo		
2003	$69,900	$233,000	0	3	64	250	89	157	496	13.5%
2004	$73,500	$245,000	0	15	126	189	93	239	521	27.1%
2005	$76,700	$255,667	0	19	137	189	93	239	521	29.9%
2006	$81,800	$272,667	1	0	108	293	100	254	647	16.8%
2007	$81,000	$270,000	0	0	3	209	80	160	449	0.7%
2008	$83,300	$277,667	0	0	4	116	47	92	255	1.6%
2009	$89,500	$298,333	0	0	8	96	23	34	153	5.2%
2010	$92,500	$308,333	0	0	17	103	35	48	186	9.1%
2011	$94,500	$315,000	1	11	27	130	30	72	232	16.8%
2012	$96,200	$320,667	4	16	29	153	47	71	271	18.1%
2013	$96,300	$321,000	2	12	27	199	75	106	380	10.8%
2014	$96,800	$322,667	1	1	33	162	56	106	324	10.8%
2015	$90,700	$302,333	1	1	17	178	82	114	374	5.1%
2016	$85,800	$286,000	0	0	10	185	74	118	377	2.7%
2017	$91,400	$304,667	0	0	4	192	82	114	388	1%
All Sales 2003–17			10	78	614	2,644	1,006	1,924	5,574	12.6%
All Sales 2013–17			4	14	91	916	369	558	1,843	5.9%
% at or under Affordability Threshold: 2003–17			0.2%	1.4%	11%					12.6%
% at or under Affordability Threshold: 2013–17			0.2%	0.8%	4.9%					5.9%

HH = Household; SFD = Single Family Detached; SFA = Single Family Attached

Source: Clarion Associates, 2018.

TABLE 22.3 Gross and Living Floor Area of Workforce Housing Projects, Teton County, 2018

	Gross Area (in square foot)	Living Area	Units	per Unit	
				Gross Area	Living Area
174 N. King St.	31,531	21,286	30	1,051	710
Redmond Street Rentals	35,078	18,645	26	1,349	717
Grove Phase 2	42,141	33,252	24	1,756	1,386
Totals	108,750	73,183	80		
Averages				1,359	915

Source: Clarion Associates, 2018.

housing. The records for their most recent developments are shown in Table 22.3. Table 22.4 shows the Housing Authority's costs to build the projects. (We note that land cost as a share of total cost is 22 percent or higher than typical.)

Table 22.4 shows that at a gross cost of $377 per foot of floor area, the average cost of a 1,359 square foot unit would be $512,758, which includes $112,836 for land and $399,922 for construction. This cost is used as the prototypical workforce housing cost in establishing the payment in-lieu of the required dedication. These costs are the actual costs incurred by the Housing Authority to provide affordable housing. There is an expectation (perhaps hope) that units could be provided at lower costs by various private contractors.

TABLE 22.4 Land and Construction Cost of Workforce Housing
Projects, Teton County, 2018

	Land Cost	Construction	Total
174 N. King St.	$1,885,487	$13,198,409	$15,083,896
Redmond Street Rentals	$3,645,000	$9,255,000	$12,900,000
Grove Phase 2	$3,498,930	$9,549,163	$13,048,093
Totals	$9,029,417	$32,002,572	$41,031,990
per Gross Foot	$83	$294	$377

Source: Clarion Associates, 2018.

If so, the cost of the required dedication met by private contractors rather than payment in-lieu would be the preferred alternative.

Given household income at the time of $81,884 and the distribution of individual household incomes about that mean, the expectation is that 8.59 percent of employee households could afford housing at a cost of $512,758. Moreover, local sales data indicates that 5.9 percent of Teton County housing has sold at prices at or below what the median household could afford. These two data suggest that 14.5 percent of employee housing needs could be met by the market. Such calculation leaves 85.5 percent of workforce households unable to afford prototypical workforce housing in Teton County and thus, in need of some type of housing assistance if they are to have affordable housing in Teton County.

Residential and non-residential development in Jackson/Teton places a demand for labor (the workforce) and the need for affordable workforce housing in four ways:

1. The construction of the building (i.e., construction employees for both residential and non-residential development)
2. The operation and maintenance of the residential building (by employees who provide services to the residential building)
3. The use of the structure by the different types of non-residential businesses once the building is constructed
4. The critical service providers (fire and rescue personnel and law enforcement personnel) who support development (both residential and non-residential, to varying degrees)

All these activities generate employment, and because of their wage levels and existing housing prices, their employment results in a need for affordable workforce housing. The demand for labor (employees) that both residential and non-residential development creates and the demand these employees place on the need for affordable housing is outlined in the following sections.

22.4.1 Nexus for Construction Employment–Based Workforce Housing

Construction employees are essential for the construction of both residential and non-residential buildings. As a consequence, construction employment is common to both residential and non-residential workforce housing programs. Table 22.5 correlates the

TABLE 22.5 Construction Employee Years per
1,000 ft² of Floor Area

Non-Residential	
Lodging	1.234
Office	1.234
Retail	1.234
Industrial	0.514
Institutional	0.927
Food & Drinking Places	1.234

Source: Clarion Associates, 2018.

TABLE 22.6 Construction Employee Housing Needs by Industry and per 1,000 Square Feet

	Residential per 1,000 ft²	Retail per 1,000 ft²	Eating & Drinking per 1,000 ft²	Office per 1,000 ft²	Industrial per 1,000 ft²	Institutional per 1,000 ft²	Lodging per Room
Construction Employees per 1,000 ft²	0.041	0.041	0.041	0.041	0.017	0.031	0.041
Employees per Household	1.774	1.774	1.774	1.774	1.774	1.774	1.774
Construction Employee Households per 1,000 ft²	0.023	0.023	0.023	0.023	0.01	0.017	0.023
Households able to Afford Market Housing	0.005	0.005	0.005	0.005	0.002	0.003	0.005
Available Affordable Housing per 1,000 ft²	0.001	0.001	0.001	0.001	0	0.001	0.001
Net Affordable Housing Need per 1,000 ft²	0.017	0.017	0.017	0.017	0.007	0.013	0.017

Source: Clarion Associates, 2018.

amount of construction employment by type of building, with the size of building (employee years it takes to build 1,000 square feet of the building). Data for this analysis originated from (1) building permit records for both the County and the Town of Jackson for a 10-year period, 2001–2011, and (2) information on construction employees from the Quarterly Report on Employment and Earnings.

Table 22.6 shows construction employee housing needs by industry per 1,000 square feet of floor area of development, given 30 years of economic activity by the employee and 1.774 employed persons per household.

After the affordable housing needs are determined for construction employees, the subsidy needed to make a prototypical unit is determined and summarized in Table 22.7. A construction employee's earned income for 2018 was $50,163. As noted earlier, census data report that the households of construction

TABLE 22.7 Construction Employee Affordability Gap

Construction Worker Earned Income	$50,163
Income from Others in Household	$36,310
Average Seasonal Income	$1,152
Total Household Income	$87,625
Affordability Threshold (333% of Household Income)	$292,087
Average Cost for Prototype Workforce Housing Unit	$512,758
Workforce Housing Gap per Construction Employee	$220,671

Source: Clarion Associates, 2018.

employees will, on average, have 0.774 additional employed persons in that household. Because nothing is known about those other employees, it is assumed that they will earn the average employee salary of $44,281. Moreover, local experience and employment records show that many employees have second seasonal jobs. Employment and earnings data suggest that seasonal second income would be approximately13 percent of base income.

22.4.2 Nexus for Non-residential Workforce Housing

The next step is to estimate the workforce housing demand created by new residents (including seasonal residents) to Jackson/Teton. A survey of Jackson and Teton County businesses with respect to their employees was conducted to assist in determining the number of employees at different types of

businesses in the community, presented in Table 22.8. The data sets were organized by industry and by land use. This data was then converted to employee households by industry and land use. This is shown in Table 22.9. The number of construction employee households was then added to the employee households from the different industries and land uses for non-residential total employment. This is reported in Table 22.10.

Because Jackson/Teton was also concerned about affordable workforce housing availability for critical employees (law enforcement and firefighting, including emergency medical personnel), as well as those directly employed

TABLE 22.8 Summary of Survey Results, Employees by Land Use

Land Use	Floor Area	Employees		Employees per 1,000 ft²	
		Year Round	Peak Season	Year Round	Peak Season
Retail	505,677	619	3,304	1.224	6.534
Bar/Restaurant	45,000	88	411	1.956	9.133
Office	957,065	841	1,940	0.879	2.027
Industrial	111,342	182	114	1.635	1.024
Hotel/Lodging	1,233,200	78	503	0.063	0.408
Special	41,000	109	151	2.659	3.683
Other	96,399	277	312	2.873	3.237
		Employees		**Employees**	
Hotel/Lodging	**Rooms**	**Year Round**	**Peak Season**	**Year Round**	**Peak Season**
Hotel/Lodging per Room				0.487	0.958

Source: Clarion Associates, 2018.

TABLE 22.9 Employee Households by Land Use

Land Use	Employees per Household	Households per 1,000 ft²	
		Year Round	Peak Season
Retail	1.706	0.718	3.83
Bar/Restaurant	2	0.978	4.568
Office	1.678	0.524	1.208
Industrial	1.652	0.99	0.62
Hotel/Lodging	2	0.032	0.204
Special	1.713	1.552	2.15
Other	1.713	1.677	1.889
	Employees per Household	**Households per Room** **Year Round**	**Peak Season**
Hotel/Lodging per Room	2	0.244	0.479

Source: Clarion Associates, 2018.

TABLE 22.10 Non-Residential Employees and Employee Households by Land Use

	Construction		Permanent		Total	
	Employees	Households	Employees	Households	Employees	Households
Retail per 1,000 ft²	0.041	0.023	1.224	0.718	1.265	0.741
Eating & Drinking per 1,000 ft²	0.041	0.023	1.956	0.978	1.997	1.001
Office per 1,000 ft²	0.041	0.023	0.879	0.524	0.92	0.547
Industrial per 1,000 ft²	0.041	0.023	1.635	0.99	1.676	1.013
Institutional per 1,000 ft²	0.017	0.01	0.063	0.032	0.08	0.042
Lodging per Room	0.031	0.017	2.659	1.552	2.69	1.569

Source: Clarion Associates, 2018.

TABLE 22.11 Non-Residential Employee Households by Land Use

	Construction	Permanent	Critical	Total
Retail per 1,000 ft²	0.023	0.718	0.00224	0.743
Eating & Drinking per 1,000 ft²	0.023	0.978	0.00224	1.003
Office per 1,000 ft²	0.023	0.524	0.00224	0.549
Industrial per 1,000 ft²	0.023	0.99	0.00224	1.015
Institutional per 1,000 ft²	0.01	0.032	0.00224	0.044
Lodging per Room	0.017	1.552	0.00224	1.571

Source: Clarion Associates, 2018.

on new development, Jackson/Teton County calculated a need for critical employee housing of 0.00224 units per 1,000 square feet of non-residential development. This is shown in Table 22.11.

22.4.3 Nexus for Residential Workforce Housing

The methodology for assessing the need for workforce housing resulting from residential development is similar to the approach used for non-residential development. A survey of residential occupants, homeowners' associations, and property managers was conducted by RRC Associates to determine the number of construction and operations and maintenance employees used at different types and sizes of home. The survey requested the number of employees hired or retained to operate and maintain the residential properties or the amounts paid to services or managers to operate and maintain the property (e.g., property owners' association employees).

Respondents were also asked for the type and size of the residence in square feet of floor area. Residences were divided into four groups based on whether they were detached or attached dwellings:

- Detached dwelling
  - Occupied by local resident
  - Non-local seasonal, vacation, or part-time occupied

- Attached dwelling (referred to in documents as "Other")
  - Occupied by local resident
  - Non-local seasonal, vacation, or part-time occupied

Table 22.12 summarizes the responses from the residential survey.

The results from the survey and the analysis of the results demonstrate that employment proved to be non-linear, because operational and maintenance employment at residences grew at a greater rate than unit size. As might be expected, units occupied

TABLE 22.12 Residential Survey Responses

Respondents Answering Employment Question	**648**
Full-Time Equivalent Employees Employed by Respondents	
Home Owner's Association (HOA) Employees	10
Property Management Employees	9
Onsite Caretakers	13
Contract Employees	26
All Other Employees	29
Total	**87**
Full-Time Equivalent Conversions per Year	
Full-time Equivalent Employees per Year	0.134
Employee Hours per Year	279

Source: Clarion Associates, 2018.

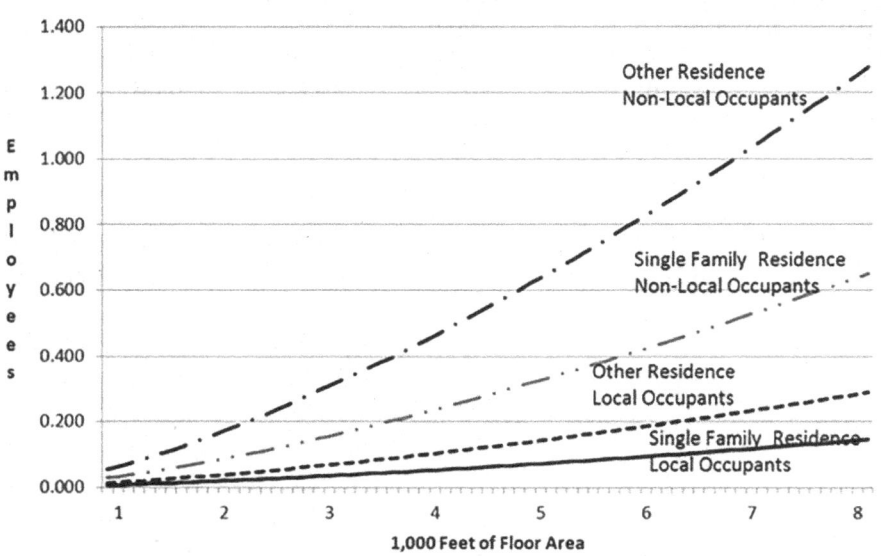

FIGURE 22.2 Operations and maintenance workers. (From Clarion Associates, 2018.)

by non-local residents employed more operational and maintenance employees than units occupied by local residents. This expectation is based on the presumption that local residents would perform more operational and maintenance functions themselves simply because they are present and able to do them. Additionally, detached residences tended to employ fewer operational and maintenance employees than other residences. Regression analysis was used to determine employment by type, size, and occupancy of residence, as shown in Figure 22.2. The data for the regression analysis graphic are shown in Table 22.13.

As with non-residential development, residential development will also require construction and critical service employees. As outlined earlier, construction employment for residential development requires 1.243 employee years and 0.023 construction employee households per 1,000 ft^2 of a residential unit built. Critical employees serving the residential development amount to 0.008

TABLE 22.13 Operations and Maintenance Employees by Residential Unit Type and Size

| | Non-Local | | | | Local | | | |
| | Other Unit | | Single Family Detached (SFD) Unit | | Other Unit | | SFD Unit | |
ft^2	Employees per Unit	Housing Units Needs for Employees	Employees per Unit	Housing Units Needs for Employees	Employees per Unit	Housing Units Needs for Employees	Employees per Unit	Housing Units Needs for Employees
500	0.013	0.007	0.004	0.002	0.007	0.004	0.004	0.002
1,000	0.04	0.022	0.011	0.006	0.021	0.012	0.011	0.006
1,500	0.076	0.042	0.02	0.011	0.04	0.022	0.02	0.011
2,000	0.12	0.067	0.032	0.018	0.063	0.035	0.032	0.018
2,500	0.171	0.095	0.046	0.025	0.09	0.05	0.046	0.025
3,000	0.228	0.127	0.061	0.034	0.12	0.067	0.061	0.034
3,500	0.292	0.162	0.078	0.043	0.153	0.085	0.078	0.043
4,000	0.292	0.162	0.096	0.054	0.153	0.085	0.096	0.054
4,500	0.292	0.162	0.116	0.065	0.153	0.085	0.116	0.065
5,000	0.292	0.162	0.137	0.076	0.153	0.085	0.137	0.076
5,500	0.292	0.162	0.137	0.076	0.153	0.085	0.137	0.076
6,000	0.292	0.162	0.137	0.076	0.153	0.085	0.137	0.076
6,500	0.292	0.162	0.137	0.076	0.153	0.085	0.137	0.076
7,000	0.292	0.162	0.137	0.076	0.153	0.085	0.137	0.076

Source: Clarion Associates, 2018.

and 0.004 households per 1,000 ft². This is shown in Table 22.14.

Table 22.15 summarizes the total number of employee households required to construct and operate/maintain a residential unit by type and size of unit. These data are for all employee households, some of which can obtain housing in Jackson/Teton County without assistance.

22.4.4 Proportionality Analysis

We come now to the proportionality analysis. The RRC survey obtained data by type and size of development, thus providing a basis for the nexus between development and workforce housing for each type and size of development. The nexuses were the employee households needed to serve the residential or non-residential developments. These needs were apportioned to individual types and sizes of both residential and non-residential developments based on localized survey research in conjunction with census, state, and local data for the community. The proportional need for workforce housing for residential development and non-residential development are summarized in Table 22.16 and Table 22.17.

Income and sales data show that 14.7 percent of employee households should be able to obtain housing in Teton County without assistance. This reduction in need is shown in the previous tables. The net need shown is the employee households expected to be in need of housing assistance. This is reported in Table 22.18.

While the goal of the workforce housing program is private provision of such housing, private provision may not be desirable in all situations. Therefore, a payment in-lieu option was provided. The payment in-lieu is based on the net need for workforce housing multiplied by the affordability gap calculated for each group of employee households by land use type. The employee housing affordable gap is multiplied by the net need for workforce housing by land use type to establish the payment in-lieu. This is shown in Tables 22.19, 22.20, and 22.21 for each group of impacted households analyzed previously.

Housing costs and prices, together with employee household income, show that housing availability is severely constrained. This is also true for critical employees. The goal of the Jackson/Teton County workforce housing program is to increase the availability of housing affordable to Teton County employees. The preferred means of attaining the goal is to have private parties assist their employees in obtaining housing in Teton County. If private provision is impractical, a payment in-lieu is available.

22.5 WORKFORCE HOUSING MITIGATION AS A PROJECT IMPROVEMENT

Legal analysis addressed by Clarion Associates (2018) concludes that the Clarion programs do not violate takings and due process requirements. The key issue is that these programs are designed to mitigate the adverse impact of new development on Jackson/Teton with respect to workforce housing. Indeed, it is because of these impacts that local government likely has the option to deny applications for discretionary permits that would increase workforce housing demand without solving it by way of internalizing externalities through the workforce housing program.

This approach may be distinct from typical impact fees. Recall from Chapters 2 and 3 that impact fees are limited to helping with the financing of infrastructure specific on a list. No legislation includes workforce housing on its list of facilities qualifying for impact fees. The Clarion program, however, should not be labeled an impact fee even though, as already discussed, the methodology for calculating the developer provision requirement is similar to that used in impact fee formulae.

TABLE 22.14 Total Residential Employee Households by Type and Size of Unit

ft^2	Non-Local						Local					
	Other Unit			SFD Unit			Other Unit			SFD Unit		
	O & M Households	Construction Households	Critical Employee Households	Operation & Maintenance Households	Construction Households	Critical Employee Households	O & M Households	Construction Households	Critical Employee Households	Operation & Maintenance Households	Construction Households	Critical Employee Households
500	0.007	0.012	0.002	0.002	0.012	0.002	0.004	0.012	0.002	0.002	0.012	0.002
1,000	0.022	0.023	0.004	0.006	0.023	0.004	0.012	0.023	0.004	0.006	0.023	0.004
1,500	0.042	0.035	0.006	0.011	0.035	0.006	0.022	0.035	0.006	0.011	0.035	0.006
2,000	0.067	0.046	0.008	0.018	0.046	0.008	0.035	0.046	0.008	0.018	0.046	0.008
2,500	0.095	0.058	0.01	0.025	0.058	0.01	0.05	0.058	0.01	0.025	0.058	0.01
3,000	0.127	0.069	0.012	0.034	0.069	0.012	0.067	0.069	0.012	0.034	0.069	0.012
3,500	0.162	0.081	0.014	0.043	0.081	0.014	0.085	0.081	0.014	0.043	0.081	0.014
4,000	0.162	0.092	0.016	0.054	0.092	0.016	0.085	0.092	0.016	0.054	0.092	0.016
4,500	0.162	0.104	0.018	0.065	0.104	0.018	0.085	0.104	0.018	0.065	0.104	0.018
5,000	0.162	0.115	0.02	0.076	0.115	0.02	0.085	0.115	0.02	0.076	0.115	0.02
5,500	0.162	0.127	0.022	0.076	0.127	0.022	0.085	0.127	0.022	0.076	0.127	0.022
6,000	0.162	0.138	0.024	0.076	0.138	0.024	0.085	0.138	0.024	0.076	0.138	0.024
6,500	0.162	0.15	0.026	0.076	0.15	0.026	0.085	0.15	0.026	0.076	0.15	0.026
7,000	0.162	0.161	0.028	0.076	0.161	0.028	0.085	0.161	0.028	0.076	0.161	0.028

Source: Clarion Associates, 2018.

TABLE 22.15 Total Employee Households Needed to Construct and Operate/Maintain Residential Unit by Type and Size of Unit—Summary

ft^2	Non-Local		Local	
	Other Unit	SFD Unit	Other Unit	SFD Unit
	Total Employee Households	Total Employee Households	Total Employee Households	Total Employee Households
500	0.021	0.015	0.017	0.015
1,000	0.049	0.033	0.039	0.033
1,500	0.083	0.052	0.063	0.052
2,000	0.121	0.072	0.089	0.072
2,500	0.163	0.093	0.117	0.093
3,000	0.208	0.115	0.148	0.115
3,500	0.257	0.138	0.18	0.138
4,000	0.27	0.162	0.193	0.162

Source: Clarion Associates, 2018.

But, that may be the extent of similarities for several reasons.

First, impact fee legislation refers to exclusively to *public* infrastructure. The preferred method under the Clarion program for developers to meet their workforce housing responsibility is to construct and continue to own and manage the housing. As such, workforce housing would not become public infrastructure but remain private housing that serves the developers' interests in having housing for employees necessary to the success of their developments. Of course, under the Clarion program, a developer, under limited circumstances (e.g., where it is unrealistic for a developer to construct affordable workforce housing), may pay an in-lieu fee instead of constructing affordable workforce housing. Even then, the ownership would not necessarily be in the local government but perhaps a public–private entity or a non-profit, such as Habitat for Humanity or other local non-profit housing providers.

Second, the workforce housing constructed is not a system improvement but a project improvement. Recall in Chapter 3 that impact fee legislation in many states distinguishes between system improvements and project improvements. For example, the Georgia Development Impact Fee Act clearly states: "Nothing in this chapter shall prevent a municipality or county from requiring a developer to construct reasonable project improvements in conjunction with a development project" (Ga. Code § 36-71-13(a)). This point raises the possible argument that the Clarion programs are grounded in the more mitigation-oriented required dedications approach from subdivision regulation law rather than monetary impact fees. Courts generally apply less stringent reasonableness requirements to them (Juergensmeyer, Roberts, Salkin and Rowberry 2018: 7.10). In other words, if a development imposes adverse impacts such as new demands for workforce housing that the community cannot mitigate, the community may have the authority to deny the project unless it internalizes its externalities by mitigating its workforce housing impacts. In this respect, the provision of workforce housing is a project improvement exempt from impact fee legislation. But if the mitigation is based on the formula outlined earlier, it would per se meet reasonable relationship tests (see Clarion Associates 2018 and Chapter 2).

The Clarion approach presents an ideal method to provide workforce housing in new

TABLE 22.16 Summary of Workforce Employee Housing Need and Assistance by Type and Size of Residential Unit

ft²	Non-Local						Local					
	Other Unit			SFD Unit			Other Unit			SFD Unit		
	Total Employee Households	Able to Afford Housing	Net Housing Need	Total Employee Households	Able to Afford Housing	Net Housing Need	Total Employee Households	Able to Afford Housing	Net Housing Need	Total Employee Households	Able to Afford Housing	Net Housing Need
500	0.019	0.003	0.016	0.014	0.002	0.012	0.016	0.002	0.014	0.013	0.002	0.011
1,000	0.046	0.007	0.04	0.03	0.004	0.026	0.036	0.005	0.030	0.027	0.004	0.023
1,500	0.115	0.017	0.098	0.066	0.01	0.056	0.083	0.012	0.071	0.057	0.008	0.049
2,000	0.199	0.029	0.17	0.106	0.015	0.09	0.139	0.02	0.119	0.09	0.013	0.077
2,500	0.223	0.032	0.19	0.13	0.019	0.111	0.201	0.029	0.172	0.114	0.016	0.097
3,000	0.247	0.036	0.211	0.154	0.022	0.131	0.225	0.033	0.192	0.138	0.02	0.118
3,500	0.271	0.039	0.231	0.178	0.026	0.152	0.249	0.036	0.213	0.162	0.023	0.138
4,000	0.295	0.043	0.252	0.202	0.029	0.172	0.273	0.0	0.233	0.185	0.027	0.159

Source: Clarion Associates, 2018.

TABLE 22.17 Workforce Housing in Need of Assistance per 1,000 Square Feet of Non-Residential, Construction, and Post-Construction (Operation and Maintenance)

		Retail	Eating & Drinking Places	Office	Industrial	Institutional	Lodging per Room
Construction							
	Employees	0.041	0.041	0.041	0.041	0.041	0.041
	Households	0.023	0.023	0.023	0.023	0.023	0.023
	Able to Afford Units	0.002	0.002	0.002	0.002	0.002	0.002
	Available Affordable Units	0.001	0.001	0.001	0.001	0.001	0.001
	Net Affordable Units Needed	0.02	0.02	0.02	0.02	0.02	0.02
Post-Construction							
	Employees	1.202	3.911	1.598	0.71	1.598	0.487
	Households	0.705	1.956	0.952	0.43	0.952	0.244
	Able to Afford Units	0.0501	0.1555	0.0968	0.0354	0.0862	0.0214
	Available Affordable Units	0.0416	0.1154	0.0562	0.0254	0.0562	0.0144
	Net Affordable Units Needed	0.6134	1.6851	0.799	0.3692	0.8097	0.2082
Critical Service Providers							
	Employees	0.004	0.004	0.004	0.004	0.004	0.004
	Households	0.0022	0.0022	0.0022	0.0022	0.0022	0.0022
	Able to Afford Units	0.0002	0.0002	0.0002	0.0002	0.0002	0.0002
	Available Affordable Units	0.0001	0.0001	0.0001	0.0001	0.0001	0.0001
	Net Affordable Units Needed	0.0019	0.0019	0.0019	0.0019	0.0019	0.0019
Totals							
	Employees	1.2471	3.9561	1.6431	0.7551	1.6431	0.5321
	Households	0.7302	1.9812	0.9772	0.4552	0.9772	0.2692
	Able to Afford Units	0.0518	0.1573	0.0987	0.0372	0.088	0.0232
	Available Affordable Units	0.0431	0.1169	0.0577	0.0269	0.0577	0.0159
	Net Affordable Units Needed	0.6353	1.707	0.8209	0.3912	0.8316	0.2302

Source: Clarion Associates, 2018.

residential and commercial developments. Rather than following the common approach of set-asides through inclusionary zoning, Clarion offers a formula to calculate the exact need for workforce housing units generated by a new development. Using this formula avoids an arbitrary percentage of units being set aside for workforce housing. Additionally, by precisely calculating the number of employees generated by a development and then the

TABLE 22.18 Affordability Gap per Employee Household,
Residential and Non-Residential Development

	Household Income	Affordability Limit	Housing Cost	Gap
Residential				
Construction	87,626	292,087	512,758	220,671
Operation & Maintenance	73,342	244,473	512,758	268,285
Critical Service	90,312	301,040	512,758	211,718
Non-Residential				
Construction Permanent	87,626	292,087	512,758	220,671
Retail	64724	215,747	512,758	297,011
Eating & Drinking	73668	245,560	512,758	267,198
Office	96368	321,227	512,758	191,531
Industrial	77758	259,193	512,758	253,565
Institutional	88213	294,043	512,758	218,715
Lodging	81165	270,550	512,758	242,208
Critical Service	90,312	301,040	512,758	211,718

Source: Clarion Associates, 2018.

TABLE 22.19 Total Workforce Housing Assistance Need Created by Local Residential Development
(Single-Family Detached and All Other Units)

Unit Size (ft²)	Local Tenancy Single-Family Detached							
	Construction		Operations and Maintenance		Critical Service Providers		Total	
	Affordable Housing Units Needed	Housing Assistance Needed	Affordable Housing Units Needed	Housing Assistance Needed	Affordable Housing Units Needed	Housing Assistance Needed	Affordable Housing Units Needed	Housing Assistance Needed
500	0.01	$2,185	0.001	$258	0.0003	$65.48	0.011	$2,509
1,000	0.02	$4,369	0.003	$775	0.0007	$130.97	0.023	$5,276
2,000	0.04	$8,739	0.008	$2,197	0.0013	$261.94	0.049	$11,198
3,000	0.059	$13,108	0.015	$4,136	0.002	$392.91	0.077	$17,637
4,000	0.079	$17,477	0.015	$4,136	0.0026	$523.87	0.097	$22,137
5,000	0.099	$21,846	0.015	$4,136	0.0033	$654.84	0.118	$26,637
6,000	0.119	$26,216	0.015	$4,136	0.004	$785.81	0.138	$31,137
7,000	0.139	$30,585	0.015	$4,136	0.0046	$916.78	0.159	$35,638

Unit Size (ft²)	Local Tenancy All Other Units							
	Construction		Operations and Maintenance		Critical Service Providers		Total	
	Affordable Housing Units Needed	Housing Assistance Needed	Affordable Housing Units Needed	Housing Assistance Needed	Affordable Housing Units Needed	Housing Assistance Needed	Affordable Housing Units Needed	Housing Assistance Needed
500	0.01	$2,185	0.003	$905	0.0003	65.4843	0.014	$3,155
1,000	0.02	$4,369	0.01	$2,714	0.0007	130.9686	0.031	$7,214
2,000	0.04	$8,739	0.03	$8,142	0.0013	261.9372	0.071	$17,143
3,000	0.059	$13,108	0.058	$15,509	0.002	392.9058	0.119	$29,010
4,000	0.079	$17,477	0.091	$24,427	0.0026	523.8744	0.173	$42,428
5,000	0.099	$21,846	0.091	$24,427	0.0033	654.8430	0.193	$46,929
6,000	0.119	$26,216	0.091	$24,427	0.004	785.8116	0.214	$51,429
7,000	0.139	$30,585	0.091	$24,427	0.0046	916.7802	0.234	$55,929

TABLE 22.20 Total Workforce Housing Assistance Need Created by Non-Local Residential Development (Single-Family Detached and All Other Units)

| Unit Size (ft²) | Non-Local Tenancy Single-Family Detached | | | | | | | |
| | Construction | | Operations and Maintenance | | Critical Service Providers | | Total | |
	Affordable Housing Units Needed	Housing Assistance Needed	Affordable Housing Units Needed	Housing Assistance Needed	Affordable Housing Units Needed	Housing Assistance Needed	Affordable Housing Units Needed	Housing Assistance Needed
500	0.01	$2,185	0.002	$517	0.0003	$65.48	0.012	$2,767
1,000	0.02	$4,369	0.005	$1,422	0.0007	$130.97	0.026	$5,922
2,000	0.04	$8,739	0.015	$4,136	0.0013	$261.94	0.056	$13,136
3,000	0.059	$13,108	0.029	$7,884	0.002	$392.91	0.091	$21,385
4,000	0.079	$17,477	0.029	$7,884	0.0026	$523.87	0.111	$25,885
5,000	0.099	$21,846	0.029	$7,884	0.0033	$654.84	0.132	$30,385
6,000	0.119	$26,216	0.029	$7,884	0.004	$785.81	0.152	$34,886
7,000	0.139	$30,585	0.029	$7,884	0.0046	$916.78	0.173	$39,386

| Unit Size (ft²) | Non-Local Tenancy All Other Units | | | | | | | |
| | Construction | | Operations and Maintenance | | Critical Service Providers | | Total | |
	Affordable Housing Units Needed	Housing Assistance Needed	Affordable Housing Units Needed	Housing Assistance Needed	Affordable Housing Units Needed	Housing Assistance Needed	Affordable Housing Units Needed	Housing Assistance Needed
500	0.01	$2,185	0.006	$1,680	0.0003	65.4843	0.016	$3,930
1,000	0.02	$4,369	0.019	$5,170	0.0007	130.9686	0.04	$9,670
2,000	0.04	$8,739	0.058	$15,509	0.0013	261.9372	0.099	$24,510
3,000	0.059	$13,108	0.11	$29,468	0.002	392.9058	0.171	$42,969
4,000	0.079	$17,477	0.11	$29,468	0.0026	523.8744	0.192	$47,469
5,000	0.099	$21,846	0.11	$29,468	0.0033	654.8430	0.212	$51,969
6,000	0.119	$26,216	0.11	$29,468	0.004	785.8116	0.233	$56,470
7,000	0.139	$30,585	0.11	$29,468	0.0046	916.7802	0.253	$60,970

TABLE 22.21 Summary of Workforce Housing and Assistance Need for Non-Residential Construction

| | Construction | | Post-Construction | | Critical Service Providers | | Totals | |
	Workforce Housing Units per 1,000 ft² or Room	Housing Assistance Needed per 1,000 ft² or Room	Workforce Housing Units per 1,000 ft² or Room	Housing Assistance Needed per 1,000 ft² or Room	Workforce Housing Units per 1,000 ft² or Room	Housing Assistance Needed per 1,000 ft² or Room	Workforce Housing Units per 1,000 ft² or Room	Housing Assistance Needed per 1,000 ft² or Room
per 1,000 Square Feet								
Retail	0.02	$4,335	0.613	$182,172	0.0019	$433	0.635	$186,940
Eating & Drinking	0.02	$4,335	1.685	$450,251	0.0019	$433	1.707	$455,020
Office	0.02	$4,335	0.799	$153,036	0.0019	$433	0.821	$157,804
Industrial	0.009	$1,885	0.369	$93,627	0.0019	$433	0.38	$95,945
Institutional	0.015	$3,204	0.81	$177,087	0.0019	$433	0.826	$180,725
per Room								
Hotel/Lodging	0.02	$4,335	0.208	$50,421	0.0019	$433	0.23	$55,189

number of those employees who need affordable housing because of their income levels, the approach complies with the nexus/proportionality test required by *Nollan/Dolan* as well as the dual rational nexus test.

NOTE

1 Portions of this chapter are excerpted and adapted from Nicholas and Juergensmeyer (2019), originally published in Vol. 52, Issue 3, *John Marshall Law Review*. 2019, with permission from the University of Illinois, Chicago.

REFERENCES

Callies, D. L. (2019). Public and private land development conditions: An overview. *John Marshall Law Review, 52,* 747–781.

Clarion Associates, in association with Dr. Nicholas, J. C., & RRC Associates (n.d.). *Employee Generation by Land Use Study: Teton County & Town of Jackson app. G (Jul. 2018) [hereinafter, "Clarion Report"].*

Juergensmeyer, J. C., Roberts, T. E., Salkin, P. E., & Rowberry, R. M. (2018). *Land Use Planning and Development Regulation Law* (4th ed.). St. Paul: West Publishing.

Nicholas, J. C., & Juergensmeyer, J. C. (2019). A rational nexus approach to workforce housing land development conditions, UIC. *Journal of Marshall Law Review, 52,* 647–675.

23 INNOVATIONS IN IMPACT FEE ADJUSTMENTS TO ADVANCE HOUSING AFFORDABILITY

23.1 OVERVIEW

There is a concern that impact fees can have adverse effects on housing prices and therefore, the ability of households to own homes or even to rent. This may be due to how impact fees are designed, such as when studio apartments, which statistically generate no students, are changed the same impact fee as mansions, which generate the most students per unit; or, charging smaller homes on smaller lots in low-cost area the same as larger homes on larger lots in high-cost areas. Many of the concerns about the effect of impact fees on housing prices and rents can be addressed by making them proportionate to the type, size, and location of the housing unit. In effect, perhaps the next stage of impact fee policy is to extend Dolan's rough proportionality to legislative actions to ensure that, to paraphrase in this context: local government "must make … (an) individual determination that the [impact fee] is related both in nature [type, size and location] and extent [proportionality] (of) the impact of the proposed development."

Moreover, we know that in competitive markets, impact fees are capitalized into the price of land, often dollar-for-dollar. When this happens, it is the seller of land that essentially pays the fee and not the developer or buyer. On the other hand, impact fees can make communities more attractive and thus, drive prices up for the interesting reason that because impact fees typically cover only part of the cost, they effectively leverage more community infrastructure investment than the impact fee itself. Nonetheless, we recognize that there will be circumstances where local governments feel compelled to do something proactive, if only symbolic, to shelter lower-cost housing from impact fees.

This chapter uses information provided by Florida Housing Finance Corporation (2017), which appears to be the nation's only survey of local government tools to offset the effects of impact fees on housing affordability to target households. It observes:

One way impact fees often intersect with affordable housing is through the granting of fee waivers or deferrals. These waivers or deferrals essentially represent a local government's commitment to subsidize and thereby incentivize the production of affordable housing. Though common, waivers for affordable housing are not ubiquitous. Like all issues related to impact fees, decisions to grant waivers for affordable housing are jurisdiction-specific and subject to local circumstances, vetting (including legal interpretation) and control.

(Florida Housing Finance Corporation 2017: 1).

This chapter summarizes the Florida Housing Finance Corporation's (FHFC) findings with respect to calculating impact fees that respect proportionate share principles in ways that reduce fees on less costly housing, reviews the rationale used by some Florida local governments to waive or exempt impact fees on qualifying housing, and presents its findings on specific techniques used by selected Florida local governments to do so.

23.2 PROPORTIONATE SHARE IMPACT FEE CALCULATIONS

The FHFC observes that flat rate or constant fees applied to houses or apartments are among the most basic methods for calculating

DOI: 10.4324/9781003336075-28

impact fees. While easy to calculate and administer, however, these fees are often regressive. A report prepared by the US Department of Housing and Urban Development (HUD) (2008), of which we were co-authors or otherwise participated in its drafting, opined that:

Flat rate impact fees compromise affordability and are socially negative to the degree they systematically overcharge purchasers in smaller, less expensive houses or apartments and undercharge others in the most valuable houses.

(HUD 2008: 43)

The HUD report (of which we were authors or peer reviewers) recommended that at a minimum, residential impact fees be calculated considering dwelling unit type (e.g., single-family detached, townhouse, condominium, apartment, etc.) and size in bedrooms or square feet.

HUD also states that "ensuring that impact fees do not charge more than the proportionate share is fair and equitable and protects affordable housing from paying a disproportionate share" (HUD 2008: ii), noting that "the simplest and most universal factor associated with actual costs is the square footage of the home" (HUD 2008: ii). The FHFC quotes further from HUD:

For certain impact fees, particularly those covering libraries, parks, open space and construction of schools, square footage of the homes may be sufficient for allocating costs. For other fees, such as those covering roads, public safety and water or drainage, additional significant variables should also be considered along with dwelling unit square footage in determining the appropriate costs and payments. Depending on the particular fee, these variables might include size of lots and the density of subdivisions or broader neighborhoods. But the key point is that basing all types of impact fees in whole or in part on house or apartment square footage rather than charging uniform rates is straightforward to implement and helps to avoid overcharging smaller units more than their true proportionate share.

(HUD 2008: ii)

23.3 MODIFYING OR WAIVING IMPACT FEES TO ADVANCE HOUSING AFFORDABILITY

The FHFC notes that regardless of how impact fees are calculated, they may still impact certain kinds of housing or housing for certain kinds of people disproportionately. To reduce the burden, some Florida local governments find various ways in which to reduce fees on certain kinds of housing, but this must be tempered. For instance, the Indian River County Affordable Housing Advisory Committee finds:

Legally, impact fees must be applied to all activities that create a demand for capital facilities. Consequently, impact fees cannot be waived or reduced. There are, however, alternative methods of fee payment to assist income eligible persons with the cost of impact fees and /or utility capacity charges.[1]

The report goes on to explain the economic rationale for doing so.

Waiving impact fees does not eliminate the cost of the infrastructure that the impact fees are designed to pay for. Either new development or existing residents must pay the cost of needed infrastructure improvements. If new development, which puts additional demand on county facilities, does not pay its fair share of infrastructure cost through impact fees, then existing residents will have to pay those costs through higher fees or taxes.[2]

With these caveats in mind, what is the practice of some Florida local governments? This is addressed next.

23.4 LOCAL GOVERNMENT IMPACT FEE ADJUSTMENTS TO ADVANCE HOUSING AFFORDABILITY

FHFC staff surveyed State Housing Initiatives Program (SHIP) administrators to learn how local governments were addressing the concern of the impact of impact fees on housing affordability. We quote examples here.

Hillsborough County assess residential impact fees using a mixture of methods including location in the County (the zone). Mobility is Type and Size; Parks is Type and Bedroom count; School is Size; and Fire is a Flat rate. Affordable Housing has a program to provide relief. Multifamily developments are provided 90% relief for Park, Fire, and Mobility fees. Single family construction is provided 100% relief for all but School Impact fees. Hillsborough County can also lower the Mobility Fee for houses with less than 1500 square feet of living area if Affordable Housing provides documentation that shows the annual household income meets select SHIP definitions (less than 50%, and between 50% and 80%).

Manatee County now utilize square footage for impact fees. Board just approved an innovative new program called Livable Manatee. Local government will pay, from a County source, the County Impact Fees, School Impact Fees, and Facility Investment Fees for new construction affordable units for both homeownership and rental up to a maximum of $500,000 per development (have resolution putting this into effect). The fund is a limited fund that once depleted, may or may not be re-established. Local government is legislatively looking into the possibility of fee waivers for affordable housing units that would help us to continue this program effectively.

City of Palm Bay annually adopts Fair Share Impact Fees by Resolution. The fees are a combination of flat fee and calculated additional fees based upon square footage. No waiver or reduction is permitted; however, the Growth Management Director retains authority to structure a payment plan.

City of Cape Coral charges impact fees by type of development/construction: 1) residential—single-family duplex; 2) commercial—multi-family over three units and non-residential uses. In the process of implementing a pilot impact fee program for affordable housing. Single-family impact fees levied by the City would be deferred until the first sale of the property. This program will be limited to non-profit housing developers. Multifamily impact fees will be bought down over a

period using a Synthetic Tax Increment Financing model.

Flagler County charges impact fees for transportation, parks and recreation, and educational facilities, with the transportation impact fee presently in a moratorium. These fees are collected for development within unincorporated Flagler County and for development within the City of Bunnell through interlocal agreement. The fees are based on type of land use and vary based on the type of unit being developed: single-family residential, multifamily residential, or mobile home residential. Currently, an exemption from educational facilities impact fee for low-income housing. In the past, the County has sporadically waived impact fees by paying them from County funds. Such waiver/payment by the County is subject to Board of County Commissioner review and approval.

City of Largo charges impact fees (sewer and water, mobility, and parkland/recreation) based on Type of Residence. A housing development that requests approval to be deemed an "Affordable Housing Development" may receive assistance with the impact fees from our SHIP program for the affordable set-aside units.

Miami-Dade County charges impact fees by type of use and region in the County. Impact fees are required to be paid prior to the issuance of any building permit for development activity within Miami-Dade County. No building permit may be issued until all required impact fees are paid in full. Miami-Dade County collects impact fees for Road, Fire and Emergency Services, Police Services, Parks, and Educational Facilities. The application is reviewed for size (a square footage maximum) and type of land use for the new development. Ordinances exempt from the required payment of impact fee housing units that provide affordable housing for low- and very low-income families.

Seminole County charges impact fees based on unit type and region of County. The largest single impact fee is the school impact fee. Seminole County has been examining ways to provide a modification of impact fee requirements, including, but not limited to, reduction, waiver, or alternative methods of payment of impact fees. To date, a funding source has not been identified to provide an alternative payment of impact fees.

The funding source, policy, and procedures to implement such a program have not been located and implemented.

City of Fort Meyers impact fees for residential structures are assessed at a flat per unit rate based on the unit type (SF, MF/SFA/Duplex, Mobile Home), while the impact fees for commercial structures are based on square footage and type of use. Currently, there are no waivers or reductions in place.

City of Port St. Lucie charges tiered impact fees based on square footage for unit. Reduction of impact fees for in-fill housing or housing in different areas of the city, such as Community Reinvestment Area (CRA), etc.

City of Ocala impact fees (water, sewer) for homes are assessed based on the square footage under air/heated space. Apartments/condos are assessed based on the number of bedrooms they have. There is no concession for affordable housing projects within impact fee ordinance, but there is an Affordable Housing Fund that can offset the development fees.

23.5 CONCLUDING OBSERVATIONS

As we noted in Chapter 9, exempting or waiving impact fees for anything, no matter how noble, can create problems. Firstly, how is the lost revenue made up? After all, the premise of impact fees is that a certain amount of money is needed to make up the shortfall in revenues needed to finance facilities required to mitigate the demands of new development, and if that money is not available, who pays? Which leads to the second issue: If foregone revenue is financed from taxes paid in part by other development that also paid impact fees, to what extent is that development paying twice, in the form of its own impact fees and impact fees for other development?

To address these concerns, some local governments use housing trust fund money to pay for impact fees on targeted housing directly. Also, federal Community Development Block Grant funds can be used for this purpose. While we know of no case law on the subject, local governments would be wise to avoid complete waivers or exemptions and identify funds or financing approaches to pay those fees from other accounts. Impact fee deferral approaches might be used, such that impact fees may be assessed but not collected until the home is sold, but if it is sold to another qualifying household, the deferral continues.[3]

Nonetheless, by far the best way in which to advance housing affordability is to calculate fees based on house size and location (see Chapter 15 and its Coda). This helps ensure that lower-cost housing pays lower fees than higher-cost housing.

NOTES

1 See Indian River County Affordable Housing Advisory Committee, *2008 Incentives Review and Recommendation Report*, available at www.ircgov.com/Boards/AHAC/AHAC2008report.pdf.
2 Ibid.
3 See HUD's (2008) description of Alachua County, Florida, for an example.

REFERENCES

Florida Housing Finance Corporation (2017). *Overview of Impact Fees and Affordable Housing.* Retrieved October 21, 2021, from www.floridahousing.org/docs/default-source/aboutflorida/august2017/october2017/TAB_3.pdf

U.S. Department of Housing and Urban Development Office of Policy Development and Research's (HUD) (n.d.). *Impact Fees and Housing Affordability: A Guide for Practitioners,* June 2008. Available at file:///U:/USER/JToman/Task%20Force/Impact%20Fees%20-%20HUD%20Guide.pdf

24 WESTERN PLACER COUNTY, CALIFORNIA

Habitat Conservation Fee

ROBERT SPENCER

24.1 BACKGROUND

24.1.1 The Endangered Species Act and Landscape-Level Conservation

Mitigating development impacts under the federal Endangered Species Act (ESA) on a project-by-project basis has significant challenges. Land developers must incur costs to estimate impacts and implement mitigation measures. Under-staffed wildlife agencies are stretched to adequately review all projects and provide consistent guidance. Environmental advocacy groups focus on large development projects and miss the cumulative impact of smaller projects. Local jurisdictions are stuck in the middle trying to accommodate the interests of all stakeholders.

Western Placer County is under development pressure due to its desirable location in the foothills adjacent to Sacramento, the California state capital. Within the Plan area, which includes the City of Lincoln and county unincorporated areas, regional projections estimate that 30,100 acres could develop over the next 50 years. The natural lands on which this development would occur contain significant habitats, including vernal pools and other wetlands, plus woodlands and grasslands that support 14 endangered species.

The *Placer County Conservation Program, Western Placer County Habitat Conservation Plan / Natural Community Conservation Plan* (2020) (HCP/NCCP or Plan) exemplifies a regional, landscape-level planning approach to endangered species conservation and mitigation of development impacts. Implementation of the Plan over the 50-year permit term will result in establishment of a reserve system to protect 47,300 acres of habitat, including an endowment to manage and monitor these lands in perpetuity after the permit term. Seventy percent of the $1.2 billion Plan is funded by a program of development fees. Under the Plan, any covered activity, such as land development projects, can minimize and mitigate negative impacts by complying with the Plan, including paying applicable development fees.

The Plan, adopted in 2020, meets the needs of all stakeholders while improving outcomes:

- Land developers gain a streamlined development process, reduced costs for habitat surveys, and certainty with regard to the time and cost of mitigation.
- State and federal wildlife agencies can focus on the implementation of a single regional plan instead of multiple, disconnected, project-by-project impact analyses and mitigation programs.
- Environmental advocacy groups are assured of landscape-level conservation, a more effective approach to endangered species protection.
- Local jurisdictions directly manage plan implementation through a new joint powers agency, including control of the development fee program.

The Placer Conservation Authority (PCA), a joint powers authority, was formed to implement the mitigation and conservation actions of the Placer County Comprehensive Program (PCCP). The PCA will be responsible for

DOI: 10.4324/9781003336075-29

maintaining and updating the development fee program.

See Figure 24.1 for a map of the Plan area. Plan Area A. labeled as the "Valley" and the "Foothills" subareas. is the focus of the HCP/NCCP and where all future growth and most impacts are anticipated to occur. Plan Area A includes the City of Lincoln and all unincorporated lands within western Placer County, approximately 209,800 acres or roughly five-sixths of western Placer County (the portion of the County that is west of the Sierra Crest). Among the many species intended to be protected through the habitat conservation fee is the Western burrowing owl (*Athene cunicularia*), illustrated in Figure 24.2.

24.1.2 Development Fee Nexus Study

A nexus study was prepared in conjunction with the Plan to provide the evidence for findings required by the Mitigation Fee Act, contained in California Government Code, sections 66000 through 66025, which guides the adoption and collection of development fees by local agencies. Placer County and the City of Lincoln are the two permittees with authority to approve development within the Plan area, so these two agencies used this study to support their adoption of the HCP/NCCP development fees.

For additional explanation of the approach and methodology as well as more detail behind the data sources and calculations presented in this chapter, please refer to Spencer (2020), known as the "Nexus Study."

The Nexus Study addresses three types of fees and integrates funding from a fourth fee adopted with a separate nexus study concurrent with the Plan:

- **Land Conversion Fee:** All development projects and other covered activities under the Plan pay the land conversion fee. The fee funds mitigation of all direct, indirect, and cumulative impacts of land conversion except impacts mitigated by special habitat fees.

- **Special Habitat Fee:** Special habitats are particularly sensitive habitats associated with watershed features such as streams including salmonid habitat, marshes, riparian woodlands, and seasonal wetlands including vernal pools. To fund the restoration and enhancement of these habitats, covered activities that affect special habitats pay special habitat fees in addition to the land conversion fee.

- **Temporary Effect Fee:** The temporary effect fee applies when direct impacts from covered activities alter land cover but the disturbed area recovers or is restored within 1 year. The temporary effect fee is determined by applying the land conversion fee and special habitat fees but at reduced fee amounts to reflect the temporary nature of the impact.

- **Open Space and Fire Hazard Management Fee:** A substantial share of development in the Foothills will occur on small lots in developed areas with little habitat value and therefore not subject to the Plan's three development fees described previously. However, this exempt development will benefit from the Plan's open space acquisition and fire hazard management. A separate nexus study was prepared for a development fee applicable to this type of development.

This chapter focuses on the land conversion fee nexus analysis that has the most complex fee structure and provides over half of the total funding required to implement the Plan.

24.1.3 Policy Objectives and Related Technical Challenges

Achieving the following policy objectives and related technical issues created a significant

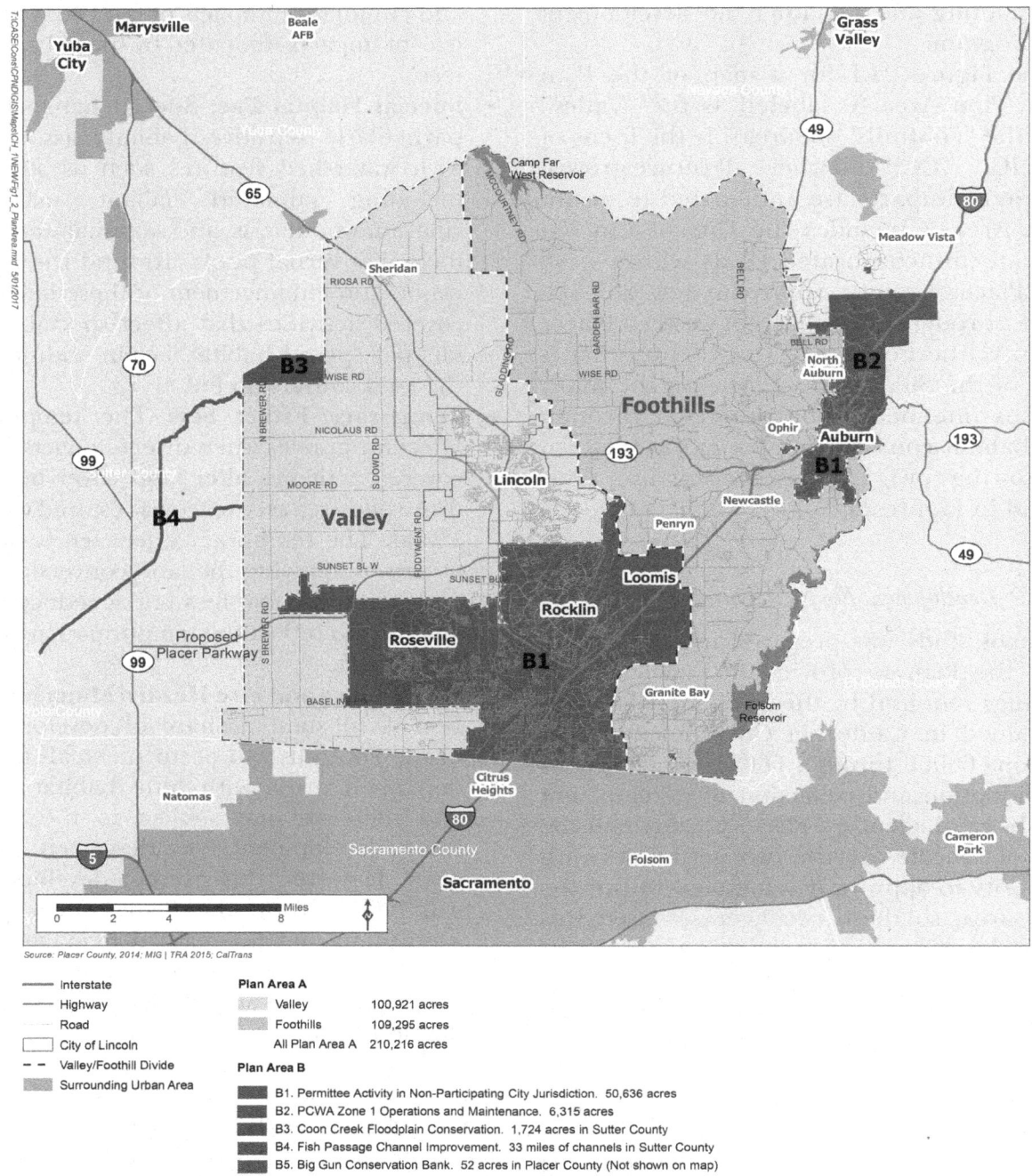

Plan Area A

	Valley	100,921 acres
	Foothills	109,295 acres
	All Plan Area A	210,216 acres

Plan Area B

B1. Permittee Activity in Non-Participating City Jurisdiction. 50,636 acres
B2. PCWA Zone 1 Operations and Maintenance. 6,315 acres
B3. Coon Creek Floodplain Conservation. 1,724 acres in Sutter County
B4. Fish Passage Channel Improvement. 33 miles of channels in Sutter County
B5. Big Gun Conservation Bank. 52 acres in Placer County (Not shown on map)

Legend:
— Interstate
— Highway
— Road
☐ City of Lincoln
- - - Valley/Foothill Divide
▨ Surrounding Urban Area

Note: For purposes of the Nexus Study and application of the land conversion fee, the Foothills includes that portion of the Valley that is the higher elevation portion of the City of Lincoln planning area roughly eastward of a line dropped due south from the intersection of Virginiatown Road and Hungry Hollow Road, and pulled west to follow the 200' elevation line which runs roughly along the NID irrigation ditch north of Hwy. 193 and Oak Tree Lane.

FIGURE 24.1 Western Placer County and the Plan area. (From Placer County, 2014; MIG | TRA 2015; CalTrans.)

FIGURE 24.2 Western burrowing owl, *Athene cunicularia hypogea*, preservation of whose habitat is a purpose of the Western Placer County Habitat Conservation Fee. (From National Nuclear Security Administration; retrieved November 27, 2021, from https://commons.wikimedia.org/wiki /File:Athene_cunicularia_hypugea.jpg.)

degree of complexity in the nexus analysis and resultant fee structure:

- **Determining Conservation versus Mitigation Funding Shares:** The Plan qualifies as a Natural Community Conservation Plan under the California Natural Community Conservation Planning Act (NCCP) Act. To qualify, the Plan must not only mitigate impacts but in addition, contribute to the recovery and continued viability of species, whether or not those

species are protected under the California ESA. Determining the share of total Plan costs associated with these "mitigation" and "conservation" components was a technical challenge.

- **Ensuring Full Mitigation Funding:** For the wildlife agencies to grant necessary permits, the Plan had to fully mitigate the impacts of covered activities (the mitigation component of the Plan). Other major potential revenue sources such as state and federal grants are restricted from being used to mitigate development impacts but can fund the conservation component of the Plan. Thus, the Plan had no flexibility but had to charge the maximum justified development fees. The technical challenge, within the bounds of the "reasonable relationship" nexus tests used for development fees, was to ensure that these maximum fees were not so high that stakeholder opposition prohibited adoption of the Plan.

- **Addressing Varied Land Use Patterns and Development Economics:** The Plan area includes a wide variety of land use patterns with differing abilities to absorb the additional cost of a habitat conservation fee. Although most anticipated development will occur in large planned unit developments, a substantial share will occur in rural residential development with much lower land values. Fortunately, the relative impact per parcel is lower for rural residential projects. The technical challenge was determining how much lower without clear metrics of the cumulative impacts on habitats and species that could be used to compare across land use types.

- **Integrating Open Space and Fire Hazard Management Fee Structure:** As mentioned earlier, a separate nexus study was prepared for development only benefiting from the Plan's open space acquisition and fire hazard management. The technical challenge was structuring the Plan's land conversion fee to integrate seamlessly with this separate fee applied in adjacent areas. Funding from the open space fee was helpful in reducing the land conversion fee on rural residential development by spreading costs across all benefiting development.

24.2 MITIGATION FAIR SHARE

A key element of the nexus analysis for the land conversion fee is determining how to fairly allocate Plan costs between mitigation and conservation components. This is accomplished by comparing the reserve acreage required to mitigate the impacts of covered activities and the total reserve acreage required by the Plan.

The amount of reserve required to mitigate the impacts of covered activities is calculated by applying landscape-scale mitigation ratios (acres of mitigation per acre of impact) to the maximum acres of permanent direct impacts from land conversion allowed over the permit term. Mitigation ratios represent a landscape-scale analysis and do not necessarily represent ratios used for a project-level analysis. The remainder of the reserve acreage not identified for mitigation is the conservation share associated with the requirements of the NCCP.

The analysis is conducted separately for the Valley and Foothills subareas (see Figure 24.1). This approach incorporates differences in the amount of land conversion by community type and related mitigation cost obligations that vary by subarea. As a result of these differences, the Valley has higher costs per acre of direct impact.

Table 24.1 shows that 30,100 acres of permanent direct impacts from land conversion

TABLE 24.1 Permit Term Limit Land Conversion and Reserve Mitigation

Natural Community	Land Conversion (Acres)			Mitigation Ratio	Mitigation Share of Reserve (Acres)
	Plan Area A	Plan Area B	Total		
Valley Subarea					
Vernal Pool Complex	12,400	50	12,450	1.35	16,807
Grassland	3,500	76	3,576	1	3,576
Aquatic/Wetland	120	7	127	1.5	191
Riverine/Riparian	150	7	157	1.52	238
Valley Oak Woodland	30	6	36	1.5	54
Oak Woodland	1,100	6	1,106	0.75	829
Agriculture	2,900	101	3,001	1	3,001
Subtotal	**20,200**	**253**	**20,453**		**24,697**
Foothill Subarea					
Vernal Pool Complex	100	0	100	1.35	135
Grassland	3,300	24	3,324	1	3,324
Aquatic/Wetland	130	3	133	1.5	199
Riverine/Riparian	330	3	333	1.52	507
Valley Oak Woodland	100	4	104	1.5	156
Oak Woodland	5,100	4	5,104	0.75	3,828
Agriculture	540	9	549	1	549
Subtotal	**9,600**	**47**	**9,647**		**8,698**
Total	**29,800**	**300**	**30,100**		**33,395**

Source: HCP/NCCP, chapter 4, table 4-1.

TABLE 24.2 Reserve Fair Shares for Mitigation and Conservation

	Valley Subarea		Foothills Subarea		Total	
	Reserve Allocation (acres)	Fair Share	Reserve Allocation (acres)	Fair Share	Reserve Allocation (acres)	Fair Share
Mitigation	24,697	72.6%	8,698	65.4%	33,395	70.6%
Conservation	9,303	27.4%	4,602	34.6%	13,905	29.4%
Total Reserve	34,000	100%	13,300	100%	47,300	100%
Subarea Share	71.9%		28.1%		100%	

Source: HCP/NCCP, appendix L (Cost Estimates and Assumptions), table A (based on HCP/NCCP, table 5-2); Table 24.1.

are allowed during the permit term within Plan Areas A and B and allocated between the Valley and Foothills subareas. The land conversion permit term limits shown in Table 24.1 are multiplied by the mitigation ratio applicable to each community type to determine the share of total reserve acreage needed to mitigate covered activities.

Table 24.2 provides the determination of mitigation and conservation fair shares by subarea. For each subarea, the total reserve acreage is split between mitigation share and conservation share, starting with the subarea mitigation acreage calculated in Table 24.1. The remainder of the reserve acreage for that subarea is the basis for the conservation share associated with the requirements of the NCCP to contribute to the recovery of natural communities and covered species over and above the mitigation of impacts from covered activities.

As shown in Table 24.2, the mitigation share for the Valley is 72.6% based on the reserve acres associated with mitigation of impacts in the Valley. The mitigation share for the Foothills is 65.4%. These shares are central to the nexus analysis, allocating total Plan costs to the land conversion fee net of mitigation costs funded by the special habitat fee.

24.3 PLAN COSTS BY SUBAREA

A detailed cost model was developed to estimate total Plan costs over the permit term (see chapter 9 of the Plan). The cost model allocated Plan costs between the Valley and Foothills subareas based primarily on per acre costs for Plan implementation and the amount of the reserve associated with each. Total Plan costs allocated by subarea are summarized in Table 24.3. All cost categories are included in the land conversion nexus analysis except:

• Special habitat restoration and enhancement, because the mitigation (versus conservation) share of these costs is funded separately by the special habitat fee.
• Investment earnings on the endowment fund, which represent a cost as part of the total endowment fund balance required at the end of the permit term, but a cost that is internally funded by earnings generated by the fund.

24.4 COST ALLOCATION APPROACH

This section describes the approach used to allocate costs to the land conversion fee by subarea. The amount of impact per acre of land conversion is the basis for assigning costs to various types of covered activities and related fee categories. The following sections apply this approach to calculate the land conversion fee for the Valley and Foothills subareas.

TABLE 24.3 Total Plan Costs for Permit Term (2019 $)

Cost Category	Valley Subarea	Foothills Subarea	Total	Include in Fee Calculation?
Establish Reserve System	$398,480,000	$94,040,000	$492,520,000	Yes
Special Habitat Restoration and Enhancement	$186,940,000	$68,210,000	$255,150,000	No[a]
Other Restoration	$44,510,000	$9,330,000	$53,840,000	Yes
Other Management and Enhancement	$70,930,000	$11,140,000	$82,070,000	Yes
Monitoring, Research, and Scientific Review	$41,530,000	$18,310,000	$59,840,000	Yes
Environmental Compliance	$18,210,000	$9,540,000	$27,750,000	Yes
Plan Administration	$60,160,000	$32,070,000	$92,230,000	Yes
Contingency	$27,000,000	$7,350,000	$34,350,000	Yes
Subtotal	**$847,760,000**	**$249,990,000**	**$1,097,750,000**	
Valley Share of Upper Salmonid Watersheds[b]	$20,840,000	$(20,840,000)	$–	Yes
Endowment Fund[c]				
Funding Sources	$29,910,000	$11,690,000	$41,600,000	Yes
Investment Earnings	$43,950,000	$17,180,000	$61,130,000	No
Endowment Fund Balance (Year 50)	$73,860,000	$28,870,000	$102,730,000	
Plan Preparation Reimbursement[d]	$12,550,000	$660,000	$13,210,000	Yes
Total Plan Costs	**$955,010,000**	**$258,680,000**	**$1,213,690,000**	

[a]Special habitat costs associated with mitigation are included in a separate special habitat mitigation fee.

[b]Cost shift from Foothills to Valley based on benefits to Valley of protecting upper watersheds for salmonids located in the Foothills.

[c]Endowment based on (1) a constant annual contribution during the permit term, (2) a real rate of return of 3.25% on the fund balance from investments in a diversified portfolio of marketable securities, net of investment management costs and inflation, and (3) no withdrawals until the end of the 50-year permit term. Endowment funding allocated to subareas based on total subarea share of total reserve (see Table 24.2).

[d]Plan preparation cost reimbursement for funding provided by Placer County general fund only. Ninety-five percent of costs allocated to Valley subarea reflecting the substantially greater planning effort associated with mitigating Valley development.

Sources: Placer County (for Plan preparation costs); Nexus Study, tables\2.3; A.1, A.2, and A.4; Table\24.2.

24.4.1 Direct Effects versus Gross Parcel Area for Low-Density Rural Residential

Low-density rural residential development tends to have project footprints and therefore, direct impacts from ground disturbance that are lower than the entire size of the parcel. Direct impacts can be substantially lower for larger parcels. Applying the land conversion fee based on direct impacts, such as actual disturbed land area, could create burdensome information requirements and incentives for under-reporting development footprints in project applications for these small projects. Greater oversight and enforcement would then also be required by Placer County and the City of Lincoln to ensure that projects conformed to the level of direct impacts anticipated when the fee was calculated.

These issues are particularly relevant in the Foothills, where a substantial amount of low-density rural residential development is anticipated. By contrast, most of the development in the Valley is anticipated to be from planned developments where direct impacts and parcel area are typically more congruent.

To avoid these application and oversight requirements, the land conversion fee is charged in most instances on gross parcel area rather than on the area of direct impacts.[1] However, to maintain a reasonable relationship between the parcel area upon which the fee is applied and the need for mitigation of direct impacts, the nexus analysis needs to consider the amount of land conversion (direct impact) per parcel and how that generally varies depending on the type of development. These considerations include:

- Larger parcels typically have larger direct impact footprints from low-density rural residential development. However, the footprint as a proportion of total parcel area typically decreases as parcel area increases.
- The direct impact footprint from low-density rural residential development as a proportion of total parcel size tends to be small on parcels in the range of 10 to 20 acres and negligible on parcels above that threshold.

The PCA will track direct impact footprint and parcel area by project to verify and adjust these assumed relationships as needed during Plan implementation.

24.4.2 Fragmentation Effects

Fragmentation is an indirect impact that occurs when patches of habitat are reduced in size and isolated by development, resulting in reduced species diversity due to lower carrying capacity and reduced habitat quality due to increased edge influence from human activity. Fragmentation of the natural landscape as larger parcels are subdivided and developed has significant indirect and cumulative impact in addition to the amount of direct impact from land conversion. The impacts of fragmentation are particularly common in the Foothills due to the dominant pattern of low-density rural residential development discussed in the prior subsection.

Developing a fee schedule that integrates the impacts of fragmentation is difficult, however, due to the many different types of development patterns that can occur. The State's Subdivision Map Act offers reasonable thresholds to indicate levels of fragmentation. The Act governs approval of subdivisions by local jurisdictions. Provisions of the Act distinguish between subdivisions that create five or more parcels ("major subdivisions") and four or fewer parcels ("minor subdivisions" or "parcel maps"). Minor subdivisions typically have a lower level of development activity, lower density, and fewer impacts per acre compared with major subdivisions, which are more likely to be more land-intensive planned unit developments. Consequently, this nexus analysis uses the threshold between minor and major subdivisions as a reasonable indicator of the degree of fragmentation impacts associated with rural residential development.

24.4.3 Fee Categories to Capture Relative Effects

The nexus analysis develops fee categories based on types of covered activities to demonstrate a reasonable relationship between the amount of the land conversion fee and the proportionate cost of mitigation attributable to the type of development paying the fee. Types of covered activities used to develop the land conversion fee categories, described in the following, reflect the considerations discussed earlier regarding the relative impacts of variation in footprint-to-parcel area and fragmentation. The fee categories are based on existing parcel size at the time of Plan adoption.

24.4.3.1 Small Lots Fee Category

The small lots fee category includes covered activities on existing parcels greater than 20,000 square feet and up to 1 acre in size. The lower threshold corresponds to a provision in the Plan that excludes parcels of 20,000 square feet and smaller from being covered under the Plan because of a lack of natural habitat due to the small parcel size. Therefore, these parcels are exempt from being subject to the Plan's development fees. The upper threshold of 1 acre corresponds to the distinction between small lots and low-density rural residential (see next subsection).

On the one hand, projects on small lots have greater impacts per gross parcel acre, because direct impacts are equal to gross parcel size. On the other hand, projects on small lots have less impact, because their small size indicates that fragmentation of the landscape has already occurred prior to Plan adoption.

24.4.3.2 Low-Density Rural Residential Fee Category

Low-density rural residential includes covered activities for single-family development on existing parcels greater than 1 acre in size that are not subdivided or are subdivided into four or fewer parcels following Plan adoption. Low-density rural residential has the lowest impact per gross parcel acre of the three fee categories because (1) land conversion direct impact tends not to

occur over the entire parcel and (2) less subdivision activity is related to a lower level of fragmentation. Unlike other covered activities, impacts per acre decline as parcel size increases. Consequently, this category has a cap of 20 acres on any individual parcel subject to the per acre fee to reflect the negligible incremental impacts from single-family development on parcels above that size.

24.4.3.3 All Other Development Fee Category

"All other development" includes all covered activities besides small lots and low-density rural residential. All other development includes the large, planned unit developments anticipated to cause much of the adverse impacts from covered activities in the Valley. These types of covered activities have the greatest impact per gross parcel acre of the three fee categories because (1) direct impact from the development footprint equals parcel size and (2) fragmentation impacts are higher compared with both small lots and minor subdivision low-density rural residential.

24.4.4 Summary of Fee Categories and Relative Impacts

Fee categories and the overall impact per gross parcel acre that guide the nexus analysis and calculate land conversion fees are shown in Table 24.4. The category numbers (1a, 1b, 2a, 2b, etc.) refer to the Valley and Foothills land conversion fees developed in the next sections of this analysis and used in the fee schedules. Based on the preceding discussion, and to maintain a reasonable relationship between the amount of the fee and the proportionate cost of mitigation attributable to the type of development paying the fee, fees per parcel acre are:

- Lowest on low-density rural residential
- Higher on small lots
- Highest on all other development

TABLE 24.4 Land Conversion Impact by Fee Category

Fee Category and Subarea		Impact per Parcel Acre		Overall Impact per Parcel Acre
Valley	Foothill	Direct Impact	Fragmentation	
Small Lots				
1a Covered activity on existing parcel greater than 20,000 square feet up to 1 acre	2a Residential project on existing parcel greater than 20,000 square feet up to 1 acre 2b Non-residential project on existing parcel greater than 20,000 square feet up to 1 acre	More	Less	**Medium**
Low-Density Rural Residential				
1b Single-family residential on existing parcel greater than 1 acre or on any parcel created by subdivision of an existing parcel into four or fewer total parcels	2c Single-family residential on existing parcel greater than 1 acre or on any parcel created by subdivision of an existing parcel into four or fewer total parcels	Less	Less[a]	**Low** Effect per parcel acre declines as parcel size increases
All Other Development				
1c All other covered activities	2d Single-family residential on any parcel created by subdivision of existing parcel into five or more total parcels and multi-family residential 2e Non-residential project on existing parcel greater than 1 acre or on any parcel created by subdivision	More	More	**High**

Source: Urban Economics.

Note: Existing parcel is a parcel at time of Plan adoption.

[a]Impacts of fragmentation are greater in the Foothills, though the overall impact per acre remains less than for small lots.

24.5 VALLEY LAND CONVERSION FEE

The following sections describe how the nexus analysis determined the Valley land conversion fee schedule. The analysis captures the variation in overall impact per parcel acre by fee category (Table 24.4) to establish the necessary reasonable relationship between the amount of the fee and the type of development paying the fee.

24.5.1 Mitigation Costs and Required Funding

The Valley land conversion fee is based on the 72.6% mitigation share of total Plan costs allocated to the Valley, as shown in Table 24.5. After a series of adjustments to total Valley costs (described later), the average mitigation cost per acre of direct impact is calculated using the total acres of direct impact allowed by the HCP/NCCP during the permit term in the Valley (see Table 24.1).

Total Plan costs are drawn from Table 24.3 and include the Valley's share of endowment contributions and Plan preparation costs. Special habitat costs are deducted because these costs are addressed through the special habitat fee. The net cost subject to the fair share allocation is multiplied by the Valley mitigation fair share from Table 24.2, and then added to the Valley share of upper salmonid watershed acquisition costs, to determine the total Valley mitigation cost share.[2] The mitigation cost share represents the amount to be funded by the Valley land conversion fee.

24.5.2 Valley Land Conversion Fee Schedule and Revenue

Table 24.6 shows how the Valley land conversion fee is determined and presents estimated revenue by fee category based on the growth scenario estimated for the permit term. Total estimated revenue is equal to the Valley mitigation cost share shown in Table 24.5.

As explained in more detail in the following, for each category, the fee calculation adjusts the cost per acre of direct impact to account for the overall impact per parcel acre based on the guidance provided in Table 24.4. The resultant fee per parcel acre is lowest for low-density rural residential (fee 1b), higher for small lots (fee 1a), and highest for all other development (fee 1c).

- **Small lots (fee 1a):** The fee is based on parcel size. The fee is set at 20% of the average mitigation cost per acre of direct impact to reflect the relatively lower level of impact associated with covered activities on existing small lots that are already part of a fragmented landscape with less habitat value.

- **Low density rural residential (fee 1b):** This fee is applied both per dwelling unit and per parcel acre, so the combined fee declines on a per acre basis as parcel size increases to reflect declining direct impacts per parcel acre. To provide for an equitable transition between fee 1a on small lots and fee 1b, fee 1b is set to equal 20% of the average mitigation cost per acre

TABLE 24.5 Valley Land Conversion Mitigation Cost per Acre of Direct Effect

Valley Costs (from Cost Model)	$847,760,000
Valley Endowment Contribution	29,910,000
Valley Plan Preparation Reimbursement	12,550,000
Total Valley Plan Costs	$890,220,000
Valley Special Habitat Costs	(186,940,000)
Costs Subject to Fair Share Allocation	$703,280,000
Valley Mitigation Fair Share	72.6%
Valley Mitigation Cost Share (unadjusted)	$510,580,000
Valley Share of Upper Salmonid Watersheds	20,840,000
Valley Mitigation Cost Share (adjusted)	$531,420,000
Valley Direct Effect (acres)	20,453
Average Mitigation Cost per Acre of Direct Effect	**$25,983**

Sources: Tables 24.2 and 24.3.

TABLE 24.6 Valley Land Conversion Fee and Revenue by Fee Category (2019 $)

Fee Category	Average Mitigation Cost per Acre of Impact	Relative Impact Factor[a]	Fee	Valley Growth Scenario (50-Year Permit Term)		
				Dwelling Units	Parcel Area (Acres)	Fee Revenue
1a[b] Covered activity on existing parcel greater than 20,000 square feet up to 1 acre	$25,983	0.2	$5,197 per parcel acre		53	$280,000
1b[c] Single-family residential on existing parcel greater than 1 acre or	$25,983	0.15	$3,897 per dwelling unit	214		$830,000
on any parcel created by subdivision of an existing parcel into four or fewer total parcels	$25,983	0.05	$1,299 per parcel acre		1,225[d]	$1,590,000
1c All other development	$25,983	1.02	$26,473 per parcel acre		19,972	$528,720,000
Total					21,250[4]	**$531,420,000**
Valley Land Conversion Fee Cost Share						$531,420,000
Difference						**$–**

Sources: Nexus Study, table 3.5; Tables 24.4 and 24.5; Urban Economics.

Notes:

Existing parcel refers to a parcel at time of Plan adoption.

Per acre fees apply to the entire parcel area excluding areas improved at time of Plan adoption and where avoidance occurs. For low-density rural development, per acre fees apply only to the disturbed area footprint of covered activities unless the project includes a new dwelling unit.

[a]See text for explanation.

[b]Existing parcels 20,000 square feet or less are not covered activities and therefore not subject to HCP/NCCP development fees.

[c]Fee per acre capped at 10 acres per parcel. Estimated acreage and revenue exclude parcel acreage above this cap.

[d]Amount is greater than acres of impact shown in Table 24.1 (20.453 acres) because parcel acreage for rural residential development (fee category 1b) is greater than acres of direct impact (1,225 versus 428 acres).

for a 1-acre project. The relative impact per dwelling unit is assumed to be 15% of the average mitigation cost per acre due to the large impact associated with a dwelling unit and associated human activities compared with land conversion, resulting in 5% of the average mitigation cost per acre being allocated to impacts per parcel acre (0.15 + 0.05 = 0.2).

- **All other covered activities (fee 1c):** The fee is based on parcel size. This category includes the large, planned developments anticipated to generate much of the impact from covered activities in the Valley. The fee is calculated as a residual to ensure full funding of the Valley mitigation cost share after deducting revenue from fees 1a and 1b. Because fee 1c includes 94% of total parcel area subject to the fee (19,972 of 21,360 acres), the data and assumptions used to calculate fees 1a and 1b have little impact on the amount of fee 1c.

24.6 FOOTHILLS LAND CONVERSION FEE

The following sections describe how the nexus analysis determined the Foothills land conversion fee schedule. The analysis captures the variation in overall impact per parcel acre by fee category (Table 24.4) to establish the necessary reasonable relationship between the amount of the fee and the type of development paying the fee.

24.6.1 Foothills Land Conversion Fee Approach

One challenge is that substantial development is anticipated on existing small lots less than 20,000 square feet that would not be subject to Plan development fees. Yet, this development would benefit from the open space acquisition and fire hazard management provided by the Plan. If the benefits and costs of these Plan actions were not spread fairly to all development in the Foothills, the Plan's land conversion fee would unfairly burden covered activities.

The nexus analysis is based on an approach that integrates impacts from development not covered by the Plan with impacts from the Plan's covered activities. The approach is summarized in Table 24.7 and in the text that follows and is described in more detail in the following subsections. Key to this approach is breaking out the Foothills land conversion fee into two parts. The Part A component is complemented by an equivalent but separate open space and fire hazard management fee that applies to all Foothills development not subject to the Plan's development fees. The Part B component only applies to activities covered by the Plan.

The approach is described in the following steps:

1. The cost of open space land acquisition and fire hazard management that benefit all new development is broken out from other Foothills costs.
2. Part A of the Foothills land conversion fee allocates land acquisition and fire hazard management costs across all new development in the Foothills, both covered

TABLE 24.7 Foothills Land Conversion Fee Approach

| | Foothills Land Conversion Fee | |
	Part A FeeAll Development	Part B FeeCovered Activities Only
Plan Actions Funded by Fee	Foothills open space land acquisitionFoothills fire hazard management	All Foothills mitigation actions except those funded by Part A fee
Fee Categories Subject to Fee	Small lotsLow-density rural residentialAll other development	Low-density rural residentialAll other development
Cost Allocation		
Land Use Scenario	All covered activities and other development not covered by the Plan	Covered activities only for categories subject to fee (low-density rural residential and all other development)
Measure of Impact	Service population (residents and workers) converted to equivalent dwelling units (EDUs)	Acres of direct impact
Application of Fee		
Residential	Per dwelling unit	Per acre
Non-residential	Per acre	Per acre

and non-covered activities, because of the open space and public safety benefits associated with those Plan costs.

3. For the Part A fee, service population (the number of residents and workers) is the measure of need for the Plan's open space acquisition and fire hazard management actions from all new development, whether a covered activity or not. Service population better reflects the level of need for these specific Plan actions than does acres of land conversion, because residents and businesses are the primary beneficiaries of open space and fire hazard management. This approach allows the Part A fee (for covered activities) and the open space and fire hazard management fee (for non-covered activities) to be applied to development at the same level and in the same manner.

4. Service population is converted to equivalent dwelling units (EDUs) to allocated costs for the Part A fee across both residential and non-residential development for covered and non-covered activities. The fee is applied per dwelling unit on residential development and per acre on non-residential development.[3]

5. All Foothills covered activities pay the Part A fee to fund open space land acquisition and fire hazard management costs. All non-covered activities in the Foothills pay the same fee supported by a separate nexus analysis for an open space and fire hazard management fee. [4]

6. For covered activities on small lots (fees 2a and 2b), the Part A fee is sufficient to reflect the overall impact per parcel acre for these fee categories based on the guidance provided in Table 24.4 and relative to other Foothills fees.

7. Part B of the Foothills land conversion fee allocates the remaining mitigation cost share across covered activities in the low-density rural residential and all other development fee categories.

8. The Part B fee is applied per parcel acre in a manner similar to the Valley land conversion fee.

24.6.2 Foothills Land Conversion Mitigation Costs, Funding, and Fee Schedule

24.6.2.1 Part A Fee

Table 24.8 shows the calculation of the 65.4% mitigation cost share for the Part A fee. After a series of adjustments to account for other funding sources and credits (see explanation in text following the table), Part A costs are allocated per EDUs across all covered and non-covered activities in the Foothills through the permit term.

Costs to establish the Foothills reserve system (land acquisition) in Table 24.8 are drawn from Table 24.3. Costs for fire hazard management are drawn from the cost model. The total cost of these Plan actions is multiplied by the Foothills mitigation fair share from Table 24.2 to determine the cost share that could be funded by Part A of the Foothills land conversion fee.

The number of EDUs shown in Table 24.8 is based on covered activities and all other development in the Foothills. One worker (and the associated business activity) is assumed to generate a need for and benefit from the open space acquisition and fire hazard management funded by the Plan at half (50%) of the level of one resident. This assumption reflects on average lower occupancy over a 24-hour period and fewer building square feet per occupant for non-residential compared with residential development.

Table 24.9 shows how Part A of the Foothills land conversion fee is determined and presents estimated revenue by fee category. For each category, the cost per EDU is adjusted for the relative impact per EDU. One dwelling unit equals one EDU, and 1 acre of non-residential development equals 1.21 EDUs based on an analysis of the Foothills land use scenario.[5] At the bottom of the table is an

TABLE 24.8 Foothills Land Conversion Mitigation Cost per Equivalent
Dwelling Unit (EDU) (Part A)

Foothills Reserve System (Land Acquisition)	$94,040,000
Foothills Fire Hazard Management	6,920,000
Part A Costs Subject to Fair Share Allocation	$100,960,000
Foothills Mitigation Fair Share	65.4%
Subtotal	$66,030,000
Bickford Ranch Open Space Funding[a]	(500,000)
Foothills Existing Reserve Credit[b]	(11,980,000)
Valley Share of Upper Salmonid Watersheds[c]	(20,840,000)
Foothills Mitigation Part A Cost Share	**$32,710,000**
Equivalent Dwelling Units (EDU)[d]	14,354
Average Mitigation Cost per EDU	**$2,279**

Sources: Michael J. Johnson, Director of Community Development, memorandum to Placer County Board of Supervisors regarding Bickford Ranch Specific Plan, December 8, 2015, p. 20; Nexus Study tables A.5, A.6, and A.7; Tables 24.2 and 24.3.

[a]Funding for open space provided by Bickford Ranch development agreement.
[b] Existing open space credited to the Plan's reserve obligation.
[c]See Tables 24.3 and 24.5.
[d]Includes activities on small parcels in urban land cover types that have no direct impact and are not subject to the land conversion fee. As explained in the text, such activities are subject to an open space and fire hazard management impact fee.

estimate of revenue from the proposed open space and fire hazard management fee, showing that the combined revenue from the two fees fully funds the Part A fee mitigation cost share.

24.6.2.2 Part B Fee

Part B of the Foothills land conversion fee is based on the mitigation share of total Plan costs allocated to the Foothills minus costs funded by the Part A fee. After adjusting total Foothills costs for funding from the Part A fee and special habitat costs, the mitigation cost per acre of direct impact is calculated using total acres of direct impact from those covered activities subject to the Part B fee (fees 2c, 2d, and 2e). See Table 24.10.

Total Plan costs are drawn from Table 24.3 and include the Foothills share of endowment contributions and Plan preparation costs. Costs allocated to the Part A fee nexus are deducted, as are special habitat costs, because

these costs are addressed through the special habitat fee. The net cost subject to the fair share allocation is multiplied by the Foothills mitigation fair share from Table 24.2 to determine the Foothill mitigation cost share for Part B. The mitigation cost share represents the amount to be funded by Part B of the Foothills land conversion fee.

Table 24.11 shows how Part B of the Foothills land conversion fee is determined and presents estimated revenue by fee category. The relative impact factor for the low-density rural residential category (fee 2c) reflects the guidance provided by Table 24.4 and the factor used for the Valley land conversion fee low density rural residential category. The per acre fee for categories 2d and 2e is calculated as a residual to ensure full funding of the Foothills mitigation cost share after deducting revenue from fee 2c. Total estimated revenue is equal to the Foothills Part B mitigation cost share shown in Table 24.12.

TABLE 24.9 Foothills Land Conversion Fee and Revenue by Fee Category (Part A)

Fee Category		Average Mitigation Cost per EDU	Relative Impact Factor[a]	Fee	Foothills Growth Scenario (50-Year Permit Term)		
					Dwelling Units	Parcel Area (Acres)	Fee Revenue
2a[b]	Residential project on existing parcel greater than 20,000 square feet up to 1 acre	$2,279	1	$2,279 per dwelling unit	1,089		$2,480,000
2b[b]	Non-residential project on existing parcel greater than 20,000 square feet up to 1 acre	$2,279	1.21	$2,757 per parcel acre		50	$140,000
2c	Single-family residential on existing parcel greater than 1 acre or on any parcel created by subdivision of an existing parcel into four or fewer total parcels	$2,279	1	$2,279 per dwelling unit	3,675		$8,380,000
2d	Single-family residential on any parcel created by subdivision of existing parcel into five or more total parcels and multi-family residential	$2,279	1	$2,279 per dwelling unit	4,639		$10,570,000
2e	Non-residential project on existing parcel greater than 1 acre or on any parcel created by subdivision	$2,279	1.21	$2,757 per parcel acre		193	$530,000
Total					**9,403**	**243**	**$22,100,000**
Open Space & Fire Hazard Management Fee							$10,610,000
Total Fee Revenue							**$32,710,000**
Foothills Land Conversion Fee (Part A) Cost Share							$32,710,000
Difference							**$–**

Notes:

Existing parcel refers to a parcel at time of Plan adoption.

[a]See text for explanation.

[b]Existing parcels 20,000 square feet or less are not covered activities and therefore not subject to HCP/NCCP development fees.

Sources: Nexus Study, tables 3.8, A.7, and A.8; Table 24.8; Urban Economics.

Table 24.12 shows the total Foothills land conversion fee based on the sum of the Part A and Part B fees. The combined Part A and B Foothills land conversion fee reflects the overall impact per parcel acre based on the guidance provided in Table 24.4, with the lowest fee for low-density rural residential (fee 2c), a higher fee for small lots (fees 2a and 2b),

TABLE 24.10 Foothills Land Conversion Mitigation Cost per Acre of
Direct Effect (Part B)

Foothills Costs	$249,990,000
Foothills Endowment Contribution	11,690,000
Foothills Plan Preparation Reimbursement	660,000
Total Foothills Plan Costs	$262,340,000
Foothills Land Conversion Fee Part A Costs	(100,960,000)
Foothills Special Habitat Costs	(68,210,000)
Part B Costs Subject to Fair Share Allocation	$93,170,000
Foothills Mitigation Fair Share	65.4%
Foothills Mitigation Part B Cost Share	$60,930,000
Foothills Direct Impact (Fees 2d, 2e, 2e) (Acres)	9,148
Average Mitigation Cost per Acre of Direct Effect	**$6,660**

Sources: Nexus Study, table 3.8; Tables 24.2, 24.3, and 24.8.

TABLE 24.11 Foothills Land Conversion Fee and Revenue by Fee Category (Part B)

Fee Category		Average Mitigation Cost per Acre of Direct Effect	Relative Impact Factor[a]	Fee	Foothills Growth Scenario (50-Year Permit Term)	
					Parcel Area (Acres)	Fee Revenue
2c[b]	Single-family residential on existing parcel greater than 1 acre or on any parcel created by subdivision of an existing parcel into four or fewer total parcels	$6,660	0.2	$1,332 per parcel acre	18,993	$25,300,000
2d	Single-family residential on any parcel created by subdivision of existing parcel into five or more total parcels and multi-family residential	$6,660	1.14	$7,560 per parcel acre	4,520	$34,170,000
2e	Non-residential project on existing parcel greater than 1 acre or on any parcel created by subdivision	$6,660	1.14	$7,560 per parcel acre	193	$1,460,000
Total					**23,706**	**$60,930,000**
Foothills Land Conversion Fee (Part B) Cost Share						$60,930,000
Difference						**$–**

Notes:

Existing parcel refers to a parcel at time of Plan adoption.

[a]See text for explanation.

[b]Fee per acre capped at 20 acres per parcel. For purposes of calculating revenue, parcel area excludes acreage above this cap (see table 3.8).

Sources: Nexus Study, table 3.8; Table 24.10; Urban Economics.

TABLE 24.12 Foothills Land Conversion Fee (2019 $)

Fee Category		Part A Fee	Part B Fee	Total Fee
2a	Residential project on existing parcel greater than 20,000 square feet up to 1 acre	$2,279 per dwelling unit	NA	$2,279 per dwelling unit (no per acre fee)
2b	Non-residential project on existing parcel greater than 20,000 square feet up to 1 acre	$2,757 per acre	NA	$2,757 per acre
2c	Single-family residential on existing parcel greater than 1 acre or on any parcel created by subdivision of an existing parcel into four or fewer total parcels	$2,279 per dwelling unit	$1,332 per parcel acre	$2,279 per dwelling unit plus$1,332 per acre up to$13,320 per parcel maximum amount[a]
2d	Single-family residential on any parcel created by subdivision of existing parcel into five or more total parcels and multi-family residential	$2,279 per dwelling unit	$7,560 per parcel acre	$2,279 per dwelling unit plus$7,560 per acre
2e	Non-residential project on existing parcel greater than 1 acre or on any parcel created by subdivision	$2,757 per acre	$7,560 per parcel acre	$10,317 per acre

Sources: Tables 24.9 and 24.11.

Notes:

Existing parcel refers to parcels at time of Plan adoption.

Per acre fees apply to the entire parcel area excluding areas improved at time of Plan adoption and where avoidance occurs. For low-density rural development, per acre fees apply only to the disturbed area footprint of covered activities unless the project includes a new dwelling unit.

For mixed use projects with multi-family residential, the project pays the higher fee of either category 2d or category 2e.

[a]Maximum amount per parcel applies to per acre fee only. Dwelling unit fee is in addition to the per acre fee.

and the highest fee for all other development (fees 2d and 2e).

24.7 LAND CONVERSION FEE SUMMARY

The land conversion fees for both subareas and all fee categories are shown in Table 24.13.

Fees are lower in the Foothills compared with the Valley due to lower mitigation costs per acre (compare the results in Table 24.5 and Table 24.10). Within each subarea, the nexus analysis resulted in less of a difference between the fees on small lots and rural residential, on the one hand, and fees on all other development, on the other hand (compare categories 1a and 1b with category 1c in the Valley, and categories 2a, 2b, 2c with categories 2d and 2e in the Foothills). This result is related to the greater benefits from fuels management and the increased impacts from fragmentation associated with small lots and rural residential development in the Foothills.

24.8 FUNDING PLAN SUMMARY

The funding plan for the HCP/NCCP is shown in Table 24.14. The funding plan demonstrates that anticipated revenues are sufficient to fund all Plan costs. Sources of funding include sources (1) dedicated to mitigating impacts of covered activities, (2) restricted to funding only the conservation component of Plan action, and (3) fungible across both the

TABLE 24.13 Land Conversion Fee Schedule (2019 $)

Plan Area A—Valley		
1a	Covered activity on existing parcel greater than 20,000 square feet up to 1 acre	$5,197 per acre
1b	Single-family residential on existing parcel greater than 1 acre or on any parcel created by subdivision of an existing parcel into four or fewer total parcels	$3,897 per dwelling unit plus $1,299 per acre up to $12,990 maximum amount[a]
1c	All other covered activities	$26,473 per acre
Plan Area A—Foothills		
2a	Residential project on existing parcel greater than 20,000 square feet up to 1 acre	$2,279 per dwelling unit
2b	Non-residential project on existing parcel greater than 20,000 square feet up to 1 acre	$2,757 per acre
2c	Single-family residential on existing parcel greater than 1 acre or on any parcel created by subdivision of an existing parcel into four or fewer total parcels	$2,279 per dwelling unit plus $1,332 per acre up to $13,320 maximum amount[a]
2d	Single-family residential on any parcel created by subdivision of existing parcel into five or more total parcels and multi-family residential	$2,279 per dwelling unit plus $7,560 per acre
2e	Non-residential project on existing parcel greater than 1 acre or on any parcel created by subdivision	$10,317 per acre
Plan Area B		
	Valley (Component B1: Roseville/Rocklin/Loomis area)	
3a	All covered activities	$26,473 per acre
	Foothills (Component B1: Auburn area and Component B2)	
3b	Covered activity on existing parcel up to 1 acre	$2,757 per acre
3c	Covered activity on existing parcel greater than 1 acre	$10,317 per acre

Notes:

Existing parcel refers to a parcel at time of Plan adoption.

Per acre fees apply to the entire parcel area excluding areas improved at time of Plan adoption and where avoidance occurs. For low-density rural development, per acre fees apply only to the disturbed area footprint of covered activities unless the project includes a new dwelling unit.

For mixed use projects with multi-family residential, the project pays the higher fee of either category 2d or category 2e.

[a]Maximum amount per parcel applies to per acre fee only. Per dwelling unit fee is in addition to per acre fee.

Sources: Tables 24.6 and 24.12.

mitigation and conservation components of the Plan.

One of the conditions for the wildlife agencies to grant permits for implementation of the Plan is that the Plan must be fully funded. Yet, the agencies also limited their "state and federal grant" revenue estimate to only the cost of land acquisition associated with the conservation component of the reserve (29.4%, see Table 24.2). This restriction is based on current eligible uses of state and federal grant revenue that exclude funding of other Plan costs such as management, monitoring, plan administration, and the endowment. The agencies were unwilling to allow the expanded use of grants to fund part of

TABLE 24.14 Funding Plan (2019 $)

	Valley		Foothills		Total	
PLAN FUNDING						
Mitigation Funding						
Land Conversion Fee	$531,420,000	56%	$83,030,000	32%	$614,450,000	51%
Special Habitat Fees	$172,840,000	18%	$60,770,000	23%	$233,610,000	19%
Temporary Effect Fees	negligible	<1%	negligible	<1%	negligible	<1%
Open Space and Fire Hazard Management Fee	$–	<1%	$10,610,000	4%	$10,610,000	<1%
Existing Reserve Credit[a]	$9,830,000	1%	$11,980,000	5%	$21,810,000	2%
Bickford Ranch Open Space	$–	<1%	500,000	<1%	500,000	<1%
Subtotal	**$714,090,000**	**75%**	**$166,890,000**	**65%**	**$880,980,000**	**73%**
Conservation Funding						
State and Federal Grants	$115,170,000	12%	$36,180,000	14%	$151,350,000	12%
Existing Reserve Credit[1]	$12,230,000	1%	$8,790,000	3%	$21,020,000	2%
Subtotal	**$127,400,000**	**18%**	**$44,970,000**	**27%**	**$172,370,000**	**20%**
Other Funding						
Interest Income	$2,100,000	<1%	$400,000	<1%	$2,500,000	<1%
Agricultural Leases	$7,990,000	<1%	$ -	<1%	$7,990,000	<1%
Other Local, State, and Federal[b]	$59,480,000	6%	$29,240,000	11%	$88,720,000	7%
Endowment Investment Earnings	$43,950,000	5%	$17,180,000	7%	$61,130,000	5%
Subtotal	**$113,520,000**	**12%**	**$46,820,000**	**18%**	**$160,340,000**	**13%**
Total PCCP Funding	**$955,010,000**	**100%**	**$258,680,000**	**100%**	**$1,213,690,000**	**100%**
PLAN COSTS						
Plan Implementation	$868,600,000	91%	$229,150,000	89%	$1,097,750,000	90%
Endowment Fund Balance, Year 50	$73,860,000	8%	$28,870,000	11%	$102,730,000	8%
Plan Preparation	$12,550,000	1%	$660,000	<1%	$13,210,000	1%
Total PCCP Costs	**$955,010,000**	**100%**	**$258,680,000**	**100%**	**$1,213,690,000**	**100%**
PLAN NET REVENUE						
Surplus/(Deficit)	**$–**	**0%**	**$–**	**0%**	**$–**	**0%**

Sources: Nexus Study, tables 2.6, 5.2, A.6, and A.9, and appendix L Table 4a; Tables 24.3, 24.6, 24.8, 24.9, and 24.11.

Notes:

[a]Existing reserve credit is an in-kind (non-cash) contribution to the Plan. Land value allocated to "Mitigation Funding" if original funding was not restricted to conservation purposes, otherwise allocated to "Conservation Funding."
[b]See text for explanation.

PCCP means Placer County Comprehensive Program.
Percentages are calculated within Plan Funding and Plan Costs groups.
Figures may not sum due to rounding.

the mitigation share of land acquisition in return for not funding the management and other costs associated with the conservation component of the Plan.

Consequently, total revenues in Table 24.14 are balanced to total costs, with revenue from "Other Local, State & Federal" sources representing 7% of total Plan revenues.

The wildlife agencies considered this revenue reasonable to anticipate given the long period represented by the 50-year permit term, the potential expansion of uses of state and federal grants to include other Plan costs, and the potential for new revenue sources, such as local tax measures and private foundations.

24.9 CONCLUSION

The policy objectives and technical issues discussed at the beginning of this chapter brought significant complexity to the nexus analysis and fee structure. The primary lesson learned from this nexus study is the appropriate use of professional judgement based on best available information to develop quantitative inputs to a nexus analysis when data is otherwise unavailable.

A quantitative measure of impact would have been relatively easy if the fee had been based solely on direct impacts measured by the amount of ground disturbance. However, as discussed in Section 24.4, the fee is applied based on gross parcel area and had to consider the significant indirect impacts of habitat fragmentation. The result is the set of professional judgements embodied in Table 24.4, which ranks types of development by relative impact. This table is significantly informed by the analysis of development impacts conducted by the Plan's environmental scientists. However, there was no data available to quantity with a single metric the "apples and oranges" effects of direct, indirect, and cumulative impacts.

The qualitative results of Table 24.4 were used to calculate the 0.2 relative impact factor for small lots and rural residential (fee categories 1a and 1b in Table 24.6 and 2c in Table 24.11). Professional judgement also had to be applied to allocate the 0.2 relative impact factor between dwelling units and parcel acres for rural residential (fee category 1b in Table 24.6). These factors also had to consider the combined Part A and Part B Foothills land conversion fee, where Part A was structured to be the only fee applicable to small lots, and to mirror the open space and fire hazard management fee developed through a service population rather than habitat impact analysis.

The outcome of this combination of thoughtful qualitative and rigorous quantitative analysis is a fee structure that achieved the policy objectives of this study while meeting the reasonable relationship tests required of a nexus analysis.

NOTES

1 Deductions from parcel area are made where documented avoidance of direct effects occurs, including land approved by the PCA set aside as habitat. HCP/NCCP, Section 6.3.1.3, *General Condition 3, Land Conversion*. Also, the fee is applied based on disturbed area footprint rather than parcel area for covered activities in low-density rural settings that do not include a dwelling unit. Finally, certain land conversion fees are applied per dwelling unit and not per parcel acre.

2 The upper salmonid watershed cost share is added after adjusting for the mitigation fair share because the upper salmonid watershed cost has already been adjusted for the mitigation cost share.

3 Many nexus studies that use a service population approach apply the fee to non-residential development based on building square feet, because this is more closely related to the number of workers than parcel acres. However, in the Foothills, fewer than 1% of covered activities are anticipated to be non-residential development (based on parcel acreage). Given this small share, and to avoid further complicating the fee schedule by adding another metric (building square feet), non-residential EDUs are converted to parcel acres as a reasonable indicator of employment for application of the Part A Foothills land conversion fee.

4 A separate open space nexus analysis determined that the maximum justified open space fee based on the existing open space standard is greater than the Part A fee calculated here. Only a fee equivalent to the Part A fee is charged to new development in the Foothills not subject to the Plan. See *Development Fee Nexus Study for the Open Space & Fire Hazard Management Fee*, Urban Economics, January 2020.

5 Nexus Study, table A.7, p. 83. Relevant inputs to this result included 2.71 persons per dwelling unit, weighting one worker at 0.5 relative to one resident to represent the relative benefit of open space and fire hazard management, and an floor-area ratio for non-residential development of about 0.1.

REFERENCES

Placer County (2020). *Placer County Conservation Program, Western Placer County Habitat Conservation Plan / Natural Community Conservation Plan*. Auburn: Placer County.

Spencer, R. D. (2020). *Development Fee Nexus Study for the Western Placer County HCP/NCCP*. Oakland: Urban Economics.

25 FLEXIBLE DEVELOPMENT FUNDING FOR LARGE-SCALE DEVELOPMENT

ALISON BOULEY

25.1 BACKGROUND

The City of Tracy, California, is situated within a triangle of Interstates 580, 205, and 5—making it an accessible suburb in the San Francisco Bay Area. With a population of almost 83,000 in the early 2020s, plus a solid base of small businesses and national retailers, the City of Tracy is a desirable home with many opportunities for growth.

When the Great Recession ended, the City established several areas for development. The largest area comprised 2,732 acres of residential, mixed-use, commercial, and light industrial land. With Harris & Associates' help, the City coordinated with the developer to ensure it could provide new residents with quality services and maintain the infrastructure required to do so.

The team established agreements that outline the funding mechanisms—including impact fees and bond funds—for the Tracy Hills specific plan area. The agreements also clarified the developer's role in bringing the critical infrastructure to life and the timeline in which it should happen.

The developer was required to pay upfront for a portion of improvements. For several of the improvements, they received a credit against their development impact fees.

The collaboration between the City and the developer illustrates the possibilities that arise when different forms of funding and financing are combined. The flexible fee programs also account for the infrastructure's future maintenance, in alignment with the City of Tracy's progressive goal of becoming the most prosperous community in California.

25.2 CONTEXT

The City of Tracy, California, experienced major growth beginning in the 1980s as people looked for affordable alternatives to Bay Area home prices. In 2000, the residents of Tracy voted for Measure A, which limited the City's growth to a maximum of 750 building permits in any given year or an average of 600 permits. Following the adoption of Measure A, the City continued to see rapid growth—until the Great Recession, when home prices dropped drastically. Meanwhile, the City of Tracy, like other California cities, faced budget deficits that forced leaders to make tough budgetary decisions.

Though growth had essentially ceased in the City, several large developments used this time to work through their entitlement process. When the Great Recession ended, they were poised for development. The largest was the Tracy Hills specific plan area, consisting of approximately 2,732 acres of residential, mixed-use, commercial, and light industrial land.

The development is nestled among the foothills on the southern edge of Tracy, providing easy access to the Bay Area. In an otherwise flat city, this area has a distinct feel. Despite its appealing location and characteristics, the Tracy Hills specific plan area presented many infrastructure challenges. It required the City to:

- Extend and improve several roads
- Build new pipelines and storage tanks to provide potable water to this new water zone

DOI: 10.4324/9781003336075-30

- Expand the wastewater treatment plant on the opposite side of town
- Extend the wastewater collection pipe
- Retain all storm drainage on-site in a series of percolation ponds
- Build a new fire station

When it came to recreation, the development was set to contain 45 acres of neighborhood parks, 30 acres of community parks, numerous walking and hiking trails, and a 180-acre open space park. The total infrastructure cost at buildout of the area was estimated at over $360 million.

With the addition of 4,700 homes, this development will add over 15,000 people to the City. Although such growth will generate property and sales tax revenue to the City, it is not enough to provide services to these new residents and maintain the infrastructure needed. Therefore, the developer and the City worked together to develop a funding strategy that ensured the timely construction of infrastructure and established a long-term funding source.

25.3 TECHNICAL ANALYSIS

Agencies can use a variety of tools to ensure that new growth pays its way. These include, among others: development impact fees, land-secured financing, public benefit payments, development agreements, and credit and reimbursement agreements. When combined, these tools can help create a flexible arrangement between the City and the developer.

In 2012, the City of Tracy adopted Citywide Impact Fees, which apply to all new developments within the City, while the older specific plan areas retained their historical localized fee programs. The Citywide fee program set the fee amounts for water, recycled water, sewer, traffic, parks, public safety, and public facilities. The City also adopted storm drainage fees by drainage shed area.

The City of Tracy and the developer worked through a series of tools, including a credit and reimbursement agreement, development agreement, and finance and implementation plan. They also formed a Community Facility District (CFD) for both maintenance and infrastructure. The agreements laid out the timing of the necessary improvements along with the funding mechanisms for each. It also established the improvements the developer was required to build.

In order to move this development forward, water and sewer service was a priority. To meet this need, the developer was required to pay upfront for a portion of its fair share of the wastewater treatment plant expansion, design of the required water improvements, purchase of necessary police equipment, and payment of a public benefit fee. The City could use this fee at its discretion for other needed infrastructure or equipment. The upfront payments are summarized in Table 25.1

In addition, the developer was required to build or secure several improvements for which it would receive a credit against its development impact fees. In order to ensure water was available, the developer was required to secure its own water supply and construct distribution lines within the project. It was also required to mitigate all its storm drainage on-site by constructing storm drainage collection facilities and percolation ponds. Because wildfires are a major concern in California, the developer agreed to design and build a fire station. The developer is also required to fund and build its neighborhood parks and open space areas.

Once 2,900 building permits have been issued, the developer is required to begin

TABLE 25.1 Upfront Developer Payments

Facility	Upfront Cost
Wastewater Treatment Plant Expansion	$2,000,000
Design of Water Improvements	500,000
Police Equipment	400,000
Public Benefit Fee	5,000,000
Total	$7,900,000

TABLE 25.2 Fees Assessed on and Credits Awarded to Developer

Facility	Fees	Credits	Deferred Fees	Fees Due at Occupancy
Transportation	$5,878	$4,996	–	$882
Water Distribution	4,801	4,801	–	–
Water Supply	2,054	2,054	–	–
Water Treatment	3,735	2,288	–	1,447
Recycled Water	3,008	–	1,594	1,414
Wastewater Treatment Plant	7,624	7,624	–	–
Wastewater Conveyance	1,824	1,824	–	–
Neighborhood Parks	6,508	6,183	–	326
Community Parks	2,057	–	–	2,057
Public Safety	1,529	1,451	–	78
Public Facilities	3,347	–	–	3,347
Total	**$42,365**	**$31,221**	**$1,594**	**$9,550**

construction of the community parks. The developer is also required to pay the community park fee, but the fees will be held in a separate account and used to reimburse the developer when it constructs the community parks. If for any reason, the developer does not build the community park, the City will have access to those funds to construct the park for the developer.

The developer negotiated with the City for deferment of about half of the recycled water fees. Those fees will be paid out of bond proceeds during later phases of the development.

Table 25.2 shows a sample of the fees and credits that are to be received for a typical residential lot in the first phase of development.

25.4 LAND-SECURED FINANCING

Proposition 13, passed in California in 1978, limited the property tax rate and the ability of local governments to increase the assessed value of real property by no more than an annual inflation factor. In 1982, the Community Facilities Act, adopted by the California State Legislature, presented a new way to fund public improvements and services. A CFD, commonly known as a Mello-Roos, is a special district, formed with a two-thirds property owner vote, which places a special tax on the property owners' tax bills to fund

ongoing services or serve as the security on which to issue land-secured municipal bonds.

Tracy Hills is forming a series of CFDs, which will reimburse the developer for infrastructure they construct, pay development impact fees, and ultimately, finance long-term maintenance. The estimated proceeds from the bond sale total $284 million. They will be completed in multiple phases and will fund developer-constructed infrastructure and development impact fees.

The maintenance CFD for a single-family home was set at $212 annually for Fiscal Year 2017–18 with a built-in escalation factor. This maintenance CFD covers maintenance of both improvements within the development as well as arterials outside the development, as shown in Table 25.3.

In negotiations between the developer and the City, they determined which improvements would be owned and funded by the

TABLE 25.3 Community Facilities District (CFD) Payments to Developer

Facility	Annual Cost
Citywide Maintenance	$62.00
City-Owned Parks	$122.60
City Roads	$3.66
Retention Basins	$23.98
Total	**$212.24**

City, along with those owned and funded through the home owners association (HOA).

The City will fund the following improvements:

- City parks
- A portion of public rights-of-way that include streets, on-street bikeways, sidewalks, curb and gutter, street signage, sewer, water, and storm drainage
- Storm retention basins
- Water storage and pumping facilities
- Sewer pump station
- Arterial road landscaping
- Typical municipal services

The HOA and/or property owners will fund the following improvements:

- All landscaping including irrigation, walls and fencing, and monuments within rights-of-way including median and roundabouts
- Fencing
- Seating areas/benches and trash receptacles
- Common area landscaping, walls and fencing, signage and monuments
- All private/HOA parks
- Open space
- Landscape utility corridors and slope easement areas
- Street lighting

The City required the developer to include a contingent special tax that will activate if the City needs to take over maintenance from the HOA. The contingent special tax was set at approximately $606 annually per single-family home for Fiscal Year 2017–18, providing assurance for the City in case the HOA fails to maintain the infrastructure.

25.5 CFD REIMBURSEMENT

The City and developer executed an acquisition agreement, which establishes the discrete components and facilities eligible for reimbursement. It also outlines the required process and timeline the developer and City must follow in processing reimbursements. The agency has fiduciary responsibility over the CFD funds and responsibility to verify eligibility for reimbursement under the Mello-Roos Act. The timeline for review is strict to ensure the developers receive reimbursement in a predictable and timely manner.

As the developer completes specific components of infrastructure, as identified in the acquisition agreement, it must submit a reimbursement package containing all contracts, change orders, invoices, checks, plans, prevailing wage, and lien releases. The documents are reviewed for completeness of documentation and eligibility. Once the review is complete, a report is issued, recommending that the City release the CFD funds to the developer and documenting the eligible costs. The City then completes a wire transfer of the funds.

Once all components within a larger facility are completed, and the City accepts the facility, the developer will receive its final reimbursement, including retention. Reimbursing for the individual, eligible components, rather than the facility as a whole, has financial advantages for the developer and the City. For the developer, it assists in the cash flow of the project. For the City, this process facilitates timely usage of the bond proceeds, which must be used within 3 years to maintain the tax-exempt status of the bonds. This well-established reimbursement process is just one of the many tools used in facilitating a large development project.

25.6 CONCLUSION

Communities in California today face a number of conflicting priorities: Provide more housing at an affordable price, and develop policies and procedures to create a financially sustainable agency. Agency staff and policymakers are constantly balancing these two imperatives.

Collaboration between the developer and the City—and the use of creative financing mechanisms—helped this large development project achieve both of those goals. Their cooperation and teamwork helped the project move forward as the state recovered from the Great Recession. The developer's willingness to take on upfront costs and fund long-term maintenance, coupled with the City's flexibility, contributed to this project's success. Their partnership serves as an example of a sustainable financial model in California and beyond.

26 RESIDENTIAL AND NONRESIDENTIAL SCHOOL IMPACT FEE NEXUS

Case Study of Fremont Union High School District, California

J. RICHARD RECHT

26.1 OVERVIEW

This chapter presents a case study conducted by Schoolhouse Services to apply school impact fees to both residential and nonresidential development in California. California's provisions for levying school impact fees require the demonstration of a needs nexus showing how all development, including nonresidential development, creates the need for school facilities. The case study is based on analysis completed in 2016, so all figures relate to that year. The case study includes background, an overall summary allowing readers to know the context of analysis in advance, and sections on establishing the nexus between residential and nonresidential development and school enrollment, housing and enrollment projections, school capacity analysis, facility costs, calculating school impact fees for residential development, and calculating impact fees for nonresidential development—called *commercial/industrial* (C/I) *development* for purposes of California's school impact mitigation legislation. The case study concludes with observations about emerging school facility financial needs and the role of proportionate share mitigation to address them.

26.2 BACKGROUND

The Fremont Union High School District ("FUHSD" or the "District") serves the communities of Cupertino and Sunnyvale, along with portions of other cities and unincorporated Santa Clara County, all located in the Silicon Valley portion of the San Francisco Bay Area. FUHSD serves grades 9 through 12, operating five comprehensive high schools with a combined enrollment of 10,700 students.

FUHSD has been experiencing steady growth, its enrollment as of 2016 having increased by 18 percent over the last 15 years. Enrollment is projected to grow another 6 percent over the next 5 years. A further examination of future enrollment, looking at both enrollment from already existing homes and students generated by new residential development, will come later in this case study.

Section 17620 of the California Educational Code[1] authorizes school districts to collect fees for mitigation of the impact of new development on enrollment in the District. In 2016, at the time of this case study, the maximum fee levels under this Section are $3.48 per square foot of residential development and $0.56 per square foot of C/I development. The State Allocation Board bi-annually updates the maximum development impact fee amounts.

Where an elementary district and a high school district both serve an area, the districts must agree on an appropriate sharing of the maximum fee amounts. Per existing fee sharing agreements with its feeder school districts, FUHSD can levy up to 38 to 40 percent of the maximum fees, with 60 to 62 percent going to the elementary school district within whose boundaries the development will occur. (The terms of the fee agreements vary slightly.)

DOI: 10.4324/9781003336075-31

In 2016, the maximum fees allocated to FUHSD are from $1.32 to $1.39 per square foot on residential development and $0.21 or $0.22 per square foot on C/I development.

To levy fees, the District requires documentation showing the nexus between development and the facilities to be funded and the cost of mitigation. (Government Code Sections 66000 *et seq.*) This case study shows how the analysis met these requirements.

26.3 CONTEXT AND OVERALL SUMMARY

This section provides the overall context for the case study and summarizes key findings used in the analysis.

- Enrollment was 10,736 students as of the fall 2015 count date, with about 10,700 of these students enrolled in the District's five comprehensive high schools. The District's demographers project that enrollment at these five schools will increase by more than 600 students by the 2020–21 school year.
- In 2016, the District housed all students from existing homes in its facilities. However, class sizes are on average a little larger than they used to be and larger than the District considers educationally desirable. The number of classrooms available at most of the schools is inadequate for the District to be able to schedule classes efficiently, and some teachers have to exit their rooms during their preparation periods. The addition of more than 400 students from homes already existing in the District will increase the need for additional capacity.
- New housing development of 3,350 housing units is projected from 2016 to the 2020–21 school year. Continued C/I development, primarily on redeveloped sites, is expected.
- Approximately 169 students are projected to live in the 3,350 new homes. This increase

will exacerbate the District's capacity shortage if new facilities are not built.

- It is assumed that the additional capacity necessary to house increased enrollment from both existing homes and new development will be in the form of additions to the existing campuses. The share of the cost of these additions appropriately allocated to the 169 students from new homes is estimated to be approximately $11.76 million.
- The cost impact per square foot of residential development is $2.76 per square foot. The District's 2016 Section 17620 maximum residential fee level is either $1.22 or $1.29 per square foot of new construction, less than half of the cost impact. Thus, the District is justified in levying the maximum fee on residential development.
- The District's share of the 2016 maximum fee for C/I space was $0.21 or $0.22 per square foot. This fee is justified on all types of C/I development except Parking Structures and Self-storage. The fees for these categories in 2016 were $0.01 and $0.02 per square foot, respectively.

The next section presents the nexus between development of all types and school enrollment.

26.4 NEXUS BETWEEN DEVELOPMENT AND ENROLLMENT

New development can be required to provide mitigation only to the extent of its impacts. For schools, the impacts are students for whom additional capacity must be provided. The mitigation is funds to offset the costs involved in providing facilities to accommodate the increased enrollment. A school district seeking mitigation from developers has the burden of documenting the nexus between development and the facilities that will be needed. This chapter describes this nexus in general terms. Its purpose is to clarify the causal chain between developments and its facility impacts, and in so doing, provide a framework for the quantification of the impacts in the remainder of the chapter.

This section begins with a description of the nature of growth in a regional economy and the associated growth in population. It then traces the effect of the construction of workplaces and homes, components of regional growth, on increases in enrollment in local schools. It concludes by discussing how the estimated cost of facilities to accommodate the increased enrollment can be allocated among the development that generates this additional enrollment.

26.4.1 Economic Growth

C/I construction and residential development (and hence, additional households and children) are related parts of economic growth. An expanding regional economy results from increased demand for the goods and services produced in the region. As economic expansion progresses, more workers are needed, and increasingly, they must be attracted from outside the region. Sometimes, the process is reversed; the availability of a productive labor force can be a key factor leading to the expansion of business activity in the region, with a resultant increase in employment.

Both the increase in business activity and the addition of new households require new development. The business activity requires new commercial and industrial space; the addition of families requires additional housing units. This is not to imply that the additional employees necessarily work in the new C/I space or that the new households occupy the new housing units; this is obviously not the case. However, when new space is constructed, and existing businesses or households move into it, the space they previously occupied is made available. Whatever the number of

shifts in the chain, space is eventually available for occupancy by new employees or residents from outside the region. In contrast, in regions where growth is not occurring, new construction is slow to occur, because there is little market for the space made available, which keeps property prices and rents below the level necessary to cover the cost of new construction.

26.4.2 Impacts on Schools

The interrelated nature of C/I development and residential development justified the California legislature's adoption of fee legislation that recognized both as contributing to enrollment growth in schools. The higher per square foot fee on residential development presumably represents the immediacy of the new home's role in generating additional students; when a new home is occupied, most of the children immediately begin attending local schools. Yet, it is clear that new homes are developed primarily in response to the need for additional housing to accommodate the growing labor force and their families, making employment growth a major contributor to the need for additional school facilities. The enrollment impacts are therefore the joint effect of local housing development and both local and regional C/I development.

The most immediate school impact of new homes is, as stated earlier, additional students enrolling in the local schools. The associated impact is the need for school facilities to accommodate these students. In fact, the school district must usually anticipate this need far in advance in order to plan for the construction of the additional facilities needed. The enrollment projections must include consideration of factors affecting enrollment other than new development. For example, rising birth rates may be resulting in increased enrollment from older homes. However, the enrollment impacts of new development must be separately identified, as mitigation can be sought from new development only for the portion of the facilities that would not have been needed in the absence of that development.

Thus, the final step in the demonstration of nexus is the determination of the facilities anticipated to be needed to accommodate the additional enrollment that would not have occurred without the new development. The facilities are often new schools, though they are sometimes wings to be added to existing schools, relocatable classrooms, or occasionally, the reconstruction or replacement of school buildings that would otherwise have reached the end of their useful life.

Once the facilities appropriate to provide the needed capacity have been identified, their cost must be estimated. It is the mitigation of this cost, and only this cost, that the district may seek from new development.

26.4.3 Determination of Mitigation

It should be noted that the task of quantifying the impacts of new development on school facility costs involves identifying the relative shares of the cost impacts attributable to each individual development project: to begin with, how much of the cost should be allocated to C/I development and how much to residential. Within these categories, how much, for example, should be allocated to office versus retail space and how much to single-family homes as compared with multi-family? The most common approach is to assume that housing development should bear the cost of mitigation up to the level set by the state legislation. If fees at that level are inadequate, fees on C/I development are then appropriate. The amount of the C/I fee is based on the portion of the cost calculated to be unfunded after the fees on residential development are paid (up to the limits set by the state). This perspective reflects the immediacy with which residential development impacts school enrollment.

In the majority of cases, the total of residential and C/I fees is inadequate to provide the facilities to accommodate the enrollment from new development. The courts earlier upheld city-imposed mitigation supplemental to the statutory developer fees in situations where the new development is a result of changes in public policy, such as annexation or rezoning. California Senate Bill 50 of 1998[2] subsequently shifted responsibility for school financing to the state and removed the basis for supplemental mitigation imposed by cities and counties. However, it provided for greater residential mitigation in the form of alternative fees if certain requirements are met.

The school enrollment resulting from C/I development is proportional to the number of employees. Thus, appropriate mitigation amounts per square foot are determined proportional to the employment density of each type of building. The approach taken in the analysis is conservative in that it assumes that only the proportion of employees residing in the local school district impact that district and ignores the impact on all the other districts in which the employees reside. If all districts use this approach in their analysis, the majority of the impact from employment is never considered, simply because on a regional basis, the majority of the labor force commutes to work in districts other than where the employees reside.

The impacts of residential development tend to be somewhat proportional to size of unit (that is, larger homes tend to generate more students). This relationship supports the implicit determination in state legislation for square feet as a measure of relative causality of school impacts. If there is evidence that student generation characteristics are different for different types of residential development, it may be necessary to determine the impacts of the different types.

Housing and enrollment projections are presented in the next section.

26.5 HOUSING AND ENROLLMENT PROJECTIONS

This section begins with a projection of housing, followed by identifying student generation rates for housing, and then, projections of new students from development as well as a comparison with students from existing development.

26.5.1 Housing Projections

FUHSD is called upon to house enrollment from new residential development. Additional enrollment occasioned by new housing is projected to continue into the foreseeable future, although the rate of enrollment growth from new housing is slowing due to land availability constraints. Enrollment from new homes is projected separately from enrollment from existing homes. This is necessary, since fee justification must identify and address the impact of students from new development, distinguishing it from the costs of housing students from existing homes. A projection of future enrollment from new development is therefore an essential aspect of the District's fee justification. This section sets forth enrollment projections and describes the analysis upon which they are based.

The analysis of enrollment from new homes begins with projections of new residential development. The FUHSD boundaries encompass essentially all of the cities of Cupertino and Sunnyvale, small portions of the several surrounding cities, and an unincorporated portion of Santa Clara County. Almost all of new residential development will occur in the Sunnyvale and Cupertino School Districts, the feeder districts that provide almost all of FUHSD's students. There are no large vacant land areas available for development within the District's boundaries. There are only a limited number of smaller vacant parcels. The majority of new residential will occur as redevelopment of existing commercial and residential properties.

The projections used here are those prepared for the District by Enrollment Projection Consultants (EPC); the firm has provided demographic information for the District and its feeder districts for many years. They are based on an extensive analysis of factors affecting enrollment in the District. The analysis includes economic and social factors, birth statistics, patterns of grade-to-grade cohort progressions, and, particular to enrollment from new homes, development in the pipeline, zoning, and other development constraints and student generation per new home. The analysis is detailed in that it analyzes and projects factors affecting enrollment in small "planning areas," allowing for the factors based on the nature of each area.

In 2016, the EPC projected the construction of 3,350 new homes in the District over the next 5 years (see Table 26.1). The forecasts separate the projected housing units between the northern (Sunnyvale Elementary School District) and southern (Cupertino Union School District) portions of the District, and between more family-friendly (mostly single-family detached [SFD]) and less family-friendly units (smaller apartments and condominiums), as student generation tends

TABLE 26.1 Projected Housing Units 2011–12 through 2021–22

City and Residential Type	Units
Sunnyvale ESD	
Single-Family Detached	50
Condominiums and Apartments	2,280
Below Market Units	120
Total Sunnyvale ESD	2,450
Cupertino Union ESD	
Single-Family Detached	80
Condominiums and Apartments	820
Below Market Units	0
Total Cupertino Union ESD	900
FUHSB Total Units	3,350

Note: The Sunnyvale and Cupertino Elementary School Districts comprise almost all of the District.

Source: Enrollment Projection Consultants.

to vary in different areas and among different types of housing.

The large majority of the projected new housing, 2,450 units, is in the Sunnyvale Elementary School District portion of the District; only 900 units are in the Cupertino Union School District portion. The large majority, 3,100 units, are apartments and condominiums, reflecting the lack of greenfield areas for development. One hundred and thirty of the units are SFD (and townhouses), units traditionally more oriented to families. The remaining 120 units are part of below market rate (BMR) projects; these are separated out because they are often oriented to families and can generate a relatively large number of young children.

A time framework of a decade was used in the analysis for the 2012 justification document. The shorter time framework here follows from EPC's decision to restrict its forecast to 5 years. New housing being completed and occupied during the school years 2015–16 through 2019–20 is forecasted. This allows a comparison of enrollment from the fall of 2015 to the fall of 2020.

The actual volume and timing of new housing within the District is not critical when determining the cost impact of new residential development for fee calculation purposes. Regardless of whether these projections are realized in 5 years or 10 years, the same number of students from new housing will have to be accommodated. Furthermore, while any unanticipated change in the *amount* of housing constructed in a given time frame will change the projected enrollment from new housing and the cost of accommodating it; it will also change by the same proportion the assessable square footage projected to be constructed over that same time period, leaving the per square foot cost of new development essentially unchanged. In other words, using a moderately lower (or higher) growth estimate than is assumed here would not affect the cost impact of an individual new housing unit.

26.5.2 Student Generation Rates

Student generation rates (SGRs or student yields), the average number of students per home, are the second key aspect of projecting enrollment from new homes. (For example, if 40 students reside in 100 homes, the SGR of these homes is 0.4.) Student generation, however, typically varies among housing types; SFD homes usually generate two to three times more students than units in multiple-family structures (apartments and condominiums). Other factors such as the sale price, the location of residential development, the characteristics of the units, and socio-economic factors are also significant in determining student generation.

EPC's work for FUHSD includes searching the District's student file for addresses matching the addresses of recently built housing. This survey provides SGRs for housing of different types in different parts of the District. The SGRs for the housing type and District sub-areas are shown in Table 26.2.

26.5.3 Enrollment from New Housing

The number of housing units of each type simply multiplied by the student generation rate of each housing type results in a preliminary

TABLE 26.2 Student Generation Rates (SGRs) for New Housing

City and Residential Type	SGR
Sunnyvale ESD	
Single-Family Detached[a]	0.1
Condominiums and Apartments	0.02
Below Market Units	0.28
Total Sunnyvale ESD	
Cupertino Union ESD	
Single-Family Detached[a]	0.21
Condominiums and Apartments	0.08
Below Market Units	0.02

[a]Some family-friendly condominiums are included with single-family.

Source: Enrollment Projections Consultants.

TABLE 26.3 Enrollment from New Housing

City and Residential Type	Units	SGR	As Built
Sunnyvale ESD			
Single-Family Detached	50	0.10	5
Condominiums and Apartments	2,280	0.02	47
Below Market Units	120	0.28	34
Total Sunnyvale ESD	2,450		86
Cupertino Union ESD			
Single-Family Detached	80	0.21	17
Condominiums and Apartments	820	0.08	67
Below Market Units	0	0.02	0
Total Cupertino Union ESD	900		84
FUHSB Total Units	3,350		169

Sources: Tables 26.1 and 26.2.

total of 169 students, as shown in Table 26.3. (EPC actually tracks the new students through the grades, and thus, the District forecasts include a slightly different count of students from new housing.)

26.5.4 Enrollment from Existing Housing

District enrollment as of the fall 2015 California Longitudinal Pupil Achievement Data System (CALPADS) (the successor to the Basic Education Data System [CBEDS]) was 10,736. Of this total, 37 students did not attend the five comprehensive high schools; the enrollment at these five schools was about 10,700 students. District enrollment has increased by 1,674 students, an increase of 25 percent, over the last 15 years. The majority of this increase has come from existing housing. From 1996 through about 2006, the presence of the baby boom echo generation into high school years fueled the increases, though the increasing efforts of parents to have their children attend high-achieving schools played a role. Since 2006, the large baby boom echo cohorts have been passing from their high school years. Yet, even with smaller high school age cohorts in California, District enrollment has increased by a small amount over the last 5 years. Now, with the baby boom echo cohorts almost all graduated, enrollment is projected

to increase by over 600 students over the next 5 years, with only about 169 of this increase being generated by students from new homes.

The enrollment would have been even larger if the District had not over the last decade undertaken a program to diminish the number of inter-district transfers attending FUHSD schools. In the middle 2000s, the District established a residency office. Since 2016, it requires that new students enrolling in the District's schools, whether entering the ninth grade or into a later grade, present evidence of residence in the District and do so again prior to their junior years. (The only significant exception is for children of the employees of the District and the feeder districts.)

The next section addresses school capacity to accommodate existing and projected demand.

26.6 CAPACITY ANALYSIS

FUHSD is a growing school district, as was made clear earlier. This increased enrollment has been accommodated in the same schools in the District. And, enrollment is projected to increase by over 600 students in the next 5 years. The intent in this section is to look at the enrollment capacity of the existing facilities of the FUHSD to house the growing enrollment.

Given the need each year to picture how the increasing enrollment will be housed, it is not surprising that District staff prepare detailed information about the capacity of the schools. It should be understood that staff are not determining long-term capacity based primarily on educational standards. Rather, the determination of capacity reflects factors such as current teacher/pupil ratios (lower than they used to be), whether teachers can stay in their rooms during their teacher preparation periods, minimal availability of rooms for meetings that are not regularly scheduled, etc. Though these are not the determination of the District's educational standards, they are the appropriate basis to begin consideration of the District's current enrollment capacity.

Per the District's recent classroom count for the space available for the 2016–17 school year, there will be a total of 457 classrooms in the five high schools (Cupertino, Fremont, Homestead, Lynbrook, and Monta Vista) that can be used for instruction; this count is up from a total of 345 classrooms 10 years ago. The total includes 405 general education classrooms and 52 classrooms used for Special Day Classes (SDCs), the program for students with special needs, which have much smaller class sizes. The count of classrooms does not include rooms used full time for academic support (e.g. libraries, computer labs, etc.) or administration.

The District's target is to schedule (non-SDC) classes for an average of 5.33 periods out of the seven periods of the day. One of the reasons for this is the presence of specialty rooms such as music rooms, computer labs, some science labs, etc., which are not scheduled for their special classes in all periods and are not arranged for general classes. Another reason is the District's policy of allowing teachers to remain in their home rooms during their two preparation periods, rather than requiring them to move out and back, and allowing them to meet with students and/or parents. (This is the policy at the great majority of California high schools.) Finally, class

attendance is lower during the first period and particularly, the last period of the day due to athletics, transportation arrangements, and student work schedules. The District estimates needed capacity per student at 6.10 classes per day. The 5.33 periods of usage of a classroom thus equals 87 percent of the need of the students in an average class.

The maximum number of students for each type of class is set by the District's contract with teachers. This often means that the number of students in a given room will differ for different periods of the day. For example, freshman English and algebra classes are counted as having 23 students, and later English and math classes have up to 28 students. Science, social science, and several other class categories have a maximum of 32.5 students. The largest class sizes are for physical education and band/choir classes. The average of all (non-SDC) classes is 30.10 students per class.

The sizes of SDCs are set by the state standards. The District averages 12 students per SDC class. Room usage is targeted for 4.5 periods per day. SDC students are also assumed to take an average of about 6.10 classes per day, meaning each room provides about 74 percent of the needs of an average class.

Using these data, the capacity of the 405 noon-SDC rooms is 10,640 students and the SDC rooms 460 students, for a total capacity of 11,100 students. This capacity is just about equal to the current enrollment.

At this point, the compromises inherent in the assumptions need to be recognized. For example, teachers are allotted 2 hours each day for teacher preparation and other school-related activities. The District's policy is that the teacher's home room will be available during that time. Yet overall, only about half of that time is made available for this purpose. Another problem is that with the rooms all assumed to be scheduled, rooms are not available for classes that pull students from their regular class schedule. A very important consideration is that the current class sizes, while now common in California, are larger than they used to be and larger than the average of high school classes nationwide. If the District moved towards the average sizes that used to be characteristic of the District and of the state, and the average of the country as a whole, its capacity would be significantly short of its enrollment.

In other words, the District is already compromising on educational standards in its provision of enrollment capacity. There is no excess capacity available for students from new homes in the District.

The cost of school facilities to meet enrollment demand is addressed next.

26.7 FACILITY COSTS

As discussed earlier, over the next 5 years, enrollment is projected to increase by over 600 students. New development is forecasted to generate 169 of these additional students. To cope with increased enrollment to this point, the District has undertaken projects over the last decade that have added 112 classrooms. (This is a net count; some classrooms, primarily portables, have been removed to make space for two-story buildings.) The enrollment of 600 more students will require the addition of even more capacity.

An additional high school campus would provide more than enough capacity. Reopening the former Sunnyvale High School campus was one possibility considered in prior justification analyses. The District is currently leasing out the site, and it could, in theory, be taken back and renovated for use as a high school. However, the condition of the campus is such that it's likely that it would be less expensive to demolish the buildings there and build anew than to renovate them. And, the campus is currently subject to multiple long-term leases; taking the campus back would, in effect, result in a large land cost. Also, very importantly, it is not in the southern portion of the District, where the additional capacity is needed. The District has decided that it would not be a good campus

for a comprehensive high school serving the Cupertino and Sunnyvale communities. And, it would probably provide more than the capacity needed.

A new, smaller high school in the southern portion of the District would appear to be ideal. However, it would be difficult to find an available site, and even if one could be found, the cost of adding capacity in the form of a new campus would be prohibitively expensive, given the cost of land. Thus, more intensive development of existing campuses appears to be the most likely option.

The District has data on its cost of construction in the building of additional classrooms funded by Measure B, authorized by the voters in 2008. One of the projects is the construction of a classroom and cafeteria building at Fremont High School. It is a two-story building with 30,000 square feet of floor space. The cost is $22 million, which is $733 per square foot for the 30,000 square feet of improvements. Similarly, a classroom and cafeteria building at Homestead High School has 17,000 square feet and cost $12.6 million, or $741 per square foot.

It is clear that infill construction on an existing campus on a tight schedule is much more expensive than construction of a new campus on an open field. The reasons include that they are designed to receive high LEED (Leadership in Energy and Environmental Design) ratings; that non-classroom space is usually more expensive than classroom space; and that they are two-story buildings, the construction of which has to be fitted into an existing campus and scheduled so as to minimize interruption of ongoing school activities.

However, they do not include any land acquisition costs. These projects call attention to the reality that expanding the enrollment capacity of schools requires expanded capacity in the educational support spaces as well as classroom space.

The California School Facility (CSF) program uses a size standard of 95 square feet per high school student. This standard

TABLE 26.4 Facilities Expansion Costs

TABLE 26.4 Facilities Expansion Costs

Calculation Step	Figure
Per Student Construction Cost	$69,600
Students from Residential Development	169
Construction Costs due to Residential Development	$11,762,000

Note: Figures rounded.

Source: General Plan Housing Element Study (2014) and Schoolhouse Services.

includes space for academic support activities. This standard times a $733 per square foot cost results in $69,600 as the cost of adding capacity to FUHSD schools. These costs per student, times the number of students generated by each alternative, project the cost of capital facilities to accommodate additional students.

This information about per student construction costs provides a basis for calculation of the cost impact of the 3,350 new homes projected in the next 5 years and the 169 students projected to reside in them. The cost is $11.76 million (see Table 26.4).

The next step of the analysis is to calculate the impact fee for residential development.

26.8 DETERMINATION OF FEE ON RESIDENTIAL DEVELOPMENT

California's legislation authorizing school districts to impose fees implicitly assumes that they will be in the form of a fee amount per square foot of new construction. It is thus necessary to calculate the total square feet of new units among which the cost will be allocated. SFD units vary widely in size. The SFD units will generally be as large as will fit on the sites, though in some cases, they will be townhouses. An average size of 3,000 square feet is assumed for these units. The apartment and condominium units will be much smaller in size; an average size of 1,200 square feet is projected, above the size of projects now being proposed. In both cases, the area estimated is as defined in Section 65995(b)(1) of the California Government Code, being the "square footage within the perimeter of a residential structure," with exclusions for garages, patios, and so forth.

Multiplying the 130 SFD units projected to be constructed by an average size of 3,000 square feet yields approximately 390,000 square feet. Multiplying the 3,220 projected units in multiunit buildings (i.e. condominiums and apartments) by an average size of 1,200 square feet yields approximately 3,864,000 square feet. The calculations are summarized in Table 26.5.

The total cost impact of new development was determined to be $11,762,000. As shown in Table 26.6, the resulting cost impact per square foot is $2.76.

The statutory fee the schools can levy on residential development per Educational Code Section 17620 is adjusted biennially by the State Department of Education. As adjusted on February 24, 2016, the maximum fee is $3.48 per square foot. Per agreements with the elementary school districts, FUHSD is entitled to 38 percent to 40 percent of this fee, if justified by this analysis. Its share is

TABLE 26.5 Square Feet of Residential Development

Calculation Step	Single-Family Detached	Condominiums, Apartments	Total
Number of New Units	130	3,220	3,350
Average Square Feet	3,000	1,200	
Total Residential Square Feet	390,000	3,864,000	**4,254,000**

Note: Figures rounded.

Source: Schoolhouse Services.

TABLE 26.6 Per Square Foot Cost of Residential Development

Facility Costs	Figure
Construction Costs due to Residential Development	$11,762,000
Total Residential Square Feet	4,254,000
Facilities Costs per Square Foot	$2.76

Note: Figures rounded.

Source: Schoolhouse Services.

therefore $1.32 or $1.39 per square foot. With a cost impact of $2.76 per square foot, FUHSD is justified in levying its share of the maximum state legislated amount on residential development.

Adjustments for the type of residential unit may be needed. Government Code Sections 66000 et seq. refer to "types of development." The type of development analyzed in this subsection is residential construction (without demolition of pre-existing structures) of new housing units. Other types of development have, or potentially have, different cost impacts. We here address several types of residential development other than new residential units on vacant land. The impacts of commercial and industrial development are addressed later.

26.8.1 Redevelopment Construction

In *Warmington Old Town Associates v. Tustin Unified School District*,[3] the court ruled that new construction that replaced pre-existing structures would be considered "redevelopment construction," and constituted a different type of development. This was because it potentially had different student generation characteristics than new construction on vacant land. In other words, the removal of existing structures potentially removed some students, which could offset at least some of the impact of the students residing in the new homes. The court's finding was that the Tustin School District's justification lacked

determination of the impacts of redevelopment construction. Therefore, we address the matter of redevelopment construction.

It should be understood that FUHSD provides a credit for structures removed in preparation for new development. In most cases, this means that in effect, only the incremental new square footage of redevelopment construction is assessed. This is not the only approach to implementing the court's decision regarding "redevelopment construction;" it is the one that generally results in lower fees.

The analysis (of new construction on vacant land) would then also apply to that portion of redevelopment construction on which fees are levied. There will be cases in which the per square foot fiscal impact of the property demolished will differ from the impact of the new development, meaning that a simple subtraction of the old square footage is incorrect. The obvious example is when a commercial building is replaced by a residential building. In this case, the fee amount the demolished building would have to pay if new is subtracted from the fee otherwise due on the new, all as determined by the implementing ordinance.

26.8.2 Residential Expansions

Additions to existing homes are another type of development that differs from the model analyzed previously. Additions to existing housing represent a permanent increase in the capacity to accommodate population in a community. Any increased population may include school-aged children, who will place a corresponding demand on schools. Thus, to maintain the educational level of service, the increase in local residential capacity from additions must be met by a corresponding availability of school facility capacity.

California state law allows school districts to collect fees on room additions to existing housing units over 500 square feet. From a legislative standpoint, additions are considered a type of new development; in so far as they generate facility impacts, they are subject to fees. Within the frame of the enrollment projections in this analysis, however, the students from additions are not included in the number of student from new development. In fact, residential additions represent a form of intensification of the existing housing stock, and the resulting enrollment growth is a component of enrollment from existing housing.

We only have data on the impacts of additions from one situation. An analysis of residential additions was conducted by Schoolhouse Services for the Santa Cruz City School Districts. Available data there showed that additions averaged 977 square feet in size, and student generation for these homes increased from 0.48 to 0.69 K–12 students. The average share for grades 9–12 was approximately 0.05. A simple calculation serves to illustrate the school facility cost impacts of additions. Earlier, it was shown that average facilities cost per student was determined to be $69,600. If each addition resulted in 0.05 students, the impact per addition would be $3,480. An average addition of 977 square feet thus produces an impact of $3.56 per square foot. This amount is well above the state's authorized Level 1 fee amounts of $1.32 or $1.39 per square foot the District is eligible to levy.

26.8.3 Senior Housing

Certain types of housing dedicated for occupancy by senior citizens may not be subject to the full residential fee because it would not house student-age residents. Pursuant to state law, it would generally be subject to the maximum fee for commercial development projects, based on its indirect contribution to student generation. Individual projects applying for such special treatment should be evaluated by the District on a case-by-case basis.

The next step in the process is calculating school impact fees for C/I development.

26.9 IMPACT FEES FOR COMMERCIAL/INDUSTRIAL DEVELOPMENT

Commercial or industrial development, along with residential development, has an impact on school enrollment. New jobs require a larger labor force, which in turn, causes new housing to be built to increase the housing supply. The families in new houses have their children enrolled in the local school district. This enrollment growth, a joint result of the C/I and the residential development, in turn impacts the facility capacities of the district.

The District levies fees consistent with California Educational Code Section 17620 to be applied to the mitigation of these impacts. Previously, it was established that current Section 17620 fees for residential development do not generate enough revenue to cover the costs of additional capacity to accommodate the students from that development. The revenue gained from the maximum allowable such fees on residential projects covers only a portion of the cost of housing the students from new homes. Therefore, the District looks to C/I development also to contribute its fair share of the cost of needed school facilities.

The 2016 maximum fee for commercial or industrial development projects is set at $0.56 per square foot. If justified by this analysis, FUHSD is entitled, depending on the elementary district, to 38 percent or 40 percent of this fee, or $0.21 or $0.22 per square foot of C/I development. The District seeks to levy this amount, where justified, to help alleviate the unfunded facilities cost per student.

26.9.1 Calculation of Cost Relationship

There are several key components in calculating a justifiable commercial or industrial development fee. The following formula is used to determine the school facility cost per square foot of development:

A Employees per Square Foot of Development
B Percentage of Employees Residing within the District
C Average Number of Homes per Resident Employee
D Average Number of Students per Home
E Unfunded Cost of School Facilities per Student

$$A \times B \times C \times D \times E$$

$$= \text{School Facility Cost per Square Foot}$$

$$\text{of Development}$$

The number of employees per square foot depends on the type of C/I development. Consequently, the result of the equation will differ for each principal C/I category. The remaining factors are approximately consistent across development types. The fact that the result is greater than zero reflects the causal relationship between C/I development and school facility needs. If the calculated impact is greater than the maximum, currently $0.21 or $0.22, for a given category of development, then the maximum fee is justified for that type of development. Each factor in this formula is discussed in the following.

26.9.1.1 *Employees per Square Foot of Development*

The estimated number of employees per square foot must reflect the wide variation among the different types of C/I development. As permitted by state law, results from an employment density survey published by the San Diego Association of Governments (SANDAG) are used to determine numbers of employees per square foot anticipated in future commercial or industrial development. (Information on warehouses, for which SANDAG lacks data, is from the Institute of Transportation Engineers.) SANDAG provides employment densities based on a series of categories ranging from retail to research and development. The densities are shown in Table 26.7.

TABLE 26.7 Employees per Square Foot of Building Area

Category	Employees/sq. ft.	sq. ft./Employee	Employees/1,000 sq. ft.
Parking Structures[a]	0.00002	50,000	0.02
Self-Storage	0.00006	15,541	0.06
Lodging	0.0011	883	1.1
Schools	0.0011	878	1.1
Warehouses[b]	0.0013	769	1.3
Auto Repair	0.0013	741	1.3
Movie Theaters	0.0015	667	1.5
Big Box Retail	0.0017	597	1.7
Regional Shopping Centers[c]	0.0019	539	1.9
Hospitals	0.0021	471	2.1
Community Shopping Centers[c]	0.0023	442	2.3
Neighborhood Retail[c]	0.0026	388	2.6
Banks	0.0028	354	2.8
Business Offices	0.0034	293	3.4
Medical Offices	0.0043	234	4.3

[a]With attendants.
[b]*Source*: Institute of Traffic Engineering (ITE) *Trip Generation* 5th ed.
[c]Regional is greater than about 35,000 sq. ft., community 10,000 to about 35,000 sq. ft., and neighborhood less than 10,000 sq. ft.

Source of other data: SANDAG Traffic Generators report, April 2002 (most recent edition).

For example, suppose an office developer wishes to build a medical office building with an area of 100,000 square feet. To determine the justifiable fee for this category, SANDAG provides a statistic of an average of 0.0043 employees per square foot, or 4.3 employees per 1,000 square feet. With an area of 100,000 square feet, this development would yield approximately 430 employees.

26.9.1.2 Percentage of Employees Residing within the District

FUHSD serves an area that includes C/I as well as residential property. A share of those employed within the District's boundary will also reside in the area. This is more likely to occur in communities where there is a substantial supply of residential properties. The Cupertino and Sunnyvale areas are fairly large, with varying degrees of affordability. However, being located in the Silicon Valley, there are also other nearby residential opportunities outside the FUHSD. Therefore, we estimate that the percentage of employees who work and reside in the District is approximately 35 percent. (This is a conservative approach in that we include no impact from employment outside the District that contributes to enrollment within the District, or from employment in the District that contributes to enrollment in other districts.)

Continuing with our example, the second step in determining the total cost of the medical office building development is to determine the number of new employees likely to also live within the District by using the ratio for current residents. In the previous section, we established that there would be approximately 430 employees for the 100,000–square foot office building. The number of employees living in the District, and therefore likely to have an impact on District facility capacity, would be 35 percent of 430, or 151 employees.

26.9.1.3 Average Number of Homes per Resident Employee

This section addresses how many homes are likely to result from new employees living in the District. A rule of thumb supported by Census data is that there are typically about 1.5 employed persons per home. This can also be stated as 0.67 homes per employee. This ratio reflects the fact that many homes have more than one worker.

In our office building example, the 151 employees living in the District will require 151 * 0.67, or 101 additional homes.

26.9.1.4 Average Number of Students per Home

A total of 3,350 new homes are forecast over the next 10 years. These homes are projected to generate 169 new students. The average SGR is therefore 0.05045 students per home.

Continuing with the medical office building example, we can now determine how many students will impact facility capacity as a result of new employees residing in the District. The approximately 101 homes (occupied by 151 employees) will in turn yield 101 * 0.05045, or about 51 students.

26.9.1.5 Unfunded Cost of School Facilities per Student

The cost of facilities for new students assigned to C/I development must not include the portion funded by residential fee revenue. As calculated in Table 26.8, the unfunded facility

TABLE 26.8 Unfunded Facility Cost per Student

Calculation Step	Figure
Total Residential Square Feet	4,254,000
Fee per Square Foot	$2.76
FUHSD's Total Residential Revenue	$5,913,000
Total Facilities Cost	$11,762,000
Total Unfunded Cost	$5,849,000
Number of Students	169
Unfunded Facility Cost per Student	$34,609

Note: Figures rounded.

Source: Schoolhouse Services.

cost, after revenue from residential fees, is $5,849,000, or $34,609 per student. (The higher residential rate of $1.39 per square foot is conservatively used for this analysis.) It is this unfunded remainder per student that drives the need to levy appropriate fees on the new commercial/industrial development.

We can now finish calculating the large medical office building example. Multiplying the unfunded facility cost for one student of $34,609 times 51 students results in a total impact of $1,765,000. At 100,000 square feet, this commercial development costs the District approximately $1.76 per square foot. This is well beyond the maximum of $0.22 per square foot fee, which is the maximum fee allowable by state law and the agreement with the feeder schools. This example illustrates the significant impact of C/I development, and specifically medical office space, on District capacity and facility costs.

Similar calculations for other categories of commercial/industrial development are shown in Table 26.9.

26.9.1.6 Development Not in Prescribed Categories

Given the District's 60/40 and 62/38 splits with its feeder districts, this analysis demonstrates that the maximum fee amounts of $0.21 and $0.22 are justifiable for all of the categories except Parking Structures and Self-Storage. These low–employment density categories can only be levied fees of $0.01 and $0.02, respectively.

However, if when using this table to determine future fees, no category directly fits the type of development in question, one can use the following analysis to determine the justifiable fee. First, determine the employment density (employees per square foot) for the project. Next, determine if the employment density is high enough to justify levying the maximum fee (the greater the number of square feet per employee, the lower the density, and the lower the impact). In this case, it is helpful to know the minimum number of square feet per worker needed to justify such a fee. A "break-even point" can be calculated

TABLE 26.9 Cost per Square Foot with Residential Offset

Building Type	Employees per sq. ft.	Employees in District	Homes per Employee	Students per Home	Cost per Student	Cost per sq. ft.
Parking Structures[a]	0.00002	35%	0.67	0.0505	$34,609	$0.01
Self-storage	0.00006	35%	0.67	0.0505	$34,609	$0.02
Lodging	0.0011	35%	0.67	0.0505	$34,609	$0.45
Schools	0.0011	35%	0.67	0.0505	$34,609	$0.45
Warehouses[b]	0.0013	35%	0.67	0.0505	$34,609	$0.53
Auto Repair	0.0013	35%	0.67	0.0505	$34,609	$0.53
Movie Theaters	0.0015	35%	0.67	0.0505	$34,609	$0.61
Big Box Retail	0.0017	35%	0.67	0.0505	$34,609	$0.7
Regional Shopping Centers[c]	0.0019	35%	0.67	0.0505	$34,609	$0.78
Hospital	0.0021	35%	0.67	0.0505	$34,609	$0.86
Community Shopping Centers[c]	0.0023	35%	0.67	0.0505	$34,609	$0.94
Neighborhood Retail[c]	0.0026	35%	0.67	0.0505	$34,609	$1.06
Banks	0.0028	35%	0.67	0.0505	$34,609	$1.15
Business Offices	0.0034	35%	0.67	0.0505	$34,609	$1.39
Medical Offices	0.0043	35%	0.67	0.0505	$34,609	$1.76

Notes:
[a]With attendants
[b]Source: Institute of Traffic Engineering (ITE) Trip Generation 5th ed.
[c]Regional is greater than about 35,000 sq. ft., community 10,000 to about 35,000 sq. ft., and neighborhood less than 10,000 sq. ft.
Sources: Table 26.8 and Schoolhouse Services

using the formula for cost per square foot of development, setting the result equal to $0.22 (assumed to apply for this calculation) and solving for A, number of square feet per worker. Again, the factors are:

A. Employees per Square Foot of Development
B. Percentage of Employees Residing within the District (0.35)
C. Number of Homes per Resident Employee (0.67)
D. Number of Students per Home (0.0505)
E. Unfunded cost of School Facilities per Student ($34,609)

Break-Even Point:

Workers/Sq. ft. = 0.22/(B * C * D* E) = 0.22/ (0.35 * 0.67 * 0.05045 * $34,609). Workers/ Sq. ft. = 0.001246
Sq. ft./Worker = 803 square feet per worker

Therefore, any commercial or industrial development that does not fit into one of the SANDAG categories but is projected over its lifetime to have less than 803 square feet per worker should still be levied the maximum $0.22/sq. ft. However, if the type of development in question typically has an employment density of more than 803 square feet per worker, the maximum fee should not be levied. Instead, a justifiable amount can be calculated using the formula outlined earlier, substituting the relevant number of employees per square feet.

For all categories above the break-even point (currently all categories except "parking structures" and "self-storage"), the fee is $0.22 per square foot.

Example:

Suppose a developer wishes to build a 10,000– square foot storage facility that by its nature, is expected typically to have about one employee. The employment density for this development is 1/10,000 or 0.0001 employees per square foot. However, the break-even point for

justifying a maximum fee is a per employee density of 803 square feet. It is therefore necessary to calculate a lower fee for this development. Using the formula for school facility cost per square foot of development, we obtain the following result:

0.0001 * 0.35 * 0.67 * 0.05045 * $34,609 = $0.08 per square foot.

We conclude with emerging school facility financial needs and the role of proportionate share mitigation in addressing them.

26.9.2 The Evolving Role of Renovation and Refurbishment in Meeting Enrollment Capacity Needs

California's original legislation reflected the assumption that the impact of growth was the need for new facilities to increase enrollment capacity. The majority of the state's districts now have decreased enrollments and capacity available to accommodate students from new development. At the same time, they face the need to refurbish facilities constructed long ago, often from the time of the baby boom echo and even the baby boom following the Second World War, if they are to maintain the district's standards as they house students. California recognized this situation and adopted legislation clarifying that such costs were an appropriate demonstration of the nexus needed to justify fees. Reinvestment in existing facilities to maintain their enrollment capacity plays the same role as investment in new facilities; depending on a district's needs, each provides the capacity to house students from both new and existing development, and each can be used to justify impact fees.

NOTES

1 See https://leginfo.legislature.ca.gov/faces/codes_displaySection.xhtml?lawCode=EDC&sectionNum=17620.
2 See www.leginfo.ca.gov/pub/97-98/bill/sen/sb_0001 -0050/sb_50_cfa_19980715_154314_sen_floor.html.
3 101 Cal.App.4th 840 (2002).

27 PARKS AND RECREATION IMPACT FEES FOR RESIDENTIAL AND NONRESIDENTIAL DEVELOPMENT

Case Study of Tucson, Arizona

CARSON BISE

27.1 OVERVIEW

Often, impact fees are assessed on only residential development, assuming that only this impacts on certain facilities, such as parks, libraries, and schools. Although there are examples where parks impact fees are assessed on nonresidential development, they are usually based on local records that enable analysts to apportion park use and therefore, demand to nonresidential land uses. To some extent, this is a double standard, because analysts do not collect and use data to apportion park impact fees to residential land uses or even to particular residential uses.

Chapter 26, relating to assessing school impact fees on nonresidential development, provides insights that are useful here. Communities actively seek economic development in the form of new office, retail, industrial, and institutional land uses. Communities often use their park systems to gain a competitive advantage in attracting economic development. Once successful, these new firms attract new workers, who may wish to live in the community. In effect, the direct source of new park demand is not the new residents themselves but the economic development attracted to the community, which creates the jobs that lure new residents.

In laying the foundation for calculating parks impact fees, our firm, TischlerBise, will start by asking clients "For whom do you build parks?" Based on the answer, we ask a series of follow-up questions. For example, some cities will tell us that both the city and unincorporated county residents are driving their park demand. We then calculate a "park population" that differs from the city's population, which captures the holistic nature of park demand. Moreover, many communities have very active business sports leagues, and there appears to be a growing presence of exercise programs that are aimed explicitly at workers. We also find that even when communities collect data on park use, such as through picnic, court, and field reservations, these data are problematic, and even the best data do not capture the totality of worker and visitor use of local parks.

Moreover, in some areas, such the Phoenix metropolitan area, the local home builders' association is assertive in ensuring that all land uses share in the burden of financing parks, in part through impact fees.

There is a final consideration. Often, parks and recreation impact fees are assessed on a per unit basis regardless of the type or size of the dwelling unit. Census and other data show clearly that there are vast differences in persons per unit by type, and those differences translate into differences in impact. For instance, age-restricted communities use public parks nearly the least of all demographic groups.[1] Even when impact fees are differentiated by type of residential unit, however, there remain important differences in impact based

DOI: 10.4324/9781003336075-32

on unit size. These issues apply to libraries for the same reasons.

We present a case study showing how we assess parks impact fees for all land uses, not just residential ones. We also show how to scale impact fees by the size of the residential unit. Our client was Tucson, Arizona. Given the specificity of Arizona's impact fee legislation, we will show how the Tucson Parks impact fee followed it. Important details on how we apportion impact by size of residential unit are offered in Appendix 25A, while details for apportioning impact to nonresidential development are offered in Appendix 25B.

We start with how the statute defines parks for impact fee purposes. ARS (Arizona Revised Statutes) § 9-463.05 (T)(7)(g) defines the facilities and assets that can be included in the Parks and Recreation Facilities Infrastructure Improvement Plan (IIP):

Neighborhood parks and recreational facilities on real property up to thirty acres in area, or parks and recreational facilities larger than thirty acres if the facilities provide a direct benefit to the development. Park and recreational facilities do not include vehicles, equipment or that portion of any facility that is used for amusement parks, aquariums, aquatic centers, auditoriums, arenas, arts and cultural facilities, bandstand and orchestra facilities, bathhouses, boathouses, clubhouses, community centers greater than three thousand square feet in floor area, environmental education centers, equestrian facilities, golf course facilities, greenhouses, lakes, museums, theme parks, water reclamation or riparian areas, wetlands, zoo facilities or similar recreational facilities, but may include swimming pools.

The Parks and Recreation Facilities IIP includes components for park amenities, recreational facilities, park land, and the cost of professional services for preparing the Parks and Recreation Facilities IIP and related impact fee analysis. An incremental expansion methodology is used for amenities, recreational facilities, and park land, and a plan-based methodology (see Chapter 7) is used for the analysis.

It is noted that the parks and recreation facilities included in this study reflect a subset of the City's parks and recreation facilities due to limitations of the Arizona Enabling Legislation.

27.2 SERVICE AREAS

The City has chosen to provide a uniform level of service and equal access to parks and recreational facilities within its City limits. Therefore, the impact fee is calculated on a citywide basis but will be expended in the three service areas corresponding to where impact fees are collected.

27.3 PROPORTIONATE SHARE

ARS § 9-463.05 (B)(3) states that the development fee shall not exceed a proportionate share of the cost of necessary public services needed to accommodate new development. TischlerBise recommends daytime population as a reasonable indicator of the potential demand for parks and recreational facilities from residential and nonresidential development. According to the US Census Bureau web application OnTheMap,[2] there were 107,223 inflow commuters in 2015, which is the number of persons who work in Tucson but live outside the City. OnTheMap is a web-based mapping and reporting application that shows where workers are employed and where they live. It describes geographic patterns of jobs by their employment locations and residential locations as well as the connections between the two locations. OnTheMap was developed through a unique partnership between the US Census Bureau and its Local Employment Dynamics (LED) partner states. OnTheMap data is used, as shown in Table 27.1, to derive functional population shares for Tucson. The estimated total City population in 2015 is 524,072, based on housing unit estimates and persons per housing unit (PPHU) ratios derived from the US Census Bureau. The study uses 2015 data for

TABLE 27.1 Proportionate Share Impact Allocation for Parks

		Cumulative Impact Hours per Year (000s)			Cost Allocation	
Tucson Residents	Inflow Commuters	Residential Hours	Nonresidential Hours	Total Hours	Residential	Nonresidential
524,072	107,223	4,590,868	171,557	4,762,425	96%	4%

Source: Tucson residents based on TischlerBise housing unit estimates and persons per housing unit (PPHU) ratios derived from the US Census. Inflow Commuters from US Census On the Map web application, 2015.

proportionate share analysis, because this the most recent year available for inflow/outflow data. Therefore, it is compared to the population estimate for the corresponding year.

As shown in Table 27.1, the proportionate share is based on cumulative impact hours per year. Tucson residents were allocated 24 hours per day at 365 days per year, for a total of 8,760 impact hours per resident. Inflow commuters were allocated 8 hours per day, 4 days per week, and 50 weeks per year, for a total of 1,600 impact hours per nonresident. Multiplying the respective impact hours by the number of residents and inflow commuters (shown in Table 27.1 in thousands of hours) yields the total annual impact hours for both residential and nonresidential categories. Residential development's proportionate share of the total impact hours is 96 percent, while the nonresidential share is 4 percent. Lacking data from the City, this was deemed to be a reasonable way in which to apportion park demand to nonresidential land uses.

27.4 RATIO OF SERVICE UNITS TO DEVELOPMENT UNIT

ARS § 9-463.05(E)(4) requires:

A table establishing the specific level or quantity of use, consumption, generation or discharge of a service unit for each category of necessary public services or facility expansions and an equivalency or conversion table establishing the ratio of a service unit to various types of land uses, including residential, commercial and industrial.

Consistently with this requirement, Table 27.2 displays the demand indicators for residential and nonresidential land uses. For residential development, the table displays the PPHU by unit size. For nonresidential development, the table displays the number of employees per thousand square feet for seven different types of nonresidential development. Appendix 25A presents the details for how residents per unit by size of unit is determined while Appendix 25B does the same for nonresidential development.

Notice that "residential" applies to all units, not just type. For the categories, we used the most recent residential population then available from the census and applied it to Pima County Assessor data for the year.[3] For nonresidential, we used data from the Institute of Transportation Engineers' *Trip Generation Manual*.[4]

27.5 ANALYSIS OF CAPACITY, USAGE, AND COSTS OF EXISTING FACILITIES

In this section, we follow Arizona statutes guiding analysis of current capacity and use, and the cost of existing facilities.

ARS § 9-463.05(E)(1) requires:

A description of the existing necessary public services in the service area and the costs to upgrade, update, improve, expand, correct or replace those necessary public services to meet existing needs and usage and stricter safety, efficiency, environmental or regulatory standards, which shall be prepared by qualified professionals licensed in this state, as applicable.

TABLE 27.2 Parks and Recreational Facilities Ratio of Service Unit to Development Unit

Residential Service Unit Ratios

Size of Housing Unit (sq. ft.)	Demand Unit	Persons per Demand Unit
750 or less	Housing Unit	1
751 to 1,250	Housing Unit	1.43
1,251 to 1,750	Housing Unit	2.03
1,751 to 2,250	Housing Unit	2.46
2,251 to 2,750	Housing Unit	2.79
2,751 to 3,250	Housing Unit	3.06
3,251 to 3,750	Housing Unit	3.29
3,751 or More	Housing Unit	3.54

Nonresidential Service Unit Ratios

Type	Demand Unit	Jobs Per Demand Unit
Industrial: Light Industrial	1,000 sq. ft.	1.63
Industrial: Manufacturing	1,000 sq. ft.	1.59
Industrial: Warehousing	1,000 sq. ft.	0.34
Commercial/Retail: General	1,000 sq. ft.	2.34
Commercial/Retail: Free Standing Discount Store	1,000 sq. ft.	2.16
General Office	1,000 sq. ft.	2.97
Institutional: Schools	1,000 sq. ft.	0.93
Institutional: Religious Facilities	1,000 sq. ft.	1.39
Institutional: Medical (Nursing Home/Assisted Living)	1,000 sq. ft.	2.28
Institutional: Medical (Clinical, Hospital)	1,000 sq. ft.	4.13
Hotel	1,000 sq. ft.	0.58

Source: TischlerBise Land Use Assumptions, Impact Fee Report to Tucson, AZ, 2021.

ARS § 9-463.05(E)(2) requires:

An analysis of the total capacity, the level of current usage and commitments for usage of capacity of the existing necessary public services, which shall be prepared by qualified professionals licensed in this state, as applicable.

27.5.1 Park Land—Incremental Expansion

As noted, ARS limits the types of parks and recreation facilities for which development impact fees can be collected. City parks that were included in the inventory include those in the Community Park, Metro Park, Neighborhood Park, and Regional Park classifications, with a limit of up to 30 acres of each park. This is in accordance with ARS § 9-463.05 (T)(7)(g). All other park types were excluded due to the limitations of the State Statute.

Tucson will use development impact fees to expand its inventory of park land. Table 27.3 shows summary of existing park land in Tucson allowable for development impact fees. The new definition of necessary public services for parks and recreational facilities includes parks or facilities on real property up to 30 acres in area. For parks and facilities larger than 30 acres, the allowable acreage per park is adjusted downward to 30 acres.

27.5.2 Existing Park Land Level of Service

To allocate the proportionate share of demand for park land to residential and nonresidential development, our analysis used the population estimate shown in Table 27.1.

TABLE 27.3 Existing Park Land

Park Land	Category	Total Acres[a]	Allowable Acres[a]
Subtotal	Neighborhood	292.2	292
Subtotal	Community	368.1	321.4
Subtotal	Metro	1,154.9	390
Subtotal	Regional	1,317.3	120
Total		3,132.4	1,123.4

[a]Impact fees for parks in Arizona are limited to those parks of 30 acres or less.

TABLE 27.4 Existing Park Land Level of Service

Level of Service (LOS) Standards	
Category	Allocation
Residential Proportionate Share	96%
Nonresidential Proportionate Share	4%
Residents in 2019	530,015
Jobs in 2019	230,007
LOS: Acres per Resident	0.00203
LOS: Acres per Job	0.0002
Cost Analysis	Figure
Land Cost per Acre[a]	$35,000
LOS: Acres per Resident	0.00203
LOS: Acres per Job	0.0002
Cost per Person	$71.05
Cost per Job	$7

[a]City of Tucson Parks and Recreation Department.

Tucson's existing level of service for residential development is approximately 0.00203 acres per person (1,123.4 acres × 96 percent residential share / 530,015 persons). For nonresidential development, the existing level of service is approximately 0.00020 acres per job (1,123.4 acres × 4 percent nonresidential share / 230,007 jobs). The results are shown in Table 27.4.

27.5.3 Recreational Facilities— Incremental Expansion

The inventory of City of Tucson facilities shows that it has eight recreational facilities comprised of community centers and other recreational buildings. The facilities total 529,987 square feet and have an average estimated cost per square foot of $350. However, ARS § 9-463.05 limits the inclusion of community centers to a maximum of 3,000 square feet in floor area. Therefore, the total allowable floor area is capped at 64,800 square feet. This results in a level of service of 0.11737 square feet per person and 0.01127 square feet per job. Multiplying the levels of service by the residential and nonresidential proportionate shares and the cost per square foot ($350) results in recreational facility costs per service unit of:

$41.08 per person
$3.94 per job

27.5.4 Development Impact Fee Report—Plan-Based

The cost to prepare the Parks and Recreational Development Impact Fees and IIP totals $34,615. Tucson plans to update its report every 5 years. Based on this cost, proportionate share, and 5-year projections of new development from the Land Use Assumptions document, the cost is:

$2.46 per person
$0.12 per job

27.5.5 Projected Demand for Services and Costs

The next step in the process is to project the demand for future parks and recreation facilities, and their costs. We are again guided by Arizona's statutes.

ARS § 9-463.05(E)(5) requires:

The total number of projected service units necessitated by and attributable to new development in the service area based on the approved land use assumptions and calculated pursuant to generally accepted engineering and planning criteria.

Land Use Assumptions included in the plan project an additional 27,295 persons and 23,329 jobs over the next 10 years.

ARS § 9-463.05(E)(6) requires:

The projected demand for necessary public services or facility expansions required by new service units for a period not to exceed ten years.

These projected service units are multiplied by the current level of service for the IIP components shown in Figure PR10. New development will demand an additional 1,035 park amenities, 60.1 park land acres, and 3,467 square feet of recreational facilities.

The park improvements, park land, and recreational facility square feet totals demanded by new development multiplied by the respective costs suggest that the City will need to spend a total of $27.2 million on new park amenities, land, and recreation center space to accommodate projected demand, as shown in the bottom of Table 27.5.

Based on levels of service and projected growth by service area, Table 27.6 shows demand for infrastructure citywide. (This demand is then allocated to each of the three service areas.)

27.6 PARKS AND RECREATIONAL FACILITIES IIP

The incremental expansion needs identified in Table 27.6 drive the identification of

TABLE 27.5 Projected Demand for Parks and Recreational Facilities

Category	Park Level of Service Standards				
	Level of Service	Impact Unit	Demand Unit	Unit Cost	
Residential	0.03505	**Amenities**	per Person	$23,100	
Nonresidential	0.00337		per Job		
Residential	0.00203	**Land (acres)**	per Person	$35,000	
Nonresidential	0.0002		per Job		
Residential	0.11737	**Recreation Centers (sq. ft.)**	per Person	$350	
Nonresidential	0.01127		per Job		

Need for Park Amenities and Recreation Facilities

Year		Population	Jobs	Park Amenities	Park Land	Recreation Center sq. ft.a
Base	2019	530,015	230,007	19,352	1,122	64,800
Year 1	2020	532,681	232,238	19,453	1,128	65,138
Year 2	2021	535,360	234,491	19,555	1,134	65,478
Year 3	2022	538,053	236,766	19,657	1,140	65,820
Year 4	2023	540,760	239,063	19,759	1,146	66,163
Year 5	2024	543,484	241,384	19,863	1,152	66,509
Year 6	2025	546,219	243,727	19,966	1,158	66,857
Year 7	2026	548,969	246,094	20,071	1,164	67,206
Year 8	2027	551,736	248,484	20,176	1,170	67,558
Year 9	2028	554,516	250,898	20,281	1,176	67,911
Year 10	2029	557,310	253,336	20,387	1,182	68,267

aArizona's impact fee legislation restricts recreation centers to 3,000 square feet for impact fee financing purposes.

TABLE 27.6 Projected Citywide Demand for Parks and
Recreational Facilities

Need for Amenities and Recreation Facilities		Citywide (Net Increase)		
Year		Amenities	Land	Recreation Center (sq. ft.)
Base	2019			
Year 1	2020	101	5.9	338
Year 2	2021	101	5.9	339.8
Year 3	2022	102	5.9	341.7
Year 4	2023	103	6	343.6
Year 5	2024	103	6	345.8
Year 6	2025	104	6	347.5
Year 7	2026	104	6.1	349.4
Year 8	2027	105	6.1	351.6
Year 9	2028	106	6.1	353.5
Year 10	2029	106	6.2	355.4
10-Year Increase		1,035	60.1	3,467
Growth-Related Expenditures		$23,919,148	$2,103,500	$1,213,450

Note: Citywide demand is allocated to each of the three service areas.

specific projects included in the Parks and Recreational Facilities IIP, as provided by Arizona statutes:

ARS § 9-463.05(E)(3) requires:

A description of all or the parts of the necessary public services or facility expansions and their costs necessitated by and attributable to development in the service area based on the approved land use assumptions, including a forecast of the costs of infrastructure, improvements, real property, financing, engineering and architectural services, which shall be prepared by qualified professionals licensed in this state, as applicable.

Parks and recreational facility improvements (not shown for brevity) include, but are not limited to, the projects listed in the plan as long as the overall allocations are met. Indeed, the City will identify projects that will serve growth as part of its annual budget process and annual capital improvement planning process.

27.7 PARKS AND RECREATIONAL FACILITIES DEVELOPMENT IMPACT FEES

The last step in the process is calculating the impacts for residential and nonresidential development. This has two elements. In the first, credit—called revenue offset in this example—must be given to the new revenues new development may generate for use of the same facilities financed in part by impact fees. The next is the actual impact fee itself.

27.7.1 Revenue Offset

A revenue offset is not necessary for the parks and recreation development impact fees, because 10-year growth costs exceed the amount of revenue that is projected to be generated by development impact fees. The impact fee calculations are thus net of dedicated funding sources.

27.7.2 Parks and Recreational Facilities Development Impact Fees

Infrastructure standards and cost factors for parks and recreational facilities, including park amenities, park land, recreational facilities, and the professional services cost for the IIP and Development Impact Fee Report, are summarized at the top of Table 27.7. Updated development impact fees for Parks and Recreational Facilities are shown in the column with green shading. The result is the "Full Adopted Fee Rates," reflecting the maximum amount allowed by Arizona law.[5]

27.8 SUMMARY AND IMPLICATIONS

This case study has presented a method to reasonably apportion the demand for parks, recreation, and similar facilities to nonresidential development. The method can also be applied to libraries, which our firm has done.

This is not the only technique, and in fact, it may be the most conservative. Where a community has data of reasonably good quality, the share of nonresidential demand may be higher. We know of instances where the share approaches a quarter or sometimes more. In that sense, our method may be considered

TABLE 27.7 Parks and Recreational Facilities Development Impact Fees

Impact Fee Component	Cost per Person	Cost per Job
Park Amenities	$810.02	$77.88
Park Land	$71.05	$7
Recreation Facilities	$41.08	$3.94
Development Fee Report	$2.46	$0.12
Total	$924.61	$88.94

Residential Development Fee (per Housing Unit)

Size of Housing Unit (sq. ft.)	Demand Unit	Persons of Demand Unit	Proposed Impact Fee
750 or less	Housing Unit	1	$925
751 to 1,250	Housing Unit	1.43	$1,322
1,251 to 1,750	Housing Unit	2.03	$1,877
1,751 to 2,250	Housing Unit	2.46	$2,275
2,251 to 2,750	Housing Unit	2.79	$2,580
2,751 to 3,250	Housing Unit	3.06	$2,829
3,251 to 3,750	Housing Unit	3.29	$3,042
3,751 or More	Housing Unit	3.54	$3,273

Nonresidential Service Unit Ratios

Type	Demand Unit	Jobs Per Demand Unit	Proposed Impact Fee
Industrial: Light Industrial	1,000 sq. ft.	1.63	$145
Industrial: Manufacturing	1,000 sq. ft.	1.59	$141
Industrial: Warehousing	1,000 sq. ft.	0.34	$30
Commercial/Retail: General	1,000 sq. ft.	2.34	$208
Commercial/Retail: Free Standing Discount Store	1,000 sq. ft.	2.16	$192
General Office	1,000 sq. ft.	2.97	$264
Institutional: Schools	1,000 sq. ft.	0.93	$83
Institutional: Religious Facilities	1,000 sq. ft.	1.39	$124
Institutional: Medical (Nursing Home/Assisted Living)	1,000 sq. ft.	2.28	$203
Institutional: Medical (Clinical, Hospital)	1,000 sq. ft.	4.13	$367
Hotel	1,000 sq. ft.	0.58	$52

the floor by which communities can allocate a proportionate share of demand for these and related facilities to nonresidential development.

APPENDIX 27A

Calculation of Persons per Residential Unit by Size of Unit

This appendix shows how we apportion parks and recreation facility impact to residential development based on persons per unit by size of unit. We start with current estimates and future projections of residential development, including population and housing units by type (single-family versus multi-family units). Current (2018) estimates of housing units were obtained using annual housing unit permit data provided by the City of Tucson's Planning & Development Services department, the 2013 Pima Association of Governments (PAG) Population Projections, the PAG 2045 Regional Mobility and Accessibility Plan (RMAP), and the PPHU ratio derived from the 2017 US Census Bureau's American Community Survey 1-year estimates.

Persons per Housing Unit

In 2010, the US Census Bureau transitioned from the traditional long-form questionnaire to the American Community Survey, which is less detailed and has smaller sample sizes. As a result, Census data now have more limitations than before. For example, data on detached housing units are now combined with attached single units (commonly known as townhouses). For development impact fees in Tucson, "single-unit" residential includes detached units and townhouses that share a common sidewall but are constructed on an individual parcel of land. The second residential category includes all structures with two or more units on an individual parcel of land.

According to the US Census Bureau, a household is a housing unit that is occupied by year-round residents. Development impact fees often use per capita standards and PPHU, or persons per household, to derive proportionate share fee amounts. When PPHU are used in the fee calculations, infrastructure standards are derived using year-round population. When persons per household are used in the fee calculations, the development impact fee methodology assumes all housing units will be occupied, thus requiring seasonal or peak population to be used when deriving infrastructure standards.

TischlerBise determined that development impact fees for residential development in the City of Tucson should be imposed according to a number of year-round residents per housing unit. For the development fee calculations, TischlerBise used the American Community Survey results shown at the top of Table 27a.1 to determine the relative number of persons per housing unit, by units in a residential structure, and the housing mix in Tucson. The ratio of PPHU across housing types is 2.24. To estimate population for future years, however, the single-family and multi-family PPHU ratios of 2.37 and 1.56, respectively, are used. The share of multi-family housing in Tucson is approximately 30 percent. In 2017, approximately 11.5 percent of the housing stock in Tucson was vacant or used by seasonal residents.

Household Size by Dwelling Unit Size

Custom tabulations of demographic data by bedroom range can be created from individual survey responses provided by the US Census Bureau in files known as Public Use Microdata Samples (PUMS). PUMS files are available for areas of roughly 100,000 persons, and the City of Tucson is covered in Public Use Microdata Areas (PUMA) 202, 205, 206, 207, 208, and 209. Table 27a.2 shows the survey results for the City of Tucson. Unadjusted PPHU, derived

TABLE 27a.1 City of Tucson Year-Round Persons per Unit by Type of Housing

Type	Persons	Housing Units	Housing Mix	Persons per Housing Unit
Single Unit[a]	395,571	166,710	70%	2.37
Two or More Units	113,089	72,289	30%	1.56
Subtotal	508,660	238,999		2.13
Group Quarters	27,016			
Total[b]	535,676	238,999		2.24

Notes:

[a]Includes detached, attached, and mobile homes.

[b] Excludes boat, RV, van, etc.

Source: US Census Bureau's American Community Survey, 2017 1-Year Estimates, Tables B25024, B25032, B25033, and B26001.

TABLE 27a.2 Average Number of Persons by Bedroom Range (All Housing Types)

Bedroom Range	Persons	Units	Unadjusted Persons per Unit	Adjusted Persons per Unit[a]
0–2 bedrooms	9,920	6,343	1.56	1.55
3 bedrooms	12,954	5,400	2.4	2.38
4 bedrooms	6,534	2,164	3.02	2.99
5 or more bedrooms	1,046	277	3.78	3.74
Totals	30,454	14,184	2.15	2.13

[a]Adjusted multipliers are scaled to the average household size from American Community Survey 2017 One-Year data for the City of Tucson.

Source: American Community Survey, Public Use Microdata Sample (2017 One-Year unweighted data).

from PUMS data, were adjusted downward to match the control totals for the City of Tucson, as documented in Table 27a.1

Average Number of Persons by Dwelling Unit Size

Average floor area and number of persons by bedroom range are plotted in Figure 27a.1, with a logarithmic trend line derived from four-unit size averages. Using the trend line formula shown in the chart, TischlerBise derived the estimated average number of

persons, by dwelling size, using four size thresholds. For the purpose of development impact fees, TischlerBise recommends a minimum fee based on a unit size of 750 square feet and a maximum fee for units 3,751 square feet or larger. Average dwelling sizes by bedroom range in the City were derived from US Census Bureau regional data.

Current Residential Estimates

To estimate the current number of housing units and residents, TischlerBise used

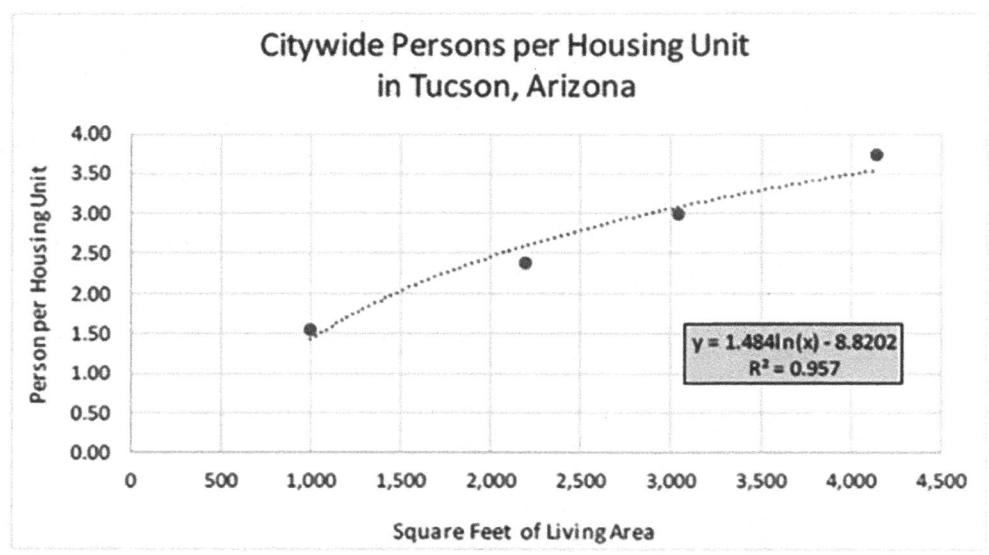

Actual Averages per Housing Unit			Persons per Housing Unit by Size	
Bedrooms	Square Feet	Persons	Sq Ft Range	Persons
0-2	1,000	1.55	750 or Less	1.00
3	2,200	2.38	751 to 1,250	1.61
4	3,050	2.99	1,251 to 1,750	2.15
5+	4,150	3.74	1,751 to 2,250	2.55
			2,251 to 2,750	2.86
			2,751 to 3,250	3.12
			3,251 to 3,750	3.34
			3,751 or More	3.53

Average persons per housing unit derived from 2017 ACS PUMS data for the area that includes Tucson. Unit size for 0-2 bedroom is from the 2017 U.S. Census Bureau average for all multi-family units constructed in the Census West region. Unit size for all other bedrooms is from the 2017 U.S. Census Bureau average for single-family units constructed in the Census Mountain division.

Citywide Persons per Housing Unit in Tucson, Arizona

$y = 1.484\ln(x) - 8.8202$
$R^2 = 0.957$

FIGURE 27a.1 Persons by square feet of living space (all housing types). (From TischlerBise, 2020.)

building permit data from 2010 through 2018 provided by the City of Tucson's Planning & Development Services department, which were added to the total housing unit count from the 100 percent 2010 Decennial Census.

Table 27a.3 shows Tucson's recent housing unit permit totals by calendar year, provided by the City of Tucson's Planning & Development Services. Single-family permits have been steadily increasing from a low of 269 at the tail end of the Great Recession to a high of 729 in 2016. Multi-family unit permits have fluctuated from year to year as buildings come online. The general trend in housing unit permits is increasing. Adding residential building permits to the 100 percent estimate from the 2010 US Census Bureau provides a current housing estimate of 238,461.

Population estimates are derived by multiplying PPHU by type of unit from information provided in Figure 27a.1 by the estimated number of housing units in 2019. These estimates are shown in Table 27a.4. Added to this is population in group quarters, estimated at 4.5 percent of total population in the City of Tucson based on trends from the last 8 years.

TABLE 27a.3 City of Tucson Residential Permits by Year and Current Housing Unit Estimate (2019)

Year	Housing Units Permitted		
	Single-Family	Multi-Family	Total
2010	344	38	382
2011	300	551	851
2012	484	487	971
2013	269	610	879
2014	546	247	793
2015	338	220	558
2016	729	60	789
2017	707	462	1,169
2018	680	176	856
Total	4,397	2,851	7,248

Year	Total Housing Units		
	Single-Family	Multi-Family	Total
2010 (April 1)	160,267	69,495	229,762
2010 (July 1)	161,412	69,992	231,404
2011	161,584	70,011	231,595
2012	161,884	70,562	232,446
2013	162,368	71,049	233,417
2014	162,637	71,659	234,296
2015	163,183	71,906	235,089
2016	163,521	72,126	235,647
2017	164,250	72,186	236,436
2018	164,957	72,648	237,605
2019	165,637	72,824	238,461

Source: City of Tucson.

TABLE 27a.4 City of Tucson Current Population Estimate (2019)

Housing Type	2019 Estimated Units[a]	Persons per Housing Units[b]	2019 Estimated Population
Single-Family	165,637	2.37	392,559
Multi-Family	72,824	1.56	113,605
Subtotal in Units	506,164		
plus Group Quarters[c]	23,851		
Grand Total	530,015		

Notes:
[a]City of Tucson.
[b]US Census Bureau's American Community Survey, 2017 1-Year Estimates.
[c]Estimated based on 3-year average of 4.5 percent total population in group quarters.

Appendix 27B shows how we apportion parks and recreation facility impact to non-residential development.

APPENDIX 27B

Calculation of Persons per Residential Unit by Size of Unit

In addition to data on residential development, the infrastructure improvements plan and development impact fees require data on nonresidential development in Tucson. Current estimates and future projections of nonresidential development are detailed in this section, including jobs and floor area by type. TischlerBise uses the terms "jobs" to refer to employment by place of work.

Jobs by Type of Nonresidential Development

To estimate the current (2018) number of jobs, TischlerBise applied most recent (2015) US Census OnTheMap Longitudinal-Employer Household statistics for the City of Tucson to industry sector growth projections from the PAG for 2045. Jobs were aggregated into one of four categories: industrial, commercial, institutional, and office & other. These estimates are shown in Table 27b.1. Analysis estimates there were 228,635 jobs in Tucson in 2018.

TABLE 27b.1 City of Tucson Job Estimates for 2018

Employment Category	2015*	Annual Growth Rate**	2018 Estimate
Industrial	28,336	6%	28,849
Commercial	52,258	100%	53,841
Institutional	84,420	106%	87,133
Office & Other	57,099	99%	58,812
Total	222,113		228,635

Notes:
[a]US Census On the Map, 2015.
[b]Pima Association of Governments, Annual Growth Rates.

TABLE 27b.2 City of Tucson Employment Projections

Employment Category	2018	2028	10-Year Change
Industrial	28,849	30,628	1,779
Commercial	53,841	59,474	5,633
Institutional	87,133	96,822	9,689
Office & Other	58,812	64,900	6,088
Total	228,635	251,825	23,190

Note: Figures may not sum due to rounding.

These industry sector growth rates are used to project employment growth to 2028. Tucson's 10-year job projections through 2028 are shown in Table 27b.2. The City is expected to add a total of 23,190 jobs by 2028.

Nonresidential Floor Area by Type of Development

Table 27b.3 provides January 1, 2019, floor area estimates for the City of Tucson, subdivided into the four aforementioned categories. Total nonresidential floor area in the aggregate was obtained through CoStar and provided to TischlerBise by the City. This estimate was further allocated by industry sector from employment data and square footage analysis (US Census, OnTheMap).

Table 27b.4 shows jobs per 1,000 square feet and average weekday vehicle trip ends per 1,000 square feet, broken down by non-residential land use category. Gray shading indicates the four nonresidential development prototypes used by TischlerBise to correlate Tucson's projected job growth with nonresidential floor area growth and vehicle trips generated by development. The last column in Table 27b.4 shows the ratio of jobs per 1,000 square feet from the Institute of Transportation Engineers (ITE) *Trip Generation Manual* (2017).

TABLE 27b.3 City of Tucson 2019 Jobs and Floor Area Estimates

2015 Jobs (on the Map)

Category	Jobs	Share
Industrial	28,336	12.8%
Commercial	52,258	23.5%
Institutional	84,420	38%
Office & Other	57,099	25.7%
Total	222,113	100%

Square Foot per Job (from ITE)

Category	Square Feet
Industrial	613
Commercial	427
Institutional	1,075
Office & Other	337

2015 Nonresidential Floor Area Breakdown

Category	Square Feet	Share
Industrial	17,370	11.6%
Commercial	22,314	14.9%
Institutional	90,752	60.6%
Office & Other	19,242	12.9%
Total	149,678	100.0%

2019 (1 J) Total Nonresidential Floor Area (CoStar)

151,268,525 Square Feet
Adjustment of 2019 CoStar to 2015 ITE-Based Estimate

Sector	2015% Allocation	2019 Square Feet (in 000s)
Industrial	11.6%	17,547
Commercial	14.9%	22,539
Institutional	60.6%	91,669
Office & Other	12.9%	19,514
Total		151,269

Notes:
Figures may not sum due to rounding.
ITE = Institute of Transportation Engineers.

TABLE 27b.4 ITE Employee and Trip Generation Ratios

ITE Code	Land Use	Demand Unit	Weekday Trip Ends per 1,000 sq. ft.	Weekday Trip Ends per Employee	Employees per 1,000 sq. ft.	Square Feet per Employee
110	Light Industrial	1,000 sq. ft.	4.96	3.05	1.63	613
130	Industrial Park	1,000 sq. ft.	3.37	2.91	1.16	8,620
140	Manufacturing	1,000 sq. ft.	3.93	2.47	1.59	629
150	Warehouse	1,000 sq. ft.	1.74	5.05	0.34	2,941
254	Assisted Living	Bed	2.6	4.24	0.61	na
320	Motel	Room	3.35	25.17	0.13	na
520	Elementary School	1,000 sq. ft.	19.52	21	0.93	1,075
530	High School	1,000 sq. ft.	14.07	22.25	0.63	1,587
540	Public/Institutional[a]	1,000 sq. ft.	20.25	14.61	1.39	721
565	Day Care	1,000 sq. ft.	47.62	21.38	2.23	448
610	Hospital	1,000 sq. ft.	10.72	3.79	2.83	353
710	General Office (average size)	1,000 sq. ft.	9.74	3.28	2.97	337
720	Medical-Dental Office	1,000 sq. ft.	34.8	8.7	4	250
730	Government Office	1,000 sq. ft.	22.59	7.45	3.03	330
750	Office Park	1,000 sq. ft.	11.07	3.54	3.13	3,190
760	Research & Development Center	1,000 sq. ft.	11.26	3.29	3.42	292
770	Business Park	1,000 sq. ft.	12.44	4.04	3.08	325
820	Shopping Center (average size)	1,000 sq. ft.	37.75	16.11	2.34	427
815	Discount Store (free-standing)	1,000 sq. ft.	53.12	24.63	2.16	464
520	Institutional—Schools	1,000 sq. ft.	19.52	21	0.93	1,075
560	Institutional—Religious	1,000 sq. ft.	6.95	n/a	1.39	721
620	Institutional—Nursing Home	1,000 sq. ft.	6.64	2.91	2.28	438
630	Institutional—Medical Clinic	1,000 sq. ft.	38.16	9.25	4.13	242
310	Hotel	Room	8.36	14.34	0.58	1,715

Note: [a]Employees per demand unit reflect proxy 540 ITE Code.

Source: *Trip Generation*, Institute of Transportation Engineers, 10th Edition (2017).

NOTES

1 This is inferred from *The First National Study of Neighborhood Parks: Implications for Physical Activity* (Cohen et al. 2016), which shows that seniors represented 4 percent of park users, but were 20 percent of the general population implying that they impact parks a fifth less than the population as a whole.

2 See https://onthemap.ces.census.gov/.

3 For details on the data and calculation methods, see Appendix A of www.tucsonaz.gov/files/pdsd/EXHIBIT_1_TO_ORDINANCE_11759.pdf.

4 See www.ite.org/technical-resources/topics/trip-and-parking-generation/.

5 Tucson, Arizona, Code of Ordinances Article III, Sec. 23A-91 ("Fee Schedule Tables").

REFERENCE

Cohen, D. A., Han, B., Nagel, C. J., Harnik, P., McKenzie, T. L., Evenson, K. R., Marsh, T., Williamson, S., Vaughan, C. A., & Katta, S. (2016). The first national study of neighborhood parks: Implications for physical activity. *American Journal of Preventive Medicine*, *51*(4), P419–426. https://doi.org/10.1016/j.amepre.2016.03.021.

28 WATER IMPACT FEES FOR RESIDENTIAL DEVELOPMENT BASED ON HOUSE SIZE

Case Study of Bozeman, Montana

CARSON BISE

Water (and sewer) impact fees are based typically on the size of the meter connection homes to those systems (see Chapter 7). This can have equity implications, as two very different homes with very different demands on water and sewer pay the same impact fee. The worry expressed in Chapter 15 is that smaller homes averaging fewer occupants (not to mention being more affordable) are charged disproportionately more than their impact on infrastructure, while larger homes averaging more occupants (not to mention being more expensive) are charged less than their proportionate share impact on infrastructure. This chapter presents a case study where a particular community, Bozeman, Montana, retained TischlerBise to craft water and sewer impact fees to address these equity and efficiency concerns. Our case study focuses on the water impact fee, though the calculation of sewer impacts followed the same conceptual steps. Moreover, although we calculated impact fees for nonresidential using the standard meter-size approach (see Chapter 7 for a review), we focus our case study on residential impact fees. As our study needs to comply with Montana Code Title 7, Chapter 6, Sections 1601–1604, addressing impacts, the case study will be framed and referenced accordingly. Our case study presents the analytic steps leading to water impact fees scaled by the size of the residential unit. We include a technical appendix showing how we estimated persons per residential unit by the size of the unit.

28.1 CONCEPTUAL IMPACT FEE CALCULATION

In contrast to project-specific improvements, impact fees fund growth-related infrastructure that will benefit multiple development projects or the entire jurisdiction (usually referred to as system improvements). The basic steps in a conceptual impact fee formula are illustrated in Figure 28.1. The first step (see the left box) is to determine an appropriate demand indicator, or service unit, for the particular type of infrastructure. The demand/service indicator measures the number of demand or service units for each unit of development. For example, an appropriate indicator of the demand for parks is population growth, and the increase in population can be estimated from the average number of persons per housing unit. The second step in the impact fee formula is shown in the middle box. Infrastructure units per demand unit are typically called Level-of-Service (LOS) standards. In keeping with the park example, a common LOS standard is park acreage per thousand people. The third step in the impact fee formula, as illustrated in the right box, is the cost of various infrastructure units. To complete the park example, this part of the formula would

DOI: 10.4324/9781003336075-33

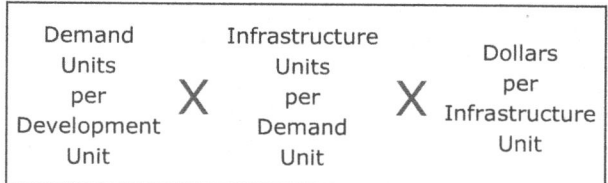

FIGURE 28.1 Typical impact fee formula.

establish the cost per acre for land acquisition and/or park improvements.

28.2 GENERAL METHODOLOGIES

Although they were reviewed in Chapter 7, we will summarize the general methods for calculating development impact fees, because they help frame our work for Bozeman. The choice of a particular method depends primarily on the timing of infrastructure construction (past, concurrent, or future) and service characteristics of the facility type being addressed. Each method has advantages and disadvantages in a particular situation and can be used simultaneously for different cost components. For example, a jurisdiction might use bond financing to oversize a water treatment plant (recoup method) and identify future water mains needed to geographically expand the service area (plan-based method).

Reduced to its simplest terms, the process of calculating development impact fees involves two main steps: (1) determining the cost of development-related capital improvements and (2) allocating those costs equitably to various types of development. In practice, though, the calculation of impact fees can become quite complicated because of the many variables involved in defining the relationship between development and the need for facilities. The following paragraphs discuss three basic methods for calculating development impact fees and how those methods can be applied.

28.2.1 Recoupment (Past Improvements)

The rationale for recoupment, often called cost recovery, is that new development is paying for its share of the useful life and remaining capacity of facilities already built, or land already purchased, from which new growth will benefit. This methodology is often used for utility systems that must provide adequate capacity before new development can take place. Montana enabling legislation specifically authorizes recoupment in 7-6-1603 (3).

28.2.2 Incremental Expansion (Concurrent Improvements)

The incremental expansion method documents current LOS standards for each type of public facility using both quantitative and qualitative measures. This approach ensures that there are no existing infrastructure deficiencies or surplus capacity in infrastructure. New development is only paying its proportionate share for growth-related infrastructure. LOS standards are determined in a manner similar to the current replacement cost approach used by property insurance companies. However, in contrast to insurance practices, the fee revenues would not be for renewal and/or replacement of existing facilities. Rather, revenue will be used to expand or provide additional facilities, as needed, to accommodate new development. An incremental expansion cost method is best suited for public facilities that will be expanded in regular increments concurrently with new development.

28.2.3 Plan-Based Fee (Future Improvements)

The plan-based method allocates costs for a specified set of improvements to a specified amount of development. Improvements are typically identified in a long-range facility plan, and development potential is identified by a land use plan. There are two options for determining the cost per demand unit: 1) Total cost of a public facility can be divided by total demand units, or 2) the growth share of the public facility cost can be divided by the net increase in demand units over the planning timeframe.

28.2.4 Credits

Regardless of the methodology, a consideration of "credits" is integral to the development of a legally defensible impact fee methodology. There are two types of "credits" with specific characteristics, both of which should be addressed in development impact fee studies. The first is a revenue credit due to possible double payment situations, which could occur when other revenues may contribute to the capital costs of infrastructure covered by the impact fee. Montana's enabling legislation requires "consideration of payments for system improvements reasonably anticipated to be made by or as a result of the development in the form of user fees, debt service payments, taxes, and other available sources of funding the system improvements" (7-6-1602 (7) (b) (ii)). This type of credit is integrated into the impact fee calculation, thus reducing the fee amount. The second is a site-specific credit or developer reimbursement for dedication of land or construction of system improvements. This type of credit is addressed in the administration and implementation of the impact fee program.

The following ten sections address all requirements of Montana's impact fee enabling legislation (see 7-6-1602) regarding the calculation of impact fees. We will use the example of water impact fees first and then summarize the extension to sewer impact fees, both of which are based on categories of residential dwelling sizes.

28.2.4.1 Service Area

Bozeman's water system is a single integrated utility that serves all customers. For the purpose of calculating and imposing water impact fees, the entire City will be treated as a single service area pursuant to MCA 7-6-1602 (1) (f).

28.2.4.2 Existing Conditions and Deficiencies

Complete documentation of existing conditions and deficiencies is contained in Bozeman's Water Facility Plan, as amended.

Impact fees will not be used to correct existing deficiencies. At the time of our analysis, the City obtained water from the Hyalite/Sourdough water treatment facility and the Lyman Creek system. The City also had three distribution storage reservoirs for a total capacity of 11.3 million gallons. Capital improvements identified in the long-range facility plan include expansion of the Hyalite/Sourdough water treatment plant to 22 million gallons per day (MGD); construction of a new 5.3 million gallon storage reservoir; identification, permitting, and design of adequate water sources, including water rights; and improvements to the transmission and distribution system to serve growth. The Water Facility Plan includes an analysis of additional water rights needed for future growth. However, water rights are not included in the impact fee program.

28.2.4.3 Operation and Maintenance

The City of Bozeman funds all operation and maintenance costs from utility user charges. Impact fee revenue will not be used for operating and maintenance expenses. Capital items are segregated operationally and for accounting purposes.

28.2.4.4 Level-of-Service Standards

To update water demand indicators in the City of Bozeman, staff provided 3 years of water billing records by customer classification and water meter size. As shown in Table 28.1, TischlerBise summarized the data into three development categories and by meter size. For nonresidential customers, the updated weighting factors are slightly different from the American Water Works Association weighting factors used by prior consultants. The weighting factors are simply multipliers derived from the average day gallons per larger meter compared with the average day gallons for the smallest size of meter. The analysis accounted for annual fluctuations in

TABLE 28.1 Average Daily Water Demand Indicators in 2012

Land Use Category	Average Gallons per Day[a]	Share	2012 Connections	Gallons per Day per Connection	Gallons per Person per Average Day[b]
Single-Unit Residential	1,774,518	35%	7,344	242	109
2+ Units Residential	1,213,029	24%	2,080	583	
Nonresidential	2,038,867	41%	1,121	1,819	
Total	5,026,413		10,545		
Average Day Water Demand from Housing Built 1990–2010				255	114

Notes:

[a]2012 linear trend projection of average day gallons based on water billing records from 2009 to 2011, increased by 11.5% for unaccounted water. Historical water billing data provided by the City of Bozeman.

[b]Single unit gallons per person per day based on an average of 2.23 persons per housing unit (Census 2010).

water billings, which are influenced by such factors as weather and irrigation demand, increased utilization of irrigation water from individual wells, and conservation.

As shown in Figure 28.2, average daily water demand indicators for residential and nonresidential customers are derived from cumulative average day gallons divided by water meter counts in January 2012. When all units (regardless of year built) are included in the analysis, single-unit residential demand averages 242 gallons per connection, or 109 gallons per person on an average day (interior and exterior demand). Using year-built data from the Montana Department of Revenue, TischlerBise was able to reanalyze billing records for housing units constructed from 1990 through 2010. Average day water demand from new housing is slightly higher at 255 gallons per unit, or 114 gallons per person on an average day. Greater water use from new units is probably due to outdoor irrigation.

Residential structures with two or more units often have more than one housing unit served by a single water meter, which explains the increased demand of 583 gallons per connection. In Bozeman, at the time of the study, 41% of the demand for potable water is for nonresidential development.

28.2.4.5 Future Additional Needs

Projected water system demand, shown in Table 28.2, is a function of the development projections (not reported here for brevity) and the water demand factors discussed earlier. This analysis assumes that all future residential units become water customers. To project future water demand from nonresidential development, the impact fee analysis assumed that the then current average of 22.59 jobs for each nonresidential water connection would remain constant over time. The water demand projection assumed that new single-unit housing requires 255 gallons per day, which is the demand factor for housing constructed in the last two decades. Based on work by prior consultants, we determined that peak day demand is 2.3 times the average day demand.

We next calculated the current replacement value of the City's water system, which was $65.65 million.

As required by Montana's impact fee enabling legislation, Table 28.3 documents the distribution system LOS standard for existing and new development. In 2010, Bozeman had 12,478 acres within the City limits, but 3,409 acres were vacant, leaving 9,069 developed acres. The impact fee analysis assumed that 10% of the future service area (3,801 acres)

TABLE 28.2 Projected Water System Demand

Year		MGD Average	Connections	Annual Increase		Cumulative Increase	
				Connections	MGD	Connections	MGD
Current	2012	5.03	10,545				
future 1	2013	5.13	10,748	203	0.1	203	0.1
future 2	2014	5.23	10,953	205	0.1	408	0.2
future 3	2015	5.33	11,164	211	0.1	619	0.3
future 4	2016	5.43	11,377	213	0.1	832	0.4
future 5	2017	5.54	11,595	218	0.11	1,050	0.51
future 6	2018	5.65	11,818	223	0.11	1,273	0.62
future 7	2019	5.76	12,043	225	0.11	1,498	0.73
future 8	2020	5.87	12,275	232	0.11	1,730	0.84
future 9	2021	5.98	12,510	235	0.11	1,965	0.95
future 10	2022	6.1	12,750	240	0.12	2,205	1.07
future 11	2023	6.22	12,994	244	0.12	2,449	1.19
future 12	2024	6.34	13,244	250	0.12	2,699	1.31
future 13	2025	6.46	13,498	254	0.12	2,953	1.44
future 14	2026	6.59	13,756	258	0.12	3,211	1.56
future 15	2027	6.72	14,019	263	0.13	3,474	1.69
future 16	2028	6.85	14,288	269	0.13	3,743	1.82
future 17	2029	6.98	14,562	274	0.13	4,017	1.95
future 18	2030	7.12	14,842	280	0.14	4,297	2.09

Note: MGD means millions of gallons per day.

TABLE 28.3 Water Distribution Cost per Acre

Calculation Step	Service Area in 2010	Future Service Area	Increase
Total Acres	12,478	38,007	25,529
	less vacant acres	less 10% POS acres	
	3,409	3,801	
Developed Acres[a]	9,069	34,206	25,137
Linear Feet of 10+-Inch Pipe	393,526	594,996	201,470
Linear Feet per Developed Acre	43.4	17.4	26.0
Current Cost Estimate for Piping			$65,651,000
5.3 MG Water Storage Reservoir[b]			$5,300,000
$ per Acre for Pipes			$2,612
$ per Acre for Storage Reservoir			$211
Total Cost per Gross Acre			$2,823
Total Cost per Net Acre (18.6% for ROW[a])			$3,468
2010 Average Dwelling Units per Net Acre[c]			7.1
Cost per DU @ Average Density w 5% Administration			$512

Notes:

[a]Bozeman 2010 Land Use Inventory, with same percentage applied to future service area.

[b]WIF03 Bozeman Approved CIP FY13-17.

[c]Census 2010 housing units divided by 2010 land use acreage for each residential category.

would be used for Parks/Open Space (POS), thus reducing the future developed area to 34,206 acres. The increase between the existing and future developed areas is 25,137 acres.

The fifth row in Table 28.3 indicates that existing water customers are being served by 43.4 linear feet of distribution system piping per developed acre. Based on improvements identified in the Water Facilities Plan, the future service area will have 17.4 linear feet of distribution system piping per developed acre. Expansion of the service area requires 26.0 linear feet of piping per developed acre.

In addition to the cost of future piping, the then Water Facilities Plan calls for a water storage tank with a capacity of 5.3 million gallons. The total estimated cost for the water distribution system (piping plus reservoir) is $2,823 per gross acre. However, building permits and site plans are based on net developable land area, excluding right-of-way (ROW) for streets. To make the impact fees easier to administer, distribution system costs are converted to $3,468 per net acre, based on the 2010 citywide average of 18.6% of land area being used for ROW.

According to 2010 data on housing units from the US Census Bureau (see Appendix) and Bozeman's land use inventory, the City averages 7.1 dwelling units per residential acre. At the average density, the future water distribution system needed to accommodate new development includes a 5% component for impact fee administration, as allowed by Montana's impact fee legislation. The result is an average cost of $512 per dwelling unit. (We note that states vary, with many being silent. Chapter 3 notes that Georgia limits these costs to 3%, for example.)

Bozeman had a water treatment plant (WTP) with a peak capacity at the time of 15 million gallons per day (MGD). The new WTP can produce 22 MGD, providing a peak day increase of 7 MGD. According to the Water Facilities Plan, peak water demand is typically 2.3 times average day demand. Applying this conversion factor yields an average day capacity increase of 3.05 MGD. As shown in

Table 28.4, the growth share of the WTP is $13.4 million, or $4.39 per gallon of capacity (average day increase).

The Water Facilities Plan also identified three future water mains that provide redundancy in service in addition to increased capacity to serve growth. As reported in the Water Facilities Plan, redundancy mains have a total cost of $28.05 million. Because redundancy increases system reliability and pressure for existing customers, previous work allocated only $10.93 million as the growth share of redundancy that is eligible for impact fee funding. The purpose of redundancy mains is primarily to improve capacity, not geographically expand the service area. Therefore, redundancy is included in the cost per gallon of capacity (average day increase), not in the water distribution cost per acre (shown in Table 28.3).

28.2.4.6 Growth Share Determination
Where specific improvements benefit existing customers and expand capacity for new development, the growth share of the capital cost is determined by an engineering analysis of the specific improvement. Individual project worksheets in the approved FY13-17 Capital Improvement Plan (CIP) contain details on the growth share determination for each line item. For example, approximately one-third of the WTP cost is growth related, with two-thirds to be funded by sources other than impact fees. The WTP growth share of $13.4 million is coming from the water impact fee (WIF) fund balance, of approximately $8.5 million at the end of FY2011, leaving a balance of $4.9 million to be paid from future WIF revenue. To avoid potential double payment for anticipated debt service on the WTP, the updated fee calculations include a credit for future principal payments, as explained further in the next section.

28.2.4.7 Proportionate Share Considerations
Not reported for brevity is the schedule of future loan payments to address the

TABLE 28.4 WTP and Redundancy Cost per Gallon of Capacity Increase

Water Treatment Plant	Cost (in Millions)		Cost Calculation
Total Cost	$40.70		
Non-Growth Share from User Charges	$27.30		
Growth Share from Impact Fees	$13.40		
	Million Gallons per Day (MGD)		
	Peak Day		**Average Day**
New WTP Capacity (MGD)	22		9.57
Existing Water Treatment Capacity (MGD)	15		6.52
Water Capacity Increase (MGD)	7		3.05
WTP Cost per Gallon of Capacity Increase			**$4.39**
Redundancy Mains	Cost (in Millions)		
Water Treatment Plant Area[a]	$21.68		
Laurel Glenn Area[a]	$2.77		
Frontage Road Area[a]	$3.60		
Total Cost	$28.05		
Non-Growth Share from User Charges	$17.12		
Growth Share from Impact Fees[b]	$10.93		
Water Capacity Increase (Average Day MGD)			3.05
Redundancy Cost per Gallon of Capacity Increase			**$3.58**

Notes:

[a]Table 5.B.3, Water Facilities Plan 2006.

[b]Exhibit 4, Water Impact Fees, HDR 2007.

Source: Bozeman approved FY13-17 CIP.

unfunded balance of the growth share of the WTP. The amortization schedule calculates principal payments on $4.9 million, with a 20-year payback, at 3.75% annual interest. The WIF update includes a revenue credit for future utility user charges that will make principal payments on the unfunded balance of the WTP growth share. Credit is not given for future interest payments, however, which were conservatively excluded from the WIF update. This approach gives the City greater flexibility to accelerate debt service payments without making adjustments to the impact fee calculations.

Principal payments over the next 5 years were divided by average day water demand to yield annual payments per gallon of capacity. To account for the time value of money, the annual revenue stream was discounted by 3.75% (see earlier) to yield a present value of $0.15 per gallon. The credit calculations do not extend beyond 5 years because the City intends to accelerate debt repayment using

impact fee revenue to minimize the financial obligation of existing utility customers, and Bozeman intends to update impact fees every 3–5 years.

28.2.4.8 Fee Calculation Methodology

WIFs included the cost of water capacity and distribution system improvements, less a credit for future principal payments, but also adding the 5% administration cost. Net capital cost per gallon of water capacity is multiplied by average daily gallons of demand to yield the impact fee for water treatment and redundancy mains. In addition, the cost of distribution system expansion will be applied to the land area of a parcel seeking a building permit. As shown in Table 28.5, all types of development will pay the water distribution system cost of $3,641 per net acre (defined as the gross land area less street ROW), though this figure is scaled to the lot size of the individual development.

TABLE 28.5 Water System Impact Fee Schedule

Input Variables	All Types	Residential	Nonresidential
Water Treatment Plant Cost per Gallon of Capacity	$4.39		
Redundancy Water Mains Cost per Gallon of Capacity	$3.58		
Principal Payment Credit per Gallon of Capacity	($0.15)		
Net Capital Cost per Gallon of Capacity	$7.82		
Gallons per Average Day per Person in new Housing Units		114	
Gallons per Average Day for Single-Unit Residential			242

Residential Impact Fee by Living Area

Square Feet	Persons per Housing Unit	Water Capacity Cost with 5% Administration	Distribution System Cost per Net Acre[a]	Current Fee
A 1,400 or less	1.03	$964	$3,641	$3,850
B 1,401–1,600	1.32	$1,235	$3,641	$3,850
C 1,601–1,800	1.58	$1,478	$3,641	$3,850
D 1,801–2,000	1.81	$1,694	$3,641	$3,850
E 2,001–2,200	2.02	$1,890	$3,641	$3,850
F 2,201–2,400	2.21	$2,068	$3,641	$3,850
G 2,401–2,600	2.38	$2,227	$3,641	$3,850
H 2,601–2,800	2.54	$2,377	$3,641	$3,850
I 2,801–3,000	2.69	$2,517	$3,641	$3,850
J 3,001 or more	2.78	$2,602	$3,641	$3,850
Group Quarters (per person)		$936	$3,641	

Nonresidential (per meter)

Meter Size (inches)[b]	Weighting Factor	Water Capacity Cost with 5% Adm	Distribution System Cost per Net Acre[a]	Current Fee
0.75	1	$1,987	$3,641	$3,850
1	2.3	$4,570	$3,641	$9,624
1.5	5	$9,935	$3,641	$19,249
2	9.3	$18,479	$3,641	$30,798
3	19.9	$39,542	$3,641	$61,597

Notes:

[a]Includes 5% for Administration. Distribution system cost component will be applied to the parcel size.

[b]Fees for meters larger than 3 inches will be based on annualized average day demand and the net capital cost per gallon of capacity for WTP (water treatment plant) and Redundancy Water Mains. Also, the water impact fee includes the distribution system cost per net acre of development.

The approach of imposing water distribution system cost per acre provides an economic incentive for the efficient use of land within Bozeman. For example, two houses with identical living space would pay the same amount for water capacity but could pay different amounts for the water distribution system if the lot size varies. An infill lot in central Bozeman with 9,800 square feet of lot area would pay $819 for the water distribution system (9,800/43,560 × $3,641 per acre). A large 1-acre lot would pay $3,641 for the water distribution system, in addition to the water capacity cost, which is based on square feet of living space.

WIFs for nonresidential development vary by meter size using weighting factors to account for the increased demand associated with larger water meters. The equivalent dwelling unit (EDU) demand factor for nonresidential development is based on average day water demand from all single-unit customers.

28.2.4.9 Impact Fee Schedule

Following Montana's ten-step mandatory impact analysis protocol, the next step applies LOS standards to derive the WIF, as shown at the top of Table 28.5. For instance, for a small housing unit (1,400 square feet or less of living space) constructed at a density of 12 units per net acre, the WIF would be equal to 1.03 persons per housing unit, multiplied by 114 gallons per person, multiplied by $7.82 per gallon of water capacity, multiplied by 1.05 for administration, or $964 per housing unit for the water capacity cost component. At a density of 12 dwelling units per acre, the cost of the water distribution system is $303 per housing unit ($3641/12 truncated). For both water capacity and distribution, the total WIF would be $1,267 per unit. To compare this amount with the current fee schedule by meter size, it is necessary to make some assumptions regarding number of units per structure and the meter size serving the structure. For a three-story apartment building with 12 units served by a 2-inch water meter, the current WIF would be $30,798 for the entire building, or approximately $2,566 per unit. In comparison, the proposed fee of $1,267 per unit would be $1,299 less than the current fee amount.

The fee for an average single-unit residence, with 2,201–2,400 square feet of living space, is equal to 2.21 persons per housing unit, multiplied by 114 gallons per person, multiplied by $7.82 per gallon of water capacity, multiplied by 1.05 for administration, or $2,068 per housing unit for the water capacity cost component. At the average citywide density of 7.1 dwelling units per acre, the cost of the water distribution system is $512 per housing unit. For both water capacity and distribution, the total WIF for the "average" housing unit in Bozeman would be $2,580, which is $1,270 less than the current fee amount of $3,850 for the smallest-size water meter.

For the largest housing unit category (3,001 square feet or more of living space) constructed at a density of two units per net acre, the WIF would be equal to 2.78 persons per housing unit, multiplied by 114 gallons per person, multiplied by $7.82 per gallon of water capacity, multiplied by 1.05 for administration, or $2,602 per housing unit for the water capacity cost component. At a density of two dwelling units per acre, the cost of the water distribution system is $1,820 per housing unit ($3641/2 truncated). For both water capacity and distribution, the total water impact fee would be $4,422, which is $572 more than the current fee amount of $3,850 for the smallest-size water meter.

28.2.4.10 Capital Improvements

Based on development projections, we projected water impact fee revenues of $7.1 million over the next 5 years. This revenue would be used to help finance debt service, line extensions, enhanced storage, and looping the system in a newer part of the City.

The appendix to this chapter reviews how we apportioned demand by size of residential unit.

28.3 PERSPECTIVES FOR ADVANCING PROFESSIONAL PRACTICE

Our method is an improvement in conventional practice, usually by engineers, in that we are able to refine proportionate share analysis to address differences in impact based on the size of residential units. We are not the first to do so, and we suspect the practice is gaining traction nationally, but we also suspect that the vast majority of communities calculate water and sewer fees in the "old fashioned way," which does little to advance equity.

Nor does the "old fashioned way" advance efficiency. As discussed in Chapter 13, if less costly development pays more than its impact, while more costly development pays less, this inefficient pricing leads to less low-cost development and more high-cost development (see also Chapter 15 and its Coda). This can lead to fiscal stress, as revenues generated from larger homes are not sufficient to cover costs.

We refer readers to the technical appendix, which shows how we apportioned population to residential units based on the size of the unit.

APPENDIX 28A

In this appendix, we present a method to apportion the mitigation of water infrastructure impacts based on the variation in size of residential units. This is a refinement over the approach introduced in Chapter 7 on impact fee methodology. The approach is based on the desire to achieve more equitable distribution of mitigation based on the principles identified in Chapter 15, on the ethics of impact fee equity, and its Coda.

Development projections and growth rates are summarized in Figure 28A.1. These projections will be used to estimate impact fee revenue and to indicate the anticipated need for growth-related infrastructure. However, impact fee methodologies are designed to reduce sensitivity to accurate development projections in the determination of the proportionate share fee amounts. If actual

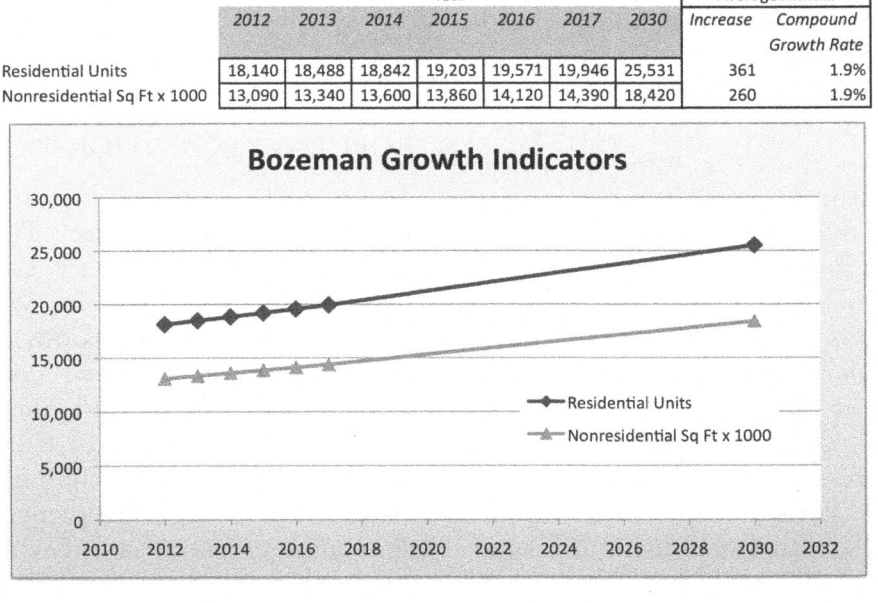

| Bozeman, Montana | | | | Year | | | | 2012 to 2017 Average Annual | |
	2012	2013	2014	2015	2016	2017	2030	Increase	Compound Growth Rate
Residential Units	18,140	18,488	18,842	19,203	19,571	19,946	25,531	361	1.9%
Nonresidential Sq Ft x 1000	13,090	13,340	13,600	13,860	14,120	14,390	18,420	260	1.9%

FIGURE 28A.1 Development projections and growth rates.

development is slower than projected, impact fee revenues will also decline, but so will the need for growth-related infrastructure. In contrast, if development is faster than anticipated, the City will receive an increase in impact fee revenue but will also need to accelerate the capital improvements program to keep pace with the actual rate of development.

While we focus on estimating persons per residential unit by unit size, we include key calculations for nonresidential development. These are needed to apportion demand first between residential and nonresidential land uses, and then within residential land uses by size unit.

Bozeman-specific base data for the demographic analysis and development projections include 2010 census counts of population and housing units, American Community Survey tables and Public Use Microdata Samples (PUMS), plus databases provided by City staff, including Montana Department of Revenue data on floor area and utility billing records. The projected increase in housing units is based on the City's population projection from the 2009 Community Plan, but instead of 54,500 residents by 2015, the projections for the impact fee analysis assume this population level will not be reached until 2030. Projected population was converted to housing units using the 2010 average of 2.13 year-round residents per housing unit. Given the 5-year update cycle for impact fees, TischlerBise did not vary this ratio over time or assume any changes to the vacancy rate in Bozeman, which was approximately 10% at the time of the 2010 census. From the 2000 to 2010 census, Bozeman had an average annual increase of 589 housing units per year. According to the City's building permits (see Year 2010 Annual Report from the Department of Planning and Community Development), 2005 was the peak year for residential construction, with 955 housing units. The low point for the past decade was 2009, with 182 housing units permitted. Residential construction increased slightly in 2010 to 208 units. Based on 54,500 residents by 2030, Bozeman would see an increase of 341 units in 2012, increasing slowly over time to 375 housing units being constructed in 2017.

Because the 2009 Community Plan does not provide job projections for Bozeman, TischlerBise assumed a constant jobs-to-housing ratio, yielding 35,647 jobs in 2030. Current ratios of floor area per job, for four general types of nonresidential development, were used to convert projected jobs into the floor area increase shown in the following. For both residential and nonresidential development, the impact fee study assumes a compound annual growth rate of 1.9%.

RECENT RESIDENTIAL CONSTRUCTION

During the 2000s, Bozeman has increased by an average of 589 housing units per year. The chart at the bottom of Figure 28A.2 indicates the estimated number of housing units added by decade in Bozeman. Consistently with the nationwide decline in development activity, residential construction has slowed significantly since 2008. Even with the recent drop in housing starts, Bozeman added more units during the past decade than in any previous decade.

POPULATION AND JOBS FORECAST

To provide context for population and job growth in Bozeman, TischlerBise prepared comparisons with Gallatin County projections published by Woods & Poole Economics for 2011. Woods & Poole annually updates a database containing more than 900 economic and demographic variables for every county in the United States. Their economic and demographic projections use an integrated projection model, so that changes in one county will affect growth or decline in other counties. The methods used by Woods & Poole to generate county

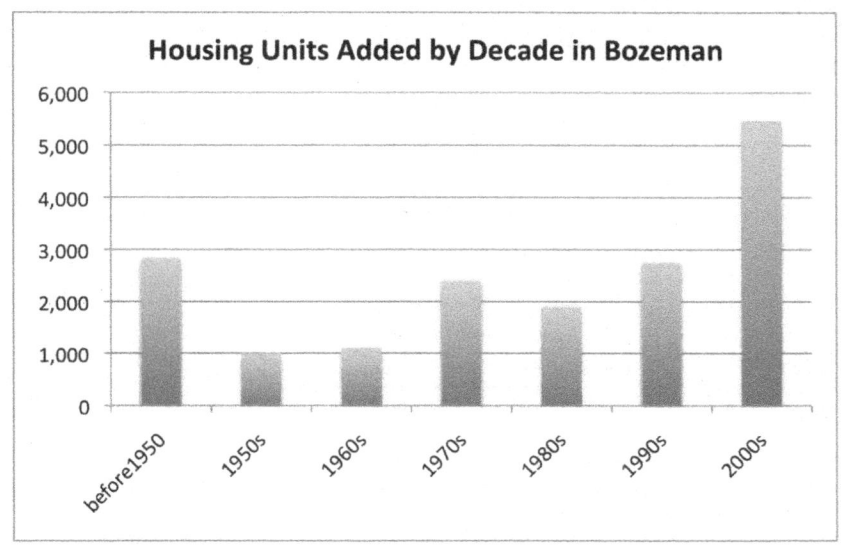

Bozeman, Montana

Census 2010 Population*	37,280
Census 2010 Housing Units*	17,464
Total Housing Units in 2000	11,577
New Housing Units	5,887

From 2000 to 2010, Bozeman added an average of 589 housing units per year.

* U.S. Census Bureau SF1.

Housing Units Added by Decade in Bozeman

Source for 1990s and earlier is Table B25034, American Community Survey, 2008-2010.

FIGURE 28A.2 Housing units by decade.

projections proceed in four stages. First, forecasts to 2040 of total US personal income, earnings by industry, employment by industry, population, inflation, and other variables are made. Second, the country is divided into 179 Economic Areas (EAs) as defined by the US Department of Commerce, Bureau of Economic Analysis (BEA). EAs are aggregates of contiguous counties that attempt to measure cohesive economic regions in the US. For each EA, a projection is made for employment using an "export-base" approach. The employment projection for each EA is then used to estimate earnings in each EA. The employment and earnings projections then become the principal explanatory variables used to estimate population and number of households in each EA. The third stage is to project population by age, sex, and race for each EA on the basis of net migration rates associated with employment opportunities. For stages two and three, the US projection is the control total for the EA projections. The fourth stage replicates stages two and three except that it is performed at the county level, using the EAs as the control total for the county projections.

Figure 28A.3 indicates the City's share of countywide population over time. Bozeman's 2009 Community Plan projected a population of 54,500 by 2015. Due to the significant decrease in housing construction in recent years, the impact fee update assumes this population level will not be reached until 2030. Given these projections of County and City population, Bozeman would experience a decrease in population share over the next 20 years. To derive annual data for the impact fee analysis, TischlerBise used an exponential growth formula to yield more conservative short-term development increases.

In addition to data on residential development, the calculation of impact fees requires data on nonresidential development.

	1990	2000	2010	2020	2030
Gallatin County (July 1)	50,811	68,369	93,268	122,726	152,522
City of Bozeman (April 1)	22,660	27,509	37,280	45,075	54,500
Remainder of County	28,151	40,860	55,988	77,651	98,022
Bozeman Share	45%	40%	40%	37%	36%

Sources: Gallatin County from Woods & Poole Economics (2011). Appendix B of the Bozeman Community Plan (2009) expected the City to reach 54,500 residents by 2015. Due to the significant decrease in housing construction in recent years, this population is not anticipated until 2030.

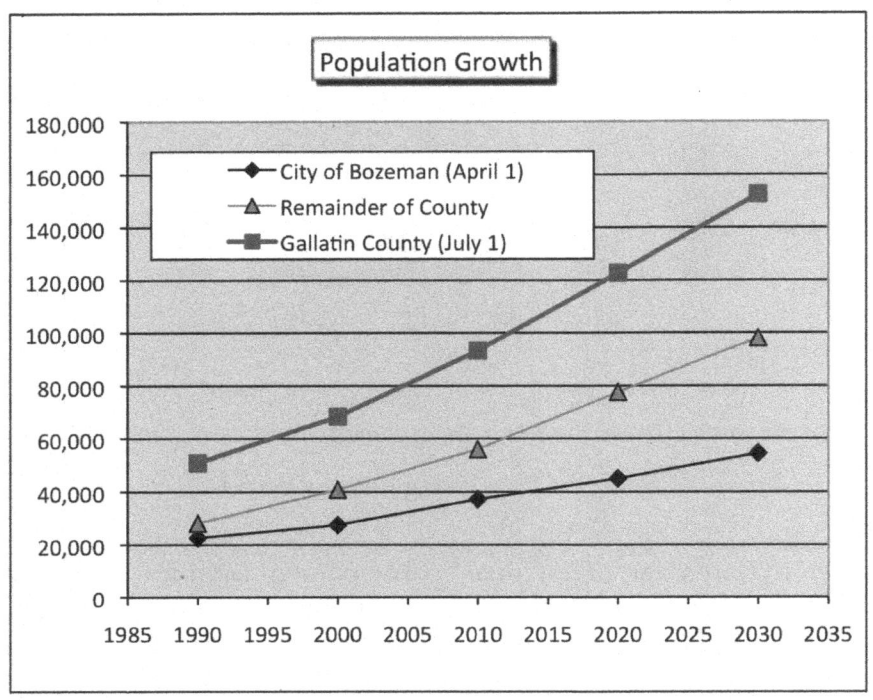

FIGURE 28A.3 City of Bozeman population share.

TischlerBise uses the term "jobs" to refer to employment by place of work. Similarly to the population share evaluation discussed earlier, countywide jobs are shown in Figure 28A.4 along with the City of Bozeman job share. Countywide jobs are from Woods & Poole Economics, scaled according to the year 2000 ratio of jobs reported by the Census Transportation Planning Package (CTPP) compared with the BEA job data used by Woods & Poole. For the purpose of transportation impact fees, CTPP data provide a better representation of the demand for journey-to-work travel. BEA includes self-employed, sole proprietors, and part-time employment. Even though 2010 CTPP data is not yet available, the methodology for deriving these two data sets has not changed significantly over the past decade.

For the City of Bozeman, TischlerBise assumed a constant jobs-to-housing ratio over time, starting from the 2010 job estimate available from OnTheMap (US Census Bureau web application). TischlerBise also used an exponential formula to derive annual jobs from 2010 to 2030, thus minimizing short-term increases in jobs and nonresidential floor area. Jobs were converted to nonresidential floor area using average square feet per employee multipliers, as discussed further later.

	2000	2003	2006	2010	2020	2030
Gallatin County	37,247	33,581	39,283	38,532	55,805	66,472
City of Bozeman	22,887	22,744	25,011	24,384	29,483	35,647
Remainder of County	14,360	10,837	14,272	14,148	26,322	30,825
Bozeman Share	61%	68%	64%	63%	53%	54%

Sources: Gallatin County and Bozeman 2000 are from Census Transportation Planning Package (CTPP). County and City data for 2003-2010 are from OnTheMap, U.S. Census Bureau web application. Gallatin County 2020-2030 projections are from Woods & Poole Economics (2011), scaled by the ratio of CTPP to W&P jobs in 2000. Projected Bozeman jobs in 2030 assumes a constant jobs-to-housing ratio over time.

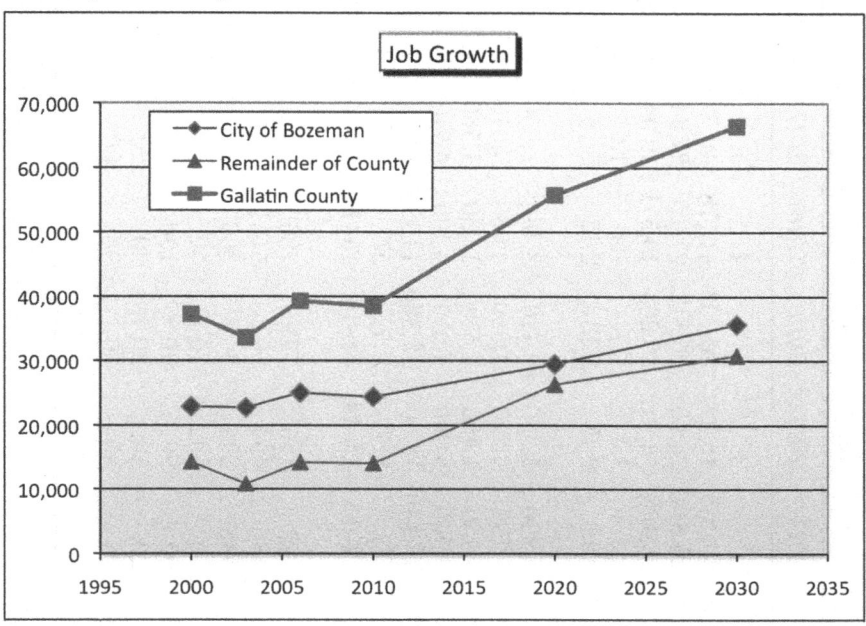

FIGURE 28A.4 City of Bozeman job share.

DETAILED DEVELOPMENT PROJECTIONS

Demographic data shown in Table 28A.1 provide key inputs for updating development impact fees in the City of Bozeman. Cumulative data are shown at the top and projected annual increases by type of development are shown at the bottom of the table. Given the expectation that impact fees are updated every 3 to 5 years, TischlerBise did not evaluate long-term demographic trends such as declining household size. As discussed in the next section, TischlerBise recommends the use of persons per housing unit to derive impact fees. Therefore, vacancy rates and number of households are not essential to the demographic analysis.

PERSONS PER HOUSING UNIT

The 2010 census did not obtain detailed information using a "long-form" questionnaire. Instead, the US Census Bureau has switched to a continuous monthly mailing of surveys, known as the American Community Survey (ACS), which is limited by sample-size constraints in areas with relatively few residents. For cities like Bozeman, data on detached housing units are now combined with attached single units (commonly known as townhouses). Part of the rationale for deriving fees by housing unit size, as discussed further later, is to address this ACS data limitation. Because townhouses and mobile homes generally have less floor area than detached units, fees by house size

TABLE 28A.1 Annual Demographic Data

Calculation Step	2010	2012	2013	2014	2015	2016	2017	2022	2030
Cumulative		Base Year	1	2	3	4	5	10	18
Year-Round Population	37,280	38,723	39,465	40,222	40,993	41,778	42,579	46,820	54,500
Jobs	24,384	25,328	25,814	26,308	26,812	27,326	27,849	30,624	35,647
Housing Units	17,464	18,140	18,488	18,842	19,203	19,571	19,946	21,933	25,531
Jobs-to-Housing Ratio	1.4	1.4	1.4	1.4	1.4	1.4	1.4	1.4	1.4
Persons per Housing Unit	2.13	2.13	2.13	2.13	2.13	2.13	2.13	2.13	2.13
Nonres. Sq. Ft. in thousands (KSF)									
Industrial		3,230	3,290	3,350	3,420	3,480	3,550	3,900	4,540
Commercial		4,610	4,700	4,790	4,880	4,980	5,070	5,580	6,490
Health Care & Social Assistance		1,420	1,450	1,480	1,510	1,530	1,560	1,720	2,000
All Other Services		3,830	3,900	3,980	4,050	4,130	4,210	4,630	5,390
Total		13,090	13,340	13,600	13,860	14,120	14,390	15,830	18,420
Average Sq. Ft. per Job		517	517	517	517	517	517	517	517
Annual Increase	**Change**	**11–12**	**12–13**	**13–14**	**14–15**	**15–16**	**16–17**	**21–22**	**2012–2030 Average Annual**
	Analysis								
Population		728	742	756	771	786	801	881	917
Jobs		476	486	494	504	514	523	577	600
Housing Units		341	348	354	361	368	375	413	430
Industrial KSF		60	60	60	70	60	70	70	76
Commercial KSF		80	90	90	90	100	90	110	109
Health Care & Social Assistance KSF		20	20	30	30	30	20	30	30
All Other Services KSF		70	70	80	70	80	80	90	91
Total Nonresidential KSF/Yr		230	250	260	260	260	270	300	309

Note: KSF = thousands of square feet. Nonres means nonresidential land uses.

ensure proportionality and facilitate the construction of affordable units.

According to the US Census Bureau, a household is a housing unit that is occupied by year-round residents. Impact fees often use per capita standards and persons per housing unit or persons per household to derive proportionate share fee amounts. When persons per housing unit are used in the fee calculations, infrastructure standards are derived using year-round population. When persons per household are used in the fee calculations, the impact fee methodology assumes all housing units will be occupied, thus requiring seasonal or peak population to be used when deriving infrastructure standards. TischlerBise recommends that impact fees for residential development in the City of Bozeman be imposed according to the number of year-round residents per housing unit. As shown at the bottom of Table 28A.2, census data indicates that Bozeman had 17,464 housing units in 2010. In 2010, dwellings with a single unit per structure (detached, attached, and mobile homes) averaged 2.23 persons per housing unit. Dwellings in structures with multiple units averaged 1.62 year-round residents per unit.

DEMAND INDICATORS BY SIZE OF HOUSING

The impact fee update recommends residential impact fees that increase with the floor area of the living space. An extensive analysis of demographic data from the US Census Bureau and unit size data from Montana Department of Revenue (DOR) supports the proportionate share methodology for the proposed cost allocation. The number of bedrooms is the common connection between the two databases, with the analysis limited to units constructed during the past two decades. In Bozeman, the average-size one-bedroom dwelling has 1,254 square feet of living area. The average size of a two-bedroom unit is 1,966 square feet of living area. Housing units with three bedrooms average 2,065 square feet of living area. Due to sample-size limitations in the demographic data (discussed further later), TischlerBise aggregated all units with four or more bedrooms. These large units average 3,189 square feet of living space. This analysis is shown in Table 28A.3.

Custom tabulations of demographic data by bedroom range can be created from individual survey responses provided by the US Census Bureau in files known as Public Use

TABLE 28A.2 Year-Round Persons per Unit by Type of Housing

2009 ACS	Persons	Households (HH)	Persons per HH	Housing Units	Persons per Unit
Single Unit[a]	20,571	8,753	2.35	9,726	2.12
2+ Units	11,793	6,813	1.73	7,642	1.54
Subtotal	32,364	15,566	2.08	17,368	
Group Quarters	4,759				
Total	37,123	15,566		17,368	**2.14**
2010 Census					
Single Unit[a]	21,770	8,871	2.45	9,780	2.23
2+ Units	12,480	6,904	1.81	7,684	1.62
Group Quarters	3,030				
Total	34,250	15,775		17,464	**2.13**

[a]Single-family includes detached, attached, and mobile homes.

Sources: Tables B25024, B25032, B25033, and B26001. 2008-2010 American Community Survey (ACS), US Census Bureau, 2010.

TABLE 28A.3 Floor Area of Living Space by Bedrooms

Bedrooms	Data	Analysis
1	Sum of Square Footage	61,450
	Count of Geocode	49
	Average Square Footage	1,254
2	Sum of Square Footage	495,355
	Count of Geocode	252
	Average Square Footage	1,966
3	Sum of Square Footage	6,282,153
	Count of Geocode	3,042
	Average Square Footage	2,056
4	Sum of Square Footage	3,125,693
	Count of Geocode	1,038
	Average Square Footage	3,011
5	Sum of Square Footage	734,637
	Count of Geocode	186
	Average Square Footage	3,950
6	Sum of Square Footage	94,336
	Count of Geocode	19
	Average Square Footage	4,965
7	Sum of Square Footage	24,173
	Count of Geocode	5
	Average Square Footage	4,835
8	Sum of Square Footage	3,772
	Count of Geocode	1
	Average Square Footage	3,772
Total Sum of Square Footage		10,821,569
Total Count of Geocode		4,592
Total Average Square Feet per Unit		2,357

Note: Universe is units built in 1990–2010.

Microdata Samples (PUMS). Because PUMS files are only available for areas of roughly 100,000 persons, the City of Bozeman is included in Public Use Microdata Area (PUMA) 00500, which includes five counties (Meagher, Park, Gallatin, Madison, and Beaverhead). As shown in Figure 27A.8, TischlerBise derived trip generation rates and average persons per housing unit by bedroom range from PUMS data. Recommended multipliers were scaled to make the average value for all housing units in PUMA 00500 match the average value derived from 2010 census data for the City of Bozeman. For example, the PUMS-derived average of 1.87 persons per housing unit was less than the actual average in Bozeman (2.13 persons per housing

TABLE 28A.4 Persons by Bedroom Range

Bedrooms	Persons per Housing Unit
0–1	0.78
2	1.44
3	2.27
4+	2.78
Total	2.13

unit, as shown in Table 28A.4). Multiplying the PUMS-derived average for each bedroom range by 2.13/1.87 increases persons per housing unit to the Bozeman-specific data. The recommended multipliers shown in the following are for all types of housing units (consolidated residential analysis of units constructed in 1990–2010).

AVERAGE NUMBER OF PERSONS BY DWELLING SIZE

Determining the average number of persons by square feet of housing requires a combination of demographic data from the Census Bureau and house size data from the local property-tax database, with number of bedrooms as the common connection between the two databases. Residential floor area, by bedroom range, is based on living space, which excludes garages.

Average floor area and number of persons by bedroom range are plotted in Figure 28A.5,

with a logarithmic trend line derived from the four actual averages in the City of Bozeman. Using the trend line formula shown in the chart, TischlerBise derived the estimated average number of persons, by dwelling size, using 200 square feet intervals. For the purpose of impact fees, TischlerBise recommends a minimum fee based on a unit size of 1,400 square feet and a maximum fee for units 3,001 square feet or larger. In Bozeman, the average size for all housing units constructed during 1990 through 2010 is 2,357 square feet of living space.

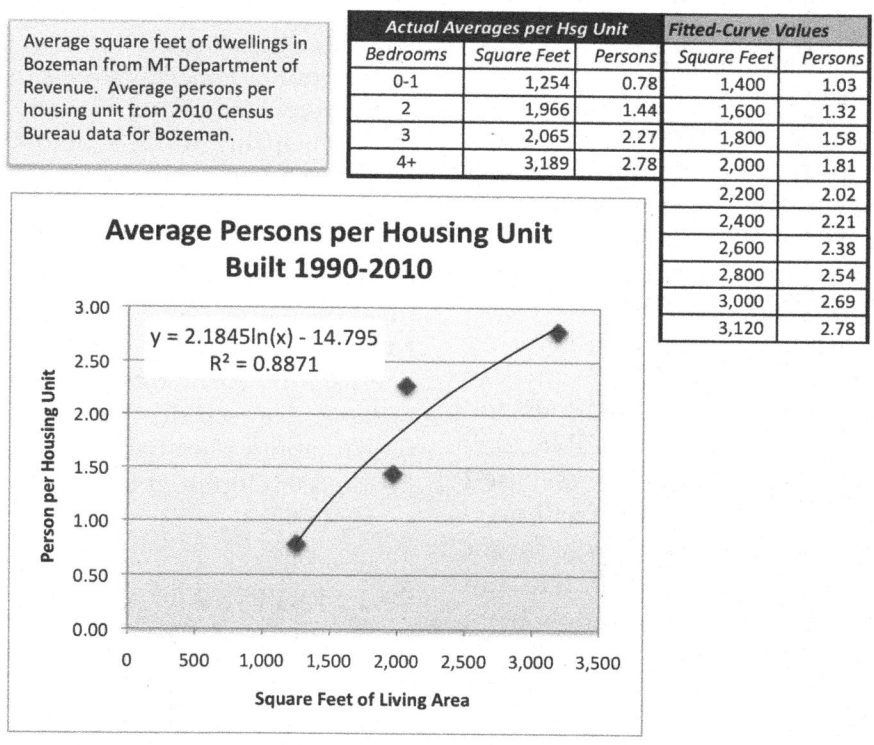

Average square feet of dwellings in Bozeman from MT Department of Revenue. Average persons per housing unit from 2010 Census Bureau data for Bozeman.

Actual Averages per Hsg Unit			Fitted-Curve Values	
Bedrooms	Square Feet	Persons	Square Feet	Persons
0-1	1,254	0.78	1,400	1.03
2	1,966	1.44	1,600	1.32
3	2,065	2.27	1,800	1.58
4+	3,189	2.78	2,000	1.81
			2,200	2.02
			2,400	2.21
			2,600	2.38
			2,800	2.54
			3,000	2.69
			3,120	2.78

Average Persons per Housing Unit Built 1990-2010

$$y = 2.1845\ln(x) - 14.795$$
$$R^2 = 0.8871$$

FIGURE 28A.5 Persons by square feet of living space.

29 TRANSPORTATION IMPACT FEES SCALED TO RESIDENTIAL UNIT SIZE IN TUCSON, ARIZONA

CARSON BISE

29.1 OVERVIEW

With few exceptions, impact fees for streets and highways use the Institute of Transportation Engineers' *Trip Generation Manual*. Chapter 18 noted several limitations of this source. A key limitation is that for residential land uses, there is no variation based on the size of the residential unit. Yet, data from such sources as the National Household Transportation Survey for 2017 show that larger households have more trips than smaller ones. This is shown in Table 29.1.

We also know from the American Housing Survey for the same year, 2017, that as the size of the dwelling unit increases, so does the number of occupants, as shown in Table 29.2.

Clearly, transportation impact fees based on the average for a residential unit will overcharge smaller units and undercharge larger ones. We know from Chapters 10, 11, and 13 that this is inefficient. We also know from Chapters 14 and 15, as well as the Coda to Chapter 15, that this is inconsistent with the ethics of equity.

TischletBise was retained by the City of Tucson, Arizona, to create transportation impact fees that were consistent with the ethics of impact fee equity. What follows is our analytic steps for both residential and nonresidential development though focusing on how we used data and reasoning to vary residential impact fees by the size of the residential unit provided in Appendix 29A.

We begin with what Arizona legislation provides. ARS (Arizona Revised Statutes)§ 9-463.05 (T)(7)(e) defines the facilities and assets that can be included in the Street Facilities Infrastructure Improvement Plan (IIP):

Street facilities located in the service area, including arterial or collector streets or roads that have been designated on an officially adopted plan of the municipality, traffic signals and rights- of-way and improvements thereon

The Street Facilities IIP includes components for arterial street improvements and the cost of professional services for preparing the Street Facilities IIP and related Development Impact Fee Report. An incremental expansion methodology is used for arterial street improvements, and a plan-based methodology is used for the Development Impact Fee Report.

29.2 SERVICE AREA

For street facilities, capacity projects for which development impact fees will be collected are anticipated to be built to serve both citywide and subarea transportation needs. Three service areas were developed based on growth patterns and location of infrastructure. For streets, a portion of the fee is based on citywide capacity needs reflected in Regional Transportation Authority (RTA) projects and other citywide capacity transportation projects and is recommended to be collected and spent citywide on those projects. The remainder of the fee is for other non-RTA/citywide capacity street improvement

DOI: 10.4324/9781003336075-34

TABLE 29.1 Trips per Household by Average Household Size

Household Size	Trips per Household
1	3.7
2	7.0
3	9.3
4	11.9
5 or more	22.7

Source: National Household Transportation Survey for 2017, https://nhts.ornl.gov/, released in 2019.

TABLE 29.2 Occupants per Dwelling Unit by Unit Size

Size of Occupied Unit	Occupants per Unit
<750 sq. ft.	1.61
750 to <1,000 sq. ft.	1.82
1,000 to <1,500 sq. ft.	2.30
1,500 to <2,000 sq. ft.	2.53
2,000 to <2,500 sq. ft.	2.71
2,500 to <3,000 sq. ft.	2.91
3,000 to <4,000 sq. ft.	3.18
4,000 sq. ft. or more	3.31

Source: American Housing Survey for 2017, www.census.gov/programs-surveys/ahs.html, released in 2018.

projects and is recommended to be collected and spent within the respective three service areas. Potential projects are identified in this chapter.

29.3 METHODOLOGY

Street facilities development impact fees use an incremental expansion methodology and allocate capital costs to residential and non-residential development based on vehicle miles of travel (VMT) using average weekday vehicle trips and average trip lengths. This methodology allows Tucson to provide additional capacity at the current level of service standard as growth occurs. Development fee revenue collected using this methodology may not be used to replace or rehabilitate existing improvements.

29.4 PROPORTIONATE SHARE

ARS § 9-463.05 (B)(3) states that the development fee shall not exceed a proportionate share of the cost needed to provide necessary public services to the development. Vehicle trip length, trip generation rates, and trip adjustment factors are used to determine the proportionate impact of residential, commercial, office, and industrial land uses on the city's street network.

29.5 RATIO OF SERVICE UNIT TO LAND USE

ARS § 9-463.05(E)(4) requires:

A table establishing the specific level or quantity of use, consumption, generation or discharge of a service unit for each category of necessary public services or facility expansions and an equivalency or conversion table establishing the ratio of a service unit to various types of land uses, including residential, commercial and industrial.

29.6 SERVICE UNITS

The appropriate service unit for the street facilities development impact fees is VMT. VMT creates the link between supply (roadway capacity) and demand (traffic generated by new development). Components used to determine VMT include: vehicle trip ends (or trip generation rates), adjustments for commuting patterns and pass-by trips, and trip length weighting factors. Each is discussed further in this section. This is shown in Table 29.3.

29.7 TRIP GENERATION RATES

For nonresidential development, trip generation rates (i.e., vehicle trip ends) are from the 10th edition of the reference book *Trip Generation* published by the Institute of Transportation Engineers (ITE) (2017). A vehicle trip end represents a vehicle either

TABLE 29.3 Summary of Service Units

Development Type	ITE Code	Weekday Vehicle Trip Ends	Development Unit	Trip Adjustment	2019 Trips
Single-Family Units	210	8.19	Housing Unit	56%	764,493
2+ Units	220	3.89	Housing Unit	56%	159,645
Industrial (KSF)	110	4.96	KSF	50%	43,780
Commercial	820	37.75	KSF	33%	282,498
Institutional (KSF)	520	19.52	KSF	33%	594,114
Office & Other	710	9.74	KSF	50%	95,611
Total					1,940,141

Sources:
Institute of Transportation Engineers (ITE) *Trip Generation*, 10th Edition, 2017; TischlerBise analysis. Derived using local traffic counts and Federal Highway Administration, 2017 National Household Travel Survey.

entering or exiting a development (as if a traffic counter were placed across a driveway). As an alternative to using the national average trip generation rate for residential development, ITE publishes regression curve formulas that may be used to derive custom trip generation rates using local demographic data. This is discussed in Appendix 29A.

29.8 ADJUSTMENTS FOR COMMUTING PATTERNS AND PASS-BY TRIPS

To calculate street facilities development impact fees, trip generation rates require an adjustment factor to avoid double counting each trip at both the origin and destination points. Therefore, the basic trip adjustment factor is 50%. As will be discussed further, the development fee methodology includes additional adjustments to make the fees proportionate to the infrastructure demand for particular types of development.

Residential development has a larger trip adjustment factor of 56 percent to account for commuters leaving Tucson for work. According to the 2009 National Household Travel Survey, weekday work trips are typically 31 percent of production trips (i.e., all outbound trips, which are 50 percent of all trips). As shown in Table 29.4, the Census Bureau's

TABLE 29.4 Inflow/Outflow Analysis

Trip Adjustment Factors for Commuters[a]	
Employed Residents	196,003
Residents Working in Tucson	114,890
Residents Commuting out of Tucson	81,113
Percent Out-Commuting	41%
All Outbound Trips	50%
Weekday Work Trip Share[b]	31%
Additional Production Trips	6%

Sources:
[a]US Census Bureau, OnTheMap Application and LEHD Origin- Destination Employment Statistics, 2015.
[b]National Household Travel Survey, 2009.

web application OnTheMap indicates that 41 percent of resident workers traveled outside the City for work in 2015. In combination, these factors ($0.31 \times 0.50 \times 0.41 = 0.06$) support the additional 6 percent allocation of trips to residential development (50 percent plus 6 percent).

For commercial development, the trip adjustment factor is less than 50 percent, because retail development and some services attract vehicles as they pass by on arterial and collector roads. For example, when someone stops at a convenience store on the way home from work, the convenience store is not the primary destination. For the average shopping center, the ITE data indicates that 34 percent of the vehicles that enter are passing by on their way to some other primary destination. The remaining 66 percent of attraction trips have the commercial site as their primary destination. Because attraction trips are half of all trips, the trip adjustment factor is 66 percent multiplied by 50 percent, or approximately 33 percent of the trips. These factors are shown to derive inbound vehicle trips for each type of nonresidential land use.

29.9 ANALYSIS OF CAPACITY, USAGE, AND COSTS OF EXISTING PUBLIC FACILITIES

ARS § 9-463.05(E)(1) requires:

A description of the existing necessary public services in the service area and the costs to upgrade, update, improve, expand, correct or replace those necessary public services to meet existing needs and usage and stricter safety, efficiency, environmental or regulatory standards, which shall be prepared by qualified professionals licensed in this state, as applicable.

The City of Tucson provided an inventory of existing arterial road segments, including segment lengths, lane quantities, and annual average daily traffic (AADT) counts. Multiplying each segment's length by the number of lanes yields the number of lane miles per segment. The City's arterial (major and minor) road network consists of 1,476 lane miles. By multiplying the traffic counts and segment lengths, daily VMT is determined. The sum of all arterial road segment's VMT is approximately 7.7 million, meaning that Tucson's arterial street network handles an average of just under 8 million daily VMT.

Table 29.5 documents the capacity of Tucson's arterial road network. Generally, the City's arterial streets operate at a level of service D, and the average number of lanes for arterials is roughly four lanes. An urbanized mile segment of a four-lane arterial street with a level

TABLE 29.5 Arterial Road Network Capacity and Usage

Analysis Step	Figure
Total Arterial Lane Miles	1,476
Vehicle Miles Capacity (VMC) per Lane Mile[a]	8,100
Total Vehicle Miles Capacity (VMC)	11,955,600
Existing Vehicle Miles of travel (VMT)	7,689,394
VMC/VMT Ratio	1.55

[a]See 2012 FDOT Quality/Level of Service Handbook Tables (LOS D, Four-Lane Arterial (Class II)).

of service D should maintain a daily volume of 32,400 vehicles, or 8,100 vehicles per lane mile over a 24-hour period. This means that the total daily lane mile capacity of the City's arterial road network of 1,476 lane miles is approximately 12 million vehicle miles of capacity.

As noted earlier, current daily volume on Tucson's arterial network is approximately 7.7 million VMT. The resulting vehicle miles of capacity (VMC) to VMT ratio is 1.55 (12 million VMC / 7.7 million VMT). The baseline VMC/VMT ratio for any incremental expansion method is 1.0 (i.e., VMC=VMT), therefore the current ratio of 1.55 exceeds current level of service ensuring that new capacity built with development impact fee funds will be at or below current level of service.

29.10 COST PER VEHICLE MILES TRAVELED (VMT)

Detailed analysis, which is not reported for brevity, shows that the total project cost per lane mile is approximately $7.5 million. However, after adjusting for other non–development fee funding sources and growth-related needs, the local cost used in the development fee calculation is a weighted average cost per lane mile of $1.2 million (rounded).

The cost per VMC is calculated based on the average cost per lane mile of $1.2 million divided by the average lane capacity of

TABLE 29.6 Cost per VMC Factors

Cost Factor	Figure
Cost per Lane Mile	$1,200,000
Vehicles Miles Capacity (VMC) per Lane Mile	8,100
Cost per VMC	$148.15
Cost per VMC, rounded	$148

8,100 average daily vehicle trips (per 1 lane mile). This results in a $148.00 cost per VMC (rounded). The incremental expansion methodology assumes the ratio of VMC to VMT is 1; therefore, the cost per VMT is also $148.00. This is shown in Table 29.6.

29.11 VEHICLE TRIPS

Table 29.7 shows the calculation of vehicle trips generated by existing development. When average weekday vehicle trip ends and trip adjustment percentages are multiplied by the development unit quantities for Tucson from the Land Use Assumption (housing units and nonresidential in square feet), the total number of vehicle trips generated by existing development is determined. As shown in Table 29.7, this totals 1,940,141 adjusted vehicle trips.

29.12 AVERAGE TRIP LENGTH

For the incremental expansion methodology, it is necessary to determine the average trip length on the City's arterial network. To do this, national trip generation rates and average trip lengths from the 2017 National Household Travel Survey are used to determine *expected* VMT on the City's transportation network. Table 29.8 shows average trip lengths from the National Household Travel Survey (2017).[1]

The national average trip length needs to be adjusted to reflect actual local demand on the City's arterial network. To do this, TischlerBise first determines expected demand (VMT) on the City's complete transportation network using the previously described national travel demand characteristics. Average daily trips from existing development in each land use category are multiplied by the applicable average trip lengths. Results are shown in Table 29.9.

Because expected VMT reflects anticipated travel demand from City development on the entire roadway system, it is therefore higher than actual VMT on the arterial system in the City. To calibrate demand on the arterial system, expected travel demand is compared with actual VMT obtained from the City of

TABLE 29.7 Vehicle Trips and Miles per Trip

Development Type	ITE Code	Weekday Vehicle Trip Ends	Development Unit	Trip Adjustment	2019 Trips	Average Trip Length
Single-Family Units	210	8.19	Housing Unit	56%	764,493	4.92
2+ Units	220	3.89	Housing Unit	56%	159,645	4.92
Industrial (KSF)	110	4.96	KSF	50%	43,780	3.07
Commercial	820	37.75	KSF	33%	282,498	3.15
Institutional (KSF)	520	19.52	KSF	33%	594,114	3.07
Office & Other	710	9.74	KSF	50%	95,611	3.07
Total					1,940,141	3.96

Sources:
Institute of Transportation Engineers (ITE), Trip Generation, 10th Edition, 2017; TischlerBise analysis.
Derived using local traffic counts and Federal Highway Administration, 2017 National Household Travel Survey.

TABLE 29.8 National Average Trip Lengths

Land Use	Trip Miles[a]
Residential	12.32
Industrial	7.70
Commercial/Retail	7.90
Institutional	7.70
Office and Other	7.70

[a]US Department of Transportation, Federal Highway Administration, 2017 National Household Transportation Survey, adjusted for land use.

TABLE 29.9 Expected VMT in the City of Tucson

Land Use	2019 Trips	National Average Trip Lengths	Expected VMT
Single Units	764,493	12.32	9,418,554
2+ Units	159,645	12.32	1,966,826
Industrial	43,780	7.70	337,106
Commercial/ Retail	282,498	7.90	2,231,734
Institutional	594,114	7.70	4,574,678
Office and Other	95,611	7.70	736,205
Total	1,940,141		19,265,103

TABLE 29.10 Local Trip Length Adjustment Factor

Calculation Step	Figure
Actual Local VMFT on Arterials[a]	7,689,394
Expected Local VMT[b]	19,265,103
Actual to Expected VMT	0.399

Notes:
[a]City of Tucson
[b]TischlerBise analysis

TABLE 29.11 Local Average Trip Lengths by Land Use

Land Use	National Average Trip Length (Miles)	Local Adjustment Factor	Local Trip Length
Residential	12.32	0.399	4.92
Industrial	7.70	0.399	3.07
Commercial/ Retail	7.90	0.399	3.15
Institutional	7.70	0.399	3.07
Office and Other	7.70	0.399	3.07

Sources: National trip length from 2017 NHTS and TischlerBise; local adjustment factor.

Using these factors, VMT per service unit is calculated, shown in Table 29.12.

29.13 SERVICE UNITS, DEMAND, AND COST FOR SERVICE

ARS § 9-463.05(E)(2) requires:

An analysis of the total capacity, the level of current usage and commitments for usage of capacity of the existing necessary public services, which shall be prepared by qualified professionals licensed in this state, as applicable.

TischlerBise created an aggregate travel model to convert development units within Tucson to vehicle trips and VMT. This includes the factors discussed earlier as well as average trip length.

29.14 TRAVEL DEMAND MODEL

ARS § 9-463.05(E)(5) requires:

The total number of projected service units necessitated by and attributable to new development in the service area based on the approved land use assumptions and calculated pursuant to generally accepted engineering and planning criteria.

Tucson's street segment database. The ratio between actual and expected VMT provides a local adjustment factor that can be applied to national average trip lengths by type of land use. The local adjustment factor is shown in Table 29.10.

As shown in Table 29.11, national average trip lengths are adjusted to reflect local conditions.

TABLE 29.12 VMT per Service Unit on Arterial Network

Development Type	ITE Code	Weekday Vehicle Trip Ends	Trip Adjustment Factor	Adjusted Trip Rate	Local Trip Length	VMT per Service Unit
Single Units	210	8.19	56%	4.62	4.92	22.70
2+ Units	220	3.89	56%	2.19	4.92	10.78
Industrial (KSF)	110	4.96	50%	2.48	3.07	7.62
Commercial (KSF)	820	37.75	33%	12.46	3.15	39.28
Institutional (KSF)	520	19.52	33%	6.44	3.07	19.80
Office & Other (KSF)	710	9.74	50%	4.87	3.07	14.97

Over the next 10 years, new development in Tucson is projected to generate 156,597 average weekday vehicle trips.

ARS § 9-463.05(E)(6) requires:

The projected demand for necessary public services or facility expansions required by new service units for a period not to exceed ten years.

Travel demand model inputs are used to derive level of service in VMT and future needs of lane miles. A VMT is a measurement unit equal to one vehicle traveling 1 mile. Based on the increase in VMT (568,845), the City of Tucson would need to construct an additional 70.22 lane miles of arterials to accommodate projected development over the next 10 years.

ARS § 9-463.05(E)(3) requires:

A description of all or the parts of the necessary public services or facility expansions and their costs necessitated by and attributable to development in the service area based on the approved land use assumptions, including a forecast of the costs of infrastructure, improvements, real property, financing, engineering and architectural services, which shall be prepared by qualified professionals licensed in this state, as applicable.

Multiplying the increase in number of lane miles (70.22) by the cost per lane mile of $1,200,000 results in a 10-year cost of $84,264,000 attributed to arterial lane miles. (For brevity, the detailed cumulative calculations are not reported.)

29.15 DEVELOPMENT IMPACT FEE REPORT—PLAN-BASED

The cost to prepare the Street Facilities IIP and Development Impact Fee Report totals $62,307. Tucson plans to update its report every 5 years. Based on this cost, proportionate share, and 5-year projections of new residential and nonresidential development from the Land Use Assumptions document, the cost was calculated at $0.22 per average weekday VMT.

29.16 STREET FACILITIES IIP

From the foregoing, the street facilities improvements for development impact fee purposes were created for each of the three service areas as well as for citywide facilities. (For brevity, the details are not reported.)

29.17 CALCULATION OF STREET FACILITIES IMPACT FEES

The final steps in the process generate street facilities impact fees. The immediate step is the calculation of revenue offsets, and then, the impact fee itself is calculated.

29.18 REVENUE OFFSET

A revenue offset is not necessary for the street facilities development impact fees, because 10-year growth costs generated by projected development exceed revenues projected to be generated by development impact fees according to the Land Use Assumptions.

29.19 PROPOSED STREET FACILITIES DEVELOPMENT IMPACT FEES

ARS § 9-463.05(E)(4) requires:

A table establishing the specific level or quantity of use, consumption, generation or discharge of a service unit for each category of necessary public services or facility expansions and an equivalency or conversion table establishing the ratio of a service unit to various types of land uses, including residential, commercial and industrial.

Infrastructure standards and cost factors for street facilities come to $148.22 per VMT (Table 29.13).

The proposed development impact fees for street facilities are shown in Table 29.14. Cost factors for streets improvements and professional services are summarized at the top of the figure. Residential development impact fees are expressed by size of unit. Nonresidential development impact fees are expressed per 1,000 square feet (KSF) of floor area and per room for lodging land uses. The street facilities development impact fees are calculated by multiplying the $148.22 net cost per VMT/VMC by the VMT per development unit for each land use type.

TABLE 29.13 Proposed Street Facilities Development Impact Fees

Fee Component	Cost per VMC		
Cost per VMT/VMC	$148		
Development Fee Report	$0.22		
Total	$148.22		
Residential (per Housing Unit)			
Size of Housing Unit (Sq. Ft.)	Demand Unit	Average Weekday VMT	Proposed Fees
750 or less	Housing Unit	9.53	$1,412
751 to 1,250	Housing Unit	14.77	$2,189
1,251 to 1,750	Housing Unit	19.48	$2,887
1,751 to 2,250	Housing Unit	22.92	$3,397
2,251 to 2,750	Housing Unit	25.63	$3,798
2,751 to 3,250	Housing Unit	27.88	$4,132
3,251 to 3,750	Housing Unit	29.79	$4,415
3,751 or More	Housing Unit	31.45	$4,661
Nonresidential (per Demand Unit)			
Type	Demand Unit	Average Weekday VMT	Proposed Fees
Industrial: Light Industrial	1,000 Sq. Ft.	7.62	$1,129
Industrial: Manufacturing	1,000 Sq. Ft.	6.04	$895
Industrial: Warehousing	1,000 Sq. Ft.	2.67	$395
Commercial/Retail: General	1,000 Sq. Ft.	39.28	$5,822
Commercial/Retail: Free Standing Discount Store	1,000 Sq. Ft.	55.27	$8,192
General Office	1,000 Sq. Ft.	14.97	$2,218
Institutional: Schools	1,000 Sq. Ft.	19.80	$2,934
Institutional: Religious Facilities	1,000 Sq. Ft.	7.05	$1,044
Institutional: Medical (Nursing Home/Assisted Living)	1,000 Sq. Ft.	6.73	$997
Institutional: Medical (Clinical, Hospital)	1,000 Sq. Ft.	38.70	$5,736
Hotel	1,000 Sq. Ft.	13.18	$1,953

TABLE 29a.1a Average Weekday Vehicle Trip Ends by Bedroom Range

Bedroom Range	Persons	Vehicles Available	Housing Units	Housing Mix	Unadjusted persons per house (PPH)	Adjusted PPH	Unadjusted vehicles per house (VPH)	Adjusted VPH
0–2	9,920	6,699	6,343	45%	1.56	1.55	16.00	0.92
3	12,954	9,773	5,400	38%	2.40	2.38	1.81	1.58
4	6,534	4,568	2,164	15%	3.02	2.99	2.11	1.84
5+	1,046	677	277	2%	3.78	3.74	2.44	2.13
Total	30,454	21,717	14,184	100%	2.15	2.13	1.53	1.34

Source: American Community Survey, Public Use Microdata Sample for AZ PUMAs area that includes Tucson (2013–2017 5-Year unweighted data).

TABLE 29a.1b National Averages According to ITE

ITE Code	AWVTE per Person	AWVTE per Vehicle	AWVTE per (housing unit) HU	Tucson Housing Mix	Persons per household	Vehicles per household
210 single family detached (SFD)	2.65	6.36	9.44	70%	3.56	1.48
220 Apartment	3.31	5.10	6.65	30%	2.01	1.30
Weighted Average	2.85	5.98	8.60	100%	3.10	1.43

TABLE 29a.1c Recommended AWVTE per Housing Unit

Bedroom Range	AWVTE per Household Based on Persons[1]	AWVTE per Household Based on Vehicles[2]	AWVTE per Household[3]
0–2	4.42	5.50	4.96
3	6.78	9.45	8.12
4	8.52	11.00	9.76
5+	10.66	12.74	11.70
Average	**6.07**	**8.01**	**7.04**

Notes:

[1]Adjusted persons per household multiplied by national weighted average trip rate per person.

[2]Adjusted vehicles available per household multiplied by national weighted average trip rate per vehicle.

[3]Average trip rates based on persons and vehicles per household.

A key element of this analysis was determining the travel demand for residential development by unit size. These details are reported in Appendix 29A (Table 29A.1a to 29A.1d).

of data showing that smaller residential units have smaller impacts on streets than larger ones. In this case, impact fees for the largest units would be $4,661, or roughly 3.3 times those of the smallest units.

29.20 CONCLUSION AND SUMMARY OBSERVATIONS

Tucson's street facilities impact fees fairly apportion impact by size of residential unit, as shown in Table 19.13. This is based on analysis

APPENDIX 29A

Refining Trips for Residential Development

Rather than rely on only the trip generation rates produced by the ITE, TischlerBise

TABLE 29a.1d Calculation of Persons per House

Bedroom Range	Persons	Vehicles Available	Housing Units	Housing Mix	Unadjusted PPH	Adjusted PPH
0–2	9,920	6,699	6,343	45%	1.56	**1.55**
3	12,954	9,773	5,400	38%	2.40	2.38
4	6,534	4,568	2,164	15%	3.02	2.99
5+	1,046	677	277	2%	3.78	3.74
Total	30,454	21,717	14,184	100%	2.15	2.13

Source: American Community Survey, Public Use Microdata Sample for AZ Public Use Micro Areas (PUMAs) area that includes Tucson (2013–2017 5-Year unweighted data).

Note: Adjusted multipliers are scaled to make the average Public Use Micro Samples (PUMS) values match control totals for Tucson, based on American Community Survey 2013–2017 5-Year Estimates.

Actual Averages per Household			Fitted-Curve Values	
Bedrooms	Square Feet	Trip Ends	Sq Ft Range	Trip Ends
0-2	1,000	4.96	750 or Less	3.44
3	2,200	8.12	751 to 1,250	5.33
4	3,050	9.76	1,251 to 1,750	7.03
5+	4,150	11.70	1,751 to 2,250	8.27
			2,251 to 2,750	9.25
			2,751 to 3,250	10.06
			3,251 to 3,750	10.75
			3,751 or More	11.35

Average weekday vehicle trips per household derived from 2017 ACS PUMS data for the area that includes the City of Tucson. Unit size for 0-2 bedroom is from the 2017 U.S. Census Bureau average for all multi-family units constructed in the Census West region. Unit size for all other bedrooms is from the 2017 U.S. Census Bureau average for single-family units constructed in the Census Mountain division.

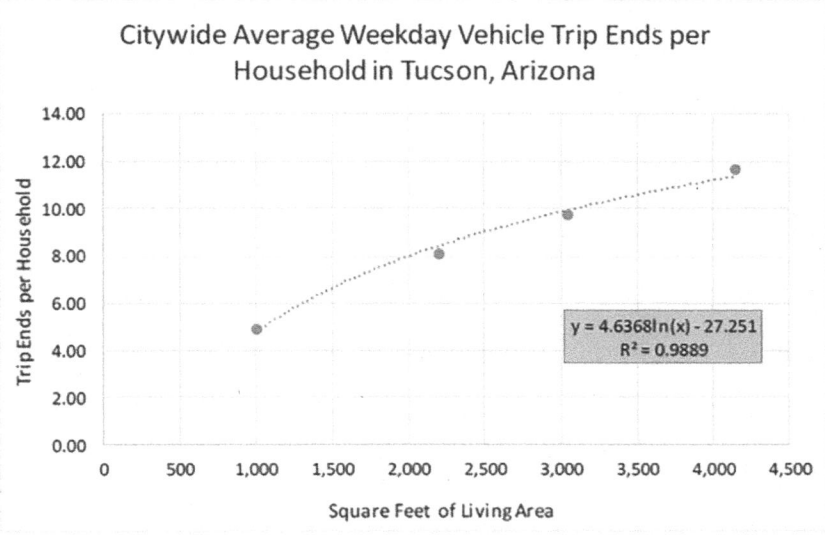

FIGURE 29a.1 Statistical attribution of street facility demand by residential unit size. (From TischlerBise, 2020.)

calculated trip generation rates based on the size of dwelling units, shown at the bottom of Table 29a.1. This helps advance the social equity concerns noted in Chapter 15 and its Coda. The area shaded gray is an average of trip rates based on persons and vehicles available for all types of households. In Tucson, each household is expected to generate an average of 7.04 Average Weekday Vehicle Trip Ends (AWVTE), compared with the national average of 9.22 trip ends per household.

To derive AWVTE by dwelling size, TischlerBise matched trip generation rates and average floor area by bedroom range, as shown in Figure 29a.1, with a logarithmic trend line derived from 2016 square footage estimates provided by the US Census Bureau (West region). Dwellings with two bedrooms or fewer average 1,000 square feet of floor area— based on multi-family dwellings constructed in West census region. Three-bedroom

dwellings average 2,200 square feet, four-bedroom dwellings average 3,050 square feet, and dwellings with five or more bedrooms average 4,150 square feet—based on single-family dwellings constructed in West census region. Using the trend line formula shown in the chart, TischlerBise derived the estimated AWVTE, by dwelling size, using the size ranges shown in Table 19.13 where the smallest floor area range (750 square feet or less) generates an estimated average of 3.44 trip ends per dwelling. The largest floor area range (3,751 square feet or more) generates an estimated average of 11.38 trip ends per dwelling.

NOTE

1 US. Department of Transportation, Federal Highway Administration, 2017 National Household Travel Survey. URL: http://nhts.ornl.gov.

30 IMPACT FEE FOCUS GROUPS

Case Study of Town of Queen Creek, Arizona

KEVIN BURNETT

30.1 INTRODUCTION

While the actual calculation of development impact fees is relatively straightforward, the political nature associated with the adoption and implementation of the fees can be difficult. Our experience shows that if the new proposed fees are unveiled to stakeholders for the first time when the governing body is preparing to consider their adoption, they are more likely to raise concerns about the assumptions and methodologies, as well as the fees themselves, largely based on their incomplete understanding of the process. This can in turn sow doubt amongst the members of the governing body regarding the validity of the fees, particularly if stakeholders raise these concerns in negative and confrontational tones at a public meeting, and implementation can be delayed as a result. By delaying implementation, the municipality may lose revenue necessary to construct facilities for which the fees are being collected, and on which the fees are based, and the entire community may be affected.

The town of Queen Creek, Arizona responded to this challenge with a proactive approach, engaging stakeholders and interested members of the community early on in the process. Willdan worked with local staff to develop an outreach strategy that provided stakeholders with insight into the process, approach, and methodology in a transparent manner. This also allows questions and potential opposition to be presented earlier in the process, often in a less public setting than at a City Council meeting. Furthermore, it provides more time for discussion and explanation with stakeholders, and any concerns or serious opposition can also be addressed earlier, so that surprises are less likely by the time Council is considering adoption. Throughout this chapter, we will present a case study that demonstrates our experience in taking an active role with stakeholders.

30.2 TOWN BACKGROUND

Queen Creek began its impact fee update process in 2017. At the time, the town was home to approximately 42,000 residents, with the population projected to double to 88,000 in 10 years. During that time, the developed non-residential square footage was projected to increase by 60% from 3,939,000 to 6,229,000 square feet. While the prior impact fee study had been completed 3 years earlier, the development projections and infrastructure needs were drastically different in 2017 than in 2014. It was deemed necessary to initiate a proactive approach from the onset of this update with both the Council and the community, including the Home Builders Association of Central Arizona and the Valley Partnership (representing commercial development interests), to explain the effects of these and other changes to the town's impact fees.

30.3 GENERAL OVERVIEW

After some initial work with town staff to understand land use assumptions (LUAs) and capital needs, preliminary fees were developed and presented during several focus group meetings

DOI: 10.4324/9781003336075-35

with citizens, staff, and the development community (residential and non-residential representatives). The purpose of these meetings was to provide an overview and discussion of how LUAs are developed, a full picture of the anticipated facility needs, and a description of the impact fee methodologies under consideration. The meetings began with a review of the LUAs. While town staff prepared the LUAs, it was important to obtain the perspective of the development community with respect to the timing and location of their anticipated development over the next 10 years. During the focus group meetings, the appropriate department head from the town provided an overview for their specific fees and required capital facilities and discussed the reasons why the capital projects were necessary to include in the analysis and fee development.

These forums provided an opportunity for participants to ask questions, share ideas and experiences from other communities, and voice concerns. The goal of the focus groups was not to achieve full support of the fees themselves but rather, to provide enough information to demonstrate that the facilities to be constructed were necessary, the fees were based on sound and reasonable assumptions, and the calculations were undertaken in an acceptable and equitable manner. The categories of fees that were discussed extensively with the focus groups, and individually with some stakeholders, included:

1. Library and town facilities
2. Parks
3. Streets
4. Water and wastewater

30.4 LIBRARY AND TOWN FACILITIES

As the library and town facility impact fee methodologies were developed, the calculated fees for both categories decreased from the amounts currently in effect. Between 2014 and 2017, the town had refinanced the outstanding debt used to finance the library and town facilities, resulting in reduced debt service requirements associated with the facilities. While it was expected that the development community would be pleased with the lowering of these fees, we felt it was necessary to explain the decrease, in part to avoid the assumption that the previous fees were too high. The reasoning for the decrease in the fees was explained to the focus group rather than simply presenting a lower fee and assuming their understanding and acceptance. The old and new debt schedules were presented, along with the calculations that we had undertaken to show why the fees decreased. It was not a result of the burden being shifted or a lower level of service being provided to new development, but simply a case of the town staff being proactive in reducing costs and passing the cost savings on to the community. As a result, all parties understood and were accepting of the new lower fees. The existing and new fees are illustrated in Table 30.1.

30.5 PARKS

The parks fee category generated substantial interest and required several components to work through. The town's original master plan identified a level of service for 61 acres

TABLE 30.1 Library and Town Facility Impact Fee Comparison

Fee	Proposed ($)	Current ($)	Difference ($)	Difference (%)
Single-Family	243	1,193	(950)	(79.6%)
Multifamily	174	878	(704)	(80.2%)
Retail	57	403	(346)	(85.9%)
Office	83	395	(312)	(78.9%)
Industrial	84	466	(382)	(81.9%)

of parkland per 10,000 residents. The recently updated master plan identified a new level of service of 51 acres of parkland per 10,000 residents, while the town had an existing level of service of 21 acres per 10,000 residents, based on actual population and park acreage.

Based on focus group discussions, three different levels of service for parks were identified. It would not have been technically defensible to develop a parks impact fee based on a level of service of 61 acres, or even 51 acres, without identifying a corresponding non–impact fee funding source to bring the existing level of service up to either 61 or 51 acres of parkland. Additional focus groups were held to discuss parks and park standards, and to receive feedback. We wanted to hear from the development community how many acres of parkland they felt would be beneficial in terms of selling homes to new residents. We also needed to identify existing residents' expectations for the parkland they expected, wanted, and were willing to fund. Over the course of several meetings, the park profile for the town was discussed and projected. It was determined that while the town should strive to achieve the identified level of service of 51 acres per 10,000 residents over the next 10 years, the impact fees would be based on 40 acres per 10,000 residents. This was an acceptable level of service for both the development community and existing residents.

30.6 STREETS

When the town's street impact fees were calculated in the prior study, they were based on the need for 68 additional lane miles at a cost of $6.5 million. However, the 2017 study reflected a need for 84 new lane miles at a cost of $72.5 million. Given the significant change in lane miles and capital costs, it was important for members of the Public Works Department to meet with the focus group and discuss the additional street needs, explain how traffic was modeled to flow through the town, and discuss the impact on existing and new development resulting from the identified capital projects.

Conversations quickly revealed that the streets capital plan included $20 million of half street improvements (right-of-way, curb and gutter, etc.) in addition to the improvements specific to arterial streets. The discussion further revealed that depending upon where development would occur, not all parcels would need and/or benefit from the half street improvements. For example, if development was proposed for the undeveloped north side of the street (with the south side already partially developed with curb and gutter), including half street improvements in the impact fee would result in parties on both side of the street paying for capital that only directly benefited the development on the north side. As the fee was initially calculated, all new development would share in the cost of the half street improvements, regardless of whether the adjacent property received direct benefit. Two options were identified to address this issue.

1. The developers themselves would be responsible for the half street (curb and gutter, etc.) improvements if their parcel of land required this type of improvement, and the half street capital costs would be excluded from the impact fee calculation.
2. Continue including the costs in the impact fee, but if a developer completed the half street (curb and gutter, etc.) improvements on their own, they would receive a monetary credit against the streets impact fee commensurate with the cost incurred for the half street improvements. As an example, if the impact fee for the development was $500,000, and the developer paid $200,000 for required half street improvements, the net impact fees paid to the town would be $300,000.

It was determined that the second option would be more of an administrative burden to the town; and while it helped those developers that had to complete half street improvements, those who did not would still be paying the full higher impact fee. All parties agreed that

TABLE 30.2 Street Impact Fee Comparison

Fee	With Half Street ($)	Without Half Street ($)	Difference ($)	Difference (%)
Single-Family	3,436	2,118	1,318	62.2%
Multifamily	2,400	1,479	921	62.2%
Retail	4,268	2,630	1,638	62.2%
Office	1,847	1,139	708	62.2%
Industrial	1,167	720	447	62.1%

TABLE 30.3 Single-Family Residential Impact Fee Comparison

Fee	Proposed ($)	Current ($)	Difference ($)	Difference (%)
Single-Family	6,966	6,794	$172	2.5%
Multifamily	4,966	4,954	12	0.2%
Retail	4,893	3,054	1,839	60.2%
Office	3,029	2,001	1,028	51.4%
Industrial	2,467	1,936	531	27.4%

the preferred option was to exclude half street improvement costs from the capital plan. The overall capital plan was reduced by $20 million, thereby reducing the streets impact fees for all new development. A comparison of the impact fee with and without the half street improvements is summarized in Table 30.2.

30.7 WATER AND WASTEWATER

The main thrust of the focus group meetings was the proposed non-utility impact fees. Water and wastewater fees are typically less controversial than their non-utility counterparts, as their connection to new growth is often more evident and easier to defend. However, there were two issues the development community wanted to explore. The first was the calculation of gallons per capita per day (GPCPD) used for planning purposes. The concern was that in some master planning documents, GPCPD is calculated by dividing total system water or wastewater use by the population. If the system provides service to one or multiple large non-residential entities, dividing total system use by population can overestimate the GPCPD, with residential developments being overcharged for water or wastewater flows not reflective of actual use. This concern was taken under

advisement, and before the focus groups, it was confirmed that the GPCPD calculations were based upon residential use and population only; non-residential use was not included.

The second concern was that many of the proposed new homes would be built with a 1-inch water meter in order to irrigate larger lots and fill swimming pools. In other words, a 1-inch meter was needed to meet outdoor water use needs, but from a wastewater perspective, the sewer flows of these homes behaved more like those with a ¾-inch meter. Upon investigation of billing data and actual sewer flows, we confirmed that there was minimal difference in indoor water use between homes with a ¾-inch meter and those with a 1-inch meter, and it was recommended that the 1-inch residential sewer fee be tied to the ¾-inch sewer fee.

30.8 SUMMARY

At the completion of the study, we had conducted eight focus group meetings, lasting 2 hours each. When the fees were presented to the Council, the overall cost to development classes increased from the prior study, with some fees increasing more significantly than others (see Table 30.3). However, even with the fee changes, the Home Builders

Association and Valley Partnership spoke favorably on behalf of the engagement process. They praised the involvement of town department heads, the staff, and the consultant for facilitating their inclusion in the process because of the transparency it provided, and because it allowed their voices to be heard.

EPILOGUE

Commentaries and Reflections on the Promise of Proportionate Share Impact Fees and Development Mitigation

COMMENTARIES BY JIM NICHOLAS, CLANCY MULLEN, JULIAN JUERGENSMEYER, AND CHRIS NELSON

COMMENTARY BY JIM NICHOLAS

On June 22, 1969, Cleveland's Cuyahoga River caught on fire. This shock to the nation was an important factor leading to the first Earth Day in 1970 and the proposal by President Nixon and the subsequent enactment of the National Environmental Policy Act (NEPA) in 1970. NEPA was quickly followed by the Clean Air Act in 1970 and the Clean Water Act in 1972. The mood of the public had changed from acceptance of a deteriorating quality of life as a "cost of progress." These acts introduced the concept of mitigation; persons, especially land developers, had first to minimize their impacts and then, mitigate those minimized impacts.

The same public sentiment led to numerous actions and acts in states and local governments. Congestion of roads or schools was no longer acceptable.[1] The public demanded change, and change resulted. The impact fee was one of those changes. Planning was the means to minimize and mitigate the negative consequences of new development. Various state enablements and judicial holdings provided local jurisdictions with the authority to plan their communities and the orderly growth of their communities. Ramapo, New York, and Petaluma, California, became famous for being among the first to hold new developments to the publicly demanded standards for adequate public infrastructure and locating development

consistent with a comprehensive plan. Others followed. The thrusts of these standards were to direct new development to designated areas and that those areas be provided with infrastructure. But, infrastructure has to be paid for. There were four ways to pay for these public facilities:

- Federal and/or state grants
- General taxation
- Require dedications by developers
- Impact fees

Federal grants were greatly reduced for two programs used by local governments to finance potable and wastewater facilities. Also, road funding was diminished due to the motor fuels tax being fixed based on cents per gallon, while road building costs grew at rates that exceeded the general rate of inflation. The other types of local infrastructure were largely funded by general taxation at the local level. The 1970s was the time of the "Taxpayers Revolt." It began in California and Massachusetts and then spread to the entire country. General taxation at the local level, mainly the property tax, was no longer going to be the financial cornucopia; thus, new development was going to have to pay for itself, first by required dedications and second by impact fees.

The first national survey of impact fees in 1990 found the average total fee for a single-family unit to be $3,886 (exclusive of water and sewer charges). In 2019, the national average was \$6,743, again excluding water and sewer.[2] In both surveys, California and Florida tend to dominate the results.

Water and sewer remain the most common impact fees, with roads, parks and recreation, and schools following in popularity. The impact fee has evolved in amount and what is included. A road or transportation impact fee now collects for constructing the road but also for utility relocations, environmental mitigation, and sidewalks. School impact fees now include furnishing, fixtures, and technology, with the last becoming an increasingly important component of education. Such would once have been thought of as a fee gone too far, but now, they are standard inclusions.

Today, there is discussion of extending impact fee methods to the environment (see an application in Chapter 24).[3] Today, there is discussion of impact fee methods being applied to workforce housing, while several jurisdictions have gone ahead and done it (see Chapter 22).[4] Today, there is a great deal of discussion of mobility (see Chapter 19). Is mobility an extension, a broadening if you will, of transportation impact fees? Are bicycling and walking a form of transportation? Are they a transportation alternative to motor vehicles? Should transportation impact fees be broadened to incorporate other means of mobility? Today, the growing concern with climate change has raised questions about how resources are used or abused. How do impact fees fit into these questions? I think that impact fees have not been static and will continue to evolve in ways that in the past some would have thought inappropriate or impossible but are now mainstream.

The modern impact fee was born one cold evening in Montreal, first following a panel discussion and then in a bar. Then and now, it harkens back to the concept of mitigation: that the community should be no worse off after the impacts of new developments are minimized and mitigated. As impact fees move forward to address new issues, mitigation must be kept as the goal of any existing or new impact fee program.

COMMENTARY BY CLANCY MULLEN

I am not going to use this space to make prognostications about the current and future state of impact fee practice. Some of my co-authors feel strongly about the need to improve the practice in ways that promote more sustainable and equitable development. There are certainly some alternative ways to structure impact fees to better align with such goals, and it is important to be familiar with them. However, I am skeptical that alternative impact fee structures can do much to significantly support such ends. More importantly, I do not feel it is my role, as a consultant to local governments, to advocate for what the community's priorities should be. My priority as a consultant is to try to ensure that the impact fee study and its implementation comply with the requirements of statutory and case law. In this space, I want to focus on the confusion and unintended consequences that can result from states' attempts to micro-manage how impact fees are implemented. Although I use Florida as a case study, my concern applies broadly to all states with impact fee legislation.

Florida was relatively late in enacting an impact fee act in 2006, when it was the last of 28 states to do so before Oklahoma became the 29th in 2011. The original statute imposed only a few requirements, which most jurisdictions with impact fees already complied with. Historically, state legislatures have rarely amended impact fee statutes once they were adopted, and indeed, only minimal changes were made to Florida's 2006 act until recently. In recent years, however, the legislature has made significant amendments to the statute. I focus here on 2021 legislation that limits how quickly impact fees can be increased to illustrate the potential for legislation to have unintended consequences.

The goal in 2021 of Florida House Bill 337 was to keep local governments from raising impact fees quickly. It was filed by a legislator who earned a six-figure salary as vice-president of residential development for a major retirement community developer in Sumter

County. In early 2021, the Sumter County Commission was planning to increase its road impact fees from 40 percent to 70 percent of the maximum fees calculated in a previous study. The fees for all land uses would increase by 75 percent. The fee for retirement homes would increase from $972 to $1,701, an increase of $729 per home. The original bill that was filed would have restricted impact fee increases to 3 percent per year.

The final legislation required any impact fee increase of less than 25 percent to be phased in over 2 years, and any increase between 25 and 50 percent to be phased in over 4 years in equal annual increments. No fee can go up more than 50 percent over 4 years. Aside from annual phasing of increases, fees can only be increased once every 4 years. It included an exemption in the case of undefined "extraordinary circumstances," but based on recent history, that could be removed in any given legislative session. The legislation does not allow annual inflation adjustments, which were previously made by many Florida jurisdictions to help avoid large jumps when fees were updated.

The simplicity of Sumter County's increase, in which the percentage increase for every land use is the same, makes it a poor model for the legislation. Most fee increases are made in conjunction with an updated impact fee study, and the percentage change differs between land use types, often significantly. The statute requires that the fees for each facility type be proportional to the impacts of each land use. This means that the fee for each land use should be assessed at the same percentage of the maximum fee each year. Yet, this is not possible if increases must be phased in with equal annual increments, as the law now requires. It would appear that the only reasonable approach is to temporarily vary from proportionality during the phase-in period.

However, it would be hard to argue that a suspension of proportionality would be "temporary" if the phase-in takes so long that the fees are likely to be updated before it is completed, in which case the fees for every land use might never be assessed at the same percentage of the maximum fee. In light of this, I am advising clients to achieve proportionality by the last year of a maximum 4-year phase-in.

Allowing fees to increase by 50 percent over 4 years does not seem highly restrictive at first glance, but that's deceptive. The land use category with the largest percentage increase will set the percentage at which all land uses can be assessed by the end of the phase-in, because that category will be assessed at the lowest percentage of the maximum fee. Assume, for example, that the fee for one land use increases 100 percent, while the other land uses increase by only 25 percent. By the fourth year of the phase-in, that one land use would be limited to 75 percent of its maximum fee, and the others would also need to be assessed at 75 percent. If you do the math, you will find that the other fees would need go down 6 percent to be proportional. While this example is highly stylized, it is often the case that the fee for a single land use increases much more than most others when impact fee studies are updated, especially if the fee schedule contains numerous land use categories. This would seem to give jurisdictions an incentive to reduce the number of land use categories they include in their fee schedules.

Florida legislators were probably not fully aware of these nuances and their effects, although they might well be pleased that they succeeded in restricting impact fee increases much more effectively than they thought at the time they approved HB 337.

This example provides a cautionary tale about the possible unintended consequences that can result from attempts to micro-manage how impact fees are assessed. Unless legislators are motivated by a desire to make it as difficult as possible for local governments to assess impact fees, they would be better advised to focus on clearly establishing the principles to be followed rather than prescribing the details.

COMMENTARY BY JULIAN JUERGENSMEYER

Permit me to first expose my perspective on impact fees. I first became involved with impact fees in 1975, published my first impact fee law review article in 1981, and over the last 45 years, have served as a consultant for the development of impact fee programs for local governments in approximately 28 states. As a law professor (currently professor of law emeritus at both the University of Florida and Georgia State University), I have taught numerous law school classes and continuing education programs for law and planning students and for lawyers and planners. Although this book contains much material that reflects my positions and experiences, I would like to take this opportunity to express some ideas, concerns, and generalizations about the past, current, and future role of impact fees.

First, we should have never gotten sucked into classifying impact fees as exactions. It is a negative, judgmental, and inaccurate word to apply to impact fees. According to the dictionary, "to exact" means "to extort." The use of the term "exaction" implies that local governments are doing something illegal or immoral by requiring developers to mitigate some of the expenses they are otherwise passing on to the public if they are not required to pay at least some of the infrastructure costs for the development that will bring them profits. Without such a requirement, the public (taxpayers) are being required to subsidize the profits reaped from development. More importantly, the use of the term "exactions" results in not recognizing the mitigation and proportionality concepts, which are essential aspects of impact fees. Perhaps, we should have never used the term "impact fees." It might have been better if they had been called "proportionate share mitigation requirements" or perhaps simply "mitigation fees." If done properly, they don't take anything from private parties; they just require the private sector to internalize costs rather than shifting them to the public sector.

Second, are impact fees the best or an overused approach to require developers to share the fiscal requirements generally placed on local government as an inevitable burden imposed on local residents by private for-profit development? In our zeal to obtain some relief for units of governments required to provide public infrastructure to serve private development, I fear we often pay too little attention to the concept of value capture—requiring the private sector to recognize the portion of its profits derived from public finance of infrastructure. Of course, it can be, and has been, pointed out that impact fees are analytically one way to approach value capture, but at best, they are a very primitive approach that results in the public being reimbursed for some of the costs of private development that it otherwise subsidizes; they are not adequate to truly recognize the gain the private sector derives from government permitting certain private development that legally and/or economically would preclude other developments.

Third, are impact fees appropriate growth management tools? Since impact fees are usually classified as a growth management technique, this question may be considered shocking. However, one should realize that even though impact fees are designed to solve some of the problems arising from the need for local governments to pay for providing the infrastructure needed to support private development and make it profitable and marketable, they are not responsive to what, if any, development should be permitted at the time and place in question. In fact, there is a much too common perception that if a development pays impact fees, that entitles it to proceed. This approach ignores the issues that two of this book's authors and I have posed in a monograph,[5] which advocates that development should be permitted only if there is adequate demand for the proposed development, and the willingness or necessity of the development community to pay part of the infrastructure bill is not responsive to the issue of whether there is a demand/need for the type of development proposed at the particular time and place.

Fourth, we have been too limiting in our definition of infrastructure. For many reasons, we have concentrated too much on traditional concepts of infrastructure rather than approaching a definition of infrastructure from an impact mitigation perspective. Most impact fee programs confine them to traditional infrastructure such as roads, parks, fire stations, libraries, and the like. What we should ask is: What mitigation is required to neutralize or make positive the proposed developments? Of course, the traditional needs—roads, parks, schools, libraries, and fire stations—will jump out, but what of the environmental needs created by new development, such as open space, wetland and aquifer recharge protection, and the social impact on the need for affordable housing and childcare facilities? Two of the "further out" suggestions can be seen in my advocacy 40 years ago of an agricultural Lands Preservation Impact Fee[6] and the recent proposal for an impact fee charged on low-performance buildings to help finance green buildings.[7]

Fifth, on a rather specific aspect of the infrastructure definition issue, I fear that we have made too great a distinction, and made it too important, between, as the Georgia Development Impact Fee Act calls them, "system" and "project" improvements. It all started when we were needing to convince judges of the legality of impact fees. The common approach to this was to point out that courts had been generally receptive to so-called "required dedications" contained in subdivision regulations. The distinction between them and impact fees was that required dedications concerned onsite (within the development) infrastructure, such as streets, and impact fees were concerned with offsite (outside of the development) infrastructure, such as highways, parks, and schools. The onsite–offsite terminology stressed the physical location of the infrastructure too much. I can remember the late Fred Bosselman constantly

urging that the terminology be changed to site related versus non-site related, which it eventually was. When Georgia adopted its Development Impact Fee Act in 1990, site related and non-site related were abandoned and replaced with project versus system improvement. The evolution of the concept was a positive development, but maybe we were mistaken to ever attempt the dichotomy. The issue is mitigation of the infrastructure needs necessitated by development in order to internalize the costs of mitigation. Shouldn't infrastructure needs created by development be addressed in regard to how and by whom they are paid for? Onsite versus offsite—later, site related versus non-site related. And as mentioned, an improvement on this was found, at least in Georgia—project versus system improvements

This discussion reminds me of how different the approaches of an academic and a practitioner are in this regard. When a practitioner—lawyer or planner—is explaining it to the judge, they stress that what they are seeking approval of is not new and different but a "very slight" extension of approaches already approved by courts. The academic stresses how new, different, and innovative the proposal is.

Finally, I would like to comment on the advantages and disadvantages of a state having a so-called impact fee enabling statute. My early impact fee work was in Florida, where we developed impact fees without any statutory provisions. I never believed it was necessary to have a state enabling act, because I believed that local governments in Florida and in most states could adopt comprehensive impact fee programs using their police power and home rule powers. I feared that adoption of state statutes would serve as impact fee limitation acts. To wit, Georgia's otherwise excellent act is designed to preclude adoption of badly needed school impact fees, and by giving a list of the only infrastructure items to which Georgia's development impact can apply, has precluded extending impact fees to a broader range of mitigation through impact fees as discussed earlier. As my co-author Clancy Mullen discusses in his contribution to the Epilogue, the second problem is that once state legislatures (he uses the Florida example) get involved, they can seldom resist the political pressures behind micro-managing impact methodology.

COMMENTARY BY CHRIS NELSON

I cut my professional planning teeth in the "privilege" era (see Prologue and Chapters 1 and 2). A leading example was where a client wanted to build smaller homes for lower–middle-income households. The day after his 50-unit subdivision was approved, the city raised its sewer connection fees from $250 to $2,500 per home without any analysis, saying only that the city's general fund needed the extra cash. Although my client could have sued and maybe won, he did not want to undermine future projects in the city. To pay the higher costs, my client scrapped building homes for lower–middle-income households and built them for middle-income ones. I thought there must be a better way to establish the nexus between development impact and proportionate mitigation.

Then, I met Jim Nicholas and Julian Juergensmeyer at the Montreal conference of the American Planning Association in 1985. They were doing a workshop on calculating impact fees consistently with legal, planning, and economic principles. We've been colleagues and friends since. Along the way, we've worked together on numerous books, articles, research projects, workshops, and consultancies.

In 1994, I was asked to help the City of Tigard, Oregon, in a case that had made its way to the US Supreme Court: *Dolan v. City of Tigard*. In exchange for a conditional use permit to expand their retail store, the City wanted the Dolans to dedicate a non-buildable easement in a floodplain connecting a residential area to downtown Tigard in front of the Dolans' store. For the City, I wrote a report that was accepted by the Library of Congress, allowing the Court to take official notice of it, which also allowed the City to use it in their argument. My analysis showed that the dedication of easements for pathways of the kind Tigard was conditioning would increase the value of the subject property by more than the value of the easement itself. Privately, I recommended that the City give the Dolans credit for a portion of the transportation impact fees they needed to pay reflecting its easement value. It seems that this never occurred to the City, but it was too late anyway. Chief Justice Rehnquist cited my report in writing his opinion, leading to the "rough proportionality" test. (On remand to the Oregon courts, the City and the Dolans settled for $1.4 million, or roughly $1,000 per linear inch of the pathway easement.)

In my practice for local governments, developers, and the occasional nonprofit, I find that too many professionals claim they have broad leeway in designing impact fees because all the Court requires is "rough proportionality," as that standard does not require "precise mathematical calculation."[8] My colleagues have it wrong in several respects. First, *Dolan* was an administrative case and not a legislative one. As impact fees are legislative actions, it is improper to extend an administrative standard to legislative actions—at least for now (more on this later). Second, and perhaps more important, is that many colleagues fail to acknowledge the totality of the *Dolan* standard:

No precise mathematical calculation is required, but the city must make some sort of *individualized determination* that the required dedication is *related both in nature and extent* to the impact of the proposed development.[9] (Emphasis added)

Notably, in claiming the relevant professional standard is "rough proportionality," some colleagues forget that this requires an individualized determination related to the nature—such as the type of residential or commercial structure, and the *extent*—such as size of the structure, density of the site or area being impacted, the extent to which new facilities are needed to accommodate the impacts of new development based on location, and so forth. Rough proportionality does not allow professionals to ignore these two prongs of the *Dolan* test. For example, rough proportionality does not mean assessing the same impact fees for each residential land use regardless of its nature and extent for reasons discussed in the Prologue, Chapter 1, and Chapter 15 as well as the Coda to that chapter.

But, *Dolan* and its ilk (*Nollan* and *Koontz*) actually have implications for such legislative actions as impact fees (see Chapter 2). Therein lies the cop-out local governments are allowed to avoid the kind of proportionate share analysis we advance throughout our book. For example, in Chapter 15, we saw that one county charged the same school impact fee for studio apartments as for large single-family detached homes, even though census data show that studios have a minuscule impact on schools, while large, detached homes have a substantial impact. As long as courts give more deference to legislative actions than administrative ones, we may continue to see what I would characterize as gross misapplications of the proportionate share principles we have spent our careers advancing. My personal sense is that the Supreme Court may be attracted to a residential land use case of the kind outlined in Chapter 15 inviting them to extend *Dolan* to legislative actions. After all, for nonresidential development, we calibrate mitigation based on the nature and extent of its impacts. For instance, for road impact fees, we do not charge a building of one million square feet as though it were 10,000 square feet just because that is the overall average in the community. Yet, we do this routinely for residential land uses. This is where courts may be interested in extending *Dolan* to such legislative actions as local impact fee ordinances. Indeed, as we noted in Chapter 2, at least one sitting Supreme Court Justice (Thomas) has invited the Court to accept a case where it can apply *Dolan* (along with *Nollan* and *Koontz*) to legislative actions. Maybe that would not be a bad thing, at least in the context of advancing proportionate share principles.

Echoing Clancy's advice, proportionate share mitigation analysis should not go outside the boundaries of its principles to advance social equity, environmental, or other policies not reasonably related to the impacts of new development. But, the genius of proportionate share mitigation is that it can do much to address social equity, environmental, and other concerns *within* the boundaries of proportionate share analysis. As we see in Chapter 22, workforce housing mitigation can be achieved substantially through proportionate share impact analysis. The same goes for environmental and habitat preservation, as seen in Chapter 24. Indeed, Part 4 reports many ways in which proportionate share mitigation can advance social equity, environmental protection, and other public policy concerns consistent with is principles.

Moreover, I often find it ironic that many communities complain about the effect of impact fees on housing affordability when the reason is their own lack of due diligence (see the Coda to Chapter 15). The reason is that many of them do not vary their fees by the nature or extent of residential development. If they did, they would find that impact fees for smaller and attached homes in higher-density, fully served areas would likely be lower, perhaps much lower, than for single-family detached units in lower-density areas farther away that need new services. In other words, making impact fees truly proportionate to the impact of new development based on its nature and extent, and location, would do much to address housing affordability concerns.

What is the future of proportionate share mitigation? In Chapter 20, on transportation operations and maintenance (O&M) and transportation utility fees, we may be seeing the future of proportionate share impact mitigation. Consider that research shows that lower-density development does not generate sufficient revenues to cover the long-term O&M costs of many facilities. Even if impact fees fully recover the cost of mitigating infrastructure investments, the long-term O&M and capital replacement costs will stress the community's budget over time. One solution is to charge an increment to impact fees reflecting the capitalized long-term O&M costs, putting those funds into an endowment. This may not be allowed in states with impact fee legislation, and it may be problematic because of calculation complications in other states. On the other hand, it may be permissible as part of discretionary land use approval processes, provided the proportionate share principles advocated in this book are followed.

What intrigues me most about the future of proportionate share mitigation is the potential to apply the transportation utility fee (TUF) concept to all infrastructure through what I call the infrastructure preservation fee (IPF). The calculation method would be the same as that for TUF but extended to all infrastructures. However, where most TUFs do not vary by location in present practice, IPFs would be based on the service area principles of proportionate share analysis outlined in Chapters 2 and 15 (including its Coda). They would also vary by the nature and extent of land uses ideally at a very fine grain, perhaps at the parcel level. We have the technology to do this. The methodologies are already available. What we need is a few demonstration projects to apply and refine the concept.

As Jim observed wisely, what were once considered novel applications of proportionate share principles have become mainstream. With this in mind, we proceed with some broad, concluding perspectives on the future of proportionate share development impact mitigation.

REFLECTIONS ON THE PROMISE OF PROPORTIONATE SHARE IMPACT FEES AND DEVELOPMENT MITIGATION

This book has addressed the history, law, theory, methods, practice, and emerging innovations of proportionate share mitigation, mostly in the context of impact fees. The modern impact fee arose in the 1970s, when constituents demanded that ever-increasing property taxes stop. Lower taxes, especially lower property taxes, have been the rallying cry of every election since. The property tax has long been a primary source of revenue for local governments, and property tax limitations and reforms have fallen particularly heavily on local governments. In the meantime, there has been no fall-off in the demand for or the cost of roads, utilities, parks, or the other items of public infrastructure that must be provided. In fact, not only has the quantity of infrastructure needed skyrocketed in recent years, but also, the quality of infrastructure that is acceptable to most citizens has also spiraled upward. For example, most parents expect public schools today to have computers, swimming pools, chemistry labs, and lighted athletic fields with modern locker rooms. These were unheard-of "luxuries" in most areas of the country in the last century when we were all public school students.

If expansion of public infrastructure is not going to be funded by traditional forms of taxes in the future to the extent that it was in the past, then it must be funded by some other means. Impact fees are one of those other means. The desirability of impact fees within the broader context of public finance is no longer an issue. Today, the issues are developing impact fee programs that are calculated based on proportionate share principles, as consistent as possible with society's goals, and at the same time, achieving meaningful investment in public infrastructure broadly defined.

Coincident with the evolution of such forms of development impact mitigation as required dedications, payments in-lieu, and impact fees came the cry of "unfair." Developers and their customers (buyers and tenants) were being required to incur costs that had been previously borne by the public. Conflict ensured. State and federal courts and many state legislatures have examined the issue and have largely concluded that impact fee programs as a form of development impact mitigation are an important component of local government finance if proportionality of burden and benefit is achieved. We now see expanded use of proportionate share development mitigation extending to workforce housing, environmental and habitat preservation, and even addressing the O&M impacts of new development.

While impact fees as a form of proportionate share mitigation are here to stay, they can be implemented in many ways, each with its own set of consequences. The law demands proportionality in impact fees, but proportionality can be achieved in a variety of different ways. One of our goals is to show some of those different ways so that communities can gain from the experiences of others as they design or redesign impact fee programs that meet their individual needs. Some of the principles of impact fees are absolute; the amounts imposed as impact fees must be proportional to the impact of the development, considering its nature (such as type of development) and extent (such as size, density, and other factors), and the payment of impact fees must result in infrastructure (broadly defined) that benefits such development proportionately to its impact.

Proportionality also means equity. We are mindful that equity is not the same as equality, and achieving equity is not typically as straightforward. Equity occurs when benefits and burdens are distributed proportionately to impact, and this results in a level playing field, even though the starting point for all those affected may not be equal. Equity does not occur when impact mitigation through such means as impact fees is applied in an equal manner, such as through a "one size fits all" approach, especially when impacts vary between and among land uses and by extension, those who occupy them, and by location.

Whether in the form of impact fees or other methods, the purpose of proportionate share impact mitigation is more than just balancing the benefits and burdens of development. As noted throughout our book, the overarching purpose is to implement local planning policy, typically the comprehensive plan. In turn, good plans have such over-arching goals as preserving public goods, minimizing adverse development impacts but maximizing positive ones, maximizing the use of existing infrastructure at minimum cost, and distributing benefits and burdens proportionately to impact. Once these goals are achieved, in part through proportionate share impact mitigation, overall community quality of life will be elevated.

NOTES

1 For an excellent discussion of this period, see William K. Riley, *The Use of Land: A Citizens' Policy Guide to Urban Growth*, New York: Thomas Y. Crowell Company, 1973.

2 1990 data from Nicholas, Nelson, & Juergensmeyer, *Practitioner's Guide to Impact Fees*, APA, 1992, p. 9. 2019 data from Mullen, "2019 Impact Fee Survey," www.impactfees.com.

3 "Market Based Approaches to Environmental Preservation: To Environmental Mitigation Fees and Beyond," *Natural Resources Journal.* 2003. Nicholas & Juergensmeyer, explored impact fees as a means of environmental preservation.

4 *A Rational Nexus Approach to Workforce Housing Land Development Covenants*, 52 UIC J. Marshall L. Rev. 647 (2019), Nicholas & Juergensmeyer.

5 Arthur C. Nelson, John T. Marshall, Julian Conrad Juergensmeyer, and James C. Nicholas, Market Demand-Based Planning and Permitting American Bar Association (2017).

6 See Julian Conrad Juergensmeyer, "Implementing Agricultural Preservation Programs: A Time to Consider a Novel Approach," 20 GONZ. L. REV. 701 (1986).

7 Nelson, Marshall, Juergensmeyer, and Nicholas.

8 *Dolan v. City of Tigard*, 512 U.S. 374 (1994) at 391.

9 Ibid.

INDEX

Page numbers **bold** indicate a table on the corresponding page

flexible fee programs 433

Florida: Aventura transportation O&M mitigation fee 377, 378, 379, 380–381; House Bill 337 504–505; impact fee revenues 10, 11, 13; impact fee waivers to advance affordable housing 409; Legislative Committee on Intergovernmental Relations (LCIR) 10; local government impact fee adjustments to advance affordable housing 409–411; proportionate-share impact fee calculation 408–409

Florida Housing Finance Corporation 408

focus group discussions 497–498, 499, 500–501

fragmentation 419

free riders 274

Fremont Union High School District (FUHSD) 438–439; capacity analysis 444–446; determination of fee on residential development 447, 448; enrollment from existing housing 444; enrollment from new housing 443, 444; facility costs 446, 447; housing projections 442, 443; impact fees for commercial/industrial development 449–450, 451, 452, 453; redevelopment construction 448; residential expansions 448–449; senior housing 449; student generation rates 443

fuel tax 194

full cost 85, 90, 182, 202, 232, 247, 248, 249

functional population approach 124, 379

funds and funding 182; capacity improvements 138; decision charts 307; dedicated 139; discretionary local 138–139; enterprise 381–382; facility 503; flexible fee programs 433; grants 139–140; mobility plans 362, 363, 364; multimodal projects 355, 356; non-local 139; social programs 258–259; Tracy Hills 433, 434; waivers 176; Western Placer County Habitat Conservation Plan and Natural Community Conservation Plan 429, 430, 431

general obligation bond 9

gentrification 191; applying the equity lens 266

geographic equity 306

George, H. 238

Georgia 62; affordable housing exemptions 57–58; appeals process 60; capital improvement 56–57; capital improvement advisory committee 58–59; capital improvements plan requirements 59; collection of impact fees when services are unavailable 58; comprehensive plans 60–61; credit provisions 60; development moratoriums 59; forms of local governments that may act 57; impact fee caps 59–60; impact fee refunds 58; intergovernmental agreements 59; project improvements vs. system improvements 60; proportionate-share calculation 61; service areas 58; time for assessment and collection of impact fees 57; types of capital improvement impact fees 57

Glass, R. 266

good planning 85, 230, 233, 238

governmental services 18

graduated impact fees 195

grants 139–140

Great Recession 67, 73, 392, 433

"green" infrastructure 35–36

growth: ability-to-pay standard 248–249; beneficiaries of 246–248; culpability standard 249–251; fair allocation question 246; indirect beneficiaries 247; projections 49–50

Gyourko, J. 208

Haar, C. M. 77–78, 78, 83, 86

hard facilities: capacity 122; consumption-based methodology 132, 133; plan-based methodology 134–135

home ownership 13

home prices: impact fees and 72, 73; over-shifting 202, 203, 217; reservation price 200, 201

"home rule" 346

homevoter hypothesis 208

horizontal equity 190

housing: bubble 67, 68; constant quality price 205–206; impact fee effects on prices 408; impact fee effects on prices, empirical evidence 202–206; impact fee effects on prices, theoretical evidence 200–202; price of 182; production effects of impact fees 207–212; workforce 328, 390; see also affordable housing

housing affordability 13, 99, 176, 179, 199, 207, 210, 212, 221, 224, 227, 279, 304, 307, 392, 408–411, 509

Ihlanfeldt, K. 200, 201, 202, 203, 204, 205, 208–209, 215, 217

impact cost calculation: adopt a LOS and project future infrastructure demand 100–101; calculate current LOS 99–100; calculate the cost to meet projected demand at adopted LOS 101; impact cost per impact unit at adopted LOS 101

impact fee(s) 1, 3, 7, 8, 9, 17, 18, 65, 304, 510–511; ability-to-pay standard 248–249; accounting 146; adjustments 409–411; administration 56; administrative fees 52, 151; advisory committees 58–59; affordable housing and 269, 270–271; affordable housing exemptions 57–58; alternatives 504; amounts 9; appeals process 60; apportioning to all development 278–279; approximations 188; assessment 145–146; backward capitalization 224; *Banberry* criteria 23, 34, 97–98; bands 283; based on conventional theories of regulation 222; benefit districts 34; binary 282; borders approach 215–216; building additions and expansions 145; calculation 193; capital improvement 32, 49, 57; capitalization effects 248; caps 59–60; categorical 283; characteristics 64; Citywide 434; collection 58, 146; comprehensive plan implementation 78; comprehensive plans 60–61; constitutionality of 19–20; construction credit 46; consultants 142–143; continuous 283; credit provisions 38, 54, 58, 60, 148–149, 159–161; criticisms 199–200; culpability standard 249–251; data maintenance 150–151; for demolition and replacement 145; design 193; differential 119–120; disbursement 146–148; discriminatory 257–258; districts 157; drafting 32–34; earmarking 146–147; economic benefits 216; economic development effects 212–216, 217; effect on capital improvement policy 147–148; effect on community priorities 307, 314; eligible facilities 46, 47; enabling acts 43, 45–46; enforcement 148; equal protection issues 23–24; equitable 267–268, 282; ethics 246, 259–260; evolution 18–19; as exactions 506; exemptions 145, 159–161, 175–176; extending across the development spectrum 35; facilities 117, 118; fallacy of assuming the present is the future 280–281; focus groups 497–498, 499, 500–501; forms of local governments that may act 57; future 13–14; goals 193–194; graduated 195; as growth management tools 506; growth projections 49–50; home prices and